Legisprudence Library

Studies on the Theory and Practice of Legislation

Volume 2

More information about this series at http://www.springer.com/series/11058

Michał Araszkiewicz • Krzysztof Płeszka
Editors

Logic in the Theory and Practice of Lawmaking

Springer

Editors
Michał Araszkiewicz
Faculty of Law and Administration
Department of Legal Theory
Jagiellonian University
Kraków, Poland

Krzysztof Płeszka
Faculty of Law and Administration
Department of Legal Theory
Jagiellonian University
Kraków, Poland

ISSN 2213-2813 ISSN 2213-2856 (electronic)
Legisprudence Library
ISBN 978-3-319-19574-2 ISBN 978-3-319-19575-9 (eBook)
DOI 10.1007/978-3-319-19575-9

Library of Congress Control Number: 2015949152

Springer Cham Heidelberg New York Dordrecht London

Printed on acid-free paper

Springer International Publishing AG Switzerland is part of Springer Science+Business Media (www.springer.com)

For Małgosia with many thanks for her patience
and Agata with many thanks for her impatience.
Editors

Preface

This volume explores the role of logic in the theory and practice of lawmaking. Clearly, the process of making law is a social phenomenon of great complexity that has been analysed from multiple scientific perspectives and methodological stances. The many elaborations of the process of lawmaking have variously emphasised its political, social or economic aspects. Yet despite strong interest in the logical analysis of law, both in legal theory and in the research domain known as "artificial intelligence and law", there remains a gap in the literature as to any systematic investigation of the role of logical tools in the process of lawmaking and especially in legislation. This volume attempts to bridge this gap, or at least to narrow it, and to indicate important research problems that remain open and in need of solutions.

How, then, is the very concept of "logic" to be accounted for in the context of lawmaking? Does the structure of statutes, and of the system of law, resemble the structure of deductive systems? What are the logical relations between the basic jurisprudential concepts that constitute the system of law? How do we infer legal norms from the formulations of the statutory text? Are legal systems consistent and complete, and how should these logical features be understood within the domain of law? How are we to formally represent changes in the system of law? What are the logical characteristics of the discourse around legislative proposals? How are theories of legal interpretation relevant to the process of legislation? How might we proceed from the statutory text through its formal representation to executable computer programs? How can legal rules be represented by means of formal calculi and visualisation techniques? How might the statutory text be analysed by means of contemporary computer programs? These and many other questions, both general and specific, are addressed in the chapters that follow.

The planning of this volume demanded active reflection on its scope. Should the concept of "logic" as understood here be confined to the theory of deductive systems? How broadly should the concept of "lawmaking" be drawn? We have opted to interpret these concepts in relatively broad terms, lending the book another (perhaps implicit) kind of value, as a compendium of the various understandings of logic and lawmaking by contemporary legal philosophers and theorists. Rather than adopting any single or imposed viewpoint, the book instead presents a multitude of approaches and perspectives within this relatively new area of research. To that extent, the present volume can be seen as a first attempt to define the scope of this domain and to characterise its methodologies. Even a preliminary glance at the present collection of chapters confirms that this characterisation is indeed complex, as the (broadly construed) subject of lawmaking may fruitfully be analysed by different logical tools in pursuit of different scientific objectives. The contributing authors come from different traditions; among them, one will find legal philosophers, theorists of argumentation, logicians and computer scientists. However, this does not in our view render the field hopelessly eclectic. The discernible streams, trends and features in this work lead us to propose three scaleable criteria (or dimensions, to borrow an expression from the computational theory of legal argument) ordering the content of the volume. Of course, this ordering should not be seen as in any way a rigid classification or systematisation; rather, the adopted criteria are typological devices that can be used by the reader as alternate "keys" to the content of the book.

The first criterion concerns the general emphasis of a given chapter as theoretical or practical. Recalling that the title of the volume is Logic in the Theory and Practice of Lawmaking, it seemed important to examine how logic can contribute in equal measure to the theoretical and practical aspects of lawmaking. Of course, both theoretical and practical elements inform these chapters in differing degree, and some embrace both approaches equally. The first criterion, then, orders the chapters from the more theoretical to the more practical, inviting the reader to participate in a journey from the (mainly) theoretical to the (predominantly) practical use of logical tools in the context of lawmaking. The weighing of this theoretical/practical component in turn prompted partition of the volume in two parts, although there is in fact no clear dividing line, and the boundary drawn exactly at the midpoint is to a great extent arbitrary. For that reason, the two parts are respectively entitled "From the Theory…" and "…to the Practice of Lawmaking".

Although the constituent chapters of the first part focus on theoretical rather than practical aspects of the role of logic in lawmaking, many include concrete examples illustrating the theoretical considerations under consideration. Taken together, these chapters embody a unique panorama of theoretical issues of relevance to the intersection of the domain of logic with lawmaking, with particular emphasis on legislation.

In the first chapter, authored by Jaap Hage, "The (Onto)logical Structure of Law. A Conceptual Toolkit For Legislators" fulfils the promise of its title, providing an extensive analysis of the most fundamental concepts of legal order, including obligation, duty and right, in their potential applicability for legislators to the development of "the world of law". In the second chapter, Lars Lindahl and David Reidhav engage with the classical problem of normative conflict, offering a detailed formal analysis. The authors investigate and precisely define normative conflicts in respect of both deontic norms and norms relating to legal power. Their findings have application in identifying both intranational and supranational normative conflicts, as, for instance, in conflicts between domestic law and EU law.

In Chap. 3, Pablo Navarro and Jorge Rodríguez discuss the classical problem of entailed norms. In discussion with two prominent legal philosophers, Joseph Raz and Andrei Marmor, they eventually claim that validity of entailed norms is compatible with the social sources thesis as advanced by legal positivism. The discussion is highly relevant for the task of the legislator, who must take account of the effects of derived norms as well as of explicitly issued rules. Chapter 4 is devoted to a cognate theoretical topic: the closure of legal system. Here, Juliano Maranhão employs the concept of coherence to elaborate a conceptual scheme that enables him to represent (some types of) reasoning related to legislative goals.

The contribution by Giovanni Battista Ratti (Chap. 5) is an analysis of the concept of negation in legislation. Having introduced a number of carefully drawn distinctions related to the problem of negation of norms, the author relates these results to legal-philosophical issues of derogation and defeasibility. In Chap. 6, Šavelka and Harašta consider another important jurisprudential problem: the open-textured character of legal provisions formulated in natural language. These last two chapters usefully illustrate the application of logical tools in the analysis of important legal-theoretical notions.

In Chap. 7, Linda Jellum addresses the perennial topic of statutory interpretation, reviewing theories of statutory interpretation developed in the USA that include textualism, intentionalism and purposivism. This contribution is among the most informative and synthetic elaborations of this subject in the present state of the art, offering an insight into problems of these theories' relevance for the legislative process. In Chap. 8, Andrzej Grabowski and Urszula Kosielińska-Grabowska present a detailed analysis of logical aspects of the Polish regulation on Principles of Legislative Technique. They highlight important interrelations between certain theses in logic and the rules governing legislative technique in Poland, yielding important insights concerning the "logical component" of the process of drafting of statutes.

Chapter 9, by Giovanni Damele and Fabrizio Macagno, offers a thorough analysis of the crucial problem of definitions in the law, with particular emphasis on underestimated issues related to the omitting of definition by the legislator and to implicit (re)definitions. Their contribution illuminates both the theory of legislative drafting and the nature of judicial decision-making and case-based reasoning. In Chap. 10, Michał Araszkiewicz and Krzysztof Płeszka's theoretical investigations of the concepts of legal system and normative consequence lead to the elaboration of a useful semiformal framework for practical assessment of actual legislative bills.

At this point, we encounter the conventional dividing line between the two parts of the book. The remaining chapters focus more on problems of legislative practice while still engaging where necessary with significant theoretical concerns. Chapter 11 by Henry Prakken presents a formalisation of debates on proposals for lawmaking, drawing on two extensive examples, respectively, involving lawmaking through legislation and by precedent. This kind of reconstruction of practical discourse can potentially enhance the quality of actual lawmaking processes in terms of clarity and transparency. In Chap. 12, Guido Governatori and Antonino Rotolo focus on important temporal features of legal rules and of legal systems in general. They present practical examples to demonstrate the expressive power of their formalism, contributing to a better understanding of the concepts so analysed and, potentially, to a better management of the process of amending the law.

Chapter 13, co-written by Vern R. Walker, Bernadette C. Lopez, Matthew T. Rutchik and Julie L. Agris, also advances the practical use of logical modelling of actual legislative provisions, emphasising the usefulness of this formalism in the application of legal rules and in assessment of this process. In Chap. 14, Layman Allen and Leon J. Lysaght Jr. investigate the problem of ambiguities arising in two extant parts of American law, identifying a need for more extensive application of hypertext representation to the legal corpus. The development of logic programmes serving multiple practical objectives is the topic of Chap. 15, authored by Adam Wyner. An important feature of this chapter is the discussion of computer programs developed in the last three decades that have actually been implemented. The next chapter, by Nitin Bilgi, is a technical report concerning a simple computer program designed to represent the rule-based structure of Indian property law.

Chapter 17, by Vytautas Čyras and Friedrich Lachmayer, has a practical focus, addressing the use of logic-based and visualisation tools to enhance the process of legislative drafting. The contribution of Burkhard Schäfer, Addi Rull, Anni Säär and Ermo Täks (Chap. 18) brings together the practical project of creating CoReO, a tool employed to support the process of legislative reform, with the theoretical viewpoint of Luc Wintgens' notion of "legisprudence". In Chap. 19, Enrico Francesconi discusses some very important practical problems concerning the management of knowledge in the lawmaking process, especially at EU level. Finally, Chap. 20 by Tomasz Pełech-Pilichowski and Wojciech Cyrul is devoted to the problem of developing new IT tools (so-called artificial immune systems) to analyse and enhance certain important features of legislative texts.

The second criterion used to organise the content of this collection relates to the various understandings of the term "logic" employed here. It is a platitude that "logic" is an ambiguous expression and may refer to different subjects and methods within the broader topic of reasoning. The literature on varying conceptions of logic is too broad to be reviewed here, even in the sole context of law. However, it is possible to distinguish at least four different approaches to the application of logic to the domain of law, forming a kind of dimension from strictly formal approaches to the broader and less formal.

First, when understood as a mathematical logic in general or as a chosen logical calculus (satisfying certain important metalogical criteria), logic may be applied in reconstructing the law itself or in legal argumentation. This may enable a researcher to more strictly determine, for instance, the deductive consequences of logical representations of legal norms, and the theses of the elaborated theory may be formally proven. Although such rigour and precision is especially valuable with regard to potential computational implementations of the designed system, it is also of value in itself.

Second, certain formal logical notions and methods may fruitfully be used to account more precisely for certain legal concepts or patterns of argumentation, albeit short of full-fledged formalisation of legal system, legal norms or legal reasoning. This type of limited application enables the researcher to develop or clarify important conceptual distinctions, which may be useful in both theoretical and practical discourses.

Third, logic may be construed more broadly as referring to all types of (possibly rational) reasoning and argumentation. This broad perspective often offers interdisciplinary insights, intersecting with research on semantics, linguistics, general epistemology or philosophy of science. This informal approach seems more germane to lawyers who have extensive training in the analysis of legal texts but favour the original natural language formulation and are reluctant to impose any formal reconstruction. The perennial issues discussed within this approach encompass, *inter alia*, problems of legal interpretation or definition.

Finally, logical analysis may be understood as the application of any systematic method yielding relevant information from the existing data. In particular, computational and quantitative methods as well as methods of visualisation should be mentioned in this context.

This second criterion, concerning the understanding of "logic", invites the following order of reading. Those interested in contemporary rigorously formal approaches might begin with Chap. 2 (Lindahl and Reidhav) and Chaps. 11–13 (Prakken, Governatori and Rotolo and Walker et al.). It is interesting to note the diversity of approach among these authors. Governatori and Rotolo adopt defeasible temporal deontic logic to represent the temporal features of legal rules and legal systems, and Prakken applies ASPIC^{+}, a formal framework for structured argumentation, to describe discourse around lawmaking proposals. These formally rigorous contributions are quite distinct from the earlier, classical work in the field of legal theory and logic, where propositional logic, first-order logic and standard deontic logic were most often applied to the modelling of law and legal reasoning. A more classical but still rigorous approach is proposed by Lindahl and Reidhav, who designed the formal COLT system for analyses of normative conflict. The logical features of this system enable them to derive theses on the basis of formal proofs. The representation adopted by Walker et al. is based on default logic and rule trees, making this a middle-ground proposal between the strictly formal and more lightweight contributions. Chapter 15 by Wyner discusses the state of the art in moving from the natural language formulation of legal provisions through formalisation to executable computer programs.

Methods of formalisation are employed to bring clarity and rigour to certain legal-theoretical concepts or patterns of legal reasoning in Chap. 1, Chaps. 4–5 and 10. Hage (Chap. 1) uses logical tools to reconstruct the most fundamental concepts of law. Maranhão (Chap. 4) employs his original notation to analyse the concept of coherence in the law, while Ratti (Chap. 5) investigates the role of negation in legislation, founding his arguments mainly on classical logic and legal-theoretical distinctions. In Chap. 10, Araszkiewicz and Płeszka develop AFLEG, a semiformal argumentation framework for investigating the actual normative consequences of normative acts and amendments thereto. The contributions by Šavelka and Harašta (Chap. 6) and Allen and Lysaght (Chap. 14) employ logical methods to investigate such phenomena as vagueness and ambiguity in legal texts.

A more informal methodological approach to issues of legal reasoning and legislation is found in Chap. 3 and Chaps. 7–9 (Jellum, Grabowski and Kosielińska-Grabowska, Damele and Macagno). Finally, certain relatively novel approaches, emerging from the intersection between research on law and various branches of computer science, are to be found in Chaps. 16–20 (Bilgi, Čyras and Lachmayer, Schäfer et al. Francesconi and Pełech-Pilichowski and Cyrul).

These alternate pathways through the book, from the strictly formal, rigorous approaches through more lightweight formalism and on to informal expositions and discussion of novel IT case techniques, are depicted in Fig. 1.

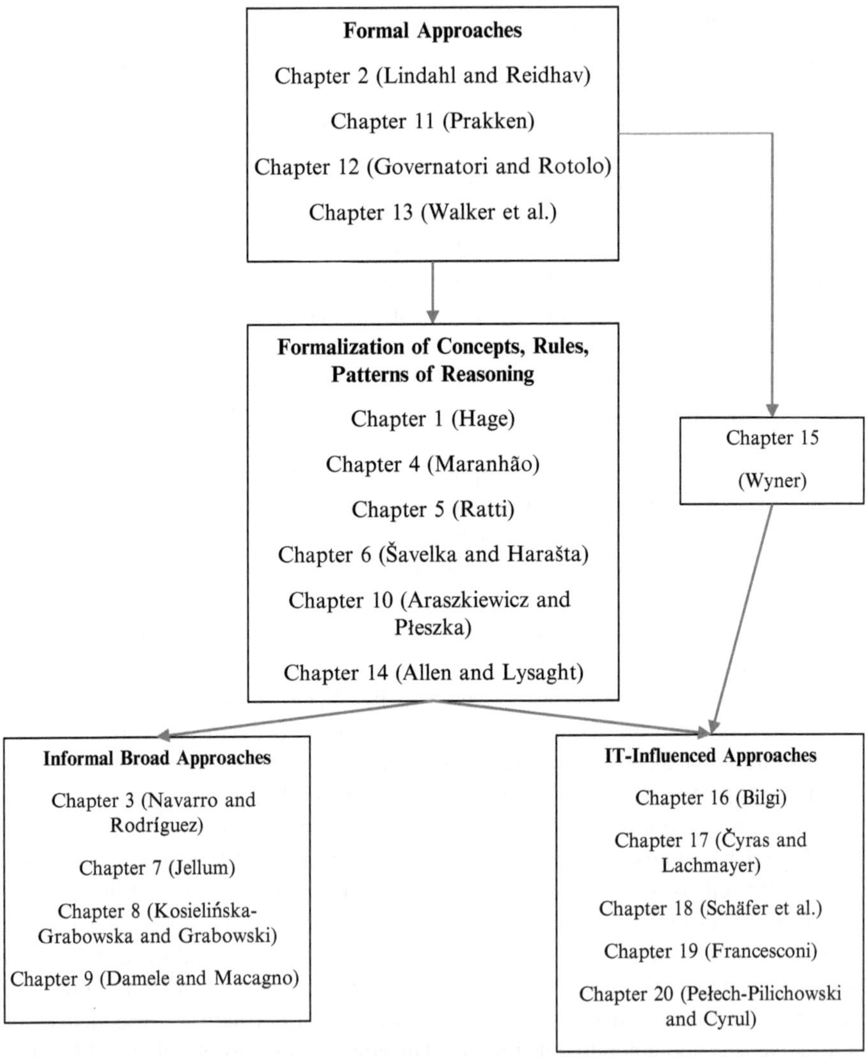

Fig. 1 The structure of the volume with regard to the understanding of the term "logic"

The third criterion governing reading order is the relative weight of the component related strictly to lawmaking and the component concerning the application of law. Clearly, these are strongly interconnected, and many of the chapters deal with both, but it is nevertheless possible in most cases to distinguish the dominant component.

This third criterion creates another reading pathway, starting from the chapters focused on logical aspects of the lawmaking process and the actual text of legislation and ending with those contributions that deal predominantly with problems of the application of law and of legal interpretation.

Chapters 15, 17, 18, 19 and 20 (Wyner, Čyras and Lachmayer, Schäfer et al. Francesconi and Pełech-Pilichowski) relate to problems of application of certain IT tools in the domain of legislation in pursuit of important goals. These authors are concerned to develop tools supporting the process of legislative drafting and management of legislative knowledge. Adam Wyner presents a broad description of the state of the art related to formalisation by means of logic of the legislative text as expressed in natural language, with the ultimate objective of developing executable logic programmes. Čyras and Lachmayer propose to supplement the legislative process with logic-oriented tools such as ontologies, thesauruses and taxonomies, as well as by deploying the methods of sequential legal visualisation to deal with semantic features of legal provisions. The tool called CoReO, devised by Schäfer and the Estonian research group, enables the legislator to collect data about the smallest possible changes in the legislation that lead to the largest possible effects. Enrico Francesconi argues for an integrated solution to enhance the process of multilingual lawmaking. Importantly, his proposal seeks to involve different actors within the democratic process: decision-makers, legal drafters and citizens. Pełech-Pilichowski and Cyrul apply immune system-like processing of legislative text for analytical description, aiming ultimately to enhance features such as consistency, coherence, uniformity and comprehensiveness.

Henry Prakken (Chap. 11) deals with the process of debate in relation to lawmaking. Interestingly, this chapter facilitates comparison between the structure of these debates in continental legal culture and in common law legal cultures. In Chap. 8, Urszula Kosielińska-Grabowska and Andrzej Grabowski analyse the regulations which govern the legislative drafting in Poland from the viewpoint of logic. They propose a typology of relationships between logic and legislative technique that contributes to the discussion concerning the logical rationality of lawmaking. Michał Araszkiewicz and Krzysztof Płeszka argue in Chap. 10 for a semiformal framework for the assessment of logical features of legislative bills, enabling the lawmaker to take the so-called argumentative consequences of legal texts into account. Authors in the next group of chapters aim to reconstruct the content of legislation, or specific parts or aspects thereof, with a particular focus on enhancing the process of application of legal rules. These papers encompass representations of concrete pieces of legislation (Vern R. Walker et al. Chap. 13; Nitin Bilgi, Chap. 16; Layman Allen and Leon Lysaght, Chap. 14) as well as reconstructions of more abstract normative concepts, structures and phenomena

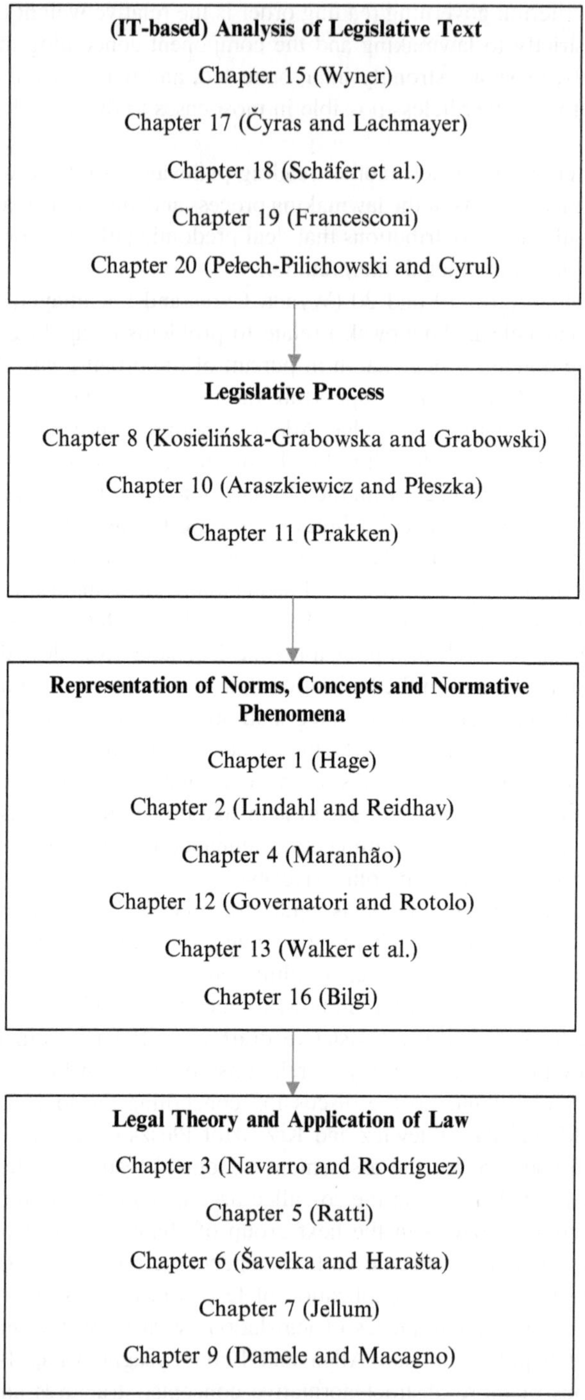

Fig. 2 The structure of the volume with regard to emphasis on legislative or law-applying issues

as illustrated by concrete examples (Jaap Hage, Chap. 1; Lars Lindahl and David Reidhav, Chap. 2; Juliano Maranhão, Chap. 4; Guido Governatori and Antonino Rotolo, Chap. 12).

The final cluster of chapters focuses on legal reasoning rather than on lawmaking in itself, at both legal-theoretical and law-applying levels. In the former domain, Chap. 3 by Pablo Navarro and Jorge Rodríguez is an extensive philosophical discussion of the validity of entailed norms, while Giovanni Battista Ratti (Chap. 5) investigates the notion of negation of norms. Chapters 6, 7 and 9 (Jaromír Šavelka and Jakub Harašta, Linda Jellum and Giovanni Damele and Fabrizio Macagno) focus on legal reasoning in the application of law and in particular on legal interpretation (Fig. 2).

There are many people whose help and support made this book possible. We would like to thank Professor Luc Wintgens and Professor Daniel Olivier-Lalana, the editors of the Legisprudence Library Series at Springer, for kindly assigning us the task of gathering relevant contributions and editing this volume. We are deeply grateful to all the chapter authors for contributing despite the many other demands of their time. We would like to thank those who participated in the "Logic and Legislation" workshop, co-organised by us as an associated event at the XXVI World Congress of Philosophy of Law and Social Philosophy (Belo Horizonte, Brazil, 21–26 July 2013), which opened a space for the discussion of the topics that have defined the scope of this volume (although we wish to stress that this volume is independent from that event). We are grateful to several people for their supportive attitude towards the very idea of this volume, including Professor Jaap Hage (one of the contributing authors), Professor Kevin Ashley and Professor Tomasz Gizbert-Studnicki. Our deepest thanks go to the people responsible for this project in Springer, particularly to Neil Olivier and Diana Nijenhuijzen. Many thanks are also due to Bartosz Janik, who was responsible for technical editing of the draft of this volume. Last but certainly not least, we would like to thank our families for their support and patience.

Kraków, Poland

Michał Araszkiewicz
Krzysztof Płeszka

Contents

Contributors

Julie L. Agris, PhD, JD, LLM, is a clinical assistant professor in the School of Health Technology and Management at Stony Brook University, an adjunct associate professor of health policy and management at the Wagner School, New York University (NYU) and a clinical assistant professor at the Hofstra North Shore–LIJ School of Medicine. Dr. Agris has professional experience in and teaches healthcare law, ethics, bioethics, policy and management and has published and presented in these areas. Prior to her academic appointments, Dr. Agris served as a healthcare attorney, representing large academic medical centres, the US Department of Health and Human Services and the Vermont General Assembly.

Layman E. Allen graduated from Turtle Creek High School in 1945. His subsequent career included the US Navy, 1945–1946; Princeton, BA, 1951; Harvard, MPA, 1952; Yale Law School, LLB, 1956; fellow, Institute for Advanced Study in the Behavioral Sciences, 1962–1963; assistant and associate professor, Yale Law School, 1957–1965; professor of law and senior research scientist, University of Michigan, 1966–2006 (emeritus); and scholar, University of Detroit Mercy Law School, 2007–present.

Michał Araszkiewicz works in the Department of Legal Theory at Jagiellonian University in Kraków (Poland). He has published extensively in the fields of legal argumentation, legal logic and AI and law and has co-edited two volumes in Springer's Law and Philosophy Library Series: Coherence: Insights from Philosophy, Jurisprudence and Artificial Intelligence (2013) and Problems of Normativity, Rules and Rule-Following (2014). He is a member of the International Association for Artificial Intelligence and Law and is also admitted to legal practice in Poland where he specialises in intellectual property law.

Nitin B. Bilgi is professor and head of the Department of Computer Science and Engineering at Maratha Mandal Engineering College, Belgaum, Karnataka state (www.mmec.edu.in), affiliated to VTU Belgaum (www.vtu.ac.in). He previously worked at the Gogte Institute of Technology, Belgaum (www.git.edu), India, for

27 years. He completed his PhD at Graphic Era University Dehradun (www.geu.ac.in). His current research interests include knowledge-based systems. He has (co-) authored six international journal papers and two national journal papers, attended more than ten conferences and presented papers at three national and two international conferences.

Wojciech Cyrul is currently an adjunct professor at the Jagiellonian University in Kraków, member of the Management Board of the European Association for Teaching Legal Theory and a member of the European Academy of Legal Theory. He has authored several articles and books about the influence of ICT and IT on law and legal practice. His research interests include legal informatics, theory and philosophy of law, ICT law and theory of legislation.

Vytautas Čyras is associate professor of computer science at Vilnius University. He graduated from Vilnius University in 1979, and in 1985 he obtained a PhD degree (candidate of physico-mathematical sciences) in computing from Lomonosov Moscow State University. In 2007, he obtained a master of laws from Vilnius University. His research interests include computer science, law and legal informatics.

Giovanni Damele is a full member of the Nova Institute of Philosophy (Universidade Nova de Lisboa). His main fields of academic interest include philosophy of law, political philosophy, argumentation theory and rhetoric. His recent publications include the papers "Rhetoric and Persuasive Strategies in High Courts' Decisions" (2011), "Legal Certainty in Europe. Legal Pluralism and Argumentative Practices of the ECJ" (2013) and "Analogia Legis and Analogia Iuris: An Overview from a Rhetorical Perspective (2014)".

Enrico Francesconi holds a master's degree in electronic engineering and a PhD in computer science from the University of Florence. He is a researcher at ITTIG–CNR, the Legal Information Institute of the National Research Council of Italy. His main activities include semantic web technologies for the legal domain, ontologies and knowledge representation, legal drafting, AI techniques for legal document classification and knowledge extraction. He is a member of the Italian and European working groups defining XML and URI standards for legal documents. He has been involved in various projects of the European Commission framework programmes, the European Parliament and the Publications Office of the European Commission. He is professor of information retrieval and semantic web technologies in the Faculty of Computer Science at the University of Florence. He is currently a temporary agent of the European Commission (DG Publications Office).

Guido Governatori is a senior principal researcher and research leader of the Software Systems Research Group and NICTA, Australia, where he leads the research activities on business process compliance. He received his PhD in legal informatics in 1997 from CIRSFID, University of Bologna. Guido's research interests are on nonclassical logics, in particular, non-monotonic logic, defeasible logic, modal and deontic logic and their applications to legal and normative reasoning, autonomous agents and business process management. He is one of the editors of the deontic logic corner of the Journal of Logic and Computation and the editor of the Agents and Law section of the Journal of Artificial Intelligence and Law. He has over 250 publications in scholarly journals and international conferences.

Andrzej Grabowski is an assistant professor in the Department of Legal Theory at the Jagiellonian University in Krakow (Poland). His scientific interests include the theory of legal argumentation, the relationship of law and morality, the postpositivist theory of law and the issues of legal validity. He has published Judicial Argumentation and Pragmatics (Księgarnia Akademicka 1999) and Juristic Concept of the Validity of Statutory Law (Springer 2013).

Jaap Hage studied both law and philosophy at Leiden University. At present, he holds the chair in jurisprudence at Maastricht University. His main scientific publications include the books Reasoning with Rules (1997) and Studies in Legal Logic (2005). His recent research focuses on basic legal concepts and on the philosophy of legal science.

Jakub Harašta is an assistant lecturer and PhD candidate at the Institute of Law and Technology, Masaryk University in Brno, Czech Republic. The main focus of his dissertation is the principle of technological neutrality in cyber security with related issues of legal theory. He is also deputy editor of Masaryk University's Journal of Law and Technology.

Linda D. Jellum is the Ellison Capers Palmer Sr. Professor of Law at Mercer University Law School. She teaches administrative law, statutory interpretation, federal income taxation and property. Professor Jellum is a prolific scholar and has written numerous articles in the areas of administrative law and statutory interpretation. In addition, she has authored two books on statutory interpretation: Mastering Statutory Interpretation (Carolina Academic Press) (2nd ed. 2013) and Modern Statutory Interpretation: Problems, Theories, And Lawyering Strategies (co-authored) (Carolina Academic Press) (2nd ed. 2009). Her articles can be found at http://ssrn.com/author=624243.

Urszula Kosielińska–Grabowska is an assistant professor in the Institute of Political Sciences at the Pedagogical University in Kraków, with a PhD from the Jagiellonian University in Kraków (2011). Her areas of research include theory of legislation, issues of legal certainty and neuroscience. She is the author of many scientific works on analytical legal theory, legal axiology and the theory of legislation.

Friedrich Lachmayer obtained a doctor Iuris from the University of Vienna in 1966. From 1967 to 1970, he worked at the Austrian Federal Law Office

(Finanzprokuratur), followed by a lengthy service at the Austrian Federal Chancellery, Constitution Service (1970–2003). In 1988, he obtained a habilitation degree at the University of Innsbruck (legal theory and theory of legislation). From 1989 to 2003, he was head of the Austrian Legal Information System (www.ris.bka.gv.at). His research interests include legal theory, legislation, legal informatics and legal semiotics.

Lars Lindahl has a background in both philosophy and law and is professor emeritus of jurisprudence in the Faculty of Law at Lund University, Sweden. His main field of research is law and logic, exemplified by normative positions (the Kanger–Lindahl theory), the logical representation of normative systems with intermediate concepts such as "ownership" (the theory of joining systems), the fine structure of conflicts of norms, the concept of legal power and the logical interrelationship between importance and value.

Bernadette C. Lopez is a law clerk at the Minnesota Court of Appeals for the 2015–2016 term. She was a member of Hofstra Law's research laboratory for Law, Logic and Technology (LLT Lab) from 2012 to 2014, where she was a senior researcher and the Lab's coordinator for the Vaccine/Injury Project. She graduated from Duke University with a bachelor of science in biology. Prior to law school, Bernadette worked as an elementary and middle school educator, specialising in teaching English as a second language, physical science and mathematics. At Hofstra Law, Bernadette was president of Hofstra Law First Generation Law Students, co-founder and vice president of the Labor & Employment Law Society, a senior staff editor at the Family Court Review and a legal intern at the Youth Advocacy Clinic.

Leon J. Lysaght, Jr. received a BA from Whitman College and a JD from the University of Chicago Law School. Now retired, he has taught law or philosophy at five universities in three countries on two continents.

Fabrizio Macagno (PhD in linguistics, UCSC, Milan, 2003) works as a researcher and auxiliary professor at the Universidade Nova de Lisboa. His current research is focused on the persuasive use of emotive language and on the dialectical dimension of discourse implicitness, applied to the fields of education and law and to political speeches. He is author of several papers on definition, informal fallacies, argumentation schemes and dialogue theory, published in major international peer-reviewed journals that include the Journal of Pragmatics, Science and Education, Argumentation, Philosophy and Rhetoric, Informal Logic and Journal of Pragmatics and Cognition. His most important publications include the books Argumentation Schemes (CUP 2008) and Emotive Language in Argumentation (CUP 2014).

Juliano S.A. Maranhão is a Donald Berman award winner (International Association of Artificial Intelligence and Law) and has been a visiting researcher at the Universities of Miami, Leipzig and Maastricht and a visiting scholar at Utrecht

University, conducting studies on artificial intelligence and law. At present, he is assistant professor in the Department of Philosophy and General Theory of Law at the University of São Paulo Law School.

Pablo E. Navarro is a professor of philosophy of law at the National University of the South and Blas Pascal University (Argentina). He is also a researcher for the National Council for Research in Science and Technology (CONICET). Navarro has published several books and has written papers on legal theory and deontic logic for journals such as Law and Philosophy, Ratio Juris, Rechtstheorie and Theoria. He has been a visiting professor at many European and Latin American universities. He obtained a Guggenheim Fellowship (2001–2002), was recognised by the Konex Foundation (2006) in the discipline of legal philosophy and has been a recipient of the Bernardo Houssay Prize (2003).

Tomasz Pełech–Pilichowski received his PhD degree in computer science from AGH University of Science and Technology, Kraków., Poland He is an assistant professor in the Department of Applied Computer Science (AGH UST, Faculty of Management). His research focuses on artificial immune systems, signal processing, event detection, similarity analysis, legal text processing, time series prediction, qualitative data processing and business intelligence. He is a member of the Board of the Polish Information Processing Society.

Krzysztof Płeszka is a professor of law in the Department of Legal Theory at Jagiellonian University in Kraków (Poland). His areas of research interest include the problems of legal systems (Hierarchy in a Legal System, 1989) and theory of legal interpretation and argumentation (The Justification of Court Decisions by their Consequences, 1996; Extensive Interpretation, 2010). He is author of numerous papers in Polish, German and English, published in monographs and journals. His current research is focused on alternative dispute resolution and theory of legislation.

Henry Prakken is a full professor of legal informatics and legal argumentation at the Faculty of Law, University of Groningen, and a lecturer in artificial intelligence at the Department of Information and Computing Sciences, Utrecht University. He holds master's degrees in law (1985) and philosophy (1988) from the University of Groningen and a PhD degree (1993, cum laude) from the Free University Amsterdam with a thesis entitled "Logical Tools for Modelling Legal Argument". Prakken's main research interests concern logical and computational models of argumentation and their application to legal reasoning, multi-agent systems, e-democracy and other domains.

Giovanni Battista Ratti is associate professor in legal philosophy in the Department of Law at the University of Genoa (Italy). He has been a Government of Canada Research Scholar (University of Toronto, 2004–2005), Government of Spain "Juan de la Cierva" Fellow in Law (University of Girona, 2008–2011), visiting professor at the Universities of Girona (Spain, 2006–2008), Pompeu Fabra (Spain, 2008–2009) and Nacional de Mar del Plata (Argentina, 2011), visiting scholar at the Law School of the University of Virginia (USA, 2015). His books include El gobierno de las normas, Madrid, 2013; Diritto, indeterminatezza, indecidibilità, Madrid, 2012, The Logic of Legal Requirements, Oxford, 2012 (with Jordi Ferrer Beltrán); Norme, principi e logica, Rome, 2009; and Sistema giuridico e sistemazione del diritto, Turin, 2008.

David Reidhav is an associate professor at the Faculty of Law, Lund University. His doctoral dissertation was on analogy-based arguments in law. His current research areas include conflicts of legal norms, the analysis of legal power and legal argumentation. He teaches inter alia philosophy of law, legal argumentation and law and economics at the University of Lund.

Jorge L. Rodríguez is professor of legal theory at the National University of Mar del Plata (Argentina) School of Law and a visiting researcher in the Department of Law at the University of Girona (Spain). He has published several books and articles in Argentina, Brazil, Canada, Colombia, Germany, Italy, Mexico, the Netherlands, UK, Spain, Uruguay and the USA on legal theory and deontic logic. Rodríguez was awarded the Young Scholar Prize by the International Association for Philosophy of Law and Social Philosophy (1999) and was recognised by the Konex Foundation (2006) in the discipline of legal philosophy. He has served as a criminal judge in Mar del Plata since 2009.

Antonino Rotolo is professor and currently deputy head of the UNIBO Department of Legal Studies. He is a board member of CIRSFID, where he conducts international research studies on legal informatics, knowledge representation in the legal domain, normative systems and game theory and normative multi-agent systems. He has written extensively on logics for artificial intelligence, artificial intelligence and law and deontic logic.

Addi Rull has worked as a lecturer at Tallinn Law School, Tallinn University of Technology since 2010. He coordinates the master's programme in law and technology and teaches several IP and IT law courses. He is working towards a PhD in informatics, in the field of AI and systematisation of legal norms. Before joining law school, Addi worked in the business sector and completed LLM degrees in European intellectual property law and law and IT from Stockholm University.

Matthew T. Rutchik is an investigator at the US Department of Labor's Employee Benefit Security Administration, where he helps to enforce the fiduciary duties of ERISA Title I through investigations of employee benefit plans and service providers. He is also an adjunct member of the New York City Bar Association's Employee Benefits and Executive Compensation Committee. He holds a JD from Hofstra University School of Law, an MA in literature from the University of Toronto and a BA in humanities from the University of Toronto.

Anni Säär has worked as a legal expert at the Estonian Human Rights Centre since 2011, representing Estonia on the EU Civil Society Platform against Trafficking in Human Beings. She is pursuing a master of arts in law and technology at Tallinn University of Technology, where she has been teaching a course on rights, obligations and liability of users on the Internet. Anni is involved in research on AI and the systematisation of legal norms.

Burkhard Schäfer is professor of computational legal theory and director of the SCRIPT Centre for IT and IP at the University of Edinburgh, where he has conducted research at the interface between law and new technologies since 1996. He is also a member of the RCUK-funded CREATE Network on Copyright and Creative Industries. With a background in logic, theory of science and computer linguistics, his main interest is in how law interacts with other fields of knowledge–how law, understood as a system, can communicate with systems external to it: the law of other countries (comparative law and its methodology) or science (evidence, proof and trial process).

Jaromír Šavelka is a graduate research student at the Intelligent Systems Program, University of Pittsburgh. His research focuses on the interdisciplinary area of artificial intelligence and law. Specifically, he is interested in applications of statistical machine learning (ML) and natural language processing (NLP) techniques to legal knowledge and information systems. Additionally, he is interested in selected areas of legal theory and legal philosophy. He has published regularly on various topics in AI and law and has participated in conferences that include JURIX and ICAIL. He has also helped to organise conferences such as Cyberspace and Argumentation, which are both held annually at the School of Law, Masaryk University in Brno, Czech Republic.

Ermo Täks, PhD, has worked since 2002 at the Faculty of Informatics of Tallinn University of Technology, teaching law students in the field of informatics, e-government solutions and automated legal processes. His main research interests originate from his experience in the public sector, deriving mainly from practical tasks as IT development manager at the Estonian State Chancellery where his main responsibility was to create the world's first Information System of Government Sessions. His current academic work further develops this and related knowledge. Ermo Täks defended his doctoral dissertation, entitled "An automated legal content capture and visualisation method", in 2013.

Vern R. Walker is professor of law at the Maurice A. Deane School of Law at Hofstra University (http://people.hofstra.edu/vern_r_walker/) and director of the school's research laboratory for Law, Logic and Technology (LLT Lab) (http://lltlab.org/). He received his PhD in philosophy from the University of Notre Dame, concentrating on knowledge theory, logic and artificial intelligence. After receiving his JD from Yale Law School, he practised law in Washington, D.C., specialising in scientific and medical expert evidence, administrative law and products liability litigation. He has taught law at Hofstra for over 25 years, particularly in the areas of scientific evidence, logic skills for legal reasoning and torts. He is a member of the Association for the Advancement of Artificial Intelligence and of the International Association for Artificial Intelligence and Law and has published and presented extensively on legal reasoning, legal technology and law.

Adam Wyner completed a PhD in linguistics (Cornell University, 1994) on the formal syntax and semantics of adverbial modification and subsequently lectured on a range of topics in linguistics at Bar Ilan University, Israel (1995–2001). Sensing the winds of change in linguistics and computational linguistics, he took up an opportunity to write a second PhD thesis in computer science (King's College London, 2008) on the representation of deontic concepts in legal contracts. He has been a research associate at the University of Liverpool, where the work focused on argumentation, case-based reasoning and policy-making. He currently is a lecturer in computing science at the University of Aberdeen. His research interests focus on the analysis of language found in argumentation and legal texts (legislation and cases), using tools from computational linguistics and text analytics.

Part I
From the Theory...

Chapter 1
The (Onto)logical Structure of Law: A Conceptual Toolkit for Legislators

Jaap Hage

Abstract The work of a legislator is to contribute to the set of rules that gives structure to the "world of law". This world of law consists of all the facts, rules and other entities that exist through the application of legal rules. Logic may well be interpreted as a theory of the (logically) necessary relations between facts in the world. This article combines these two ways of looking at legislation and logic. It analyses a number of central legal notions such as right, duty, obligation, power and competence in order to provide insight into the structure of the world of law. The relevance of this insight for legislators is illustrated by means of an example about the transfer of a piece of land, which shows how facts in the world of law are glued together by different kind of rules. It is also illustrated at the hand of the question how law can affect the "outside world" and how legislators can contribute to this impact by providing proper "pathways through the world of law".

Keywords Competence • Direction of fit • Duty • Norm • Obligation • Pathway through the world of law • Right • Rule

1.1 Introduction

The link between logic and legislation is not the most obvious one. Logic provides a standard for the validity of arguments. And although legislators have to argue like other persons that perform intellectual jobs, there is no reason why the position of legislators is in this respect different from that of other mind workers. Yet, logic is

This article is based upon, systematises, and adds to earlier publications of the author, in particular Hage and Verheij (1999), Brouwer and Hage (2007), and Hage (2005a, 2007, 2011a,b, 2012, 2013a,b, 2014). The author wants to thank Michał Araszkiewicz and Krzysztof Pleszka for valuable comments on a draft version of this article which have led to substantial changes, and hopefully improvements. Of course, the responsibility for remaining errors remains with the author.

J. Hage (✉)
Department Foundations and Methods of Law, Maastricht University, Maastricht, Netherlands
e-mail: jaap.hage@maastrichtuniversity.nl

M. Araszkiewicz, K. Płeszka (eds.), *Logic in the Theory and Practice of Lawmaking*, Legisprudence Library 2, DOI 10.1007/978-3-319-19575-9_1

particularly important for legislators, and to see why this is so we must take two steps. The first step is to adopt a particular perspective on the work of a legislator, the perspective according to which a legislator designs and constructs an abstract entity that will be described as the "world of law". The second step is to replace the interpretation of logic as a tool for the evaluation of arguments by the interpretation of logic as specification of the structure of the world. In case of legislation, the world of which the structure is specified is again the world of law. Both steps will be briefly elaborated.

1.1.1 Building the World of Law

The tasks of a legislator are manifold, because legislation can be used for many different purposes, such as founding an organisation, approving the wedding of an heir to the throne, ascribing sovereignty to the people, and validating the budget of a governmental department. The main use of legislation, however, is the creation of rules, and this use is the focus of the present article. However, even then many perspectives on legislation are possible. The creation of rules is a means to improve society, the outcome of a political process, and also an alternative for case law. Important as these perspectives may be, in this paper yet another perspective is adopted. To make the relevance of logic for legislation clear a rather abstract view of legislation is taken as starting point, namely the view of legislation as a means to (re)build the world of law. The basic idea is that law is a specialized, institutionalized part of social reality, the "world of law", and that legislation is a means to modify this part of social reality. Using terminology that will be explained in Sects. 1.2 and 1.4, the world of law can be defined as the collection of all those facts and things (individuals) that obtain or exist as the result of the application of some legal rule. The specific perspective is that legislation can be compared to building and from this perspective I will sketch the main building blocks that are used in building the world of law.

These building blocks have traditionally been studied from the perspective of the general theory of law. Important studies in this connection are Bentham's *Of Laws in General* (Bentham and Hart 1970), Austin's *The Province of Jurisprudence Determined* (Austin 1954), Hohfeld's *Fundamental Legal Conceptions as Applied in Judicial Reasoning* (Hohfeld 1920), Ross' *Directives and Norms* (Ross 1968), Kelsen's *Reine Rechtslehre* (Kelsen 1960), and Hart's *Essays on Bentham* (Hart 1982). Perhaps less known to many lawyers is that much work on Law and Artificial Intelligence and on legal logic (many contributions to the *Artificial Intelligence and Law* journal; Alchourrón and Bulygin 1971; Lindahl 1977; Lindahl and Odelstad 2013; Lodder 1999; Prakken 1997; Prakken and Sartor 1997; Royakkers 1998; Sartor 2005; Von Wright 1963) is also highly relevant from this perspective.

1.1.2 Logic and Ontology

In the logical tradition of the last 150 years, logic has usually been conceived as the study of the validity of arguments.[1] The kind of validity at stake in this connection is deductive validity. An argument is considered deductively valid if and only if it is logically impossible that all the premises of the argument are true, while the argument's conclusion is false. A characteristic of this definition is that it relates the validity of arguments to what is (logically) possible. In this way the theory of what is possible and impossible plays a role in logic and it is quite plausible to reinterpret deductive logic as the study of logically necessary relations between the truth of descriptive sentences. Moreover, since the truth of sentences depends on the facts described by these sentences, logic is also a study of the necessary relations between facts. If it is a fact that all mathematicians are rational and also a fact that Willard is a mathematician, then necessarily it is also a fact that Willard is rational. Deductive logic is as much the study of such necessary relations between facts as a study of the validity of arguments.

In this article the relevance of logic for legislators will be shown by interpreting logic as the study of the necessary relations between facts, and in the present connection particularly the necessary relations between facts in the world of law. These necessary relations are in a sense the framework that must be stuffed by means of legislation. A thorough understanding of this framework is crucial for every competent legislator.

1.1.3 Overview of the Article

Basically, this article contain a study of the logical relations between a number of the most basic concepts of law, such as the concept of rule, norm, duty, obligation, ought, and competence. The foundations of the argument of this article will be laid in Sect. 1.2, which deals with language and its relation to facts and things (individuals). Section 1.3 continues that discussion by paying attention to the two directions of fit between on the one hand linguistic or language–dependent entities like sentences and rules and on the other hand the facts. These directions are the word–to–world direction of fit and the world–to–word direction of fit. Then the emphasis moves towards the content of the world, with discussions of three kinds of facts (Sect. 1.4), three kinds of legal rules (Sect. 1.5), facts and events in the world of law (Sect. 1.6), deontic facts and norms (Sect. 1.7), and rules and regulations (Sect. 1.8). After these sections, the reader should have an impression of the framework that supports the world of law. The relevance of this framework will be illustrated in Sects. 1.9–1.11, which deal in some more detail with respectively

[1] Anybody familiar with the mainstream literature about logic will recognise this characterisation. And yet, when I tried to find references to support this claim, I found many different circumscriptions of the nature of logic.

the kinds of relations between facts in and outside the world of law, the structure of the world of law, and the interface between the world of law and the "outside world". The article is concluded in Sect. 1.12, which points to the relevance of pathways through the world of law for proper legislation.

1.2 Language, Facts, and Individuals

As a starting point we can define the world as everything that exists. Part of this world is the "world of law", the collection of everything that is based on legal rules. The only way to say something about the world, including the world of law, and about the facts and things that are in the world is by means of language. That is why the language that is used to describe the world strongly influences the kinds of entities that we recognise. Therefore, the discussion of the kinds of entities that exist, facts and things, starts with language.[2]

1.2.1 Sentences

For our present purposes the main distinction between linguistic entities is between descriptive sentences and terms. Properly speaking it is not sentences that are descriptive, but the uses of sentences. Sentences can be used for many different kinds of speech acts, including ordering, praising, asking, praying and describing (Austin 1954; Searle 1969). For the present purposes, the speech act of describing is the most important one, and in the following discussion sentences are assumed to be used for descriptive purposes. Sentences are the bearers of truth values; they are either true or false. Examples of sentences, including some that are potentially controversial, are:

(a) Jane is running.
(b) Hohfeld is the owner of Blackacre.
(c) It is forbidden to steal.
(d) This is a beautiful landscape.

1.2.2 Facts and States of Affairs

As Strawson (1950) has pointed out, facts depend on language. A fact is always the fact that ..., where the dots stand for a phrase expressed in some language. It

[2]This article is written in English, and much literature on jurisprudence has been written in English or another Indo–European language. As a consequence, the ontological presuppositions of Indo–European languages may have exerted a considerable influence on jurisprudence in general and the following discussion in particular. Although this is unavoidable, it is something to keep in mind.

is for instance a fact that "I am in Lanaken". However, facts also depend on the world, because it is the world, not language, which determines the facts that obtain. A language determines which facts can be expressed, the world determines which of the expressible facts actually obtain.

It is useful to distinguish between expressible facts and actual facts. An expressible fact will be called a *state of affairs*. States of affairs are expressed by sentences. For instance, the sentence "It's raining" expresses the state of affairs that it is raining. Which states of affairs there are depends only on the power of the language in which the states of affairs are expressed.

Some states of affairs *obtain* in the actual world; these are called *facts*. A sentence that expresses a fact is *true*. False sentences express *non–facts*, states of affairs that do not obtain. Whereas states of affairs depend on language only, facts depend both on language and the world, and – as we will see in Sect. 1.4 – sometimes also on rules and standards.

1.2.3 Terms and Individuals

Unlike sentences, terms do not have truth values, but they stand for (denote) "things" in the world. Logicians call these "things" that are denoted by terms "individuals". Examples of such individuals are President Poetin (a real individual), Mount Kilimanjaro, the house in which I live, the piece of music to which I am listening, the smallest prime number, a fleeting thought, and the moment at which the sun will rise in the year 3012 A.D.

Terms can have different grammatical shapes. *Proper names* are one such a shape, as in "John walks". Proper names can stand for persons, but also for buildings ("the Empire State Building"), cities ("Paris"), and events ("the Olympic Games").

Definite descriptions, like "the earliest possible opportunity" are a second shape of terms, as in "The form is to be completed at the earliest possible opportunity", which has two terms: "The form" and "the earliest possible opportunity". Definite descriptions are combinations of predicators[3] (in the example "earliest possible") in a construction which makes clear that one or at most a definite number of entities are denoted. Such a construction is often created by using the definite particle ("the"). A special kind of definite description that is particularly important for the present purposes denotes a rule, as in "The rule that cars count as vehicles is valid in the Netherlands".

Function expressions like "the mayor of London" are a third shape of terms. A *function expression* is a term which is defined by means of one or more other

[3]Predicators are expressions which are typically used to say something about one or more individuals. They usually are verbs or contain a verb in combination with predicates and or nouns. Examples of predicators are "bribes" as in "If a person bribes an official... ", and "is defect", as in "If the sold good is defect, the seller must replace it".

terms. "The mayor of London" is defined by means of the term "London" which is itself a proper name. Another example would be "the oldest child of the King and the Queen". In this last example, "the King" and "the Queen" are both (elliptical) function expressions too, denoting the present King and Queen of a particular country. A function expression can be used as a definite description, as is illustrated by the example about the mayor of London.

Characterizations of *action types* are a fourth kind of terms. An example is "to steal" as in "It is forbidden to steal".

Finally, sentence–like phrases such as "Medusa is ugly" can also be terms, namely when they are used to refer to states of affairs, as in "Jason believes that Medusa is ugly". States of affairs are rather peculiar individuals because of their explicit dependence on language. That they are individuals becomes clear from the phenomenon that one state of affairs may be preferred over another. For instance, Henry, who loves to jog, may prefer the state of affairs that it is raining over the state of affairs that the temperature is over 30 °C. Moreover, it is possible to quantify over states of affairs as in "Everything that Jane believed turned out not to be the case".

The terms that are most suitable to denote states of affairs involve the use of the descriptive sentence that expresses the state of affairs. One and the same sentence, for instance the sentence "It's raining", may be used to describe a part of reality, in which case it is true or false, and to refer to an individual namely the state of affairs that it is raining, in which case it singles out that state of affairs to say something about it.

1.2.4 Rules and Factual Counterparts of Rules

Rules resemble states of affairs in the sense that they also depend for their existence on language. Just as a state of affairs is always the state of affairs that ...., where the dots stand for a descriptive sentence in a particular interpretation, a rule is always the rule that ..., where the dots stand for the content of the rule, something that can be expressed in language. An example would be the rule that skate boards count as vehicles for the purpose of traffic rules.

Suppose that there exists a rule to the effect that skate boards count as vehicles in the sense of some traffic regulation. Because this rule exists, skate boards count as vehicles in the sense of this traffic regulation. To state it differently: because the rule exists, it is a fact that skate boards count as vehicles. This fact, that skate boards count as vehicles, is not the same fact as the fact that the rule "Skate boards count as vehicles" exists. The former fact is about skate boards; the latter is about a rule.

Apparently, a rule can lead to facts which can be described by re–using the formulation of the rule content. "Skate boards count as vehicles" is both a descriptive sentence that expresses a state of affairs, and expresses the content of a rule. Moreover, the existence of this rule tends to go hand in hand with the state of affairs being a fact. Because it is convenient to have a term which denotes this phenomenon, I propose to use "factual counterpart of a rule". The factual counterpart of a rule is a fact which corresponds to the content of an existing rule and which obtains because of the existence of this rule.[4]

1.3 Directions of Fit

A main, or even – as will be argued in Sect. 1.8.1 – the main, function of rules is to connect facts with each other. A proper understanding of rules requires therefore an initial understanding of the different kinds of facts that exist. However, to complicate the account, a proper understanding of the different kinds of facts requires an initial understanding of rules. To break out of the hermeneutic circle the argument of this article starts with a brief account of different kinds of facts (Sect. 1.4), builds upon that account to give a first account of rules (Sect. 1.5), and then returns to facts (Sects. 1.6 and 1.7.1–1.7.5) and then again to rules (Sects. 1.7.6 and 1.8). However, as a preliminary step it is necessary to pay some attention to the phenomenon that two "directions of fit" can be distinguished in the relation between on the one hand language dependent entities such as sentences, speech acts and rules and on the other hand the world. These directions of fit are the topic of the present section.

The distinction between the word–to–world and the world–to–word direction of fit in its modern form stems from Anscombe (1976, 56) and was made popular by Searle who used it, first to distinguish between kinds of speech acts (Searle 1979b), and later also to explain the phenomenon of constitutive or counts–as rules (Searle 1995, 43–51; 2010, 97).

The basic idea is that descriptive sentences, or rather utterances thereof, consist of words that aim to fit the world. These sentences are true and the speech acts in which they are used are successful in the sense of "true", if and only if the facts in the world "fit", presumably in the sense of "correspond to", what these sentences express. This is the word–to–world direction of fit, because the facts are assumed to be there first, and the sentence (words) are adapted to fit the facts (the world).

For the world–to–word direction of fit we must distinguish between three kinds. For all three kinds holds that somehow the facts in the world are adapted, in order to "fit" what is expressed by the words. One case is when the words function as a *directive*, as for example in "Close the door!". Such an order aims at having somebody close the door, and if the order is successful in the sense of "efficacious", the door will be closed and the facts in the world fit the content of the order: the door is closed. In this case the relation between the utterance of the order (the performance of the speech act) and the facts in the world is causal by nature.

A second case concerns constitutive speech acts, such as "I hereby baptise you the Herald of Free Enterprise". If such an act of baptising is successful, the facts in

---

[4]Often it is not easy to tell a factual counterpart of a rule from the rule itself, but if it is an appropriate reaction to say "That is (not) true" then what was said should be interpreted as the expression of a factual counterpart, and otherwise not.

the world come to match the content of the speech act and the ship bears the name "Herald of Free Enterprise". In this case the relation between the *performance* of the speech act and the facts in the world is rule–based by nature (see Sect. 1.4). The third case concerns the effects of rules. If a rule exists, it affects the facts in the world. Take for instance the rule that mayors are competent to issue emergency regulations. If this rule exists, it makes the mayor of Sun City competent to issue emergency regulations. This world–to–word direction of fit will be discussed in more detail in Sect. 1.8.1. For the present purposes if suffices to note that some facts, as in this example the fact that the mayor of Sun City is competent to issue emergency regulations, obtain as the result of the application of a rule.

1.4 Kinds of Facts

When it comes to facts, we often take some form of ontological realism for granted. We assume that facts exist independent of what we believe about them or whether we accept them as being facts. This may be a good approach for facts such as that the Pacific Ocean is mostly filled with water, but for many facts this is not adequate. Think for instance of the facts that the United Nations have their seat in New York city, and that tortfeasors are liable to pay damages.

In this connection it is useful to distinguish between three kinds of facts.[5] This usefulness reflects the phenomenon that we tend to distinguish between different ways in which something can be a fact. This tendency is reflected in natural language, which allows constructions like "It is a fact that Brussels is the capital of Belgium", "It is a fact that Clarence chairs this meeting", "It is a fact that John has the obligation to pay damages to Charlotte", and perhaps even "It is a fact that chocolate tastes better than spinach". However, the possibility to distinguish between categories of facts does not commit to the view that all of these categories have members.

The first category consists of facts of which it is assumed that they are mind–independent. These facts exist, if they exist, no matter whether anybody is aware of them, knows what they are, or believes in their existence. They include – at least, that is what most people assume – that the highest mountain on Earth is Mount Everest, that computers were invented after 1700 AD, that there are Higgs particles and that the amount of solar systems in the universe equals some as yet unknown number. We will call them *objective facts*. Notice that the issue whether a particular fact belongs to the type "objective facts" may be disputed. Somebody may be sceptical about the "objective" existence of particles the existence of which can only be inferred from

[5]This distinction was inspired by a distinction made by Leiter (2002, 969–989), between different kinds of objectivity.

other facts, and then it is questionable whether the existence of the Higgs particle would count as an objective fact for this person.[6]

The second category consists of facts that derive their existence from being recognised as facts. These *recognition–based facts* exist because they are recognised or accepted as facts by sufficiently many and sufficiently relevant members of some social group. The precise conditions of existence of these facts are still object of discussion,[7] but typical examples from Belgium are that sunny weather is good weather, that there is nothing wrong with gay marriages, and that legislation is a source of law. The existence of facts in social reality depends on what the members of a social group believe or accept to be the case, but they do not depend on the beliefs or acceptance of single persons. For example, the seat of the United Nations is New York city, whether some particular person believes it or not. However, if nobody believes this anymore, New York city has stopped being the seat of the UN.

The third category consists of facts the existence of which is attached by rules or standards to the existence of other facts, or to the occurrence of events. Examples of such *rule–based* facts are that in chess the person who has check–mated his opponent's king has won the game, that nobody can chair the hockey club for more than two subsequent periods, that $3 + 5$ equals 8, that in the EU, states are in general not allowed to subsidize local industries, and that a car that enables the driver to drive more than 500 miles without becoming tired is a good car. All facts in the world of law are by definition rule–based facts. More in particular they are based on *legal* rules.[8]

Seemingly there is a fourth category of facts, exemplified by the "facts" that chocolate tastes better than spinach and that Peter Green is a better blues guitarist than Joe Bonamassa. However, many people consider "facts" like these to be mere expressions of personal preference or taste, and for that reason not as "real" facts. For the present purposes, this fourth category will be ignored.

1.5 Three Kinds of Legal Rules

This section discusses three kinds of legal of legal rules: counts–as rules (Sect. 1.5.1), fact–to–fact rules (Sect. 1.5.2), and dynamic rules (Sect. 1.5.3). It is neither claimed that these three kinds exhaust the space of legal rules, nor that rules that belong to one of these kinds are always legal rules. As a matter of fact a fourth kind, how–to rules, will be briefly mentioned in the discussion of counts–as

[6] Even more fundamentally, one may wonder whether adoption of the view that the world as set of all facts is language–dependent does not commit to the view that there are no objective facts at all. In the present article, that line of thought will not be explored any further.

[7] See for instance Searle (2010) and Tuomela (2010).

[8] Arguably, also acts based on legal values, legal standards, or legal principles belong to the world of law. This is a line of thought that will not be explored here, however.

rules. However, the possibility to distinguish between counts–as, fact–to–fact, and dynamic rules already increases our insight into the world of law considerably.

1.5.1 Counts–as Rules

Counts–as rules as they are used in law make that some kinds of individuals, including events, legally also count as individuals of some other kind.[9] For instance, under suitable circumstances, the delivery of a good counts as the transfer of the ownership of this good, or a vote in parliament may count as the adoption of a Bill. Typically, the operation of a counts–as rule makes that one and the same "individual" has two or more different statuses. Something is not only a vote, but also the adoption of a Bill; not only a delivery, but also a transfer.

Sometimes several individuals together count as one new individual. Moreover, counts–as rules can be applied in a chain, building one status on top of another. For instance, the individual votes of the members of parliament together count as a vote in parliament; this vote of parliament also counts as the adoption of a Bill, and the adoption of the Bill counts as the creation of legal rules.

An important function of counts–as rules is to include individuals into the world of law. In Sect. 1.10 we will consider an example about the transfer of a piece of land that includes the transformation of signing a piece of paper into engaging into a sales contract, and the transformation of an event at a notarial office into the delivery of the land to the new owner. The former events do not belong to the world of law, since they are not based on a legal rule; the latter events do.

Often it is necessary to follow a particular procedure to make one thing count as something else. A parliamentary vote is a case in point; drafting a sales contract for a house is another example. These procedures are specified by means of *how–to rules*, and only if these how–to rules are complied with the execution of the procedure counts as something else, for instance as adopting a Bill, or as engaging into a contract, or as undertaking contractual obligations.[10]

---

[9]Counts–as rules can also bring about that some facts count as other facts, but most of the times this is derivative from some kinds of individuals also counting as individuals of another kind. For instance the fact that a book was delivered counts as the fact that the ownership of the book was transferred, because the delivery counts as a transfer. This theme is explored a little more in Hage (2005d).

[10]The relation between how–to rules and counts–as rules is the same as that between respectively rules of change and rules of recognition in Hart's theory of Law ((Hart 2012, 94–96),). As a matter of fact, rules of change are a kind of how–to rules, while rules of recognition are a kind of counts–as rules.

1.5.2 Fact–to–Fact Rules

Fact–to–fact rules make that one kind of fact tends to go together with some other kind of fact, where the latter fact depends on the former. The relation between the kinds of facts is timeless, in the negative sense that the one kind of fact is not the occurrence of an event after which the second kind of fact comes into existence.[11]

Typical legal examples of fact–to–fact rules are the rules that

- the owner of a good is allowed to use this good;
- the mayor of a municipality has the competence to issue emergency regulations for that municipality;
- house owners must keep the pavement before their houses clean;
- the king of Belgium is the commander in chief of the Belgian army.[12]

Characteristically, all the example rules attach legal consequences to the possession of a certain legal status. Important legal examples of fact–to–fact rules are rules that impose legal duties and rules that confer competences on people with a particular status. We will return to this point in Sect. 1.11.3.

1.5.3 Dynamic Rules

Dynamic legal rules determine, in combination with the events that take place, how the world of law develops in time. They attach new facts, or modify or take away existing facts, as the consequence of an event. Examples of events to which a dynamic rule attaches consequences are that:

(a) Jane formally promised Gerald to give him €500, which makes that Jane incurred the obligation towards Gerald to pay him €500;
(b) Eloise was appointed as chair of the French parliament, which makes that from the new term on, Eloise chairs the French parliament;
(c) a creditor informed his debtor that the latter will not have to repay the money before next year, which makes that the debtor only has to repay his debt next year;
(d) the legislator derogated a legal rule, which makes that the derogated rule is not valid law anymore.

Important kinds of dynamic rules are the rules that lead to obligations (see Sect. 1.7.3) and the rules that make it possible to modify the law by means of legislation (see Sect. 1.8.3).

---

[11]Notice that this timeless relation between the conditions and the consequences of a fact–to–fact rule is compatible with the existence in time of the rule. Only as long as the rule exists, the condition facts and the conclusion facts go together in a timeless fashion.

[12]This last rule may also be interpreted as a counts–as rule.

In opposition to dynamic rules, counts–as rules and fact–to–fact rules might be classified as static rules. This opposition between static and dynamic rules corresponds to respectively the *Rechtsstatik* and the *Rechtsdynamik* as described by Kelsen (1960, Ch. IV and V).

1.6 Facts and Events in the World of Law

The three mentioned kinds of rules fulfil an important role in connecting the facts in the world of law, both statically (counts–as and fact–to–fact rules) and dynamically. To obtain a better picture of how these rules fulfil their functions it is useful to take a closer look at some facts and events as they obtain, respectively take place, in the world of law.[13]

If somebody acted unlawfully and thereby caused damage to somebody else in a legally protected interest, the tortfeasor incurs the liability to compensate the damage. This connection between the damage causing event and the resulting liability is brought about by a dynamic legal rule. Before the event there was no liability, and after the event the tortfeasor has become liable. A new fact in the world of law, the fact that the tortfeasor is under an obligation to compensate the damage, has come about.

Dynamic rules can be used by agents to bring about legal consequences. For example, a person may migrate from one municipality to another municipality to pay less real estate tax. Some dynamic legal rules are especially meant to empower agents to intentionally bring about legal consequences. In private law there are rules that make it possible for fathers to legally recognize children born outside a marriage, and rules that empower agents to create legal obligations through contracting.

A particularly interesting case of rules that empower agents to bring about intentional changes in the world of law are the rules to govern legislation and that make it possible to create, modify or abrogate legal rules by means of it. Legislation is governed by how–to rules that specify how to create law by means of legislation and what counts as a valid statute or by–law, and by dynamic rules that attach changes in the set of valid legal rules to a valid legislative event. (See also Sect. 1.8.3.)

Contracts, the recognition of children and legislation are all examples of "juridical acts", acts to which the law by means of dynamic rules attaches legal consequences for the reasons that the agents intended to bring about these legal effects through their juridical acts (Hage 2011a,b). In order to bring about particular legal consequences by means of a juridical act, the agent must have the competence to do so. This competence is a legal status, assigned by a fact–to–fact rule.

[13]This section runs ahead of a more extensive discussion in Sects. 1.9 and 1.10.

Legal duties and competences are attached to the possession of a particular legal status. The minimal status to which these can be connected is the status of legal subject. This status tends to be assigned by law to human beings – "natural persons" – and also to some organisations which are then called "legal persons".

The possession of a legal status may be the result of an event and then it is attached to this event by a dynamic rule. An example is the status of mother of a child, which is assigned to a woman as the consequence of giving birth to this child (or some earlier event). Another example is the status of president of a state which is the result of being appointed as president.

Legal status can not only pertain to persons but also to things. For example, The city of The Hague has the status of being the seat of the International Court of Justice.

Legal status is often attached to another legal status by means of a fact–to–fact rule or a counts–as rule. We have already seen the examples of a delivery that counts as a transfer, and the king of Belgium who is also the commander in chief of the Belgian army. The possession of a right is perhaps the most prominent example of a legal status to which other statuses are attached by means of fact–to–fact rules. For example, the right of ownership brings with it the competence to alienate the owned good, and also the permission to use this good. Arguably the function of many rights is to be a stepping stone for attaching other legal statuses (Ross 1957). See also Sect. 1.11.3.

1.7 Deontic Facts and Norms

Arguably, the ultimate function of law is to guide human behaviour (Fuller 1963, 46). Law uses different techniques to perform this function, but possibly the most important amongst these techniques is to prescribe behaviour and to attach sanctions to non–compliance. Therefore duties, obligations and the legal ought that follows from duties and obligations, as well as the norms by means of which law creates duties and obligations deserve special attention.

1.7.1 Preliminaries

Before going into details concerning obligations and duties, two preliminaries must first be dealt with. The first one is terminological. Law uses different ways to prescribe behaviour, and these different ways will be discussed in some detail in the following subsections. To that purpose a terminological distinction will be made between duties, obligations, what is legally obligated and what legally ought to be done. Although the ways these notions are distinguished has *some* basis in actual English usage, it must be conceded on beforehand that this basis is weak. The words "duty", "obligation", obligated", and "ought" are often used interchangeably. When the present article makes terminological distinctions, these distinctions are therefore to a large extent stipulative where the word use is concerned. Nevertheless it is claimed that the different words denote real differences.

The second preliminary concerns the possibility of deontic facts. Many academics have been raised with the fundamental distinction, if not the gap, between is and ought. And it is true that for instance the fact that people do not lie is different from the fact that people ought not lie. However, as this example already indicates, the gap between is and ought does not preclude us from speaking of the fact that people ought not lie. Of course, it is possible that argue that this "fact" is not a real fact, and that the sentence is merely a means to emphasize that people ought not lie. However, it is also possible to take the opposite view and to admit that it can be a fact that people ought not lie. This fact would most likely not be an objective fact, but rather a rule–based fact, but rule–based facts are arguably also facts. In the present article this opposite view is adopted, and it is assumed that there can be rule–based deontic facts, which include the presence of legal duties and obligations, and the facts that, for example, somebody is legally obligated or legally ought to compensate somebody else's damage.[14]

1.7.2 Duties

Mandatory rules create either duties or obligations, and in that way obligate people to act in a particular way. Duties and obligations are not the same things.

1.7.2.1 What Is a Duty?

A *duty* to do something is what one is obligated to do as a consequence of a particular status, position or role (White 1984, 21–26). It is for instance, the duty of a judge to apply the law, and the duty of a house–inhabitant to clear away the snow from the pavement before the house. The most general duty is a duty that holds for "everyone"; this duty (as are many other duties) is connected to the role of being human. A duty can also be a duty to refrain from doing something, such as the duty not to disturb the peace in church. These duties are also connected to roles and positions, as in the duty for all traffic participants not to create dangerous situations.

Apart from duties to do something or to refrain from doing something, there can also be duties to do things in a particular way, or to refrain from doing things in a particular way. Let us call them "how–to–duties". How–to–duties are also connected to roles or positions. Examples are the duty to drive on the right hand side of the road, which holds for all drivers, and the duty not to score exams too strictly. Notice that these latter duties are compatible with permissions not to drive, respectively the

[14]For more extensive arguments why there can be deontic facts, see Hage 2013a and Draft.

duty to score exams. It is for example permitted not to drive a car, but also a duty to drive cars on the right hand side of the road.

1.7.2.2 The Elements of a Duty

A duty contains three elements:

1. the addressee(s) of the duty;
2. the modality of the duty;
3. the object of the duty.

The addressee of a duty may be:

(i) one or more specific agents (e.g. John, or Mary and Harold);
(ii) all agents that belong to a particular category (e.g. car drivers, or – more specific– left handed burglars who were born on a Sunday);
(iii) everybody (as in "everybody must love his neighbour").

The modality of the duty is either that something is obligated or that something is forbidden. If the modality is that something is forbidden, the duty is also called a prohibition.

The object of the duty is:

(a) either the action type to which the duty commits,[15]
(b) or the mode of performance on an action type.

The modality combines with the action type or action mode that is obligated, respectively forbidden, which leads to four possible combinations:

1. the performance of some action type is obligatory ("pay taxes", "tell the truth" or "pay Gerald €100");
2. the obligatory nature of performing some action in a particular way ("drive on the right");
3. refraining from some type of action is obligatory ("do not steal"); or
4. the obligatory nature of refraining from doing something in a particular way ("do not score exams malevolently") (Fig. 1.1).

1.7.2.3 Duty/3 and Duty/4

The structure of duties can also be made explicit by linguistic means. To this purpose we will introduce the predicators Duty/3 and Duty/4.[16] The former is used for duties

[15]This action type may be the realisation of some state of affairs, as in "killing", or "closing the door". It may also be attempting to realise a state of affairs as in "promoting optimal health care".

[16]The 3 and the 4 stand for the number of parameters of the predicator Duty.

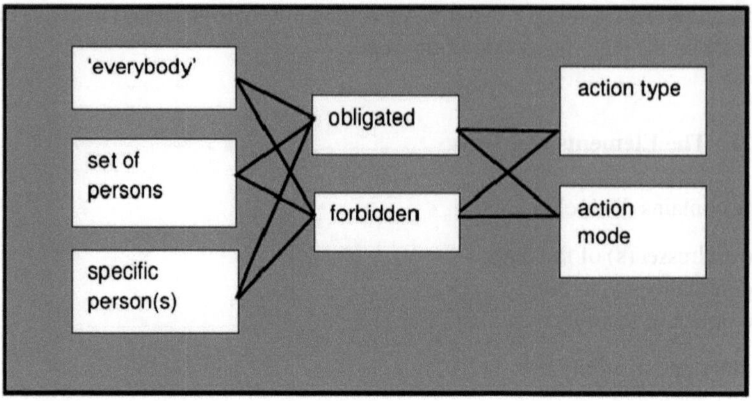

Fig. 1.1 The structure of duties

to perform some kind of action or to refrain from doing so; the latter for duties to perform some kind of action in a particular way, or to refrain from doing so.

The predicator Duty/3 goes with parameters for the addressee(s) of the duty, for the duty modality (perform or refrain), and for the action type that should be performed or refrained from. The following three sentences express that respectively that John has the duty not to murder SuzyQ, that car drivers have the duty to carry a driver's license, and that everybody has the duty not to lie[17]:

- Duty(john, refrain, murder(SuzyQ));
- (x)Car_driver(x) ⊃ Duty(x, perform, carry_driver's_license);
- (x)Duty(x, refrain, lying).

The predicator Duty/4 goes with parameters for the addressee(s) of the duty, for the duty modality (perform or refrain), for the action type that should be performed in a particular way or not, and for the way (mode) in which the action type should (not) be performed.

1. The formalisation of the first three parameters is the same as for Duty/3.
2. The action mode is denoted by a term (e.g. "carefully", or "cruelly").[18]

The following example sentences express the presence of a duty to do something (not) in a particular way:

Duty(john, refrain, murder(SuzyQ), cruelly);
(x)Car_driver(x) ⊃ Duty(x, perform, drive, on_the_right).

[17]The operator ⊃ stands for the material conditional.

[18]As Michał Araszkiewicz pointed out to me, there may be a series of modes, as in murdering somebody particularly cruelly. As we will see later, there are reasons to treat conditional duties as duties with a modification of the action type.

1.7.2.4 Duties for Conditional Action

Some duties need only be complied with if certain conditions are fulfilled. An example is the duty for car driver's to turn on the car lights when it is dark. This duty exists always, also when it is not dark, but the situation for complying with it is not always present. Therefore the following formalisation will *not* do:

(x)(Dark & Car_driver(x) ⊃ Duty(x, perform, turn_on_car_lights))

Perhaps the best way to represent conditional duties is by including the condition as a modifier on the action type, analogous to the action mode. Since this is essentially a formalisation problem, the issue will not be explored here any further.

1.7.2.5 Some Logical Characteristics of Duties

It is possible to have two (or more) duties that conflict in the sense that it is (logically) impossible to comply with all of them. For example, it is possible that Caroline has the duty to vote in her hometown on Sunday. To fulfil that duty, she must travel home on Saturday evening. However, she must also stay with her mother who is seriously ill, and who lives at quite some distance from Caroline's hometown. Although it is not the case that Caroline both ought to stay with her mother and to go home (see Sect. 1.7.5), she does have two duties that she cannot both comply with.[19]

To allow for the possibility of conflicting duties, the following two sentences should be considered consistent:

Duty(agent, perform, action_type)
Duty(agent, refrain, action_type)

Since the sentences

Duty(agent, perform, action_type)
¬Duty(agent, perform, action_type)

should still be considered inconsistent, it should be impossible to derive

¬Duty(agent, refrain, action_type)

from

Duty(agent, perform, action_type).

[19]That it is possible to have such conflicting duties can be seen from the fact that the violation of one of these duties may be considered unlawful and lead to liability for damages. This is particularly the case if the presence of conflicting duties is to be blamed on the person who suffers the conflict (*culpa in causa*). Interestingly, the existence of a conflicting duty is sometimes regarded as a reason why non–compliance is not considered unlawful, because of *force majeure*.

A duty to perform an act in a particular way does not imply the duty to perform that kind of act. Therefore it should not possible to derive Duty(john, refrain, murder(suzyq)) from Duty(john, refrain, murder(suzyq), cruelly).

In fact, the two sentences

Duty(john, perform, murder(suzyq), gently)

and

Duty(john, refrain, murder(suzyq))

should be considered consistent.[20]

1.7.3 *Obligations*

1.7.3.1 What Is an Obligation?

Where a duty is connected to a position or role, *obligations* are the consequences of events. Some obligations are undertaken voluntarily, most notably by contracting or promising. For example the event that Peter promised Quintus to do A leads to the fact that Peter is under an obligation towards Quintus to do A.

Other obligations are not undertaken voluntarily. An example would be that Brad by accident caused damage to Cecile. This event results in the obligation to compensate the damage.

As these two examples illustrate, obligations are always *directed*. A person P is under an obligation towards person Q to do A. Normally this goes together with a *claim* of Q against P that the obligation is performed.[21]

1.7.3.2 The Elements of an Obligation

Because obligations are by definition the results of concrete events, they are deontic relations between specific persons.[22] The distinction between specific persons, categories of persons and everybody as the addressees of duties does not apply to

[20]Here and in the following subsections I write that some sentences "should be" (in)consistent. The reason why I chose this vague terminology is that I do not want to limit the value of the analysis to a particular formal system. My point is that logical systems adequate for modelling the deontic relations analysed here should *represent* the sentences as (in)consistent.

[21]The law knows some exceptional circumstances where such a claim is lacking, for instance in the case of *obligationes naturales* and *stipulationes alteri*. Cf. Zimmerman (1996, 7–10 and 34–45).

[22]Michał Araszkiewicz pointed out that one can promise a reward to, for instance, whoever brings back my lost dog. This would lead to an "undirected obligation". I am not completely sure that this is correct. Possibly the obligation only comes into existence as soon as somebody brought the dog back, and then the claimant is individualised.

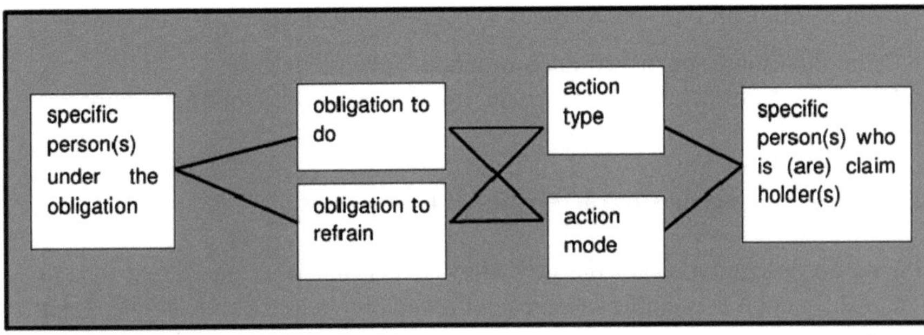

Fig. 1.2 The structure of obligations

obligations. However, obligations can both be obligations to do something and to refrain from doing something, and this something may both be an action type or an action mode. This is graphically represented in Fig. 1.2: The structure of obligations.

1.7.3.3 Obligation/4 and Obligation/5

The logical structure of obligations can also be represented by linguistic means. To this purpose we will introduce the predicators Obligation/4 and Obligation/5. The former is used for obligations to perform some kind of action or to refrain from doing so; the latter for obligations to perform some kind of action in a particular way, or to refrain from doing so.

The predicator Obligation/4 goes with parameters for the addressee(s) of the obligation, also called the "debtors", for the beneficiaries of the obligation, also called the "claim holders", for the obligation modality (perform or refrain), and for the action type that should be performed or refrained from. The following two sentences express respectively that John is under an obligation (contractual, we shall assume) toward SuzyQ's husband not to flirt with SuzyQ, and that Eric is under an obligation toward Jack to play guitar on his new album:

Obligation(john, husband(suzyq), refrain, flirt_with(suzyq));
Obligation(eric, jack, perform, play_guitar)

The predicator Obligation/5 goes with parameters for the addressee(s) of the obligation, for the beneficiaries of the obligation, for the obligation modality, for the action type that should be performed in a particular way or not, and for the way (mode) in which the action type should (not) be performed.

1. The formalisation of the first four parameters is the same as for Obligation/4.
2. The action mode is denoted by a term (e.g. "carefully", or "cruelly").

The following example sentences express respectively that John is under an obligation towards SuzyQ not to murder her cruelly and that the president of France is under an obligation to Van Rompuy to support him timely:

Obligation(john, suzyq, refrain, murder(suzyq), cruelly)
Obligation(president_of(france), van_rompuy, perform, support, timely)

1.7.3.4 Some Logical Characteristics of Obligations

Having an obligation is not the last word concerning what one ought to do (see Sect. 1.7.5) and it is possible to have conflicting obligations. An example would be the case that Jane promised her new friend that she would spend the evening with him and promised her old friend to collect her clothes that same evening. Therefore the following two sentences should be considered consistent:

Obligation(agent, claim_holder, perform, action_type)
Obligation(agent, claim_holder, refrain, action_type)

An obligation to perform an act in a particular way does not imply an obligation to perform that kind of act. So it should not be possible to derive

Obligation(john, suzyq, refrain, murder(suzyq))

from

Obligation(john, suzyq, refrain, murder(suzyq), cruelly).

In fact, the two sentences

Obligation(john, suzyq, perform, murder(suzyq), gently)

and

Obligation(john, suzyq, refrain, murder(suzyq))

should be considered consistent.

1.7.4 Being Obligated

Although being under an obligation and having a duty are different things, they have in common that they both provide a reason why something ought to be done. This common element in obligations and duties will be expressed by the word "obligated". This is an artificial term, since it seems that the English language does not have a word to denote the common element of duties and obligations.[23]

To facilitate the following discussion of being obligated, we will ignore duties and obligations to do something in a particular way. For the same reason it is also assumed that duties and obligations address a single individual called "Agent" and concern the performance of an action type "Action".

[23]We will see in Sect. 1.7.5 that "ought" does not represent this common element.

1.7.4.1 Having a Duty and Being Obligated

Being under an obligation and having a duty both involve that the addressee of the duty or the obligation is obligated to do what she is under the obligation or has the duty to do.

The operator Obligated/3 is used to express that an agent is obligated to perform (or refrain from) some action type.

Logically, the relation between being under a duty and being obligated can then be expressed by the following axiom:

(*agent*)(*action*) Duty(*agent*, perform, *action*) ⊃ Obligated(*agent*, perform, *action*)

1.7.4.2 Being Under an Obligation and Being Obligated

The relation between being under an obligation and being obligated is expressed by the following axiom:

(*agent*)(*action*)(*claimant*) Obligation(*agent*, *claimant*, perform, *action*) ⊃ Obligated(*agent*, perform, *action*)

As becomes clear from this example, the Claimant drops out in the step from having an obligation to being obligated. The reason is that being obligated is not directed towards a claimant.

1.7.4.3 Being Obligated and Deontic Inheritance

Deontic inheritance is the phenomenon that if performing some kind of action involves or otherwise necessitates performing some other kind of action, being obligated to perform the first kind of action implies being obligated to perform the second kind. Deontic inheritance occurs between cases of being obligated, but not between duties or between obligations. Let us consider some examples.

Joan contracted to deliver her house to Gerald. As a consequence she is under an obligation and also obligated to deliver her house to Gerald. Delivery of real estate takes place by signing a notarial deed. Joan did not contract to sign the deed, and therefore she is not under an obligation to sign it. But she is obligated to do so, because signing the deed is the only way to perform what she was obligated to do, namely to deliver the house.

A man is chased by members of the Mafia who want to kill him. He fleas into Tom's house and begs Tom to hide him. Let us assume that Tom is under a duty to save human lives where possible, and therefore obligated to protect this man. When the Mafia gang asks Tom whether he has seen anybody, Tom is obligated because of this duty to lie and tell the Mafia that he did not see anybody. But Tom is not under a duty to do so; he has no duty to lie, because there is no deontic inheritance between duties. In fact, Tom is under a duty not to lie, and therefore also obligated not to lie.

Let us introduce the relation Involves/2 which has two action types as its parameters.

Involves(actiontype1, actiontype2)

means that performing an act that belongs to ActionType1 necessitates performing an act that belongs to ActionType2[24]:

N(x)Performs(x, actiontype1) ⊃ Performs(x, actiontype2)

This involvement may be based on conventions, as in the example of the notarial deed. It may also be based on causal relations, as in the example of the Mafia. With the help of this relation, deontic inheritance can be characterised as follows:

N(x)(Obligated(x, perform/refrain, y) & Involves(y, z) ⊃ Obligated(x, perform/refrain, z))

1.7.4.4 Conflicts in Being Obligated

Since the logical step from a duty or an obligation to being obligated is without exceptions, and since duties and obligations can conflict amongst each other, there can be conflicts in being obligated without inconsistency. So the sentences

Obligated (agent, perform, action)

and

Obligated (agent, refrain, action)

can be true simultaneously. A case in which such a dilemma occurs is for instance when an agent has made a promise to do something, which leads to an obligation to do what was promised, while the circumstances of the situation involve a duty to do something else. Then there is a conflict between an obligation and a duty, and the agent who faces this conflict is both obligated to do what she promised and obligated to refrain from doing it. This is a practical conflict, but not an inconsistency. Regrettably, practical conflicts sometimes occur.

1.7.5 Ought to Do

It is not possible that somebody morally or legally both ought to do something and ought or even is permitted to refrain from doing it. But it is possible that somebody legally ought to do something while he is morally permitted to do it, or even morally ought to refrain from doing it.

[24]The N at the beginning of the formula stands for the necessity operator. The precise characteristics of this modal operator are left unspecified on purpose.

Judgments of the ought–to–do type are summaries of the reasons why an agent has to do something or has to refrain from doing it. In that sense, ought–to–do judgements are always relative to sets of reasons. If these reasons coincide with the set of all reasons from a particular point of view, such as the legal or the moral point of view, the ought judgment expresses what legally or morally ought to be done.

For the purpose of the present discussion we will confine ourselves to the legal ought only.

The following equivalences, where "Od" stands for "ought to do", "Pd" stands for "permitted to do" and "Fd" for "forbidden to do", are true by definition:

Od(*agent*, perform, *action*) ≡ ¬ Pd(*agent*, refrain, *action*)
Od(*agent*, refrain, *action*) ≡ ¬ Pd(*agent*, perform, *action*)
Fd(*agent*, perform, *action*) ≡ Od(*agent*, refrain, *action*)
Fd(*agent*, refrain, *action*) ≡ Od(*agent*, perform, *action*)

Ought–to–do judgments are true on the balance of reasons. A reason why somebody is under an obligation or has a duty to do something is also a reason why this person is obligated to do it and also a reason why this person ought to do it and a reason against the state of affairs that this person ought not to do it. A reason why somebody is under an obligation or has a duty not to do something is a reason why this person is obligated not to do it and also a reason why this person ought not do it and a reason against the state of affairs that this person ought to do it.[25]

Since it is impossible that both the reasons for an ought–to–do judgement outweigh the reasons against it and the reasons against an ought–to–do judgment outweigh the reasons for it, it is logically impossible that an agent both ought to perform and to refrain from performing an action type. So the following two sentences should be inconsistent:

Od(*Agent*, perform, *Action*)

and

Od(*Agent*, refrain, *Action*).

With regard to actions that ought to be performed or refrained from deontic inheritance is also possible. This is because an ought, just as being obligated, is not strictly tied to the duties or obligations from which it stems. Therefore the following holds:

N(Od(x, perform/refrain, y) & Involves(y, z) ⊃ Od(x, perform/refrain, z))

[25]Readers who are interested in a formal elaboration of these ideas are referred to Chapter 3 of Hage (2005a).

1.7.6 Norms

In the legal theoretical literature, the terms "rule" and "norm" are often used interchangeably. For instance, Kelsen et al. (1979, 82–84) writes about power conferring norms, which suggest that some norms do not tell agents what to do; they do not have to be "deontic". On the other hand, Kelsen et al. (1979, 15) also writes about individual norms, which suggests that not all norms are rules.

More in general, the terminology around norms leaves much to be desired, and the best way to continue here may therefore be to propose precise terminology.

My proposal is to use the word "norm" only for rules that lead to deontic facts. There are two main categories of such rules. There are dynamic rules that lead to obligations, such as the rule of tort law that imposes on tortfeasors the obligation to pay damages. And there are duty–imposing fact–to–fact rules, such as the rule that nobody is allowed to kill human beings, and the rule that car drivers must carry a driver's license. Since rules are general and do not mention individuals as bearers of duties or obligations, there cannot be individual norms under the proposed word usage. Neither can there be power conferring norms, since a power is not a duty or obligation.

Notice that rules impose duties or obligations, and only bring about in an indirect fashion, via a duty or an obligation, that somebody is obligated to do something or ought to do something. Let us have a look at a simple example how the fact that Basil ought to pay €100 damages to Cedric follows from the fact that Basil unlawfully caused €100 damage to Cedric.[26]

1. Valid(*unlawfuly_caused(*tortfeasor, victim, damage*) ⇒ *duty(*tortfeasor, victim*, perform, *pay(victim, damage)*))
2. Unlawfully_caused(basil, cedric, €100)

---

3. Obligation(basil, cedric, perform, pay(cedric, €100))
4. (x)(y)(z)Obligation(x, y, perform, z) ⊃ Obligated(x, perform, z)

---

5. Obligated(basil, perform, pay(cedric, €100))
6. Reason(*obligated(x, perform, z), *od(x, perform, z))

---

7. Reason(*obligated(basil, perform, pay(cedric, €100)), *od(basil, perform, pay (cedric, €100)))
8. ¬∃*r*(Reason(r, *¬ od(basil, perform, pay(cedric, €100))))

---

[26]Strictly speaking, the operation of obligation creating rules involves an element of time. This is discussed, in the context of juridical acts, in Hage (2011a,b). For the present purposes this temporal element is not important and to keep the example relatively simple, it has been ignored in the formalisation.

9. Od(basil, perform, pay(cedric, €100)))

Line 1 of this argument states that the basic rule of tort law is valid.
Line 2 states that Basil satisfied the conditions for being liable for damages.
Line 3 formulates the conclusion from 1 and 2 that Basil is under an obligation toward Cedric to pay €100.
Line 4 expresses that being under an obligation implies being obligated.
Line 5 formulates the conclusion from 3 and 4 that Basil is obligated to pay €100.
Line 6 expresses that being obligated is a reason why the obligated person ought to do what (s)he is obligated to do.
Line 7 formulates the conclusion from 5 and 6 that the fact that Basil is obligated to pay €100 is a reason why Basil ought to pay €100.
Line 8 formulates that there is no reason why Basil ought not to pay the €100. (This would be a default conclusion, based on the fact that the information about the case does not provide any clue suggesting that there would be such a reason.)
Line 9 formulates the final conclusion that Basil ought to pay €100. (This conclusion can be drawn on the assumption, which was not formulated explicitly, that if there is a reason pleading for a conclusion and no reason against this conclusion, the conclusion follows.)

1.7.7 Some Implications for Legislation

As the last example illustrated, the road from an obligation creating rule to what an agent legally ought to do is not as simple as a subsumption argument, but nevertheless quite straightforward. It becomes slightly more complicated if there are not only reasons why an agent ought to do something, but also reasons why he ought to refrain from doing this. Then the reasons need to be balanced against each other, and additional information about the relative weight of the reasons is required (Hage 1997, Section III.13).

A legislator who can make rules can create duty imposing rules and obligation creating rules, and also rules that deal with the conflicts that result if an agent is both obligated to perform and to refrain from some action. A legislator cannot make a rule that tells legal subjects what they legally ought to do, since such an ought is by definition the result of interacting reasons. This has two implications:

1. In formulating duty imposing or obligation creating rules, a legislator should not worry about possible conflicts. It is desirable to avoid unsolved conflicts of norms, but conflicts should not be prevented on the level of duty imposing or obligation creating rules, but solved on a higher level.
2. Legislators should pay serious attention to the possibility that the duties and obligations they (indirectly) create, conflict and they should do that by adding rules for conflict resolution to the duty imposing or obligation creating rules they create. The best strategy for handling conflicts of norms is a topic that falls

outside the scope of the present article, but the traditional principles for handling rule conflicts such as *Lex Specialis* and *Lex Superior* give an indication of the direction in which a solution might go.

1.8 Rules and Regulations

In the previous sections, rules were frequently mentioned, but mostly to say something about the structure of the world of law. This section is devoted to a more detailed discussion of rules, their operation, and their mode of existence.

1.8.1 Legal Rules as Constraints on Legally Possible Worlds

The idea of a rule is traditionally associated with the guidance of behaviour. Rules prescribe behaviour, they can be followed, obeyed and disobeyed, and after the behaviour has taken place, rules can be used to evaluate behaviour as correct or incorrect. This association between rules and the guidance of behaviour is reflected in philosophical discussions about rule following (Brożek 2013; Kripke 1982; Wittgenstein 1953), and in jurisprudential accounts of the nature of law (Aquinas S. Th. I, II, qu. 90 sect. 4; D'Entréves 1959, 57; Kelsen 1960; Hart 2012, 94). And yet many rules seem not to guide behaviour at all, or only in the marginal sense that they allow the evaluation of behaviour as correct (in agreement with the rule) or incorrect. Examples of rules that seem not to aim at guidance at all are the rules that confer competences, or define the institutions of the European Union. Apparently the nature of rules cannot be found in the fact that rules prescribe behaviour.

Legal rules are often analysed as a kind of conditionals that attach facts, the legal consequences, to other facts, the operative facts of the rule. The operative facts are mentioned in the condition part of the rule, while the legal consequences are mentioned in the conclusion part. This structure can also be found back in counts–as, fact–to–fact, and dynamic rules. The condition for the application of a counts–as rule is that some individual belongs to a particular kind (e.g. a delivery), and the conclusion that follows is that this individual also belongs to some other kind (a transfer). The condition for the application of a fact–to–fact rule is that some fact obtains (e.g. that somebody is the mayor of a city), and the conclusion that some other fact obtains (that this person is competent to issue emergency regulations for this city). The condition for application of a dynamic rule is that some event occurred (e.g. a Bill was adopted), and the conclusion is that some fact obtains (some new legal rules exist).

The talk of conditions and conclusion is a bit deceptive, though, because they suggest arguments. As a matter of fact, rules can be used in arguments and that justifies this terminology, but rules are also constitutive. They *make it the case* that the facts of the rule conclusion enter into existence if the facts of the rule conclusion obtain. If an event is the delivery of a good, the counts–as rule makes that it is also a transfer of ownership. If somebody is the King of Belgium, the fact–to–fact rules makes that he is also the commander in chief of the Belgian army. And if a person contracted to deliver a car, a dynamic rule makes that he is under an obligation to deliver the car. This is the world–to–word direction of fit of rules, that was mentioned in Sect. 1.3.

Even this "makes it the case that" talk is somewhat deceptive, as it suggests that the rule undertakes some active action. Perhaps it is even better to talk about legal rules as constraints on legally possible worlds. Take again the rule that the mayor of a city is competent to issue emergency regulations for this city. If we ignore the possibility of exceptions to rules, the existence of this rule makes that facts of two types, being the mayor and being competent to issue emergency regulations, go together. Moreover, this relation is not contingent; it has a ring of necessity in the sense that it supports conditionals, including counterfactual conditionals: it is not only that the actual mayor of a city is competent to issue emergency regulations, but also that if P were to be the mayor, P would have the competence to issue emergency regulations.

To state it in the terminology of logicians: in all legally possible worlds, mayors are competent to issue emergency regulations. Which worlds count as legally possible is defined by the existing legal rules. These rules function as constraints on legally possible worlds.[27] A world in which the mayor of Sun City has the competence to issue emergency regulations is to that extent legally possible. A world in which the mayor would not have had this competence would not have been legally possible. Another example would be the following. Purely logically, the states of affairs that P is a thief and the state of affairs that P is not punishable are compatible. Formulated in the technical jargon of logicians: there exist logically possible worlds in which both P is a thief and at the same time not punishable. If the rule that thieves are punishable is added, a legal constraint on what is possible is introduced. In legally (as opposed to merely logically) possible worlds being a thief and not being punishable have become incompatible. It is in this sense that the rule functions as a constraint on legally possible worlds.[28] Not all logically possible worlds are also legally possible ones. Only those worlds which (also) satisfy the constraints imposed by the existing legal rules count as legally possible. The rule that mayors are competent to issue emergency regulations also functions as a constraint on legally possible worlds, because if this rule is valid a world does not count as legally possible if it contains a mayor who is not competent to issue emergency regulations.[29]

---

[27] A possible world is in this connection defined as a maximal set of states of affairs (possible facts), where being maximal means that it is not possible to add new states of affairs to the world that are compatible with the states of affairs that already exist in this world.

[28] Rules would be "weak" constraints in the sense that although they necessitate connections between facts of particular types, their existence and therefore also the presence of this necessity is contingent. See for more details Hage (2005b, 2014).

[29] This idea is elaborated philosophically in Hage (2014) and formally in Hage (2005b).

For legislators this means that they influence which worlds are legally possible – and that is not the same as legally permitted – by making, modifying, and derogating legal rules.

1.8.2 Regulations, Rules, and Rule Content

There are basically two different ways in which a legal rule can exist. A legal rule can exist because it is accepted as a legal rule. This mode of existence characterises customary law, and also judge–made law in the civil law tradition, where the rule of *stare decisis* does not exist.

A legal rule can also exist because another rule attaches its existence to an event. Typical events to which the existence of a legal rule is attached are judicial decisions (in legal systems where *stare decisis* holds), and all forms of legislation, including statutes, by–laws, treaties and general decisions of international organisations. Many legal rules are created by means of legislation. In this connection it is possible to distinguish between the text of the regulation by means of which a rule was created, the rule itself, and the content of the rule.

1.8.2.1 Regulations

A *regulation* may be defined as a (part of a) legislative product by means of which a single legal rule is made. An example of such a regulation is Article 29 Section 1 of the Common European Sales Law (CESL), which reads:

> A party which has failed to comply with any duty imposed by this Chapter is liable for any loss caused to the other party by such failure.

Regulations may be divided over more than one article in a statute. This is for instance the case in the Dutch Penal Code which contains a number of articles that define several variations of theft. The more complex variations, such as theft by means of burglary or theft during the time meant for sleeping, are defined in terms of simple theft which is defined in a separate article. It is also possible that one article or even one section of an article is used to make more than one rule.[30]

Regulations are linguistic entities and are therefore by definition phrased in a particular language, such as English or Portuguese. The regulations are not the legal rules themselves. To the extent that statutes consist of regulations, statutes therefore do not contain law. They are means to create (or modify or derogate) law, but that is not the same thing.

[30]The individuation of legal rules ("laws") is discussed extensively in Raz (1980, Chapter IV).

1.8.2.2 Rule Content

Every rule has a *content*. This content is determined by the rule conditions and the rule consequence in the sense that if two rules have the same conditions and the same consequence, these two rules have the same content. Both conditions and consequence are defined in terms of states of affairs; the rule has as content that it connects the condition state(s) of affairs to the consequence state of affairs. States of affairs are language–dependent, but they are not linguistic entities themselves. As a consequence the rule content is not a linguistic entity either. This means that a regulation may determine the contents of rules, but that regulations do not contain the rule contents. For example, the regulation of Article 29 Section 1 CESL determines under which conditions the rule that was made by this regulation is applicable, and what the consequences are if the rule is applied. However, this regulation is not identical to these conditions and consequences because the conditions and consequences do not depend on a particular language, while the regulation does. Moreover, the relation between a regulation and the content of the rule made by means of that regulation is not straightforward. Usually the content of the rule is determined by the text of the regulation, but it may happen that in legal practice it is assumed that a rule has more, or fewer, or slightly different, conditions than those mentioned in the regulation. Then we can still say that the rule was created by means of the regulation, even though the content of the rule is not completely determined by the text of the regulation.

1.8.2.3 Rules

The precise nature of rules is hard to nail down. On the one hand there is a strong temptation to identify rules with the regulations by means of which they were created. It is for instance very well possible to speak of the rule of Article 29 Section 1 CESL, and if this Article would be modified, it makes sense to say that its rule has changed too. And yet, there are several reasons not to identify a rule with either its underlying regulation, or with its content. If a rule would coincide with its regulation it would be a linguistic entity. However, contrary to linguistic entities such as sentences, rules exist in time, can be created, modified and derogated, have a scope of application, and they can bring about facts such as the punishability of criminals, and the existence of obligations.

On the other hand is also tempting to identify a rule with its content. We have no problems in saying that two different countries have the same rule governing the side of the road on which car drivers must drive. Most likely we mean by that that the rules of the countries have the same content, and not that they were made by the same regulation. The relation between a rule and its content is a bit like the relation between a book and its content. We need to know the content in order to know with which book we are dealing, but it is possible to talk about a book with a particular content, even if this book does not actually exist ("If this book were ever to be written, it would become a bestseller."). Similarly it is possible to talk about rules as defined by a particular content, even if these rules do not actually exist. ("It would not be wise to introduce a rule that makes visiting pornographic websites punishable.") However, if a rule is identified with its content, it is not possible to modify the content of a rule, because such a modification would lead to a new rule. Modification of a rule would boil down then to the replacement of one rule by another rule.

Most likely the best solution to this problem of identifying the nature of a rule is to treat the concept of a rule as a stereotype (Putnam 1975a). A typical rule is made by a particular regulation (or a judicial decision) and has a particular content. A change in either one of them does not necessarily lead to a different rule, for instance if the "same" rule is moved from one statute to a more recent statute, or if a minor condition is added to the rule. However, if the changes are too "big", however "big" may be defined in this connection, the rule has been replaced by a different rule. If this analysis is by and large correct, it suggests that a rule is neither to be identified by its underlying regulation nor by its content, but is nevertheless dependent on both of them in the sense that major changes in either regulation or content may lead to a different rule.

1.8.3 Modifying the World of Law by Means of Legislation

If legal rules function as constraints on legally possible worlds, this implies that legislation leads to new facts in the world of law in perhaps even four different ways. First, legislation is a juridical act to which existing dynamic rules attach changes in the set of valid legal rules: new rules are added, existing ones derogated or modified.

Second, the modification in the set of valid legal rules affects other facts and individuals in the world of law. Suppose for instance that adultery used to be punishable, and that Xaviera is an adulteress. Then the rule that makes adultery punishable adds the fact to the world of law that Xaviera is punishable. If new legislation derogates this rule, the fact that Xaviera is punishable is also removed from the world of law.

Third, it is also possible that legislation modifies priority relations between existing rules. Suppose that a rule made by the municipality council for a particular municipality conflicts with national law. Under present law, national law has priority over municipal law. If this priority relation is modified by new legislation, the new priority makes that the already existing municipal law enters into force, which has again implications for still other facts in the world of law.

And fourth, it is possible that legislation leads to the recognition of a new source of law. Suppose that the national legislator of an EU member state creates the rule that recommendations by the EU also count as valid law. If that happens, suddenly a lot of new law is introduced into the legal system of that member state, new law which itself may also have impact on other facts and individuals in the world of law.

1.9 Interrelations

In the previous sections a rather abstract view of law was sketched. Moreover, in the introduction it was claimed that this abstract picture constituted the framework of law that was to be stuffed by means of legislation and that therefore it is important for legislators to grasp this framework. The time has arrived to substantiate this claim. Sections 1.9–1.12 will illustrate how insight into the structure of the world of law can assist legislators in building that part of the world of law with which they have to deal.[31] To that purpose, it will sketch a picture of what legislators can and cannot do and what they should keep in mind when they try to do what they can do as well as possible. The key issue in this connection that law, and legislators as persons who want to make law, strive to influence actual, physical, human behaviour, but can do little more than make, modify and abrogate rules. Legislators can influence the world of law, but their objective is to influence the "real" world. Somehow, the facts in this real world and the facts in the world of law should be interrelated. What should be the impact of this condition on the work of a legislator?

To facilitate the following discussion some conventions will be recapitulated and introduced. The world of law is defined as the set of all facts and things (individuals) whose existence is the result of the application of some legal rule. Examples are that the fact that the Euro is the currency of many European countries, the fact that the Bundesverfassungsgericht is a German court of law, and the fact that Jane is under an obligation to pay her landlord the rent as facts in the world of law, and the Bundesverfassungsgericht, and the rent contract between Jane and her landlord as individuals in the world of law. All entities in the world of law are rule–based in the sense of Sect. 1.4, and more in particular based on legal rules.

The world of law is part of the world that consists of all facts and individuals. The part of the world that does not belong to the world of law will be referred to as the "outside world".

The facts in the world are often interrelated. These relations are either based on causal laws, or on rules. The former will be called "causal relations", and the latter "rule–based relations".

Causal relations exist first and foremost between objective facts. For instance, there can be a causal relation between the fact that a piece of metal is heated, and the fact that it expands, or there can be a causal connection between the fact that a car is hit by a stone and the fact that it is dented.

The question may be raised whether there can also be a causal relation from objective facts to recognition–based facts. A seeming example of such a relation is that there is an event which makes that most people start to accept a particular rule. But this example is complicated, because there are two steps involved. First the purely causal one between the event and the acceptance of the rule, and second the conceptual step between this acceptance and the existence of the rule. Arguably

[31] Sections 1.9–1.12 have been adapted from Hage (2013b).

this conceptual step is based on the convention (rule) that social rules exist by being accepted and then the social fact is not brought about by the objective fact alone.

No matter how the step from objective facts to social facts is seen, the causal direction goes at most one way only; the existence of a social fact cannot directly cause an objective fact to exist. This impossibility deserves some attention, because it has direct implications for the interface between the world of law and the outside world. It may seem possible that a recognition–based fact causes an objective one. A seeming example would be that the fact that somebody is the Secretary–General of the United Nations causes her to be proud. This appearance is deceptive, however, because it is not being the Secretary–General that makes her proud, but believing (knowing) to be the Secretary–General which has this effect.

Since rule–based facts are by definition brought about by rules, there cannot be a direct causal relation from objective facts to rule–based facts. An indirect connection is possible if the last step in the chain is rule–based. For instance, a car accident causes damage to a car, and a rule attaches an obligation to compensate damages to the presence of this damage. But then the rule–based fact is directly based on the operation of a rule, and only indirectly on a causal relation. Moreover, this causal relation holds between two objective facts. Because rule–based facts are immaterial, they cannot causally influence facts in the outside world, so there exist no causal relations from rule–based facts to the outside world either.

Only rule–based facts can be brought about by rules. Actually, rule–based facts must be brought about by rules, because that is how they were defined. Most kinds of facts can trigger rules to make them generate rule–based facts. For instance, the fact that it rains may obligate taxi drivers to take along passengers for free (if there is a rule to that effect). Recognition–based facts can also trigger rules, such as the fact that somebody chairs a charitable society can give her the right to open the annual ball of the society. And the law contains an endless list of illustrations of the phenomenon that rule–based facts can trigger rules and in that way lead to new rule–based facts. It is this very possibility which makes the idea of a world of law interesting.

1.10 The Structure of the World of Law

The world of law consists of rule–based facts (and individuals), and most of these facts derive their relevance from legal rules which attach consequences to them. For instance, the fact that somebody can be classified as a thief derives its legal relevance from a rule that attaches the legal consequence that this person is liable to be punished. The fact that somebody has received a building permit has as consequence that this person now has the permission to build, which would otherwise not have been allowed.

Often the legal consequences of some legal status are (parts of) the conditions for other rule–based facts. The transfer of ownership in a piece of land, which makes amongst many other things that the original owner loses the permission to cultivate the land while the new owner obtains this permission, illustrates this well. Let us have a closer look at an example case in which Alice sells her land to Charles. We assume that the sale takes place in the Netherlands, a jurisdiction that works with a tradition system, where a notarial deed is required to transfer the ownership of real estate.[32] Then the following will occur.

Alice and Charles draw up a document which they both undersign. Under some assumptions concerning the content of this document, the document counts as a sales contract and the event of signing the document counts as entering into a sales contract. Both the facts that the document counts as a sales contract and that the signing counts as entering into a contract are rule–based facts. The rules which make that the document counts as a contract and that the signing counts as entering into a contract are counts–as rules, rules which make that something legally also counts as something else. The facts that result as consequence of the application of a counts–as rule are rule–based facts.

The event that Alice and Charles entered into a sales contract leads to two new facts. One is that Alice is from that moment on under an obligation to transfer the ownership of the land to Charles, and the other is that Charles is under an obligation to pay Alice the price of the land. Both legal consequences are the result of a dynamic rule which attaches new facts to the occurrence of an event, in this case the sales contract. The existence of both obligations is a rule–based fact.

In order to fulfil Alice's obligation to transfer the ownership of the land to Charles, Alice and Charles visit a notary who makes up a deed according to which Alice declares to transfer the ownership and Charles declares to accept the ownership. This event counts, on the basis of a counts–as rule, as the delivery of the ownership.

Moreover, this delivery in its turn counts as the transfer of the ownership. The delivery can, according to Dutch law, only count as a valid transfer of ownership because of Alice's obligation to make the transfer, which counts as the title for the transfer.

There is another precondition for the delivery to count as a valid transfer and that is that Alice had the competence to transfer ownership of the land. This competence is attached to Alice's ownership of the land by a fact–to–fact rule.

If the transfer of ownership is valid, a dynamic rule attaches to this event the consequences that Alice has lost the ownership of the land and that Charles has become the new owner. A fact–to–fact rule attaches to this latter fact that Charles has permission to cultivate the land if he wants to.

Figure 1.3 below pictures the described events and their consequences. Horizontal arrows represent the operation of dynamic rules. Solid vertical arrows represent fact–to–fact rules, and dotted vertical arrows represent counts–as rules. The facts within the dotted box are rule–based and since all the relevant rules belong to the law, the facts are also part of the world of law.

[32]For an exposition of the difference between consensual and tradition systems, see van Vliet (2012).

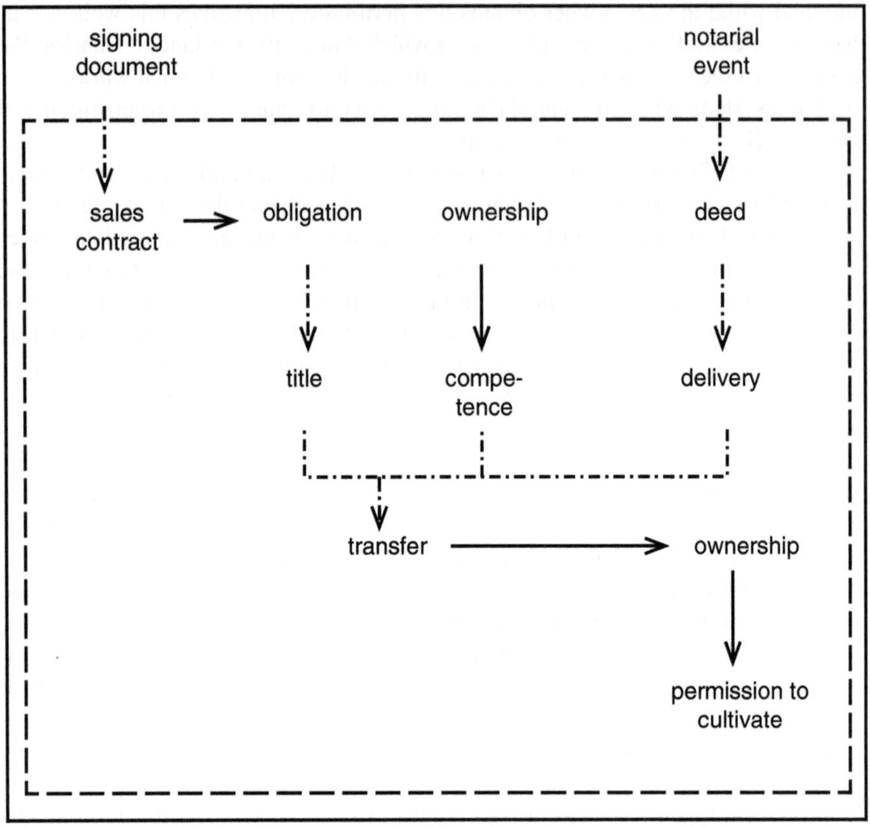

Fig. 1.3 The transfer of real estate

1.11 Interfacing the World of Law and the Outside World

1.11.1 The World of Law and the Outside World

The world of law is not a goal in itself; it is meant to have impact on the "outside world", the world that consists of facts which are not the result of the operation of legal rules. In very broad lines, the operation of the world of law can be sketched as follows[33]:

Some facts in the outside world count, on the basis of legal rules, as facts in the world of law. See Fig. 1.4: Interfaces with the world of law. In that quality, these

[33]To make the picture easier to understand, the input facts and the output facts have been positioned outside the world of law. Since both categories of facts are defined in the next subsection as parts of the world of law, be it on the border with the outside world, the picture is not fully accurate. Figure 1.5 will be more precise in this respect.

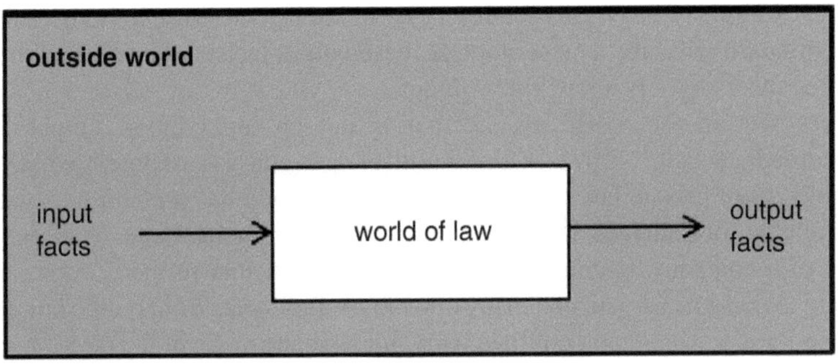

Fig. 1.4 Interfaces with the world of law

facts play a role in the world of law, usually by leading to other facts in the world of law. For example, signing a letter may, under certain circumstances, count as granting a building permit, and lead to the permission for a legal subject to raise a building. At the end of the chain the facts in the world of law should affect the outside world again.

1.11.2 Input, Intermediate, and Output Facts

The facts inside the world of law are interconnected by rules. Together the facts and the rules in the world of law form a network of interrelated rules and facts. To answer the question how elements of this network can affect the outside world it is useful to have a closer look at the facts in the world of law and more in particular to distinguish between input facts, intermediate facts and output facts.

Input facts are facts in the world of law which also exist in the outside world, be it under a different name such as "signing a letter" rather than "contracting". In the world of law they have a special status that is specified by fact–to–fact and dynamic rules. In our example about the sale of a property right in real estate, the signing of a document is a fact in the outside world. This same fact counts in the world of law as entering into a sales contract. What happened at the notarial office counts as the delivery of the sold land. The facts that Alice and Charles entered into a sales contract and that Alice delivered the land to Charles are entry points into the network of the world of law.[34]

Output facts are those facts in the world of law which affect the outside world. One example is the duty – or is it a permission? – of the public prosecution to take away the money that constitutes a fine, or to imprison a criminal convict.

[34]The idea that facts in the outside world are interpreted as facts in the world of law can already been found in the first (1934) edition of the *Reine Rechtslehre* (Kelsen 1934/1992, 10). Basically the same idea can also be found in the work of John Searle (1995, 43–51).

Another example is the permission for the owner of a good to use it. In the following subsections we will take a closer look at these output facts and then it will become clear that there are only a few kinds of them.

Every fact in the world of law that is not an input or an output fact is an intermediate fact.[35] Most of the world of law consists of intermediate facts. Examples from private law are the facts that somebody has a claim on somebody else, is liable for damages, is married, has a particular name, is the chief executive officer of a company, is competent to transfer a particular property right, has the capacity to make a last will, and many other facts. Examples from public law are that some entity is a state, that a political party got so many votes in the elections, that a judge is competent to review laws against the constitution, that a public officer has the competence to grant building permits, that individuals have the right to freedom of expression, and that some particular intergovernmental organisation exists.

The intermediate facts can be subdivided into facts which lead to new facts through the application of dynamic rules and facts which only fulfil a role in argument chains concerning facts which are connected in an a–temporal fashion. Examples of the former are the facts that somebody was granted a subsidy, caused a car accident, or that a Bill was adopted. Examples of the latter are the facts that somebody is the mayor of a city, is under a contractual obligation, or has a particular name.

Some facts are on the borderline. An example is the fact that somebody has a competence to perform some juridical act such as to enter into a contract, to pass a Bill, or to pronounce a verdict. The fact that someone has a competence does not lead to anything new, but it is a kind of fact which is a necessary precondition for some other events to lead to new legal consequences. For instance, having the competence to transfer ownership in some good is a necessary precondition for a delivery to lead to a transfer of ownership. The competence to legislate is a necessary precondition for a vote to lead to new legislation and therefore to new rules.

Figure 1.5: Input, intermediate and output facts, depicts the relation between input, intermediate and output facts in the world of law. For reasons that will become clear later, there are no arrows from the output facts to the outside word.

1.11.3 The Transition from the World of Law to the Outside World

Legal consequences are brought about by legal rules and legal rules can only have effect in the world of law. Counts–as rules can bridge the gap from the outside world

[35] An output fact may at the same time function as an intermediate fact. For instance, a legal duty may lead to behaviour of the person under this duty, but it may also be a precondition for the existence of another intermediate fact, such as the unlawfulness of the behaviour which violates this duty. This possibility is also indicated in Fig. 1.5: Input, intermediate and output facts.

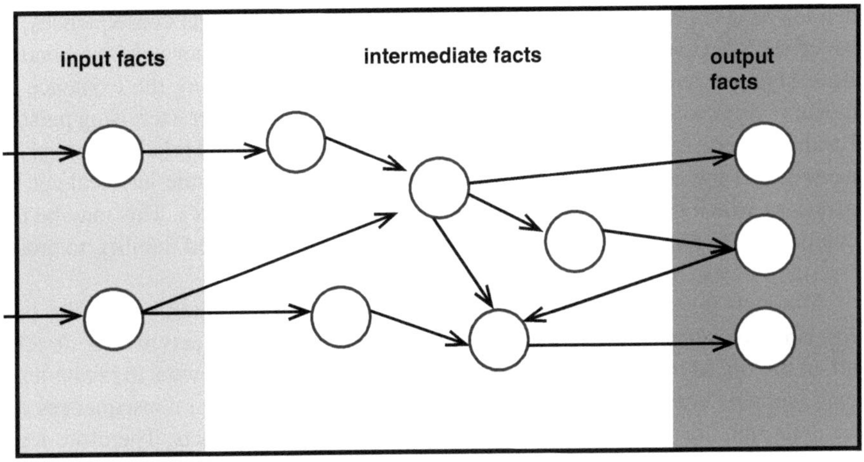

Fig. 1.5 Input, intermediate and output facts

to the world of law, but only in the direction of the world of law, because the facts in the world of law are, in contrast to those in the outside world, rule–based. Legal rules cannot bring about that facts or events in the world of law count as facts or events in the outside world. In a sense, therefore, the world of law has no exit; it cannot directly influence the outside world.

Does this mean that the world of law does not affect the outside world at all? Clearly not, but the impact can only be indirect, namely by motivating people to act by changing their legal status. There are at first sight four kinds of status which are candidates for bringing about changes in the outside world, that is legal duties, prohibitions, permissions and powers. We will discuss these four in turn and will then consider the possibility of other legal positions being similarly connected to the outside world.

1.11.3.1 Legal Powers

Legal powers can be taken in a broad and in a narrow sense. Somebody has a legal power in a broad sense if he can perform some kind of act to which a dynamic legal rule attaches a legal consequence. An example would be that somebody can bring about that she has to pay less municipality taxes by moving to another municipality. Another example is that somebody can make himself liable for damages by defaulting on a contract.

Although legal powers in a broad sense include the power to bring about legal consequences by means of so–called juridical acts (e.g. entering into a contract), juridical acts are not necessarily involved in the exercise legal powers in this broad sense. This is different for legal powers in the narrow sense: they can by definition only be exercised by means of juridical acts. In this connection juridical acts may be defined as acts performed with the intention to bring about legal consequences, to which the law attaches these consequences for the reasons that they were intended.[36] Both legal powers in the broad and in the narrow sense require the existence of dynamic rules which are triggered by the behaviour of the power exercising person. For the exercise of legal powers in the narrow sense an additional requirement exists, namely that the acting person has the competence to perform the juridical act by means of which he intends to bring about the legal consequences. This may be the competence to make a last will, to found a company with limited liability, to create legislation, or to pronounce a judicial verdict.[37]

Although the existence of a legal power may be a precondition for the performance of some acts, these acts will by definition not be acts which directly affect the outside world. The reason is that legal powers are powers to create legal consequences with the help of dynamic legal rules. These legal consequences are by definition consequences in the world of law, rule–based facts. Therefore legal powers do not provide the bridge from the world of law to the outside world that we are looking for.

1.11.3.2 Legal Duties and Obligations

The point of legal duties and obligations is that the persons who have these duties or are under such obligations comply with them. A legal system can only exist if its participants by and large voluntarily comply with the duties and obligations they are under.[38] So, if the world of law contains a duty or obligation for somebody to do something, this embodies at least the beginnings of a bridge to the outside world. The connection is not necessarily strong, though, because there is no guarantee that the obligated person will transform this requirement into actual behaviour. For instance, if somebody acted unlawfully and caused damage, he will normally be under an obligation to pay damages. If she violates this obligation by doing nothing, there is still no change in the outside world.

Of course there is the threat of the sanction in case of non–compliance, but this sanction only affects the outside world if some legal official applies it. The bridge to the outside world should then be looked for in the rule that obligates or permits the

[36] More elaborate on the nature of juridical acts is Sartor (2005, Chapters 23 and 24) and Hage (2011a,b).

[37] Here I distinguish between powers and competences, which are seen as different phenomena which exist next to each other. This follows the discussion of this subject in Hage (2013c). The terms "power" and "competence" are sometimes seen as alternative ways of designating the same phenomenon. See for instance Spaak (1994, 1).

[38] This is the seemingly obvious point that Kelsen made by his demand that legal systems must be effective because otherwise the presupposition of the basic norm would not make much sense. See Kelsen (1960, 204). Hart made a similar point by claiming that participants in a legal system should by and large take the internal point of view towards the rules of the system. See Hart (2012, 103/4).

official to apply this sanction, rather than in the duty or obligation which is backed up by the sanction.

The bridge from a duty to behaviour in the outside world may become stronger if it is the duty of a legal official. Judges are, we may take it, under a duty to apply the law. Moreover, as a matter of fact, they normally comply with this duty and actually apply the law. If they do not, the reason is most likely that they are mistaken about what the law demands from them. Downright refusal to apply the law is highly exceptional. So if a judge must decide a case, the probability is high that her verdict will be in agreement with the law. However, a judicial verdict is a juridical act, and has consequences attached to it by a dynamic rule. These consequences are still facts in the world of law.

If duties and obligations are to bridge the world of law to the outside world, it is better to look at the duties of sanction applying public officers. Bailiffs provide a good example. They may be assumed to comply with the legal rules that impose the duty upon them to apply legal sanctions. So if a judge has convicted a tortfeasor to pay damages and the person entitled to the compensation hires a bailiff to enforce this legal requirement, the bailiff is under a duty to take the money away from the convicted person. Most likely he will comply with this duty and this compliance bridges the gap between the world of law and the outside world. However, in the end, the question whether duties of officials are more effective than duties and obligations of "ordinary" legal subjects is an empirical one.

1.11.3.3 Legal Prohibitions

A prohibition is nothing else than a duty not to do something. Compliance with a prohibition means that nothing happens. It may therefore seem unlikely that legal prohibitions constitute bridges to the outside world. And yet it is possible, namely in case something was likely to happen if the prohibition were lacking. For instance, if people normally, that is if there were no prohibition, would walk on the lawn, the existence of the prohibition might affect the outside world by making that fewer people tread on the lawn.

1.11.3.4 Legal Permissions

Legal permissions are only likely to affect the outside world in case the permitted behaviour would otherwise be prohibited and if this prohibition would mostly be efficacious in the sense that it is complied with for the reason that the behaviour was prohibited. The lawn example can also illustrate this point: if people would not set foot on the lawn for the reason that it is prohibited, then a permission to walk on the lawn may lead more people to tread on the lawn.

1.11.3.5 Legal Status

Legal rules, whether they be dynamic or static, often attach the presence of some legal status to an event or a fact in the world of law. Examples of such statuses are being the president of the US, being the mayor of a city, being a criminal suspect, being the head of police, being a vehicle in the sense of the Traffic Law, being the owner of Blackacre, having the capacity to make last wills, land, and so on … Arguable, even such deontic facts as being under a duty or not being allowed to do something are examples of legal statuses.

It is not doable to run through the list of all kinds of legal status, but a superficial inspection of the examples mentioned above already indicates that the possession of most of these statuses by itself does not lead to any changes in the outside world. That does not mean that the possession of the status of, for instance, criminal suspect has no impact at all, but the impact is indirect. For instance, if P is suspected of having committed a serious crime, police officers may have the permission to search the body of P on weapons. It is not unlikely that the officers will perform such a search when P has incurred the status of suspect, where they would not have done so if P would not have incurred this status. However, it is not the status of criminal suspect in itself that changes the behaviour of the police officers, but the permission attached to this status, or – perhaps even more precise – the knowledge of this status or this permission.

In general, the presence of most legal statuses is either an entry or an intermediate fact in the world of law. Legal status may be important for the impact of the world of law on the outside world, but if so, only in an indirect fashion.

1.11.3.6 Claims

Having a legal right, such as the claim to be paid €100, the title to some real estate such as Blackacre, the copyright to a song text, the right to vote, the right not to be wounded, and the right to education, is a special case of possessing a legal status. For these statuses holds what holds for most legal statuses: they function as intermediate facts in the world of law, and do not have immediate impact on the outside world. Since rights take a special place in law and legal thinking this general point will be elaborated in a short discussion of the nature of different kinds of rights.

Claims are rights in private law which one person holds against another person.[39] If A holds a claim against B, then B is under an obligation *towards* A to do something, or to refrain from doing something. Typical examples are that somebody has a claim to the payment of some amount of money, to the delivery of some good, or to the performance of some service. The use of the term "obligation" in

[39] To keep the exposition relatively simple, the possibilities that claims are held by more than one person or organisation, or against two or more persons or organisations, are ignored. For the main argument line these possibilities hardly make a difference.

connection with claims is telling, because claims are the result of an event which brought about the relation between two parties according to which the one party has a claim against the other and the other is under an obligation towards the one. Typical examples of such events are contracts and torts.

Claims as defined here differ in several aspects from claim rights as defined by Hohfeld (1920). A Hohfeldian claim right is the counterpart of a duty, and nothing else. If A has a claim right against B that B will do X, this means the same as that B is under a Hohfeldian duty towards A to do X.

The first difference to be noticed is that Hohfeld does not use the word "duty" to express a way of being obligated because of some status, but rather for (more or less) the same purpose as the word "obligation" is used in the present article. That is merely a terminological difference and does not have to have any practical implications.

A more important difference is that a Hohfeldian claim right is exhausted by the Hohfeldian duty of the person against whom the claim is held. A claim in tort law or in contract law involves more than merely the mirror side of a Hohfeldian duty. Normally the holder of the claim has the power (in the narrow sense) to enforce the performance of the corresponding obligation, the power to waive the obligation and thereby end the existence of the claim, and the power to transfer and pledge the claim and thereby change the content of the corresponding obligation. (If A transfers her claim on B for the payment of €100 to P, then B is from then on under an obligation *towards P* to pay him €100.)

A person who holds a claim against somebody else has a set of powers which allow him to bring about intentional changes in the world of law. If these powers are exercised, the only changes that are brought about involve the world of law. To this extent, claims have no direct impact on the outside world.

This is different for the obligations that necessarily go together with claims. If the law is by and large efficacious in the sense that legal obligations and duties tend to motivate people to act in accordance with them, the obligation of a person B, or rather the awareness thereof, will normally motivate this person to fulfil this obligation. Moreover, obligations tend to be enforceable, which means that if the appropriate steps have been taken, legal officials have the duty the apply sanctions. Obligations are on the interface between the world of law and the outside world. But these obligations are not identical to the claims, although they necessarily go together with them.

1.11.3.7 Property Rights

Claims are rights against some other person. The other main category of rights in private law consists of right on some "good". The good can be material, such as land or something movable. It can also be immaterial such as a claim, an invention, or the result of artistic creativity. Since these rights are not directed towards one or more concrete persons, they are called "absolute rights", where "absolute" does not mean "unlimited", but "non–directed". To keep the discussion relatively straightforward, it will be confined to property rights on material goods, with the right of ownership to a movable good as the prime example.[40]

Suppose that Andrew owns a book. This implies that Andrew is permitted to damage the book and even to destroy it. Other persons, who do not own the book, are not permitted to damage or destroy the book. In other words, they have the legal duty not to damage or destroy the book. This duty rests on non–owners because of their quality of being a non–owner. Andrew can make an exception to this duty by giving permission to damage or destroy the book. Moreover, Andrew has the powers to forbid any non–owner to use the book and to transfer the ownership of the book to somebody else.

More in general, if A has the ownership of a material good G, amongst others the following legal consequences hold:

- all other persons have *ceteris paribus* the legal duty not to damage or destroy G, or to interfere with A's use and enjoyment of G;
- A is permitted to damage or destroy G;
- A has the competence to grant other persons the permission to damage or destroy G and to forbid them to use G;
- A has the competence to transfer the ownership of G to somebody else.

A person who holds a property right on some good has a set of competences which empower him to bring about intentional changes in the world of law. In the case of ownership of movables, these include the power to alienate the good, to forbid others to use the good, and to grant them permission to damage or even destroy the good. If these powers are exercised, the only changes that are brought about involve the world of law. To this extent, property rights have no direct impact on the outside world. However, if permissions are granted, the existence of these permissions may lead to behaviour which would not have taken place otherwise. For instance, if somebody was given permission to take away the bell of a bicycle owned by somebody else, the person may exercise this permission by taking away the bell.

Property rights do not lead to obligations or duties, but the existence of property rights as a legal institution presupposes a background of general legal duties not to damage or destroy an owned good and not to interfere with the owner's use and enjoyment of the good. If somebody becomes the holder of a property right, this does not create the legal duties, but it gives the pre–existing duties a focus which they did not have before. For example, an arbitrary person P is under the general duty not to destroy goods that have a different person as owner. If a particular car belongs to Sheryl, this duty becomes more focused because it now includes the duty not to destroy Sheryl's car. By giving pre–existing duties focus, the existence of property rights may indirectly affect the outside world . If somebody catches a bird that was

[40]The following analysis is based on Brouwer and Hage (2007), but deviates from it in a number of details.

previously free, other persons may be withheld from catching the bird themselves, because that would now amount to interference with the existing ownership of the bird.

1.11.3.8 General Observations

For purely logical reasons, there cannot be direct bridges from the world of law to the outside world on the basis of causal laws or legal rules. What is possible is that the awareness of a fact in the world of law influences (on the basis of a causal law) the behaviour of human beings. Legal rules attach legal consequences to facts, and human reasoners can mentally reconstruct this constitution of new facts, and if they do so they will know which new facts are present in the world of law. This knowledge can stand in causal relations to other objective facts. The "bridge" from the world of law to the outside world is made if such a causal relation exists. As argued above, this is most likely with regard to "deontic" facts such as duties, obligations, prohibitions and permissions, in particular but not exclusively if these deontic facts address legal officials. Where there is no knowledge of facts in the world of law, the world of law cannot affect the outside world.

1.12 Conclusion

Arguably it is the main function of law to guide human conduct by providing mandatory rules. And yet, by far most of the law does not consist of mandatory rules, and most legal rules have not as their primary function to guide conduct. Legal rules are the cement of the world of law, just like causal laws may be seen as the cement of the physical universe.[41] Legislators should not see it as their primary task to guide human conduct by means of mandatory rules, but rather to build the world of law and to provide this world with structure by means of rules. And yet, this world of law has a purpose outside itself, and this purpose is to affect the outside world by influencing human behaviour.

To make the world of law fulfil its purpose, legislators should not only pay attention to the internal structure of the world of law; they should also have eye for the interface of the world of law with the outside world. Neither self–defined legal statuses, such as that of legal suspect, or of mayor, nor legal rights, powers or competences will normally provide the necessary direct interface from the world of law to the outside world. This interface is mainly given by deontic facts such as the facts that somebody is under a duty or obligation to do something, or to refrain from doing something. Permissions which make exceptions to duties or obligations can

[41] Cf. the title of Mackie (1980).

also fulfil this function of interface. It is these deontic facts that are the main "output facts" of the world of law.

The world of law can itself be treated as a kind of black box, which takes in facts from the outside world, transforms them by means of counts–as rules into "input facts", processes them, and provides them with legal consequences in the form of "output facts". In order to do so, there must be "pathways" through the world of law, consisting of facts which are linked by means of rules, either cotemporary, or through a development in time, which connect the input facts to the output facts. The example about the transfer of a piece of land from Alice to Charles in Sect. 1.10 illustrates not only the structure of the world of law, but also such a pathway from the signing of a document and a transaction at the office of the notary to the permission for Charles to cultivate the land of which he became the owner. If the world of law is to fulfil its function, there must be pathways through the world of law from every input fact to some output fact. Input that does not lead to any output could just as well be disregarded by the world of law. Output which cannot be reached by any input makes little sense. To speak of the world of law and of pathways through it is only a metaphor. But it is a metaphor which provides the legislator with a useful perspective on his tasks: he must create a well–structured world, and one aspect of a good structure is that there are rule–defined pathways through the world of law from every input fact and to every output fact. Insight into the structure of the world of law as provided by the logical tools discussed in this article is crucially important in this connection.

References

Alchourrón, C.E., and E. Bulygin. 1971. *Normative systems*. Wien: Springer.

Anscombe, G.E.M. 1976. *Intention*, 2nd ed. Oxford: Basil Blackwell.

Aquinas, Thomas. Summa Theologica, many editions.

Austin, John. 1954. *The province of jurisprudence determined*. London: Weidenfeld and Nicholson. Reprinted in 1998 by Hackett Publishing Company.

Austin, John L., O. Urmson, and Marina SbisÃ, eds. 1975. *How to do things with words*, 2nd ed. Oxford: Oxford University Press.

Bentham, Jeremy. 1970. *Of laws in general*. London: The Athlone Press.

Brouwer, Bob., and Jaap Hage. 2007. Basic concepts of European private law. *European Review of Private Law* 1–2007:3–26.

Brożek, Bartosz. 2013. *Rule–following*. Kraków: Copernicus Center Press.

Coleman, Jules, and Scott Shapiro, eds. 2002 *The Oxford handbook of jurisprudence and philosophy of law*. Oxford: Oxford University Press.

D'Entréves, Alessandro P. ed. 1959. Aquinas. *Selected political writings*. Trans. J.G. Dawson. Oxford: Basil Blackwell.

Fuller, Lon L. 1963. *The morality of law*, rev. ed. New Haven: Yale University Press.

Gabbay, Dov, John Horty, Xavier Parent, Ron van der Meyden., and Leendert van der Torre, eds. 2013. *Handbook of deontic logic and normative systems*. London: College Publications.

Hage, Jaap. 1997. *Reasoning with rules*. Dordrecht: Kluwer.

Hage, Jaap. 2005a. *Studies in legal logic*. Dordrecht: Springer.

Hage, Jaap. 2005b. Rule consistency. In Hage 2005a, 135–158.

Hage, Jaap. 2005c. What is a norm?. In Hage 2005a, 159–202.
Hage, Jaap. 2005d. Legal statics and legal dynamics. In Hage 2005a, 203–226.
Hage, Jaap. 2007. Building the world of law. *Legisprudence* 1:359–379.
Hage, Jaap. 2011a. A model of juridical acts: Part 1: The world of law. *Artificial Intelligence and Law* 19:23–48.
Hage, Jaap. 2011b. A model of juridical acts: Part 2: The operation of juridical acts. *Artificial Intelligence and Law* 19:49–73.
Hage, Jaap. 2012. Conceptual tools for legislators. Part I: Rules and norms. *Legisprudence* 6(1):77–98.
Hage, Jaap. 2013a. The deontic furniture of the world. In *The many faces of normativity*, ed. J. Stelmach, B. Brożek, and M. Hohol, 73–114. Kraków : Copernicus Center Press.
Hage, Jaap. 2013b. Conceptual tools for legislators. Part 2: Pathways through the world of law. *The Theory and Practice of Legislation* 1:277–304.
Hage, Jaap. 2013c. Can legal theory be objective? In Husa and Van Hoecke, 23–44.
Hage, Jaap. 2014. Separating rules from normativity. In *Problems of normativity, rules and rule-following*, ed. M. Araszkiewicz, P. Bana, T. Gizbert-Studnicki, and K. Peszka, 13–30. Cham: Springer.
Hage, Jaap. (Draft). *Facts and Meaning,* draft paper that can be downloaded from: http://www.jaaphage.nl/FactsAndMeaning.pdf.
Hage, Jaap, and H.B. Verheij. 1999. The law as a dynamic interconnected system of states of affairs: A legal top ontology. *International Journal of Human–Computer Studies* 51:1043–1077.
Hart, Herbert L.A. 1982. *Essays on Bentham*. Oxford: Clarendon Press.
Hart, Herbert L.A. 2012. *The concept of law*, 4th ed. Oxford: Oxford University Press. 2012, 1st ed. 1961.
Hohfeld, Wesley N. 1920. *Fundamental legal conceptions as applied in judicial reasoning; and other legal essays*. New Haven: Yale University Press.
Husa, Jaakko, and Mark Van Hoecke, eds. 2013. *Objectivity in law and legal reasoning*. Oxford: Hart.
Kelsen, Hans. 1960. *Reine Rechtslehre*, 2nd ed. Vienna: Franz Deuticke.
Kelsen, Hans. 1979. *Allgemeine Theorie der Normen*. Wien: Manzsche Verlags– und Universitats-buchhandlung.
Kelsen, Hans. 1992. *Introduction to the problems of legal theory, translation of the first (1934) edition of the Reine Rechtslehre by Bonnie Litschewsky Paulson and Stanley Paulson*. Oxford: Clarendon Press.
Kripke, Saul A. 1982. *Wittgenstein on rules and private language*. Oxford: Blackwell.
Leiter, Brian. 2002. Law and objectivity. In Coleman and Shapiro, 969–989.
Lindahl, Lars. 1977. *Position and change. A study in law and logic*. Dordrecht: Reidel.
Lindahl, Lars, and Jan Odelstad. 2013. The theory of joining systems. In Gabbay 2013, 545–634.
Lodder, A. 1999. *Dialaw. On legal justification and dialogical models of argumentation*. Dordrecht: Kluwer.
Mackie, John L. 1980. *The cement of the universe*. Oxford: Clarendon Press.
Prakken, Henry. 1997. Logical tools for modelling legal argument. In *A study of defeasible reasoning in law*. Dordrecht: Kluwer.
Prakken, Henry, and Giovanni Sartor, eds. 1997. *Logical models of legal argumentation*. Dordrecht: Kluwer.
Putnam, Hilary. 1975a. The meaning of meaning. In *Language, mind and knowledge*, Minnesota studies in the philosophy of science vii, ed. K. Gunderson. Minneapolis: University of Minnesota Press. Also in Putnam 1975b, 215–271.
Putnam, Hilary. 1975b. *Mind language and reality*, Philosophical papers, vol. 2. Cambridge: Cambridge University Press.
Raz, Joseph. 1980. *The concept of a legal system*, 2nd ed. Oxford: Clarendon Press.
Ross, Alf. 1957. Tû tû, Harvard Law Review 70, 812.
Ross, Alf. 1968. *Directives and norms*. London: Routledge and Kegan Paul.

Royakkers, Lambert M.M. 1998. *Extending deontic logic for the formalisation of legal rules*. Dordrecht: Kluwer.
Sartor, Giovanni. 2005. *Legal reasoning, a cognitive approach to the law*. Dordrecht: Springer.
Searle, John. 1969. *Speech acts*. Cambridge: Cambridge University Press.
Searle, John. 1979a. *Expression and meaning: Studies in the theory of speech acts*. Cambridge: Cambridge University Press.
Searle, John. 1979b. A taxonomy of illocutionary acts. In Searle 1979a, 1–29.
Searle, John. 1995. *The construction of social reality*. New York: The Free Press.
Searle, John. 2010. *Making the social world*. Oxford: Oxford University Press.
Smits, Jan M., ed. 2012. *Elgar encyclopedia of comparative law*, 2nd ed. Northampton: Edward Elgar Publishing.
Spaak, Torben. 1994. *The concept of legal competence: An essay in conceptual analysis*. Aldershot: Darthmouth.
Stelmach, Jerzy, Bartosz Brożek, and Mateusz Hohol, eds. 2011. *The normativity of law*. Kraków: Copernicus Press.
Strawson, Peter F. 1950. Truth. *Proceedings of the Aristotelian Society, Supplementary Volume*. Also in Strawson, 190–213.
Strawson, Peter F. 1971. *Logico–linguistic papers*. London: Methuen.
Tuomela, Raimo. 2010. *The philosophy of sociality*. Oxford: University Press.
van Vliet, Lars. 2012. Transfer of movable property. In Smits 2012, 886–897.
von Wright, and Georg Henrik. 1963. Norm and action: A logical enquiry. London: Routledge and Kegan Paul.
White, Alan R. 1984. *Rights*. Oxford: Clarendon Press.
Wittgenstein, Ludwig. 1953. *Philosophical investigations*, 2nd ed. Trans. G.E.M. Anscombe. Oxford: Basil Blackwell.
Zimmerman, Reinhard. 1996. *The law of obligations: Roman foundations of the civilian tradition*. Oxford: Oxford University Press.

Chapter 2
Conflict of Legal Norms: Definition and Varieties

Lars Lindahl and David Reidhav

Abstract As emphasized by Jeremy Bentham and the analytical school, logical consistency is a requirement for rational legislation. For understanding consistency between norms, a logical scrutiny of normative conflicts is needed. In our paper, a framework for the fine structure of such conflicts is introduced and explained. "Normative conflict" is defined relative the framework and different types of conflict distinguished. The framework consists of a formal language in which norms of a legal system can be represented, accompanied by a set of logical rules and general principles. These rules and principles are such that their application to sentences describing the contents of a legal system discloses conflicts within legal systems. Important elements in legislation are capacitative norms, relating to legal power, or "legal competence," to achieve a valid legal result by an act–in–the–law (for example a promise, a conveyance, or a judicial decision). The analysis encompasses conflicts between deontic norms relating to obligations and permissions, on one hand, and norms relating to legal power, on the other. The analysis is applicable both to conflicts within a national legal system and to supranational normative conflicts, for example conflicts between national law and EU law.

Keywords Normative conflict • Conflict of legal norms • Normative systems • Deontic logic • Normative logic • Normative proposition • Legal power • Compliance conflict • Contradiction • Ground for

---

The authors wish to thank Michał Araszkiewicz and Krzysztof Płeszka for helpful comments and suggestions on this chapter.

L. Lindahl (✉) • D. Reidhav
Faculty of Law, University of Lund, Lund, Sweden
e-mail: lars-lindahl@live.se; david.reidhav@jur.lu.se

M. Araszkiewicz, K. Płeszka (eds.), *Logic in the Theory and Practice of Lawmaking*, Legisprudence Library 2, DOI 10.1007/978-3-319-19575-9_2

2.1 Introduction

2.1.1 Subject Matter of the Chapter

Conflict of legal norms is an important and frequent phenomenon. In national law, two statutory provisions can be in conflict, or a clause in a private contract can be in conflict with a statutory provision. Conflicts can occur between national law and international law, or between national law and the law of a supranational organization such as the European Union. Conflicts can be of different kinds. They can be deontic, i.e., in terms of obligations and permissions, they can be capacitative, i.e., in terms of legal power (competence) and legal disability, they can, moreover, be "cross–conflicts" between deontic and capacitative norms.

The theory of normative conflict expounded in the present chapter exhibits three distinctive features:

(1) It is a theory concerning the *definition* of normative conflict. A complete theory of conflicts of norms involves two stages both of which are central but which should be distinguished in the analysis. A first stage consists in the definition of conflict, i.e. in an elucidation of what it means that two or more norms are in conflict. A second stage is the analysis of ways of *solving* an existing conflict, for example by applying a norm of higher order prescribing that of two conflicting norms one is to take precedence over the other. In the scientific analysis of conflict, it is essential that definition and solution are kept apart (Pauwelyn 2003, 169 f.; Ratti 2013, 129 f.). A theory of conflict resolution presupposes that it is clear what it means that there is a conflict. If definition and solution are mixed up, the analysis will be muddled. The theory set out herein is exclusively concerned with the definition of conflict, as well as with ways of exhibiting conflicts and how types of conflict can be systematized.[1] All issues concerning conflict resolution are disregarded. For example, the chapter does not deal with any issues concerning preference among conflicting norms, or defeasibility of a norm in a conflicting set. Such issues belong to the theory of the resolution of conflict, not to the theory of defining conflict.

(2) It is a theory devised so that it extends to *capacitative* norms, i.e., to norms expressing legal power (competence) or non–power. Most theories of normative conflict entirely disregard conflicts involving capacitative norms (Hamner Hill 1987, 230 and 237; Elhag et al. 2000, 212 f.). In our view, neglect of such conflicts results in an incomplete picture of the phenomenon of normative conflict. In the formal framework developed, conflicts involving both deontic and capacitative norms are disclosed. As will appear subsequently, the action notion "Do" plays an essential role in the framework and the logic of action is extensively exploited. "Do" will be combined with both deontic and capacitative notions.

[1]The authors pursue a larger project involving as well a theory of conflict resolution.

(3) It is a theory based on a logical system for *descriptive* sentences containing a number of operators and concepts suitable for representing legal norms. In contrast, analyses of conflict within the literature, predominantly, rely on deontic logic and, moreover, do not introduce any special operator for legal implication in the representation of legal norms. In our view, unless such an operator is introduced, legal norms are misrepresented, since, as we argue, normative discourse has a certain direction.

The theory, to be presented, is developed in two principal phases. In Sects. 2.2 and 2.3, the logical system, consisting of a formal language and a set of logical rules, is devised. Then, in Sect. 2.4, the system is used to define normative conflict in a designated set *J* of legal norm–sentences.

With a view to the introduction and development of the logical system (Sects. 2.2 and 2.3), it proceeds in two steps. In a first step (Sect. 2.2), a framework of notions is introduced, so as to provide a common ground for the deontic notions of obligation and permission, on one hand, and the capacitative notions of legal power (competence) and non–power, on the other. In order to obtain such a common ground for the two groups of notions, we do not rely on the deontic logic of "Ought" or "Shall" devised by Jeremy Bentham, G. H. von Wright and others, and exemplified by what is called "Standard Deontic Logic." Instead, the logical system devised and relied on herein includes a vocabulary of action concepts, a relation "Ground for" expressing legal implication, and a notion "Wrong is committed," similar to A. R. Anderson's constant "S" (Anderson 1956).

In a second step (Sect. 2.3), the formal system, called COLT, is developed.[2] Here, the analysis targets logical consequences of true statements that such and such norm–sentences belong to a designated set *J* of norm–sentences. Derivability proceeds by the notion H_J expressing "Holds as a consequence for system *J*." The logic of H_J is related to the logic of Carlos Alchourrón's so–called "normative logic" for statements that such and such norms are enacted by a legislator (Alchourrón 1969). The COLT system is used in this chapter only to elucidate normative conflict; however, it is submitted that it has several other uses.

In Sect. 2.4, using the COLT system, the subject matter of normative conflict is addressed. The expression "normative conflict in system *J*" is defined in terms of derivability of certain consequences from true sentences stating that a set of deontic and capacitative norm–sentences belong to *J*. Two main types of conflict in a system *J* are defined: compliance conflict and contradiction. Furthermore, conflicts are classified as deontic conflicts, capacitative conflicts, and cross–conflicts, i.e. conflicts between the deontic and capacitative modes.

[2]COLT is an abbreviation for Conflicts On Levels Theory. This study is part of a more comprehensive study on normative conflicts. In the more comprehensive study, the interrelationships between norms on the level of public officials, enforcing the legal system, and norms on the level of citizens are analyzed. This is why the system is called COLT. In the present chapter, due to space limitations, we do not distinguish between these levels and do not analyze the interrelationships between these levels.

Finally, in Sect. 2.5, the COLT theory of conflicts is illustrated by a few practical cases, two of which concern conflicts between national legal provisions and the law of the European Community. Focus, in the present chapter, is on conflicts in a set of *legal* norms, in particular, norms that are issued by an authority or some authorities. In a wide sense, such norms can be called norms issued by legislation. It is submitted, however, that the theory, or part of it, can be applied as well to sets of norms that are not strictly legal, for example, norms of a private club or norms issued in a formal multi–agent system.

The subject matter of the present chapter is complex leading into much debated issues of legal theory and philosophical logic. However, we maintain that the analysis is of considerable practical relevance for legislation and other forms of norm–giving. In practical application, the starting point can be a set of (legal) texts. Our analysis does not presuppose that this set of texts is chosen from a single legal "system."[3] For example, the set of texts can consist of some rules of national law and a rule of international law, or of a national rule and an article in the EEC Treaty or in the European Convention on Human Rights (ECHR).

Delimitations. In this chapter, we do not deal with "practical conflicts." These are conflicts due to contingent practical impossibility, which is a vague concept. The theory presented here abstracts from such problems that need a much–enlarged framework. Another delimitation is that the chapter does not develop a framework for "relational rights" in the sense of Hohfeld's fundamental jural relations, for example that X has an obligation (or a permission) versus Y but not versus Z, etc. (for some suggestions on this topic, see Lindahl 2001, 163 ff.; cf. Sergot 2013, 401 f.). Developing a logical theory of relational rights presupposes as well a much–enlarged framework (Hohfeld's logic is very rudimentary). Finally, "axiological conflicts," where different legal "values," "purposes," "goals," "policies" or "ends" underlying legal rules clash, in the sense of favoring different sets of legal rules, also fall outside the scope of the present study.

2.1.2 Recent Legal Work on Conflicts

The subject of normative conflict has attracted attention in recent work on public international law, echoing earlier discussions in legal theory.[4] In particular, the contributions of Joost Pauwelyn (2003) and Erich Vranes (2006, 2009) should be mentioned. Here, only a few topics, relating to the present chapter, will be addressed.

---

[3]For convenience, we will often use the word "system," like "system J," for a set S of norms under consideration. This way of speaking is not meant to imply any assumptions about S's constituting a system in the sense of being organized in a specific way.

[4]In legal theory, the literature on normative conflicts is vast. Comments are to be found in the works of legal theorists such as Jeremy Bentham, Hans Kelsen, Lon Fuller, Herbert Hart, Ronald Dworkin, Torstein Eckhoff, Åke Frändberg, Stephen Munzer, H. Hamner Hill, Carlos Alchourrón and Eugenio Bulygin. See as well, Sartor (1992) and Hage (2000).

Narrow and wide definition of "conflict." As exposed by Pauwelyn and Vranes, in the modern legal literature on conflicts of norms, there are two views on the definition of conflict, one of which is narrower and the other wider. Pauwelyn and Vranes maintain the wider definition.[5] Wilfred Jenks and Wolfram Karl adopt the narrower definition. According to the narrow definition, conflict is present when there are two mutually exclusive obligations (impossibility of joint compliance). Thus, in Jenks' definition: "conflict in the strict sense of direct incompatibility arises only where a party to the two treatises cannot simultaneously comply with the obligations under both treaties" (Jenks 1953, 426); similarly, in Karl: "there is a conflict between treaties when two (or more) treaty instruments contain obligations which cannot be complied with simultaneously" (Karl [1984] 2000, 936).[6]

To the narrow definition Pauwelyn and Vranes object that it rules out there being a conflict between a prohibition to do X and a permission to do X, in spite of that there is a potential breach of the prohibition, namely in case the agent makes use of the permission.[7] According to Pauwelyn, the conflict becomes an actual conflict only if the permission is used. As long as the permission is not used, the conflict itself is not actual but only potential (Pauwelyn 2003, 176). Vranes' criteria for conflict also include potential violation: There is a conflict if "in obeying or applying one norm, the other norm is necessarily or potentially violated" (Vranes 2006, 418 and 2009, 35).

The standpoint adopted in the present chapter is as well that there are conflicts between prohibitions and permissions. Our argument, though, does not depend on potential breach. If it is prohibited to do X, this means the same as that it is not permitted to do X. Thus, in the case under consideration, a consequence of the set of norms is that it is both permitted to do X and not permitted to do X. As this conjunction is contradictory, there is a conflict in the set of norms. With respect to the simple cases in view now, no distinction is made herein between potential and actual conflicts: in these cases, if there is conflict, it is conflict *tout court*. In case of prohibition, N_1, and permission, N_2, the existence of conflict is independent of whether someone makes use of the permission or not. The consequence of a list containing both N_1 and N_2 is a contradiction. This exemplifies one basic type of conflict: contradiction.

The other basic type of conflict can be described as follows. Suppose that in a list of official documents there is one command N_1 saying that it is obligatory to buy the supply of medicine from company X and another command N_2 saying that it is obligatory *not* to buy the supply of medicine from company X (but from company

[5] For references to Czaplinski, Danilenko, Neumann, and Kelly and partly diverging readings of these writers with respect to whether they maintain the wide or narrow definition, see Pauwelyn (2003, 168 f.) and Vranes (2006, 402).

[6] For this standpoint in legal philosophy, see references in Hamner Hill (1987, 227 ff.).

[7] A similar objection to the stricter definition ("the impossibility–of–joint–compliance test") was raised earlier by Herbert Hart ([1968] 1983, 326 f.).

Y). A list of N_1 and N_2 implies that the norm–subject cannot avoid doing wrong. This is not contradiction in the set of norms, but the list of norms is such that avoiding doing wrong is logically impossible.

Both Pauwelyn and Vranes adopt a criterion based on the notion of breach or violation. According to Pauwelyn: "Essentially, two norms are [...] in a relationship of conflict if one constitutes, has led to, or may lead to, a breach of the other" (Pauwelyn 2003, 175 f.). Pauwelyn's definition of *inherent* conflict needs a comment, since it concerns the very notion of *breach*. The authors of the present chapter use the following terminology: If a prohibition is broken, the breach is a relation between the prohibition and the prohibited *act* or *omission*. Suppose that an authority issues a norm and there is another norm prohibiting the act of issuing this norm.[8] (Pauwelyn 2003, 175 ff.) seems to maintain that in this case, the issued *norm* constitutes a breach of the prohibitive norm. We do not use the term "breach" in this way. In our view, in a prohibition to issue a norm, the addressees are norm–givers, while, in the issued norm, the addressees are the subjects of the issued norm. The two norms, therefore, are on different levels. The breach is the act of issuing the norm.

Legal Power (competence). One specific kind of conflict is that between one norm enacting legal power and another enacting legal disability for an agent with respect to the same subject–matter; another type of conflict is that between one norm prescribing an obligation to exercise legal power and another imposing legal disability to do this. The classifications by Pauwelyn and Vranes do not include conflicts involving legal power or legal disability.[9] Their classifications are restricted to deontic conflict, i.e., in their terminology, conflict involving commands, prohibitions, permissions and exemptions (in Pauwelyn's sense of "need not," i.e., permission not to do). In the present chapter, the authors endeavor to incorporate norms on power and disability and their interrelationships with deontic norms (i.e., norms on obligations and permissions).

The role of logic. In the works of Pauwelyn and Vranes, the use of logic is strictly limited. Both use the classical so–called "square of opposition" from scholastic logic for exhibiting the interrelationship between deontic notions, but they do not go much further than that. In the present chapter, it is submitted that a richer logical framework is apt to throw more light on the various kinds of conflict.

---

[8]There being such a prohibition is compatible with that the enacting authority has the legal power (competence) to enact the norm. An authority's legal power can be wider than its permission. In that case the enacted norm is valid in spite of its enactment being prohibited.

[9]Vranes writes: "By norm of competence is meant a norm which enables the state or person holding the competence to *transform* the legal situation of persons/states subjected to this power: in the exercise of this competence, new norms of conduct (prohibitions, obligations, and permissions) as well as subordinate norms of competence can be brought into existence. This is the reason why competences have to be distinguished from "mere" permissions. [...] What is crucial, however, is the fact that exercising competences may create incompatible prohibitions, obligations and permissions" (Vranes 2006, 417). Vranes does not develop these ideas further and focuses on the deontic norms following from exercises of legal competence.

2.1.3 Recent Logical Work on Normative Conflict

In a couple of recent papers, Lou Goble has addressed the issue of normative conflict. Goble's preliminary characterization of conflict is as follows:[10]

> Generally speaking, there is a normative conflict when an agent ought to do a number of things, each of which is possible for the agent, but it is impossible for the agent to do them all (Goble 2013, 242).

Goble's point of departure for his treatment of normative conflicts is as follows: "On one hand, they [normative conflicts] appear to be commonplace. [. . .] On the other hand, common principles of deontic logic entail that normative conflicts are literally impossible" (Goble 2013, 242). The principle of deontic logic that Goble refers to is primarily the axiom of standard deontic logic: $Op \supset \neg O \neg p$, i.e., if Ought p, then not: Ought not p. In our terminology, this is a principle for *ideal* normative systems, not for a set of norms selected from various legal texts. Thus, the sentence:

(1) "On list L there is both the norm "Ought p" and the norm "Ought not p" "

can be perfectly true. If true, the sentence means that (it is true that) in list L there is a conflict of norms. The difference between (1) and

(2) "Ought p and Ought not–p"

yields a difference between two kinds of logic. One kind is systems of logic for *genuine norms* expressed by sentences (2).[11] This kind is *deontic logic*, and is exemplified by Standard Deontic Logic (SDL). The other kind is systems of logic for *descriptions* of norm–enactments, i.e., sentences (1). Carlos Alchourrón (1969, 242) has baptized this kind of logic "normative logic" which is a logic of descriptive sentences, primarily for the description of a legal system J. Another term used to designate this latter kind of logic is "logic of normative propositions" (Alchourrón 1969, 242; von Wright 1982, 4; Bulygin 1985, 148).[12]

Goble deals with a logical framework for sentences of the kind (2), whereas the present chapter, for defining and exhibiting conflict, uses a logic for the kind

[10] For references to the work of other moral philosophers, in particular, G. H. von Wright, E. J. Lemmon, Risto Hilpinen, Bernard Williams, C. L. Hamblin, R. Barcan Marcus, F. Jackson and M. Nussbaum, see as well Lindahl (1992).

[11] Regarding the distinction between genuine norms and descriptions of norm–enactments, there is a long tradition, emanating from Bentham, maintained by Fenno–Scandian philosophers (Hedenius, Wedberg, Stenius, von Wright) and stressed by Alchourrón and Bulygin, see references in Sect. 2.2.3.

[12] Alchourrón establishes his terminology as follows: "I use the expression "deontic logic" to identify the logical properties and relations of norms, and "normative logic" to identify the logic of normative propositions" (1969, 242). By "normative proposition," Alchourrón means a proposition "to the effect that a norm has been issued." In Alchourrón (1969) a system of "normative logic" is presented for descriptions of the kind (1) above. We note that the name "normative proposition" might be misleading as ambiguous between kind (1) and (2), see, for example, Goble (2013, 241) where the expression is used for kind (2).

(1); in fact, it relies on a generalized version of Alchourrón's normative logic. Next, Goble's work concerns another problem area than the issue of definition and exposition of conflicts to be dealt with in the present chapter. Goble presents an elaborate logical framework for different varieties of *prima facie* obligations and obligations *all–things–considered.*

We note that the difference between sentences (1) and (2) does not correspond to the difference between "legal" and "moral" norms. Insofar as a number of norms (legal or moral or even of some third kind) are put down in a list L (think of the list of The Ten Commandments), it is possible to state in true sentences what list L describes. Then, with regard to list L, it is possible as well to define what constitutes a conflict between the norms in list L.

Goble takes great care to develop his framework in such a way that it avoids so–called "deontic explosion." By many systems of logic, from an inconsistent set of premises, any arbitrary sentence results as a consequence. For example, if a set of deontic Ought–sentences is inconsistent, then "Ought p" can be derived in Standard Deontic Logic for any arbitrary p (Goble 2013, 344, et passim, on the principle *ex contradictione quodlibet*).

In the present chapter, deontic logic (SDL) is not used. The problem of "explosion," however, might be present as well in a logic for descriptive sentences of kind (1). We endeavor to cope with the problem of "explosion," by distinguishing two kinds of descriptive statements with different logic. One set states what is expressed in a list L considered. For this set, since very little logic is assumed, the problem of explosion is absent. The other set of descriptive sentences state conflict–exhibiting consequences of L. For this set a richer logic is assumed and explosion may occur. We submit, however, that explosion in the conflict–exhibiting set is innocuous, since this set does not state what the list prescribes but only has the object of exhibiting conflict.

Turning to the main part of the chapter, we begin with the issue of the representation of norms and norm–descriptions. Then the system devised for exposing conflicts is set out in Sect. 2.3. The notion "normative conflict" is defined in Sect. 2.4, where its varieties also are exhibited. Finally, the theory is illustrated in Sect. 2.5.

2.2 Norms and Norm–Descriptions

2.2.1 Logical Tools for Representing Norms

A formal framework suitable for explicating normative conflict must be sufficiently rich to account for the wide variety of legal norms contained in legal systems. Devising logical tools adequate for representing legal norms is an important task in its own right. To this purpose, we now introduce a number of concepts.

2.2.1.1 Ground For

A central concept in law is "ground for." If *A* is ground for *B*, *A* is said to be operative fact for legal consequence *B*. In legal theory, a norm to the effect that *A* is ground for *B* is often called a legal conditional and the relation between *A* and *B* described as "implicative" or as a relation of "legal causality" (Zitelmann 1879, 222 ff.).[13]

What facts are grounds for legal consequences is a contingent matter. It depends on the contents of the norms issued by agents having been conferred legal power (legislators, judges, private individuals with respect to their own affairs, etc.). However, in well–known systems, a promise is ground for an obligation to fulfill the promise, a breach of contract ground for damages, a purchase ground for ownership, etc.

In legal texts, the relation "ground for" can be expressed in several different ways, for example by "If *A*, then *B*," "*B* is legal consequence of *A*," "Any person *X* shall do *B*," "*X*–objects are not permitted in *Y*–places," etc. (See examples below in Sect. 2.5) Truth–functional implication is too weak to accurately represent this relation. The so–called paradoxes of truth–functional implication make a stronger connective desirable in the representation of legal sentences.

In normative discourse, the "ground for"–relation has a specific direction. The direction is *from* grounds *to* consequences, not the other way around. Consider the following sentence:

(1) John's lending 50€ to Paul is ground for an obligation for Paul to repay 50€.

In (1) John's lending legally causes the obligation to repay and has the characteristic direction from fact to consequence. Sentence (1) is not equivalent to:

(2) Paul's not having an obligation to repay 50€ is ground for John's not lending 50€ to Paul.

Sentence (2) is not equivalent to (1), because it has the "wrong" direction. Even if (1) is true; it is not true that the absence of obligation is legal ground for John not lending the money (cf. input/output logic, Makinson and van der Torre (2000), and the theory of "joining systems" in Lindahl and Odelstad (2013)). This means that so–called contraposition (which holds for the truth–functional implication "$\supset$") does not hold for "Ground for."

As is well–known, terms such as "ownership" are ambiguous with respect to the distinction between grounds and consequences. Intermediaries (e.g. ownership, contract, will, letter of attorney, etc.) are legal consequences relative to a set of

---

[13] In recent philosophical literature, there is an increasing interest in the general phenomenon called "grounding," exemplified by statements of the kind "*A*–facts obtain because of *B*–facts," "*A*–facts are grounded in *B*–facts," "*A*–properties are due to *B*–properties," and so on. See the various essays in Correia and Schneider (2012). There are interrelations between the analysis of "grounding" and the relation "ground for" expressing legal conditionals. However, the scope of the present chapter, where focus is on legal systems, legal implication and normative conflict, does not leave room for entering on the vast subject of grounding dealt with in this literature.

grounds and grounds relative to further legal consequences (see, e.g. Wedberg 1951; Ross 1957; Lindahl and Odelstad 2013). Consider the following sentences:

(1) John's purchasing object *o* from Paul is ground for John's ownership of object *o*,
(2) John's ownership of object *o* is ground for John's liberty to dispose of object *o*.

"Ownership" is legal consequence in (1) and ground in (2). Since transitivity holds for the "ground for"–relation, it is warranted to infer:

(3) John's purchasing object *o* is ground for John's liberty to dispose of object *o*.

In this way, an intermediary such as "ownership" functions as a "vehicle of inference" in legal inferences from facts to consequences (Wedberg 1951, 272 ff.).

Since truth–functional implication ($\supset$) misrepresents the "ground for"–relation, an operator GF is introduced into the formal framework. This operator is supposed to be read, "is legal ground for." Any GF–sentence then warrants inferring its legal consequence, when the ground is fulfilled. Accordingly, the following principle holds for operator GF:

(Inf $\supset$) Inferred material implication: $(\alpha \text{ GF } \beta) \supset (\alpha \supset \beta)$.

In general, the principle (Inf $\supset$) holds for all plausible understandings of a conditional sentence (Edgington 2001, 387). It holds, for example, for an interpretation of "If, then" in terms of C. I. Lewis' notion "strict implication," since Lewis' "$A \prec B$" implies "$A \supset B$" (Lewis and Langford 1932, 137). However, (Inf $\supset$) will not be assumed among the axioms of the subsequent system COLT in the present chapter. Instead, we assume a bridging axiom (see, Sect. 2.3.2.4).[14]

A full–fledged theory of operator GF is beyond the scope of the present chapter. In accordance with the foregoing, transitivity and inferred material implication are assumed to be valid for GF. Moreover, it is assumed that contraposition is not valid for GF, though, of course, it is valid for "$\supset$." Thus, "A GF B" implies "$\neg B \supset \neg A$," while it does not imply "$\neg B$ GF $\neg A$." "Nested" occurrences of GF in sentences will be allowed; so, sentences of the form "A GF (B GF C)," where A is ground for a "ground–for"–sentence, are meaningful sentences.

These principles are sufficient for the notion GF in the context of conflict analysis. In system COLT, subsequently to be developed, operator H_J (see Sect. 2.1.1) focuses on the logical consequences in COLT on the assumption that a set of GF–sentences (norms) belong to a normative system J.

[14]As is well–known, Lewis' theory of strict implication ($\prec$) emerged as a reaction against truth–functional implication, which, in his view, was not "in accord with any ordinary or useful meaning of the term "implies" " (Lewis 1912, 529). Strict implication is defined as: $A \prec B =_{Def.} \neg \Diamond (A \wedge \neg B)$ (Lewis and Langford 1932, 124). Equivalently, it can be defined as: $A \prec B =_{Def.} \Box(A \supset B)$ from which it is immediately seen that the principle (Inf $\supset$) holds for it.

2.2.1.2 Action: Operator "Do"

So far, we have not introduced any symbols for individuals. In subsequent sections, such symbols will be employed; therefore, some conventions are in order. Letters $x, y, z, \ldots, x_1, x_2, x_3, \ldots$ will be used either as variables or as parameters for agents. If x is a parameter, the reference of x is assumed to be constant throughout the specific context. Then x replaces devices such as using names "Mary," "Paul," etc. for imaginary persons. Letters $A, B, C, \ldots A_1, A_2, A_3, \ldots$ will be used similarly as variables or parameters for states of affairs (see, further, Appendix 1).

Normative systems regulate human action. Norms require that certain acts be performed, omitted, etc. For the representation of action, the operator "Do" is employed. It is supposed to be read, "sees to it that" (for the concept "sees to it that" see, Kanger (2001), Pörn (1970), Lindahl (1977), Belnap and Perloff (1988), Segerberg (1992), Holmström–Hintikka (1997), and Horty (2001)). By the introduction of action operator "Do," several forms of action become distinguishable within the formal framework. The distinctions go back at least to St. Anselm who referred to them as different styles of doing (Anselm of Canterbury [c. 1100] 1998, 489).

Let symbol $\pm$ stand for affirmation or negation of the sentence that it precedes. Then the general possibilities with respect to action can be written as:

$$\pm \text{Do}(x, \pm A).$$

The four possibilities are:

1. Pro–action: $\text{Do}(x, A)$ "x sees to it that A."
2. Not Pro–action: $\neg$ $\text{Do}(x, A)$ "Not: x sees to it that A."
3. Counter–action: $\text{Do}(x, \neg A)$ "x sees to it that not A."
4. Not Counter–action: $\neg\text{Do}(x, \neg A)$ "Not: x sees to it that not A."

To exemplify (1)–(4):

1. John sees to it that Paul has possession of object o.
2. John does not see to it that Paul has possession of object o.
3. John sees to it that Paul does not have possession of object o.
4. John does not see to it that Paul does not have possession of object o.

2.2.1.3 Doing *A* by Means of Doing *B*

In what follows, much use will be made of the notion "seeing to it that A by seeing to it that B" (see, Goldman 1970, 20 ff.; Lindahl 1977, 69 ff.).

Obligations must usually be fulfilled in a specified fashion; not any act achieving the obligatory state of affairs is adequate. A contractual obligation for John to see to it that Paul acquires possession of a bushel of apples is likely fulfilled by handing the bushel to Paul in his house but not by dumping the bushel on the street outside. Similarly, a permission to achieve A is not a permission to achieve A by any means

B whatever. Paul, having a firm, can be permitted to enlarge his profits by increasing the quality of goods sold but not by threatening to thrash his competitors.

The concept of doing A by doing B is important as regards legal power and disability. For achieving legal artefacts (e.g. a contract, a will, a verdict, a legislative act, etc.) by the exercise of power, the law specifies validity requirements. Consider the following sentences:

(1) By oral consent, John accepts Paul's proposal to buy the piece of land Greenacre.
(2) By signing a written contract, John accepts Paul's proposal to buy Greenacre.

In well–known legal systems, John achieves a valid contract by the action described in (2), but not by the action described in (1).

In order to have a formal apparatus sufficiently rich to explicitly represent the distinction between (1) and (2), operator "Do (./.)" is introduced into the formal framework and supposed to be read as "sees to it that by seeing to it that." Thus, in the sequence,

$$\mathrm{Do}(x, A_2/\mathrm{Do}(x, A_1)), \mathrm{Do}(x, A_3/\mathrm{Do}(x, A_2)), \ldots, \mathrm{Do}(x, A_n/\mathrm{Do}(x, A_{n-1})),$$

each act is achieved by the preceding act. In the representation of legal sentences, operator "Do (./.)" will be employed.

2.2.2 *Types of Norms of the Model*

As is well known, W. N. Hohfeld distinguished the following legal relations (Hohfeld 1913, 30):

1. Right – Duty.
2. Privilege – No-Right.
3. Power – Liability.
4. Immunity – Disability.

We will say that 1 and 2 are *deontic* concepts while 3 and 4 are *capacitative*; our theory will include both kinds. Therefore, the norm typology is wider in scope than deontic logic, which is confined to obligations and permissions. We now introduce definitions of the different types of norms that the theory embraces. Four concepts are defined, *viz*. obligation, permission, power and disability. The theory is confined to conflicts between norms instantiating these types.

2.2.2.1 Deontic Norms

Constant "W" for "Wrong is committed" is a deontic concept that will be used to define deontic norms. This approach is not a novelty (see, e.g., Anderson (1956) on the constant S and Henry (1967, 10) on St. Anselm and on *Corpus Iuris Civilis*, also cf. Lindahl (2001), pp. 163 ff. on the notion of a right).

The deontic concept *obligation* or *duty* is defined as follows:

Obligation to do:

$$\text{Obligation}(x, \text{Do}(x, A)) =_{Def.} (\neg\text{Do}(x, A) \text{ GF Do}(x, \text{W}/\neg\text{Do}(x, A))).$$

Obligation not to do:

$$\text{Obligation}(x, \neg\text{Do}(x, A)) =_{Def.} (\text{Do}(x, A) \text{ GF Do}(x, \text{W}/\text{Do}(x, A))).$$

By letting $\pm$ stand for either affirmation or negation and $\mp$ stand for the opposite of $\pm$, the following definition is acquired:

$$\text{Obligation}(x, \pm\text{Do}(x, A)) =_{Def.} (\mp\text{Do}(x, A) \text{ GF Do}(x, \text{W}/\mp\text{Do}(x, A))).$$

An obligation not to do is a prohibition to bring about a specified state of affairs. For example, an obligation not to disclose a certain kind of information is a prohibition to disclose it; disclosing the information is then ground for committing wrong by disclosing the information.

The deontic notion of *permission* is understood as follows:

Permission to do:

$$\text{Permission}(x, \text{Do}(x, A)) =_{Def.} (\text{Do}(x, A) \text{ GF } \neg\text{Do}(x, \text{W}/\text{Do}(x, A))).$$

Permission not to do:

$$\text{Permission}(x, \neg\text{Do}(x, A)) =_{Def.} (\neg\text{Do}(x, A) \text{ GF } \neg\text{Do}(x, \text{W}/\neg\text{Do}(x, A))).$$

If we let $\pm$ stand for either affirmation or negation, we obtain the following definition:

$$\text{Permission}(x, \pm\text{Do}(x, A)) =_{Def.} (\pm\text{Do}(x, A) \text{ GF } \neg\text{Do}(x, \text{W}/\pm\text{Do}(x, A))).$$

Permission guarantees that wrong is not committed by an act. Consider the following sentence:

(1) Disclosing information of kind k is ground for not committing wrong by disclosing information of kind k.

Sentence (1) is to the effect that disclosing information of kind k is sufficient for concluding that wrong is not committed by disclosing information of kind k.

2.2.2.2 Note Concerning General Rules and Instantiation

We assume that if a norm–sentence is to the effect that:

(1) $\text{Do}(x, A)$ GF $\text{Do}(x, \text{W}/\text{Do}(x, A))$,

then (1) is a general rule applying to any x (the expression "For any" is tacitly presupposed). On the other hand, if instead of agent–variable x, we have an individual constant i, the norm–sentence,

(2) $\text{Do}(i, A)$ GF $\text{Do}(i, \text{W}/\text{Do}(i, A))$,

expresses a norm that holds for the particular individual i.

The relation between (1) and (2) is that (2) is an instantiation of (1). In general terms, let $\alpha(x_1, \ldots, x_n)$ be a general rule. Then the set of individual norms instantiating this rule is denoted $\text{IN}(\alpha(x_1, \ldots, x_n))$. This set is obtained by substituting individual constants $i_1, \ldots, i_n$ for the variables $x_1, \ldots, x_n$ in $(\alpha(x_1, \ldots, x_n))$ (cf. Hansson and Makinson 1995, 42 f.). Accordingly, if (2) belongs to the instantiation set of the general rule (1), then we assume that (1) implies (2).

When we use variables rather than individual constants, we tacitly assume "For any" preceding a GF–formula (norm) of the form "$\alpha(x)$ GF $\beta(x)$." Since what is said in the present chapter does not hinge on existential quantification and quantification within quantification, we will not introduce the complex calculus of first order predicate logic in the object language of the formal system COLT. As just mentioned, the expression "For any" preceding a formula means that the formula holds for all instantiations of the formula. By the incorporation of the notion of an instantiation set, $\text{IN}(\alpha(x_1, \ldots, x_n))$, into the formal framework, subsequent derivations do not depend on predicate calculus.

2.2.2.3 Capacitative Norms

Legal power conceptually implies ability to change legal relationships. However, the concept is construed too broadly if simply defined as that ability (cf. Brinz (1873), 211 f., Moritz (1960), 100 ff. on "Befugnis," Lindahl (1977), 51, 194 ff. on the traditional concept "Rechtliches Können," MacCormick (1981), 74 ff.). Any act having a legal effect achieves a legal result. For example, if x assaults y, the result ensues that x is liable to punishment and paying damages. So, equating legal power with the ability to achieve a legal result does not distinguish such power from other legal concepts whereby legal consequences are attached to actions.

In our view, drawing on a long tradition especially within continental law, the characteristic feature of legal power is that legal powers are exercised by behavior of a special kind. A necessary part of any behavior exercising a legal power is *manifestation of intention* to achieve the very legal result that the exercise achieves.

Let A be a legal result which can be characterized in terms of legal relationships, i.e. obligations, permissions etc. and M be a measure that implies manifestation of the intention to achieve legal result A. Then, legal power is defined as follows:

Legal power:

$$\text{Power}(x, \text{Do}(x, A/\text{Do}(x, M))) =_{Def.} \text{Do}(x, M) \text{ GF } \text{Do}(x, A/\text{Do}(x, M)).$$

A notable difference between the deontic concepts previously defined and legal power is that legal power always is positive. Legal power not to achieve a legal result is either trivial or not meaningful (cf. David Makinson's "triponodo" principle, which is short for "trivial power not to do," Makinson (1986, 412)).

In the case of legal disability, regardless of measure M being performed or not, an individual does not achieve the legal result. Legal disability is defined as follows, where $\top$ stands for tautology:

Legal disability:

$$\text{Disability}(x, \text{Do}(x, A/\text{Do}(x, M))) =_{Def.} \top \text{ GF } \neg\text{Do}(x, A/\text{Do}(x, M)).$$

In most legal systems, there is a *closure rule* for legal power: If legal power is not conferred on an individual by a rule of the system in view, it can be inferred that disability holds for that individual in this system. For example, legal power to adjudicate is explicitly conferred on appointed judges and then from the silence of the law it is supposed to be inferred that disability holds for others.

2.2.2.4 Meaning Postulates

In addition to deontic and capacitative norms, there are conceptual rules in the sense of norms that are stipulations about the meaning of particular words, phrases, or sentences. Such rules are auxiliary in the sense that they do not, like deontic and capacitative norms, themselves determine legal effects of action; instead, they are concerned with the meaning of terms occurring in other norms. Within the present framework, they perform the function of *meaning postulates* (for this term, see Carnap (1952), 65 ff., cf. Lindahl (1977), 296 ff.).

Within our framework, one kind of meaning postulate is represented as:

Double–edged meaning postulate:

$$\text{As for the meaning of } B\text{: } A \text{ GF } B \text{ and } \neg A \text{ GF } \neg B.$$

This is not a definition of double–edged meaning postulate; it only shows how postulates of this kind are represented in terms of operator GF. Double–edged meaning postulate is not the only kind of meaning postulate (see, Lindahl 1997, 297).

A weaker form is single–edged meaning postulate where, as a matter of meaning, one concept merely is included in another (e.g. chattel conceptually implies property, car conceptually implies vehicle, etc.). This kind of legal classification has the following form within the framework:

Single–edged meaning postulate:

As for the meaning of B: A GF B and not $\neg A$ GF $\neg B$.

We observe, since "Ground for" is directed, that meaning postulates, as represented above, exhibit the characteristic direction from ground, A, to consequence, B. For example, as for the meaning of "minor," being less than fifteen years old is ground for being a minor, but not conversely, and this holds even if the postulate is double–edged.

In the literature, what is here called meaning postulates are often divided into subgroups, such as definitions or classifications adopted by the law from ordinary language, and postulates that are instituted by legal rules themselves. According to the so–called theory of "Counts–as," some "Counts–as" relations instituted by legal rules are constitutive and others are hybrids of different kinds, for example, a combination of a constitutive rule and a generally acknowledged classification (see Grossi and Jones (2013), with further references, and the comment in Lindahl and Odelstad 2013, 627 ff.).

In the theory of conflict developed in the present chapter, as will appear subsequently, the division of legal norms into deontic/capacitative, on one hand, and meaning postulates, on the other, plays no role for the definition of conflict. The divisions and subdivisions above are of interest from a philosophical perspective and for understanding the function of various norms. The theory of conflict as developed here, however, does not depend on them: In the derivation of conflict, norms of different kinds can function as premises on equal basis. In contrast, an essential tool used here for covering the whole ground of various norms is the notion of "ground for."

What is said above about meaning postulates is mentioned as a reminder that there are norms that do not regulate behavior in a direct way. Even if the distinction between meaning postulates and other norms has no impact on the actual definition of conflict, meaning postulates are often crucial in the derivation of conflict. Frequently, normative conflict hinges on a certain meaning relation holding between the terms occurring in the regulatory norms assessed for conflict (see, Sect. 2.5.1, Case 1).

2.2.3 *The Path from Crude Legal Texts to the Formal Description of a Legal System*

2.2.3.1 Disambiguation and Formal Representation

The formal derivation and exposition of conflict in a normative system presupposes a formal representation of the norms. A first and preparatory step in achieving such a representation is disambiguation of a set I of norm inscriptions (legal texts). It is from such a set I, consisting of inscriptions expressed in ordinary language, that norms stem. Disambiguation generates a new set J of disambiguated legal sentences. For example, an inscription i_1 in set I of inscriptions that is ambiguous between one meaning and a different meaning, yields two different norms N_1, N_2 in set J. The collection of *disambiguated* norms so established will be denoted J:

$$J = \{N_1, N_2, N_3, \ldots, N_n\}.$$

Each member of this set will be referred to as a J–norm and it is such a set of norms that is assessed for conflict. The assessment, as will be shown, proceeds in several steps. For convenience, we will often refer to J as a "system." However, as will be emphasized subsequently, by a legal "system" J, we understand simply a set J of legal norms; so, "normative system" shall be understood as "set of norms." A set J can refer to an entire national legal system, or to the norms in a private contract, or to part of such a set. Or, set J can contain norms belonging to different systems (e.g. norms of a national legal system and norms belonging to EU–law).

For the members of J, it is presupposed that each member: (i) is a sentence having a normative content (norm), (ii) is expressed in informal language, (iii) is an "interpreted" sentence in the weak sense of disambiguation, which doesn't preclude it from containing vague terms. Moreover, as for the relationship between members of set J, (iv) no relations between norms N_1 and N_2 are presupposed for both being members of J. Thus, N_1, N_2 can be members of J, without regard to whether they are contradictory or whether one N_1 is superior to N_2 (in the sense of *Lex superior derogat inferiori*), and so on.

Obviously, from (i)–(iv), it follows that set J is not an interpreted set in the strong sense of conflict–resolving interpretations and conflict–resolving rules (meta–rules) having been applied to the norms. This standpoint is taken to ensure that the theory, in fact, can disclose conflicts within a legal system, since a consistency requirement on J would muddle the distinction between definition and solution of normative conflict.

Next, the sentences in J are represented in terms of Do, GF, Obligation, Permission, Power and Disability. This representation is a function from J into a set of well–formed formulas (wffs) of the formal framework (for this language and its formation rules, see Appendix 1, Sect. 1):

Rep(N) = the expression of norm N within the language of the formal framework.

The representation of set J, obtained by this operation, will be denoted J^* and is a set of GF–sentences. So, each member of J is associated with one, and only one, member of J^*. The step from J to J^* is to be regarded merely as a translation of informal legal sentences to the formal language of COLT. We observe that logical system COLT is not applied to the sentences in this step; therefore, the translation does not imply anything concerning whether two norms are contradictory or whether one norm follows from another, etc.

2.2.3.2 Descriptive Sentences About Norms

As is well known, a *norm expression N* is an entity that is different from a descriptive sentence stating that *N has been issued* by the legislator of a specific legal system. Alchourrón and Bulygin (1971) express the distinction as that between "norms" and "normative propositions," a terminology that is frequently used. Generalizing the distinction, we can distinguish between a norm expression *N* and a sentence stating that (in the set–theoretical sense) *N* is a member of set *S* of norms on a list that is under consideration. This distinction is implicit in the work of Bentham ([1780] 1970, 294), it is emphasized by Hedenius ([1941] 1963, 58), Wedberg (1951, 252 ff.), Stenius (1963, 250) and von Wright (1963, 104 ff., 1991, 273) and, moreover, a corner stone in the work of Alchourrón and Bulygin (see, e.g., Alchourrón and Bulygin 1971, 121).[15]

In the present chapter, descriptive sentences regarding membership in set J^* will be referred to as *J^*–membership sentences*. Such a sentence affirms that a GF–sentence (norm) belongs to set J^*, i.e., to the formal representation of *J*. The collection of J^*–membership sentences will be denoted $\mathrm{E}(J^*)$. Obviously, since, for any norm expression "α GF β," it holds that:

> (α GF β)$\in J^*$ if and only if ((α GF β)$\in J^*$)$\in \mathrm{E}(J^*)$, where α, β are meta–variables for wffs,

there is a one–one correspondence between J^* and $\mathrm{E}(J^*)$. The set $\mathrm{E}(J^*)$ has a pivotal role within the theory, because the system devised for disclosing normative conflicts is applied to such a set of *descriptive* sentences.

2.2.3.3 Overview

Before we move to the formal logical system COLT for sentences describing J^*–membership, the four stages in procedure so far introduced will be schematically exposed in Fig. 2.1 below.

With respect to Fig. 2.1, a caveat is appropriate. An obligation, permission or power can be *conditional* in the sense that it is the legal consequence of some condition. For example, expressed in ordinary language,

> If *x* has promised to pay 100€ to *y*, then *x* has the obligation to pay 100€ to *y*.

That is, *x* has the obligation to pay 100€ to *y in the case that x* has promised to pay 100€ to *y*. Transcribed into J^*, this norm becomes:

$$\mathrm{Do}(x, x \text{ promises to pay } 100\,€ \text{ to } y) \text{ GF } [\neg \mathrm{Do}(x, x \text{ pays } 100\,€ \text{ to } y) \text{ GF } \mathrm{Do}(x, \mathrm{W}/\neg \mathrm{Do}(x, x \text{ pays } 100\,€ \text{ to } y))].$$

[15]For comments on the distinction, see also Frändberg (1987, 85 f.) and Åqvist (2008).

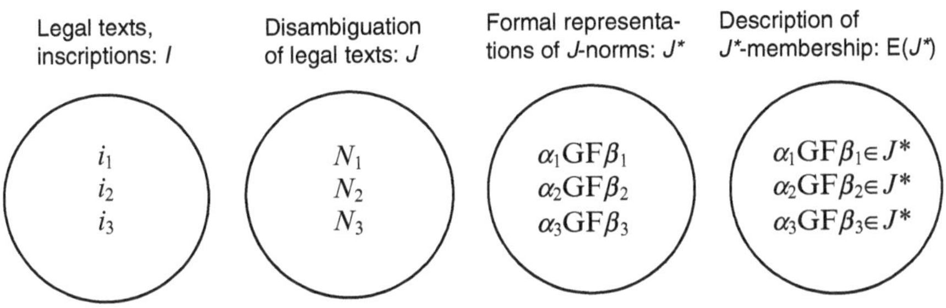

Fig. 2.1 Illustration of successive steps involved in assessing J for normative conflict

In general form:

(*) α GF (β GF γ),

where (β GF γ) expresses the obligation, as expressed in J^*. Similarly, a permission to do in case α or a power to do in case α is of the general form (*).

Sentence (*) expresses a nesting of GF in the sense that (β GF γ) is present within the scope of another GF occurrence. In (*), γ, in turn, can be a sentence (δ GF ϕ) so that the result is (α GF(β GF (δ GF ϕ))). As indicated previously (Sect. 2.2.1.1), there can be any number of successive nestings. Due to the possibility of conditions and nestings, in any sentence α_i GF β_j, in set J^* of Fig. 2.1, it can be the case that β_i is itself a GF–expression or a chain of GF–expressions. As a consequence, the same holds for any sentence ((α_i GF β_j)$\in J^*$) in Fig. 2.1 for E(J^*).

The final step in assessing set J of norms for conflict consists of applying the COLT–system, now to be introduced, to collection E(J^*). By this operation, a set of consequences ensues. This derivational step is crucial to conflict analysis proper where logical consequences of sentences to the effect that norms belong to the normative system are brought out and analyzed.

2.3 The COLT–System

2.3.1 *Introductory Remarks on the System*

System COLT is designed to disclose conflicts within normative systems such as legal systems. The system is comprised of a language and a set of axioms and inference rules. A complete listing of the system including its language, formation rules, etc. is found in Appendix 1. The following formation rules are adopted for language L_{COLT}:

Formation rules, well–formed formulas:

All variables/parameters for state of affairs and the constant W are wffs.
If α, β are wffs, then $\neg\alpha$, $\alpha \wedge \beta$, $\alpha \vee \beta$, $\alpha \supset \beta$, $\alpha \equiv \beta$ are wffs.

If α, β are wffs, then Do(s, α) and Do(s, α/ $\pm$Do(s, β)) are wffs.
If α, β are wffs, then (α GF β) is a wff.
If α is a wff, then $H_J(\alpha)$ is a wff.
Let δ be $\pm$Do(s, α) or $\pm$Do(s, α/$\pm$Do(s, β)) and α, β be wffs. Then Obligation(δ) and Permission(δ) are wffs.
Let δ be Do(s, α) or Do(s, α/Do(s, β)) and α, β be wffs. Then Power(δ) and Disability(δ) are wffs.
If α is a wff and Γ is a set, then ($\alpha \in \Gamma$) is a wff.

In the present section, focus will be on axioms and inference rules of the system, since it is by these axioms and rules that consequences of J^*–membership sentences are derived. As emphasized in the Introduction, system COLT devised for defining and disclosing conflicts, is a "normative logic" or "logic of normative propositions."

2.3.2 *Axioms and Rules of the System*

Different parts of the system are discernable. When expounding the system, Greek letters α, β, and γ are used as meta–variables, letter s as meta–symbol for agent–variables, constants or parameters and "$\vdash$" used to stand for "provable within COLT."

At basis is propositional logic. Any tautology of propositional logic is provable within the system. This is the Rule of Tautology, RT. In order to infer sentences from axioms of the system, the Rule of Modus Ponens, RMP, is adopted. Moreover, for the move from a general rule to its instances (individual norms) to be warranted, an Instantiation axiom, Ax0, is adopted. Thus, the following axiom and general rules of inference are part of the system:

RT, If α is a tautology of propositional logic, then $\vdash \alpha$.
RMP, If ($\vdash \alpha$ and $\vdash (\alpha \supset \beta)$), then $\vdash \beta$.
Ax0, $(\alpha(x) \wedge (\alpha(i) \in \mathrm{IN}(\alpha(x)))) \supset \alpha(i)$, where IN($\alpha(x)$) is the instantiation set of $\alpha(x)$.

2.3.2.1 Logic for Action

For "Do" and "Do(./.)," several axioms and inference rules are adopted. By their adoption, a comprehensive logic for action emerges. The axiom schemata and inference rules making up this logic are, where, in Ax3, RD2, RD3, $\pm$ stands for affirmation or negation uniformly in the context and, in RD4, the value of $\pm$ is constant preceding Do(s, α) and constant preceding Do(s, β):

Ax1, Do(s, α) $\supset \alpha$.
Ax2, (Do(s, α) $\wedge$ Do(s, β)) $\supset$ Do(s, $\alpha \wedge \beta$).
Ax3, Do(s, α/$\pm$Do(s, γ)) $\supset$ (Do(s, α) $\wedge$ $\pm$ Do(s, γ)).

RD1, If $\vdash \alpha \equiv \beta$, then $\vdash (\text{Do}(s, \alpha) \equiv \text{Do}(s, \beta))$.
RD2, If $\vdash \alpha \equiv \beta$, then $\vdash (\text{Do}(s, \alpha / \pm \text{Do}(s, \gamma)) \equiv \text{Do}(s, \beta / \pm \text{Do}(s, \gamma)))$.
RD3, If $\vdash \alpha \equiv \beta$, then $\vdash (\text{Do}(s, \gamma / \pm \text{Do}(s, \alpha)) \equiv \text{Do}(s, \gamma / \pm \text{Do}(s, \beta)))$.
RD4, If $\vdash \pm \text{Do}(s, \alpha) \supset \pm \text{Do}(s, \beta)$, then $\vdash [(\pm \text{Do}(s, \beta) \supset$
$\text{Do}(s, \gamma / \pm \text{Do}(s, \beta))) \supset (\pm \text{Do}(s, \alpha) \supset \text{Do}(s, \gamma / \pm \text{Do}(s, \alpha)))]$.

We take it that these axioms and rules appear straightforwardly as logical truths why they will not be dwelled upon. For discussions of the logic of action see, Kanger (2001, 123 and 148 ff.), Pörn (1970, 1 ff.), Lindahl (1977, 69 ff.), Segerberg (1992), Horty and Belnap (1995), Holmström–Hintikka (1997), and Horty (2001).

Relying on Ax1, to the effect that "Do" is a "success"–operator, the following can be proved as theorems within the system:

Theorem 1, for Do: $\text{Do}(s, \alpha) \supset \neg\text{Do}(s, \neg\alpha)$.
Theorem 2, for Do: $\text{Do}(s, \neg\alpha) \supset \neg\text{Do}(s, \alpha)$.

Proof for Theorem 1, for Do:

(1)	$\text{Do}(s, \alpha) \supset \alpha$.	(Ax1)
(2)	$\text{Do}(s, \neg\alpha) \supset \neg\alpha$.	(Ax1)
(3)	$\alpha \supset \neg\text{Do}(s, \neg\alpha)$.	(Contraposition of (2))
(4)	$\text{Do}(s, \alpha) \supset \neg\text{Do}(s, \neg\alpha)$.	(By (1), (3) and transitivity of truth–functional implication)

2.3.2.2 Transitivity for Norm–Descriptions of GF–Sentences

Though transitivity holds for operator GF, we do not assume this as an axiom in COLT. Instead, the following norm–descriptive analogue is adopted within the system:

Ax4, $[(\alpha \text{ GF } \beta) \wedge (\beta \text{ GF } \gamma)] \in J^* \supset (\alpha \text{ GF } \gamma) \in J^*$, where J^* is the set of wffs of L_{COLT} representing normative system J.

Ax4 warrants inferring that a norm (GF–sentence) belongs to the normative system. For example, from the truth of (i) it being part of the normative system that purchase is ground for ownership and (ii) ownership being ground for permission to dispose of an object, it is warranted to infer that it belongs to the system (iii) that purchase is ground for permission to dispose of an object. A legislator issuing (i) and (ii), in effect, also issues (iii).

2.3.2.3 Operator H_J

A sentence $\text{H}_J[\alpha]$ or $\text{H}_J[\alpha \supset \beta]$ means that α or $[\alpha \supset \beta]$, respectively, holds for J as a consequence of what is expressed in $\text{E}(J^*)$.

With respect to the sentence $\text{H}_J[\alpha \supset \beta]$ a distinction should be emphasized. $\text{H}_J[\alpha \supset \beta]$ is not a descriptive sentence about J^*–membership of a norm, since

$[\alpha \supset \beta]$ is not a GF–sentence. In this respect, the sentence is different from the sentence $(\alpha \text{ GF } \beta) \in J^*$, which describes such membership. Accordingly, there is a difference between two kinds of descriptive sentences, *viz.*, those of the form $(\alpha \text{ GF } \beta) \in J^*$ and those of the form $H_J[\alpha \supset \beta]$. The sentence $(\alpha \text{ GF } \beta) \in J^*$, or equivalently, $[(\alpha \text{ GF } \beta) \in J^*] \in E(J^*)$ is to be read:

$(\alpha \text{ GF } \beta)$ is expressed in J^*.

In contrast, the sentence $H_J[\alpha \supset \beta]$ is to be read:

$(\alpha \supset \beta)$ holds for J as a COLT–logical consequence of $E(J^*)$.

This difference is important since not every consequence of $E(J^*)$ belongs to $E(J^*)$. (See further below, Sect. 2.3.3, the remark that $E(J^*)$ is not closed under Cn_{COLT}, meaning that not all members of $Cn_{COLT}(E(J^*))$ need be members of $E(J^*)$.) While the logic for $E(J^*)$ assumed in the present chapter (incorporating the norm–descriptive analogue of transitivity for GF) is poor, the logic for H_J, as will appear subsequently, is richer.[16] As adumbrated above, Sect. 2.1.1, the logic of H_J may be compared with the so–called "normative logic" developed in Alchourrón (1969, 245 ff.) and Alchourrón and Bulygin (1989, 665 ff.), where an operator N_x is introduced (cf. above, Sect. 2.1.3).[17] In the words of Alchourrón, " "NxO*p*" means "x has ruled (issued a norm to the effect) that it is obligatory that *p*" " (1969, 245). However, the framework in Alchourrón (1969) is different and there is no distinction corresponding to the one made here between $H_J[\alpha \supset \beta]$, on one hand, and $(\alpha \text{ GF } \beta) \in J^*$, on the other.

2.3.2.4 The Bridging Axiom

The system contains an axiom creating a "bridge" between descriptive sentences with operator GF and H_J–sentences. This so–called "bridging axiom" is:

Ax5, $(\alpha \text{ GF } \beta) \in J^* \supset H_J[\alpha \supset \beta]$.

From $(\alpha \text{ GF } \beta) \in J^*$, i.e., that $(\alpha \text{ GF } \beta)$ is expressed in J^*, we can, by the meaning of H_J, infer that $[\alpha \supset \beta]$ holds for J as a logical consequence in the COLT logic. As appears from the formulation of Ax5, the implication goes only one way. Thus,

[16]We do not here address the issue of application to $E(J^*)$ of *relevance logic* as developed in the system R of relevant implication, by Anderson and Belnap (1975). Cf. Goble (2009).

[17]Lennart Åqvist's System NL of normative propositions is inspired by the normative logic NO of Alchourrón (1969, 245 ff.), and NL of Alchourrón and Bulygin (1989, 685 ff.). (See Åqvist 2008, 233 ff.) The construction of Åqvist's NL, however, is different, with a necessity operator □, and axioms different from those of Alchourrón and Bulygin. Having developed the semantics of NL in terms of frames, accessibility, and models, Åqvist proves the soundness and completeness of NL. (This is done in accordance with the methodology developed in Chapters III and IV of Åqvist 1987.) The scope of the present chapter does not permit going into the problem area of semantics for the complex system COLT here introduced in Sect. 2.3.

from $H_J[\alpha \supset \beta]$ it does not follow that $(\alpha \text{ GF } \beta) \in J^*$. This is due to our standpoint that not every logical consequence of what is expressed is itself expressed (cf. Ross' paradox, Ross 1944, 38). The contraposition of Ax5, i.e., $\neg H_J[\alpha \supset \beta] \supset (\alpha \text{ GF } \beta) \notin J^*$, proceeds by the same argument. Thus, if $\alpha \supset \beta$ is not a logical consequence of what is expressed, then α GF β is not expressed.

As pointed out in Sect. 2.2.1.1, the principle of inferred material implication, (Inf $\supset$), is not introduced among the axioms and rules of COLT. However, the principle is part of the explanation and justification for Ax5. The argument for the bridging axiom is as follows:

Argument for Ax5

(1) $(\alpha \text{ GF } \beta) \in J^* \supset H_J[\alpha \text{ GF } \beta]$.
(2) $H_J[\alpha \text{ GF } \beta] \supset H_J[\alpha \supset \beta]$.
(3) $(\alpha \text{ GF } \beta) \in J^* \supset H_J[\alpha \supset \beta]$.

Premise (1) is true in virtue of the definition of set J^* and the meaning of H_J. Every sentence implies itself. Therefore, if a norm–sentence belongs to the formal representation of J, the sentence holds for J as a logical consequence. Premise (2) is true in virtue of the principle (Inf $\supset$) for GF and the meaning of H_J. Part of the meaning of operator GF is that it implies $\neg(\alpha \wedge \neg\beta)$, i.e. $(\alpha \supset \beta)$. Accordingly, if $(\alpha \text{ GF } \beta)$ holds for J as a logical consequence, then $(\alpha \supset \beta)$ holds as well for J as a logical consequence.[18] Because (3) expresses the bridging axiom and follows deductively from (1) and (2), which are premises true in virtue of the meaning of the terms contained in them, the argument establishes the bridging axiom as a conceptual truth.

A remark concerning general rules and instantiations is in order here. Suppose that α,β are one–place predicates and that the sentence $\alpha(x)$ GF $\beta(x)$ expresses a general rule such that $\alpha(i) \in \text{IN}(\alpha(x))$ is ground for $\beta(i) \in \text{IN}(\beta(x))$, i.e., $\alpha(i)$ GF $\beta(i)$, where i is a meta–variable for individual constants. Furthermore, suppose that it is true that $(\alpha(x) \text{ GF } \beta(x)) \in J^*$, i.e., that $\alpha(x)$ GF $\beta(x)$ is expressed in J^*. Then it is true that the general sentence $(\alpha(x) \supset \beta(x))$, holding for the same instantiations, is a consequence that holds for J. This means that in the sentence $H_J(\alpha(x) \supset \beta(x))$, the expression $(\alpha(x) \supset \beta(x))$ is to be understood as a general sentence such that $\alpha(i) \in \text{IN}(\alpha(x))$ truth–functionally implies $\beta(i) \in \text{IN}(\beta(x))$, i.e., $\alpha(i) \supset \beta(i)$.[19]

---

[18]If the principle of inferred material implication, (Inf $\supset$), were adopted within the axioms and rules of the system, the sentence expressed in premise (2) would be derivable as follows (the proof presupposes the logic of H_J to be introduced):

(1) $(\alpha \text{ GF } \beta) \supset (\alpha \supset \beta)$.	(Inf $\supset$)
(2) $H_J(\alpha \text{ GF } \beta) \supset H_J(\alpha \supset \beta)$.	(From (1), by RH1)

[19]As stated previously, in the present chapter we do not introduce predicate logic in the object language (we do not need predicate logic for the derivations accomplished). It can be of interest to see, however, that if we were to use predicate logic, the standpoint maintained above would amount to the following variety of the Bridging Axiom: $[(\forall x\colon \alpha(x) \text{ GF } \beta(x)) \in J^*] \supset H_J[\forall x\colon \alpha(x) \supset \beta(x)]$. Furthermore, note that if we were to use predicate calculus in the object language, we would bring

2.3.2.5 Logic for the H_J–Operator

The following axiom schemata and inference rule are adopted for operator 'H_J':

Ax6, $(H_J(\alpha \supset \beta)) \supset (H_J\alpha \supset H_J\beta)$.
RH1, If $\vdash (\alpha \supset \beta)$, then $(H_J\alpha \supset H_J\beta)$.

In the establishment of normative conflict, a set of H_J–sentences is first inferred from J^*–membership sentences, by Ax5. It is then seen, if normative conflict is derivable from the inferred set, by use of H_J–logic together with action logic. The logic for H_J is a comprehensive logic, which becomes apparent if some samples of significant theorems are made explicit.

The following list contains a sample of theorem schemata for H_J:

Theorem 1, for H_J: $H_J[(\alpha \supset \beta) \wedge (\beta \supset \gamma)] \supset H_J[\alpha \supset \gamma]$.
Theorem 2, for H_J: $H_J[(\alpha \vee \beta) \supset \gamma] \supset H_J[\alpha \supset \gamma]$.
Theorem 3, for H_J: $H_J[(\alpha \supset \gamma) \wedge (\beta \supset \gamma)] \supset H_J[(\alpha \wedge \beta) \supset \gamma]$.
Theorem 4, for H_J: $H_J[\alpha \supset \beta] \supset H_J[(\alpha \wedge \gamma) \supset \beta]$.
Theorem 5, for H_J: $H_J[(\alpha \supset \beta) \wedge (\alpha \supset \gamma)] \supset H_J[\alpha \supset (\beta \wedge \gamma)]$.
Theorem 6, for H_J: $H_J[\alpha \supset (\beta \wedge \gamma)] \supset H_J[(\alpha \supset \beta) \wedge (\alpha \supset \gamma)]$.
Theorem 7, for H_J: $H_J[\alpha \supset \beta] \supset H_J[\neg\beta \supset \neg\alpha]$.
Theorem 8, for H_J: $H_J[\alpha] \supset H_J[\alpha]$.
Theorem 9, for H_J: $H_J[\alpha \supset \beta] \supset H_J[\alpha \supset (\beta \vee \gamma)]$.
Theorem 10, for H_J: $H_J[(\alpha \supset \beta) \wedge (\gamma \supset \beta)] \supset H_J[(\alpha \vee \gamma) \supset \beta]$.
Theorem 11, for H_J: $H_J(\alpha \wedge \beta) \equiv (H_J\alpha \wedge H_J\beta)$.

Each of the proofs for Theorem 1–10 has the same structure; all of them rely on the rule of inference RH1. Theorem 11 relies on a longer proof (for the proofs, see Appendix 2).

2.3.2.6 Comments on Some Theorems in COLT

The Principle of Greater Wrongdoing

An important theorem with respect to conflict analysis is the so–called *principle of Greater Wrongdoing* which allows inferring that a greater wrong is committed by Pro–action or Counter–action when it holds that the omission entailed by such action implies wrongdoing. The two versions of this principle are respectively, where + indicates that Pro–action is the greater wrong and - indicates that Counter–action is the greater wrong:

Theorem 12+: $H_J[\neg Do(s, \neg\alpha) \supset Do(s, W/\neg Do(s, \neg\alpha))] \supset H_J[Do(s, \alpha) \supset Do(s, W/Do(s, \alpha))]$.

---

in a dual C_J for H_J, defined as $C_J\alpha =_{Def.} \neg H_J\neg\alpha$. Then, the expression $\neg H_J[\forall x\colon \alpha(x) \supset \beta(x)]$ would be equivalent to $C_J[\exists x\colon \alpha(x) \wedge \neg\beta(x)]$. In this chapter, since existential quantifiers do not occur, no such dual is introduced.

Theorem 12–: $H_J[\neg Do(s, \alpha) \supset Do(s, W/\neg Do(s, \alpha))] \supset H_J[Do(s, \neg\alpha) \supset Do(s, W/Do(s, \neg\alpha))]$.

These theorems follow from the logic of Do in combination with the logic for H_J. Proof for theorem 12+:

(1)	If $\vdash(Do(s, \alpha) \supset \neg Do(s, \neg\alpha))$, then $\vdash [(\neg Do(s, \neg\alpha) \supset Do(s, W/\neg Do(s, \neg\alpha))) \supset (Do(s, \alpha) \supset Do(s, W/Do(s, \alpha)))]$.	(By RD4)
(2)	$\vdash(Do(s, \alpha) \supset \neg Do(s, \neg\alpha))$.	(By Ax1)
(3)	$\vdash[(\neg Do(s, \neg\alpha) \supset Do(s, W/\neg Do(s, \neg\alpha))) \supset (Do(s, \alpha) \supset Do(s, W/Do(s, \alpha)))]$.	(From (1) and (2), by RMP).
(4)	$H_J[\neg Do(s, \neg\alpha) \supset Do(s, W/\neg Do(s, \neg\alpha))] \supset H_J[Do(s, \alpha) \supset Do(s, W/Do(s, \alpha))]$.	(From (3) by RH1)

To exemplify, suppose it is mandatory for businesses within the food industry to supply consumers with adequate information concerning the nutritional characteristics of their products, for the purpose of furthering consumer protection. Accordingly, it holds for the legal system that John & Sons omitting to supply adequate information concerning the nutritional characteristics of their products implies wrongdoing. It can then be inferred by the principle of Greater Wrongdoing that it holds for the legal system that John & Sons misleading consumers with respect to the nutritional characteristics, i.e., "actively" seeing to it that there is not adequate information, implies wrongdoing by the company.

The Theorem of Monotony

In the present chapter, there is not room for an extensive discussion of all the theorems, which may be relied on in the derivation of normative conflict. We will be content with a short example, elucidating Theorem 4, for H_J: $H_J[\alpha \supset \beta] \supset H_J[(\alpha \wedge \gamma) \supset \beta]$. This is the theorem of Monotony for H_J. Some remarks on this theorem are in order, since its results bring to light the importance of carefully separating the different stages of defining and resolving normative conflict.

Suppose that a legal system J contains the following norms:

N_1: Anyone at least Eighteen years old and Called to serve on a jury, has the obligation to Serve.
N_2: Anyone having only Foreign citizenship is forbidden to serve on a jury.
N_3: Anyone seriously ill is permitted not to serve on a jury.

Since J contains N_1, N_2, N_3, the following is true for $E(J^*)$:[20]

[20]The expressions E(x), C(x), F(x), I(x), S, are assumed to be self–explanatory. Thus, E(x) is "*at least Eighteen years old*", and so on.

N_1^*: [E(x) ∧ C(x) GF Obligation(x, Do(x, S))]∈ J^*.
N_2^*: [F(x) GF Obligation(x, ¬Do(x, S))]∈ J^*.
N_3^*: [I(x) GF Permission(x,¬Do(x, S))]∈ J^*.

First, let us look at the pair of N_1^* and N_2^*. Applying Monotony, as a consequence of this conjunction, in COLT it holds that if x is at least eighteen years old, called to serve and has only foreign citizenship, then x *cannot avoid doing wrong*. Formally, we obtain (recalling that W stands for: Wrong is committed):

H_J[E(x) ∧ C(x) ∧ F(x) ⊃ (¬Do(x, S) ⊃ Do(x, W/¬Do(x, S)))], and
H_J[E(x) ∧ C(x) ∧ F(x) ⊃ (Do(x, S) ⊃ Do(x, W/Do(x, S)))].

Proof

(1) H_J[E(x) ∧ C(x) ⊃ (¬Do(x, S) ⊃ Do(x, W/¬Do(x, S)))]. (From N_1^* by Ax 5)
(2) H_J[F(x) ⊃ (Do(x, S) ⊃ Do(x, W/Do(x, S)))]. (From N_2^* by Ax 5)
(3) H_J[E(x) ∧ C(x) ∧ F(x) ⊃ (¬Do(x, S) ⊃ Do(x, W/¬Do(x, S)))]. (From (1), by H_J Th 4)
(4) H_J[E(x) ∧ C(x) ∧ F(x) ⊃ (Do(x, S) ⊃ Do(x, W/Do(x, S)))]. (From (2), by H_J Th 4)

Next, we look at the pair of N_1^* and N_3^*. As a consequence of this conjunction, in COLT it holds that if x is at least eighteen years old, called to serve, seriously ill and x does not serve, then x both commits a wrong and does not commit a wrong. That is, the regulation is contradictory for this case, since in this case, from N_1^* and N_3^* we obtain the following statement (where ⊥ stands for the contradiction):

H_J[(E(x) ∧ C(x) ∧ I(x) ∧ ¬Do(x, S)) ⊃ ⊥].

Proof

(1) H_J[E(x) ∧ C(x) ⊃ (¬Do(x, S) ⊃ Do(x, W/¬Do(x, S)))]. (From N_1^*, by Ax 5)
(2) H_J[I(x) ⊃ (¬Do(x, S) ⊃ ¬Do(x, W/¬Do(x, S)))]. (From N_3^*, by Ax 5)
(3) H_J[E(x) ∧ C(x) ∧ I(x) ⊃ (¬Do(x, S) ⊃ Do(x, W/¬Do(x, S)))]. (From (1), by H_J Th 4)
(4) H_J[E(x) ∧ C(x) ∧ I(x) ⊃ (¬Do(x, S) ⊃ ¬Do(x, W/¬Do(x, S)))]. (From (2), by H_J Th 4)
(5) H_J[E(x) ∧ C(x) ∧ I(x) ⊃ (¬Do(x, S) ⊃ ⊥)]. (From (3), (4) by H_J Th. 5)
(6) H_J[(E(x) ∧ C(x) ∧ I(x) ∧ ¬Do(x, S)) ⊃ ⊥]. (From RH1 and (5))

In order to avoid misunderstandings concerning the stage of formal conflict definition (i.e., the stage of the COLT theory, addressed in the present chapter), it is essential to have in mind that when a set J of norms is considered for exposing conflict, the set J is taken as given, without prejudice to any questions concerning the status of the norms in J from a wider perspective of a legal system. At this stage, the "conflict defining" stage, it is disregarded whether J simply is a set of legal texts, or a set of texts that have been subjected to a systemic interpretation (concerning whether some norms are exceptions to some other norms), or even have been subjected to some meta–rules concerning the solution of conflicts. Whether one or more norms in J are "defeasible" in the presence of other J–norms (and what defeasibility means) is disregarded as well. This standpoint results from our strict adherence to the principle of not merging questions of solution of conflict into the theory of defining and exposing conflict.

To elaborate on this point, in the example just given, it is possible that a system of norms finer than $\{N_1, N_2, N_3\}$ can be constructed by interpretation, a system giving detailed regulation concerning obligation/non–obligation to serve/not to serve on a jury for different Boolean combinations of E(x), C(x), F(x) and I(x).[21] Or, by a theory of "exceptions," N_2 and N_3 might be considered as exceptions to N_1. Or, by a theory of defeasibility, N_1 might be considered "defeasible" by N_2 and N_3. Any questions of this kind are disregarded here, since these issues belong to the subsequent stage of conflict resolution, while this chapter is only concerned with the definition of conflict.

2.3.3 *Consequence Sets*

In the assessment of normative conflict as developed below in Sect. 2.4, the COLT–system is applied to sentences (premises) to the effect that norms belong to a normative system. This application returns a set of consequences. In other words, the system takes a set of J^*–membership sentences as "input" and returns a set of consequences as "output." Each set of sentences is associated with exactly one set of consequences. As before, E(J^*) is the collection of norm–descriptive sentences (wffs of $\mathrm{L_{COLT}}$) affirming that norms belong to the formal representation of J. Then the consequence operation is:

$\mathrm{Cn_{COLT}}(\mathrm{E}(J^*))$ = The set of consequences obtained by the application of COLT to E(J^*).

Like most consequence operations (see, Tarski [1930a] 1983, 30–37), $\mathrm{Cn_{COLT}}(\mathrm{E}(J^*))$ satisfies T1–T3 below:

T1) $\mathrm{E}(J^*) \subseteq \mathrm{Cn_{COLT}}(\mathrm{E}(J^*))$.

Since sentences entail themselves, the set of consequences includes the set of norm–descriptive sentences E(J^*). Moreover, consequences derivable from consequences are consequences:

T2) $\mathrm{Cn_{COLT}}(\mathrm{Cn_{COLT}}(\mathrm{E}(J^*))) = \mathrm{Cn_{COLT}}(\mathrm{E}(J^*))$.

[21] On "fineness," cf. Alchourrón and Bulygin (1971, 97 f.).

Furthermore, adding norm–descriptive sentences to a set, $E(J^*)$, so that a larger expanded set, $E_{EXP}(J^*)$, ensues does not result in the previous consequences no longer being inferable. That is, the consequence operation is *monotonous*:

T3) If $E(J^*) \subseteq E_{EXP}(J^*)$, then $Cn_{COLT}(E(J^*)) \subseteq Cn_{COLT}(E_{EXP}(J^*))$.

As will be discussed subsequently (see, Sect. 2.4.2), monotony is a characteristic of the consequence operation that facilitates disclosing conflicts within normative systems.

It does not hold generally that:

$Cn_{COLT}(E(J^*)) \subseteq E(J^*)$.

This means that $E(J^*)$ is *not closed* under Cn_{COLT}: Not all members of $Cn_{COLT}(E(J^*))$ need be members of $E(J^*)$ (cf. above, Sects. 2.1.3, 2.3.2.3 and 2.3.2.4).[22]

As will appear subsequently, for a set $E(J^*)$ of descriptive sentences, a contradiction can be involved in $Cn_{COLT}(E(J^*))$, the result being that an arbitrary (well–formed) sentence can be inferred as a member of $Cn_{COLT}(E(J^*))$. Thus, to use Goble's terminology (above Sect. 2.1.3), "explosion" can occur within $Cn_{COLT}(E(J^*))$. However, since $E(J^*)$ is not a closed system with respect to $Cn_{COLT}(E(J^*))$, the inferred arbitrary sentence is not an element of $E(J^*)$ and, in this sense, does not belong to the legal system J. Thus, "explosion" within $Cn_{COLT}(E(J^*))$ does not imply "explosion" in $E(J^*)$.[23]

If "explosion" occurs with respect to $Cn_{COLT}(E(J^*))$, this shows that J is in need of revision so that arbitrary sentences no longer are derivable in $Cn_{COLT}(E(J^*))$. Revision is part of the solution of normative conflict, not its definition.

2.4 Conflicts of Norms According to COLT

2.4.1 Introductory Remarks

The analysis of normative conflict presupposes the series of steps that successively have been developed in this chapter (i.e., the steps of Fig. 2.1 together with the final step consisting of the application of the COLT–system to set $E(J^*)$ whereby the set of consequences is obtained). Whether there is conflict within a subset S of J (of course including a conflict within J itself), depends on the contents of the consequence set $Cn_{COLT}(E(S^*))$, which is a subset of $Cn_{COLT}(E(J^*))$.

---

[22]A closed system is a set of sentences that includes each and every one of its consequences, see Tarski ([1930a] 1983, 33 and [1930b] 1983, 69 f.).

[23]The phenomenon of "explosion," in the sense of getting as a theorem *ex contradictione quodlibet*, $(\alpha \wedge \neg\alpha) \rightarrow \beta$, is avoided within relevance logic as developed in the system **R** of Anderson and Belnap (1975). Cf. Goble (1999).

2.4.2 *The Definition of Normative Conflict*

We begin by defining compliance conflict. Let α be a meta–variable for Do(s, β) or Do(s, β/Do(s, γ)) where β, γ are contingent. We say that there is *compliance conflict* within a subset S of J if:[24]

(I) $H_J[\delta \supset (\alpha \supset \mathrm{Do}(s, W/\alpha))] \in \mathrm{Cn}_{\mathrm{COLT}}(E(S^*))$, and
$H_J[\delta \supset (\neg\alpha \supset \mathrm{Do}(s, W/\neg\alpha))] \in \mathrm{Cn}_{\mathrm{COLT}}(E(S^*))$.

(Obviously, the definition applies if $S = J$.) The situation described in (I) is to the effect that, for s, wrongdoing is logically unavoidable, either absolutely or in a contingent case δ.

Compliance–conflict is present in cases where it follows from E(S^*) that, in a certain circumstance, x does wrong both in the case that x does A and in the case that x does not do A. (For analogous cases in deontic logic, cf. Hamblin (1972), 74, and Hilpinen (1985), 195, on "quandaries", and von Wright (1968), 67, and 78 ff., on "predicaments." Also, see above, Sect. 2.1.3, on Goble.)

Depending on whether circumstance δ is the tautology, i.e., $\delta \equiv \top$, or not, two special cases of compliance conflict can be distinguished.[25] Let α be as indicated under (I). Then, we say that a compliance conflict within S is *unconditional* if (I) is true for δ such that $\delta \equiv \top$. In this case, (I) reduces to:

(I*) $H_J[\alpha \supset \mathrm{Do}(s, W/\alpha)] \in \mathrm{Cn}_{\mathrm{COLT}}(E(S^*))$, and
$H_J[\neg\alpha \supset \mathrm{Do}(s, W/\neg\alpha)] \in \mathrm{Cn}_{\mathrm{COLT}}(E(S^*))$.

On the other hand, we say that a compliance conflict is *conditional* if it is not unconditional but (I) is true for a contingent δ (i.e., where $\delta \neq \bot$, $\delta \neq \top$).

Unconditional compliance conflict depicts the situation where avoidance of wrongdoing occurs regardless of any (contingent) conditions being fulfilled (e.g. if x has the unconditional duty to serve on a jury and the unconditional duty not to serve). For an example of a conditional compliance conflict, see the first of the two examples illustrating the Theorem of Monotony in Sect. 2.3.2.6, where it could be derived that avoidance of wrongdoing was logically impossible for x on the condition of x's being at least eighteen years old, called to serve on a jury and only having foreign citizenship, which is a contingent matter.

The second main type of conflict is *contradiction*. The definition is as follows. We say that there is *contradiction* within a non–empty subset S of a normative system J if there is a non–contradictory α (i.e., $\alpha \neq \bot$) such that:

(II) $H_J(\alpha \supset \bot) \in \mathrm{Cn}_{\mathrm{COLT}}(E(S^*))$.

---

[24]Instead of writing "if and only if," we simply write "if," when it is clear from the context that a definition is made and thus that the relation between *definiendum* and *definiens* is a bi-conditional.

[25]We observe that, by propositional logic, $\delta \equiv \top$ if and only if $\top \supset \delta$, and that $\delta \equiv \bot$ if and only if $\delta \supset \bot$.

In this situation, it follows from E(S^*) that α implies contradiction (i.e., $\perp$).[26] In this case, there is contradiction for the case that α. An example is where it follows from E(S^*) that, in case α, both x does wrong and x does *not* do wrong.

Depending on whether case α is contingent or not, once more we distinguish between two cases. We say that a contradiction within S is *absolute* if (II) is true for α such that $\top \supset \alpha$. In this case, (II) reduces to:

(II*) $H_J(\top \supset \perp) \in Cn_{COLT}(E(S^*))$.

On the other hand, we say that the contradiction is *contingent* if it is not absolute but (II) is true for a contingent α (i.e., α such that $\alpha \neq \perp, \alpha \neq \top$).

Absolute contradiction might be exemplified by norms to effect that x both does wrong and not if x serves on a jury as well as that x both does wrong and not if x does not serve.[27] As an example of a contingent contradiction, we take the second of the two examples illustrating the Theorem of Monotony in Sect. 2.3.2.6.

Having defined the two main types of conflict, "normative conflict" is defined as follows:

> There is *normative conflict within S* if there is compliance conflict or contradiction within S.

We observe that normative conflict is defined for norms belonging to a (non–empty) subset S of a normative system J, but *definiens* refers to the *descriptive sentences* in $Cn_{COLT}(E(S^*))$. According to the COLT theory, norms in S do conflict when there is a chain going from the norms *via* a description to a consequence set, $Cn_{COLT}(E(S^*))$, to the effect that it holds that wrongdoing is unavoidable or action implies contradiction.

As a sequel to the definition of conflict within a subset S of J, the binary relation "conflicts with" for two norms in J is defined as follows: Let $N_1, N_2 \in J$. Then N_1 *conflicts with* N_2 if there is normative conflict in the subset $\{N_1, N_2\}$ of J.

If N_1 conflicts with N_2, then N_2 conflicts with N_1; so, the relation "conflicts with" is *symmetric*. Self–conflicting norms stand in the relation "conflicts with" to themselves, but norms that are not self–conflicting do not; so, the relation is *non–reflexive*. There are instances such that if N_1 conflicts with N_2 and N_2 conflicts with N_3, then N_1 conflicts with N_3 but also instances where this is not the case; so, the relation is *non–transitive*.[28]

---

[26]We note that the restriction $\alpha \neq \perp$ is necessary. If $\alpha = \perp$, we get $H_J(\perp \supset \perp) \in Cn_{COLT}(E(S^*))$, i.e., since $(\perp \supset \perp) = \top$, $H_J(\top) \in Cn_{COLT}(E(S^*))$, which does not signify conflict. Also, we note that, in (II), α can be a complex condition. For example, if $\alpha = \beta \wedge \gamma$, the H_J–part of (II) is equivalent to $H_J(\beta \supset (\gamma \supset \perp)) \in Cn_{COLT}(E(S^*))$.

[27]Expressed in the COLT language: $H_J[Do(x, S) \supset (Do(x, W/Do(x, S)) \wedge \neg Do(x, W/Do(x, S))] \wedge H_J[\neg Do(x, S) \supset (Do(x, W/\neg Do(x, S)) \wedge \neg Do(x, W/\neg Do(x, S))]$. It follows: $H_J[(Do(x, S) \vee \neg Do(x, S)) \supset (Do(x, W) \wedge \neg Do(x, W))]$, i.e. $H_J(\top \supset \perp)$.

[28]The following examples illustrate "conflicts with" being non–transitive. First, let N_1 be the obligation to bring about A, N_2 be the obligation to bring about not A and N_3 be the permission to bring about A. Then N_1 conflicts with N_2 and N_2 has conflict with N_3, but N_1 does not conflict with

Since Cn_{COLT} is *monotonous* (see, T3 in Sect. 2.3.3), if norms N_1 and N_2 are in conflict, it follows that there is conflict within any subset of J containing N_1, N_2 as a subset. Therefore, the result that there is normative conflict in a large set of J–norms can simply be established by establishing conflict for a pair of J–norms.

2.4.3 *Types of Conflict*[29]

2.4.3.1 Deontic Conflict

By deontic norms in J^*, we mean norms of the form:

Obligation(s, $\pm$ Do(s, β)),
Permission(s, $\pm$ Do(s, β)),
δ GF Obligation(s, $\pm$ Do(s, β)),
δ GF Permission(s, $\pm$ Do(s, β)), where δ can be a compound, for example, $\delta = \phi \wedge \lambda$.

Let S be a non–empty subset of J, and S_{DEON} be the subset of *deontic sentences* in S, so that: $S_{DEON} \subseteq J_{DEON}$ and $S^*_{DEON} \subseteq J^*_{DEON}$. Then one variety of conflict is between deontic norms in a set $S_{DEON} \subseteq J$. We say that there is *deontic* conflict within a subset S of J if there is compliance conflict or contradiction within S_{DEON}. (Of course, deontic conflict in a subset of J does not exclude that there are as well other types of conflict in J.)

One example of deontic conflict is where $S^*_{DEON} \subseteq J^*$, and,

(i) Obligation(x, Do(x, A))$\in S^*_{DEON}$,
(ii) Obligation(x, $\neg$Do(x, A))$\in S^*_{DEON}$.

As a variation, suppose that:

(i) Obligation(x, Do(x, A))$\in S^*_{DEON}$,
(ii) Obligation(x, Do(x, $\neg A$))$\in S^*_{DEON}$,

where the negation sign is moved into the Do–formula. Then by use of Theorem 12, for H_J, i.e. the principle of Greater Wrongdoing, compliance conflict is once more derivable in COLT.

An example of a different kind is where

(i) Obligation(x, Do(x, A))$\in S^*_{DEON}$,
(ii) Permission(x,$\neg$Do(x, A))$\in S^*_{DEON}$.

N_3. Second, let N_1 be the self–conflicting norm to the effect that it is obligatory to bring about A and obligatory not to bring about A, N_2 be the permission to bring about A and N_3 be the obligation not to bring about A. Then the consequences of N_1 (second conjunct) conflicts with N_2, N_2 conflicts with N_3 and, finally, the consequences of N_1 (first conjunct) conflicts with N_3.

[29]We recall that the present chapter does not deal with so–called practical conflicts (see, above, Sect. 2.1.1).

Here, contradiction is derivable in COLT:

Proof

(1) $H_J[\neg Do(x, A) \supset Do(x, W/\neg Do(x, A))]$. (From (i) by Ax 5)
(2) $H_J[\neg Do(x, A) \supset \neg Do(x, W/\neg Do(x, A))]$. (From (ii) by Ax 5)
(3) $H_J[\neg Do(x, A) \supset \bot]$. (From (1) and (2) by H_J Th 5)

We note that if α,β are contingent, sentences of the form Permission(s, $\pm$Do(s, α)) and Permission(s, $\pm$Do(s, β)) are never in conflict. And so, if a subset S of J *only* consists of such permissions, then there is no conflict in S. This agrees with Standard Deontic Logic where the conjunction of a set of sentences of this form never violates the axioms of SDL. However, it disagrees with Munzer (1973, 1146 ff.) and Hamner Hill (1987, 237).

2.4.3.2 Capacitative Conflict

By capacitative norms in J^*, we mean norms of the form:

Power(s, Do(s, β/Do(s, γ))),
Disability(s, Do(s, β/Do(s, γ))),
δ GF Power(s, Do(s, β/Do(s, γ))),
δ GF Disability(s, Do(s, β/Do(s, γ))).

Let S be a non–empty subset of J and S_{CAP} be the subset of *capacitative norms* in S, so that: $S_{CAP} \subseteq J_{CAP}$ and, consequently, $S^*_{CAP} \subseteq J^*_{CAP}$. We now turn to the definition of capacitative conflict. We say that there is a *capacitative conflict within* S if there is contradiction in S_{CAP}.

For example, let

(i) Power(x, Do(x, A/Do(x, M)))$\in S^*_{CAP}$,
(ii) Disability(x, Do(x, A/Do(x, M)))$\in S^*_{CAP}$.

Then there is capacitative conflict, since it is derivable by COLT that[30]:

$H_J(Do(x, M) \supset \bot) \in Cn_{COLT}(E(S^*_{CAP}))$.

Proof

(1) $H_J[Do(x, M) \supset Do(x, A/Do(x, M))]$. (From (i), by Ax 5)
(2) $H_J[(Do(x, M) \vee \neg Do(x,M)) \supset \neg Do(x,A/Do(x,M))]$. (From (ii), by Ax 5)
(3) $H_J[Do(x, M) \supset \neg Do(x, A/Do(x, M))]$. (From (2), by H_J Th 2)
(4) $H_J[Do(x, M) \supset \bot]$. (From (1) and (3) by H_J Th 5)

[30]Since the norms are capacitative, it follows that A is a legal result and M a measure manifesting the intention to achieve A.

Note that any reference to compliance conflict (above Sect. 2.4.2) is redundant and, consequently, omitted in the definition of capacitative conflict. A characteristic of capacitative norms is that such norms express the conditions of achieving a legal result, not the conditions of wrongdoing.[31]

Because the framework discloses capacitative conflicts, it is wider in scope compared to accounts in legal and logical writing, based on deontic notions. As pointed out in the Introduction, one of the purposes of the present chapter is to establish a formal framework that extends to capacitative norms and is capable of disclosing conflicts between such norms. In actual legal systems, capacitative conflicts are frequent and often concern important issues (see, Case 3 of Sect. 2.5.3 for an example of this kind of conflict).

2.4.3.3 Cross–Conflict

A common view is that unavoidability of wrongdoing is a sign only of pure deontic conflict; but, as we will now show, there are "cross conflicts" between capacitative and deontic norms. This variety is conflict *across* the deontic and capacitative sphere. A cross conflict is defined as follows.

Let $E(J^*_{DEON})$ and $E(J^*_{CAP})$ be as before, with $[E(S^*_{DEON}) \cup E(S^*_{CAP})]$ a non–empty subset of $E(J^*)$. We say that there is cross–conflict within J if there is a non–empty subset S of J such that there is neither deontic conflict nor capacitative conflict in S, but compliance conflict can be derived in COLT from $[E(S^*_{DEON}) \cup E(S^*_{CAP})]$.

For convenience, we state explicitly what compliance conflict means in the case of cross conflict. Let α be a meta–variable for $\mathrm{Do}(s, \beta)$ or $\mathrm{Do}(s, \beta/\mathrm{Do}(s, \gamma))$ where β, γ are contingent. Then there is *cross conflict within J* if it is derivable:

$$H_J[\delta \supset (\alpha \supset \mathrm{Do}(s, W/\alpha))] \in Cn_{COLT}[E(S^*_{DEON}) \cup E(S^*_{CAP})], \text{ and}$$
$$H_J[\delta \supset (\neg\alpha \supset \mathrm{Do}(s, W/\neg\alpha))] \in Cn_{COLT}[E(S^*_{DEON}) \cup E(S^*_{CAP})].$$

As a simple example, suppose that A is a legal result (a valid contract, a valid marriage etc.) and M a measure manifesting the intention to achieve A. Furthermore, suppose that subsets S^*_{DEON}, S^*_{CAP}, of $S^* \subseteq J^*$, are such that it is true:

(i) $\mathrm{Obligation}(x, \mathrm{Do}(x, A/\mathrm{Do}(x, M))) \in S^*_{DEON}$,
(ii) $\mathrm{Disability}(x, \mathrm{Do}(x, A/\mathrm{Do}(x, M))) \in S^*_{CAP}$,

where A, M are contingent. Then there is compliance conflict within S.

Proof

(1) $H_J[\neg \mathrm{Do}(x, A/\mathrm{Do}(x, M)) \supset \mathrm{Do}(x, W/\neg \mathrm{Do}(x, A/\mathrm{Do}(x, M)))]$. (From (i), Ax5)
(2) $H_J[\top \equiv \neg \mathrm{Do}(x, A/\mathrm{Do}(x, M))]$. (From (ii), Ax5)

[31] As we will see, in a so–called "cross conflict," capacitative norms are involved together with deontic norms.

(3)	$\vdash [\top \equiv \neg \mathrm{Do}(x, A/\mathrm{Do}(x, M))] \equiv$ $[\bot \equiv \mathrm{Do}(x, A/\mathrm{Do}(x, M))]$.	(Propositional logic)
(4)	$\mathrm{H}_J[\top \equiv \neg \mathrm{Do}(x, A/\mathrm{Do}(x, M))] \equiv$ $\mathrm{H}_J[\bot \equiv \mathrm{Do}(x, A/\mathrm{Do}(x, M))]$.	(From (3), RH1)
(5)	$\mathrm{H}_J[\bot \equiv \mathrm{Do}(x, A/\mathrm{Do}(x, M))]$.	(From (2), (4))
(6)	$\vdash [[\bot \equiv \mathrm{Do}(x, A/\mathrm{Do}(x, M))] \supset$ $[\mathrm{Do}(x, A/\mathrm{Do}(x, M)) \supset$ $\mathrm{Do}(x, \mathrm{W}/\mathrm{Do}(x, A/\mathrm{Do}(x, M)))]]$.	(Propositional logic)[32]
(7)	$\mathrm{H}_J[\bot \equiv \mathrm{Do}(x, A/\mathrm{Do}(x, M))] \supset$ $[\mathrm{H}_J[\mathrm{Do}(x, A/\mathrm{Do}(x, M)) \supset \mathrm{Do}(x, \mathrm{W}/\mathrm{Do}(x, A/\mathrm{Do}(x, M)))]]$.	(From (6), RH1)
(8)	$\mathrm{H}_J[\mathrm{Do}(x, A/\mathrm{Do}(x, M)) \supset$ $\mathrm{Do}(x, \mathrm{W}/\mathrm{Do}(x, A/\mathrm{Do}(x, M)))]$.	(From (5) and (7))
	Let $\alpha = \mathrm{Do}(x, A/\mathrm{Do}(x, M))$. Then:	
(9)	$\mathrm{H}_J[\neg\alpha \supset \mathrm{Do}(x, \mathrm{W}/\neg\,\alpha)] \wedge \mathrm{H}_J[\alpha \supset \mathrm{Do}(x, \mathrm{W}/\alpha)]$.	(From (8) and (1))
(10)	There is compliance conflict within S.	(From (i), (ii), (9) per def. compl. conflict)

We observe that a cross conflict in the sense defined does not follow from the conjunction of a legal power to achieve a legal result and an obligation not to bring about that result. For example, a public official x can have the legal power to achieve a legal result A by a certain act M, even if, by instructions, he is forbidden to do so. This means that if x performs act M, the result A (a valid contract, a valid marriage etc.) ensues and is legally valid. However, since x was forbidden to achieve A by M, x can be subjected to legal sanctions (x can be liable to dismissal, punishment, payment of compensation etc.) In this case, we can derive:

$$\mathrm{H}_J[\mathrm{Do}(x, M) \supset \mathrm{Do}(x, \mathrm{W}/\mathrm{Do}(x, A/\mathrm{Do}(x, M)))] \in \mathrm{Cn}_{\mathrm{COLT}}\,[\mathrm{E}(S^*_{\mathrm{DEON}}) \cup \mathrm{E}(S^*_{\mathrm{CAP}})].$$

From this sentence, however, it does not follow that there is a compliance conflict: x can avoid doing wrong by not performing act M.

We note that in the example above with:

(i) $\mathrm{Obligation}(x, \mathrm{Do}(x, A/\mathrm{Do}(x, M))) \in S^*_{\mathrm{DEON}}$,
(ii) $\mathrm{Disability}(x, \mathrm{Do}(x, A/\mathrm{Do}(x, M))) \in S^*_{\mathrm{CAP}}$,

the notions Obligation and Disability refer to $\mathrm{Do}(x, A/\mathrm{Do}(x, M))$, i.e., to achieving A by means of measure M, which expresses that Obligation and Disability here are *means–related*. Another version of the example is obtained if, instead of (i) and (ii), we suppose simply:

[32]In propositional logic it holds: $\vdash \gamma \supset \beta \supset ((\alpha \equiv \gamma) \supset (\alpha \supset \beta))$. Therefore, $\vdash \bot \supset \beta \supset ((\alpha \equiv \bot) \supset (\alpha \supset \beta))$. Furthermore, for arbitrary β: $\vdash \bot \supset \beta$. Consequently: For arbitrary β: $\vdash (\alpha \equiv \bot) \supset (\alpha \supset \beta)$.

(iii) Obligation(x, Do(x, A))$\in S^*_{\mathrm{DEON}}$,
(iv) Disability(x, Do(x, A))$\in S^*_{\mathrm{CAP}}$,

where there is no reference to a specific means M for achieving A. In this case as well, there is cross conflict in $S^*_{\mathrm{DEON}} \cup S^*_{\mathrm{CAP}}$. (The proof is analogous to the one just given.)

2.4.3.4 Overview of the Varieties of Conflict

For the previous varieties of conflict, related to the two main types *compliance–conflict* and *contradiction*, the following holds. There are instances of pure deontic conflict that are contradictions (obligation conflicting with permission) but also instances that are compliance–conflicts (obligation conflicting with obligation). Pure capacitative conflicts are contradictions, while deontic–capacitative cross–conflicts are compliance–conflicts. The kinds of conflict analyzed in the present chapter can be called "system–inherent" conflicts, since they relate merely to the contents of a system of norms (including legal definitions and meaning postulates): Whether a conflict is present or not does not depend on the truth of sentences external to the system, for example whether it is practically possible or not practically possible to do both A and B. An overview of the types of conflict analyzed is given in Fig. 2.2 below.

2.5 Three Cases: Exemplifying the Theory

Two court cases and an imaginary case will be used to illustrate the theory of normative conflict set out in this chapter. The cases have been chosen so that all varieties of normative conflict that COLT discloses, exhibited in Fig. 2.2, become illustrated.

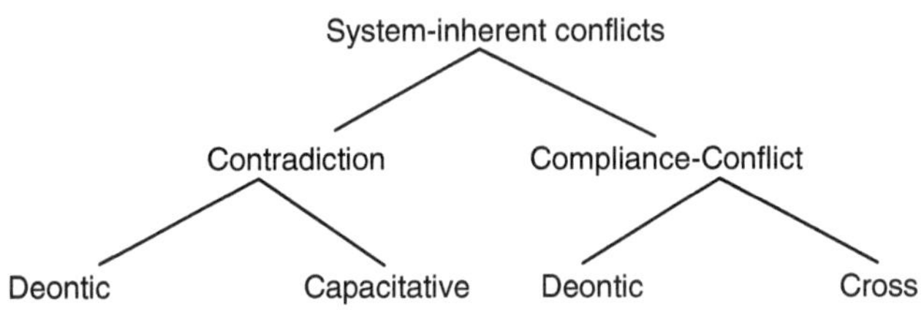

Fig. 2.2 Varieties of system–inherent conflict

2.5.1 Case 1: No–Vehicles in the Nature Reserve

Herbert Hart's well–known "no–vehicle"–example (Hart 1994, 124 ff.) will be used to exemplify contradiction involving a meaning postulate.[33] Suppose that the interpretation of norm–inscriptions of legal sources are to the effect that there is a rule, N_1, prohibiting vehicles in a nature reserve and a rule, N_2, permitting motorcycles in the nature reserve. Let V and C be as follows:

V: A vehicle is placed in the nature reserve.
C: A motorcycle is placed in the nature reserve.

Then the formal representations of these norms are the following well–formed formulas:

Prohibition: Do(x, V) GF Do(x, W/Do(x, V)).
Permission: Do(x, C) GF ¬Do(x, W/Do(x, C)).

Furthermore, suppose, that the normative system contains a conceptual rule, N_3, to the effect that "motorcycle" conceptually implies "vehicle" (legal classification/single–edged meaning postulate) and that, therefore, placing a motorcycle in the nature reserve is ground for placing a vehicle in the reserve:

Conceptual rule: Do(x, C) GF Do(x, V)

Let the members of E(S^*) $\subseteq$ E(J^*) be:

N_1^*: [Do(x, V) GF Do(x, W/Do(x, V))]$\in S^*$.
N_2^*: [Do(x, C) GF ¬Do(x, W/Do(x, C))]$\in S^*$.
N_3^*: [Do(x, C) GF Do(x, V)]$\in S^*$.

Then, there is conflict in subset S of J, in the sense that:

H_J[Do(x, C) $\supset \bot$]$\in \mathrm{Cn_{COLT}}$(E(S^*)).

Proof

(1) [Do(x, C) GF Do(x, W/Do(x, C))]$\in S^*$. (From N_1* and N_3^*, Ax 4)
(2) H_J[Do(x, C) $\supset$ Do(x, W/Do(x, C))]. (From (1), Ax5)
(3) H_J[Do(x, C) $\supset$ ¬Do(x, W/Do(x, C))]. (From N_2*, Ax5)
(4) H_J[Do(x, C) $\supset \bot$]. (From (2), (3), Th 5 for H_J)

Having brought out the logical consequences in terms of membership mediated by the meaning postulate, it is clear that there is a deontic conflict within subset S of the system. Line 4 of the proof shows that the conflict is an instance of *contradiction*. And, since $\mathrm{Cn_{COLT}}$(E(S^*)) $\subseteq \mathrm{Cn_{COLT}}$(E($J^*$)), it holds as well that J is contradictory.

We note that the norm [Do(x, C) GF Do(x, W/Do(x, C))], referred to in line (1) of the proof, expresses a norm, N_4, to the effect that motorcycles are prohibited in the nature reserve. The normative system is expanded by this norm.

[33] Hart uses the "no–vehicle"–example for the different purpose of showing the possibility of open texture or vagueness of rules.

2.5.2 Case 2: The Late Application of the Farming Company

In the Swedish case RÅ 1997 ref 65, the Swedish Board of Agriculture had taken a decision to the effect that the application of a farming company (Lassagård AB) for area aid, funded by the EU, was late and thus inadmissible.[34] According to the company, the decision was in error. The company appealed arguing that working days, instead of calendar days, should be used in estimating whether or not the application was late. Relevant domestic law (article 33 of decree SFS (Swedish Code of Statutes) 1994:1715) was to the effect that a decision concerning area aid by the Swedish Board of Agriculture was final and not subject to appeal. As noted in the case by the Swedish Supreme Administrative Court, this was contrary to Community law, since domestic law deprived the company of its right to a court. In the case *Borelli v. Commission*, the ECJ had pronounced: "the requirement of judicial control of any decision of a national authority reflects a general principle of Community law [. . .]" (Case C–97/91, 1992, paragraph 14).

An interpretation of domestic law and Community law yields a prohibition and an obligation in the case. For the Swedish court having jurisdiction, there was a prohibition, N_1, under domestic law to try the case. But, there was as well an obligation, N_2, to try the case under Community law. Let i be the Swedish Court having jurisdiction to hear the appeal, and let R be that the case is tried by i. Then the following wffs are representations of the two norms:

Swedish law, Prohibition: $\text{Do}(i, \text{R})$ GF $\text{Do}(i, \text{W}/\text{Do}(i, \text{R}))$.
Community law, Obligation: $\neg\text{Do}(i, \text{R})$ GF $\text{Do}(i, \text{W}/\neg\text{Do}(i, \text{R}))$.

Let $\text{E}(S^*_{\text{DEON}}) \subseteq \text{E}(J^*_{\text{DEON}})$ be the set of the following sentences:

N_1*: $[\text{Do}(i, \text{R})$ GF $\text{Do}(i, \text{W}/\text{Do}(i, \text{R}))] \in S^*_{\text{DEON}}$.
N_2*: $[\neg\text{Do}(i, \text{R})$ GF $\text{Do}(i, \text{W}/\neg\text{Do}(i, \text{R}))] \in S^*_{\text{DEON}}$.

Then there is deontic conflict between the pair of norms N_1 and N_2. Here, a *deontic compliance–conflict* is derivable in COLT.

Proof

(1) $\text{H}_J[\text{Do}(i, \text{R}) \supset \text{Do}(i, \text{W}/\text{Do}(i, \text{R}))]$. (From N_1*, by Ax 5)
(2) $\text{H}_J[\neg\text{Do}(i, \text{R}) \supset \text{Do}(i, \text{W}/\neg\text{Do}(i, \text{R}))]$. (From N_2*, by Ax 5)

2.5.3 Case 3: The Italian Border Fees

One of the several issues raised in the case of *Simmenthal* (Case 106/77, 1978) was whether an Italian court had legal power to order repayment of charges, collected by Italian authorities at the Italian border, for inspection of beef imported from another

[34]RÅ is the Year Book of the Swedish Supreme Administrative Court.

Member State. The charges were in agreement with Italian law but in violation of Community law; so, ordering repayment would mean that the national court trying the case would set aside Italian law. From the reports submitted by Italy, it was clear that Italian law did not "*empower* their national courts not to apply the law" (Reports of Cases before the Court (ECR) 1978 part I, 637). Setting aside domestic rules in conflict with Community law was the prerogative of the Italian constitutional court. As a matter of Community law, the ECJ declared that in order to give Community rules "full force and effect" any national court had legal power to set aside domestic rules conflicting with Community law (Case 106/77, paragraph 22).

An interpretation of the legal sources is that there is, N_1, (Italian domestic law) disability for Italian courts other than the constitutional court to order repayment, while N_2 (Community law) is to the effect that these courts have legal power. Let O, M and x be as follows:

O: A valid order to repay charges is delivered.
M: A verdict is pronounced ordering repayment.
x: A variable for any of the Italian national courts of lower rank than the constitutional court.

Then the following formulas represent the norms:

Italian law, Disability: $(\mathrm{Do}(x, \mathrm{M}) \vee \neg\mathrm{Do}(x, \mathrm{M}))$ GF $\neg\mathrm{Do}(x, \mathrm{O}/\mathrm{Do}(x, \mathrm{M}))$.
Community law, Power: $\mathrm{Do}(x, \mathrm{M})$ GF $\mathrm{Do}(x, \mathrm{O}/\mathrm{Do}(x, \mathrm{M}))$.

Let the members of $\mathrm{E}(S^*_{\mathrm{CAP}}) \subseteq \mathrm{E}(J^*_{\mathrm{CAP}})$ be:

N_1*: $[(\mathrm{Do}(x, \mathrm{M}) \vee \neg\mathrm{Do}(x, \mathrm{M}))\ \mathrm{GF}\ \neg\mathrm{Do}(x, \mathrm{O}/\mathrm{Do}(x, \mathrm{M}))] \in S^*_{\mathrm{CAP}}$.
N_2*: $[\mathrm{Do}(x, \mathrm{M})\ \mathrm{GF}\ \mathrm{Do}(x, \mathrm{O}/\mathrm{Do}(x, \mathrm{M}))] \in S^*_{\mathrm{CAP}}$.

Then there is *capacitative* conflict, since it is derivable that:

$\mathrm{H}_J[\mathrm{Do}(x, \mathrm{M}) \supset \bot] \in \mathrm{Cn}_{\mathrm{COLT}}(\mathrm{E}(S^*_{\mathrm{CAP}}))$.

Proof

(1)	$\mathrm{H}_J[(\mathrm{Do}(x,\mathrm{M}) \vee \neg\mathrm{Do}(x,\mathrm{M})) \supset \neg\mathrm{Do}(x,\mathrm{O}/\mathrm{Do}(x,\mathrm{M}))]$.	(From N_1*, by Ax5)
(2)	$\mathrm{H}_J[\mathrm{Do}(x, \mathrm{M}) \supset \mathrm{Do}(x, \mathrm{O}/\mathrm{Do}(x, \mathrm{M}))]$.	(From N_2*, by Ax5)
(3)	$\mathrm{H}_J[\mathrm{Do}(x, \mathrm{M}) \supset \neg\mathrm{Do}(x, \mathrm{O}/\mathrm{Do}(x, \mathrm{M}))]$.	(From (1) by Th 2 for H_J)
(4)	$\mathrm{H}_J[\mathrm{Do}(x, \mathrm{M}) \supset \bot]$.	(From (2), (3) by Th 5 for H_J)

In the *Simmenthal* case, the ECJ declared that national courts, besides power, had an obligation to enforce Community law. The ECJ pronounced, in its opinion, that a national court "*must*, in a case within its jurisdiction, apply Community law in its entirety and protect rights which the latter confers on individuals and *must* accordingly set aside any provision of national law which may conflict with it [...]" (Case 106/77, 1978, paragraph 21 [Italics added]).

An interpretation of Community law is then that there is an obligation, N_3, for the Italian court hearing the case to order repayment of charges collected in violation of

Community law. But, under Italian law, there is disability, N_1, for that court to order repayment. Let O and M be as before and i be the Italian court hearing the case. Then these legal positions can be represented as follows:

Italian law, Disability: $\top$ GF $\neg$Do(i, O/Do(i, M)).
Community law, Obligation: $\neg$Do(i, O/Do(i, M)) GF Do(i, W/$\neg$Do(i, O/Do(i, M))).

Let the following descriptive sentences be $[E(S^*_{DEON}) \cup E(S^*_{CAP})] \subseteq E(J^*)$:

N_1*: [$\top$ GF $\neg$Do(i, O/Do(i, M))]$\in S^*_{CAP}$.
N_2*: [$\neg$Do(i, O/Do(i, M)) GF Do(i, W/$\neg$Do(i, O/Do(i, M)))]$\in S^*_{DEON}$.

Then there is *compliance conflict* in J in the form of *cross–conflict* (compare line (2) and (8) in the proof; cf. the proof in Sect. 2.4.3.3).

Proof

(1)	$H_J[\top \equiv \neg$Do(i, O/Do(i, M))].	(From N_1*, by Ax5)
(2)	$H_J[\neg$Do(i, O/Do(i, M)) $\supset$ Do(i, W/$\neg$Do(i, O/Do(i, M)))].	(From N_2*, by Ax5)
(3)	$\vdash [\top \equiv \neg$Do(i, O/Do(i, M))] $\equiv$ [$\bot \equiv$ Do(i, O/Do(i, M))].	(From RT)
(4)	$H_J[\top \equiv \neg$Do(i, O/Do(i, M))] $\equiv$ H_J [$\bot \equiv$ Do(i, O/Do(i, M))].	(From (3) and RH1)
(5)	$\vdash$[$\bot \equiv$Do(i, O/Do(i, M))]$\supset$[Do(i, O/Do(i, M)) $\supset$ Do(i, W/Do(i, O/Do(i, M)))].	(From RT)
(6)	$H_J[\bot \equiv$ Do(i, O/Do(i, M))] $\supset$ H_J[Do(i, O/Do(i, M)) $\supset$ Do(i, W/Do(i, O/Do(i, M)))].	(From (5) and RH1)
(7)	$H_J[\bot \equiv$ Do(i, O/Do(i, M))].	(From (1) and (4))
(8)	H_J[Do(i, O/Do(i, M))) $\supset$ (Do(i, W/Do(i, O/Do(i, M))))].	(From (6) and (7))

2.6 Concluding Remarks

As is well–known, Jeremy Bentham, Lon Fuller and others have argued that a vital property of a legal system to be constructed is the absence of inconsistency. Bentham spoke of inconsistency as an "evil" recommending that a "single hand" drew up the legal code for its avoidance (Bentham [1822] 1998, 279 and 286). Fuller took it as one of the "distinct routes to disaster" for legal systems (Fuller 1969, 38 f.). If the legal system makes contradictory determinations for the same act, the principle of formal justice is violated, since relevantly similar cases are not treated alike. Such a system, moreover, fails to achieve predictability, since it does not regulate action unequivocally.

The framework developed in the present chapter can be used, in the legislative process, as a tool for avoiding conflicting provisions. The framework can be employed to answer whether or not the enactment of a legislative proposal results in normative conflict. To the extent that the series of steps (starting with norm–inscriptions and ending with a large consequence set) yields that conflict would result from the enactment, the proposal must be retracted or revised, or pre–existing laws abolished prior to its enactment; otherwise, conflict enters the system.

For the judiciary, the framework can, instead, be used as a tool in the application of the law. If the analysis discloses conflict between the norms that the outcome of a litigated case turns on, the deciding court has to resolve the conflict before it can reach a decision on basis of the system. The court, then, has to resort to interpretation, weighing and balancing, application of meta–rules etc. until a construction of the system is reached such that the final step of the analysis exhibits a consequence set to the effect that the system is conflict–free. The theory, concerning the definition of conflict, set out herein, implies nothing with respect to such conflict resolution being difficult or not.

The formal framework of the present chapter discloses where conflicts are present and whether, after a process of solution, previously existing conflicts have been resolved successfully. Therefore, it can be viewed as a logical device in the pursuit of constructing a rational legal system in agreement with Rule of Law and principles for ideal normative systems.

In addition to the present stage of disclosing conflicts and showing whether conflicts have been successfully resolved, a complete theory of normative conflict includes a theory on how normative conflicts are resolved. Conflict–resolution raises a whole new set of questions and problems having to do, *inter alia*, with interpretation, weighing and balancing, values and policies. It also raises important issues having to do with Separation of Powers, for example the power of the judiciary to invalidate legislation *vis–a–vis* the more limited power to merely eliminate conflicts by interpretation, when deciding concrete litigated cases. These issues, as we argue, belong to a subsequent stage, different from the definition of normative conflict. Conflict–resolution will be dealt with in a separate study.

Appendix 1: Overview of the COLT–System

1 *Language* L_{COLT}

Symbols:

(1) Variables/parameters for:

  (i) Individuals (persons, objects, times etc.):
  $x, y, z, \ldots, x_1, x_2, x_3, \ldots$

  (ii) States of affairs:
  $A, B, C, \ldots, A_1, A_2, A_3, \ldots, B_1, B_2, B_3, \ldots, A(x_1, \ldots, x_n), \ldots,$
  $A(i_1, \ldots, i_n), \ldots$

(2) Constants.

(i) Meta-variables for individual constants (from a set I of individuals) "$i, j, k, i_1, i_2, \ldots$".
(ii) Sentence constant:
W for "Wrong is committed."
(iii) Relational constant:
$\in$ for "is a member of the set" (set–membership).
(iv) Brackets, signs for negation, conjunction, disjunction, material implication, and material equivalence:
(,), [,], $\neg$, $\wedge$, $\vee$, $\supset$, $\equiv$.

(3) Operators.
In (i)–(v) below, s, α and β are meta–variables for symbols: s for (1) (i) and (2) (i), and α, β for (1) (ii) and 2 (ii). Symbol $\pm$ signifies the possibilities of affirmation and negation respectively.

(i) Action operators:
Do(s, α) for "s sees to it that α."
Do(s, α/Do(s, β)) for "s sees to it that α by seeing to it that β."
(ii) Binary operator GF, where α GF β is read: "α is ground for β."
(iii) Monadic operator $H_J(\alpha)$ for "it holds as a consequence for J that α."
(iv) Deontic operators:
Obligation(s, $\pm$ Do(s, α)).
Obligation(s, $\pm$ Do(s, α/ $\pm$ Do(s, β))).
Permission(s, $\pm$ Do(s, α)), indicating strong permission.
Permission(s, $\pm$ Do(s, α/ $\pm$ Do(s, β))).
(v) Capacitative operators:
Power(s, Do(s, α)).
Power(s, Do(s, α/Do(s, β))).
Disability(s, Do(s, α)).
Disability(s, Do(s, α/Do(s, β))).

(4) Abbreviations:

$\bot$ (falsum) = $\alpha \wedge \neg\alpha$ (contradiction).
$\top$ (verum) = $\alpha \vee \neg\alpha$ (tautology).

Formation rules, well–formed formulas:

All variables/parameters for state of affairs and the constant W are wffs.
If α, β are wffs, then $\neg\alpha$, $\alpha \wedge \beta$, $\alpha \vee \beta$, $\alpha \supset \beta$, $\alpha \equiv \beta$ are wffs.
If α, β are wffs, then Do(s, α) and Do(s, α/ $\pm$ Do(s, β)) are wffs.
If α, β are wffs, then (α GF β) is a wff.
If α is a wff, then $H_J(\alpha)$ is a wff.
Let δ be $\pm$ Do(s, α) or $\pm$ Do(s, α/$\pm$ Do(s, β)) and α, β be wffs. Then Obligation(δ) and Permission(δ) are wffs.

Let δ be Do(s, α) or Do(s, α/Do(s, β)) and α, β be wffs. Then Power(δ) and Disability(δ) are wffs.
If α is a wff and Γ is a set, then ($\alpha \in \Gamma$) is a wff.

2 Axioms and Inference Rules of COLT

In the axiom schemata and rules of inference below, α, β, and γ are meta–variables for wffs of L_{COLT}. Symbol "$\vdash$" is relative COLT and stands for "provable within COLT."

(1) Axioms and inference rules for action (where, in Ax3, RD2, RD3, $\pm$ stands for affirmation or negation uniformly in the context, and, in RD4, the value of $\pm$ is constant preceding Do(s, α) and constant preceding Do(s, β)):

Ax1, $\text{Do}(s, \alpha) \supset \alpha$.
Ax2, $(\text{Do}(s, \alpha) \wedge \text{Do}(s, \beta)) \supset \text{Do}(s, \alpha \wedge \beta)$.
Ax3, $\text{Do}(s, \alpha/\pm\, \text{Do}(s, \gamma)) \supset (\text{Do}(s, \alpha) \wedge \pm\, \text{Do}(s, \gamma))$.
RD1, If $\vdash \alpha \equiv \beta$, then $\vdash (\text{Do}(s, \alpha) \equiv \text{Do}(s, \beta))$.
RD2, If $\vdash \alpha \equiv \beta$, then $\vdash (\text{Do}(s, \alpha/\pm\, \text{Do}(s, \gamma)) \equiv \text{Do}(s, \beta/\pm \text{Do}(s, \gamma)))$.
RD3, If $\vdash \alpha \equiv \beta$, then $\vdash (\text{Do}(s, \gamma/\pm\, \text{Do}(s, \alpha)) \equiv \text{Do}(s, \gamma/\pm\, \text{Do}(s, \beta)))$.
RD4, If $\vdash \pm\, \text{Do}(s, \alpha) \supset \pm\, \text{Do}(s, \beta)$, then $\vdash [(\pm\, \text{Do}(s, \beta) \supset \text{Do}(s, \gamma/\pm\, \text{Do}(s, \beta))) \supset (\pm\, \text{Do}(s, \alpha) \supset \text{Do}(s, \gamma/\pm\, \text{Do}(s, \alpha)))]$.

(2) Axiom for GF:

Ax4, $[(\alpha \text{ GF } \beta) \wedge (\beta \text{ GF } \gamma)] \in J^* \supset (\alpha \text{ GF } \gamma) \in J^*$, where J^* is the set of wffs of L_{COLT} representing normative system J.

(3) Bridging axiom:

Ax5, $(\alpha \text{ GF } \beta) \in J^* \supset H_J[\alpha \supset \beta]$.

(4) Axioms and inference rules for H_J:

Ax6, $(H_J(\alpha \supset \beta)) \supset (H_J\alpha \supset H_J\beta)$.
RH1, If $\vdash (\alpha \supset \beta)$, then $\vdash (H_J\alpha \supset H_J\beta)$.

(5) Additional axiom and inference rules of the system:

RT, If α is a tautology of propositional logic, then $\vdash \alpha$.
RMP, If ($\vdash \alpha$ and $\vdash (\alpha \supset \beta)$), then $\vdash \beta$.
Ax0, $(\alpha(x) \wedge (\alpha(i) \in \text{IN}(\alpha(x)))) \supset \alpha(i)$, where IN($\alpha(x)$) is the instantiation set of $\alpha(x)$.

3 A Sample of Theorem Schemata for H_J

Theorem 1, for H_J: $H_J[(\alpha \supset \beta) \wedge (\beta \supset \gamma)] \supset H_J[\alpha \supset \gamma]$.
Theorem 2, for H_J: $H_J[(\alpha \vee \beta) \supset \gamma] \supset H_J[\alpha \supset \gamma]$.

Theorem 3, for H_J: $H_J[(\alpha \supset \gamma) \wedge (\beta \supset \gamma)] \supset H_J[(\alpha \wedge \beta) \supset \gamma]$.
Theorem 4, for H_J: $H_J[\alpha \supset \beta] \supset H_J[(\alpha \wedge \gamma) \supset \beta]$.
Theorem 5, for H_J: $H_J[(\alpha \supset \beta) \wedge (\alpha \supset \gamma)] \supset H_J[\alpha \supset (\beta \wedge \gamma)]$.
Theorem 6, for H_J: $H_J[\alpha \supset (\beta \wedge \gamma)] \supset H_J[(\alpha \supset \beta) \wedge (\alpha \supset \gamma)]$.
Theorem 7, for H_J: $H_J[\alpha \supset \beta] \supset H_J[\neg\beta \supset \neg\alpha]$.
Theorem 8, for H_J: $H_J[\alpha] \supset H_J[\alpha]$.
Theorem 9, for H_J: $H_J[\alpha \supset \beta] \supset H_J[\alpha \supset (\beta \vee \gamma)]$.
Theorem 10, for H_J: $H_J[(\alpha \supset \beta) \wedge (\gamma \supset \beta)] \supset H_J[(\alpha \vee \gamma) \supset \beta]$.
Theorem 11, for H_J: $H_J(\alpha \wedge \beta) \equiv (H_J\alpha \wedge H_J\beta)$.

4 *Principles for $Cn_{COLT}(E(J^*))$*

T1) $E(J^*) \subseteq Cn_{COLT}(E(J^*))$.
T2) $Cn_{COLT}(Cn_{COLT}(E(J^*))) = Cn_{COLT}(E(J^*))$.
T3) If $E(J^*) \subseteq E_{EXP}(J^*)$, then $Cn_{COLT}(E(J^*)) \subseteq Cn_{COLT}(E_{EXP}(J^*))$.

Appendix 2: Proofs for the Sample of H_J–Theorems

Theorem 1, for H_J: $H_J[(\alpha \supset \beta) \wedge (\beta \supset \gamma)] \supset H_J[\alpha \supset \gamma]$.

Proof

(1) $\vdash (((\alpha \supset \beta) \wedge (\beta \supset \gamma)) \supset (\alpha \supset \gamma))$. (By RT)
(2) $H_J[(\alpha \supset \beta) \wedge (\beta \supset \gamma)] \supset H_J[\alpha \supset \gamma]$. (By RH1, from (1))

Theorem 2, for H_J: $H_J[(\alpha \vee \beta) \supset \gamma] \supset H_J[\alpha \supset \gamma]$.

Proof

(1) $\vdash (((\alpha \vee \beta) \supset \gamma) \supset (\alpha \supset \gamma))$. (By RT)
(2) $H_J[(\alpha \vee \beta) \supset \gamma] \supset H_J[\alpha \supset \gamma]$. (By RH1, from (1))

Theorem 3, for H_J: $H_J[(\alpha \supset \gamma) \wedge (\beta \supset \gamma)] \supset H_J[(\alpha \wedge \beta) \supset \gamma]$.

Proof

(1) $\vdash (((\alpha \supset \gamma) \wedge (\beta \supset \gamma)) \supset ((\alpha \wedge \beta) \supset \gamma))$. (By RT)
(2) $H_J[(\alpha \supset \gamma) \wedge (\beta \supset \gamma)] \supset H_J[(\alpha \wedge \beta) \supset \gamma]$. (By RH1, from (1))

Theorem 4, for H_J: $H_J[\alpha \supset \beta] \supset H_J[(\alpha \wedge \gamma) \supset \beta]$.

Proof

(1) $\vdash ((\alpha \supset \beta) \supset ((\alpha \wedge \gamma) \supset \beta))$. (By RT)
(2) $H_J[\alpha \supset \beta] \supset H_J[(\alpha \wedge \gamma) \supset \beta]$. (By RH1, from (1))

Theorem 5, for H_J: $H_J[(\alpha \supset \beta) \wedge (\alpha \supset \gamma)] \supset H_J[\alpha \supset (\beta \wedge \gamma)]$.

Proof

(1) $\vdash (((\alpha \supset \beta) \wedge (\alpha \supset \gamma)) \supset (\alpha \supset (\beta \wedge \gamma)))$. (By RT)

(2) $H_J[(\alpha \supset \beta) \wedge (\alpha \supset \gamma)] \supset H_J[\alpha \supset (\beta \wedge \gamma)]$. (By RH1, from (1))

Theorem 6, for H_J: $H_J[\alpha \supset (\beta \wedge \gamma)] \supset H_J[(\alpha \supset \beta) \wedge (\alpha \supset \gamma)]$.

Proof

(1) $\vdash ((\alpha \supset (\beta \wedge \gamma)) \supset ((\alpha \supset \beta) \wedge (\alpha \supset \gamma)))$. (By RT)
(2) $H_J[\alpha \supset (\beta \wedge \gamma)] \supset H_J[(\alpha \supset \beta) \wedge (\alpha \supset \gamma)]$. (By RH1, from (1))

Theorem 7, for H_J: $H_J[\alpha \supset \beta] \supset H_J[\neg\beta \supset \neg\alpha]$.

Proof

(1) $\vdash ((\alpha \supset \beta) \supset (\neg\beta \supset \neg\alpha))$. (By RT)
(2) $H_J[\alpha \supset \beta] \supset H_J[\neg\beta \supset \neg\alpha]$. (By RH1, from (1))

Theorem 8, for H_J: $H_J[\alpha] \supset H_J[\alpha]$.

Proof

(1) $\vdash (\alpha \supset \alpha)$. (By RT)
(2) $H_J[\alpha] \supset H_J[\alpha]$. (By RH1, from (1))

Theorem 9, for H_J: $H_J[\alpha \supset \beta] \supset H_J[\alpha \supset (\beta \vee \gamma)]$.

Proof

(1) $\vdash ((\alpha \supset \beta) \supset (\alpha \supset (\beta \vee \gamma)))$. (By RT)
(2) $H_J[\alpha \supset \beta] \supset H_J[\alpha \supset (\beta \vee \gamma)]$. (By RH1, from (1))

Theorem 10, for H_J: $H_J[(\alpha \supset \beta) \wedge (\gamma \supset \beta)] \supset H_J[(\alpha \vee \gamma) \supset \beta]$.

Proof

(1) $\vdash (((\alpha \supset \beta) \wedge (\gamma \supset \beta)) \supset ((\alpha \vee \gamma) \supset \beta))$. (By RT)
(2) $H_J[(\alpha \supset \beta) \wedge (\gamma \supset \beta)] \supset H_J[(\alpha \vee \gamma) \supset \beta]$. (By RH1, from (1))

Theorem 11, for H_J: $H_J(\alpha \wedge \beta) \equiv (H_J\alpha \wedge H_J\beta)$.

Proof

(1) $\vdash ((\alpha \wedge \beta) \supset \alpha)$. (By RT)
(2) $H_J(\alpha \wedge \beta) \supset H_J\alpha$. (By RH1, from (1). Similarly for β.)
(3) $H_J(\alpha \wedge \beta) \supset (H_J\alpha \wedge H_J\beta)$. (From 2.)
(4) $\vdash (\alpha \supset (\beta \supset (\alpha \wedge \beta)))$. (By RT)
(5) $H_J\alpha \supset H_J(\beta \supset (\alpha \wedge \beta))$. (By RH1, from (4))
(6) $H_J(\beta \supset (\alpha \wedge \beta)) \supset (H_J\beta \supset H_J(\alpha \wedge \beta))$. (By Ax6.)
(7) $H_J\alpha \supset (H_J\beta \supset H_J(\alpha \wedge \beta))$. (From (5) and (6), by propositional logic.)
(8) $(H_J\alpha \wedge H_J\beta) \supset H_J(\alpha \wedge \beta)$. (From (7), by propositional logic.)
(9) $H_J(\alpha \wedge \beta) \equiv (H_J\alpha \wedge H_J\beta)$. (From (3) and (8))

References

Alchourrón, C.E. 1969. Logic of norms and logic of normative propositions. *Logique et Analyse* 12: 242–268.
Alchourrón, C.E., and Eugenio Bulygin. 1971. *Normative systems*. New York: Springer.
Alchourrón, C.E., and Eugenio Bulygin. 1989. von Wright on deontic logic and the philosophy of law. In *The philosophy of Georg Henrik von Wright*, ed. P.A. Schilpp and L.E. Hahn, 665–693. La Salle: Open Court.
Anderson, A.R. 1956. The formal analysis of normative systems. In *The logic of decision and action*, ed. Rescher Nicholas, 147–213. Pittsburgh: University of Pittsburgh Press.
Anderson, Alan R., and Nuel Belnap. 1975. *Entailment: The logic of relevance and necessity*. Princeton: Princeton University Press.
Anselm of Canterbury. [c. 1100] 1998. *The major works*, ed. Brian Davies and G.R. Evans. Oxford: Oxford University Press.
Åqvist, Lennart. 1987. *Introduction to deontic logic and the theory of normative systems*. Napoli: Bibliopolis.
Åqvist, Lennart. 2008. Alchourrón and Bulygin on deontic logic and the logic of norm–propositions: Axiomatization and representability results. *Logique & Analyse* 203: 225–261.
Belnap, Nuel, and Michael Perloff. 1988. Seeing to it that: A canonical form for agentives. *Theoria* 54: 175–199.
Bentham, Jeremy. [1822] 1998. Codification proposal, adressed by Jeremy Bentham to all nations professing liberal opinions. In *The collected works of Jeremy Bentham – "Legislator of the World": Writings on codification, law and education*, ed. Philip Schofield and Jonathan Harris, 243–388. Oxford: Clarendon Press.
Bentham, Jeremy. [1780] 1970. *An introduction to the principles of morals and legislation*, ed. J.H. Burns and H.L.A. Hart. London: The Athlone Press.
Brinz, Alois. 1873. *Lehrbuch der Pandekten*. Erster Band, 2nd ed. Erlangen: Verlag von Andreas Deichert.
Bulygin, Eugenio. 1985. Norms and logic: Kelsen and Weinberger on the ontology of norms. *Law and Philosophy* 4: 145–163.
Carnap, Rudolf. 1952. Meaning postulates. *Philosophical Studies* 3(5):65–73.
Correia, Fabrice, and Benjamin Schneider. eds. 2012. *Metaphysical grounding: Understanding the structure of reality*. Cambridge: Cambridge University Press.
Edgington, Dorothy. 2001. Conditionals. In *The Blackwell guide to philosophical logic*, ed. Lou Goble, 385–414. Oxford: Blackwell Publishing.
Elhag, Abdullatif, Joost Breuker, and Bob Brouwer. 2000. On the formal analysis of normative conflicts. *Information & Communications Technology Law* 9(3):207–217.
Frändberg, Åke. 1987. An essay in the systematics of legal concepts. *Scandinavian Studies in Law* 31: 83–115.
Fuller, Lon. 1969. *The morality of law*. New Haven: Yale University Press.
Goble, Lou. 1999. Deontic logic with relevance. In *Norms, logics and information systems*, ed. P. McNamara and H. Prakken, 331–346. Amsterdam: ISO Press.
Goble, Lou. 2009. Normative conflicts and the logic of "Ought". *Nous* 43(3):450–489.
Goble, Lou. 2013. Prima facie norms, normative conflicts, and dilemmas. In *Handbook of deontic logic and normative systems*, ed. Dov Gabbay et al., 241–351. London: College Publications.
Goldman, A.I. 1970. *A theory of human action*. Englewood Cliffs: Prentice-Hall.
Grossi, Davide, and Andrew J. I. Jones. 2013. Constitutive norms and counts-as conditionals. In *Handbook of deontic logic and normative systems*, ed. Dov Gabbay, et al., 407–441. London: College Publications.
Hage, Jaap. 2000. Rule consistency. *Law and Philosophy* 19: 369–390.
Hamblin, Charles L. 1972. Quandaries and the logic of rules. *Journal of Philosophical Logic* 1: 74–85.

Hamner Hill, H. 1987. A functional taxonomy of normative conflict. *Law and Philosophy* 6(2): 227–247.

Hansson, Sven O., and David Makinson. 1995. Applying normative rules with restraint. In *Logic for a change – essays dedicated to Sten Lindström on the occasion of his fiftieth birthday*, ed. S.O. Hansson and Wlodek Rabinowicz, 40–60. Uppsala: Uppsala Prints and Preprints in Philosophy 1995:9, Department of Philosophy, Uppsala University.

Hart, Herbert L.A. [1968] 1983. Kelsen's doctrine of the unity of law. In *Essays in jurisprudence and philosophy*, ed. H.L.A. Hart, 309–342. Oxford: Clarendon Press.

Hart, Herbert L.A. 1994. *The concept of law*, 2nd ed. Oxford: Oxford University Press.

Hedenius, Ingemar. [1941] 1963. *Om rätt och moral*. Stockholm: Wahlström & Widstrand.

Henry, Desmond P. 1967. *The logic of Saint Anselm*. Oxford: Oxford University Press.

Hilpinen, Risto. 1985. Normative conflicts and legal reasoning. In *Man, law and forms of life*, ed. Eugenio Bulygin, 191–208. Dordrecht: D. Reidel Publishing Company.

Hohfeld, W.N. 1913. Some fundamental legal conceptions as applied in judicial reasoning. *Yale Law Journal* 23(1):16–59.

Holmström–Hintikka, Ghita. 1997. Actions in action. In *Contemporary action theory*. Volume I: Individual action, ed. Ghita Holmström–Hintikka and Raimo Tuomela, 109–134. Dordrecht: Kluwer Academic.

Horty, John F. 2001. *Agency and deontic logic*. Oxford: Oxford University Press.

Horty, John F., and Nuel Belnap. 1995. The deliberative stit: A study of action, omission, ability and obligation. *Journal of Philosophical Logic* 24: 583–644.

Jenks, Clarence Wilfred. 1953. The conflict of law–making treaties. *British Yearbook of International Law* 30: 401–453.

Kanger, Stig. 2001. Collected papers of Stig Kanger with essays on his life and work, vol. I, ed. Ghita Holmström–Hintikka, Sten Lindström, and Rysiek Sliwinski. Dordrecht: Kluwer Academic.

Karl, Wolfram. [1984] 2000. Conflicts between treaties. In *Encyclopedia of public international law*, ed. Rudolf Bernhardt, 935–941. Amsterdam: Elsevier.

Lewis, Clarence I. 1912. Implication and the algebra of logic. *Mind* 21: 522–531.

Lewis, Clarence I., and Cooper H. Langford. 1932. *Symbolic logic*. New York: Dover Publications.

Lindahl, Lars. 1977. *Position and change*. Dordrecht: D. Reidel Publishing Company.

Lindahl, Lars. 1992. Conflicts in systems of legal norms: A logical point of view. In *Coherence and conflict in law*, ed. P.W. Brouwer et al., 39–64. Deventer: Kluwer.

Lindahl, Lars. 1997. Norms, meaning postulates, and legal predicates. In *Normative systems in legal and moral theory – festschrift for Carlos E. Alchourrón and Eugenio Bulygin*, ed. Ernesto Garzón Valdés et al., 293–307. Berlin: Duncker & Humblot.

Lindahl, Lars. 2001. Stig Kanger's theory of rights. In *Collected papers of Stig Kanger with essays on his life and work*, vol. II, ed. Ghita Holmström–Hintikka, Sten Lindström, and Rysiek Sliwinski, 151–171. Dordrecht: Kluwer Academic.

Lindahl, Lars, and Jan Odelstad. 2013. The theory of joining systems. In *Handbook of deontic logic and normative systems*, ed. Dov Gabbay et al., 545–634. London: College Publications.

MacCormick, Neil. 1981. *H. L. A. Hart*. London: Edward Arnold Publishers Ltd.

Makinson, David. 1986. On the formal representation of rights relations. *Journal of Philosophical Logic* 15: 403–425.

Makinson, David, and Leendert van der Torre. 2000. Input/output logics. *Journal of Philosophical Logic* 29: 383–408.

Moritz, Manfred. 1960. *Über Hohfelds System der Juridischen Grundbegriffe*. Library of Theoria, No. 7. Lund: Gleerup.

Munzer, Stephen. 1973. Validity and legal conflicts. *The Yale Law Journal* 82(6):1140–1174.

Pauwelyn, Joost. 2003. *Conflict of norms in public international law: How WTO law relates to other rules of international law*. Cambridge: Cambridge University Press.

Pörn, Ingmar. 1970. *The logic of power*. Oxford: Basil Blackwell.

Ratti, G.B. 2013. Normative inconsistency and logical theories: A first critique of defeasibilism. In *Coherence: Insights from philosophy, jurisprudence and artificial intelligence*, ed. Michal Araszkiewicz and Jaromir Savelka. Dordrecht: Springer.

Ross, Alf. 1944. Imperatives and logic. *Philosophy of Science* 11(1):30–46.

Ross, Alf. 1957. Tû–Tû. *Harvard Law Review* 70: 812–825.

Sartor, Giovanni. 1992. Normative conflicts in legal reasoning. *Artificial Intelligence and Law* 1: 209–235.

Segerberg, Krister. 1992. Getting started: Beginnings in the logic of action. *Studia logica: An international Journal for Symbolic Logic* 51(3/4):347–378.

Sergot, Marek. 2013. Normative positions. In *Handbook of deontic logic and normative systems*, ed. Dov Gabbay et al., 353–406. London: College Publications.

Stenius, Erik. 1963. The principles of a logic of normative systems. *Acta Philosophica Fennica* 16: 247–260.

Tarski, Alfred. [1930a] 1983. On some fundamental concepts of metamathematics. In *Logic, semantics, metamathematics – papers from 1923–1938*, ed. John Corcoran, 30–37. Indianapolis: Hackett Publishing Company.

Tarski, Alfred. [1930b] 1983. Fundamental concepts of the methodology of the deductive sciences. In *Logic, semantics, metamathematics – papers from 1923–1938*, ed. John Corcoran, 60–109. Indianapolis: Hackett Publishing Company.

von Wright, Georg H. 1963. *Norm and action*. London: Routledge & Kegan Paul.

von Wright, Georg H. 1968. *An essay in deontic logic and the general theory of action*. Amsterdam: North–Holland Publishing Company.

von Wright, Georg H. 1982. Norms, truth and logic. In *Deontic logic, computer linguistics and legal information systems*, vol. II, ed. A.A. Martino, 3–20. Amsterdam: North–Holland Publishing Company.

von Wright, Georg H. 1991. Is there a logic of norms? *Ratio Juris* 4(3):265–283.

Vranes, Erich. 2006. The definition of "Norm Conflict" in international law and legal theory. *European Journal of International Law* 17(2):395–418.

Vranes, Erich. 2009. *Trade and the environment: Fundamental issues in international and WTO law, and legal theory*. Oxford: Oxford University Press.

Wedberg, Anders. 1951. Some problems in the logical analysis of legal science. *Theoria* 17:246–275.

Zitelmann, Ernst. 1879. *Irrtum und Rechtsgeschäft: Eine Psychologisch–Juristische Untersuchung*. Leipzig: Duncker & Humblot.

Chapter 3
Entailed Norms and the Systematization of Law

Pablo E. Navarro and Jorge L. Rodríguez

Abstract The validity within legal systems of entailed norms, that is, those norms that are logically derivable from explicitly issued rules, has been called into question with different arguments. To take two examples from distinguished figures, Joseph Raz has claimed that what he calls the "incorporation thesis" cannot account for law's claim of authority, and Andrei Marmor believes that the admission of entailed norms in a legal system would imply the mistaken view that it is necessarily coherent. In this paper we show that these two arguments are, at the very least, highly controversial; that the positivist social sources thesis, though not committed to it, is compatible with the validity of entailed norms, and that taking into account the whole set of logical consequences of explicitly issued norms is an unavoidable step in explaining the dynamic character of legal systems.

Keywords Conventionalism • Legal positivism • Logical consequences • Legal systems

3.1 Introduction

One of the most important tasks performed by legal science is to make explicit a set of implicit norms that are hidden in the conceptual content of a certain legal system. Therefore, a legal system is more than a set of explicitly issued norms in so far as

---

We are deeply indebted to the editors of this volume and to Stanley L. Paulson, for their careful reading and comments on an earlier version of the manuscript.

P.E. Navarro (✉)
CONICET, Buenos Aires, Argentina
e-mail: pabnav@hotmail.com

J.L. Rodríguez
University of Mar del Plata, Mar del Plata, Buenos Aires, Argentina
e-mail: jorgerodriguez64@yahoo.com

M. Araszkiewicz, K. Płeszka (eds.), *Logic in the Theory and Practice of Lawmaking*, Legisprudence Library 2, DOI 10.1007/978-3-319-19575-9_3

the logical consequences that follow from them are regarded as valid norms, too. According to Alchourrón and Bulygin (1971, 67–68):

> . . . the description of the law is not a mere transcription of statutes and other legal norms, but . . . it also involves the operation which jurists refer to under the vague term "interpretation" and which fundamentally consists in the determination of the consequences that can be derived from such norms. Jurists are particularly interested in discovering the solutions that the law provides for certain cases. . . Thus a great part of what jurists call "interpretation" in this context may be reformulated as a determination of the normative consequences of a set of legal sentences for a certain problem or topic. And this, in our terminology, means the construction of an axiomatic system, adopting these sentences as axioms. . .

The normative consequences of a set of legal sentences are often called "entailed norms" ("implicit norms" or "derived norms" are also offered as alternative names). However, the incorporation of entailed norms in a legal system seems to be at odds with other central ideas advanced by contemporary legal theorists, in particular, the social sources thesis defended by legal positivists who assume a conventional foundation of law. Entailed norms extend the limits of law beyond both conventions and norms explicitly issued by legal authorities, challenging the central place assigned to them by positivism in the explanation of the nature of law. For example, exclusive positivists like Joseph Raz (1994a, 210–214) or Andrei Marmor (2001, 69–70) reject the validity of entailed norms. Raz maintains that the idea that the law incorporates norms entailed by source–based law cannot account for law's claim of authority. Marmor, from a perspective very close to Raz, thinks that accepting the validity of entailed norms would be tantamount to assuming coherence as a necessary property of legal systems.

Our main purpose in this paper is to examine this kind of argument in order to determine the place of entailed norms within our legal practices. We will emphasize that the reconstruction of the dynamic character of legal systems (that is, the fact that legal systems are changed by explicit acts of legislation) cannot be properly explained without taking into account the logical consequences of expressly issued norms. In this respect, it is worth stressing that the analysis of entailed norms also provides a conceptual scheme for explaining the nature of legislation. By "legislation" we refer to general norms that have been deliberately issued by legal authorities. This kind of norms may be viewed as a conditional relation between abstract circumstances or properties with deontic consequences. These properties are often called "cases", but they are generic cases, which must not be confused with individual cases. While a generic case is a class of circumstances (for example, "the case of political murder"), an individual case is a particular event, like when we speak of "the case of the murder of John F. Kennedy". All individual cases regulated by a certain norm are the immediate range of such a norm, and the relation between norms and individual cases is internal or conceptual, and this means that, like the truth of a proposition, it does not depend on the beliefs, attitudes or decisions of judges.

The analysis of the logical consequences of general norms is necessary in order to determine their scope, i.e. the individual cases regulated by them. Logical consequences of norms are part of their conceptual content; they "project" the normative solution of a generic case to every individual case that belongs to it. Consequently, it may be said that individual cases are solved even if such individual norms have not been anticipated by authorities; their solutions are implicit in the regulation of generic cases. Thus, the analysis of entailed norms plays an essential role in the explanation of the nature and limits of legislation.

3.2 Authority and Entailed Norms

Joseph Raz claims that what he calls the *incorporation thesis*, that is, that all law is either source–based or entailed by source–based law, has to be rejected if the law does indeed necessarily claim authority (Raz 1994a, 229). According to Andrei Marmor, Raz's criticism of the acceptance of entailed norms may reflect at least two different interpretations, depending on the notion of entailment one assumes (Marmor 2001, 69). Under a first interpretation, the incorporation thesis says that if norms N1 and N2 belong to a certain legal system S1, and they logically entail another norm N3, then N3 also belongs to S1. Under the alternative version, the incorporation thesis says that if norms N1 and N2 belong to a certain legal system S1, and they exemplify a general normative principle P that justifies both norms, and P entails another norm N3, then N3 also belongs to S1. Here we will only take into account the first of these two alternatives, that is, henceforth we only deal with "logically entailed norms" and we also assume a "normal" o "classic" notion of deontic consequence as developed by the most common systems of deontic logic, e.g. the standard system. (A brief analysis of the main systems of deontic logic could be found in Navarro and Rodríguez 2014, 24–33.)

Why does Raz reject the validity of entailed norms? It is somewhat surprising that, parallel to the alleged superiority of a restricted version of the sources thesis – all law is source–based – over the incorporation thesis, in analyzing legal rights Raz suggests that a legal system can be regarded as a system of practical reason, in the sense that its rules are nested in justificatory structures in which some of them legally justify others (Raz 1994b, 242–253). According to Raz, some legal norms provide content–independent justifications of other legal norms. To exemplify this, he proposes to consider the following two statements (Raz 1994b, 247):

(a) Everyone has a legal right to his good name.
(b) Jimmy has a legal right to his good name.

And he wonders whether the fact that (b) is legally justified by (a) is the only way in which its truth can be established. In Raz's thinking, Kelsen would deny this, for he did not grant that a content–independent justification could ever establish the truth of the justified legal statement. The opposite view would be Dworkin's, according to which all successful legal justifications establish the truth of the justified statements. Raz, in turn, claims that a successful content–independent legal justification can establish the truth of the justified statement only if it does not involve moral premises, that is, if there are no moral premises between those that would have to be added for a complete justification of the justified statement.

Raz believes that, in its strongest version, the social sources thesis not only claims that the existence and content of law can be determined without recourse to moral justifications but that, in more general terms, it would also determine the truth of all (pure or applied) legal statements. So there would be no problem in accepting the idea that content–independent legal justifications determine the validity of entailed norms, insofar as this does not demand that one appeal to moral premises.

It is not obvious how these latter considerations can be reconciled with Raz's explicit rejection of the incorporation thesis. A possible way out is to think that, in Raz' s account, only *some* of the logical consequences of source–based legal norms can be admitted as members in a legal system. Raz believes that since the law claims to have legitimate authority, its addressees should be better placed to act in each case according to the result of the balance of underlying reasons applicable to them following the prescriptions of the law rather than calculating for themselves what the result of that balance comes to. If this idea is to be accepted, it should be possible to identify the law without any evaluation of those underlying reasons. Hence, this mediating role performed by the law involves, in Raz' s view, that its authoritative directives are confined to what the legal authority can be said to have held.

From this perspective, and based on his conception of the authority of law, Raz would be restricting the set of all logically derived norms to those that could be justifiably attributed to the authority. This restriction would not go beyond the limits of the attribution of beliefs (Raz 1994a, 228):

> People do not believe in all that is entailed by their beliefs. Beliefs play a certain role in our lives in supporting other beliefs, in providing premises for our practical deliberations ... Many of the propositions entailed by our beliefs do not play this role in our lives. Therefore they do not count amongst our beliefs. One mark of this is the fact that had people been aware of some of the consequences of their beliefs, rather than embrace them they might have preferred to abandon the beliefs which entail them ... This consideration explains why we cannot attribute to people belief in all the logical consequences of their beliefs.

Under this interpretation, Raz's ideas face a challenge designed following the lines of Schauer's analysis of the role of language in rule–based decision–making (Schauer 1991, 62–64). According to Schauer, a rule can only be used as a ground for a decision if it is treated as not being completely transparent with respect to its underlying justification, that is, if its linguistic expression is not taken as "entrenched" in relation to the reasons that could justify its formulation. The verbal expression of any general rule will necessarily have cases of under– and over–inclusion facing its background justification, and if in such cases the option favored is the solution dictated by the reasons justifying the rule, the decision to be taken will not be grounded on the rule itself but on those underlying reasons. Hence, concerning general rules deliberately formulated in a certain language, the authority must be assigned to the text and not to its author, to the law and not to the legislator, on pain of ignoring completely the role that rules play in decision–making environments.

Analogously, Marmor claims that opponents to intentionalism may argue that it is not accidental to democratic procedures that they result in authoritative texts, that is, in statutes (Marmor 1992, 175). And he cites Ely, who thinks that one of the main objectives motivating parliamentary debates to come to a vote on a particular text is to establish, as precisely as possible, what it is that, agreed upon, is sufficient to gain majority support (Ely 1980, 17).

On such a basis, the idea that a legal system is exclusively integrated by those norms that can be justifiably attributed to the legislator seems controvertible. We do not intend to develop at length such an argument here, but its basic idea would be that since authority should be assigned to the verbal formulations expressed by the legal authority, the fact that she has foreseen, admitted or wished certain logical consequences of the norms she issued would become completely irrelevant to determining whether those norms have to be taken as part of the law. Whether logically derived norms have any relevance in the identification or application of the law depends on the possibility of deriving them from the explicitly issued norms with the aid of certain rules of inference, and not on the fact that someone (even the legislator) performs the concrete act of inferring them. This latter idea seems to rest in a quite common and widespread confusion between logic and psychology (Alchourrón 1995, 11–48). The difference between a logical consequence and a psychological fact is clearly remarked by Ota Weinberger in the following paragraph (1995, 263):

> If there is a general rule of law that all human beings are persons in the sense of the legal order then a newborn child – *ipso facto*, without any act of an organ of the state – becomes a person in law. And if there is a general rule that nobody (no human being) is allowed to murder, then the human being NN must not murder. And this is valid regardless of whether the legislator anticipated the existence of NN or not, and independently of any decision of an organ of the state.

Even accepting the proposed reading of Raz's claim, it would be wrong to conclude from his arguments that the social–sources thesis is incompatible with the admission of logically derived norms as part of the law, for they only show that Raz's conception of the authority of law – and not the social–sources thesis – forces to restrict the set of derived norms.

3.3 Coherence and Entailed Norms

In his book *Positive Law and Objective Values*, Andrei Marmor (2001) devotes a couple of pages to the problem of conventionalism and entailed norms. As we saw in the previous section, Marmor rightly considers that Raz's rejection of the incorporation thesis can be interpreted in at least two different versions, for entailment may be viewed as a logical relation or as a moral–evaluative relation. Notwithstanding, Marmor holds that both versions presuppose coherence as necessary properties of legal systems. In his words (Marmor 2001, 69):

> [S]uppose a legal system, say, Si contains the norms Ni. . .n. Suppose further, that norms Ni. . .n entail the truth of a further norm, say, Nx. May we not conclude, then that Nx is also legally valid in Si? But what would it mean to say that Nx is entailed by Ni. . .n? There are several possibilities here. On the most restricted notion of entailment, one would think of it only in terms of logical entailment. (Coupled, I presume, with certain truths about facts.) On the least restricted notion, one could also think of it as moral–evaluative entailment. If it is the case, for instance, that the norms Ni. . .n embody, or manifest, a moral principle M, and M morally requires Nx, then Nx is also part of Si. Despite the considerable differences between these two views of entailments and perhaps other possible views in between these two extremes, they share a crucial assumption: namely that the law is necessarily coherent.

The first thing to note here is that in Marmor's analysis, validity is not clearly distinguished from truth. At least in legal discourse, validity is a property of both norms and legal acts, but truth is predicated of legal propositions, that is, propositions *about* norms. For this reason, contrary to Marmor's idea, it is difficult to grant that a set of norms "entails the truth" of another norm. The difference between truth and validity is important, for a logic of norm–propositions is not isomorphic with a logic of norms (Alchourrón 1969, 242–268). It seems beyond dispute that, like any other theoretical field, *legal science* – concerned with the identification, interpretation and systematization of legal norms – is committed to the acceptance of the logical consequences of its true explicitly formulated assertions, that is, legal propositions. However, as Marmor maintains, it is possible to defend the idea that the validity of explicitly issued legal norms is not adequate for grounding the validity of entailed norms, for entailed norms would only show what a legal system *ought to be*. It would be a fallacy to infer from this ideal normative state of affairs a conclusion about what positive law actually is. Therefore, the problem concerning which propositions of law are true in a certain legal system has to be clearly distinguished from the problem of which norms are admitted as valid within that system.

After emphasizing that he is not referring to coherence as a value in legal interpretation, Marmor remarks that the thesis of the validity of entailed norms presupposes the necessary coherence of law. According to Marmor (2001, 69):

> Therefore, the only question we should ask now is whether it makes any sense to assume that the law is necessarily coherent, logically or otherwise. A negative answer is hardly deniable.

Once these premises have been accepted, Marmor's conclusion is hardly surprising: there is no reason to assume that entailed norms are valid legal norms simply in virtue of such an entailment relation (Marmor 2001, 70).

The argument has two crucial premises: on the one hand, that the validity of entailed norms presupposes the coherence of a legal system; on the other, that law is not necessarily coherent. We have no objection to the latter. The problem, in our view, rests on the former premise. Imagine a normative system containing norm N1: "It is obligatory to perform action x", norm N2: "It is forbidden to perform action x", and all the logical consequences of these two norms. Such a system would be incoherent despite the fact that it contains all norms entailed by N1 and N2. Contrary to what Marmor thinks, the admission of the logical consequences of a normative set does not presuppose its coherence. Moreover, coherence or incoherence of a normative set is only analyzable under the assumption that there are logical relations between norms. And though this is not equivalent to saying that all logical consequences of a normative set also belong to it, the identification of possible inconsistencies in a normative set gets its full significance if logical consequences are taken into account.[1]

The incorporation of entailed norms in a legal system is sometimes rejected because they can conflict with other explicitly issued norms, and this fact seems to deprive other criteria of validity, for example, genetic criteria, of their practical function.[2] Since legal systems are dynamic orders, legal authorities can promulgate norms that are incompatible with some of the elements of a previously coherent legal set. If such a legal system does not contain rules of priority like *lex posterior derogat priori* – the argument goes –, there will be a normative conflict and, in this case, the motivational force of explicitly issued norms would be frustrated.

However, this line of reasoning is no more convincing than the absurd claim that explicitly issued norms are not valid because legislators can promulgate norms in conflict with them. As a matter of fact, neither entailed norms nor explicitly enacted norms prevent authorities from introducing normative conflicts. The importance of identifying entailed norms is not with an eye to limiting to limit the competence of normative authorities, but rather in order to find a solution to cases not explicitly considered by legislators. For example, if legal authorities prescribe that murderers should be punished, this norm will implicitly solve cases of murder committed on both working days and holidays, even though legislators never considered the possible relevance of this distinction. Moreover, this norm regulates the individual case of Brutus killing Cesar even though normative authorities never anticipated this particular fact. Thus, the main function of identifying entailed norms is not to preclude normative inconsistencies but to make explicit the conceptual content of formulated norms.

A precise reconstruction of the notion of normative incoherence would require the introduction of the refined tools developed by deontic logic.[3] However, in order to avoid technicalities, an explicit definition of normative incoherence will not be offered here. We will restrict ourselves to the platitude that incoherent normative systems demand incompatible modes of conduct. The problem with an

---

[1]A further problem in Marmor's view is that, after distinguishing different possible conceptions of entailment, he rejects entailed norms with the argument that all views of entailment share the assumption that the law is necessarily coherent. Now, it seems obvious that under different notions of entailment, "coherence" will mean different things. Consequently, despite the use of the same expression, there is not a unique argument for the rejection of all kinds of entailed norms.

[2]Contrary to Marmor, Tecla Mazzarese (1993, 166) suggests that what she calls "the logical criterion of validity" must be rejected because it allows the possibility of incoherent normative systems.

[3]On the notion of normative incoherence or normative conflicts, see, for example, Von Wright (1963, 203), Alchourrón and Bulygin (1971, 62–64 and 186–187), Hilpinen (1987, 37–40; 1985, 191–208), and Lars Lindahl (1992, 39–64).

incoherent normative set is that any norm can be derived from it as a solution to the conflicting case. Therefore, from an incoherent regulation no useful information can be obtained for the normative guide of behavior, but this is just another way of saying that the normative system is incoherent.

It is worth pointing out that in the legal domain the notion of inconsistency seems to work as a *relational* concept. Legal norms correlate certain abstract cases or circumstances with deontic solutions, and thus a legal inconsistency arises when the same case is correlated by two or more valid norms with different and logically incompatible deontic solutions. Under this idea of legal inconsistency, legal conflicts may be only *partial*, for two incompatible norms in this sense may preserve an area of univocal application. If norm N1 contradicts another norm N2 in a legal system in this partial sense, it may still be possible to derive from each of them some information for those cases not implicated by the normative conflict.

An example shed some light on this idea. Consider the case involving the principles of bargained–for consideration and estoppel presented by Susan Hurley (1989, chapter 11). The doctrine of consideration demands an element of bargain or exchange in order for a valid and enforceable contractual relationship to arise. A promise not motivated by consideration has no legal consequences in contract, and that is a reason to hold that the promisor is not legally obligated. The doctrine of estoppel prevents a party from taking unfair advantage of a situation in which that party's own bad behavior has placed his adversary in a compromised position. Suppose that a promise was made gratuitously and the promisee acts in reliance on it, such that she will be injured if the promise is not kept. Suppose further that the promisor should reasonably have expected it to induce action on the part of the promisee, but has no particular interest in this being so. Under such premises, something of value passes from the promisor to the promisee if the promise is enforceable, but nothing of value passes back to the promisor, and thus the consideration requirement is not met. The promisor is not under a contractual obligation, but has acted irresponsibly in making and then breaking a promise that she should reasonably have expected to induce reliance, and so the principle of estoppel seems to support holding that the promisor should not be permitted to take advantage of her own wrongdoing.

The conflict here is only relative to the gratuitous promise under the premises listed above, and does not affect other cases in which the principles of consideration and estoppel are applied. Thus, even if the considered case appears incoherently regulated, this does not eliminate the practical relevance of the principles for other cases. In other words, the normative conflict is *encapsulated* in the gratuitous–promise case.

Some important conclusions can be drawn from this example. First – as was already pointed out –, it is not the case that logically derived norms cannot appear in incoherent normative orders. Moreover, conflicts in legal systems can only be analyzed in their full significance if the entailed norms are considered. Second, inconsistencies are not always explicit; in some cases a practical conflict is only implicit in the conceptual content prescribed by normative authorities. Consequently, contrary to Marmor's suggestions, coherence is not presupposed in the attribution of validity to entailed norms. Rather, the identification of entailed norms is an unavoidable step to determining whether a legal system is coherent or not.

Marmor rightly stresses that some norms can only be inferred once certain facts have been established. For instance, from a general legal norm, (for example, "F → OR") we can deduce an *individual* norm only if some particular fact f instantiates the abstract property F constituting the antecedent of the first norm (Marmor 2001, 69). However – and though Marmor says nothing about this possibility –, there are also general norms that can be deduced from other *general* norms in a legal system. From "F → OR" we can deduce, by means of the law of strengthening the antecedent, a norm such as "(F&G) → OR".[4] So, even if norms "F → OR" and "G → ¬OR" are not directly incoherent, by means of the law of strengthening the antecedent it follows that "(F&G) → (OR & ¬OR)".

Finally, the idea that there is a close relation between coherence and entailed norms might be thought to lead to conclusions similar to those drawn by Kelsen in his analysis of normative conflicts. Kelsen believes that particular duties cannot be inferred from general prescriptions and he finds no problem in accepting conflicting general norms in a legal system. As Kelsen puts it, "No imperative without imperator, no command without a commander" (1991, 3). Raz has rightly criticized this approach with these words (1976, 503):

> This is quite plainly a wholly unacceptable solution to the problem of practical conflict. It leads directly to the conclusion that practical reasoning is impossible and practical discourse either equally impossible or at any rate completely pointless. Parliament may legislate that everyone must pay a percentage of his income as a tax. It does not follow according to the new kelsenian doctrine that I ought to pay tax. Only if and when an official will order me to pay will I have to pay it. But there is no reason why the official should order me to do so. True, there is a law requiring officials to demand payment from defaulters, but by the same mad logic neither this official nor any other official is obliged to demand payment from me.

Only a "mad logic" can demand specific normative acts to ground each and every legal obligation. In other words, it may be true that there is a legal obligation to do action A even if it is false that an explicitly issued norm prescribes A.

3.4 Social Conventions

We have tried to show, *contra* Raz, that the incorporation of entailed norms as valid legal norms is not incompatible with the social sources thesis, and *contra* Marmor, that the necessary coherence of legal systems need not to be assumed. Yet, we have

[4]The rejection of the law of strengthening of the antecedent is a characteristic trait of both defeasible logics and antipositivism in contemporary legal theory. See Andrei Marmor (2001, 78–81; 1992, 135–138).

neither made a case for the incorporation thesis, nor we have examined what the idea of recognizing entailed norms as valid legal norms would amount to.

Valid legal norms make a practical difference in our deliberations. They offer specific reasons to justify our decisions and actions. Although the notion of legal validity is central both to legal practice and to the philosophy of law, there is still considerable disagreement concerning its true nature. The basic intuition is that legal validity is connected with the justification of legal decisions as well as with the systematic reconstruction of law (Raz 1979b, 146–153). Valid legal norms are institutionally binding in the sense that law–applying organs cannot ignore them in the justification of their decisions.[5]

Legally valid norms belong to a legal system; and their membership in the legal system depends on the satisfaction of certain relations with other norms, relations that give the set its systematic character. The task of identifying the criteria of validity for legal systems may be performed at different levels of abstraction. One who is engaged in a philosophical reconstruction will be interested in validity criteria shared by every legal system (for example genetic relations among norms), leaving aside idiosyncratic differences. By contrast, a report of the criteria of validity in force in a particular legal community will individualize the peculiarities accepted within it in their full detail. For example, in Argentina a complete description of the sources of law cannot ignore the Federal Constitution, the nature of judicial review enforced by their judges, and so forth. At this level, substantial differences are likely to be found between any two distinct legal systems, for the identity of a legal system is defined by these specific criteria.

The detailed analysis of specific practices and conventions of validity can be used to construct a simple argument in favor of the validity of entailed norms, parallel to the one advanced in defense of inclusive legal positivism. To the extent that legal validity depends on conventions, nothing would preclude the possibility that in a certain legal community the social conventions in force render morality as a criterion of legal validity. Following the same line of thought, nothing would preclude the possibility that in a certain legal community the social conventions in force render logically derived norms legally valid. The validity of entailed norms from this perspective would be a contingent fact, depending on the existence of a social practice among individuals and officials within a concrete legal system that grounds legal claims on entailed norms.

In Argentina, for example, it is a well–established doctrine that norm–applying organs are legally bound by norms that follow logically from general explicitly issued norms and certain factual premises. Otherwise, their decisions would be regarded as arbitrary (that is, legally unjustified) and should be revoked by higher norm–applying organs.

[5]For a thorough analysis of the differences between validity and institutional force – trying to show that they can be regarded as independent properties, see Moreso and Navarro (1997, 203–204).

As for the question of the admission of explicitly issued norms as valid in a legal system, Raz answers affirmatively and offers the following reason (1979a, 68):

> The answer is that this is so because the rules practiced by the courts of a legal system are rules of that system according to the doctrine of identity. Here (as in the case of all ultimate rules) the court's practice is what makes the rule a legal rule and is thus its source.

This being so, similar considerations may be cited to ground the claim that logically derived norms are valid in those systems where a judicial practice enforces them.

Although this argument at first sight appears sound and convincing, to ground the conclusion that logically derived norms may contingently belong to a legal system on premises such as these is highly debatable, just as it seems highly debatable to use similar premises to defend inclusive positivism. The problem is that though it is correct that the criteria of legal validity depend on social practices, they do not depend *solely* on social practices. They also depend on the way such practices are theoretically reconstructed. An exclusive positivist has different theoretical alternatives to explain the relevance of moral arguments in the justification of judicial decisions, without conceding to the inclusive positivist that legal validity may sometimes depend on moral merits (Coleman 2000, 171–183, 2001, 103–119). Analogously – as will be analyzed in the following section – it is possible to offer different interpretations of those social practices that appear to assign validity to logically derived norms without conceding that in the legal systems where those practices are in force logically derived norms are part of the law.

The weakness of the argument lays in the fact that, contrary to appearances, it is not the existence of contingent practices but a certain reconstruction of those practices that is at stake here, concealed in the formulation of its premises. If an inclusive positivist asserts "In the community C there is a contingent social practice according to which the legal validity of certain norms depends on their moral merits", how are we to ascertain the truth or falsehood of such a claim? Simply in virtue of an empirical proof? Definitely not: Its truth or falsehood depends on an empirical proof but also on the elucidation of the meaning of "validity". It may be true that citizens and norm–applying organs in community C consider that certain norms must be followed and applied in virtue of their moral merits. Still, this in itself does not prove the truth of the claim that those norms are part of the law in C and, in any case, it does not prove that they are part of the law in C *for that reason*. It may well be the case that those norms do not belong to the law in C, though they are considered binding norms. It may also be the case that they are part of the law in C, but not owing to their moral merits. The formulation of the argument hides the fact that the conclusion purportedly drawn does not actually follow solely from the existence of contingent social practices unless they are supplemented by a conceptual stipulation. The only thing the argument shows by itself is that binding force may be assigned to certain norms in a given community in virtue of their moral merits. If the only possible explanation of that binding force derives from their membership in the legal system, then it would be true to say that they are part of the system. But that is not the only available explanation of their binding force.

If only valid norms, that is, those that are part of the legal system, have binding force, and accepting that some norms may have binding force in virtue of their moral merits, then legal validity will sometimes depend on moral value. Analogously – and this is what matters here – if only valid norms have binding force, and accepting that logically derived norms may have binding force, then those entailed norms would be valid. If you offer a systematic reconstruction of the set of norms that have binding force and you call any norm of that set "valid", then logically derived norms with binding force will be valid – but this simply in virtue of a plain conceptual stipulation.

3.5 The Open Character of Legal Systems

There is still another way to accommodate the intuition that logically derived norms have legal relevance, while also preserving the intuition that the content of the law depends on certain normative acts identified through contingent practices. Judges are not bound exclusively to apply valid norms. Legal systems can be regarded as *open* normative systems, for one of their main functions is to confer binding force on norms and principles that do not belong to them (Raz 1990, 152–154; see also Raz 1979c, 119–120, and 1979b, 149). According to this idea, the relevance of entailed norms could be explained by assimilating them to foreign norms that judges are often bound to apply in order to justify their decisions. In a given legal system, foreign norms may be applicable in certain cases, though they are not usually regarded as valid norms, that is, they do not belong to the legal system in which judges have adopted them as premises for their decisions. Therefore, even if lawyers sometimes ground their arguments on logically derived norms, this fact by itself cannot be taken as a proof of their validity. In other words, the open nature of legal systems may be used to explain the binding character of entailed norms without assuming that they are part of the legal system from which they are derivable.

A legal system may adopt norms of different types and we cannot rely only on formal criteria alone in order to distinguish valid norms from merely adopted ones. As Raz stresses, the distinction must be based on the different reasons that justify the application of valid norms and adopted norms (Raz 1979c, 120, 1990, 153). However, Raz also claims that a certain norm is "adopted" by a legal system *if and only if* either (i) it is a valid foreign norm, or (ii) it is a norm that was made by or with the consent of its norm–subjects (Raz 1979c, 120. A criticism of this distinction can be found in Moreso and Navarro 1998, 287).

The distinction between legally valid norms and merely adopted ones reflects two different roles that law plays in contemporary societies. On the one hand, law operates as an *initiating* system by means of norms created by legal authorities. These norms are introduced with the aim of motivating behavior, that is, to guide actions that authorities regard as socially relevant. On the other hand, law also plays a *supportive role*, that is, it recognizes and reinforces existing norms, practices, and institutions (Raz 1982, p. 933). In this case, legal authorities are not interested in specific actions, and it is left open to individuals to decide what forms of behaviors are more useful in order to achieve certain private ends.

Logically derived norms cannot be included in either of these two categories of adopted norms cited by Raz. Since the expression "if and only if" he uses suggests that the two classes exhaust the set of adopted norms, one can wonder whether it is appropriate to regard entailed norms as "adopted norms" at all. However, it may be the case that Raz's classification fails to capture other norms which are legally binding without being part of a legal system. Derogated norms, which retain their applicability to certain classes of cases; and unconstitutional norms which likewise retain their applicability, until judges declare them to be unconstitutional, may also be offered as examples of binding but not valid norms, and in order to take them into account Raz's classification should be expanded. Once the class of adopted norms is expanded in this way, logically derived norms can receive a proper place within this category.

Following Raz's idea, a certain norm will belong to the set of adopted norms in a legal system according to the reasons that justify their legal relevance. The fact that a norm belongs to a legal system is a reason for judges to take it into account in the process of decision–making with respect to all those cases to which it is relevant. In this case, the reason why judges have the duty to apply those norms is that they belong to the legal system. By contrast, the reason to apply foreign norms to certain cases is not that they belong to the system in force. Rather, the reason here lays in the fact that other valid norms empower judges to use them as legal standards.

Facing now the question of why logically derived norms are legally relevant, the answer seems clearly to be more analogous to the second than to the first of the previous two cases. Judges are undoubtedly bound to take into account the logical consequences of legal norms. But the thesis that they belong to legal systems just like any explicitly promulgated norm is controversial. Hence, the reason why judges are bound to take into account logically derived norms is not that they belong to the legal system but that they are logical derivations of norms that belong to a legal system, and that if we accept the norms of that system, we cannot reject their logical consequences – or, at the very least, we should not reject them. And if we do reject them, we should seek for a change in those norms from which they are derivable.

Although this alternative seems more plausible in dealing with the legal relevance of logically derived norms, we have defended in section II the view that the admission of logically derived norms as part of the law is not incompatible with legal positivism. In other words, from a positivistic conception, law can be reconstructed as a set that is integrated by all those norms identifiable by their social sources along with all their logical consequences, or as solely composed of the former. A defense of the social sources thesis does not by itself compel us to set aside either of those two possible alternatives. But even if the option favors the more restrictive reconstruction, excluding logically derived norms as part of the law, it should be granted that whoever accepts certain norms as grounds for decision–making is bound to accept the logical consequences that follows from them as well. Consequently, the idea that only those norms that have an appropriate social source are part of the law is feasible when we are dealing with the problem of the identification of the set of norms that belong to a certain legal system. But when we are dealing with legal reasoning and the identification of those norms judges are bound to apply to legal cases, the set that has to be taken into consideration is not restricted to the norms that have the appropriate social source but encompasses all their logical consequences.

It is interesting to note how a similar problem is dealt with in the logical studies of belief revision. In this domain, two different strategies are employed: belief bases and theories. According to this distinction, A is a belief base for a theory K if and only if K=Cn(A). In other words, a theory is a belief set closed under logical consequence, while a belief base is a set that is not closed under logical consequence (Hansson 1999, 17–18; Gärdenfors 1992, 195–200). The use of belief bases offers certain advantages over theories, for belief bases are finite – what allows their computational treatment – and they have greater expressive power than theories. However, the framework of belief bases has the disadvantage that it is quite difficult to distinguish between basic and derived beliefs. This latter problem does not arise in the analysis of legal systems, for there are conventionally accepted criteria for distinguishing between explicitly issued norms and logically derived ones.

3.6 Legal Dynamics

We saw in the previous section that the social sources thesis is compatible with two different reconstructions of the relevance of entailed legal norms. Now, the social sources thesis is supposed to restrict the elements that may be admitted as members in the law. Thus, it is concerned with the identification of a legal system. But the phrase "legal system" is ambiguous: sometimes it is used, from a *static* point of view, to refer to a set of norms, and sometimes it is used, from a *dynamic* point of view, to refer to a sequence of sets of norms within a certain period of time.

Explicitly issued norms provide the normative basis for a *momentary* legal system LS (henceforth, for the sake of simplicity we ignore customary norms). Since the identity of a normative set depends on its elements, the incorporation or elimination of norms generates a *new* momentary system, for example LS1. According to this idea, two consecutive momentary systems, for example LS and LS1, have different normative bases. The results of the promulgation or derogation of norms cannot be studied at the level of momentary legal systems; it requires taking into account a succession of momentary legal systems (a non–momentary legal system or *legal order*). Joseph Raz has presented this approach as follows (1980, 184–185):

> The genetic structure of a legal system. . .reveals how legal systems underwent change during their existence. The development of the theory of the genetic structure is essential for the understanding of the structure of non–momentary legal systems, i.e. of legal systems existing in a period of time. Indeed, it is tempting to say that the genetic structure is the structure of non–momentary legal systems.

Raz believes that the operative structure of legal systems, based on punitive and regulative relations, is the structure of momentary legal system; and he assigns no relevance to logically derived norms in order to determine the structure either of momentary or of non–momentary legal system.

However, it is easy to show that the normative basis of a momentary legal system cannot be properly identified without taking into account the logical consequences of legal norms. Promulgation and derogation of norms are different sides of the same coin, at least in the sense that it would be pointless to say that authorities can only promulgate, but not derogate, legal norms or vice versa. Therefore, in order to explain the notion of legal authority, that is, the possibility of deliberate legal change, we need to analyze the effects that both promulgation and derogation have over legal systems.[6] When a normative authority has the power to change the deontic status of a certain action, a subsequent normative act performed by the same authority concerning the same action but with an incompatible deontic status prevails over the previous one, according to the familiar principle *lex posterior derogat priori*. As Eugenio Bulygin writes (1986, 212–213):

> This rule is conceptually linked to the notion of competence, if by "competence" we understand the faculty to change the normative status of certain actions. Therefore, the rule "lex posterior" is not a contingent rule, but is conceptually necessary insofar as there is a norm authority with competence to change the deontic qualifications of certain actions... without the rule "lex posterior" there would be no competence at all and so there would be no possibility of normative change emerging from acts of authority.

The conceptual relevance of implicit derogation performed by principles like *lex posterior* can be shown by the following example. Let us assume a legal system LS containing two norms:

(1) Buenos Aires is the Capital of Argentina.
(2) The President of Argentina must reside in the Capital of the State.

Both (1) and (2) have been explicitly promulgated by the legal authority, but while (1) is a legislative definition, which does not prescribe any action, (2) is actually a rule that imposes specific obligations on a class of individuals. (1) and (2) constitute the *normative basis* of LS, and from this basis it can be easily inferred:

(3) The President of Argentina must reside in Buenos Aires.

Now, suppose the legal authority promulgates a new norm:

(4) The President of Argentina must reside in Córdoba.

Assuming that (4) has been promulgated by the same authority, and, being later in time, it has priority over (1) and (2) in cases of conflict. However, (4) contradicts neither (1) nor (2), but is incompatible with (3), a logical consequence of the conjunction of (1) and (2). This implies that the basis of our new momentary system

[6] As Hart (1994, 175–178) has shown, a normative order incapable of deliberate change would not qualify as a legal system.

(LS1), resulting from the promulgation of (3), cannot contain the new norm together with both (1) and (2); one of these two norms has to be modified or eliminated in order to prevent the derivation of (3). But this means that the new momentary system cannot be identified without taking into account, not only (1), (2) and (4) – the explicitly issued norms – but also (3), a logical consequence of the issued norms. Therefore, when principles like *lex posterior* are operative (and at least a minimal form of such principle must be operative in order to make sense of legal authority), the promulgation of a new norm may lead to a revision of the basis of our normative system, and this revision necessarily has to take into account the logical consequences of explicitly enacted norms (Alchourrón and Bulygin 1981, 398–406. See also Alchourrón and Makinson 1981, 125–148, and Alchourrón 1982, 53–55).

To summarize the argument, the concept of legal authority is closely related to the deliberate change of legal systems. A paradigmatic legal practice consists in giving priority to new issued norms over older ones, and this is not a merely contingent feature of the dynamics of legal systems. Consequently, principles like *lex posterior* are conceptually linked to the notion of legal authority. We cannot fully understand the results of the application of principles like this without taking into account the logical consequences of explicitly issued norms. It follows that the identification of entailed norms is a necessary step in the conceptual reconstruction of legal authority and the dynamics of legal systems.

3.7 Conclusions

In this paper we have mainly dealt with the problem of the logical consequences of legal norms. In particular, we have analyzed the compatibility between certain conceptions of legal positivism and the validity of logically entailed norms. We have defended that the recognition of entailed legal norms as part of a legal system is not at odds with a positivistic approach to law. According to our reconstruction, the legal relevance of entailed norms actually stems from explicitly issued norms, conventions and other social sources. For this reason, even conventionalism, understood as a specific conception of legal positivism, is compatible with the validity of entailed norms. We have pointed out that the arguments provided by Joseph Raz and Andrei Marmor against the validity of entailed norms are not conclusive. On the one hand, we have stressed that the problem of the validity of the logical consequences of legal norms is entirely different from the incorporation of moral norms. Thus, it is not necessary to defend inclusive legal positivism in order to admit that entailed norms are valid in a certain legal system. Contrary to the tension generated by the incorporation of moral norms in the explanation of the nature of law and authority, the entailed norms are implicit in the norms explicitly issued by legal authorities. On the other hand, we have rejected the existence of a conceptual connection between the validity of entailed norms and the logical coherence (consistency) of legal systems. Logical coherence is a contingent formal property of normative systems and, for this reason, if the incorporation of entailed norms involved that legal systems are necessarily coherent, then the validity of such norms should be rejected. However, we have shown that there are no reasons for maintaining that entailed norms guarantee that legal norms cannot be in conflict.

We have also claimed that some of the central features of law, like its hierarchical nature and the institutional force of legal norms, can only be adequately explained through a systematic reconstruction of legal materials. Legal systems are dynamic normative orders, susceptible of change in virtue of normative acts performed by legal authorities. Legislation is a paradigm of legal change, and any sound theory of law must offer a reconstruction of this process. As we have attempted to show in this paper, legislation cannot be fully understood without taking into account the logical consequences of explicitly issued norms. For this reason, the explanation of the dynamic aspect of law cannot be divorced from an analysis of its static nature, and from, the role played by the logical consequences of valid laws. Finally, we have offered no positive argument in order to show that entailed norms are necessarily valid in legal systems. This is still an open question. (See, for example, Navarro and Rodríguez 2014, 214–240.)

References

Alchourrón, Carlos E. 1969. Logic of norms and logic of normative propositions. *Logique et Analyse* 12:242–268.

Alchourrón, Carlos, E. 1982. Normative order and derogation. In *Deontic logic, Computational linguistics and legal information systems*, vol. II, ed. Antonio Martino, 51–63. Dordrecht: North Holland.

Alchourrón, Carlos, E. 1995. Concepciones de la lógica. In *Lógica*, Enciclopedia Iberoamericana de Filosofia, ed. Carlos Alchourrón, et al., 11–48. Madrid: Trotta.

Alchourrón, Carlos E., and Eugenio Bulygin. 1971. *Normative systems*. New York/Wein: Springer.

Alchourrón, Carlos E., and Eugenio Bulygin. 1981. The expressive conception of norms. In *New studies in deontic logic*, ed. Risto Hilpinen, 95–124. Dordrecht: Reidel.

Alchourrón, Carlos, E., and David Makinson. 1981. Hierarchies of regulations and their logic. In *New studies in deontic logic*, ed. Risto Hilpinen, 125–148. Dordrecht: Reidel.

Bulygin, Eugenio. 1986. Permissive norms and normative systems. In *Automated analysis of legal texts*, Logic, informatics, law, ed. Antonio Martino, 212–213. North Holland: Elsevier.

Coleman, Jules. 2000. Constraints on the criteria of legal validity. *Legal Theory* 6:171–183.

Coleman, Jules. 2001. *The practice of principle*. Oxford: Oxford University Press.

Ely, John Hart. 1980. *Democracy and distrust*. Cambridge: Harvard University Press.

Gärdenfors, Peter. 1992. The dynamics of normative systems. In *Expert systems in law*, ed. Antonio Martino, 195–200. North Holland: Elsevier.

Hansson, Sven Ove. 1999. *A textbook of belief dynamics: Theory change and database updating*. Dordrecht: Kluwer Academic.

Hart, Herbert L.A. 1994. *The concept of law*, 2nd ed., rev. ed. Raz, Joseph et al. Oxford: Oxford University Press.

Hilpinen, Risto. 1985. Normative conflicts and legal reasoning. In *Man, law and modern forms of life*, ed. Eugenio Bulygin, et al., 191–208. Dordrecht: Reidel.

Hilpinen, Risto. 1987. Conflict and change in norm systems. In *The structure of law*, ed. Ake Frändberg, et al., 37–49. Upsala: Förlag.

Hurley, Susan. 1989. *Natural reason*. New York/Oxford: Oxford University Press.

Kelsen, Hans. 1991. *General theory of norms*. Oxford: Oxford University Press.

Lindahl, Lars. 1992. Conflicts in systems of legal norms: A logical point of view. In *Coherence in law*, ed. B. Brouwer, et al., 39–64. Boston: Kluwer Law and Taxation.
Marmor, Andrei. 1992. *Interpretation and legal theory*. Oxford: Oxford University Press.
Marmor, Andrei. 2001. *Positive law and objective values*. Oxford: Oxford University Press.
Mazzarese, Tecla. 1993. Normological scepticism and legal dynamics. Weinberger and Kelsen confronted. In *Rechtsnorm und Rechtswirklichkeit*, ed. Aulis Aarnio et al., 155–169. Berlin: Duncker & Humblot.
Moreso, José Juan, and Pablo E. Navarro. 1997. Applicability and effectiveness of legal norms. *Law and Philosophy* 16:201–219.
Moreso, José Juan, and Pablo E. Navarro. 1998. The reception of norms, and open legal systems. In *Normativity and norms: Critical perspectives on Kelsenian themes*, ed. Stanley L Paulson and Bonnie Litschewski Paulson. Oxford: Oxford University Press.
Navarro, Pablo E., and Jorge L. Rodríguez. 2014. *Deontic logic and legal systems*. New York: Cambridge University Press.
Raz, Joseph. 1976. Kelsen's general theory of norms. Critical study. *Philosophia* 6:495–504.
Raz, Joseph. 1979a. Legal reasons, sources and gaps. In *The authority of law*, 53–77. Oxford: Oxford University Press.
Raz, Joseph. 1979b. Legal validity. In *The authority of law*, 146–162. Oxford: Oxford University Press.
Raz, Joseph. 1979c. The institutional nature of law. In *The authority of law*, 103–121, Oxford: Oxford University Press.
Raz, Joseph. 1980. *The concept of a legal system*, 2nd ed. Oxford: Oxford University Press.
Raz, Joseph. 1982. Promises in morality and law. *Harvard Law Review* 95:916–938.
Raz, Joseph. 1990. *Practical reason and norms*, 2nd ed. Princeton: Princeton University Press.
Raz, Joseph. 1994a. Authority, law and morality. In *Ethics in the public domain*, 194–221. Oxford: Oxford University Press.
Raz, Joseph. 1994b. Legal rights. In *Ethics in the public domain*, ed. Joseph Raz, 238–260. Oxford: Oxford University Press.
Schauer, Frederick. 1991. *Playing by the rules. A philosophical examination of rule–based decision–making in law and in life*. Oxford: Oxford University Press.
Von Wright, Georg H. 1963. *Norm and action*. London: Routledge & Kegan, Paul.
Weinberger, Ota. 1995. Normological inferences and the generation of legal norms. *Ratio Iuris* 8:261–270.

Chapter 4
Conservative Coherentist Closure of Legal Systems

Juliano S.A. Maranhão

Abstract The present paper has two main goals: (i) to provide a logical representation of a coherentist closure of normative systems; (ii) use this model to clarify a concept of coherence in law, which is faithful to a theory of legal validity as source based law. Source based law is taken here as the "evidential base" for the reconstruction of the normative system, therefore guiding both interpretation and legislation activities even when implicit legislative purposes are taken into account. Such reconstruction is given by the minimal assumption of "conservative" changes in the base of the original normative system so that it becomes coherent with legislative purposes. I use a belief revision model to provide a logical and abstract characterization of what I mean by "conservative changes", without providing any material criteria for conservative choices (to be made by the legal interpreter or legislator).

Keywords Normative systems • Belief revision • Logical closure • Coherence • Teleological interpretation

4.1 Introduction

Legislation is a complex activity, which requires a reflexive attitude by the law-maker. The product of his law making activity is a set of sentences in ordinary language whose content expresses a set of rules. But to reach the content of these rules from the text (rule–formulations) involves a series of interpretive operations which the lawmaker must be concerned with, not only to control the fidelity of the rule–formulation with the envisaged rule–content, but also to control possible alternative rule–contents compatible with that same rule–formulation. This happens not only in the case of semantic vagueness but also in the case of gaps and inconsistencies where the interpreter must make choices to reconstruct the

---

J.S.A. Maranhão (✉)
Department of Philosophy and General Theory of Law, University of São Paulo Law School, São Paulo, Brasil
e-mail: julianomaranhao@usp.br; jm@sampaioferraz.com.br

M. Araszkiewicz, K. Płeszka (eds.), *Logic in the Theory and Practice of Lawmaking*, Legisprudence Library 2, DOI 10.1007/978-3-319-19575-9_4

normative system. Thus, the lawmaker should be concerned not only with the relation of the employed syntax with its semantic content, but also with systematic relations among rule contents. Besides, on the minimal assumption that legislation is intended to guide conduct of individuals to an envisaged state of affairs, the very rule–content, even if precisely drawn from the rule–formulation, should be an adequate means to the intended goals.

Therefore, the lawmaker must work back and forth. First, to adjust her text to the intended rule–content, avoiding ambiguities, vagueness, gaps, inconsistencies (specially, with higher order rules) and undesired logical consequences. Secondly, to adjust the rule–content to the envisaged goals, trying to foresee circumstances where the content might not fit her intentions (what may demand the inclusion of new conditions to the application of the rule or ancillary definitions restricting the scope of that rule). To make things worse, the semantic identification of the rule–content, departing from the text, usually demands pragmatic considerations on the purported goal. So these two steps, although conceptually distinct, are actually imbricated in its interpretation and therefore, in the very design of the statute. Actually, the legislator is the first interpreter of his own lawmaking.

It would be to hard a demand on the lawmaker to deliver a precise product, immune to interpretive challenges (both by unforeseen circumstances and unforeseen interpretations). Still, if one abstracts from the semantic and pragmatic dimensions of legal interpretation, it is possible to render a syntactic description of the normative system derived from the set of fixed rule–contents, thus providing a valuable tool to check the consequences of an sketched set of rules.

Alchourrón and Bulygin (1971) have worked out this conception to a precise definition of a logically closed legal system. Given a set of conditional rules (syntactically expressed), the normative system is built by unfolding all the normative solutions to every possible combination of the conditions expressed in the antecedent of these conditional rules (assuming an underlying deontic logic). They define then the legal system as the set of logical consequences from the base of enacted rules. As a result, gaps and inconsistencies may be revealed and the legal operator may overcome these inconveniences by changing the original rule–contents (what would mean to change a previously attributed meaning for the text, in the case of an interpreter, or to change the very rule–formulation, in the case of the legislator). Alchourrón and Makinson have also provided models to represent the impact of such interventions in the normative system, by the promulgation of new rules or derogation of original ones, using logics of revision (actually creating this field) (Alchourrón and Makinson 1981; Alchourrón et al. 1985).[1]

The effort has proven fruitful not only for a conceptual clarification of the concept of a legal system, but also as an analytical tool to model both legal interpretation and legislation. Of course, the model has limitations when confronted to the complexity of legislative and interpretive activity and Bulygin replied to critics by lowering

[1]More recent applications within artificial intelligence and law may be found at Maranhão (2001) and Governatori et al. (2013).

expectations.[2] Both Alchourrón and Bulygin have later conceded that not all logical consequences of a set of rule–contents may be part of the legal system, since they admit that the inquiry into the objective reasons of the rules (Bulygin 2005) or into the dispositional attitude of the lawmaker (Alchourrón 1996) may defeat derived norms inconsistent with those reasons or subjective intention.

Hence, logical closure (even assuming fixed rule–contents) is not enough to represent *what the legal system is* out of the material given by legal texts. Legal reasoning based on legislative goals may have the effect of deleting some normative consequences of the original system as well as adding new solutions. This balance implies that *coherence* of rule–content with its goals is at stake. The question is whether this second dimension could be subject to logical modeling. While Haack states it can't and Bulygin that it doesn't have to, some researchers dedicated to artificial intelligence and law have tried to face the challenge.

Some attempts to provide an account of teleological legal reasoning have focused on modeling coherence in legal argumentation (Bench–Capon et al. 2013; Bench–Capon and Sartor 2003; Prakken 2002; Żurek and Araszkiewicz 2013). The products are systems that are able to select sets of arguments or rules, which maximize coherence or are justified based on appreciation of the relation between rules and goals (or associated values).

While these works focus on the dynamics of legal argumentation based on a system of rules, one of my goals in this paper is to sketch an abstract definition of what the system of rules is, based on a set of fixed rule–contents and a set of goals, with which it coheres. The idea pursued here is that the set of goals or values is also a set of rules which serves as a parameter and constraint to revisions of the base B of explicit rules so that it becomes coherent with the set of principles P (which represents goals or underlying reasons). Assuming the set of rules, the definition of its closure is given by the basic operations of revision in order to make rules and principles cohere, so that solutions may be derived to address cases involving gaps (here called novelties) and cases where the normative solution by the normative system conflicts with legislative intent (here called abnormalities). Although the model is abstract, it helps to advance goal of this paper, which is a substantial claim for a conservative approach to legal coherence. That is one of the reasons some pages are spent discussing legal theory; the other being the fact that such discussion illustrates the explanatory setting of legal interpretation, thus being useful for the reader to understand the logical model here developed.

Years of dispute between foundationalists and coherentists in epistemology have gradually produced if not convergence, at least the weakening of the main thesis on each side.[3] Foundationalists have accepted the idea that basic beliefs (which do not need justification and justify all other within a linear system of beliefs) may be corrigible and that coherence reasons may play a role in justification. In

[2]See Bulygin's reply to an early criticism by Aarnio at Bulygin (1986) and the controversy between Haack (2007) and Bulygin (2008), commented by Maranhão (2009a). See also Alchourrón (1996).

[3]See Amaya (2006) for a survey and relations of this discussion to the field of law.

particular, if basic beliefs are corrigible, there must be a selection of basic beliefs (which cannot be justified by incorrigible ones). If this is true, the selection should be guided by some system of evaluations determining which of our beliefs is most conductive to truth. This may itself lead to a coherentist selection of basic beliefs (Lehrer 2000, 95). Coherentists, by their turn, have been more flexible with respect to the demand of holism (that our beliefs are justified in terms of a global relation of mutual support) and have accepted both a local dimension of coherence and also the idea that some of our beliefs may have a privileged status or may be psychologically arrived at without support by other beliefs (even though they all insist that no belief may be kept in our system of knowledge without reference to other beliefs) (Bonjour 1985; Harman 1989; Lehrer 2000).

So for *soft foundationalists* and *soft coherentists* the edifice of knowledge would be built out of a preliminary basis of beliefs which are "*innocent until proven guilty*" (Reid 1895; Lehrer 2000, 73). In this softer environment of converging thesis, theories of explanatory coherence are promising candidates for an adequate account of coherence, at least not repulsive to foundationalists (for instance, Harman 1989; Sellars 1963; Thagard 2000). Faithful to coherentism these theories keep the idea that no belief may be held independently and all beliefs are corrigible, but admit that the set of beliefs may be supported by a relatively stable belief base. Such supporting relation is given by explanatory connections. It is the ability of other beliefs to better explain or be explained by "basic" beliefs that increases their chance of being legitimately held. But note that those "basic" beliefs are also unstable and may be challenged in the same explanatory grounds.

Transplanting these notions to the field of legal theory one should look for the conditions that legitimate one's belief that a normative standard is a member of the legal system. Within the explanatory setting, the relevant questions are, first, "Which set of rules would play the role of the explanatory base of coherence in law?" and second "In what would consist the explanatory relation among the rules in the legal system?"

Given that the preliminary base is indeed *preliminary*, to the first question "what would it be?" it should be added the question "*how conservative should we be about it?*". Excess of conservatism may lead to foundationalism but excess of liberalism may undermine the very base. This paper will focus on the inferences involved in the expansion or contraction of the legal system. In other words, my second inquiry will actually be: *what are the logical operations in the constructive explanation of the base?*

To explore the questions here proposed the paper will first expose difficulties around the identification of the base of legal interpretation which is linked to the very question of identification of the law (Sect. 8.2). Then it will be argued that the relation between rules in the explanatory base and legal principles may be seen as a relation of inference to the best explanation (Sect. 8.3). Such discussion form the background on which the model presented in Sect. 8.4 is based.

4.2 Coherence and the Explanatory Base of Legal Justification

The inquiry on the explanatory base of legal interpretation refers to the very identification of law: what are the rules that may be counted as immediate (but possibly unstable) evidences of legality? In the perspective of the legal subjects, the question is reduced to what actions (in a particular set of circumstances) are plainly legally right or wrong.

Actually, such questions are very close to the project of legal positivism. Its whole quest departed from a simple observation: there are prototype cases where the legal demand seems quite clear. For instance, the proposition "*according to the law it is forbidden to kill someone who commits adultery*". This proposition is surely true if referred to the Brazilian law, but it may be false if referred to other jurisdictions. But this perception of certainty indicates some form of knowledge behind the identification of the law. To disclose it, legal epistemology should identify what are the criteria that make such a proposition about law true in a given community.

The positivist answer could not rely on the discovery of any sort of moral facts or in anything that could depend on the moral evaluation of the content of law. The key was the finding of an *"external observational input"* to law, which would fit the *"perception"* that the truth or falsity of the same proposition about law may vary according to each society: the thesis of the *social sources*. So there are particular instances of actions that are obligatory simply because that type of action was the object of a rule by the conventional authority.[4]

The next step was to convert this implication into a definition of what law is. We do not have to do the same and may restrict ourselves to use the idea that there is an objectively identifiable source of legal rules, which is independent from the appreciation of the rule's content.

But an objectively identifiable source of rules is not enough if no clearly identifiable instances of these source–based rules are available (otherwise the convergence of behavior which is the very base of the rule of recognition would not be possible).[5] So what could be the criteria to identify the set of objective instances of standards derived from the objective social source? In other words, what are the clear cases that could make the role of the explanatory base?

An initial suggestion would be to consider as clear the cases immediately derived from the text without resource to interpretation (Marmor 2005). Let us see if this proposal works.

---

[4]I will avoid complex discussions about the factual or normative character of the rule of recognition as proposed by Hart (1961) or the *Grundnorm* as proposed by Kelsen (1960) which are the product of this convention or convergent behavior of approval/disapproval of actions in conformity/disconformity to authoritative rules. See Himma (2002) for an introductory discussion on Hart's rule of recognition. For Kelsen's Grundnorm see Vernengo (1960).

[5]Hart (1961). Marmor (2005) contains a more recent statement of this point. See Ratti (2008) for criticism.

The Brazilian Penal Code,[6] art. 124, commands *"abortion is forbidden"*. A few steps later, another rule, art. 128, says, *"It is permitted to abort upon consent if the woman's life is endangered or if pregnancy is the result of sexual abuse"*. Some years ago, these two rules were the center of a polemic decision by the Brazilian Supreme Court about the right of abortion of anencephalic fetuses. Although there was discrepancy on several points, no one ever questioned the *"linguistic fact"* that according to art.124* *abortion is prohibited if there is no life threat to the pregnant and no sexual abuse.*

How is such settled understanding possible? The reader may think my reaction is awkward, but notice that the content of art.124* is not exactly what art.124 says. Actually, art. 124 and 128 are inconsistent. We just do not see it because implicit inference mechanisms apply. These inferences may be grasped by reference to some immemorial principles of legal interpretation like *lex specialis derogat generalis* (to delete 124) and *exceptio firmat regulam in casibus non exceptis* (to introduce 124*).

It is worth noticing that the inference from 124 to 124* is not deductive and is related to a change of the legal system. It is a transition from an inconsistent system $K0 = \{124, 128\}$ to a consistent $K1 = \{124^*, 128\}$. In the regulation of abortion all seemed to have naturally done the same choice with respect to the set $K1 = \{124, 128\}$. Two immediate alternatives would be: to delete art. 124, or to delete art. 128. We discard these possible choices because they are too radical and offend an entrenched principle of legal interpretation of maximal conservatism of the legal material – *nihil facile mutandum in solemnibus* (Digest 4, 11.7). Instead, we all decided to weaken or "refine" art. 124, restricting the original general prohibition to the conjunction of two factors (absence of life threat and absence of sexual abuse). We have chosen K1 because it seemed the best alternative to make sense of a reasoned legislation.

Hence, to define "clear cases" as those in which the rule need no interpretation seems to be misguided.[7] Clear cases may be the result of "obvious" changes of the normative system through interpretation.

Maybe the qualification "clear" is misguided and the demand for "objectivity" has to do with the instantiation of the rule and not with its semantic content. Instead of clear cases, we should talk of clear instances or easy cases: those whose instantiation is easy. Following this line of thought, MacCormick defines easy cases as those where the *decision is legally justified by means of a purely deductive argument* (MacCormick 1994). Atria (1999) opposes this suggestion to Alexy's thesis that a sufficiently justified legal argument must contain not only an *internal justification* (deduction from legal premises) but also an *external justification* (a defense of the normative premises based on legality, morality, social consequences,

---

[6]Available at http://www.planalto.gov.br/ccivil03/decreto--lei/del2848.htm.

[7]I cannot fully develop the argument within the limits of this paper and will limit myself to indicate counter examples challenging each thesis. For a more detailed account, see Maranhão (2012).

legislative intent, etc.).[8] Therefore, another reading of this proposal would be that easy cases are those where there is no need of external justification.

This suggestion also seems inadequate. Let me quote art. 128 of the Brazilian Penal Code:

> Art. 128 Abortion practiced by a physician shall not be punished if:
>
> (i) There is no other way to save the pregnants life;
> (ii) The pregnancy results from sexual abuse and the pregnant consents with the abortion.

Nobody in the Brazilian legal community would deny that the text above means, *"It is permitted to abort upon consent if the pregnant's life is endangered **or** if pregnancy is the result of sexual abuse"*. However, there is no explicit indication that the propositions (i) and (ii) should be read as an inclusive disjunction or as a conjunction. Given that these propositions are not mutually exclusive, what renders the inclusive disjunction reading undisputable in the legal community?

The explanation must take steps towards the values protected by such rules. The theme "abortion" involves a central opposition between the fetus being subject of moral worth (right to live) and woman's freedom. Art. 124, which generally forbids abortion, clearly prefers the fetus' right to the woman's freedom. It would be difficult to make sense of this prohibition should the legislator consider fetuses were not subject of moral worth. The reference to sexual abuse and danger to the pregnant easily suggests two other relevant values: woman's dignity and woman's right to live. This hypothesis is strengthened when one considers its power to explain other rules of the penal code such as the forbearance of sexual abuse and the "state of necessity" as a condition which excludes the culpability of a crime (the protection of one's own life justifies harm to others and even murder).

It is reasonable then to explain the disjunctive reading as the best effort to make the fetus' right compatible with these two implicitly endorsed values. The fragility of the conjunctive reading becomes evident. What sense could one make of the difference between the value of a woman's life and the life of a woman who was subject to sexual abuse? If only violated women whose life is in danger may be submitted to abortion (and not all those whose life is in endangered), how could one explain the right of killing for those who are in state of necessity? The disjunctive reading, by its turn provides a harmonious preference relation between underlying values: in the case of sexual abuse, *woman's freedom* (the law demands her consent) in conjunction with her dignity prevails over the *fetus' life*; and, alternatively, her right to live prevails over the fetus' right to live.

---

[8]Atria's reading is based on MacCormick's position expressed at the first edition of Legal Reasoning and Legal Theory. In the second edition of that book MacCormick already marked his disagreement with his previous statement: *"That shows why deductive reasoning from rules cannot be a self–sufficient, self–supporting, mode of legal justification. It is always encapsuled in a web of anterior and ulterior reasoning from principles and values, even although a purely pragmatic view would reveal many situations and cases in which no one thinks it worth the trouble to go beyond the rules for practical purposes."* (MacCormick 1994, xiii).

The example above shows that a case of easy instantiation (such as the right of a sexually abused but healthy woman to abort) may involve external justification even though it is not explicit in an apparently immediate instantiation. This is specially true when the external argument is undisputable within the legal community. As Fuller puts it, sometimes the purpose behind the rule is so obvious that we lose track of its use in the identification of its meaning or in its instantiation (Fuller 1958).

So the ideas of "settled meaning of law" or of "easy case" neither can be captured as a semantic quality of the normative formulation nor as a property of its instantiation. Hart has warned against the oversimplification to see the agreement on cases that fall in the scope of a rule with the agreement on shared linguistic conventions (Hart 1983, 106). Clear cases may be the result of interpretation involving both argument about the rule's goals and values and choices based on preferences among alternative legal systems. What is characteristic of them is that the interpretation or the external argument is *undisputable* within the legal community, which means that a divergent interpretation or argument is not only considered wrong or bad, but not a legal interpretation or argument at all. Hence, we may say that clear or easy cases are those where the internal and external justification of a rule are *undisputable*.

We may think of prototypical situations from which "clear cases" emerge as those where a valid rule, objectively identified by its source, has a clear normative formulation whose instantiation to the case at hand is purely deductive. That would be an ideal for the law giving activity. However, this may provide a very restricted set, which certainly does not exhaust the "explanatory basis" of legal interpretation. Nevertheless, given that it is neither a sufficient nor a necessary condition for "clarity", the very acceptance of the meaning given by linguistic convention without external argument also involves a choice within a system of evaluation in the context of interpretation.

Three points in this discussion seem of particular importance.

First, the fact that the very "preliminary" basis of law involves the support of a system of evaluation is a good reason to believe that the construction of a normative system is of a coherentist nature. The external input given by the sources cannot stand without some clearly identifiable instances of the content of rules. In addition the identification of this set of objective instances of the rules derived from the sources involves the support of an evaluation system. This evaluation system guides the choices by which we reach a stable set of instances of legal rightness and legal wrongness explained by settled meanings of rules.

Second, the discussion above indicated that even the "clear instances" of legality presuppose relations of support with other contents of accepted rules. This is also true for those cases in which they correspond to the immediate instantiation of the clear meaning of a rule objectively identified as source–based. This suggests there is no completely external input of legality whose content is independent of any support relation with other contents accepted as law.

Somehow, we know, even if we cannot set clear criteria of identification, that there is this core of settled instantiations. In the end of the day, and that is the third point, the stability of this set is reached by a consensus within the legal community (legal scholars, officials and practitioners). Some instances of application of rules and their meanings are simply accepted given that internal and external justification find no objections and cannot be disputed. This suggests a relation between *coherence* and *argumentation* in the identification of the basis of a normative system.

4.3 Legal Principles or Legislative Goals as the Product of Local Abductive Inferences from the Base of Rules

As we have seen above coherence in legal interpretation is of a particular sort and very difficult to handle, given that there is no clarity about what are the criteria to identify the very base to be explained. We only know that it exists as a set of source–based rules whose fixed meaning immediately explain undisputed instantiations. Therefore, we have to abstract from it and take the base as a "given" if we intend to advance on the idea of defining a coherentist closure of a normative system.

So suppose we depart from a set of source–based rules and a set of clear instantiations explained by those rules. We may close this set by logical consequence providing further normative solutions. It is clear that this restricted set is limited and does not reflect the resource to values that are endorsed by the rules. The coherentist expansion and specification of the base depends on this relation between the rules and its underlying values.

The inclusion of moral values and public policies related to the settled rules has to be carefully handled; otherwise, the very base may be lost. Although principles are usually seen as justifications of legal rules, we are going to take them here the other way around.

It is interesting to differentiate *explanation* from *justification* as relations between normative standards. A normative standard is justified by another one if it is *deductively derived* from the latter in the model. Differently, a normative standard *explains* the other by a *counterfactual* relation: if it were valid then the other would be deductively derived. In this perspective, the relation of explanation is a step within an abductive inference, taken here as an inference to the best explanation. Following Harman, this method of reasoning has three steps: (a) recollection of evidences; (b) hypothesis that if were true, based on our knowledge, would explain those evidences; and (c) comparison and selection of the best explanatory hypothesis (Harman 1965).

Therefore, a valid general rule *justifies* the validity of its instantiation (individual rule) to the extent that the instantiation is deduced from it. However, a legal principle may be interpreted as the best explanation of the legislative purpose of the rule or a set of rules, what means that the principle is derived from the accepted rule by abduction.[9] It is the acceptance of the base of rules that *justifies* the acceptance of a legal principle (as a valid legal standard) to the extent that the latter provides the best explanation to the former.

The link between rules and their goals is based on some background knowledge about actions and their general consequences or its moral import. This relation is nicely captured by Schauer's description of the observational generalizations underlying rules (Schauer 1991). For instance, a rule imposing a speed limit is based on a generalized observation that driving cars beyond that limit increases the risks of fatal accidents and on an evaluation that fatal accidents are bad (human life is a value worth pursuing). This value is the *background explanation* of the speed limit rule.

The abductive inference is sensitive to variations of the base of accepted beliefs. If it expands, new elements may contradict previously accepted explanations. Hence, there is a great difference between the abduction of a principle from a rule and the abduction of a principle from a set of rules (or the whole base of rules). Here lies a decisive step. Should we consider coherence as a relation between the whole base and its explanatory principles (global coherence) or between a set of specific rules related to a particular action and its explanatory principles (local coherence)?[10]

MacCormick defends coherence as a value in Law based on two central factors: *universalism* (rules based on general principles that cohere with each other are less arbitrary) and *intelligibility* (if the law is intended to guide individuals, then its organization based on a few and coherent principles is more efficient). His idea of universalism leads to an increasing scale of principles. Precedents or rules are vehicles to satisfy principles, which by their turn are instances of more general principles or goals, leading to a set of a few principles of the *highest order* (MacCormick 2005, 193). The legal order has then to be coherent with those highest order principles.

Such a large scope to universalism may turn the explanation trivial or lead to arbitrary choices by the interpreter. The explanation of a broad base of rules related to various themes may have two consequences: either it will demand principles which are too general to have any explanatory power or, worse, it will arbitrarily delete rules of the base which are incoherent with previously accepted principles.

---

[9]In the last two decades, abductive reasoning received considerable attention of Artificial Intelligence and many models were suggested to capture its rationality. These models help to clarify how the conclusion of an abductive inference is *warranted* by its evidences and background assumptions. Given that this method of inference is *content increasing*, a central concern is how to confer *epistemic warrant* to its conclusion (Psillos 2002). This concern is faced by the development of *standards of comparison* of competing theories which are highly informed by a coherentist aesthetics (the winner hypothesis is consistent, the one which explains the greatest amount of evidences, the one which is more adherent to one's background assumptions, the simplest, without ad hoc restrictions, the more unified, the most precise, etc.). This links the justification of abduction in causal explanations to coherence theories of justification.

[10]Global coherence may be also defined as an specific case of local coherence (Hage 2013).

Savigny (1886) has warned against the second problem. He conceived the relation between the rule and its purpose as a *"logical concatenation"* leading from the rule to its *ratio (ratio legis)*. Such relation also holds between motives, establishing a gradation among rules, purposes and purposes that are more distant. The coherence among higher purposes, legal institutes, rules and legal sources provides the "organic" character of the legal order and its unity as the expression of the "spirit of the people". But he had a clear concern that the direct application of a purpose whose link were too distant with respect to the rule could be misleading, given that different specific and conflicting purposes (of inferior order), may be held under the same general and superior purpose (Savigny 1886, 246–247). Thus, the direct application of this superior purpose may betray the specific guidance contained in the *"true thought"* of the rule. According to Savigny, the use of the general purposes of law instead of the specific purposes of the rule would be an oblique modification of the content of law that does not deserve the name interpretation (Savigny 1886, 245).

The same concern is expressed by Raz (1994), arguing that the ideal of coherence, for instance, pursued by Dworkin's theory of law as integrity, transfers the base of coherence from the concrete set of rules to an abstractly articulated set of principles (linked to the interpreter's moral evaluations). The result is that the principles gain a priority status instead of playing a secondary explanatory role (that is why he rejected law as integrity as a coherence theory).

My vote for a local coherentist inference of legal principles from accepted legal rules is led both by Savigny's warning and by the intuition that the demand of coherence in the description of the whole set of valid norms does not reflect our actual practice of understanding the law. Practical questions about *"what the law is?"* are usually asked in order to know *"what the law says about such action in such circumstance?"*. To provide an adequate answer, only a small source-based subset of rules needs to be active. As Harman defends, actual reasoners are resource bounded and have no cognitive capacity to process the whole set of beliefs or to keep track of its justifications when deriving a theoretical or practical conclusion (Harman 1989). He also advances that a sensible epistemology should not aim to assume such ideal of completeness in order to justify our actual beliefs and our dispositions to change them.

4.4 Dynamic Local Inferences From the Base

The search for the background explanation of a set of local rules by a coherentist or abductive inference is not dependent on the claim that coherence is likely to warrant the truth of legal propositions. The very practice of interpretation in the legal community is carried out with the idealization of a coherent and rational legislator. Hence, in Lipton's terms (Lipton 2004), the goal is not the *likeliest* or more probable explanation of the rules, for we are not pursuing actual legislative intent. It is the best or *loveliest* explanation that we care, by the reconstruction of reasoned and coherent choices in the name of a rational lawmaker.

Just as in scientific inquiry the search of new theories or explanations are consequences of what Peirce called *"surprising observations"*, so in law the appeal to the background explanation of a rule by means of an "inference to the best legislative purpose" is provoked by some sort of surprise given by a case which was allegedly "unpredicted" with respect to the accepted base of rules. An observation is surprising if it is a novelty, i.e. our current beliefs do not explain the observation. It is an *abnormality* if our beliefs derive an explanation that contradicts the observation (Aliseda 2000). Here we take as analog to observation the set of undisputed instances of rules.

The set of legislative purposes (or principles) P is a set of rules which serves as a parameter and constraint to revisions of the base B of explicit rules. It is assumed that this set of principles *"explain"* the set of rules in the sense that it derives the set of explicit rules in presence of some background knowledge K (i.e. $B \subseteq Cn(P \cup K)$). The coherentist closure of the set of explicit rules B based on the set of principles P is then the logical closure of a revised set *B to become coherent with P*. Maxims of completeness, consistency and coherence with background principles guides the basic revision operations:

(a) expansion of the set B so that, in the case of gap, it derives a rule consistent with $Cn(P \cup K)$;
(b) refinement of B (substitution of a conflicting sentence by a logically weaker one) so that it becomes consistent with P in the case of normative conflict. The resulting expanded and refined B is included in $Cn(P \cup K)$.

It is also assumed that the set P is obtained by abduction from the very set B, given a background knowledge K, what is also modeled by belief revision tools. The connection with AI&Law approaches which model teleological reasoning relating rules with values is intuitively grasped by a simple example. For instance take a rule to the effect that *"it is forbidden to drive if you exceed 100 mph"*. One may assume that the value protected is "safety", guided by a generalization that *"exceeding 100 mph is unsafe driving"* (background knowledge). Now, instead of attaching the value "safety" to the rule, one may assume that it is explained by the principle according to which *"It is forbidden to drive unsafely"*, which, taking into account the background knowledge, derives the original rule. The abduction of the principle from the rule comes from this reversed deduction.

In the present paper, I will focus on the definition of the operations of "adjustment" of the base of explicit rules with respect to its underlying set of principles.

4.4.1 Novelties

We include in the concept of *novelties* both the cases where there is no rule related to some action (naive gap) the cases where the rule does not define the deontic status of the action in at least one relevant circumstance and the cases where due to semantic vagueness of the rule the normative solution is not determined In these cases of "gap" there seems to be no justification provided by the accepted base of rules for a solution to a particular description of action in a possible or relevant circumstance. To cope with them I propose two guiding principles:

Coherentist expansion (COH): the expansion should incorporate rules or definitions, which are coherent with the base.

Minimal expansion (MIN): the expansion should not exceed what is needed to justify the solution for the new case.

Minimality is based on the idea that the closer we keep to the accepted and settled base the stronger is the acceptance of the new normative standard. We are most likely to meet both requirements if we succeed to explain/justify the deontic status of the relevant action in the novel situation, by showing that it is explained by normative standards that are "implicitly" endorsed by the base. That is, if the background explanatory principles of the relevant subset of the base provide a normative solution. For instance, take as "novelty" the action of entering in the park with a bicycle, given a rule *"vehicles are forbidden in the park"*. If we infer as the best explanation that the concern is to protect unaware users of the park from accident, then if we accept that bicycles offer such a risk, entering with bicycles should be forbidden. From these considerations, I propose a derived principle:

Conservative expansion (CON): the expansion of the base should not exceed what is needed to justify the normative solution derived from the principles endorsed by the base.

How could we logically describe such reasoning? Two main lines[11] of representing abductive inference appeared in artificial intelligence. First, the inferential models see it as a reversed deduction based on a background theory where the inference satisfy some constraints (Josephson and Josephson 1996) – such as consistency of the hypotheses with the background theory, *minimality* in the derivation of the *explananda*, and non derivation of the *explananda* by the background theory itself. Second, it may be represented from the point of view of an epistemic process of expansion of our belief set (Pagnucco 1996).

The discussion above naturally hints to the use of a belief revision framework. In Pagnucco's model (Pagnucco 1996), for instance, the resulting abductive expansion of a set K with respect to a belief *a* is given by a choice among the minimal extensions of this set that derive *a*. Wassermann and Dias (2001) have applied Pagnucco's model to sets which are not necessarily closed by logical consequence. Olsson (1997) proposes a model of coherence where a belief revision model is constrained by a referential set he called "stability set" (a class of belief sets). The original belief base is expanded by a new belief, which is then "consolidated", that

[11]One may also refer to Thagard's (2000) method of measuring coherence by constraint satisfaction as a tool to abductive or coherentist inference if we take a belief that increases the level of coherence of a belief set (with respect to its own negation) as derivable from this set.

is it is made consistent given that the choice among the consistent alternatives is constrained by the stability set. If the new belief is already consistent with the base, we may take Olsson's model as a constrained abductive expansion.

As Amaya rightly points out (Amaya 2006), the belief revision models are too abstract and do not indicate how the resulting coherent set should be achieved. It only assumes that it is achieved and then represents the logic of change from the original to the resulting coherent set by stipulating minimal conditions that such modification should satisfy. The whole "interesting work" which is the definition of criteria of choice of the most coherent expansion is abstracted by a "choice function". So the most coherent outcomes are chosen but nothing is said about how this function makes its choices.

Anyway, such abstract enterprise is useful to clarify the field on which any choice (by any criteria) of a "best coherent explanation" may be grounded. Using the *"vehicles in the park"* example, suppose we depart from a base containing one rule related to the action of entering in the park (e). The base B is composed by the rule *"if you are driving a vehicle it is forbidden to enter in the park"* ($\forall_x(v_x \Rightarrow O_x\neg e)$) – where O is the modal operator for obligation, $\Rightarrow$ is *strict* implication and the symbols for predicate logic are as usual with variables for normative individuals. Assuming a set of settled background beliefs K, including sentences such as "John's Ferrari is a vehicle" ($f_j \Rightarrow v_j$) – using j as a name for the individual John – we may close the base with undisputed instantiations such as *"It is forbidden for John to enter in the park driving his Ferrari"* ($f_j \Rightarrow O_j\neg e$).

The belief base also contains information such as *"vehicles increase the risk of accidents in the park"* and *"John's Ferrari increases the risk of accident in the park"*, *"Paul's Mercedes increases the risk of accident in the park"*, etc. Based on the idea that the link of vehicles with the risk of accident is a generalization of these instances and that the lawmaker intends to prevent accidents, one may best explain the base B by the principle that it is forbidden to enter the park with whatever increases the risk of accidents ($\forall_x(r_x \Rightarrow O_x\neg e)$). This rule is part of the abductive closure of the set B, which is given by all the abductively inferred normative standards from B. Now suppose our base of accepted beliefs also includes the belief that bicycles increase risk of accidents in the park (as a generalization of instances of bicycle accidents), that is $\forall_x(b_x \Rightarrow r_x)$. Then the abductive closure of B, assuming K, derive $\forall_x(b_x \Rightarrow O_x\neg e)$ i.e. that based on the accepted rules it is forbidden to enter in the park riding a bicycle.

The example is assumedly simple–minded. I will not explore the complexities involving these inferences, such as the criteria of assessment of alternative explanations and further background beliefs demanded for this comparison.

It is enough to notice that the reasoning above involves three steps. First, an abductive inference which makes explicit a new standard given the base and a set of background beliefs about actions and their results. Second, the expansion of the base by the incorporation of this new standard. Finally, a deduction using the new explicit normative standard and the set of background beliefs.

First, I suggest some preliminary and rough definitions, taking *Cn* as a tarskian consequence operator:

Let *B* be a set of rules that are relevant with respect to an action whose deontic status is under scrutiny in the interpretation of the legal order. The base *B* is a subset of the legal order and it is assumed to be consistent with the background knowledge (if the set of rules associated to an action is inconsistent, one may work with a consolidation of it, that is, maximal consistent subsets, but I will avoid this complication).

The definition below is intended to be applied to the naive notion of gap which may be described as $\Delta a \notin Cn(B \cup K)$, where Δ is any deontic modality and "*a*" a sentence representing an action or an state of affairs resulting from an action. The sketch here developed can be easily adapted to cope with the notions of normative and recognition gaps.

Definition 1. *Hermeneutic theories.* Let *B* and *K* be sets of sentences and *a* a sentence. Then we define the set of $Ab_{Ka}(B)$ as the set of minimal sets of sentences which explain *B* and define a normative solution for *a* based on *K*, i.e. the set of all *Y*, such that:

(i) $B \subseteq Cn(Y \cup K)$
(ii) $\Delta a \in Cn(Y \cup K)$
(iii) $\bot \notin Cn(Y \cup K)$
(iv) there is no $Y' \subset Y$ satisfying (i)–(iii)

The best hermeneutic theory *Best* is a choice function which selects a member of $Ab_{Ka}(B)$. It constitutes the set of constraints on which both the expansions and refinements of the set *B* will be based.

I will not try to specify here the criteria involved in this choice, but it may involve coherentist considerations (such as simplicity, maximization of support constraints, etc.) besides explanatory power and consistency which are incorporated in the definition. Now we may define the abductive expansion of a local base of rules.

Definition 2. *Conservative Extensions.* Let *B* and *K* be sets of sentences and a *a* sentence. Then we define the set $CON_{Ka}(B)$ as the minimal set of rules which derive the same normative solution given by the best hermeneutic theory for the base, i.e. the set of all *X* such that:

(i) $B \subseteq X$
(ii) $\Delta a \in Cn(X \cup K)$ if $\Delta a \in Cn(BestAb_K(B))$
(iii) $\bot \notin Cn(X \cup K)$
(iv) There is no $X'' \subset X$ satisfying (i)–(iii)

Note that an extension of the local base in order to derive the same normative solution given by its endorsed principles does not need to incorporate any of those principles. Returning to the example above it may be a simple normative definition such as *"Bicycles are vehicles"* considering a suitable set of background beliefs.

The conservative expansion of the legal system is then just the incorporation of one of the conservative extensions into the original legal system:

Definition 3. *Conservative expansion.* Let B be a set of sentences and Ch be a choice function on $CON_{Ka}(B)$. Then the conservative expansion $+$ of a base B with respect to an action a and a background set of beliefs is defined as $+_{Ka}(B) = Ch(CON_{Ka}(B))$

4.4.2 Abnormalities

There is an abnormality if there is a possible case where the normative solution derived from the settled rules is inconsistent with the normative solution derived from the background explanatory principles of this set. Schauer calls these cases "recalcitrant experiences" which are a result of the over or under–inclusiveness of the rule (Schauer 1991). Alchourrón and Bulygin call them "axiological gaps" (Alchourrón and Bulygin 1971). In these cases, the principles may defeat a logical consequence derived from the base of explicit rules.

An example may help to identify what are the steps involved in reasoning with legal abnormalities. Let us take the example of abortion. According to the article 124 of the Brazilian Penal Code abortion is generally forbidden. The cases of pregnancy resulting from sexual abuse and life danger are explicit exceptions. Now suppose a case of pregnancy where the fetus is anencephalic. An inquiry into the legislative purposes suggests that the dignity of the pregnant is superior to fetus' right to live, since in the case of sexual abuse, abortion is permitted. Now if the background set of beliefs include the belief that carrying the pregnancy of a fetus diagnosed with anencephaly implies an offense to her dignity, then the best hermeneutic theory of explanatory principles associated with the background set of beliefs would derive that abortion of an anencephalic fetus is permitted. However, since anencephaly is not a relevant condition named by the BPC's rules as an exception, there is a conflict between the rule's direct instantiation and the instantiation provided by the rule's underlying reasons.

To restore coherence, a contraction should take place in the set of settled rules. Again, we assume two principles:

Coherentist contraction (COH): the contraction should restore the consistency of the base of rules with respect to its underlying explanatory principles.

Minimal contraction (MIN): delete only those rules in the local base that are responsible for the inconsistency with the set of underlying explanatory principles.

Note that once we handle sets that are not necessarily closed, the exclusion of a rule from the base will exclude all rules logically derived from it and this may be undesirable. It is possible that some of the logical consequences of the rule that conflict with the rule's underlying reasons may still be consistent with those reasons. For instance, take the set containing just the rule 124: *"Abortion is forbidden"*. Consequently, we have both that *"Abortion is forbidden if the fetus is anencephalic"* and *"Abortion is forbidden if the fetus is not anencephalic"*. Now if the explanatory principles provide the solution that *"Abortion is permitted if the fetus is anencephalic"*, then it is only a part of the rule 124 that needs deletion. If one excludes it *simpliciter*, then none of its derived beliefs will be kept, what would mean another sort of incoherence with the set of principles (it would create a gap in the set of explicit rules). The principle of minimality is satisfied in this form of contraction, given that the original rule was inconsistent with the principles and it was the only rule responsible for such inconsistency. This happens because the principle of minimal change applied on non–closed sets has no proviso for the adequacy of derived rules. As we have seen, the derived rule *"Abortion is forbidden if the fetus is not anencephalic"* is still coherent with the set of explanatory principles and we should keep it in order to avoid another gap.

Again, I propose a conservative attitude with respect to the base of settled rules. Just as the expansion should be conservative in the sense that it respects implicitly endorsed principles derived from the rules by abduction, the contraction should be conservative in the sense that it preserves implicit rules derived by deduction.

So instead of minimal change, we should use a stronger principle of conservatism (Harman 1989), according to which one is still justified to keep a belief in the absence a special reason not to (if there is no specific reason to abandon it). We may interpret this principle as saying that we should keep logically derived beliefs not specifically contradicted (Maranhão 2009b).

Conservative contraction (CON): only rules derived from the local base that are specifically responsible for the inconsistency with the set of underlying explanatory principles should be deleted from the set of consequences of the base.

A revision operator called refinement that qualifies (instead of deleting) one of the sentences of the original set has been developed at (Maranhão 2001, 2007, 2009b). I will use Greek letters to refer to any arbitrary rule. So suppose the rule α is a member of the local base of consistent rules B. Then we have, for any arbitrary condition b, that $b \Rightarrow \alpha$ and $\neg b \Rightarrow \alpha$ *are derived from* B. Now suppose that a conflicting solution is derived from the set of background principles of this base (not from the base) for that very condition. That is suppose $b \Rightarrow \neg\alpha \in Cn(BestAb(B))$. This means that the original rule is defeated by the relevant background principles given a specific condition, namely the *refuting condition*. So only $b \Rightarrow \alpha$ should be excluded. If the refuting condition is absent, then the solutions provided by the original rule should still hold for in this case they are not specifically contradicted. This means that the original rule should not be deleted, but only qualified by further conditions of application,in order to restore coherence with the background principles $\neg b \Rightarrow \alpha$.

The operation of internal refinement (notation #) satisfies the principle of conservative contraction. Provided a set of rules B, a rule $\alpha \in B$, a function Cn^* selects part of the set of non–tautological consequences of α, i.e. $Cn^*(\alpha) \subset Cn(\alpha)/Cn(\varnothing)$ and the contraction function operates on $B \cup Cn^*(\alpha)$. The selection is indicated by the best hermeneutic theory, that is, if $b \Rightarrow \neg\alpha \in Cn(BestAb(B))$, then $Cn^*(\alpha) = \{\neg b \Rightarrow \alpha, b \Rightarrow \alpha\}$. Hence the operator will delete only the sentence $b \Rightarrow \alpha$, which was specifically contradicted, and incorporate sentence $\neg b \Rightarrow \alpha$ in the set of explicit settled rules. In other words, given a normative system B, a rule $\alpha \in B$, and the choice of a relevant defeating condition b with respect to α, the internal refinement of B by α with respect to b (notation: $B\#_b\alpha$) is characterized by the following properties: *Root–cutting* warrants that not all originally derived

Root–cutting	$b \Rightarrow \alpha \notin Cn(B\#_b\alpha)$
Inclusion	$B\#_b\alpha \subset B \cup \{\neg b \Rightarrow \alpha, b \Rightarrow \alpha\}$
Core–retainement	If $\gamma \in B/B\#_b\alpha$ then there is $\Gamma'' \in \Gamma \cup \{\neg b \Rightarrow \alpha, b \Rightarrow \alpha\}$ such that $\alpha \notin Cn(B'')$ but $\alpha \in Cn(B'' \cup \gamma)$
Preservation	$\neg b \Rightarrow \alpha \in B\#_b\alpha$

rules are valid, since the derived rule that was specifically refuted has been deleted. *Inclusion* enables the operator to satisfy conservatism, i.e. $B\#_b\alpha \in Cn(B)$. *Core–retainement* is a version of the minimal change principle applied to a set larger than the original. It says that only those norms that are somehow responsible for the derivation of the specifically defeated norm should be deleted. *Preservation* provides the desired qualification of the original rule with respect to the *confirming* condition (which is the negation of the refuting condition). The internal refinement operator just qualifies the original rule so that its detachment is dependent on the *confirming* condition and therefore the base of settled rules becomes coherent with the set of background explanatory principles. The complementary move is to incorporate the rule or normative solution derived by the set of endorsed principles into the base of rules. This new rule detaches the opposite solution in presence of the *refuting* condition. The definition of such operator is immediate:

Let B be a set of rules, $\alpha \in B$, $b \Rightarrow \neg\alpha \in Cn(BestAb(B))$ and # the internal refinement operator. Then, the *global refinement* of B by $b \Rightarrow \neg\alpha$ (notation $B\cdot(b \Rightarrow \neg\alpha)$) is such that: $B \cdot (b \Rightarrow \neg\alpha) = S\#_b\alpha \cup \{b \Rightarrow \neg\alpha\}$.

4.5 Conclusions

The present paper had two main goals: (i) to sketch a logical representation of a coherentist closure of normative systems; (ii) use this model to clarify a concept of coherence in law, which is faithful to a theory of legal validity as source based law. Source based law is the evidential base of the reconstruction of the normative system, therefore guiding both interpretation and legislation activities even when implicit legislative purposes are taken into account. Such reconstruction is given by the minimal assumption of "conservative" changes in the base of the original normative system so that it becomes coherent with legislative purposes. The belief revision model provides a logical characterization of what "conservatism" means, without providing criteria for conservative choices (to be made by the legal interpreter or legislator).

With respect to the logical characterization, I have defined conservatism for basic operations of expansion and refinement of the base of rules, which are reactions of the legal operator to novelties (gaps) or abnormalities (incoherence among rules and underlying principles). Such reasons or "principles" are the result of an abductive expansion from the very set of rules, with reference to a specific action a and a set of background beliefs K.

The definition of conservative expansion provides the logical characterization of conservatism with respect to novelties. Its main points are, first, the principles endorsed by the base are those which best explain the original base of settled rules; second, the modification of the base of settled rules is minimal, i.e. it is only added what is needed to derive a normative solution to the identified gap; third, the solution provided by the expanded base of rules is the same as that provided by the legal principles endorsed by the base.

The refinement operator (internal or global) captures the characterization of conservatism with respect to abnormalities. Its main points are, first, the principles endorsed by the base are those which best explain the original base of rules; second, the modification of the base of rules is not only minimal but conservative: it is removed only what is needed to restore coherence with the set of endorsed principles; derived rules which are not specifically in conflict with those principles are kept, even if they lose the support existing in the original set; third, the rule conflicting with the set of endorsed principles in a particular refuting condition is not deleted but weakened; it becomes qualified and holds in the absence of the refuting condition.

Given the set of principles, which works as a set of constraints for expansions and refinements of the set of explicit rules, one is tempted to define its coherentist closure as the logical closure of any set resulting from conservative expansions and conservative contractions applied on the local base.

The problem is that for any new context (a set of conditions) in which the deontic status of an action is inquired, there will be a potential conflict between the set of explicit rules and its underlying reasons, thus demanding new revision. Therefore, either one is satisfied with the definition of the "process of adjustment" by conservative changes as defined here, or the definition of coherent closure should be indexed by a given context. That is, the coherentist closure would be an operator defined on a set of rules not only with respect to a certain action and based on a background knowledge, but also with respect to a given context, or set of sentences which describe a possible case under which the deontic status of the action is evaluated. I leave this challenge for future developments.

With respect to the theoretical goal on the suitable concept of coherence in Law, I remark, firstly, that the set of legal principles is dependent on its ability to explain the set of enacted rules; secondly, that only minimal additions which are coherent with endorsed principles are accepted in the case of novelties; and lastly that in case of conflict with endorsed principles, the base of settled rules suffers not properly derogations but refinements, i.e. some of its rules have their condition of application further specified. Hence, by *"conservative attitude"* towards coherence I mean maximal fidelity to the original base of settled rules. I admit that the identification of this base already involves operations of change and arguments about coherence. But once the base is settled or hypothetically assumed in the design of a legislative text, one can reconstruct (by conservative operations) a coherently closed normative system – sensible to legislative purposes – satisfying the demand of minimal change of the assumed settled rules.

The main concern here is to control the role of principles in deleting incompatible rules of the base, a move that may lead to a shift of the base from the set of settled rules to the set of basic legal principles, thus undermining the rule's authority and therefore the very legislative practice.[12] There is a cost of gaining explanatory power within a theory of legal interpretation by means of deletion of rules of the base. We may construct a coherent interpretation of a base of settled rules and accepted instantiations with great explanatory power if we simply delete what is incompatible and include what is convergent to a set of elected legal principles. It is also undesirable to seek universal principles which are too general to explain the whole base of norms since it may lead to a level of abstraction which may undermine the ability to explain the specific local base of settled rules (general principles may explain many – possibly incompatible – sets of rules). The drive of coherence should not lie in the explanatory principles but in the very base to be explained.

References

Alchourrón, Carlos. 1996. On law and logic. *Ratio Juris* 9:331–348.

Alchourrón, Carlos, and Eugenio Bulygin. 1971. *Normative systems*. New York: Springer.

Alchourrón, Carlos, Peter Grdenfors, and David Makinson. 1985. On the logic of theory change. *Journal of Symbolic Logic* 50(2):510–530.

Alchourrón, Carlos, and David Makinson. 1981. Hierarchies of regulations and their logic, new studies in deontic logic. *Synthese Library Volume* 152:125–148.

Aliseda, Atocha. 2000. Abduction as epistemic change: A Peircean model in artificial intelligence. In *Abduction and induction: Essays on their relation and integration*, ed. Peter A. Flach and Antonis C. Kakas, 45–58. Dordrecht/Boston: Kluwer Academic.

Amaya, Amalia. 2006. An inquiry into the nature of coherence and its role in legal argument. PhD thesis at European University Institute.

Atria, Fernando. 1999. Del Derecho y el Razonamiento Jurdico. *Doxa* 22:79–119.

Bench–Capon, Trevor, H. Prakken, A. Wyner, and K. Atkinson. 2013. Argument schemes for reasoning with legal cases using values. In *Proceedings of the 14th international conference on artificial intelligence and law*, Rome (Italy) 2013, 13–22. New York: ACM.

Bench–Capon, Trevor, and G. Sartor. 2003. A model of legal reasoning with cases incorporating theories and values. *Artificial Intelligence* 150(1–2):97–143.

Bulygin, Eugenio. 1986. Legal dogmatics and the systematization of law, Rechtstheorie, Beiheft 10: Vernunft und Erfahrung im Rechtsdenken der Gegenwart/Reason and Experience in Contemporary Legal Thought, 193–210.

[12]This was Raz's criticism to Dworkin's integrity, what explains why Raz considers, after all, integrity not as coherentist theory of law, but a foundationalist one (the base would be the set of normative standards which constitute the political morality of a community). See Raz (1994).

Bulygin, Eugenio. 2005. En Defensa de El Dorado. Respuesta a Fernando Atria. In *Lagunas em el Derecho*, ed. Fernando Atria et. al., 73–86. Madrid: Marcial Pons.

Bulygin, Eugenio. 2008. What can one expect from logic in the law? (Not everything, but more than something: A reply to Susan Haack). *Ratio Juris* 21:150–156.

Bonjour, Laurence. 1985. *The structure of empirical knowledge*. Cambridge: Harvard University Press.

Fuller, Lon L. 1958. Positivism and fidelity to law: A reply to professor Hart. *Harvard Law Review* 71(4):661–664.

Governatori, Guido, Antonino Rotolo, Francesco Olivieri, and Simone Scannapieco. 2013. Legal contractions: A logical analysis. In *Proceedings of the 14th international conference on artificial intelligence and law*, Rome (Italy) 2013, 63–72. New York: ACM.

Haack, Susan. 2007. On logic in the law: 'Something but not all'. *Ratio Juris* 20(1):1–31.

Hage, Jaap. 2013. Three kinds of coherentism. In *Coherence: Insights from philosophy, jurisprudence and artificial intelligence*, ed. Michal Araszkiewicz and Jaromir Savelka. Dordrecht: Springer.

Harman, Gilbert. 1965. The inference to the best explanation. *Philosophical Review* 74:88–95.

Harman, Gilbert. 1989. *Change in view: Principles of reasoning*. Cambridge: MIT.

Hart, H.L.A. 1961. *The concept of Law*. Oxford: Clarendon Press.

Hart, Herbert L. A. 1983. *Essays in jurisprudence and philosophy*. Oxford: Oxford University Press.

Himma, Kenneth Einar. 2002. Inclusive legal positivism. In *The Oxford handbook of jurisprudence and philosophy of law*, ed. Jules L. Coleman and Scott Shapiro, 125–165. Oxford: Oxford University Press.

Josephson, John, and Susan Josephson. 1996. *Abductive inference: Computation, philosophy, and technology*. Cambridge: Cambridge University Press.

Kelsen, Hans. 1967. *Pure theory of law*, 2nd ed. (trans: Knight, Max). Berkeley: University of California Press.

Lehrer, Keith. 2000. *Theory of knowledge*, 2nd ed. Boulder: Westview Press.

Lipton, Peter. 2004. *Inference to the best explanation*, 2nd ed. London/New York: Routledge.

MacCormick, Neil. 1994. *Legal reasoning and legal theory*. Oxford: Clarendon.

MacCormick, Neil. 2005. *Rhetoric and the rule of law: A theory of legal reasoning*. Oxford: Oxford University Press.

Maranhão, Juliano S. A. 2001. Some operators for refinement of normative systems. In *Proceedings of the JURIX 2001: The fourteenth anual conference on legal knowledge and information systems*, ed. Bart Verheij, Arno R. Lodder, Ronald P. Loui, and Antoinette Muntjewerff, 103–116. Amsterdam: IOS Press.

Maranhão, Juliano S. A. 2007. Refining beliefs. In *Perspectives on universal logic*, ed. Jean–Yves Bziau, and Alexandre Costa–Leite, 335–349. Monza: Polimetrica International Scientific.

Maranhão, Juliano S. A. 2009a. La lógica en el Derecho: Grandes expectativas e algunas desilusiones. *Doxa* 32:229–254.

Maranhão, Juliano S. A. 2009b. Conservative contraction. In *The many sides of logic*, Studies in logic, ed. Walter Carnielli, tala D'Ottaviano, and Marcelo Coniglio, 465–479. London: King's College Publications.

Maranhão, Juliano S. A. 2012. *Positivismo jurdico lógico–inclusivo*. São Paulo: Marcial Pons.

Marmor, Andrei. 2005. *Interpretation and legal theory*, 2nd ed. Oregon: Hart Publishing.

Olsson, Erik. 1997. *Coherence: Studies in epistemology and belief revision*, Comprehensive summaries of Uppsala dissertations. Uppsala: Acta universitatis Upsaliensis.

Pagnucco, Maurice. 1996. The role of abductive reasoning within the process of belief revision. Phd thesis, Department of Computer Science, University of Sydney.

Prakken, Henry. 2002. An exercise in formalising teleological case–based reasoning. *Artificial Intelligence and Law* 10:113–133.

Psillos, Sthatis. 2002. *Simply the best: A case for abduction*, Computational logic, LNAI 2408, 605–625. Heidelberg: Springer.

Raz, Joseph. 1994. The value of coherence. In: *Ethics in the public domain*, ed. Joseph Raz. Oxford: Oxford University Press.
Ratti, Giovanni B. 2008. The consequences of defeasibility. *Analisi e diritto* 2007:261–277.
Reid, Thomas. (1895). Essays on the active powers of man. In *The works of Thomas Reid, D.D.*, ed. Sir William Hamilton, 617. Edinburgh: James Thin.
Savigny, Friedrich Karl. 1886. *Sistema del Diritto Romano attuale*. Trans. Vittorio Scialoja. Torino: Unione Tipografico Editrice.
Schauer, Frederick. 1991. *Playing by the rules: A philosophical examination of rule based decision–making in law and in life*. Oxford: Clarendon Press.
Sellars, Wilfred. 1963. *Science perception and reality*. New York: Humanities.
Thagard, Paul. 2000. *Coherence in thought and action*. Cambrigde: MIT.
Vernengo, Roberto J. 1960. La función sistemtica de la norma fundamental. Revista Jurdica de la Universidad de Buenos Aires. [S.I.: s.n.].
Wassermann, Renata, and Wagner Dias. 2001. Abductive expansion of belief bases. In *Proceedings of the IJCAI workshop on abductive reasoning*, Seattle.
Żurek, Tomasz, and Araszkiewicz Michał. 2013. Modeling teleological interpretation. In *ICAIL 13 proceedings of the fourteenth international conference on artificial intelligence and law*, Rome, 160–168. New York: ACM.

Chapter 5
Negation in Legislation

Giovanni Battista Ratti

Abstract The paper is divided into two parts. In the first part, it surveys the different ways norms can be conceptually negated, by addressing, inter alia, categorical negation, conditional denial, and denied conditional, and establishing when two norms may be regarded as conflicting. In its second part, the paper analyzes the possible relations negation has with two important legal phenomena, such as derogation, and defeasibility.

Keywords Negation • Derogation • Defeasibility • Normative conditionals • Logical form

5.1 Introduction

Negation is a quite neglected topic in current practical philosophy, deontic logic, and theory of legislation. However, negation is a key concept for the logical analysis of any purportedly rational discourse. So, it is quite dismaying to see that almost no investigation about the use of negation by lawgivers is available.[1] This essay is conceived of as a first, tentative, attempt to change this state of affairs.

However, an abundant literature exists on topics which are related, more or less directly, to negation, such as derogation and defeasibility. As we shall see, derogation has some interesting relations with negation and sometimes is erroneously equated with it. In turn, defeasibility, which has been very fashionable in recent legal theory, has some aspects which necessarily refer to negation, especially concerning

The Author thanks Michał Araszkiewicz and Riccardo Guastini for their very helpful remarks on a previous version of the present paper.

[1]Not very recent exceptions are: Mazzarese (1989) and Wróblewski (1984). A foundational essay is provided by Weinberger (1957).

G.B. Ratti (✉)
Department of Law, Taretto Institute for the Philosophy of Law, University of Genoa, Genova, Italy
e-mail: gbratti@unige.it

M. Araszkiewicz, K. Płeszka (eds.), *Logic in the Theory and Practice of Lawmaking*, Legisprudence Library 2, DOI 10.1007/978-3-319-19575-9_5

the phenomenon of implicit exceptions to expressed norms.[2] Consequently, some features of the use of negation in legal discourses might be clarified by analyzing such topics.[3]

Accordingly, the present paper will have the following structure: first of all, I shall survey and analyze some ways in which norms can be conceptually negated, by pointing to some particular features of negation in the legal domain. The following section will deal with some of the possible relations between derogation and negation, while the third section will revolve around the notion of defeasibility and its mutual associations with negation.

5.2 Negation

5.2.1 Negation as a Logical Operator

In propositional logic, negation inverts the truth–value of a (descriptive) proposition. The proposition

[1] Snow in white

is negated by asserting

[2] Snow is not white

If [1] is true, [2] is false, and vice versa.[4]

When a certain proposition and its negation belong to the same set of sentences, such a set is said to be inconsistent. It is also trivialized according to the *ex falso quodlibet* (EFQ) principle, in the sense that it contains any proposition whatsoever among its consequences.

This may be easily proved. Let "p" be any proposition whatsoever. If we have a contradiction, say "$p\&\neg p$", as our starting assumption, we can articulate the following reasoning, by means of the classical rules of inference of bivalent logic:

[3]	$p\&\neg p$	ASS.
[4]	p	[3], elimination of conjunction

[2]See Caracciolo (2012), Chiassoni (2012), and Mendonca (2012).

[3]Before carrying out the proposed task, I must first introduce a general caveat. By "legislation" (and related concepts, such as "legislator", "legislature", "lawgivers", etc.), here I shall mean, broadly, the production of general and abstract norms by a prima facie legally competent authority (Guastini 2011a, 140). Consequently, when referring to instances of legislation, I shall mainly point to constitutional and statutory provisions alike.

[4]In bivalent logic, the conjoined truth of [1] and [2] is logically avoided by embracing the principle of non–contradiction: "$\neg(p\&\neg p)$". This principle in turn is propositionally equivalent to the principle of bivalence "$(p \vee \neg p)$": one of two propositions, of which one is the negation of the other, must be true in that they are exhaustive of a certain universe of discourse. As is easy to see, both principles are equivalent to (one of the possible formulations of) the principle of identity: "$p \supset p$".

[5]	$p \vee q$	[4], introduction of disjunction
[6]	$\neg p$	[3], elimination of conjunction
[7]	q	[5], [6], disjunctive syllogism

As is widely known, the classical logical operators – negation, conjunction, disjunction, conditional, and equivalence – can be reduced to negation plus just one operator between disjunction and conjunction.[5] For example, conditionals may be taken as shorthand for the following sentences:

[8] $\neg(p\&\neg q)$

Or – what is the same –

[9] $\neg p \vee q$

This helps explaining the notion of a denied conditional, i.e. the negation of a conditional sentence. Indeed, in propositional logic, denied conditionals are very simply reconstructed as "$\neg(p \supset q)$" or, more often, as "$p\&\neg q$" – which, in turn, is of course equivalent to "$\neg(\neg p \vee q)$".

There is a contradiction between conditionals whenever the same set allows one to derive, at the same time, "$p \supset q$" and "$\neg(p \supset q)$" – or equivalent sentences such as those mentioned above. Any sentence will follow from a set containing such two conditionals.

One must be careful in distinguishing denied conditionals from so–called "conditional negations", whose logical form is that of a negated atomic proposition conditionally connected to an affirmative atomic proposition: in short, "$p \supset \neg q$". The conjunction of the two conditionals "$p \supset q$" and "$p \supset \neg q$" is consistent and equivalent to the negation of the common antecedent: i.e., "$\neg p$".[6] It is a well–known fact that this feature of denied conditionals constitutes the structural basis for the inference which is normally called "reductio ad absurdum".

5.2.2 Negation and Categorical Norms

Norms are neither true nor false.[7] So, it is not clear which is the logical value (if any) that is to be inverted by negation. Deontic logicians and legal theorists have

[5]Indeed, they can be reduced to just *one* operator: alternative denial or joint denial.

[6]This is easily seen from the following truth–table:

$p \supset q$	&	$p \supset \neg q$	≡	$\neg p$
1 1 1	0	1 0 0	**1**	0
1 0 0	0	1 1 1	**1**	0
0 1 1	1	0 1 0	**1**	1
0 1 0	1	0 1 1	**1**	1

[7]For discussion, see the seminal von Wright (1963) and, more recently, Rodríguez (2006).

often referred to the value of “validity”.[8] However, validity is a highly contested concept, liable to be reduced to other, more nuanced, notions, such as membership, applicability, obligatory force, “being in force”, efficacy, etc.[9]

Here I will use a quite abstract notion of efficacy as the logical value of norms. By a “norm”,[10] I shall here understand a sentence discharging a prescriptive function, i.e. a sentence the primary function thereof consists in guiding human behavior.[11]

I will hold a rule efficacious if its propositional content is always true in so far as commands are concerned, and sometimes true when authorizations are concerned. In other terms, a command may be said to be efficacious if it is always used during its normative existence (i.e. its membership in a normative system), whereas an authorization is efficacious if it is sometimes used during its normative existence.

More precisely, a norm qualifies a certain action or state of affairs as obligatory or prohibited in case of commands; and as facultative or permitted, in case of authorizations. I shall assume obligatory (“O”) as the primitive operator, i.e. the one used to provide definitions for all the others. Authorizing norms are usually represented as “$\neg Op$” (or “$P\neg p$”, when a special permission operator is introduced into the calculus), in so far a permission of refraining from a certain conduct is concerned, or “$\neg O\neg p$” (or “Pp”), when the carrying out of a certain action “p” is expressly permitted. An action is facultative whenever one has, at the same time, the permission to perform it and the permission not to perform it (“$\neg O\neg p \& \neg Op$”).

In so far as categorical norms are concerned, negation seems to be easily applied. If the norm “Op” is efficacious, its internal negation “$O\neg p$” and external negation “$\neg Op$” (viz. “$P\neg p$”) cannot be efficacious, and vice versa. This is so because if “p” is always the case (what makes, by definition, “Op” efficacious), it is not the case that “$\neg p$” is sometimes true, and with more reason, that it is always true (and so “$\neg Op$” is not efficacious, as well as “$O\neg p$”).

More precisely, “Op” and “$O\neg p$” are dubbed “contrary” in that they can be both inefficacious, but not both efficacious. “Op” and “$\neg Op$” are contradictory in that if one is efficacious, the other one cannot be efficacious, and vice versa. As a matter of course, the same relation holds for “$O\neg p$” and “$\neg O\neg p$”. Moreover, “Op” implies “$\neg O\neg p$” because if “p” is always the case, “$\neg p$” cannot sometimes be the case. The same holds for “$O\neg p$” and “$\neg Op$”. The members of the relation of implication are usually called “subalterns”. Finally, “$\neg Op$” and “$\neg O\neg p$” are called “subcontraries”: they can be both efficacious, but not both inefficacious.

On a monotonic setting,[12] when two conflicting (i.e. contrary or contradictory) categorical norms belong to the same system, such a system is usually regarded

[8]Cf. Mazzarese (1989, 59 ff.) and Soeteman (1989, 132 ff.).

[9]The *locus classicus* is Bulygin (1982). More recently, see Grabowski (2013) and Rodríguez (2014, especially ch. 7).

[10]Here I will use the terms “norm” and “rule” interchangeably.

[11]Cf. von Wright (1963), Ross (1968), Alchourrón and Bulygin (1971), and Tarello (1974).

[12]For criticism of some non–monotonic conceptions, see Ratti (2013a).

as trivialized, i.e. any norm whatsoever will be a consequence of it. This is easily provable, in analogy to propositional calculus:

[10]	$Op\&\neg Op$	ASS.
[11]	Op	[10], elimination of conjunction
[12]	$Op \vee Oq$	[11], introduction of disjunction
[13]	$\neg Op$	[10], elimination of conjunction
[14]	Oq	[12], [13], disjunctive syllogism

5.2.3 The Negation of Conditional Norms

Hypothetical, or conditional, norms connect a certain normative solution to a determinate (non–empty) set of conditional operative facts or properties: e.g. "If it rains, you ought to close the window", or "Any act whatever of man, which causes damage to another, obliges the one by whose fault it occurred, to compensate it"[13] (the basic logical form thereof can be reconstructed as "If one faultily causes a damage to another, then one ought to compensate it").

Legal theorists and deontic logicians have discussed at length about the best way of reconstructing the logical form of such norms.

Some authors – like Ross (1968), Soeteman (1989) and von Wright[14] – have favored the so called "insular conception", which places conditions within the scope of deontic operators.[15] Consequently, the logical form of hypothetical norms is represented by means of the following sentence: "$O(p \supset q)$".

By contrast, other writers – such as Alchourrón and Bulygin (1971), Kelsen (1960), and Guastini (2011b) – prefer the so called "bridge conception", which places conditions outside the scope of deontic operators. Consequently, the logical form of hypothetical norms is represented in the following way: "$p \supset Oq$".

Both representations present several logical shortcomings. Just to name a few, one may point to the following ones.

[13]This is the English translation of section 1382 of the French Civil Code: "Tout fait quelconque de l'homme, qui cause a autrui un dommage, oblige celui par la faute duquel il est arrive a le reparer." Available on line at http://www.legifrance.gouv.fr/affichCode.do?cidTexte=LEGITEXT000006070721.

[14]As Moreso (1996, 94, note 4) observes: "The position of von Wright [...] has, on this point so central to the logical representation of norms, been one of vacillation". In 1980, von Wright admitted "mixed" formulas (such as "$p \supset Oq$") formed of propositional variables, sentential connectives, and deontic expressions. However, later on, von Wright (1983, 151) stated "that if the standard connective in question is a truth–connective, then this "linguistic hybrid" is a monster with no place in meaningful discourse".

[15]The dichotomy "insular conception"/"bridge conception" is borrowed from Alchourrón (1996). A recent defender of the bridge conception is Zuleta (2008).

According to the standard definition of the conditional we have referred to before, the sentence "$O(p \supset q)$" is equivalent to the sentence "$O(\neg p \vee q)$". This, in turn, would make, under the insular conception, any conditional norm equivalent to a disjunctive obligation (which places the norm–addressees in a situation where they can choose freely between two states of affairs in order to comply with the norm). This, in turn, is quite unsatisfactory if we want to reconstruct those states of affairs, when the norm–addresses cannot control the conditions of application of the norm. Take for instance the previously mentioned norm "If it rains, one ought to close the window". Representing it by means of the sentence "$O(\neg p \vee q)$" suggests the idea that who receives the norm is able to choose freely between the states of affairs "not raining" ($\neg p$) and "closing the window" (q), but this is clearly not the case, since he or she cannot create or control the states of affairs consisting, respectively, in "raining" or "not raining". In the event of raining, there is an obligation to "q". But the norm does not provide anything regarding the case when it does not rain ("$\neg p$"). So, the proposed formalization is unsuitable for situations of this sort. By contrast, the insular conception is useful in reconstructing the norms' antecedents which are under the control of the norm addressees, as happens in such norms as "If you go and visit your granny, you ought to bring her flowers" or "If you are to comply with a contract, you ought to do it in good faith".[16]

The bridge conception fares better in representing the above–mentioned situations (where norm–addresses cannot control the state of affairs on which the antecedent bears upon). However, it has, at least, one main difficulty. Indeed, under Hume's principle, it does not allow *modus tollens* as a valid schema of reasoning, since from two norms it would allow one to derive a factual proposition. In fact, from the hypothetical norm "$p \supset Oq$" and the categorical norm "$\neg Oq$", one would be entitled to derive "$\neg p$": what manifestly constitutes the inverse of the naturalistic fallacy (Martínez Zorrilla 2010, 241–243).

At any rate, and leaving the just mentioned logical problems aside, contemporary literature suggests that a complete reduction to just one logical form of all conditional (duty–imposing) norms is not viable.[17] Both logical forms are necessary to reconstruct different kinds of norms. However, what is of the utmost importance here is that, whatever form one assigns to such conditional norms, there are problems concerning their negation. Indeed, if one applies to such norms the *classical* properties of conditional negation, one obtains remarkable results.

On the bridge conception, the negation of a conditional rule like "$p \supset Oq$" would apparently be expressed by the formula "$\neg(p \supset Oq)$". By contrast, the conditional sentences "$p \supset Oq$" and "$p \supset \neg Oq$" would not bring about any inconsistency. If this were the case, some remarkable consequences would follow: (1) There would be a contradiction between conditional norms, whenever the same set of rules allowed one to derive, at the same time, "$p \supset Oq$" and "$\neg(p \supset Oq)$". From such a set any rule would follow. (2) Analogously to what happens in propositional logic, the

[16] This is a norm one may derive from combining articles 1372 and 1375 of the Italian Civil Code.

[17] The seminal discussion is Moreso and Rodríguez (2010).

conjunction of the conditional norms "$p \supset Oq$" and "$p \supset \neg Oq$" would be equivalent to the negation of the common antecedent: that is "$\neg p$".[18] A set containing such two rules would *not* be inconsistent or trivialized.

This twofold view is questionable, in that it does not faithfully reconstruct ordinary juristic views and practices.

Indeed, on the one hand, nobody interprets "$\neg(p \supset Oq)$" as the genuine negation of a conditional norm: such a formula is rather construed as a proposition stating that such a conditional norm does not exist (in one of the many senses in which a norm may be said to "exist").[19] So, sentences "$p \supset Oq$" and "$\neg(p \supset Oq)$" does not collide, since they belong to different levels of discourse. In turn, the norm–negation of "$O(p \supset q)$" – that is, "$\neg O(p \supset q)$", amounting, in turn, to "$P(p\&\neg q)$" – is well–formed, but seems to lose any feature of conditionality. Indeed, it amounts to a categorical norm permitting to bring about simultaneously states of affairs "p" and "$\neg q$".

On the other hand, it is a matter of course that normative conditionals show a quite different behavior from material conditionals. In particular, in juristic reasoning, the antecedent of a norm is taken, as it were, as a "world–identifier" condition (Moreso and Rodríguez 2010). The normative consequences provided by hypothetical norms generally apply only to the "world" (i.e. the set of operative facts) singled out by the antecedent. When the norm antecedent does not materialize, the consequence does not follow, since the norm is simply not applicable: but, unlike propositional logic (where the conditional is true when both the antecedent and the consequent are false), this does not render the normative conditional, as it were, "true" or "satisfied". Consequently, an antinomy within a hypothetical normative system – i.e. an inconsistency between conditional norms – materializes whenever a certain world "p" is connected to two categorical norms which are contrary or contradictory. Unlike in propositional logic, then, the simultaneous membership in a certain sentential set of "$(p \supset Oq)$" and "$\neg(p \supset Oq)$" brings about no inconsistency, since, as we have seen, the second sentence is better regarded as a meta–linguistic sentence bearing on some possible attributes of a normative system. By contrast, the simultaneous membership of "$O(p \supset q)$" and "$\neg O(p \supset q)$" in a certain normative system bring about a normative inconsistency, but this does not seem a correct reconstruction of actual antinomies between *conditional norms* which are found in normative documents and the way they are read by jurists.

As mentioned before, ordinary antinomies between conditional norms consist in the connection of two incompatible normative solutions (viz. categorical norms) to a certain set of conditions. In other words, a certain world "p" is inconsistently qualified by different norms. The current reconstruction of this phenomenon is correctly provided by the bridge conception, by stating that we have an antinomy whenever a normative system contain norms like "$p \supset Oq$" and "$p \supset \neg Oq$".

[18]Ross (1968, §36) for a very interesting critical discussion. See also Hage (2000, 371).

[19]Wróblewski (1984, 466 ff.).

More precisely, following Ross's (1958, 128 ff.) treatment of antinomies, we may distinguish between different kinds of inconsistency, taking into account the possible relations of complete overlapping, inclusion, or intersection, between the antecedents of the conflicting norms. We have a total–total antinomy whenever a certain normative system α contains two norms of the sort we have just mentioned ("$p \supset Oq$" and "$p \supset \neg Oq$"), since their antecedents completely overlap. We have a total–partial antinomy whenever normative system α contains norms like "$p \supset Oq$" and "$p\&r \supset \neg Oq$", since α is inconsistent only regarding the whole antecedent of the more specific norm (which is totally included in the antecedent of the more generic norm), so that α is partially free from contradictions regarding case "p", in the partition "$p\&\neg r$". Finally, we have a partial–partial antinomy whenever normative system α contains two norms like "$p \supset Oq$" and "$r \supset \neg Oq$", since α is inconsistent only regarding the intersecting case "$p\&r$", and is free from contradictions when the antecedents of both do not intersect (i.e. in cases "$p\&\neg r$", "$\neg p\&r$", and of course "$\neg p\&\neg r$").[20]

To sum up, we may say that jurists (and legal theorists) usually call a *normative inconsistency* (*or conflict*) a sentence of the kind "$(p \supset Oq)\&(p \supset \neg Oq)$" – or "$(p \supset Oq)\&(p \supset O\neg q)$" – which, as we have seen, is not a contradiction at all in propositional logic, but the conjunction of a material conditional and the corresponding conditional denial. We may add that they also hold that it is not the case that from such a contradiction, "$\neg p$" follows. And this for an intuitive reason: if, say, the case of "raining" is connected to inconsistent normative consequences (e.g. "it is obligatory to close the window" and "it is not obligatory to close the window"), nobody would derive from that that the normative authority has asserted that it is not raining.

Moreover, according to the received view, EFQ – or, better, the *ex contradictione quodlibet* principle – would not affect normative systems in their whole, since a normative contradiction would at most trivialize only the case referred to by the antecedent to which two incompatible consequences are connected.[21] There are (conceptual) reasons to think that this view is too optimistic, and that the effects of a normative conflict exceed the trivialization of the case referred to in the antecedent of the conflicting norms, but the articulation of these reasons is far beyond the scope of this paper.[22] Here, it suffices to notice that, according to lawyers, only relevant

[20]A more nuanced analysis is provided by Araszkiewicz (2013, 19–20), who systematically discusses seven different types of relations between the scopes of rules' antecedents.

[21]See Atienza (1992).

[22]For a first articulation of these reasons, see Ratti (2013b, 81–93).

norms must be taken into account in order to solve a certain legal question and this allows one to limit the destructive effects of conflicts between norms.[23]

5.3 Negation and Derogation

Negation is sometimes equated with derogation, in that, on a certain reading, denying a norm would substantially amount to repealing it from the legal order.[24] However, this is a conceptual error, since there is no one–to–one correspondence between acts of negation and acts of derogation.[25] Moreover, their logical behavior is different under many aspects.

First, double negation and "double derogation" have different effects. While double negation equates to affirming the "original" atomic proposition ($\neg\neg p \equiv p$), it is controversial that double derogation, i.e. the derogation of the derogatory norm, revivifies the original derogated norm. The formal counterpart of propositional double negation is not to be found in double derogation, but probably in what we could dub "deontic double negation", i.e. $\neg\neg Op \equiv Op$.

However, it is worth noticing that the latter sentence is ambiguous, since it may be interpreted, alternatively, as a genuine norm or as a normative proposition.

In the first case, the equivalence is indeed sound: a norm prescribing that "It is not that (It is not obligatory to pay taxes)" logically equates to the norm which prescribes that "It is obligatory to pay taxes".

In the second case, it is not sound, since to state that a certain norm permitting "$\neg p$" does not belong to a certain normative system obviously does not equate to stating that a certain norm that commands "p" belongs to that normative system. For instance, from the statement that a certain norm authorizing not to pay taxes does not exist in the legal system S, one cannot infer, obviously, that another norm, imposing to pay taxes, exists in that very system.

By contrast, double derogation has a diachronic dimension which is unknown to classical propositional logic operations.[26] Indeed, double derogation and its effects are relevant only regarding sequences of normative sets. Some qualifications are in order here.

[23]This idea is perfectly epitomized by Alchourrón and Makinson (1981, 134): "Now imagine the situation of a judge or administrative officer who is called upon to apply an inconsistent code and reach a verdict on a specific question. What ways are open to him to mitigate or transcend the contradiction? One idea is to distinguish between those parts of the code that are directly relevant to the case in hand, and those which are not".

[24]For discussion, see Bacqué (1964) and Carrió (1964).

[25]As Gioja (1964, 62) observes, "to derogate a norm" may mean two different things: (1) to repeal it from the legal order; or (2) to enact the norm–negation of a pre–existing norm. Moreover, both acts would be essentially different: see Mazzarese 1989, 97–100.

[26]Kelsen (1973, 261–263).

Let us assume that, at time t1, the norm N1 (bearing on a certain conduct) is enacted by the lawgiver. At time t2, the lawgiver enacts the derogatory norm N2, according to which "N1 is derogated". At time t3, the lawgiver enacts norm N3, according to which "N2 is derogated". Now, does the enactment of N3, as it were, "revivify" N1, in the sense that N1 now belongs again to the legal order after the repealing of N2 by means of N1? This is the intuitive impression one may have if one considers the legal order in its whole. Indeed, it is the impression jurists commonly have when they face such situations.

However, the legal order is better regarded, from an analytical point of view, as a diachronic sequence of momentary systems composed of the norms which have been enacted at different times and not yet repealed. So, the legal order is better seen as the *sequence* of all the momentary systems which are produced by normative authorities by means of acts of enactment and repealing of norms.[27]

Consequently, the normative system NS1 – brought about by the enactment of N1 – includes of course N1, while the normative system NS2 – being in force after the enactment of N2, which in turn provides the repealing of N1 – includes N2, but not N1. Now, the normative system NS3 – in force after the enactment of N3 – includes N3, but neither N2 nor N1. From a logical point of view, then, it seems that there is no reason to think that N1 belongs to NS3, because of the enactment of N3 (this latter norm does not provide anything on the validity of N1). The repealing of N2 has the *only direct* effect of eliminating N2 from the list of norms which are valid from the system NS3 on.

On a pragmatic stance, it can well be argued that the enactment of N3 may have as its principal goal that of re–validating N1. But, reversely, it can also be argued that had the lawgiver manifested the intention of re–validating N1, it should have re–enacted N1 (Carrió 1964, 14–15), so that what the legislator really does (and may expressly want to do) is just creating a gap. Indeed, the case in which a derogatory provision is read (as it normally is) by jurists as tacitly implying the re–enactment of a previous norm is a clear case of so–called "juristic construction": i.e. the creation of an implicit norm by means of inferences which are not strictly deductive and/or the introduction into the lawgiver's discourse of doctrinal theses which constitute "hidden" premises of juristic reasoning (see Guastini 2013, 153 ff.).

It is worth observing that the case is different if N2 is *declared invalid ab initio* by a competent judicial organ.[28] Indeed, in that case, N2 would be annulled from the moment of its enactment, and then it would *have never been* a member of any momentary system composing the legal order.[29] Consequently, N1 has never lost its validity due to a derogatory act, since such an act was invalid.

Second, and more importantly for the present paper, the enactment of a norm which is the negation of another norm, already belonging to the normative system

[27]On the topic, see the seminal works by Alchourrón and Bulygin (1979) and Ferrer Beltrán and Rodríguez (2011).

[28]See the decisions 107/1974 and 108/1986 of the Italian Constitutional Court.

[29]Guastini (2010, 315).

at hand, does not bring about, *per se*, the repeal of the latter norm. This effect mainly materializes in two cases: (1) when the *lex posterior* principle is expressly provided by a (meta)norm of the system; (2) when a normative power is conferred permanently (i.e. without temporal limitations): in such a case, the *lex posterior* principle is implicit in the power–conferral, because the invested authority would have no entire normative power if it could not modify pre–existing norms (Guastini 2010, 319).

The case of so–called "tacit derogation" or "implied repeal" is particularly relevant here. This case obtains whenever two incompatible norms belong to the same momentary normative system, but one of these two norms is "older" than the other. More precisely, a certain norm N1 was introduced into a normative system NS1 which is chronologically previous to the normative system NS2, to which both incompatible norms N1 and N2 now belong. From a logical point of view, lawgivers that tacitly repeal a previous norm introduce the negation of a certain norm into the system, so that the older norm is derogated in virtue of the *lex posterior* derogatory principle. It is interesting to observe that, strictly speaking, no act of derogation is carried out here. On the contrary, there is a double promulgation at play, which creates an inconsistency which, in turn, is later solved by means of the *lex posterior* principle. The effects, still, are normally those of an explicit act of derogation, since the older norm is repealed in the very moment when the new one is introduced into the legal order.

Especially significant here are the interferences that the *lex posterior* principle may have with other criteria currently used to solve legal antinomies[30]: (a) the *lex superior* or hierarchical criterion, and (b) the *lex specialis* or criterion of specificity. In particular, the chronological criterion may interfere with these two other criteria at least in two senses: (1) it may conflict with them, but (2) it also may concur with them. In both cases, it is worth stressing the main legal consequences.

5.3.1 Interference of Lex Posterior and Lex Superior

The *lex superior* principle solves a conflict between norms, by giving priority to the norm having a higher rank: for instance, by giving priority to a constitutional norm over a (supposedly unconstitutional) statute. Usually, the contrast between a superior norm and an inferior one must be identified, and the subsequent invalidity of the lower norm declared, by a competent organ. Unlike the *lex posterior* principle – which is mainly a legislative "systematizing" device and tends to work, as it were, rather straightforwardly[31] – the *lex superior* principle is mainly a judicial device, which needs some more nuanced activities of the competent judicial organ

[30]Here I follow closely Guastini (2011b, 116 ff.). See also Ross (1958, 128–132).

[31]Obviously, this is a rough simplification, since norms are the meaning of normative provisions (viz. norm–formulations) attached to them by jurists. As a matter of course, in many cases, jurists

to be applied (which may decide to reinterpret provisions from which norms are drawn from to avoid the annulment of the lower sources). Moreover, when a law is implicitly repealed by means of the *lex posterior* principle, its repealing occurs when the new conflicting norm is laid down by the legislator and the effects of the repealing are generally not retroactive. By contrast, when the *lex superior* principle is applied to a conflict between norms of different rank, the repealing intervenes with the declaration of the competent judges, the effects thereof are generally retroactive.

In those legal orders with a rigid constitution, where judicial review is carried out *a posteriori* by a special Constitutional Court, and the annulment of an unconstitutional norm has an *erga omnes* effect (such as Germany, Italy, or Spain), *lex posterior* and *lex superior* are ordered in a way that the hierarchical principle always takes priority over the chronological one. Indeed, this is the kernel of the design of "fully constitutionalized" legal orders: norms are regarded as invalid when they conflict with higher–ranked norms. But when the two criteria concur, i.e. when a certain norm N1 is at the same time higher–ranked and posterior to another conflicting norm N2, the latter norm may be, alternatively, regarded as derogated by means of *lex posterior* or invalidated by means of *lex superior*. The effects, as has been mentioned, are quite different. As we have seen, the chronological principle is used to cancel *ex nunc* the validity of a norm N1 which has been enacted before norm N2, which has the same hierarchical level as N1 and attaches an incompatible solution to the same set or subset of the cases referred to in the norms' antecedents. By contrast, the hierarchical principle is used to solve antinomies between norms of different hierarchical levels, by invalidating (normally *ex tunc*) the inferior norm. Moreover, within orders with a rigid constitution and a specialized Constitutional Court, the annulment of an unconstitutional statute may only be carried out by such a Court, whereas the derogation of an older norm by an earlier norm can also be declared by ordinary courts.

From a logical point of view, it is interesting to observe that while *lex posterior* presupposes that the norm–negation N1 of a new norm N2 was valid within the legal order prior to the enactment of N2, *lex superior* presupposes that an inferior norm N3, contrasting the superior norm N4, has never been fully valid in the relevant legal order, precisely because it somehow negated (viz. contrasted) N4. In this sense, *lex posterior* applies to the conflict between two valid norms, enacted by the competent organ in its full capacity, whereas *lex superior* is a criterion to establish that a certain norm is invalid (since it clashes with a norm the content thereof it may not contradict) and, in a sense, was enacted by a certain organ by exceeding its proper competence.

---

can interpret provisions so that they express conflicting norms, but they can also avoid normative conflicts by choosing different meaning–ascriptions to legal sources.

5.3.2 Interference of Lex Posterior and Lex Specialis

Lex specialis is a device, as it were, for "rearranging" normative systems, in that it is used to reshape a general norm in such a way that it does not conflict with a more specific norm. A norm is more specific than another, when its antecedent contains at least one key operative factor which is not contemplated by the antecedent of the more general norm. For instance, a norm N1 which imposes to citizens to pay taxes (in symbols: "$c \supset Op$") is more general than a norm N2 which permits to citizens, who are unemployed, to avoid paying taxes (in symbols: "$c \& \neg e \supset \neg Op$"). The conflict between both norms arises because the more general norm implies, by strengthening the antecedent, the norm N1′ according to which "Unemployed citizens are obliged to pay taxes" (which may be reconstructed in symbols as: "$c \& \neg e \supset Op$"), which is clearly contradictory to the norm N2 according to which unemployed citizens are not obliged to pay taxes. *Lex specialis* recommends reshaping the norm N1 as N1″ "Employed citizens are obliged to pay taxes" (in symbols: "$c \& e \supset Op$"), which does not conflict with N2. It is worth observing that such a reshaping is merely temporary, because if the more specific norm is repealed at a certain time, N1 may be again taken as implying both N1′ and N1″. In this sense, *lex specialis* is, so to speak, an "inference–hampering" device, in that it temporarily "deletes" some logical consequences of the more general norm.

It can happen that *lex specialis* and *lex posterior* interfere, in the sense that they may conflict, as well as they may concur.

They conflict whenever a more specific norm N1 was laid down earlier than a more general norm N2. If *lex posterior* is applied, N2 repeals N1. By contrast, if *lex specialis* is applied, N1 hampers the application of some logical consequences of N2. What generally happens, at least in civil law legal orders, is that *lex specialis* supersedes *lex posterior.* This is mainly due to the influence of the so–called "principle of conservation of normative texts", according to which normative texts should be as far as possible preserved and so reinterpreted and systematized in a way that none of them needs to be repealed from the legal order.

Both criteria concur when a more specific norm N2 is laid down after the enactment of a more general norm N1. Here the jurists may follow two different paths: either to apply *lex specialis*, hamper some of its logical consequences, and "save" N1 from repealing, or to apply *lex posterior* and derogate N1. In this latter case, what is usually called for is the identification of some reasons underlying N2, general enough to justify the repealing of N1.

As it is easy to see, in *lex specialis* negation plays a fundamental role. This is so because the hampering of the consequences of the general norm is to be determined by deleting those inferences which are carried out by strengthening the antecedent of such a norm regarding the key condition which is expressly negated by the more specific norm. Following up in our example, the fact that the more specific norm contemplates unemployment as a factor that allows citizens not to pay taxes, is a reason that "deletes" the consequence of the more general norm, according to which unemployed citizens ought to pay taxes.

5.4 Negation and Defeasibility

A recent trend in legal philosophy has consisted in explaining law through one of its presumed attributes: defeasibility.[32] In particular, legal norms are said to be defeasible in that all legal standards are *potentially overridable* in certain cases where they bring about results which are regarded, for some reasons, as unsatisfactory.[33] This, in turn, implies that, from this perspective, a determination must be made about when legal standards are indeed *defeated*. Here at least two contrary options are apparently available: (1) we can count on a set of rationally discoverable ordering hierarchies which determine the defeasance of a certain legal standard in some given circumstances; (2) such a set does not exist or is not completely knowable, and for this reason the applicators have to make a (more or less partially) discretional decision as for the defeasance of the legal standard at hand. In the relevant literature on the topic, the first option is dominant, although epistemic problems of incomplete knowledge of objective ordering amongst norms are regarded as fundamental in the characterization of defeasibility as a matter of *implicit* exceptions. However, here I shall assume the second perspective and analyze defeasibility as a factor regarding legislator's tacit intentions or goals underlying expressed rules. In order to do so, I shall refer to a so far unsurpassed theory of legal norms: the one deployed, in more than 20 years of joint collaboration, by Carlos Alchourrón and Eugenio Bulygin.

In their famous book *Normative Systems*, Alchourrón and Bulygin, by embracing the bridge conception, paradigmatically regard legal norms as conditional sentences, connecting a generic case (i.e. a class of particular cases) with a normative solution (i.e. the union of a normative operator and a normative content). Generic cases are identifiable by means of combination of the relevant properties (viz. the operative key factors) of the norms. Relevance is thus a predicate of properties, regarded as the operative factors of the norms, i.e. as the conditions the occurrence thereof makes the norms applicable.[34]

According to Alchourrón and Bulygin, a certain property is relevant, within a certain normative system, if: (a) at least a norm of the system mentions such a property; (b) this property (say, p) and its complementary ($\neg p$) have different normative status. This occurs either if they are attached to different normative solutions, or if one of them is connected to a certain normative solution while the other is connected to no solution.

A normative system is the set of all the relevant logical consequences which follow from a certain set of norms. Such relevant logical consequences are obtained by applying the logical rule of *strengthening the antecedent* to the relevant norms,

[32] See Ferrer Beltrán and Ratti (eds.) 2012b.

[33] See, for instance, Schauer (1991, 73 ff.).

[34] If relevant properties increase in number, the scope of a norm becomes narrower, and vice versa: if they diminish, the scope of the corresponding norms becomes wider. The sentence by which relevant properties are identified is called "thesis of relevance".

i.e. by connecting more specific relevant cases (say: "$p\&q$") to the solution provided for a less specific case (say "p").

As just noted, many of the theorems derived in *Normative Systems* are based on the application of the rule of strengthening the antecedent. Given a certain normative conditional "$p \supset Oq$", any property which is not relevant according to the normative conditional at hand does not change its outcome if it is added to the antecedent. And it is exactly such a feature of the logical development of normative sets which makes it possible to spot inconsistencies and gaps within a normative system (i.e. a fully logically–developed set of normative sentences).

Let us give a sketchy example. Take the norm N1 which provides that "If one owns a real estate, one ought to pay tax q on its possession" ("$r \supset Oq$") and the norm N2, which provides that "If one has more than three children, one may waive the payment of tax q" ("$c \supset \neg Oq$"). By developing the consequences of such norms, we can build the following normative system: more precisely, by means of strengthening the antecedent, N1 applies to all the cases where "r" appears, and N2 applies to all the cases where "c" appears.

Cases/Norms	N1	N2
1. $r\&c$	Oq	$\neg Oq$
2. $r\&\neg c$	Oq	
3. $\neg r\&c$		$\neg Oq$
4. $\neg r\&\neg c$		

As its matrix shows, the normative system is gappy regarding the case 4 (since no normative consequence is attached to the case at hand), and is inconsistent regarding the first case (since two incompatible solutions are attached to the case at hand). It can be made complete and consistent only by reshaping the norms which composes its normative basis. As this succinct analysis shows, such operations can be made in so far as norms are regarded as sorts of material conditionals.

From the early nineties on, however, Alchourrón and Bulygin became increasingly interested in the study of defeasible conditionals and begun to regard legal norms as a paradigmatic case of such conditionals.

In an encyclopedic entry bearing on the concept of legal norm,[35] Alchourrón and Bulygin (1995, 144–146) maintain – with a significant change with regards to *Normative Systems* – that most of legal standards are defeasible and that, for this reason, admit neither strengthening the antecedent nor *modus ponens*. In this entry, they defend a "normality–based" view of defeasibility: (normative) conditionals are defeasible because they hold only for "normal" circumstances.

In a slightly later paper, Alchourrón (1996, reprint 2012) holds the view that legal defeasibility may be fruitfully approached from a pragmatic standpoint about

[35] Alchourrón and Bulygin (1995, 144–146).

the counterfactual intentions of the lawgiver: that is, what the lawgiver would have done if it had considered some circumstances which it could not (or would not) have taken into account. Such considerations on the counterfactual intentions of the lawgiver bring about the defeasibility of legal standards. More precisely, at least three dispositions or attitudes of the lawgiver about the defeat of a certain conditional normative standard "If *p* then *Oq*", on the grounds of a certain implicit circumstance "*r*", can be envisaged[36]: (1) the lawgiver may have a disposition to accept both "If *p* then *Oq*" and "If *p* and *r* then *Oq*": in this case "*r*" counts as an implicit non–exception; (2) the lawgiver may have a disposition to accept "If *p* then *Oq*" whilst rejecting "If *p* and *r* then *Oq*": the circumstance "*r*" is thus to be regarded as an implicit exception; (3) the lawgiver may have no disposition at all about whether considering "*r*" as an exception (like in case 2) or a non–exception (like in case 1): accordingly, "*r*" is undetermined as an exception.

Years later, Bulygin (2005) concurred, although on partially different grounds. Unlike in *Normative Systems* where an "opaque" model of normative relevance is maintained, he now defends a "transparent" model, according to which a property might be relevant when, though not being strictly relevant in the sense illustrated above, is relevant according to the system of values underlying the activities of the legislatures. So, the model is "transparent" regarding norms' underlying values: it allows one to go beyond norms and reach the values and the goals which have inspired their enactment. According to such a model, expressed norms are to be considered as defeasible in that, in the application of law, they can be defeated by the justificatory level of reasons.[37]

Of course, so conceived defeasibility has a bearing on negation. On the one hand, conditional norms the logical form thereof is "$p \supset Oq$" are rendered defeasible by substituting the material conditional with the defeasible conditional (symbolized by the corner "$>$"). However, the corner is just a compendious way for concealing the role of negation. Defeasible conditionals such as "$p > Oq$" may be more fully reconstructed by introducing negation into the sentence. Let "*r*" stay for any defeater whatsoever. So, a fully developed defeasible conditional rule – provided that there is

---

[36]Alchourrón (2012, 47–48).

[37]The model elaborated in *Normative Systems* seems to be jeopardized by at least three features of defeasible norms, as presented in Alchourrón's and Bulygin's above–mentioned papers. First, the full logical development of a normative set would be pointless: to develop a system of norms one should resort instead to supposed lawgiver's attitudes or goals in enacting the norms at hand. However, since many circumstances would turn out be undetermined as exceptions, one should derive the conclusion that the complete logical development of a normative basis is hardly possible. Secondly, since modus ponens is not allowed by defeasible conditionals, norms would lose most of their inferential power especially regarding judicial application. Finally, the distinction between thesis and hypothesis of relevance (i.e. the latter being the sentence which identifies the properties that should be, or have been, regarded as relevant) would be obscured by the fact that one always should not confine oneself to detecting the literal understanding of a rule–formulation and always resort to something beyond it, in order to identify a rule. Consequently, also the distinction between a normative gap and an axiological one becomes fuzzy. For discussion and possible ways out from these predicaments, see Ferrer Beltrán and Ratti (2012a, 29).

only one defeater – would amount to the conjunction of the following two sentences: "$p\&r \supset \neg Oq$" and "$p\&\neg r \supset Oq$". This operation, in turn, has the outcome of reestablishing the possible transition from conditional to negation–plus–disjunction (or conjunction). Indeed, on this reading, the sentence "$p\&r \supset \neg Oq$" would amount to the sentence "$(\neg p \vee \neg r) \vee \neg Oq$", while the sentence "$p\&\neg r \supset Oq$" would equate to "$(\neg p \vee r) \vee Oq$".

Thanks to this logical reconstruction, and to other conceptual resources we may now want to introduce, it becomes clear that defeasibility may receive different interpretations.

The first interpretation reconstructs defeasibility as a phenomenon of (tacit) inconsistency within the normative system at hand. In particular, there is a conflict between a logical consequence of an expressed rule and a norm which can be derived (in a strictly logical manner or, more frequently, by means of unsound reasoning) from some lawgiver's goals or counterfactual intentions. Let us again assume that "$p \supset Oq$" is the lawgiver's expressed norm N1 and "r" is the defeater (the implicit exception, as Alchourrón would have it) which can be "derived" by (or justified on the basis of) the lawgiver's goals or unspoken intentions. From so envisaged goals or intentions, one can construe that the lawgiver intended another norm N2 which provides that "$p\&r \supset \neg Oq$". This implicit norm is clearly at odds with the implicit norm N3, logically derived from N1, according to which "$p\&r \supset Oq$". On this reading, defeasibility consists in giving priority to the norm derived from the implicit norm over the one derived from the expressed norm (Mendonca 2012). Of course, such a priority can be more or less frequently at play depending on the institutional design of a certain legal order. As Schauer (2012, 87) has recently shown, the resistance of expressed rules to implicit exceptions (or, more broadly, to underlying justifications) depends on "how some decision–making system will choose to treat its rules". In this sense, it all depends on a meta–rule (or a set of meta–rules) imposing a certain defeasible or indefeasible treatment of (some or all of) the other rules of the system.

A second possible interpretation – analyzed in depth by Ferrer Beltrán and Ratti (2010) – is that defeasibility amounts to the fact that not all the strictly logical (viz. deductive) consequences of expressed legal rules are treated as valid or applicable, but only some of them. On this reading, norms are defeasible in the sense that we can "legally derive" from them only those logical consequences which conform, cumulatively or disjunctively, to norms' underlying reasons, lawgivers' real intentions, or counterfactual dispositions. All the logical consequences which do not so conform would be connected to the negation of the normative consequence originally provided, so that from "$p \supset Oq$" *plus* a "non–conforming" condition "r" added to the antecedent, one may derive "$p\&r \supset \neg Oq$".

A third option – presented in greater detail in Ferrer and Ratti (2012a) – elaborates on the relations underpinning the notions of validity, applicability, and defeasibility of legal norms. As we shall see, negation has a fundamental bearing on these issues. Within this compass, at least three situations, broadly referred to in literature as "defeasibility of legal norms", must be distinguished.

(i) Sometimes a norm is said to be defeasible in the sense that, so to speak, its validity (i.e. its membership to the legal system) is defeasible. The defeasibility of norms, in this case, really refers to the indefinite character of the criteria of identification of the system. To hold that N1 is defeasible in this sense means, actually, that it is the criteria of identification, by means of which N1 is selected as a presumed valid norm of the system, that are liable to being revised, integrated or left aside.

(ii) Some other times, when one affirms that a norm is defeasible, one means that the so called "external applicability" of a norm is subject to defeat. Provided that the expression "external applicability" of a norm N1 denotes the situation where another norm N2 provides that N1 ought to be applied, the defeasibility of the external applicability of N1 is a consequence of the defeasibility of the norm N2.That is to say that, in spite of the fact that the norm N1 provides a solution for the case under decision,[38] the question whether it must be applied by officials is not determined once for all, since its conditions of applications – laid down in N2 – may contain implicit exceptions the scope thereof is regarded as not fully determined.

(iii) Finally, on other occasions, when one affirms that a norm N1 is defeasible, one refers to the fact that its very normative content is defeasible. This is to say that the operative facts identified in the antecedent of the norms are only a contributory condition for the normative consequence to follow: the norm's antecedent contains implicit exceptions which may not be exhaustively identified. In this third case, the defeasibility of N1 is neither necessarily a consequence of another norm N2 nor of the criteria of identification of the system. On the contrary, it is the result of the construction of N1 as allowing non–completely determinable implicit exceptions (as happens in Alchourrón's proposal).

We might say that, in cases (i) and (ii), the defeasibility affecting N1 is external, since what is being defeated is, respectively, either the criteria of identification of the legal order or the norm N2, which obliges the officials to apply N1. Contrariwise, in the case (iii), the very normative content of N1 is defeasible (what can be represented by the defeasible conditional "$p > Oq$"). In this occurrence, we can affirm that the defeasibility of N1 is "internal".[39]

[38]It is, in other words, "internally applicable".

[39]The notions of internal and external defeasibility must not be confused. However, they have mutual relations which are worth exploring. The external defeasibility of a norm N1 affects either its validity or its external applicability and is a consequence of the internal defeasibility of another norm N2 or of the criteria of identification of the system. By contrast, the internal defeasibility of a norm N1 affects its internal applicability, i.e. we cannot determine whether a certain case C can be subsumed under the antecedent of the norm, since it is not a closed antecedent. In turn, the internal defeasibility of N1 brings about the external defeasibility of the norms derived from it. In other words, if N1 ("$p > Oq$") is a valid norm, and if one accepts that the norms which are logical consequences of other valid norms are also valid, then we do not know whether N3 ("$p\&r \supset Oq$") is also valid *qua* a logical consequence of N1. This is so because, until the antecedent of N1 is (or

Negation affects all of these cases in that the full transformation of a defeasible (or weak) conditional into a material (or strong) conditional requires the complete identification of all the negative conditions which may revoke the validity or hinder the application of the conditional at hand.

Nonetheless, the way this operation works varies from case to case. In particular, in case (i), the defeasibility of N1 cannot be represented by using the defeasible conditional ($p > Oq$), if our aim consists in representing its content. The correct form of representing N1 is by using the material conditional ($p \supset Oq$). This is so for it is not the normative content of N1 that is (necessarily) defeasible, but rather its qualification as a valid norm. In other words, it is not the conditional contained in N1 the one to be weakened, but the other conditional contained in the criteria of identification of the valid norms of the system, which will provide that "$(x)\varphi x > Vx$" ("For any norm x, if x satisfies conditions φ, then x is presumably a valid norm of the system"). The full reformulation of such criteria entails the introduction of a clause bearing on the implicit defeaters. Consequently, the revised criteria will be better reconstructed as follows: "$(x)\varphi x \& \neg\{E\} \supset Vx$".

Analogously, the defeasibility of the external applicability of a norm N1 cannot be represented by using the defeasible conditional, if we want to account for its normative content. The correct form of representing N1 is by means of the material conditional "$(p \supset Oq)$". This is so because it is not the normative content of N1 that is defeasible, but rather the normative content of N2, which imposes the application of N1 "$(S > O(Apply\ N1)$". Again, the full reconstruction of N2 involves the use of a negative clause, representing the absence of all the possible defeaters, like in the following formula: "$S \& \neg E \supset O(Apply\ N1)$".

Finally, as we have already seen, the full reformulation of a defeasible norm of conducts involves making all the implicit defeaters explicit.[40] And this only can be made by introducing (at least) a negative clause into the conditional.

5.5 Some Conclusions

Negation plays a very important role in normative and legal discourses. However, it also has a peculiar logical behavior, which needs to be analyzed in great detail. This contribution is a first attempt in this direction, but a more thorough examination is

is treated as) closed, it is not possible to determine whether N3 is a logical consequence of N1 or not.

[40]This view has been frequently criticized as a scholastic fiction. Cf. Sartor (1995, 143–144). What is argued is that: (1) perfect conditional norms are not linguistic structures that concretely exist in the legal world, but rather represent the ideal result of the synthesis of many norms belonging to a certain legal order; (2) the rewriting of the entire legal system in the form of a set of perfect conditional norms can never be completed due to human limitations, both epistemological and practical. This line of criticism is untenable, though, in so far as juristic reasoning is concerned, as is argued in Ferrer Beltrán and Ratti (2012a, 15–16).

needed in order to determine whether this feature leads to the need of building an "extended" or even "deviant" logic for normative and legal conditionals.

In addition to this, one of the main results of the present investigation is that negation must be neatly distinguished from some phenomena – such as derogation and defeasibility – which are often considered as equivalent or analogous to it. As we have seen, negation plays a crucial role in both phenomena, but there is no one–to–one correspondence between negating norms and regarding them as derogated or defeated.

References

Alchourrón, Carlos Eduardo. 1996. Detachment and defeasibility in deontic logic. *Studia Logica* 57:5–18.

Alchourrón, Carlos Eduardo. 2012. On law and logic. In *The logic of legal requirements. Essays on defeasibility*, ed. Jordi Ferrer Beltrán and Giovanni Battista Ratti. Oxford: Oxford University Press.

Alchourrón, Carlos Eduardo, and Eugenio Bulygin. 1971. *Normative systems*. Wien/New York: Springer.

Alchourrón, Carlos Eduardo, and Eugenio Bulygin. 1979. *Sobre la existencia de las normas juridicas*. Valencia (Venezuela): Universidad de Carabobo.

Alchourrón, Carlos Eduardo, and Eugenio Bulygin. 1995. Norma juridica. In *Enciclopedia Latinoamericana de Filosofia*. El Derecho y la Justicia, 11, 133–147. Madrid: Trotta.

Alchourrón, Carlos Eduardo, and Makinson David. 1981. Hierarchies of regulations and their logic. In *New studies in deontic logic*, ed. R. Hilpinen, 125–148. Dordrecht: Reidel.

Araszkiewicz, Michał. 2013. Towards systematic research on statutory interpretation in AI and law. In *Legal knowledge and information systems*, ed. K.D. Ashley, 15–24. Amsterdam: IOS.

Atienza, Manuel. 1992. Sobre los limites de la lógica en el derecho. *Theoria – Segunda época* VII:1007–1018.

Bacqué, Jorge A. 1964. Doble negación y doble derogación. *Notas de filosofia del derecho* 1:10–13.

Bulygin, Eugenio. 1982. Time and validity. In *Deontic logic, computational linguistics and legal information systems*, ed. Antonio Anselmo Martino, 65–81. Amsterdam: North Holland.

Bulygin, Eugenio. 2005. En defensa de El Dorado. Respuesta a Fernando Atria. In *Lagunas en el derecho*, ed. F. Atria et al., 73–85. Madrid: Marcial Pons.

Caracciolo, Ricardo 2012. Acts, normative formulations, and defeasibile norms. Ferrer Beltrán, Jordi, and Giovanni Battista Ratti, eds. 2012b. *The logic of legal requirements. Essays on defeasibility*, 209–222. Oxford: Oxford University Press.

Carrió, Genaro R. 1964. Un supuesto principio absoluto en jacque. *Notas de filosofia del derecho* 1:14–17.

Chiassoni, Pierluigi. 2012. Defeasibility and legal indeterminacy. In ed. Ferrer Beltrán, Jordi, and Giovanni Battista Ratti, eds. 2012b. *The logic of legal requirements. Essays on defeasibility*, 151–181. Oxford: Oxford University Press.

Ferrer Beltrán, Jordi, and Giovanni Battista Ratti. 2010. Validity and defeasibility in the legal domain. *Law and Philosophy* 29:601–626.

Ferrer Beltrán, Jordi, and Giovanni Battista Ratti. 2012a. Defeasibility and legality: A survey. Ferrer Beltrán, Jordi, and Giovanni Battista Ratti, eds. 2012b. *The logic of legal requirements. Essays on defeasibility*, 11–38. Oxford: Oxford University Press.

Ferrer Beltrán, Jordi, and Giovanni Battista Ratti, eds. 2012b. *The logic of legal requirements. Essays on defeasibility*. Oxford: Oxford University Press.

Ferrer Beltrán, Jordi, and Jorge Luis Rodríguez. 2011. *Jerarquias normativas y dinámica de los sistemas juridicos*. Madrid: Marcial Pons.

Gioja, Ambrosio. 1964. Von Wright y la derogación. *Notas de filosofía del derecho* 1:62–63.

Grabowski, Andrzej. 2013. *Juristic concept of the validity of statutory law*. Dordrecht: Springer.

Guastini, Riccardo. 2010. *Le fonti del diritto. Fondamenti teorici*. Milan: Giuffrè.

Guastini, Riccardo. 2011a. *La sintassi del diritto*. Turin: Giappichelli.

Guastini, Riccardo. 2011b. *Interpretare e argomentare*. Milan: Giuffrè.

Guastini, Riccardo. 2013. Juristenrecht: Inventing rights, obligations, and powers. In *Neutrality and theory of law*, ed. J. Ferrer Beltrán et al., 147–159. Dordrecht: Springer.

Hage, Jaap 2000. Rule consistency. *Law and Philosophy* 19:369–390.

Kelsen, Hans. 1960. *Reine Rechtslehre*. Wien: Deuticke.

Kelsen, Hans. 1973. Derogation. In *Essays in legal and moral philosophy*, ed. O. Weinberger, 261–275. Dordrecht: Reidel.

Martínez Zorrilla, David. 2010. *Metodologia juridica y argumentación*. Madrid: Marcial Pons.

Mazzarese, Tecla. 1989. *Logica deontica e linguaggio giuridico*. Padua: Cedam

Mendonca, Daniel. 2012. Exceptions. Ferrer Beltrán, Jordi, and Giovanni Battista Ratti, eds. 2012b. *The logic of legal requirements. Essays on defeasibility*, 202–208. Oxford: Oxford University Press.

Moreso, José Juan. 1996. On relevance and justification of legal decisions. *Erkenntnis* 44:73–100.

Moreso, José Juan, and Jorge L. Rodríguez. 2010. Carlos E. Alchourrón y la máxima de la mutilación minima. In *Fundamentos para una teoria general de los deberes*, ed. C.E. Alchourrón, 11–38. Madrid: Marcial Pons.

Ratti, Giovanni Battista. 2013a. Normative inconsistency and logical theories: A first critique of defeasibilism. In *Coherence: Insights from philosophy, jurisprudence and artificial intelligence*, ed. M. Araszkiewicz, and J. Šavelka. Dordrecht: Springer.

Ratti, Giovanni Battista. 2013b. *Studi sulla logica del diritto e della scienza giuridica*. Madrid: Marcial Pons.

Rodríguez, Jorge L. 2006. La tensión entre dos concepciones del sistema juridico. *Análisis filosófico* 26:242–276.

Rodríguez, Jorge L. 2014. *Teoria del diritto e analisi logica*. Madrid: Marcial Pons.

Ross, Alf. 1958. *On law and justice*. London: Stevens & Sons.

Ross, Alf. 1968. *Directives and norms*. London: Routledge & Kegan Paul.

Sartor, Giovanni. 1995. *Defeasibility in legal reasoning. Informatics and the foundation of legal reasoning*, ed. Z. Bankowski et al. Dordrecht: Kluwer.

Schauer, Frederick. 1991. *Playing by the rules. A philosophical examination of rule-based decision-making in law and in life*. Oxford: Clarendon.

Schauer, Frederick. 2012. Is defeasibility an essential property of rules? Ferrer Beltrán, Jordi, and Giovanni Battista Ratti, eds. 2012b. *The logic of legal requirements. Essays on defeasibility*, 77–88. Oxford: Oxford University Press.

Soeteman, Arendt. 1989. *Logic in law*. Dordrecht: Kluwer.

Tarello, Giovanni. 1974. *Diritto, enunciati, usi*. Bologna: Il Mulino.

Weinberger, Ota. 1957. Uber die Negation von Sollsatzen. *Theoria* 23:102–132

Wright, Georg Henrik, von. 1963. *Norms and action. A logical enquiry*. London: Routledge & Kegan Paul.

Wright, Georg Henrik, von. 1983. Norms, truth and logic. In *Practical reason*. Philosophical papers, vol I., 130–209. Oxford/Basil: Blackwell.

Wróblewski, Jerzy. 1984. Negation in law. In *Theorie der Normen*, ed. W. Krawietz et al., 457–471. Berlin: Duncker & Humboldt.

Zuleta, Hugo. 2008. *Normas y justificación. Una investigación lógica*. Barcelona: Marcial Pons.

Chapter 6
Open Texture in Law, Legal Certainty and Logical Analysis of Natural Language

Jaromir Šavelka and Jakub Harašta

Abstract In this paper we use logical analysis of natural language to analyse a dilemma every legislator faces. This dilemma presents itself as a gap between what is literally prescribed by a legal rule and what goal had the legislator in mind when enacting it. First, we describe this dilemma in detail. We use Hart's example of a rule prohibiting vehicles from entering the park to show how the dilemma could pass to a decision maker if it is not sufficiently addressed by a legislator. Then, we discuss how logical analysis of natural language could be used in order to mitigate, or at least assess, severity of the dilemma passed from a legislator to a decision maker. In general, we advocate usefulness of logical analysis of natural language in legislature as well as in legal decision making.

Keywords Open texture • Logical analysis of language • Legal certainty • First-order logic • Natural language

6.1 Introduction

In his seminal work Endicott (2000) describes what he calls "the standard view of adjudication". In this view the judge's task is just to give effect to the legal rights and duties of the parties. Endicott challenges the view with the well-known "indeterminacy claim". The claim states that the requirements of the law in particular cases are frequently indeterminate. In this context the judge's task fundamentally differs from the standard view of adjudication (Endicott 2000, 1–2). The grounds for the indeterminacy claim were first laid down when Jeremy Bentham attempted to explain the nature of law through linguistic acts to find a basis for his legal positivism (Bentham 1970; Endicott 2014). With this attempt he formed a firm

J. Šavelka (✉)
Intelligent Systems Program, University of Pittsburgh, Pittsburgh, PA, USA
e-mail: jas438@pitt.edu

J. Harašta
Institute of Law and Technology, Masaryk University, Brno, Czech Republic
e-mail: jakub.harasta@law.muni.cz

M. Araszkiewicz, K. Płeszka (eds.), *Logic in the Theory and Practice of Lawmaking*, Legisprudence Library 2, DOI 10.1007/978-3-319-19575-9_6

bond between philosophy of law and philosophy of language that has been there ever since. Language certainly is a phenomenon that receives special fascination in the philosophy of law (Endicott 2014).

In the early 1950s Friedrich Waismann formulated the concept of open texture of language (Bix 1991, 51–52; Waismann 1951). This concept was later used by Herbert L. A. Hart when he formulated his well-known position on judicial interpretation. Hart's thoughts on open texture in law, widely popularized in his "Concept of Law" (Hart 1994, 124–135), became the common starting point for philosophy of law to address language phenomena. Hart's account of open texture in law can be understood from many different viewpoints. One can assume that he was presenting an argument for judicial discretion based on the nature of language. Or he can be read as putting forward a policy argument for why rules should be applied in a way, which would require that discretion (Bix 1991, 51). The main idea remains simple: there are cases in which it is not completely clear if a specific legal norm should apply and what exact effects should it have. This is not a flaw in legal regulation but its inherent feature, which stems from the open texture of language (Hart 1994, 124–135). These reflections are far from being just academic. They directly relate to the function law performs in society. Niklas Luhmann investigates what is the function of law in relation to the social system in terms of which of the problems of the social system law solves. In his work he refuses traditional sociological doctrine that the function of law is related to "social control" or "integration". He claims that the main function of law subsists in securing certain expectations of individuals as stable over time (Luhmann 2008, 147–148). In taking this particular stance he clearly relates the main function of law to legal certainty, a value traditionally promoted by law. This in turn means that any phenomenon threatening to undermine legal certainty threatens the function of law in whole.

Open texture in law has direct influence over legal certainty. It is of key importance to reflect on proper approaches to tackle the phenomenon of open texture. The main aim is to maximize promotion of legal certainty while harnessing the benefits open texture has to offer. This essentially means finding approaches that facilitates communication of general standards and reference to classes of persons, to classes of acts, and circumstances (Hart 1994), in a way that is understandable, transparent and open to rigorous assessment that leads to persuasive interpretations of that communication.

Logical analysis of natural language addresses questions such as "What do we talk about?" and "How do we talk about it?" By careful analysis of a given expression it attempts to uncover its exact meaning and represent it within the framework of established notation. We will use philosophical underpinnings of procedural semantics for hyperintensional logic as used by Marie Duži et al. (2010, 133). For the sake of simplicity we will use first-order predicate logic for the analysis of selected natural language expressions. We analyze only simple expressions which do not require heavy machinery of the transparent intensional logic notation as used in Duži et al. (2010).

In this chapter, we first present brief overview of the concept of open texture in law and selected insights into the relation that exists between the function of law and legal certainty. We argue that legislator should be aware of the effects emulated by open texture of concepts present in newly enacted legal rule and should use that awareness to decide how exactly should the rule be formulated. Specifically, we describe the dilemma a legislator deals with when creating a new rule. First of all, a rule should be able to pursue a certain goal. On the other hand, it must provide clear guidance for the addressees of a rule with respect to their expectations. These can often be in conflict and legislator must strike proper balance between the clarity of a rule and its adherence to a goal it pursues. Depending on how a legislator succeeds in the task the dilemma is transferred to a decision maker (a judge) who must repeatedly strike the balance in the light of concrete circumstances.

6.2 Open Texture in Law

Hart (1994, 124) claims that law could not exist if it would not be possible to *communicate* general standards and refer to classes of persons, and to classes of acts, things, and circumstances. On the other hand, the successful operation of law depends on a capacity to *recognize* particular acts, things, and circumstances as instances of the general classifications which the law makes. The general standards are primarily communicated through legislation and precedent. Hart relates communication by precedent to explaining through example and communication by legislation to explanation using explicit forms of language. Although, it may seem that the communication is clear Hart warns that when verbally formulated general rules are used, uncertainties as to the form of behavior required by them may break out in particular concrete cases. Even more, canons of "interpretation" cannot eliminate, though they can diminish, these uncertainties (Hart 1994, 124–126).

Hart provides an example of a rule prohibiting use of vehicles in a park. While there could be little doubt as to whether a car, a bus, or a motor-cycle are vehicles, it is much more challenging to decide about inline skates, a bike or an airplane. This means that there are objects which are clearly prohibited from entering the park and no doubt with respect to this can be entertained by any reasonable person. But there are also objects in case of which it cannot be easily, if at all, determined whether they are prohibited from entering the park. In Hart's opinion this uncertainty is the price to be paid for the use of general classifying terms in any form of communication concerning matters of fact. And it is indeed the price that must be paid because human legislators cannot have knowledge of all the possible combinations of circumstances which the future may bring (Hart 1994, 126–128). In this respect open texture can be seen not as a curse haunting law with indeterminacy but as a cure to the limited knowledge of the legislator.

Hart recognizes fundamental clash of two values that is inherent to every legal system. All legal systems, in different ways, compromise between two social needs: the need for certain rules which can, over great areas of conduct, safely be applied by private individuals to themselves without fresh official guidance or weighting up of social issues, and the need to leave open, for later settlement by an informed, official choice, issues which can only be properly appreciated and settled when they arise in a concrete case. Hart uses this claim as an argument for the existence and necessity of judicial (or other rule-making authority) discretion. He rejects the view that there is one uniquely correct answer to be found in each case. This rejection is the key ramification stemming from the open texture in law (Hart 1994, 129–134).

6.3 Function of Law and Legal Certainty

Future is inherently uncertain. But one wants to be certain about the future because operations in society take time (Luhmann 2008, 143 and 146). For example, there may be an individual who could immediately use fixed sum of money, which he does not have at the moment, to generate a profit amounting to 10 % of that sum. There may be another individual who has that sum of money but has no use for it. He cannot transfer the money to the first individual, wait for him to generate the profit, return the money and share the profit because he cannot be certain about the future. Specifically, there is no guarantee that the first individual is not going to keep the money as well as the whole profit for himself. This is an obvious problem, which prevents both individuals from using their resources (opportunity in the case of the first individual and money in the case of the second individual) efficiently. This problem is related to time as it is caused by uncertainty about the future. It is the main goal of law to solve this problem.

Law enables an individual to direct his expectations at society instead of individuals. It offers the possibility of communicating expectations and having them accepted in communication. And obviously, there are substantial consequences if expectations can be secured as stable expectations over time. Thus, legal norms can be understood as structure of *symbolically* generalized expectations. By stabilized usage of this symbolization society produces specific stabilities and specific sensibilities (Luhmann 2008, 142–146). In case of the above described example the second individual can temporarily transfer the possession of the money to the first individual because he can reliably expect that the society will acknowledge his entitlement to get the money back with a share of profit they both agree on in advance. And if necessary, the society will help him in enforcing the legitimate claim.

In performing its function law stabilizes normative expectations by regulating how they are generalized in relation to their temporal, factual, and social dimensions. Law makes it possible to know which expectations will meet with social approval and which not. Given this certainty of expectations, one can take on the disappointments of everyday life with a higher degree of composure. This means that one can afford a higher degree of uncertain confidence or even of mistrust as long as one has confidence in law. This in turn means that one can live in a more complex society (Luhmann 2008, 147–148).

Now, let us suppose that the second individual from our example lends the money to the first individual. They both agree that after a fixed period of time the money will be returned together with the half of the profit. Furthermore, let us suppose that when the time comes the second individual refuses to provide both, the money he borrowed as well as the profit he promised to deliver. As the entitlement of the second individual to receive the money and the profit is acknowledged by the society (enforceable by law) he can turn to the society for help in enforcing his claim. This would usually mean that he can file a claim with the court of justice.

How does the court address the claim, i.e. how does it acknowledge the legitimate expectations of the first individual, is of vital importance with respect to legal certainty. Brian Bix offers an interesting example of a judge deciding cases on the basis of a coin-flip (Bix 1993, 106). One can imagine how much trust in law would be generated in the society if the court dismisses the claim of the second individual on the basis of a coin flip which turns out to be unfavorable for him. With respect to this, Luhmann adds, that where law is no longer respected, or is no longer enforced as far as it is possible so to do, the consequences extend much further than what amounts to breach of law, and the system has to retreat to much more basic forms of securing confidence (Luhmann 2008, 148). If law fails to provide members of the society with sufficient amount of legal certainty, i.e. fails to persuade them that their legitimate expectations will be acknowledged, it fails to perform its function altogether. And as it no longer serves its purpose it can be dismissed since it has no value at all.

The example with a coin-flipping is extreme and it would be immediately recognized as unacceptable. However, there can be more subtle forms of coin-flipping that are more difficult to recognize. One of them is closely connected with open texture in law. If open texture is misunderstood in a way that in certain cases it gives a judge total freedom to decide a case that appears to be unclear, a special kind of coin-flipping is being introduced in law. And, as has been shown above, this may have far reaching consequences outgrowing breaches of law and dismissal of legitimate claims in individual cases.

6.4 No Vehicles in Park Revisited

In this section we use first-order predicate logic to analyse a rule expressed in natural language. We take an existing rule and analyse it from the viewpoint of a decision maker that must determine an effect of the rule in a given context. We analyse Hart's rule prohibiting use of vehicles in a park (Hart 1994, 127). For the analysis, let us assume that the goal of the legislator is to maintain serenity in a specific park. Furthermore, let us assume that it is widely believed that primary source of disturbances of serenity in the park are motorized vehicles such as cars, motorcycles and buses. There is a whole multitude of possibilities how exactly a rule promoting the goal should be expressed in natural language. For example, the rule may state the goal explicitly in the following way:

It is forbidden to disturb serenity in the park.

Such a rule may be considered too vague. Persons that are subjected to the rule can hardly tell what is forbidden from what is permitted. Therefore, it would be very difficult for each person to form legitimate expectations corresponding with the expectations of others. Therefore, it might seem reasonable to be more specific in requiring the desired behavior and express the rule in the following way:

Cars, buses and motorcycles are forbidden to enter the park.

As opposed to the previous example this rule may be considered too specific. If this rule is enacted it would be much easier to form universally accepted expectations. But not only cars, buses and motorcycles are vehicles which may disturb serenity in the park. For example, let us consider motorized bicycles or karts. Thus, it seems that the rule would be very weak in promoting the goal. Following this line of reasoning the legislator may come up with the following rule:

Any vehicle is forbidden to enter the park.

Let us suppose that there are no doubts as to which exact geographical unit constitutes the park. Furthermore, let us suppose that there are no indeterminacies with respect to what constitutes entering the park. To be more precise, it can be clearly recognized if the object entered the park. In case it was a vehicle we know that the rule was violated. Let us establish a predicate *forbidden*, which can be understood as assigning selected objects with the property of being forbidden from entering the park. This in our case amounts to nothing more or less but to assigning the object with the quality of being in breach of the rule should it enter the park. The predicate forbidden is too simplifying and by no means presents a good analysis of the expression:

x is forbidden to enter the park.

However, the predicate allows us to hide all the constituents of the rule which we consider clear and fixed under its realm. A predicate *vehicle* assigns an object with the property of being a vehicle. It is the concept of the property of being a vehicle that will be subject to our analysis, i.e. we accept that this concept is open-textured. Finally, we analyse the rule itself in the following way:

(i) *"Any vehicle is forbidden to enter the park."*

$$\forall_X vehicle(X) \rightarrow forbidden(X)$$

In addition let us have three objects X, Y, and Z. Also, let us have three additional predicates *car*, *bus* and *motorcycle* each of which assigns an object with the property of being a car, a bus or a motorcycle respectively. Let us use these to define the following:

(ii) *"x is a car."*

$$car(x)$$

(iii) *"y is a bus."*

$$bus(y)$$

(iv) *"z is a motorcycle."*

$$motorcycle(z)$$

At this point, there is the rule and three objects with known properties of being a car, a bus and a motorcycle. Now, let us have one more predicate *entered* which assigns objects with the property of entering the park at least once since the rule was adopted. With the use of this predicate let us define the following:

(v) *"x entered the park at least once since the rule was adopted."*

$$entered(x)$$

(vi) *"y entered the park at least once since the rule was adopted."*

$$entered(y)$$

(vii) *"z entered the park at least once since the rule was adopted."*

$$entered(z)$$

Let us accept that if any object that has the property of being forbidden from entering the park and that at the same time entered the park at least once since the rule was adopted then that object violated the rule ad (i). For this, we introduce yet another predicate *violated* which assigns objects with the property that they violated the rule ad (i).

(viii) *"If an object which is forbidden from entering the park entered the park it violated the rule forbidding it from entering the park."*

$$\forall_X forbidden(X) \wedge entered(X) \rightarrow violated(X)$$

The main issue at this point is if a reasonable person knowing ad (i)–(viii) could arrive at a conclusion that any of x, y and z violated the rule ad (i). Although, our intuition could easily mislead us to answer each of the questions in affirmative there is no other way but to conclude that none of x, y and z is known to violate the rule ad (i). This can be easily proven on case of x while the line of reasoning for y and z would be the same. Trying to infer that x is known to violate the rule ad (i) we do the following:

Premise 1: $\forall_X vehicle(X) \rightarrow forbidden(X)$
Premise 2: $\forall_X forbidden(X) \wedge entered(X) \rightarrow violated(X)$
Premise 3: $car(x)$
Premise 4: $entered(x)$

Conclusion: $violated(x)$

It requires nothing more but operations of elementary logic to prove that the conclusion does not follow from premises 1–4. However, as the importance of this observation is at the heart of the presented method it is worth providing detailed explanation. Duži et al. (2010, 134) give the example of the following sentence: "The biggest planet is smaller than Sun." They maintain that the sentence does not talk about Jupiter. Furthermore, they explain that whenever the impression that the kind of conclusions we talk about arise from the discussed kind of premises, it is because we happen to have background knowledge which we employ. By doing this we ignore that the premise, which is obviously not logically trivial and is necessary for deriving the conclusion, is missing (Duži et al. 2010, 134). In our case we miss the premise that any car is at the same time a vehicle.

In case of the example above this ignorance would not cause much harm. Soon, we will show that the conclusion could indeed be reached with the help of premises we take for granted which is probably the reason why we do not consider them necessary. However, it is precisely awareness for such details that sets firm limits for harnessing the benefits of open texture in law and help us prevent harm it may potentially cause. To continue with our example we can use what we already have to define the following:

(ix) *"Car is a vehicle."*

$$\forall_X car(X) \rightarrow vehicle(X)$$

(x) *"Bus is a vehicle."*

$$\forall_X bus(X) \rightarrow vehicle(X)$$

(xi) *"Car is a vehicle."*

$$\forall_X motorcycle(X) \rightarrow vehicle(X)$$

By doing this we just follow Hart (1994, 127) and the general intuition in saying that everybody would agree that cars, buses and motorcycles are vehicles. From (ii), (iii), (iv), (ix), (x) and (xi) it logically follows that x, y and z are vehicles.

At this point we can finally express logically valid inference that goes as follows:

Premise 1: $\forall_X car(X) \rightarrow vehicle(X)$
Premise 2: $car(x)$

Conclusion 1: $vehicle(x)$

Premise 3: $\forall_X vehicle(X) \rightarrow forbidden(X)$
Premise 4: $vehicle(x)$

Conclusion 2: $forbidden(x)$

Premise 5: $\forall_X forbidden(X) \wedge entered(X) \rightarrow violated(X)$
Premise 6: $forbidden(x)$
Premise 7: $entered(x)$

Conclusion 3: $violated(x)$

By conclusion 1 we have established that x is a vehicle. By conclusion 2 we have shown that x is forbidden from entering the park and finally by conclusion 3 we have shown that x at least once violated the rule, which provides that vehicles are forbidden to enter the park. The same line of reasoning could be applied to prove the same for y and z. Let us accept what was established up till now. Intuitively we agree that cars, buses and motorcycles are vehicles, which means that they are forbidden from entering the park. That in turn means that any object, which is a car, a bus or a motorcycle is forbidden from entering the park and in case it enters the park the rule that forbids vehicles from entering the park is being violated. We used plain and clear cases to establish the core meaning of the open textured concept of a vehicle. This allows us to move forward and apply the method on a case, which is in Hart's words at the borderline (Hart 1994, 127). Let us decide if an inline skater violates the rule ad (i) by entering the park on his inline skates. Hart maintains that in this case the decision-making authority would have discretion to arrive at the conclusion, which it considers reasonable. This means that the decision-making authority could theoretically arrive at the conclusion that the rule is indeed violated as well as at the conclusion that the rule is not violated in this case – whichever it considers more reasonable. Let us suppose that the goal of the rule is to promote serenity in the park. In the considered case the inline skater who entered the park behaves very noisy and clearly disturbs serenity in the park. There is no doubt that he interferes with the goal of the rule. Therefore, it may seem reasonable to arrive at the conclusion that he violates the rule and impose a sanction for that violation (provided there is one). From the previous work we know that we must first establish that inline skater i is a vehicle.

Premise 1': $\forall_X inlineSkater(X) \rightarrow vehicle(X)$
Premise 2': $inlineSkater(i)$

Conclusion 1': $vehicle(i)$

After that we must show that i is forbidden from entering the park.

Premise 3': $\forall_X vehicle(X) \rightarrow forbidden(X)$
Premise 4': $vehicle(i)$

Conclusion 2': $forbidden(i)$

Finally, it remains to infer that i violated the rule ad (i).

Premise 3': $\forall_X forbidden(X) \wedge entered(X) \rightarrow violated(X)$
Premise 4': $forbidden(i)$
Premise 5': $entered(i)$

Conclusion 3': $violated(i)$

Conclusion 3' is logically valid and it was reached because we accepted that inline skater is sufficiently similar to car, bus and motorcycle so that we can consider him a vehicle.

Now, let us reconsider the case. The inline skater does not behave noisily. In fact, he behaves in a way which could by no means interfere with the goal of keeping serenity in the park. Therefore, it may seem reasonable not to use the rule ad (i) to prevent him from entering the park. This can be done if we can show that at least one of the premises that we require for our rule to fire is not true. It should not be difficult to see that the only way how we can prevent the rule from firing is by arriving at the conclusion that inline skater is not a vehicle. Otherwise, we would have to change or dismiss the rule.

Premise 1": $\forall_X inlineSkater(X) \rightarrow \neg vehicle(X)$
Premise 2": $inlineSkater(i)$

Conclusion 1": $\neg vehicle(i)$

From conclusion 1" we already know that we cannot establish that inline skater is a vehicle. Therefore, at least one of the premises necessary for the rule to fire is not true. Both conclusion 3' and conclusion 3" were reached properly and in lights of their respective circumstances they both seem reasonable. The question that immediately appears is if it is, indeed, the case that due to the open texture in the concept of "vehicle" a decision-making authority has discretion to decide each time whichever way seems reasonable. This view is certainly correct if each of the case is treated separately. However, when considered together, for example one preceding the other, much more complexity is involved. Of course, within one legal system individual cases must be considered in the light of the similar cases that were decided before them.

Let us assume that the first case precedes the second. Altogether, there are four different possible outcomes:

1. First case would be decided in a way that the rule was violated while the second one in a way that it was not violated.

2. Both cases would be decided in a way that the rule was violated.
3. Both cases would be decided in a way that the rule was not violated.
4. First case would be decided in a way that the rule was not violated while the second one in a way that it was violated.

If we would be free to pick whichever of the above we should probably opt for ad 1. However, there is one issue surrounding ad 1 as well as ad 4. Let us get back to premises 1' and 1''. The first one is true in the first case while the second one is true in the second case. Logically, it is possible to accept them both at the same time. Intuitively, the decision-making authority would have absolute discretion to decide if the inline skater violated the rule when entering the park. In each case the decision could go either way. In this way the rule can be used very effectively in promoting the goal of keeping serenity in the park. However, it would be very difficult (if at all possible) for anyone to hold any legitimate expectations related to inline skaters violating the rule by entering the park.

Difficulties in formation of legitimate expectations have very damaging effect within the legal system. In Sect. 6.3 we explained that there could be subtle forms of coin-flipping in legal decision-making that are more difficult to recognize. This is precisely one of them. It appears when open texture is misunderstood in a way that in certain cases it gives decision-making authority total freedom to decide a case that appears to be borderline. And, as was shown in Sect. 6.3, this may have far reaching consequences outgrowing breaches of law and dismissal of legitimate claims in individual cases.

Promotion of legal certainty directly translates to the capability of law to perform its function (as described in Sect. 6.3) properly. In consequence, it is difficult to imagine any situation in which it would seem advisable to sacrifice this value in order to achieve better fit between decisions in individual cases and goals of the rules to which they relate. For this reason, we maintain that outcomes ad 2 and ad 3 are to be preferred in most of the cases over outcomes ad 1 and ad 4. This has very serious implications with respect to the discretion of the decision-making authority, which is based on open-texture. When deciding the first borderline case of its kind the authority must also take into consideration future cases of that kind which may be reasonably expected to appear. Of course, this pertains exclusively to that part of discretion, which stems from the open texture of concepts that are involved in the current case. Although, these could have not been expected by the legislator they could be foreseen by the decision-making authority on the grounds of the current case.

6.5 Implications for Legislation

Our analysis shows that a rule that was enacted by a legislator to promote serenity in the park challenges a decision-making authority to strike a proper balance between legal certainty and promotion of the goal for which the rule was adopted at the first place. Initial responsibility to avoid creation of the above mentioned trade-off is with the lawmaker. A legislator aiming to secure serenity in the park should be aware of the above described constraints placed on the decision-making authority. In the example given above, the legislator should be aware that the rule in consideration would allow the decision-making authority to exercise discretion with respect to what is and what is not a vehicle for the purpose of the rule. This could lead the legislator to an understanding that the decision-making authority would be able to use the rule to prohibit certain kinds of objects from entering the park. However, distinguishing vehicles from non-vehicles can be done solely on the basis of the objects resembling other objects in the property of being a vehicle. The decision-making authority cannot evaluate each object directly on the basis of interfering with the goal of the rule.

There may be certain objects that could be considered both vehicles and non-vehicles. At the same time there may be no reason to prohibit these objects from entering the park in general as only a small portion of them interferes with the goal of the rule. If such objects exist the rule may be very harmful for the legal system as a whole. The decision making authority is forced to choose between being unreasonably restrictive, unpredictable or incapable of using the rule to promote the goal it pursues. Clearly, none of those outcomes is desirable.

This brings us to the two fundamental qualities we believe each rule must both have in order to be considered beneficial for the legal system:

1. It must be capable of promoting the goal for pursuance of which it was enacted.
2. It must allow formation of universally accepted legitimate expectations.

Legislators can use techniques of logical analysis of natural language to assess the rule with respect to those qualities.

6.6 Conclusion

In this chapter, we first presented brief overview of the concept of open texture in law in its original sense as it was presented by Hart (1994, 124–135). Following Hart we explained that open texture is necessary for any legal system to function. On the other hand, if it is not handled carefully its adverse effect on legal certainty can be significant far beyond what can be accepted. Niklas Luhmann claims that the main function of law subsists in securing certain expectations of individuals as stable over time (Luhmann 2008, 147–148) creating firm link between legal certainty and overall functioning of any legal system. If open texture is misunderstood in a way that in certain cases it gives a judge total freedom to decide a case that appears to be unclear, the legislator may fundamentally misunderstood its position in enacting new rules. By careful analysis of a given expression logical analysis of natural language attempts to uncover its exact meaning and represents it within the framework of established notation. We showed that logical analysis of natural language can be used as a powerful tool to tame open texture. Its techniques can clearly guide the legislator as regards the exact contours of the discretion the decision-making authority would have as an effect of open-texture. In effect the legislator can better anticipate the position of the decision-making authority and provide it with rules that would not require decisions cluttering legal system with uncertainty.

References

Bentham, Jeremy, ed. H.L.A. Hart, 1970. *Of laws in general*. London: Athlone Press.

Bix, Brian. 1991. Herbert L.A. Hart and the "open texture" of language. *Law and Philosophy*. Retrieved from http://www.springerlink.com/index/rqg480g8674nrpq1.pdf

Bix, Brian. 1993. *Law, language, and legal determinacy*. New York: Oxford University Press.

Duži, Marie, Bjoern Jespersen, and Pavel Materna. 2010. *Procedural semantics for hyper-intensional logic. Foundations and applications of transparent intensional logic*. Dordrecht/Heidelberg/London/New York: Springer.

Endicott, Timothy. 2000. *Vagueness in the law*. Oxford/New York: Oxford University Press.

Endicott, Timothy. 2014. Law and language. In *The Stanford encyclopedia of philosophy*. Retrieved from http://plato.stanford.edu/archives/spr2014/entries/law-language/.

Hart, Herbert. 1994. *The concept of law*, 2nd ed. Oxford/New York: Clarendon Press.

Luhmann, Niklas. 2008. *Law as a social system*. Oxford/New York: Oxford University Press.

Waismann, Friedrich. 1951. Verifiability, XIX(1945). Retrieved from http://philpapers.org/rec/WAIV.

Chapter 7
The Theories of Statutory Construction and Legislative Process in American Jurisprudence

Linda D. Jellum

Abstract This chapter will introduce the building blocks underlying statutory interpretation in American jurisprudence: the sources of evidence American judges use to find the meaning of statutory language and the theories of interpretation American judges use when approaching an interpretation question. While at first glance this chapter may seem to be one designed for academics and theorists who argue about which theory is best, it is also designed for lawyers. Grasping the building blocks of statutory interpretation is essential for anyone wishing to make statutory arguments in an American court. Theory matters, but it matters in unusual ways. The sources and theories enable lawyers to "talk the talk", so to speak. Lawyers do not win cases simply because they argue text to a textualist judge or purpose to a purposivist judge, but a textualist judge will listen more carefully to textual arguments, while a purposivist judge will want to know the statutory purpose. Finally, theory impacts the legislative process, from drafting to enactment; thus, this chapter will examine the role legislative history has had both now and in the past.

Keywords Statutory interpretation • Statutory construction • Textualism • Purposivism • Intentionalism

---

I would like to thank Eka Lomtatidze for her thoughtful comments, James Walsh for his excellent research assistance, and Dianna Lee for her helpful editing suggestions. Information in this chapter appeared originally in Jellum, 2013. Used, as revised, with the permission of Carolina Academic Press.

L.D. Jellum (✉)
Mercer University School of Law, Macon, GA, USA
e-mail: Jellum_l@law.mercer.edu

M. Araszkiewicz, K. Płeszka (eds.), *Logic in the Theory and Practice of Lawmaking*, Legisprudence Library 2, DOI 10.1007/978-3-319-19575-9_7

7.1 Introduction

Statutory interpretation is the process of determining the meaning of a legislative act called a statute. The appropriate way to interpret a statute in American jurisprudence is far from settled. Indeed, statutory interpretation has become the focus of scholarly debate as legal experts disagree about the importance to be placed on the ordinary meaning of the text, the legislative history surrounding enactment, and the purpose of the statute. United States Supreme Court Justice Antonin Scalia can be credited for the reemergence of this controversy; he adheres to a strict approach to interpretation that ignores legislative history and unexpressed purpose. He has been recognized for returning judicial focus to the text of a statute.

Interpreting a statute involves more than simply reading its words. Depending on the interpreter, the process of interpretation includes finding the legislative intent, the statutory purpose, the ordinary meaning of the words, or perhaps a combination of some or all of these. This chapter will introduce the process of statutory interpretation in the United States. It includes a discussion of the sources of evidence American judges use to find the meaning of words in a statute and the theories of interpretation judges use when approaching interpretation questions. While at first glance this topic may seem to be one designed for academics and theorists, it is also useful for lawyers and judges, as grasping the foundation of statutory interpretation is essential for anyone wishing to understand and argue about statutory language.

Theory and sources matter, but they matter in unusual ways. They enable lawyers and judges to "talk the talk", so to speak. In one sense, learning the law involves learning a new language; however, the process is more confusing because some words are entirely new (e.g., summary judgment), while others are familiar from common language, but have a different meaning in the law (e.g., assault or property). Like all languages, the law has its own grammatical rules as well (e.g., "shall" means mandatory, while "may" means permissive). These sources and theories are a part of this language; they provide order and structure to statutory interpretation arguments and reasoning. Simply put, theory impacts every aspect of statutory life from the enactment process to judicial application.

Statutory interpretation is an art, not a science; a language, not a set of rules. Legislatures do not draft perfectly; ambiguity, vagueness, omissions, and mistakes are all common elements in the final product. Knowing how to interpret statutes in light of these imperfections is critical, because most of the work lawyers do today centers on legislative enactments, whether international, federal, state, or local. While interpreting statutes is not an exact science, there are canons, or rules of thumb, that guide interpretation. Today's lawyers simply cannot practice law without knowing the art of statutory interpretation. Because statutes and regulations have proliferated, reading and understanding statutes is a basic legal skill.

7.2 Common Law v. Civil Law

While the United States, England, and Australia, for example, have common law systems, common law is not the only, or even most common, legal system. There are other legal systems as well, including Islamic Law, Socialist Law, and Civil Law. Indeed, most European Union countries, Brazil, China, Japan, Mexico, Russia, Switzerland, Turkey, Quebec, Georgia, and Louisiana, among others, have adopted "civil" or "civilian" law, making it the most common legal system in the world.

The civil law and common law systems developed quite differently. In a civil law system, principles and rules of law are embodied in legislative enactments. In contrast, in a common law system, principles and rules of law are embodied in case law rather than, or in addition to, legislative enactments. In early common law jurisdictions, statutes were uncommon and thus were viewed with suspicion. In England, for example, the King and Parliament ran the country and only rarely enacted statutes to modify judge – made common law. Similarly, in early American jurisprudence, statutes were uncommon; those statutes that did exist were private (meaning they applied only to specific individuals) not public (meaning they would have applied to all individuals). Legislators, who worked primarily part–time, were considered to be uneducated, unsophisticated, and vulnerable to political pressures. It was during this time, when judges viewed statutes with hostility and suspicion, that the judiciary developed the canon that statutes in derogation of the common law should be strictly construed. Also, a holdover American custom from these early days is that a bill must be read three times in the legislature before it is enacted to ensure that any representatives who are illiterate know what they are enacting.

Against this backdrop, legal disputes arose, but because it was rare for a statute to resolve a controversy, judges had to look elsewhere for guidance; they looked to other cases and general principles and then explained their holding. The common law developed as judges decided cases in this piecemeal fashion. These cases became judicial precedents, which were then synthesized into legal doctrines (or norms), such as the common law tort of assault. While some of these legal doctrines were eventually codified, even when codified they retained the echo of their judicial development. Thus, in a common law system judicial opinions are controlling and play a strong role, even in statutory interpretation.

7.3 Common Law v. Statutory Interpretation

Statutory interpretation differs greatly from common law analysis. They differ, in part, because the creation of statutes is so different from the creation of case law and, in part, because the reasoning for the enactment of the statute is mostly absent. Legislatures do not always include reasons for enacting laws. Rather, statutes are the product of a time – consuming, political, and often controversial legislative process that balances competing interests. While process is never relevant to common law interpretation, process is often relevant to statutory interpretation.

American lawyers who practiced in the 1800s would have spent the majority of their time reading and analyzing cases. For example, if a client wanted to know whether he could sue his neighbor for cutting down a tree located on the property border, the lawyer would study a number of cases to understand the parameters of the law. Common law reasoning involves inductive forms of reasoning, both generalization and analogy. By generalizing, common law lawyers reason from particular cases to identify case law legal principles. Let's look at a simple example. Assume that a lawyer is trying to determine whether a client's contract is void. After reading a number of cases, the lawyer notes that in case one, the court held that a contract with a vague term was void; in case two, the court held that a contract with a vague term was void; and in case three the court held that a contract with a vague term was void. Thus, the lawyer might conclude, or generalize, that all contracts with vague terms are void. Thus, in this form of reasoning, a lawyer examines the facts, reasoning, and holdings of prior cases to identify the normative principle of law to apply to the facts of a client's case.

By analogizing, common law lawyers use previous cases to identify similarities and dissimilarities and then encourage a court to rule in the same way. Let's look at a simple example. Assume the same lawyer is still trying to determine whether the client's contract is void. After reading the same cases above, the lawyer notes that case one involved vague term A, fact B, and fact C. Case two involved vague term A1, fact C, and fact D. In both cases, the court held that the contracts were void. The lawyer's case involves vague term A2 and fact C; hence, the lawyer would argue that the contract in the lawyer's case is void because it is similar to the two prior cases and the holding should be the same. Thus, in this form of reasoning, a lawyer analyzes the facts, reasoning, and holdings of prior cases and compares the facts of those cases to the facts of a client's case.

Beginning in the late nineteenth century, however, legislation's role began to change as legislatures became more prolific and legislation became more generally applicable. As legislation flourished, statutes began to abrogate common law. This evolution intensified during the New Deal era when the United States Congress began to solve social and economic problems using legislation. Additionally, as legislators became more skilled at their jobs, distrust of legislators started to fade. By the mid–twentieth century, the United States Supreme Court regularly heard cases involving statutes, and statutory interpretation consequently became an increasingly important legal skill. Initially, statutes were written broadly, allowing for judicial contouring.

Today, legislation in the United States is pervasive and much more detailed. For example, let's compare the Sherman Act, which was enacted in 1890, with the Patient Protection and Affordable Care Act (known pejoratively as "Obamacare" or the "Health Care Act"), which was enacted in 2010. The Sherman Act is a comprehensive and expansive act regulating United States federal antitrust activity, and yet the entire Act fits onto a single page. Congress left significant room for judicial development. In contrast, the Affordable Care Act spans 906 pages. Congress left little room for judicial development.[1]

If the client concerned about his neighbor's tree came to a lawyer's office today, the lawyer would not start with case law. Rather, the lawyer would check first to see if there was a local, state, or federal statute (or regulation) addressing the issue. Assuming a statute or regulation applied, the lawyer would read it. But that would not be the end of the process, for even if a statute appears clear, it may not be. Reading a statute's text is only the first step to understanding what that statute means. Because language is inherently ambiguous (for example, is "blue" a state of being or a color? Is "dust" a verb or noun?), interpreting statutes is more complex than it would seem.

7.4 Separation of Powers and Statutory Interpretation

Separation of powers is central to statutory interpretation. Separation of powers refers to the allocation of power and function among the branches of the government; it is the concept that the functions of a government should be split between two or more independent groups so that no one branch holds too much power. No one branch should be more powerful than any other. The theory of statutory interpretation a judge adopts is based, in large part, on that judge's view of the proper power distribution of the judiciary and the legislature–in other words, on that judge's view of separation of powers. For this reason, separation of powers plays a strong supporting role in interpretation, despite the fact that standing alone, it does not directly elucidate the meaning of words in a statute.

In the United States (and many other countries), governmental power is divided among the legislative, executive, and judicial branches. Pursuant to the United States Constitution, Congress makes laws, the executive enforces those laws, and the judiciary interprets them.[2]

Yet these well–ordered categories are far from exact. The core legislative function is to make law, yet the judiciary also makes law by creating common law and by interpreting statutes. The dividing line between making law and interpreting law is ill–defined. To illustrate, one might ask whether implying a cause of action in a statute is "making" or "interpreting" law.[3] Similarly, when judges

---

[1]McNally v. United States, 483 U.S. 350, 372–73 (1987) (Stevens, J., dissenting) ("Statutes like the Sherman Act, the civil rights legislation, and the mail fraud statute were written in broad general language on the understanding that the courts would have wide latitude in construing them to achieve the remedial purposes that Congress had identified. The wide open spaces in statutes such as these are most appropriately interpreted as implicit delegations of authority to the courts to fill in the gaps in the common–law tradition of case–by–case adjudication.").

[2]U.S. Const. art. I, §1; U.S. Const. art. II, §1; U.S. Const. art. III, §1.

[3]In *Alexander v. Sandoval*, 532 U.S. 275 (2001), the U.S. Supreme Court held that there was no private cause of action to enforce disparate–impact regulations promulgated under Title VI of the

interpret statutes, judges make policy choices by filling statutory gaps, by resolving statutory ambiguity, and by identifying statutory boundaries. Indeed, every statutory interpretation case requires a judge to make a policy choice by adopting one statutory meaning and thereby rejecting at least one other meaning. Further, this choice will affect future cases because of *stare decisis*–the concept that similar cases should be decided similarly. Thus, judges do not simply interpret law; judges act in concert with the legislature to develop law; while legislatures make law, judges inevitably assist them in the process.[4] It "is emphatically the province and duty of the judicial department to say what the law is."[5]

The proper relationship between the legislature and judiciary in this area is at the heart of the debate about the appropriate theory. There is a theoretical continuum, if you will. At one end of this continuum is the view that only the enacted text of a statute is relevant to interpretation. This view places the role of the legislature above that of the judiciary. At the other end of the spectrum is the view that unexpressed statutory purpose is the most relevant. This view places the role of the judiciary above that of the legislature. Neither view is entirely accurate; the truth lies somewhere in the middle.

7.5 The Art of Statutory Interpretation

Because judges approach statutory interpretation issues in different ways, no one can definitively predict how a judge will interpret a statute. But knowing how to make statutory arguments, how to speak this new language, and how to anticipate the way statutes are likely to be interpreted is essential to the practice of law.

In its most basic form, statutory interpretation is the art of discerning the intent of the enacting legislature, for it is the enacting legislature that has the authority to make law, Jellum (2013, 22). "[L]egislation is an act of communication to be understood on the simple model of speaker and audience, so that the commanding question in legislative interpretation is what a particular speaker or group "'meant'

Civil Rights Act of 1964. *Id.* at 285. Justice Scalia, writing for the majority, said: "We therefore begin (and find that we can end) our search for Congress's intent with the text and structure of Title VI." *Id.* at 288. In other words, even though the statute at issue had been enacted during a time when the Court easily implied private rights of action, even though the enacting legislature might thus have anticipated that the Court would imply a cause of action in this statute, and even though implied rights are by their very nature non–explicit, Justice Scalia used a textualist approach to determine whether Congress intended the act in question to allow private causes of action. In essence, Justice Scalia obliterated the concept of implied private causes of action. In his dissent, Justice Stevens noted: "[T]oday's decision is the unconscious product of the majority's profound distaste for implied causes of action rather than an attempt to discern the intent of the Congress that enacted Title VI of the Civil Rights Act of 1964." *Id.* at 317 (Stevens, J., dissenting).

[4]For a more detailed discussion of this topic, see Jellum (2009).

[5]Marbury v. Madison, 5 U.S. (1 Cranch) 137, 177 (1803).

in some canonical act of utterance." (Dworkin 1986, 348). This particular "speaker or group" is the enacting legislature. Theoretically then, judges should interpret statutes as the enacting legislature intended. But discerning an enacting legislature's intent is extremely difficult; how does one discern the intent of a group of individuals all having potentially different goals? One cannot simply contact the legislators after the fact and ask them what they intended to accomplish. Even if they were still alive, even if they remembered having a specific intent on the issue before the court, and even if they remembered accurately, such after–the–fact rationalizations are generally not considered valid evidence of the intent of the legislature as a whole.

Realistically, the idea that there is one, unified "meeting of the minds" is nonsense. While members of the legislature may share the goal of passing a bill to address a particular problem, rarely will all members have the same reason for voting in favor of a bill or even the same expectations regarding the bill's effects. Rather, bills are the result of committee work and political compromise. A bill "emerges from the hubbub of legislative struggle, from the drafts of beginning lawyers, from the work of lobbyists who are casual about clarity but forceful about policy, from the chaos of adjournment deadlines." (Davies 2007, 307–08). Because of this chaotic enactment process, bills are filled with ambiguity, absurdity, lack of clarity, obscurity, mistakes, and omissions. Legislators rarely intend to be ambiguous, absurd, unclear, obscure, mistaken, or incomplete, but they often are.

Because of the difficulty of discerning legislative intent, judges have adopted a number of ways to resolve statutory interpretation issues. Some judges focus on the words of the text, believing that by giving words their ordinary, public meaning, the judge will best further the legislative agenda. Other judges focus on the stated or unstated purpose of the bill, believing that by furthering that purpose, they will best further the legislative agenda. And yet other judges focus on the piecemeal nature of the legislative process, believing that by comparing various versions of the bill and the legislators' statements accompanying the bill's enactment, they will best further the legislative agenda. Legal scholars have named these approaches the "theories of interpretation" and have exhaustively argued about which approach best interprets statutes. Practicing lawyers are mostly oblivious to the differences in the theories and so approach interpretation questions based on the theory that is most intuitive to them. Moreover, different theories predominate in different countries. For example, theories based on the text are paramount in England and many civil law countries.

Perhaps more than in any other area of law, understanding theory is critical to understanding statutory interpretation because theory drives every aspect of statutory interpretation. A judge's theory of interpretation determines what information a judge will consider when searching for a statute's meaning. For example, some judges will not look at the statute's legislative history or expressed purpose for meaning unless the text of the statute is unclear or absurd. To argue to one of these judges that the legislative history of the statute supports your client's position, you must first explain why it is necessary to go beyond the text to look for meaning. In other words, you need to learn to "talk the talk" of statutory interpretation.

7.6 The Evidentiary Sources of Meaning

The sources of statutory interpretation and the theories of statutory interpretation are interrelated but different. The theories are based on the relevance of the three sources of information, or evidence, judges consider in construing statutory language: (1) intrinsic sources of evidence, (2) extrinsic sources of evidence, and (3) policy–based sources of evidence.

Intrinsic sources are materials that are part of the official act being interpreted. The first step in the interpretation process for all judges is always "Read the statute. Read the Statute. Read the Statute." (Kernochan 1976, 338). Clearly, the words of the statute at issue are the most important intrinsic source. But the words alone are not the only intrinsic source a judge consults to discern meaning. Other intrinsic sources, such as the grammar and punctuation of the statute; the components of the act, including purpose and findings clauses, titles, and definition sections; and the linguistic canons of statutory construction may also be important to interpretation. All of these are intrinsic sources of meaning.

A second category of sources that judges may consider to discern meaning is the extrinsic sources–materials outside of the official act but within the legislative process that created the act. The following are all examples of extrinsic sources and the canons related to them: (1) legislative history, which includes the statements made during the enactment process; (2) legislative acquiescence, the canon that legislative silence in response to a judicial interpretation of a statute means legislative agreement with that judicial interpretation; (3) the borrowed–statute canon, the presumption that a legislature, by borrowing another state's statute, intended to adopt the other state's judicial opinions regarding that statute in effect at the time; and (4) the canon of deference to agency interpretations, by which the judiciary presumes that the legislature meant to defer to interpretations agencies give to ambiguous statutes.

These sources are all related at some level to the enactment process. The use of some of these sources–such as deference to agency interpretations–is relatively non–controversial. The use of others–such as reference to legislative history–is highly controversial. Historically in the United States, intrinsic sources were regularly used to aid interpretation, while extrinsic sources were used more sparingly. After the New Deal era (1933–1936), this historical custom relaxed, and judges turned to extrinsic sources, especially legislative history, more readily. Today, as a result of the reemergence of textualism, consideration of extrinsic sources has once again become controversial.

Third, and finally, are policy–based sources. These sources are separate from both the statutory act and the legislative process, and they are unique to each country. In the United States, policy–based sources reflect important social and legal choices derived from the U.S. Constitution, common law, or prudence. The following are examples of policy–based sources and the canons that relate to them: (1) the constitutional avoidance doctrine, which directs that if two reasonable or fair interpretations exist, one of which raises constitutional issues, the other interpretation should control; (2) the rule of lenity, which states that in cases involving a penal component, if two reasonable interpretations exist, the court should adopt the less penal interpretation; (3) the remedial and derogation canons, which require that statutes in derogation of the common law be strictly construed, while remedial statutes be broadly construed; and (4) the clear statement rules, which are presumptions that in some situations, such as cases raising federalism concerns, Congress would not intentionally alter the status quo absent a clear statement to that effect.

In the United States, reliance on policy–based sources has come in and out of vogue. For example, the rule of lenity, which arises from the U.S. Constitution's Due Process requirement that individuals receive adequate notice of conduct that has been penalized,[6] has been relegated to a rule of last resort with America's current focus on penalizing criminals. Some state's legislatures, such as California's, attempted to abolish the rule of lenity by statute[7]; however, because the rule of lenity is derived, in part, from federal constitutional procedural due process concerns, these state legislatures had limited success. Typically, courts continue to apply the rule of lenity in these states, just less liberally.[8]

While it would be nice if the above categories were consistently defined in American judicial opinions and academic circles, they are not. What one person calls a policy–based source, another might identify as an extrinsic source. Understanding exactly which category a source falls within is less important than understanding (1) that there is a breadth of informational sources available to judges, and (2) that some judges are more willing to look beyond intrinsic sources for meaning than other judges. What sources a judge will consider depends on that judge's theory of, or approach to, statutory interpretation.

7.7 The Theories of Interpretation

> Do not expect anybody's theory of statutory interpretation ... to be an accurate statement of what courts actually do with statutes. The hard truth of the matter is that American courts have no intelligible, generally accepted, and consistently applied theory of statutory interpretation (Eskridge and Frickey 1994, 1169).

---

[6]United States v. Gonzalez, 407 F.3d 118, 125 (2d Cir. 2005) ("[I]ndividuals should not languish in prison unless the legislature has clearly articulated precisely what conduct constitutes a crime.").

[7]California's statute provides, "The rule of the common law, that penal statutes are to be strictly construed, has no application to this Code." Cal. Penal Code §4 (West 2013).

[8]E.g., People v. Superior Court, 926 P.2d 1042, 1056 (Cal. 1996) (stating, "while ... [the rule of lenity] has been abrogated ... it is also true that the defendant is entitled to the benefit of every reasonable doubt, whether it arises out of a question of fact, or as to the true interpretation of words or the construction of language used in a statute.") (citations omitted).

This famous quote is still accurate today even though it is almost 50 years old. Even though there is no generally accepted and consistently applied theory of statutory interpretation, lawyers need to understand the various competing theories. Understanding theory is important because lawyers need a way to approach statutes to determine, among other things, whether to rely more heavily on the text and linguistic canons, or on other, extra–textual sources of meaning; whether to examine legislative history and if so, which history; whether to try to discern unexpressed purpose; and how to argue each of these sources in court.

The theories of, or approaches to, statutory interpretation vary in their emphasis on the sources identified above. Adherents of the different approaches differ in what they believe best shows the intent of the enacting legislature and, thus, the meaning of the statute. They also differ about what role the courts and legislature should play in resolving statutory ambiguity. In other words, they disagree about the role of separation of powers. At bottom, adherents of the approaches differ in their willingness to consider sources other than statutory text. For example, textualists believe that the text of the statute is central, while purposivists believe that the purpose of the statute is equally, if not at times more, important.

Lawyers can and do blend these approaches for a variety of reasons. A lawyer may generally prefer one approach, but may find that for a specific case, or even a specific issue, that the preferred approach does not work. Hence, that lawyer may adopt a different approach or meld a variety of approaches. Within the judicial system, one judge, who may approach statutory interpretation in one way, may want another judge, who may approach statutory interpretation differently, to join his or her decision; hence, appellate opinions rarely exemplify consistency in this area. Thus, the approaches that are described below are neither exclusive nor exhaustive.

Finally, all of the approaches have failings. Perhaps because of the imperfections, the preferred approach has varied with time and across jurisdictions. An approach that dominated during one era often falls out of favor in the next. For example, very early in Anglo–American jurisprudence, judges preferred to look at the purpose of the statute; today, the text has gained currency. Debate over the appropriate approach has raged; indeed, the battle over the appropriate approach has left the pages of academic law journals and become center stage in judicial opinions and in legislative debates. For example, in *State v. Courchesne*,[9] the Connecticut Supreme Court examined the various approaches and selected purposivism, an approach that focuses on the purpose of the statute. The Connecticut legislature disagreed, however, and, in a direct rebuke to the judges deciding that case, passed a statute requiring its courts to use textualism. Below, the more prevalent approaches are explained in some detail, beginning with textualism.

[9] 816 A.2d 562, 587 (Conn. 2003).

7.7.1 Textualism

As noted earlier, a judge's view of separation of powers affects interpretation. Textualists believe that a judge's role is to be faithful to the U.S. Constitution by protecting the power distribution identified within that document: The legislature has the power to enact laws, while the judiciary has the power to interpret laws. For enactment of statutes, the U.S. Constitution requires a specific process: bicameral passage and presentment to the executive. Only the statutory text goes through this process; thus, textualists believe that looking beyond the enacted text raises constitutional concerns. They "would hold Congress to the words it used.... [T]o do otherwise would permit Congress to legislate without completing the required process for enactment of legislation." (Chomsky 2000, 951). Moreover, textualists believe that the text best shows the compromises reached during the enactment process.

Textualism is a theory under which its adherents, textualists, look for the public meaning of the words used in the statute as of the time the statute was drafted rather than look for the legislature's intent. Textualists look for meaning in a relatively linear fashion, turning from one source to another in hierarchical order until an answer is found. Of all the theorists, textualists examine the fewest and the most concrete sources, focusing primarily on intrinsic sources, especially the text and its relationship to the U.S. Code as a whole.

Textualism is sometimes called the "plain meaning" theory of interpretation because textualism is based on the "plain meaning" canon of interpretation. The plain meaning canon instructs that the ordinary, or plain, meaning of the words of a statute should control interpretation. The plain meaning canon nicely matches textualists' interpretative goal of discerning the public meaning of the statute. Specifically, textualists presume that a legislature used words, grammar, and punctuation to communicate this meaning. Thus, textualists will look at the text of the statute at issue (including grammar and punctuation), the statute in its context as being part of an act, the linguistic canons, and the text of other statutes (the statute in its entire legal context). Textualists are not completely text focused; they are willing to use contemporaneous dictionaries and the linguistic canons of construction–canons explaining how a native speaker understands words–to find the ordinary meaning of the language at issue. But textualists generally refuse to look at other non–text sources unless the language of the statute continues to be ambiguous, meaning it has more than one reasonable interpretation, or absurd, meaning that the legislature could not have intended the plain meaning. In other words, textualists look beyond intrinsic sources for meaning only when intrinsic sources fail to resolve the meaning of the language definitively.

Textualism comes in gradations. While all textualists, indeed all theorists, rely foremost on the text of a statute to discern meaning, the different forms of textualism differ in the willingness of their adherents to consider some of the non–intrinsic sources. For example, there are the "soft plain meaning" theorists–those who view the text as the primary, but not the exclusive, evidence of meaning. Soft plain meaning theorists are willing to consider legislative history and context in most cases. These theorists do not need a finding of ambiguity or absurdity to consider extra–textual evidence. Soft plain meaning is the oldest form of textualism, one that views the text as the central, but not as the solitary source of meaning.[10]

Next are the moderate textualists, for whom the plain meaning canon controls. When the meaning of the statutory text is clear from the text alone, interpretation is complete; no other sources are consulted.[11] When, however, the meaning is ambiguous[12] absurd,[13] or contains a scrivener's error,[14] moderate textualists will consider other, intrinsic sources and non–intrinsic sources of meaning, including legislative history. Most textualists today are moderate textualists.[15]

---

[10]See, e.g., *State v. Grunke*, 752 N.W.2d 769, 775 (Wis. 2008) ("If the words chosen for the statute exhibit a plain, clear statutory meaning, without ambiguity, the statute is applied according to the plain meaning of the statutory terms. However, if a statute is capable of being understood by reasonably well–informed persons in two or more senses[,] then the statute is ambiguous, and we may consult extrinsic sources to discern its meaning. While extrinsic sources are usually not consulted if the statutory language bears a plain meaning, we nevertheless may consult extrinsic sources to confirm or verify a plain–meaning interpretation.") (internal quotation marks omitted).

[11]Textualism is similar to clara non sunt interpretanda (meaning transparent text requires no interpretation).

[12]Jurisprudentially, ambiguity is not consistently defined across jurisdictions. One common articulation of ambiguity is that statutory language is "ambiguous if it is capable of being understood by reasonably well–informed persons in two or more senses." State ex rel Kalal, 681 N.W.2d 110, 124 (Wis. 2004). Although the "reasonable people disagree" standard is oft–articulated, it is inaccurate. Ambiguity more likely "means that there is more than one equally plausible meaning." Fla. Dep't of Revenue v. Piccadilly Cafeterias, Inc., 554 U.S. 33, 41 (2008) (stating that although both sides presented "credible" interpretations, there was no ambiguity because "two readings of the language that Congress chose [were] not equally plausible. . . ."); Mayor of Lansing v. Michigan Pub. Serv. Comm'n., 680 N.W.2d 840, 847 (Mich. 2004); (stating that "a provision of the law is ambiguous only if it irreconcilably conflicts with another provision, or when it is equally susceptible to more than a single meaning.").

[13]The absurdity doctrine was first introduced in 1892 in the famous case *Church of the Holy Trinity v. United States*, 143 U.S. 457 (1892). This exception allows judges to look beyond the ordinary meaning of the text to extra–textual sources when the statute would be absurd if interpreted as written. If, after reviewing the extra–textual evidence, a judge determines that the legislature did intend the absurd result, then that intention should control. But if, after reviewing the extra–textual evidence, the judge determines that the absurdity was not intended, then the absurdity exception gives the judge the option to ignore the ordinary meaning. *See, e.g.*, Green v. Bock Laundry Machine Co, 490 U.S. 504, 509 (1989) (rejecting the ordinary meaning of the word "defendant" in Rule 609(a) (1) of the Federal Rules of Evidence as absurd).

[14]The scrivener's error exception to the plain meaning rule allows judges to correct obvious clerical or typographical errors. *See, e.g.*, U.S. Nat'l Bank of Or. v. Indep. Ins. Agents of Am., Inc., 508 U.S. 439, 462 (1993).

[15]*See, e.g.*, Fla. Dep't of Highway Safety & Motor Vehicles v. Hernandez, 74 So. 3d 1070, 1074–75 (Fla. 2011) ("When the statute is clear and unambiguous, courts will not look behind the statute's plain language for legislative intent or resort to rules of statutory construction to ascertain intent. In such instance, the statute's plain and ordinary meaning must control, unless this leads to an unreasonable result or a result clearly contrary to legislative intent. However, if the statutory intent

Moderate textualism is appealing, in part, because of its inherent simplicity: Textualists simply examine the text with a dictionary in hand and then finish interpreting. Textualists turn to other sources only when absolutely required. But moderate textualism may favor simplicity over accuracy. One problem with the plain meaning canon is that language that seems clear to one person can be ambiguous or even mean something completely different to another person. For example, does "defendant" include only criminal defendants or all defendants?[16] Does "labor" include intellectual labor or only physical labor?[17] Does "using a firearm" include the act of bartering a gun for drugs?[18]

While textual context often resolves which particular meaning the legislature intended, litigation arises precisely because litigants and their lawyers disagree about a statute's meaning. Theoretically, the plain meaning canon should never resolve an issue in any litigated case involving statutory interpretation unless one party is being unreasonable. If the meaning were that clear, the litigants would not be in court, paying money to attorneys to litigate meaning.

Moreover, the meaning of words can vary with context and audience. For example, the word "assault" might mean one thing in a statute aimed at the general public but mean something completely different in a statute aimed at lawyers.[19] Similarly, the word "tomato" may mean one thing to someone making a salad and another thing to a botanist or linguist.[20] In addition, the linguistic capability of readers (including judges) may affect meaning. To illustrate, some readers know grammar rules well, while others do not (consider the proper use of the word "which" and "that" in the English language). For all these reasons, non–textualists argue that the consideration of non–textual sources of meaning is essential to interpretation. The New Mexico Supreme Court put it this way:

> [Textualism's] beguiling simplicity may mask a host of reasons why a statute, apparently clear and unambiguous on its face, may for one reason or another give rise to legitimate (i.e., nonfrivolous) difference of opinion concerning the statute's meaning.... [T]his rule is deceptive in that it implies that words have intrinsic meanings. A word is merely a symbol which can be used to refer to different things. Difficult questions of statutory interpretation ought not to be decided by the bland invocation of abstract jurisprudential maxims.... The

is unclear from the plain language of the statute, then we apply rules of statutory construction and explore legislative history to determine legislative intent.") (internal quotation marks omitted).

[16]Green v. Bock Laundry Machine Co, 490 U.S. 504 (1989).

[17]Church of the Holy Trinity v. United States, 143 U.S 457 (1892).

[18]*Compare* Smith v. United States, 508 U.S. 223, 228–29 (1993) (holding that exchanging a gun for drugs was "use" of a firearm), *with* Watson v. United States, 128 S. Ct. 579, 586 (2007) (holding that receiving a gun in exchange for drugs was not "use" of a firearm).

[19]*Compare* Patrie v. Area Coop. Educ. Serv., 37 Conn. L. Rptr. 470, 473 (Conn. Super. Ct. 2004) (using the ordinary meaning of the word "assault" for an indemnification statute, which was written for lay people), *with* Dickens v. Puryear, 276 S.E.2d 325 (N.C. 1981) (using a legal meaning of the word "assault" for a limitations statute, which was written for lawyers).

[20]Nix v. Heddon, 149 U.S. 304, 307 (1893) (holding that a tomato is a vegetable not a fruit).

> assertion in a judicial opinion that a statute needs no interpretation because it is "clear and unambiguous" is in reality evidence that the court has already considered and construed the act.[21]

Thus, despite its intuitive appeal, the plain meaning canon (the very essence of moderate textualism) is imperfect.

Finally, strict, or new, textualists round out the textualist continuum. New textualists are theorists who, like moderate textualists, require ambiguity or absurdity to look beyond text, but who, unlike moderates, refuse to look at some types of non–textual sources, such as legislative history, legislative acquiescence, and unexpressed purpose. New textualists are unique in their refusal to allow any consideration of legislative history and unexpressed purpose. These theorists believe that it is simply unconstitutional to consider any source that was not subject to the enactment process outlined in the U.S. Constitution: namely, bicameralism and presentment.

The most famous proponent of new textualism is U.S. Supreme Court Justice Antonin Scalia, who was appointed to the Court in 1986. He first articulated this approach in 1985–1986 during a series of speeches in which he urged judges to ignore legislative history, especially committee reports. Once he was appointed to the Supreme Court, he brought his criticism of the Court's use of legislative history into its jurisprudence.[22] At that time, many members of the Court regularly examined legislative history to glean evidence of legislative intent, and the Court's opinions reflected that fact.

Justice Scalia criticizes the use of legislative history for a number of reasons. Foremost, Justice Scalia says that the concept of legislative intent is irrelevant to interpretation because the objective indication of the words is what constitutes the law. For him, legislative history is irrelevant precisely because legislative intent is irrelevant. He argues further that even if an interpreter were seeking legislative intent, legislative history would still be irrelevant in 99 % of the cases that reach the court, because the interpreter would not be able to find it. "If one were to search for an interpretive technique that, *on the whole*, was more likely to confuse than to clarify, one could hardly find a more promising candidate than legislative history."[23]

Justice Scalia has raised other concerns as well. He points out that legislators do not read committee reports, which staff members often write, and thus, the reports

---

[21] State *ex rel.* Helman v. Gallegos, 871 P.2d 1352, 1359 (N.M. 1994).

[22] *See, e.g.*, INS v. Cardoza–Fonseca, 480 U.S. 421, 452 (1987) (Scalia, J., concurring) ("[The majority] attempts to justify this inquiry by relying upon the doctrine that if the legislative history of an enactment reveals a clearly expressed legislative intention contrary to (the enactment's) language, the Court is required to question the strong presumption that Congress expresses its intent through the language it chooses. Although it is true that the Court in recent times has expressed approval of this doctrine, that is to my mind an ill–advised deviation from the venerable principle that if the language of a statute is clear, that language must be given effect–at least in the absence of a patent absurdity.") (internal quotation marks omitted).

[23] Conroy v. Anskoff, 507 U.S. 511, 519 (1993) (Scalia, J., concurring).

cannot be relied upon as articulating the intent of a body that did not read or write them. As Justice Scalia once wrote:

> The meaning of terms on the statute books ought to be determined, not on the basis of which meaning can be shown to have been understood by a larger handful of the Members of Congress; but rather on the basis of which meaning is (1) most in accord with context and ordinary usage, and thus most likely to have been understood by the whole Congress which voted on the words of the statute (not to mention the citizens subject to it), and (2) most compatible with the surrounding body of law into which the provision must be integrated–a compatibility which, by a benign fiction, we assume Congress always has in mind.... [I]it is natural for the bar to believe that the juridical importance of [legislative history] matches its prominence in our opinions – thus producing a legal culture in which, when counsel arguing before us assert that "Congress has said" something, they now frequently mean, by "Congress," a committee report; and in which it was not beyond the pale for a recent brief to say the following: "Unfortunately, the legislative debates are not helpful. Thus, we turn to the other guidepost in this difficult area, statutory language."[24]

Likely, legislators do not read the committee reports or other provisions of legislative history, at least not in full. However, the legislative staff do read the reports and other relevant documents, then describe the relevant details in the statute to their employers. Thus, legislators use legislative history to understand the legislative bargain that was struck when they do not have the time or inclination to examine in detail the technical language of the bill (Katzmann 2012, 653–54). Thus, his criticism is overblown.

Professor William Eskridge coined the term "new textualist" for Justice Scalia's approach to show that this "new" form of textualism differed from the soft plain meaning textualism in that it was based on a strict view of separation of powers, ideological conservatism, and public choice theory. Justice Scalia's approach brought life back to textualism, which had largely disappeared, while simultaneously narrowing the sources that could be considered. Although Justice Scalia had suggested that he was simply using the Supreme Court's pre–World War II approach, his approach was a radical, not marginal, critique of his Court's approach to interpretation, especially its use of legislative history. It was a bold rethinking of the Court's role (Eskridge 1990).

Justice Scalia initially gained a following for both his approach and his criticism of the use of legislative history. Indeed, Judge Easterbrook of the United States Court of Appeals for the Seventh Circuit promoted a similar agenda (Easterbrook 1983, 544–51). And to be fair, Justice Scalia has positively altered the dialogue in the United States regarding statutory interpretation. While many of the other Justices explicitly rejected Justice Scalia's suggestion that legislative history can never be relevant to statutory interpretation,[25] the text–based approach has certainly gained currency, even if new textualism has fewer steadfast supporters.

---

[24]Green v. Bock Laundry Mach. Co., 490 U.S. 504, 529 (1989) (Scalia, J., concurring).

[25]Wis. Pub. Intervenor v. Mortier, 501 U.S. 597, 610 n.4 (1991). Currently, only Justice Thomas seems to be completely onboard with this approach.

Some judges and academics praise new textualism, believing that it curtails judicial discretion, increases predictability and efficiency, encourages more careful legislative drafting, and limits inappropriate uses of legislative history. New textualists believe that when judges and litigants are constrained to the text of statutes, meaning becomes more assured and litigation decreases. When legislative history cannot be considered as relevant to meaning, the cost of discerning meaning lessens and certainty increases. In addition, when legislators are held to the words they use in a statute, the argument continues, they will be more likely to choose those words with care.

While there is little doubt that an important contribution of Justice Scalia and new textualism is the judiciary's renewed focus on the primacy of the text, new textualism can also be faulted. First, it can be faulted for the complete unwillingness of its adherents to consider legislative history and unexpressed purpose. It makes little sense to prohibit all evidence generated during the legislative process simply because that evidence was not enacted. Non–textualists do not claim that legislative history is the law. While the statute is authoritative and has the force of law, legislative history and purpose provide evidence of what the text of the statute means. In other words, legislative history and purpose can help illuminate the meaning of the words that were enacted. In short, new textualists' refusal to consider legislative history or unarticulated purpose in any case is rigid and inflexible.

Additionally, it is not clear why new textualists are willing to consult dictionaries and the linguistic canons, which similarly do not go through the constitutionally prescribed legislative process. While it might be a good idea for legislators to use dictionaries or the canons when drafting, there is no proof that they do so. If the Constitution allows judges to consider some non–textual sources, then why does it not allow consideration of other non–textual sources? What makes legislative history so untrustworthy and dictionaries so trustworthy? Dictionaries are not the nirvana that textualists believe. A dictionary definition of a word is broader than the ordinary meaning of a word, for dictionaries are intended to include all possible uses of that word. Surrounding text narrows the broad dictionary meaning.

Yet sometimes judges rigidly adhere to the broader dictionary definition. For example, if a statute increases the sentence of anyone who "uses or carries a firearm" in relation to a drug offense, an ordinary reading of this language would suggest that a defendant must use the gun as a weapon to incur the additional penalty, not use the gun as an item of value to barter. However, a dictionary definition of "use" is sufficiently broad to include bartering a gun for drugs. In *Smith v. United States*,[26] a majority of the Supreme Court justices adopted the dictionary definition of "use" to find that the statute covered bartering a gun for drugs, while the dissent strongly objected and noted that "[t]he Court does not appear to grasp the distinction between how a word can be used and how it ordinarily is used."[27] Interestingly, Justice

[26] 508 U.S. 223 (1993).

[27] *Smith,* 508 U.S. at 242 (Scalia, J., dissenting).

O'Connor, who is not a textualist, wrote the majority opinion broadly interpreting "use," while Justice Scalia wrote the dissent.

In a subsequent case interpreting the same word in the same statute, the Court held that "use" denoted active employment, not mere possession.[28] Then, and as a direct result of this second interpretation, the Court rejected a claim that a drug dealer who received a firearm for drugs "used" that firearm.[29] Thus, in the United States, one who barters a gun for drugs uses that gun, but one who merely receives a gun in exchange for drugs does not use the gun. These cases show that the plain meaning canon, though appealing in its simplicity, does not always resolve the issue, especially when dictionaries are used without discretion. Dictionaries define words broadly; thus, definitional meanings will always be broader than ordinary meanings, which textual and other context limit.

Regardless of his unwillingness to use legislative history and unexpressed purpose, Justice Scalia properly returned judicial focus to the text of the statute as the focus of interpretation. As a result of his and others' influence, the text of the statute has gained importance and, likely, will retain this importance in the years to come. Importantly though, legislative history remains an important source for interpretation for most lawyers in the United States.

7.7.2 Intentionalist–Based Theories

Intentionalist–based theorists reject textualism for a variety of reasons. Before discussing the different intentionalist–based theories, a discussion of the underlying basis for these theories is necessary. Three arguments have been advanced to support intentionalist–based theories. First, some note that the Constitution vests Congress with the exclusive power to create law and policy; thus, courts must carry out the intent or purpose of the enacting congress. In other words, the policies the elected, representative body chose to enact should govern society. Second, some suggests that statutes are no more than compromises reached among interest groups during the legislative process; thus, courts must act as agents of the legislature to carry out these compromises. Third, some argue that it is simply illegitimate in a majoritarian political system for nonelected judges to change the original meaning of a statute thereby making policy choices (Eskridge 1987, 1481). In short, intentionalist–based theorists believe it is their duty to discern the intent of that representative body and interpret statutes to further that intent. Thus, intentionalist–based theorists interpret statutes by asking how the enacting legislature originally intended the interpretive question to be resolved or by asking what would the enacting legislature have intended had it thought about the issue when passing the statute. Although

---

[28]Bailey v. United States, 516 U.S. 137 (1995) (holding that a defendant who carried a gun in the trunk of his car did not "use" a firearm within the meaning of the statute).

[29]Watson v. United States, 128 S. Ct. 579, 586 (2007).

intentionalists agree that the intent of the enacting legislature controls, they disagree on how to identify that intent.

There are two kinds of intent: specific intent and general intent. Specific intent can be defined as the intent of the enacting legislature on the specific issue presented. For example, if a judge had to determine whether affirmative action programs were allowable under a statute that says that "no person shall be discriminated against on the basis of race," a judge looking for specific intent would search the text, related statutes, and legislative history to determine whether the enacting legislature intended the word "discriminate" to apply to affirmative action programs that promote the hiring of racial minorities. If the legislative history for this statute showed that the legislators actually discussed affirmative action programs positively or negatively during, for example, the House or Senate floor debates, then a judge looking for specific intent would conclude that the legislature intended the word "discriminate" to include or to not include affirmative action programs, depending on the tenor of the debate. Thus, for a judge seeking specific intent, it matters whether the enacting legislature had a specific intent as to the language in dispute, in this case the word "discriminate."

In contrast, general intent refers to the overall goal or purpose of the legislature as a whole. For example, if we return to the discrimination statute in the last paragraph, a judge looking for general intent would search the text, related statutes, social context, and legislative history to determine whether the enacting legislature's purpose was to make society color–blind or was to improve the plight of racial minorities. In other words, whether the legislators actually thought about whether the word "discriminate" included affirmative action programs would not be the question for a judge seeking general intent. For a judge seeking general intent, it matters not whether the legislature had a specific intent as to the language in dispute. Instead, what matters is the ultimate goal, or purpose, behind the legislation; judges seeking general intent ask what a reasonable legislator would have intended.

The two prominent intentionalist–based theories are (1) intentionalism, which focuses on specific intent, and (2) purposivism, which focuses on general intent. Each of these theories will be explored in detail below.

7.7.2.1 Intentionalism

Intentionalists, sometimes referred to as originalists, seek out the *specific intent* of the legislature that enacted the statute: What did that legislature have in mind in regard to the specific issue before the court when the legislature enacted the statute? To find specific intent, intentionalists start with the statutory language. But intentionalists do not stop with the text even if the text is clear, as most textualists would do; rather, intentionalists move on and examine other sources of meaning. Unlike a textualist, an intentionalist does not need a reason, such as ambiguity or absurdity, to consider sources beyond the text. In perusing other sources, intentionalists are looking for help in discerning the specific intent of the enacting legislature. Thus, intentionalists often find statements made during the legislative process and early draft versions of the bill enlightening. If these extrinsic sources demonstrate that the ordinary meaning was not what was intended, intentionalists will reject the ordinary meaning for a meaning that furthers the specific intent, as discovered in these other sources. Intentionalists will also examine policy–based sources.

As noted earlier, adherents of the competing approaches differ regarding their view of the appropriate role for the judiciary when interpreting statutes. Intentionalists believe that the judicial role is to be a faithful agent of the legislature, working to ensure that the legislature's choices are implemented. They believe that examining sources other than the text helps constrain the judiciary and helps maintain its separate function–that of interpreting–by providing more information for a fully informed decision. Further, intentionalists believe that intentionalism furthers separation of powers because it protects the legislature's power to legislate from judicial interference. Judges must implement the *enacting* legislature's intent, not impose their own policy preferences.

Like textualism, intentionalism has strengths; but it too has weaknesses. For example, consider whether the Senate, a group of 100 individuals, all with different constituencies, can have one, unified intent. Some say not. Each legislator may have a unique reason for voting for a bill. For example, Title VII, which prohibits discrimination in the workplace, was a compromise among various competing interests: The liberal, Northern and Eastern legislators (who sponsored the bill) wanted to help African–American workers; the conservative Southern legislators wanted to ensure that African–American workers were not helped at the expense of Caucasian workers; and finally the conservative Midwestern legislators, the pivotal voters, wanted to limit government interference in business. With so many different interests, it is unlikely that each of these legislators would share a specific intent as to whether affirmative action programs should be allowed. The liberal Northern and Eastern legislators would likely have said "yes," while the more conservative Southern and Midwestern legislators would likely have said "no." In *United Steelworkers v. Weber*,[30] the case in which this issue was addressed, the majority and dissent disagreed on whose intent was central. The majority focused on the liberal, Northern and Eastern legislators, while the dissent focused on the conservative, Southern and Midwestern legislators.

Of course, intentionalists respond to that criticism by arguing that a group can have common intent. While the individual members may have different, private motives for their own actions, the existence of private motives does not necessarily eliminate the possibility that the group has a common goal or agenda. For example, consider a sports team as it takes the field, a political party as it enters an election, or the board of a company preparing its annual strategy. The group's agenda and the members' motives might not be identical, but each group has one, overarching intent: to out–perform the competition. Intentionalism is thus less about the *reality* of always finding a unified intent and more about the *possibility* of finding one.

---

[30]443 U.S. 193 (1979).

To find specific intent, intentionalists start with the text, but then commonly rely on legislative history in addition to the draft versions of the bill. Intentionalists' use of legislative history raises a second criticism of intentionalism: Some argue that legislative history can be manipulated to support any result a judge or a legislator wants. Judges may choose which legislative history might be relevant and consequently reject any contradictory history. "[T]he trick is to look over the heads of the crowd and pick out your friends." (Scalia 1997, 36). Additionally, legislators can manipulate legislative history; they may decide to add information to the legislative record to influence future litigation, although relatively recent procedural rules have abated this practice. Finally, legislative history is not subject to bicameral passage and presentment, the constitutionally proscribed process for enactment. Thus, the criticism continues, even if a single, unified intent exists, that intent should not be ascertained from anything other than the language of the statute, for it is only that language that goes through the enactment process.

Intentionalists accept these criticisms as valid but only suggest caution, not wholesale rejection, of the use of legislative history. True, legislative history is not enacted law, but it can offer insight into what some or all of the legislators may have been thinking when the bill, which did go through the constitutionally prescribed process, was enacted. Thus, legislative history simply offers a fuller picture of legislative intent for a particular bill.

To summarize, intentionalism is an approach that is focused on finding the specific intent of the enacting legislature in regard to the language at issue in the statute. The approach focuses first on text and then on a review of the legislative history and draft versions of the bill, as well as all other relevant sources of meaning.

7.7.2.2 Purposivism

Purposivists believe that law, both generally and specifically, is designed to solve specific problems; thus, every statute has a purpose or objective for its enactment. Purposivists strive to discern and then implement this purpose. To do so, they will look broadly to search for meaning, but the text, including enacted purpose clauses, is always the starting point. Purposivists and intentionalists differ in what they seek by examining the extra–textual sources of meaning. As we saw above, intentionalists seek specific intent: What did the enacting legislature intend regarding the precise issue presented to the court. In contrast, purposivists seek general intent, or purpose: What problem was the legislature trying to redress, and how did it redress that problem? Once the purpose and remedy have been identified, purposivists interpret the statute to further that purpose, subject to two caveats: judges should not give words (1) a meaning those words cannot bear, nor (2) a meaning that would violate generally prevailing policies of law unless the statute includes a clear statement to that effect.

Purposivism[31] is perhaps the oldest form of interpretation. In the middle ages, detailed statutes were difficult to produce, and it was hard to develop and circulate multiple drafts. Copiers did not exist. Thus, early legislators voted based on the general goal, or purpose, of the law, not on the precise language. Purposivism permitted judges to focus on the spirit of the legislation rather than on the exact wording of a statute.

Like early English statutes, early American statutes were also very general. As mentioned, the Sherman (Antitrust) Act, which was enacted in 1890, fits on only one page, while the Patient Protection and Affordable Care Act, which was enacted in 2010, is 906 pages long. In the past, the legislature drafted broad statutes to allow reasoned judicial development of a particular area of law. Because there was so little textual guidance, judges needed something other than the text to guide and unify their interpretations. Purpose provided that guiding and unifying factor. Judges could easily test their decisions by discerning which interpretation best furthered the statutory purpose. Thus, by focusing on the purpose of the statute, judges believed they were better able to fit the statute into the legal system as a whole and make public policy coherent.

In the United States, purposivism made a reappearance in 1892 in *Church of the Holy Trinity v. United States*.[32] In that case, a statute made it unlawful for anyone to import any alien into the United States to "perform labor or service of any kind."[33] Holy Trinity Church had hired a rector from England. Despite the clarity of the text–rectoring is "labor or service"–the Court held that the statute did not apply because the purpose of the Act was to "stay the influx of . . . cheap unskilled labor. . . ."[34] Rectoring was not unskilled labor. The Court derived this purpose from the legislative history and title of the Act. Famously stating that "[i]t is a familiar rule that a thing may be within the letter of the statute and yet not within the statute, because not within its spirit nor within the intention of its makers," the Court rejected the ordinary meaning of the text.[35]

After a lull, purposivism came back into vogue shortly after World War II, during a time of "relative consensus sustained economic growth, and burgeoning optimism about government's ability to foster economic growth by solving market failures and creating opportunities." (Eskridge et al. 2001, 727). The Supreme Court followed this approach, for the most part, throughout the 1950s and 1960s. By the 1970s, however, the United States was changing. Economic growth had faltered and issues relating to war, family, and government were much more controversial. Government became the enemy rather than the savior. Additionally, statutes became more complex and comprehensive. With those changes came a change in the

---

[31] Purposivism is also known as the legal process theory.

[32] 143 U.S. 457 (1892).

[33] *Id.* at 458.

[34] *Id.* at 465.

[35] *Id.* at 459.

judicial approach to statutory interpretation. Intentionalism garnered favor with such Supreme Court justices as former Chief Justices Warren Burger and William Rehnquist. Today, Justice Stephen Breyer and Judge Richard Posner adhere to this approach.[36] To many judges, purposivism appears to be a relic from early statutory development that has little application in a world in which complex statutes are the norm. In this new norm, there is a renewed emphasis on the importance and primacy of the text.

Like intentionalism, purposivism begins with the text but does not end there:

> There is, of course, no more persuasive evidence of the purpose of a statute than the words by which the legislature undertook to give expression to its wishes. Often these words are sufficient in and of themselves to determine the purpose of the legislation. In such cases we have followed their plain meaning. When that meaning has led to absurd or futile results, however, this Court has looked beyond the words to the purpose of the act. Frequently, however, even when the plain meaning did not produce absurd results but merely an unreasonable one plainly at variance with the policy of the legislation as a whole this Court has followed that purpose, rather than the literal words. When aid to construction of the meaning of words as used in the statute is available, there certainly can be no rule of law which forbids its use, however clear the words may appear on superficial examination.[37]

While intentionalists view themselves as faithful agents of the legislature, purposivists view themselves as "faithful agent[s] of a well–functioning regulatory regime." (Eskridge et al. 2006, 7) (emphasis omitted). For this reason, purposivists attempt to discern the evil, or mischief, the legislature meant to address when enacting the statute. To do so, purposivists are willing to examine text and legislative history, as well as other relevant sources, such as social and legal context. To a purposivist, a statute makes sense only when understood in light of its purpose: a rule without purpose is meaningless. For example, consider a hypothetical city ordinance prohibiting "vehicles" in a park. Is a non–motorized scooter a vehicle? To decide this issue, a purposivist judge might ask why the city council enacted the ordinance in the first place. If the council's purpose was to limit air and noise pollution, then "vehicle" should not be interpreted to include scooters. If, instead, the city's purpose was to increase pedestrian safety, then, perhaps, "vehicle" should be so interpreted. Thus, purposivists believe that knowing the mischief at which the statute was aimed aids interpretation.

One benefit of purposivism is that it permits flexibility. While purposivism and intentionalism are somewhat similar, purposivism has one advantage over intentionalism: Purposivists can interpret statutes in situations the enacting legislature never contemplated. "Purposivism ... renders statutory interpretation adaptable to new circumstances." (Eskridge et al. 2006, 221). For example, in the hypothetical city ordinance prohibiting "vehicles" in the park, a purposivist judge could determine

---

[36]For an interesting and heated debate between Justice Scalia and Judge Posner regarding statutory interpretation, *see* Posner (Sept. 18, 2012) and Shim (Sept. 18, 2012) ("Scalia transformed his response from a defensive to an offensive one, calling Posner's accusation that he had an inconsistent judicial record, to put it bluntly, a lie."); Posner (Sept. 20, 2012).

[37]United States v. Am. Trucking Ass'ns, Inc., 310 U.S. 534, 543–44 (1940) (citations omitted).

that the ordinance applied to electric scooters even though these "vehicles" may not have been around when the ordinance was adopted. But an intentionalist judge might have trouble with this issue because the city council could not have intended to regulate something not in existence when the ordinance was adopted. Therefore, purposivism allows for laws to change with technological, social, legal, and other advances–something true intentionalism is incapable of doing.

There are fair criticisms of purposivism. The most troublesome aspect of purposivism is, of course, legitimately discerning a statute's purpose. Ideally, legislatures would include a findings or purpose provision in the enacted text of every statute. Unfortunately, they do not. And even when they do, the purpose clause may have been written to aid the legislative bargaining rather than the interpretation process. Thus, judges often look for a statute's *unexpressed* purpose. To find such unexpressed purpose, purposivists consider the text, the legislative history, the legal history, the social context, and other sources. But these sources may not be conclusive. What then? Some legal scholars have suggested that to figure out a statute's primary purpose, a judge should posit various situations. In other words, a judge should start with the situations clearly covered and radiate outward. In doing so, courts should presume that legislatures are "made of reasonable persons pursuing reasonable purposes, reasonably." (Hart and Sachs 1994, 1378). As you might expect, the subjectiveness of this approach would concern a textualist.

There are other criticisms as well. For example, even if a particular purpose is discernible, there may be competing ideas of how to further that purpose. For example, is affirmative action or color–blindness the best way to achieve racial parity? A related criticism of purposivism is that statutes often have more than one purpose, and these purposes can conflict. For example, one purpose of Title VII of the Civil Rights Act of 1964[38]–which prohibits racial discrimination in the workplace–was to increase the number of African–Americans in the workforce. Another purpose was to make hiring and other work related decisions color–blind. Voluntary affirmative action programs further the first purpose but not the second. Is the fact that one purpose is furthered enough to sustain an interpretation? Purposivism does not answer the question of whether an interpretation is appropriate when one, but not another, purpose is furthered.

Similarly, a statute may have one purpose, while an exception to that statute may have a conflicting purpose. For example, the purpose of the Freedom of Information Act[39] is to encourage open government. But some of the exceptions within the Act, such as the one prohibiting the disclosure of personnel files, exist to protect individual privacy. If a judge interprets an exception, which purpose should control: the purpose of the act or the purpose of the exception? In other words, should the judge interpret the exception in the Freedom of Information Act narrowly to better further the purpose of the Act as a whole, or broadly to better further the purpose of the exception? Again, purposivism does not answer this question.

[38] 42 U.S.C. §§2000e *et. seq.* (2012).

[39] 5 U.S.C. §552 (2012).

Finally, judges are constitutionally required to interpret statutory language. They are not appropriate policy–makers, because they often are not elected and they are not expected constitutionally to perform this function. When judges make decisions based on their own policy choices, legitimized as purpose, they aggrandize their constitutional power and intrude into the legislative arena.

7.7.3 The Sliding Scale Approach

All of the approaches have shortcomings. For this reason, the state of Alaska's judiciary rejected all of the above approaches (especially textualism) and created its own compromise approach. This approach, the "sliding scale approach," blends textualism, intentionalism, and purposivism. It allows judges to consider a statute's meaning without first finding ambiguity or absurdity by applying a sliding scale of clarity. The sliding scale approach states simply that all sources of meaning are always relevant; however, the clearer the statutory language, the more convincing the evidence of a contrary legislative purpose or intent must be.[40] In other words, Alaska adopted textualism with a twist. Much like a sliding door that can be opened a little or a lot to control the airflow, the sliding scale approach allows a little or a lot of contrary evidence of meaning to flow into the analysis. The size of the opening depends on the clarity of the text: the clearer the text, the smaller the opening.

The Alaska judiciary considered moderate textualism but rejected it, because that approach overly restricted the inquiry. Because words are necessarily inexact and ambiguity is inherent in language, other sources of meaning often prove helpful in construing a statute. Thus, even if the statute under consideration is facially clear, the legislative history can be considered, because it might reveal an ambiguity not apparent on the face of the statute.[41]

Alaska's sliding scale approach has inherent appeal. The approach is a kissing cousin to the soft plain meaning approach; under the sliding scale approach, the plainer the text, the more convincing the contrary indications of meaning must be to trump the text. This soft version of textualism turns the plain meaning canon into a rebuttable presumption: the plain meaning will control absent convincing evidence that the legislature intended a different meaning. In many ways, this approach blends the best of the theories above, while avoiding the difficulties; the text is the primary, but not exclusive, evidence of meaning. But this approach shares many of the problems of textualism and, thus, is not the perfect compromise it may appear to be.

[40] LeFever v. State, 877 P.2d 1298, 1299–1300 (Alaska Ct. App. 1994).

[41] Anchorage v. Sisters of Providence in Wash., Inc., 628 P.2d 22, 27 n.6 (Alaska 1981).

7.7.4 Legislative Process Theories

In addition to the statutory interpretation theories discussed above, there are several theories that relate to the legislative process. For example, *pluralist theories* focus on the role special interest groups play in setting legislative policy. Interest group politics leads to "pluralism"–the spreading of political power across multiple political actors. The legislative process is one area in which conflicting interest groups' desires are resolved. Examples of special interest groups include political parties, churches, unions, businesses, and environmental organizations, among others. Interest groups can often accomplish what an individual cannot. Because there is strength in numbers, interest groups offer individual citizens the best possibility of meaningful participation in the legislative process. Theoretically, one benefit of a robustly pluralist system should be moderate, balanced, and well–considered legislation.

One pluralist theory is *bargaining theory*, which proposes that statutes are a compromise between various interest groups. Interest groups want a particular benefit or protection from government but often lack the clout to enact legislation absent support from other interest groups. Hence, interest groups work with other interest groups to increase their political power and get bills enacted; yet, in doing so, the groups must compromise their goals. Pursuant to bargaining theory, judges should focus on furthering the compromises that produced the necessary votes for passage of the compromise legislation. For example, for Title VII, which prohibited discrimination in the workplace on the basis of race, the compromise necessary to ensure passage was that white workers would not be disadvantaged to further black workers' plight. Bargaining theorists would interpret the statute not to allow voluntary affirmative action programs because such programs disadvantage white workers even while helping black workers.

Public choice theory is another pluralist theory. Public–choice theorists rely on economics to explain legislators' behavior. These theorists believe that statutes are the result of compromises among legislators that come about as a result of private interest groups bargaining. These private interest groups seek the best result for their members without regard for others. Access to the political process is disparate. Business interests tend to be overrepresented, while the broad public interest and the less advantaged tend to be underrepresented. Thus, public choice theory helps explain the success of distributive legislation, legislation that rewards multiple special interests simultaneously. For example, tax bills that offer loopholes to many specialized groups or defense appropriation bills that send money to a variety of districts are both likely to be enacted for this reason. Under public choice theory, special–interest legislation and pork–barrel projects should enjoy limited support because very few special interest groups are rewarded. However, legislators may choose to support special projects for a variety of reasons, such as to gain political capital with other legislators for the future, to pay back special interest groups for financial or other support, or to increase the chances of reelection or movement within the party. Hence, contrary to intentionalist thought, public–choice theorists believe that there can be no single legislative intent; rather, each legislator may have a multitude of reasons for voting for particular legislation. Given the possibility of multiple reasons, public–choice theorists urge narrow interpretation of statutes. Additionally, these theorists suggest that judges should not fill in the statutory gaps because legislatures do not act for the public as a whole, but rather act to reward special interest groups and maximize their own reelection potential. As for legislative history, public–choice theorists agree with new textualists that such history should be ignored when determining statutory meaning, because it shows nothing relevant. Legislation is a compromise of intentions; therefore, we cannot know exactly why legislators vote the way they do.

Public choice theory can be criticized for its skepticism. Not all legislators are opportunists looking for financial rewards from special interest groups; many are honest and have independent beliefs and goals that direct their legislative behavior. Thus, interest groups may be less effective at changing lawmakers' minds than public choice theory would have us believe. Finally, interest groups are better at blocking legislation than passing it, especially when legislation has low visibility. Hence, the theory may be inapposite for enacted legislation.

A second group of legislative theories, *proceduralist theories*, focuses on the legislative process and the political obstacles a bill must hurdle to become law. One such theory focuses on the "vetogates" of the legislative process (Eskridge et al. 2006, 190). The American legislative process is complex, but you need only know that it is easier to kill a bill than to pass one because of the many steps a bill must go through before it can become law. At any one step, the bill might be stopped, or choked, from passage. Vetogates are the chokepoints that can prevent a bill from becoming law. For example, each chamber sends bills to standing committees, such as the Senate Judiciary Committee. The bill must be referred out of the committee to the full chamber, the Senate, before continuing the enactment process. The committee is a vetogate, while the members of the committee (especially the chair) are gatekeepers. "Gatekeepers" are legislators that hold power at these vetogates.

Vetogates are important for two reasons. First, gatekeepers can simply block a bill's passage at any vetogate. Second, courts often reason that statements gatekeepers made reflect the intent of the legislative body because the gatekeepers' support would have been essential to the bill's passage. Yet this reasoning may be flawed. Because these gatekeepers have such power, they can abuse their position. For example, the Alaska National Interest Lands Conservation Act altered the rules for access to all nonfederally owned land within the boundaries of the National Forest System. In *Montana Wilderness Ass'n v. U.S. Forest Service*,[42] the question for the Court was whether a subsection of the Act applied nationwide or just in Alaska.[43] Congressman Udall, a key gatekeeper at the time the bill was enacted, had claimed in the legislative record that the subsection of the Act applied only to

[42]655 F.2d 951 (9th Cir.), *cert. denied*, 455 U.S. 898 (1981).

[43]*Id.* at 953.

Alaska.[44] However, other factors suggested that it was more likely that Congress intended the Act to apply nationally; thus, the Court rejected the argument that Udall's comments showed Congressional intent to limit the Act's application to Alaska.

Another legislative theory, the "Best Answer Theory," urges judges to interpret statutes to promote an "optimal state of affairs." Such a theory views judges as protectors of the minority, those individuals not in political power. Pursuant to this theory, a judge would likely find that Title VII did allow voluntary affirmative action programs because such programs would remedy employment practices that had had a disparate impact on a less powerful group, racial minorities. Allowing an employer to enact voluntary affirmative action programs, rather than wait for possible litigation, would promote harmony, lead to positive social change, and protect minority interests. Thus, in this example, promoting the "optimal state of affairs" would support allowing limited types of affirmative action programs.

7.7.5 Does Theory Matter?

Perhaps, but no one theory is better at discerning the "right" meaning than any other theory. "[T]here is no empirical way to show that one of these [theories] is better' than the others, in the sense that one [theory] more often than the others captures the true meaning' of a statute."[45] Only if we knew what the "right" interpretation was without applying a theory could we determine which theory most often leads to that "right" interpretation. But of course, we do not know which interpretation is right, nor do we even know what sources we are supposed to use to evaluate the correctness of the choice. Hence, the superiority of each theory will continue to be debated. In particular, academics love to debate the pros and cons of each of these theories. For example, in the famous hypothetical *Case of the Speluncean Explorers*, Professor Lon Fuller explored a hypothetical situation in which a group of explorers were trapped in a cave (Fuller 1949). While there, they killed one of their group and ate him to survive. After they were rescued, they were tried and convicted of murder. The hypothetical statute provided simply: "Whoever shall willfully take the life of another shall be punished by death." A judicially created self–defense exception also existed.

Professor Fuller had each judge considering the explorers' appeal draft a separate opinion, using a different statutory approach to explore the role that morality should play within the law. Theory dictated the outcome: the textualist judges imposed the rigid law, while the intentionalist judges crafted an exception.

Despite the Speluncean Explorers hypothetical, the reality is that few judges rigidly adhere to just one theory. Even Justice Scalia admits, "I play the game

---

[44] *Id.* at 956 n.9 (citing 127 Cong. Rec. 10376).

[45] Jellum and Hricik (2009, 44).

like everybody else. . . . I'm in a system which has accepted rules and legislative history is used. . . . You read my opinions, I sin with the rest of them." Easterbrook (1990, 442 n.4) (quoting Katzmann 1988, 174–75). Professors Eskridge, Frickey, and Garrett best summed up the reality of today's doctrine:

> We do not think the Supreme Court has entirely returned to the pre–Scalia days and suggest the following generalities about where it is today. First, the text is now, more than it was 20 or 30 years ago, the central inquiry at the Supreme Court level and in other courts that are now following the Supreme Court's lead. A brief that starts off with, "The statute means thus–and–so because it says so in the committee report," is asking for trouble. Both advice and advocacy should start with the statutory text. Because the Court frequently uses the dictionary to provide meaning to key statutory terms, the advocate should incorporate this methodology as well. . . . Second, the "contextual" evidence the Court is interested in is now statutory as much as or more than just historical context. Arguments that your position is more consistent with other parts of the same statute are typically winning arguments. Similarly, as [one case] indicates, the Court today goes beyond the "whole act" rule to something like a "whole code" rule, searching the United States Code for guidance on the usage of key statutory terms and phrases.
>
> Third, the Court will still look at contextual evidence and is very interested in the public law background of the statute. If a statute seems to require an odd result . . . , the Court will interrogate the background materials to find out why. . . . It remains important to research and brief the legislative history thoroughly. The effective advocate will appreciate that the presence of such materials in the briefs may influence the outcome more than the opinion in the case will indicate (Eskridge et al. 2001, 770–71).

While academics will continue rigorously to argue the legitimacy of the various approaches, few judges remain so dogmatic. Judges regularly mix approaches, fail to identify their approach, and even change approaches. Ultimately, judges want to further justice, not be dogmatically rigid. Professors Eskridge and Frickey call this the pragmatic theory. "In deciding a question of statutory interpretation in the real, as opposed to the theoretical, world, few judges approach the interpretive task armed with a fixed set of rigid rules." (Walker 2001, 232). Professor Farber demonstrated that theory made little difference in the rulings of two judges who are at the forefront of the theoretical debates: Richard Posner (a leading purposivist) and Frank Easterbrook (a leading textualist). Farber concluded that their theoretical difference did not matter: "Like other federal appellate judges, they agree on the outcome in the vast majority of the cases on which they sit." (Farber 2000, 1411).

Perhaps, as legal realists suggest, none of this theory stuff matters. The reality is that judges decide cases based on their own personal notions of justice and the underlying equities of the case. For this reason, lawyers should not expect to win their case simply because they select a particular theory. To win the case, a lawyer must prove to the judge that a ruling for the lawyer's client would be the just and right result. But knowing a judge's preferred approach can make the job easier. For example, if a lawyer is arguing before a purposivist judge, the lawyer need not raise ambiguity and absurdity before discussing legislative history or context, as the lawyer must do when arguing before a textualist judge. Thus, the theories provide legal language and seemingly impartial reasoning to help lawyers argue their case. In this world, the Ancient Greek aphorism "Know thyself" could be "Know thy judge's approach."

7.8 Theory and Its Relationship to Legislative Process

What role, if any, do the judicial theories of statutory interpretation play in American legislative drafting? Surprisingly little it appears. For the past several decades, American scholars have exhaustively debated how courts should and do interpret federal statutes; yet, the little empirical work that exists examining the relationship, if any, between the theories judges use and the process Congress uses does not support current judicial practice (Gluck and Bressman 2013; Nourse and Schacter 2002).

As noted earlier, some judges believe that a particular theory might encourage Congress to draft more precisely or act in other ways that the judges think would be preferable. Other judges believe that a particular theory best advances constitutional values or furthers the "rule of law" by coordinating systemic behavior or imposing coherence on the U.S. Code. Finally, still other judges believe that a particular theory accurately reflects how Congress drafts legislation so that applying that theory best effectuates legislative supremacy. Indeed, scholars often claim that their preferred interpretive method best reflects actual congressional practice. It appears they and the judges are wrong.

Members of Congress do not draft most statutory language.[46] Rather, they and their staff focus on policy, while a nonpartisan agency (the Offices of Legislative Counsel) drafts most statutory text.[47] Because the enacted statutory text is not drafted by Congress or its staff, while legislative history is, theorists might want to reconsider the relevance and primacy of legislative history. In short, if the judicial theories were actually designed to mirror how members of Congress and their staff actually participate in the drafting process they would certainly be less text based.[48] For example, "despite the decades of judicial [and scholarly] squabbling over the role of legislative history, it was overwhelmingly viewed by Democratic and Republican [congressional staff members] alike as the most important tool of interpretation after statutory text."[49] Moreover, because legislative history plays a different role in ordinary statutory drafting than in the drafting of omnibus or appropriations statutes, arguably judges should treat legislative history differently based on this fact. Yet neither intentionalist nor purposivist judges, who regularly consult legislative history, make any such distinction. Similarly, the identical words presumption, which is beloved by textualists, presumes that statutory words are used consistently within and across statutes. This presumption promotes consistency within the United States Code. Yet the presumption does not reflect the reality that multiple congressional committees draft different sections of bills and that those committees do not generally communicate with each other during the drafting

---

[46] *Id.* at 906.

[47] *Id.* at 908.

[48] *Id.*

[49] *Id.* at 907.

process. In short, the empirical research that exists does not support any existing theory as best reflecting the drafting process. Congress may wish to pay more attention to the ways judges interpret statutes when it drafts.

> I do not think that any of the canons of statutory construction can be defended on the theory that they are keys to deciphering a code. There is no evidence that members of Congress, or their assistants who do the actual drafting, know the code or that if they know, they pay attention to it. Nor, in truth, is there any evidence that they do not; it is remarkable how little research has been done on a question that one might have thought lawyers would regard as fundamental to their enterprise. Probably, though, legislators do not pay attention to it, if only because, as Llewellyn showed, the code is internally inconsistent. We should demand evidence that statutory draftsmen follow the code before we erect a method of interpreting statutes on the improbable assumption that they do (Posner 1983, 806).

References

Chomsky, Carol. 2000. Unlocking the mysteries of Holy Trinity: Spirit, letter, and history in statutory interpretation. *Columbia Law Review* 100:901.

Davies, Jack. 2007. *Legislative law and process in a nutshell*, 3rd ed. St. Paul: Thompson/West.

Dworkin, Ronald. 1986. *Law's empire*. Cambridge: Harvard University Press.

Easterbrook, Frank. 1983. Statutes' domains. *University of Chicago Law Review* 50:533.

Easterbrook, Frank H. 1990. What does legislative history tell us? *Chicago–Kent Law Review* 66:441.

Eskridge, Jr., William N. 1987. Dynamic statutory interpretation. *University of Pennsylvania Law Review* 135:1481.

Eskridge, Jr., William N. 1990. The new textualism. *U.C.L.A. Law Review* 37:624.

Eskridge, Jr., William N., and Philip P. Frickey. 1994. Introduction to Henry M. Hart, Jr. & Albert M. Sacks, the legal process. In *The legal process: Basic problems in the making and application of law*, ed. William N. Eskridge, Jr. and Philip P. Frickey. New York: Foundation Press.

Eskridge, Jr., William, Philip P. Frickey, and Elizabeth Garrett. 2001. *Cases and materials on legislation: Statutes and the creation of public policy*, 3rd ed. Eagen: West Group.

Eskridge, Jr., William, Philip P. Frickey, and Elizabeth Garrett. 2006. *Legislation and statutory interpretation*, 2nd ed. New York: Foundation Press.

Farber, Daniel A. 2000. Do theories of statutory interpretation matter? A case study. *Northwestern University Law Review* 94:1409.

Fuller, Lon L. 1949. The case of the Speluncean explorers. *Harvard Law Review* 62:616.

Gluck, Abbe R., and Lisa Schultz Bressman. 2013. Statutory interpretation from the inside–an empirical study of congressional drafting, delegation, and the canons: Part I. *Stanford Law Review* 65:901.

Hart, Henry M., and Albert M. Sachs. 1994. *The legal process: Basic problems in the making and application of law*, ed. William N. Eskridge, Jr. and Philip P. Frickey. New York: Foundation Press.

Jellum, Linda D. 2009. "Which is to be Master," the judiciary or the legislature? When statutory directives violate separation of powers. *U.C.L.A. Law Review* 56:837.

Jellum, Linda D., and David C. Hricik. 2009. *Modern statutory interpretation: Problems, theories, and lawyering strategies*, 2nd ed. Durham: Carolina Academic Press.

Katzmann, Robert A. 1988. Summary of proceedings. In *Judges and legislators: Toward institutional comity*, ed. R. Katzmann, 174–175. Washington, DC: Brookings Institution Press.

Katzmann, Robert A. 2012. Statutes. *New York University Law Review* 87:637.

Kernochan, John M. 1976. Statutory interpretation: An outline of method. *Dalhousie Law Journal* 3:333.

Nourse, Victoria F., and Jane S. Schacter. 2002. The politics of legislative drafting: A congressional case study. *New York University Law Review* 77:575.

Posner, Richard A. 1983. Statutory interpretation–in the classroom and in the courtroom. *University of Chicago Law Review* 50:800.

Posner, Richard A. Sept. 13, 2012. The spirit killeth, but the letter giveth life. *New Republic* 18.

Posner, Richard A. Sept. 20, 2012. Richard Posner responds to Antonin Scalia's accusation of lying. *New Republic*. http://www.tnr.com/blog/plank/107549/richard-posnerresponds-antonin-scalias-accusation-lying. Accessed 11 Nov 2013.

Scalia, Antonin. 1997. *A matter of interpretation: Federal courts and the law*. Princeton: Princeton University Press.

Shim, Eileen. Sept. 18, 2012. Yet another round of the Scalia–Posner fight. *New Republic*. http://www.tnr.com/blog/plank/107429/scaliaposner-fight-supreme-court. Accessed 11 Nov 2013.

Walker, John M. 2001. Judicial tendencies in statutory construction: Differing views on the role of the judge. *New York University Annual Survey of American Law* 58:203.

Chapter 8
Logic and the Directives of Legislative Technique: Some Logical Remarks on the Polish "Principles of Legislative Technique"

Urszula Kosielińska-Grabowska and Andrzej Grabowski

Abstract Connections of various types exist between logic and legislation. Among them, the relationships between logic and the directives of legislative technique are particularly important for the practice of lawmaking. Logic unquestionably provides the foundation for a number of the directives of legislative technique; however, to precisely determine the role that logic plays therein is not an easy task. In this paper, we examine the aforementioned relationship by analysing an example of Polish "Principles of Legislative Technique" from 2002. Our principal objective was to identify the connections between logic and legal provisions that are contained in this normative act. We also discuss the logical correctness of the directives of legislative technique that are based on logic. Finally, we propose a provisional typology of the relationships between logic and the directives of legislative technique, and make some comments on the logical rationality of lawmaking.

Keywords Legislative technique • Logic • Lawmaking • Rational legislator

8.1 Preliminary Remarks

Many and varied connections exist between logic and legislation. Among them, the relationships between logic and the directives of legislative technique are particularly important for the practice of lawmaking. In Poland, the tradition of issuing the directives of legislative technique in the form of normative acts is relatively long (Wierczyński 2010, 20–22; Brożek and Zyzik 2012, 82–83). The first "Principles of Legislative Technique" [hereafter: PLT] were enacted as early as 1929, as the Annex to the Circular Letter of the Minister of Internal Affairs of the

U. Kosielińska-Grabowska (✉)
Institute of Politology, Pedagogical University, Kraków, Poland
e-mail: grabowska@up.krakow.pl

A. Grabowski
Department of Legal Theory, Jagiellonian University, Kraków, Poland
e-mail: andrzej.grabowski@uj.edu.pl

M. Araszkiewicz, K. Płeszka (eds.), *Logic in the Theory and Practice of Lawmaking*, Legisprudence Library 2, DOI 10.1007/978-3-319-19575-9_8

Republic of Poland.[1] This regulation was followed by the PLT of 1939,[2] 1962[3] and 1991.[4] The currently valid PLT is also an Annex; this time attached to the Ordinance of the Prime Minister of 20 June 2002 [hereafter: PLT2002]. Despite the fact that the present PLT2002 is formally binding only for governmental agencies (and also partially for self-governing agencies, pursuant to Paragraph 143), the principle of correct legislation is frequently used in the jurisdiction of the Polish Constitutional Tribunal, in reference to the statutes issued by the Polish parliament (Zalasiński 2008, 41–54). The Tribunal stated in the 2013 decision concerning *inter alia* the violation of the principle of correct legislation:

> The appraisal of the correctness [of legislative acts - U.K-G, A.G] is being made on the basis of the accepted principles of writing in the Polish language, the formal logic, and the valid "Principles of Legislative Technique".[5]

The problems of correct legislation and proper lawmaking are often analysed, not only by Polish dogmatics of constitutional law, but also from the more general perspective of legal theory. At this point, the works of Ziembiński (1985), Wróblewski (1989) and Wronkowska and Zieliński (1993) are particularly important for Polish legal culture. Undoubtedly, the Polish theory of legislation is grounded on the doctrine of legal positivism (Brożek and Zyzik 2012, 77–78, 80), and is based on the jurisprudential fiction of a "rational legislator" (Nowak 1973; Wróblewski 1989, 45–48; Wróblewski 1990). The latter concept was characterised by Ziembiński (1985, 140), as follows:

> One assumes the rationality of such an idealised "legislator' in order to enable the reconstruction of a coherent system of legal norms justified by some officially accepted system of values and knowledge.

The methodological idea of a "rational legislator' also plays the crucial role in determination of the directives of legal interpretation (Nowak 1969). It is worth noting that, in Polish legal culture, the thesis on the correspondence of the directives of legislation, and the directives of legal interpretation, is taken for granted (Piszko 2002; Wróblewski 1978; Wronkowska and Zieliński 1985). In addition, the Polish Constitutional Tribunal frequently makes use of the analogous thesis on the correlation between the directives of legislative technique and legal interpretation as

[1]Zbiór zasad i form techniki legislacyjnej [The Collection of the Principles and Forms of Legislative Technique], published in the Official Journal of the Ministry of Internal Affairs from 1929, No. 7, Item 147.

[2]Issued by the Prime Minister of the Republic of Poland and published as a book entitled Zasady techniki prawodawczej [Principles of Legislative Technique], Warszawa 1939.

[3]Issued by the Prime Minister of the Republic of Poland and published as a book entitled Zasady techniki prawodawczej [Principles of Legislative Technique], Warszawa 1962.

[4]Issued by the Council of Ministers of the Republic of Poland and published in Monitor Polski [Official Gazette of the Republic of Poland] from 1991, No. 44, Item 310.

[5]Postanowienie Trybunału Konstytucyjnego z dnia 10 stycznia 2013 r. [Decision of the Constitutional Tribunal from 10 January 2013]. sign. K 36/11.

a justification for its rulings.[6] Therefore, the hypothesis of a "rational legislator" is an important element of juristic reasoning in many domains of Polish legal practice. We can also observe its influence in the case of the creation of PLT2002. The aforementioned Ordinance of the Prime Minister of 20 June 2002 concerning "The Principles of Legislative Technique" was issued as a governmental implementation act on the legal basis of Article 14, Section 4, Point 1 of the Statute of 8 August 1996 on the Council of Ministers.[7] According to the second sentence of the Section 5 of this Article:

> In particular, the application of the principles of legislative technique ought to secure the coherence and completeness of the legal system and the transparency of normative legal acts, by accounting for scientific achievements and practical experience.

As we can easily notice, the concepts of coherence and completeness of the legal system, and the transparency of legal texts, are closely connected with the positivistic views of lawmaking, and express legal values closely related to the regulative idea of a "rational legislator".

8.2 The Directives of Legislative Technique Based on Logic

Our principal objective is to examine the relationships between logic and the directives of legislative technique by analysing an example of the Polish Principles of Legislative Technique from 2002.[8] In the following subsections we identify the connections between logic and the content of legal provisions that are contained in this normative act. We will also make some comments on the logical correctness of the directives of legislative technique, as indicated below. We must add that we restricted the scope of analysis to these legal provisions, in which the connection with formal logic, deontic logic or the logical theory of language appears to be evident.

---

[6]Cf. Wyrok Trybunału Konstytucyjnego z dnia 30 października 2001 r. [Ruling of the Constitutional Tribunal from 30 October 2001], sign. K 33/00 and Wyrok Trybunału Konstytucyjnego z dnia 2 lipca 2007 r. [Ruling of the Constitutional Tribunal from 2 July 2007], sign. K 41/05.

[7]Published in Dziennik Ustaw [Journal of Statutes] from 1996, No. 106, Item 492, with amendments.

[8]English translation of PLT2002 is available at http://legislationline.org/download/action/download/id/827/file/e97fe90c34b1af6904e1e511809b.pdf. We often amend this translation in the text.

8.2.1 Prohibition of the Repetition of Legal Provisions (§§4.1–4.2, 23.1, 118) and Prohibition of the Use of Pleonasms in Penal Provisions (§76)

Firstly, we will analyse provisions, which exclude repetitions in the texts of legislative acts. With regard to so-called external repetitions, that is, the repetition of identical legal provision in different statutes or normative acts (Wronkowska and Zieliński 2004, 31–32), the question is directly regulated in two Sections of Paragraph 4 and in Paragraph 118:

§ 4.1. A statute shall not repeat the provisions of other statutes.

2. A statute shall also not restate the provisions of international treaties ratified by the Republic of Poland and the directly applicable provisions of normative acts passed by international organisations or bodies, upon which the Republic of Poland has conferred the powers of state authorities in certain matters.

§ 118. An ordinance shall not repeat any provisions of the authorising statute or other normative acts.

Furthermore, with regard to the so-called internal repetitions, that is, the repetitions of legal provisions (or the identical normative contents) in the same normative act, the issue is regulated in Section 1 of Paragraph 23:

§ 23.1. Specific provisions shall not regulate issues that have already been comprehensively regulated in the general provisions.

Both types of repetitions of legal provisions are instances of pragmatically redundant expressions (Kłodawski 2012, 128). The literature on the subject has emphasised that such repetitions can create problems for the interpreters of legal texts (Wronkowska and Zieliński 2004, 32; Wierczyński 2010, 66–67, 180). In particular, we cannot ignore the risk that the identical legal provision contained in different legislative acts can be interpreted along different lines (for instance, because of their systemic context). Conversely, the possibility of repetitions cannot be entirely excluded. Sometimes, especially in the normative acts of a lower range, the repetition of statutory provisions may be useful for the comprehensibility and coherence of these acts (Wronkowska and Zieliński 2004, 32–33).

We must also add that, in the Polish judiciary, the problem of statutory superfluity (*ius superfluum*) is treated in different ways. In some cases, the Polish Supreme Court recognises certain legal provisions as a statutory *superfluum*,[9] while in other, more frequent judicial decisions, it does not do so, mainly because the interpretation

[9]Cf. Uchwała Sądu Najwyższego z dnia 7 września 1995 r. [Resolution of the Supreme Court from 7 September 1995], sign. I PZP 23/95; Postanowienie Sądu Najwyższego z dnia 20 czerwca 2002 r. [Decision of the Supreme Court from 20 June 2002], sign. WZP 1/02; Postanowienie Sądu Najwyższego z dnia 29 listopada 2006 r. [Decision of the Supreme Court from 29 November 2006], sign. I KZP 28/06.

per non est of the repeated legal provisions is obviously contradictory with the assumption of a "rational legislator".[10]

When dealing with pragmatically redundant expressions, we must remark on a special regulation concerning the use of pleonasms in penal provisions. According to Paragraph 76 of PLT2002:

> § 76. When describing the criteria for a prohibited action in a penal provision, the expressions "unlawfully", "consciously" and similar shall not be used.

This particular legislative directive refers to the phenomenon of pleonasm, since the features of unlawfulness and consciousness are already included in the very notion of criminal offence. Therefore, the use of the terms indicated in the quoted provision within criminal provisions concerning the particular types of offences (crimes) can be classified as introducing the so-called tacit pleonasms (Kłodawski 2012, 129–130) into legal texts. It is worth noting that this directive of legislative technique was first formulated in Paragraph 19, Section 1 of the PLT1939 (Wierczyński 2010, 484), thus the Polish doctrine of penal law to which it refers is definitely unchanging on this point.

According to Article 1, Paragraph 1 of the Polish Penal Code,[11] one of the necessary conditions of criminal liability is the unlawfulness of an action, that is, the violation of the valid norms of penal law by a perpetrator. The content of Articles 29[12] and 30[13] of the Polish Penal Code directly show that unlawfulness is an indispensable element of the concept of a criminal offence. By placing the aforementioned legal provisions in the general part of the Penal Code, the lawmaker decided that each criminal offence must be unlawful. Therefore, when determining the particular types of offences, the use of the feature of unlawfulness is completely redundant in effect.

In the case of a lawmaker's use of the word "consciously", we address the analogous situation, which is correlated with the penal concept of guilt accepted by Polish doctrine and expressed in penal law. According to Article 1, Paragraph

---

[10]Cf. Wyrok Sądu Najwyższego z dnia 5 marca 2003 r. [Ruling of the Supreme Court from 5 March 2003], sign. II UK 194/02; Postanowienie Sądu Najwyższego z dnia 24 czerwca 2008 r. [Decision of the Supreme Court from 24 June 2008], sign. II CNP 55/08; Wyrok Sądu Najwyższego z dnia 18 maja 2009 r. [Ruling of the Supreme Court from 18 May 2009], sign. IV KK 459/08; Wyrok Sądu Najwyższego z dnia 2 października 2009 r. [Ruling of the Supreme Court from 2 October 2009], sign. SNO 56/09.

[11]Article 1 § 1. Penal liability shall be incurred only by a person who commits an act prohibited under penalty by the law in force at the time of its commission.

[12]Article 29. Whoever commits a prohibited act in the justified, but mistaken, conviction that a circumstance has occurred that excludes unlawfulness or guilt, shall not commit an offence; if the mistake of the perpetrator is not justifiable, the court may apply the extraordinary mitigation of the penalty.

[13]Article 30. Whoever commits a prohibited act while being justifiably unaware of its unlawfulness, shall not commit an offence; if the mistake of the perpetrator is not justifiable, the court may apply the extraordinary mitigation of the penalty.

3 of the Polish Penal Code,[14] the necessary (but not sufficient) condition of the conviction is the ascription of guilt to the accused person. Thus, in order to commit an offence the perpetrator must be conscious of her/his behaviour at the moment of a delinquent act. For instance, committing a punishable offence while sleeping is conceptually excluded. The guilt must be attributed to the perpetrator and her/his consciousness at the very moment of action.

There is no doubt that the aforementioned directives of legislative technique, which prohibit repetitions of legal provisions and the use of pleonasms in legislative acts (in the domain of penal law), are correct from the logical point of view. The pragmatically redundant expressions contained in legal acts are practically useless for the logical reconstruction of a given legal system. Moreover, the superfluous legal provisions and pleonasms may provoke contradictions in juristic interpretative reasoning. The most important problem lies in how the jurists can distinguish the legal provisions, which constitute a statutory *superfluum*, from those that are meaningful and must be considered during legal interpretation. This problem is caused by the fact that logic (and the logical theory of language in particular) does not provide any precise criteria for such a differentiation. Moreover, the consequences are devastating for the logical consistency of interpretative reasoning, because, in the case of a meaningful repetition of legal provision, the interpreter must violate one of the most fundamental directives of legal interpretation; the prohibition of the homonymous interpretation of legal texts (Morawski 2002, 145–150; Wronkowska and Zieliński 1985, 310–311; Wróblewski 1991, 264). According to the formulation proposed by Wróblewski (1992, 99), this directive prescribes that:

> One should not ascribe different meanings to identical linguistic expressions [...].

Therefore, in the case of the repetitions of legal provisions and the use of pleonasms in legislative acts, the jurists must choose the lesser of two evils: either to violate the prohibition of the homonymous interpretation of legal texts, or to disregard the equally important directive of legal interpretation - the prohibition of legal interpretation *per non est* (Morawski 2002, 150–152). Of course, we can argue that, in the case of the genuine statutory *superfluum*, the interpreter does not violate the prohibition of interpretation *per non est*, as, in such a case, we address an exceptional situation: the interpretation of ius *superfluum* is pointless, since superfluous legal provisions are legally meaningless and must indeed be interpreted *per non est*. However, even if such an argument is correct, the thesis on the logical inconsistency of interpretative reasoning remains valid in reference to legally meaningful repetitions. Hence, we arrive at the conclusion that, due to the logical requirements of the consistency and coherence of legal reasoning, the directives of legislative technique expressed in Paragraphs 4.1, 4.2, 23.1, 76 and 118 of PLT2002 must be strictly followed by the lawmaker.

[14]Article 1 § 3. The perpetrator of a prohibited act does not commit an offence if the guilt cannot be attributed to her/him at the time of the commission of the act.

8.2.2 *Prohibitions of the Iteration of Legal Obligations (§4.4) and Prohibition of the Use of "Soft" Meta-normative Directives (§11)*

Secondly, let us take a look at two provisions of PLT2002, which prohibit the iteration of legal obligations and the use of "soft" meta-normative directives:

> § 4.4. A statute shall not include provisions that order the application of other normative acts, including treaties and acts referred to in Section 2.
>
> § 11. A statute shall not contain any utterances that are not intended to express legal norms, in particular any appeals, demands, recommendations, warnings or justifications of the formulated norms.

When discussing the logical correctness of these directives of legislative technique, it is useful to recall how Ross and Hart criticised Kelsen's normative conception of legal validity, founded on the concept of *Grundnorm*. According to Ross, we cannot comprehend the concept of legal validity in such a way that it stands for a legal duty to obey the law (Ross 1961, 78–82; 1968, 156–157). The normative redundancy of iterated legal obligations can best be pointed out by quoting his famous question, which concludes his argument against Kelsen's normative conception of legal validity (Ross 1961, 80):

> [...] the norm itself, according to its immediate content, expresses what the individuals ought to do. What, then, is the meaning of saying that the individuals ought to do what they ought to do?

In effect, when we interpret a validity utterance of a logical form $V(Op)$ normatively, that is, by means of an utterance of a form $O(Op)$, we see that we eo ipso multiply legal obligations *praeter necessitatem*. It appears that the only solution that makes such a normative interpretation meaningful must be based on the differentiation of the two kinds of obligation: one that is legal and one that is extra-legal (Grabowski 2013, 403–405). It means that we can interpret $O(Op)$ as $O_X(O_Lp)$, when O_X stands for some extra-legal (for instance, moral or religious) obligation. However, it is arguably an insufficient solution as far as the procedure of legislative technique is concerned. Certainly, it is not the role of the lawmaker to establish moral or religious obligations through legislative acts.

A similar conclusion stems from Hart's critique of Kelsen's theory of basic norm. In *The Concept of Law*, Hart claimed that *Grundnorm* is a "needless reduplication", because we do not need any additional rule under which the constitution "is to be obeyed", and speaking of "the rule that this rule be obeyed" is mystifying (Hart 1961, 246). Therefore, despite the fact that some authors have defended Kelsen's theory (Alexy 2002, 98–102; cf. Grabowski 2013, 407–409, 411–413), we take for granted that, from the logical point of view, the iteration of legal obligation makes no sense. As von Wright stated (1963, ix):

> [The] iteration of deontic operators to form complex symbols, such as *OO* or *PO* or $O\neg P$ etc., does not yield meaningful results.

Therefore, the prohibition of the "provisions that order the application of other normative acts", established in Paragraph 4, Section 4 of PLT2002 is logically well-founded. Naturally, we cannot completely exclude the possibility of reasonable legal provisions, which prescribe the obligation to obey or to apply the law. For example, Article 83 of the Polish Constitution[15] prescribes that:

> Everyone shall observe the law of the Republic of Poland.

This legal provision is redundant from the logical point of view, since it adds nothing to the other legal provisions that constitute the Polish legal system (the only element, that presumably has a normative legal value is the use of the word "everyone"). Nonetheless, this article appears to be quite reasonable and meaningful, because of its educational and suggestive function.

The above analysis is also applicable, mutatis mutandis, to the directive of legislative technique expressed in Paragraph 11 of PLT2002. We can maintain that a lawmaker's use of "soft" meta-normative directives, such as appeals, demands, recommendations or warnings, is pointless in the very same way as the use of the meta-rules that produce the "needless reduplication" of legal obligations. Some commentators even treat such "soft" directives of a legislator as "non-normative" utterances, from the legal perspective (Wronkowska and Zieliński 2004, 48). At this point, we can apply *a maiori ad minus* reasoning: if legal provisions of a logical form $O_L(O_L p)$ are meaningless, then the provisions of a logical form $D_S(O_L p)$ are also meaningless, since D_S (a normative operator of a "soft" directive, for instance an appeal or a recommendation) is something less than O_L (a normative operator of a rigid legal rule). In other words: if it is pointless to order the application of legal norms, or the obedience to them, then it is equally pointless for a legislator to express appeals, demands, recommendations or warnings related to the observance or application of legal norms. However, we must emphasise that this argument does not apply to the "justifications of the formulated norms", because justifications do not belong to the category of directives. Therefore, in reference to these, the logical basis for the prohibition established in Paragraph 11 of PLT2002 is unavailable. From a logical point of view the justifications of formulated legal norms, for instance, contained in the preambles to the legislative acts, are not redundant and, at least *prima facie*, are acceptable. Moreover, we may even maintain that a legislator has an obligation to justify his legislative decisions; because society has a "right to know" why the personal freedom of individuals has been limited through legislative acts (Wintgens 1999, 208). In any case, the legislator's justifications of formulated legal norms can be very helpful for the interpreters of legislative acts, despite the lack of normative dimension.

[15]Published in Dziennik Ustaw [Journal of Statutes] from 1997, No. 78, Item 483, with amendments.

8.2.3 *The Postulate of Conceptual Consistency (§10)*

Next, the provision referred to the postulate of conceptual consistency:

> § 10. Equivalent concepts shall be expressed by the same terms and different concepts shall not be expressed by the same terms.

The postulate of conceptual consistency (introduced by Wronkowska and Zieliński (1985, 310–311) in a form of the "directive of consistency"), is an important consequence of the assumption of a "rational legislator", which strongly influenced the content of PLT2002. A fulfilment of this postulate is not a unique way to make legal text precise, but it is one of the most useful. When a lawmaker uses the same legal terms in the way prescribed in Paragraph 10, a legal interpreter is obliged to ascribe the same meaning to them, according to the prohibition of the homonymous interpretation of legal texts, already discussed in Section 8.2.1. Furthermore, when a lawmaker uses different legal terms, they then, even if they are synonyms in ordinary language, nevertheless have to be interpreted differently, according to the complementary prohibition of the synonymous interpretation of legal texts (Wróblewski 1991, 286; Morawski 2002, 144–145). For example, as Banaszak (2009, 667–668) observed, with respect to the interpretation of the provisions of the Polish Constitution:

> The use of the term "time of war" by the legislator indicates an intentional emphasis on the terminological difference in relation to the "state of war' and "martial law". [...] If a rational lawmaker did not intend to differentiate all these concepts, he would apply uniform terminology.

Undoubtedly, it is not a lawmaker's task to show erudition. The use of synonyms is greatly appreciated in poetry, but a lawmaker's basic legal duty is to issue legal provisions that are clear and precise. Ambiguous terms and synonyms, so common in everyday language, should be avoided in the language of law. A lawmaker should be aware that the more clear and precise is the legal text, the fewer the problems that will arise during its interpretation. Moreover, the clarity of legal provisions facilitates the uniform interpretation of law.[16]

According to the judicial decisions of the Polish Constitutional Tribunal, if legal provisions are unclear and their linguistic forms could lead to diverse juristic interpretations, they can be acknowledged as being inconsistent with the principle of the democratic law-governed (rule of law) state, expressed in Article 2 of the Polish Constitution. This principle comprises the more particular principle of trust in the state and its positive law, which in turn entails the requirement of the appropriate quality of legal provisions, including the demand for the linguistic consistency of legal regulations.[17] Therefore, from the legal point of view, a lawmaker has a duty

---

[16] Wyrok Trybunału Konstytucyjnego z 2 lipca 2007 r. [Ruling of the Constitutional Tribunal from 2 July 2007], sign. K 41/05.

[17] Wyrok Trybunału Konstytucyjnego z dnia 6 maja 2008 r. [Ruling of the Constitutional Tribunal from 6 May 2008], sign. K 18/05.

to formulate legal provisions pursuant to Paragraph 10 of PLT2002, that is, he must use the same terms to express equivalent concepts, and different terms to express different concepts in legal texts. If he does not observe this directive of legislation, a legal provision, or even the entire statute, can be recognised as unconstitutional.[18]

However, the postulate of conceptual consistency is not absolute. For instance, sometimes identical legal terms must be interpreted differently. As stated in one of the rulings of the Polish Supreme Administrative Court[19]:

> [. . .] although practice of this sort is not advisable, a lawmaker may ascribe different content to the same term in different legal acts. [. . .] Just then one shall use not only the grammatical interpretation of a given provision, but, while seeking out its ratio legis, make use of the other kinds of interpretation, in particular, those that are systemic and teleological.

Conversely, the prohibition of the synonymous interpretation of legal texts is also defeasible.[20] In addition, the possibility of exceptions from the postulate of conceptual consistency is accepted in Polish legal theory; both a homonymous and a synonymous interpretation of legal texts are acceptable, provided that the formulation of legal provisions requires such an exceptional interpretation (Wróblewski 1991, 286; 1992, 99).

However, from the point of view of the constitutional principle of correct legislation, we cannot evaluate these exceptions positively.[21] If a lawmaker intends to introduce different legal concepts, the simplest, and a fully acceptable, legislative method consists of using various legal terms in legal texts. Moreover, if a lawmaker wants to change the legal interpretation of a given legal term, he has to write it down distinctly, for example, by defining it anew. The Polish Constitutional Tribunal determines the appropriate legislative *modus operandi* in such a case as follows[22]:

> If legislator wants to change the meaning of expressions already used in other statutes, it should be clearly noted in the new statute.

We must add, *per analogiam* to the famous Perelman's principle of inertia (Perelman and Olbrechts-Tyteca 1969, 105–108; Atienza 1993, 72), that the change of an established meaning of a legal term must be properly justified. Moreover, the possibility of a homonymous interpretation (of the same legal term) can be justified exclusively by extra-linguistic reasons (for example, by an argument from ratio legis), whereas the possibility of a synonymous interpretation (of different legal

[18]Wyrok Trybunału Konstytucyjnego z dnia 17 grudnia 2002 r. [Ruling of the Constitutional Tribunal from 17 December 2002], sign. U 3/02.

[19]Wyrok Naczelnego Sądu Administracyjnego z dnia 6 grudnia 1996 r. [Ruling of the Supreme Administrative Court from 6 December 1996], sign. III SA 1091/91.

[20]Uchwała Trybunału Konstytucyjnego z dnia 5 września 1995 r. [Resolution of the Constitutional Tribunal from 5 September 1995], sign. W 1/95.

[21]Uchwała Naczelnego Sądu Administracyjnego z dnia 20 marca 2000 r. [Resolution of the Supreme Administrative Court from 20 March 2000], sign. FPS 14/99.

[22]Uchwała Trybunału Konstytucyjnego z 21 stycznia 1992 r. [Resolution of the Constitutional Tribunal from 29 January 1992], sign. W 14/91.

terms) can be justified by using linguistic arguments (for instance, by an argument from ordinary meaning). In the context of the principle of legal certainty, the possibility of homonymous interpretation of legal terms is worse than synonymous interpretation, because the individuals can be very surprised with the new meaning of a legal term to which they have already become accustomed. Furthermore, the change of meaning of a legal term constitutes a violation, only sometimes well-justified, and therefore acceptable, of the abovementioned principle of inertia; a principle so important for people's certainty in the practical sphere of human life:

> Inertia makes it possible to rely on the normal, the habitual, the real, and the actual and to attach a value to them, whether it is a matter of an existing situation, an accepted opinion, or a state of regular and continuous development. Change, on the other hand, has to be justified; once a decision has been taken, it cannot be changed except for sufficient reasons (Perelman and Olbrechts-Tyteca 1969, 106).

Generally speaking, we must evaluate the ambiguity of (legal) terms completely negatively from the logical point of view, whereas the evaluation of a linguistic phenomenon of synonymy can be diverse, depending on the context. Similarly, the occurrence of the homonymous legal interpretation is unjustified from a logical perspective, while the synonymous interpretation is less questionable. People are used to synonyms in everyday language, and are educated to know and apply them, for instance, in order to formulate (nominal) definitions. Therefore, despite the logical correctness of the directive of legislative technique expressed in Paragraph 10 of PLT2002, an obvious *de lege ferenda* postulate is to emphasise the unexceptional character of the rule that prohibits the use of the same legal term for different legal concepts, thus excluding the possibility of a homonymous legal interpretation.

8.2.4 The Directives of Legislative Technique Concerning Legal Definitions (§§146–153)

The issue of legal definition is regulated by eight provisions of PLT2002. In the context of our analysis, the most important of these are paragraphs 146, 151 and 153. The first of these determines the conditions for the enactment of legal definitions:

> § 146.1. A statute or another legislative act shall provide the definition of a certain term if:
> 1) The term is ambiguous;
> 2) The term is vague and it is advisable to define it precisely;
> 3) The meaning of such a term is not generally understood;
> 4) Considering the area of the regulated matters, it is necessary to define a new meaning of the term.
>
> 2. If an ambiguous term appears only in one provision of law, its definition shall be provided only if it is impossible to eliminate such ambiguity by placing the term in the relevant linguistic context.

These conditions are coherent with the general principles of precision and comprehensibility of legal texts, established in Paragraph 6 of PLT2002.[23] From the logical point of view, the difference between the conditions for legal definitions of ambiguous terms and vague terms is particularly important. In the case of ambiguous legal terms, the lawmaker is generally obliged to provide a legal definition; the only exception to this is stipulated in Section 2. The case of vague legal terms is more complex. We must note that, in PLT2002, the legislative technique of using vague terms in legal texts is regulated quite laconically:

> § 155.1. If it is necessary to ensure a certain flexibility of a normative act, then vague terms and general clauses may be used [. . .].

Commentators on PLT2002 unanimously agree that the use of vague legal terms by a lawmaker is a legally acknowledged legislative tool for ensuring the flexibility of legal provisions (Zieliński 2002, 169–171; Wronkowska and Zieliński 2004, 293–294; Andruszkiewicz and Kosielińska-Grabowska 2007, 18; Malinowski et al. 2009, 309–313; Wierczyński 2010, 761). Similarly, in many judicial decisions, the Polish Constitutional Tribunal emphasised the fact that the use of vague legal terms is not constitutionally unacceptable.[24] To quote one instructive example[25]:

> [. . .] the use of vague terms in the law cannot be *a priori* treated as a legislative infringement, because the construction of a certain legal norm with their use is often the only reasonable way out.

However, we must note the important difference. The obligation to provide a definition of ambiguous legal terms is unconditional (except in the situation indicated in Section 2 of Paragraph 146), whereas a lawmaker's decision on whether or not a legal definition of a vague term will be provided is discretional. In PLT2002, we do not even find a hint (not to mention a firm rule) on when "it is advisable" to define a vague legal term. Hence, it depends solely on the lawmaker's will and wisdom. This legal gap in PLT2002 is only partially and indirectly filled by the judicial decisions of the Polish Constitutional Tribunal. In one of the decisions concerning the question of the constitutionality of legal provisions, the Tribunal ruled that only such vagueness, or lack of clarity of statutory legal provisions that cannot be removed with the use of the accepted methods of legal interpretation, renders these provisions unconstitutional.[26] Thus, it follows that the legal definition

[23]§ 6. Statutory provisions shall be edited to express the legislator's intention in a way that is precise and comprehensible for the addressees of the regulations set forth therein.

[24]Cf. Postanowienie Trybunału Konstytucyjnego z dnia 27 kwietnia 2004 [Decision of the Constitutional Tribunal from 27 April 2004], sign. P 16/03; Wyrok Trybunału Konstytucyjnego z dnia 8 maja 2006 r. [Ruling of the Constitutional Tribunal from 8 May 2006], sign. P 18/05.

[25]Uchwała Trybunału Konstytucyjnego z dnia 6 listopada 1991 r. [Resolution of the Constitutional Tribunal from 6 November 1991], sign. W 2/91. This thesis was entirely confirmed in Wyrok Trybunału Konstytucyjnego z dnia 27 października 2010 r. [Ruling of the Constitutional Tribunal from 27 October 2010], sign. K 10/08.

[26]Postanowienie Trybunału Konstytucyjnego z dnia 27 kwietnia 2004 [Decision of the Constitutional Tribunal from 27 April 2004], sign. P 16/03.

of a vague term is sometimes legally necessary, despite the fact that PLT2002 is silent on this specific issue.

Paragraphs 151 and 153 focus on the nature and linguistic stylisation of legal definitions:

§ 151.1. A definition shall be phrased so as to clearly indicate that it refers to the meaning of respective terms, in particular it shall be in the following form: "The term ⟨⟨a⟩⟩ shall mean objects b." or "The term ⟨⟨a⟩⟩ shall mean the phrase ⟨⟨b⟩⟩.".

2. If, for stylistic reasons, a different form of a definition should be applied, the connecting phrase "it is" shall be used.

§ 153.1. An extensional definition [. . .] shall be contained in one legal provision and cover the entire extension of the defined term.

2. If it is impossible to enumerate all elements of the extension of the defined term in one provision, the definition shall clearly state that the text of the same or another statute also comprises elements supplementing the definition, in particular by using the expression ". . .. and others indicated in the provisions. . ..".

3. If it is impossible to formulate a definition referred to in Section 1 or 2, the meaning of an expression may be elucidated by an exemplary enumeration of the extension, expressly indicating the exemplary nature of such enumeration by using the phrases: "including without limitation" or "in particular".

These provisions determine two relationships of preference for lawmaking acts. Firstly, the extensional legal definitions take precedence over those that are intensional. The legislator shall prefer legal definitions that determine the extension of a defined legal term by enumerating all or, at least, some of its most important *designata* ("objects", "elements"). Secondly, the priority is conferred upon the meta-linguistic definitions.

Both relationships are based on jurisprudential reasons. The priority of extensional legal definitions is founded on the thesis that the primary task of the lawmaker is to provide extensional definitions of legal terms, whereas the primary task of legal dogmatics is to elaborate on their intensional definitions (Zirk-Sadowski 2000, 218), usually in the form of a so-called classic (Aristotelian) definition; *per genus proximum et differentiam specificam* (Patryas 1997, 13–20, 127–128). The priority of the meta-linguistic definitions is meant to be a solution to the problem of the proper identification of legal definitions in legal texts, which is one of the most complicated issues of legal interpretation (Bielska-Brodziak 2008, 162–166). It is obvious that meta-linguistic definitions, in which *definiendum* and (sometimes) *definiens* are put in quotation marks, are easy to recognise in legal texts.

Although the justification of the above-discussed paragraphs is not based on logic, we can observe that the formulation of these provisions is logically correct. In the context of various types, forms and stylisations of definitions, provided by the contemporary logical theory of definition (Ziembiński 1976, 51–66; Kotarbińska 1990; Gupta 2014), we can state that the authors of PLT2002 have selected appropriate types and stylisations for legal definitions. The differentiation of the conditions for the enactment of legal definitions of ambiguous and vague legal terms, and the preference for the extensional and meta-linguistic legal definitions, do not raise any logical objections. It appears that the only deficiency in the regulation of PLT2002 concerning legal definitions consists in too narrow formulation of the exception in Section 2 of Paragraph 146. The meaning of an ambiguous legal term can be clearly determined by placing it in a "relevant linguistic context" also when it appears in more than one legal provision (Wronkowska and Zieliński 1985, 311).

8.3 A Provisional Typology of Relations Between Logic and the Directives of Legislative Technique

Before we propose a provisional typology of relationships between logic and the directives of legislative technique, let us focus for a moment on the general problem of the logical rationality of lawmaking. According to Atienza (1992, 273):

> [. . .] in any cognitive or practical problem a logical dimension is involved - an argumentative dimension - so it can be said that logical rationality is the most basic level of rationality and it is of an instrumental nature in relation to theoretical rationality and practical rationality.

In his analysis of the problem of the rationality of lawmaking, Atienza distinguished as many as five levels of rationality. However, in the context of the directives of legislative technique, only two of these are of interest to us: linguistic rationality and legal-formal rationality. Linguistic rationality concerns clarity and precision of normative messages issued by the author of legislative acts and the underlying value is to guarantee good communication between the legislator and the addressees of legal norms (Atienza 1992, 277–279). This level of rationality appears to be closely connected with the presumption of the perfect linguistic competence of "rational legislator" (Wróblewski 1989, 48; Wronkowska 1990, 123). On the level of legal-formal rationality, the question at hand is the systemic quality of a legal order; while issuing legal provisions, the lawmaker must avoid normative contradictions, legal gaps and superfluity in a particular legal system created by him (Atienza 1992, 277, 279). Of greater importance, the level of legal-formal rationality is precisely the level on which the directives of legislative technique are applied:

> What is sometimes called legislative technique in the strict sense operates basically on this second level of rationality, which, as has been seen, presupposes the first (Atienza 1992, 279).

Therefore, we may ascertain that the relationships between logic and the directives of legislative technique belong to the domains of the linguistic and the legal-formal rationality of lawmaking. This observation takes us closer to explaining the nature of these relationships, yet we must proceed very cautiously, because the achievement of the linguistic and the legal-formal rationality of lawmaking constitute only the end of the directives of legislative technique. Thus, the question that remains open is: What role does logic (and logical theory of language in particular) play in the creation and formulation of the directives of legislative technique?

The analysis of the examples taken from the PLT2002 shows that the role in question can be diverse. With the help of the theoretical distinction (Bobbio 1988; Lang 2002; Wróblewski 1990) of the substantive (strong) reasons (rationality) concerning the content of a rule or decision, the formal (weak) reasons (rationality) related to the structure of reasoning, and the instrumental (technical) reasons (rationality) based on the relationship between means and ends, we can characterise the relationship between logic and the directives of legislative technique.

First, we can observe that in the cases of the prohibition of the repetition of legal provisions (§§ 4.1–4.2, 23.1, 118), of the prohibition of the iteration of legal obligations (§ 4.4) and of the requirement of conceptual consistency (§ 10) in reference to the homonymous legal terms, the logic fulfils the role of the substantive (strong) reason for the mentioned provisions of PLT2002. The repetitions of legal provisions (*ius superfluum*), the normative iteration of legal obligations and the introduction of ambiguous legal terms into legal texts, are all explicit logical errors, as demonstrated by the logical theory of normative systems, deontic logic and the logical theory of meaning (respectively). Thus, we can claim that the regulations of PLT2002 listed above are substantively founded on logic. We propose calling this relationship between logic and the directives of legislative technique "strong justification".

Second, in the cases of the prohibition of the use of meta-normative "soft" directives (§ 11), the prohibition of the use of pleonasms in criminal provisions (§ 76), and the requirement of conceptual consistency (§ 10) in reference to the use of synonyms in legal texts, the role of logic is somewhat weaker. The logical theory of meaning, which supports the formulation of the mentioned provisions, does not permit classification of linguistic phenomena, to which these provisions of PLT2002 refer, as logical errors. At most, the lawmaker's use of meta-normative "soft" directives, pleonasms and synonyms can be qualified as logically not recommendable. Since the justification of these provisions is directly connected with the analysis of legal interpretative reasoning, it appears that we can regard the logical theory of meaning as a formal (weak) reason for the indicated provisions. Therefore, we propose calling this type of relationship between logic and the directives of legislative technique "weak justification".

Third, with respect to the directives of legislative technique concerning legal definitions (§§ 146–153), the role of logic, the logical theory of definition, is primarily instrumental. These directives are directly justified by jurisprudential reasons, and the role that logic plays therein is fairly supplementary; the purpose of the use of logical concepts and terminology is the appropriate formulation of the indicated provisions of PLT2002. Thus, in this case, we address an instrumental relationship between logic and the directives of legislative technique, which can be called "instrumental justification".

8.4 Conclusions: The Directives of Legislative Technique and the Logical Rationality of Lawmaking

The knowledge of logic, and of the logical theory of language in particular, constitutes one of the most important elements of legal education. It is also very useful in legal practice and legal science, as emphasised by Bulygin (2008, 151):

> Law is an extremely complex cultural phenomenon. Its study must draw on the resources of many disciplines, including history, sociology, economics, etc. But as a cultural and intellectual institution, it also needs structural analysis and this is where the tools of logic and set theory are required. [...] What logic, or rather logical analysis, can do [...] is to clarify legal concepts and thus introduce greater order, thereby deepening our understanding of legal phenomena.

Without any doubt, logic is an instrument that is often used during the creation of law, the systematisation of law, the application of law and legal interpretation. In our opinion, it is exactly the parallelism of the directives of correct legislation and the directives of legal interpretation that form the best examples of the role that logic plays in law and legal reasoning.

The logical rationality of law is arguably a fundamental legal value, for the legislator, for legal scholars and for practicing lawyers. In order to achieve it, the process of lawmaking that is legally regulated by the directives of legislative technique, must be logically correct. In this paper we have demonstrated that the logic justifies the content of some legislative directives formulated in PLT2002, and that it constitutes a supplementary foundation for several others. The second decisive factor in the rationality of lawmaking is the legislator's rationality in the domain of the politics of law (Lang 2002, 282; Wróblewski 1983, 26–28). Both elements, only loosely connected, produce the effect of synergy. In any case, the logical rationality of law appears to be hardly possible without the logical rationality of the lawmaking process and the rational politics of law.

The idea of the logical rationality of lawmaking has influenced the authors of the Polish "Principles of Legislative Technique", the basic goal of which was to improve the quality of Polish legislation. To strive for the perfection of legislative acts is an obvious aim of lawyers and legal science, especially in such numerous states (including Poland), wherein the legislative technical quality of the statutory law leaves a lot to be desired (Goetz and Zubek 2005; Wronkowska 2009). As shown in the abovementioned jurisdiction of the Polish Constitutional Tribunal, the lawmaker's violation of the directives of legislative technique, formulated in PLT2002, has often resulted in the Tribunal's decision on unconstitutionality of the legislatively defective statutory legal provisions. The lawmaking of a poor legislative quality has a very negative impact on the judicial application of law. Legislatively defective normative acts also ruin the predictability of legal decisions, which is very important for the addressees of legal norms.

The scientific research on the logical fundamentals of the directives of legislative technique and the principles of rational lawmaking are especially important as far as the improvement of the quality of legislation is concerned. In the education of law students, the specific relationship between logic and the directives of correct legislation should also be considered. In this context, the scientific works on logic and legislation, for example, Patryas' textbook (2001), must be welcomed with full approval. Nonetheless, it appears that there is still a great deal to be accomplished. The importance of good quality legislation must be reflected in jurisprudential investigations. Incorrect legislation, and the violation of the directives of legislative technique in particular, has a devastating effect on legal practice and the perception of positive law in society.

References

Alexy, Robert. 2002. *The argument from injustice. A reply to legal positivism* (trans: Litschewski Paulson, B., Paulson, St.L.). Oxford: Clarendon Press.

Andruszkiewicz, Marta, Urszula Kosielińska-Grabowska. 2007. Prawodawca w labiryncie definicji legalnej [The Lawmaker in the Labyrinth of Legal Definition]. *Studia Prawno-Ekonomiczne* LXXV:9–36.

Atienza, Manuel. 1992. Practical reason and legislation. *Ratio Juris* 5:269–287.

Atienza, Manuel. 1993. *Las Razones del Derecho. Teorías de la argumentatión jurídica*, 2nd ed. Madrid: Centro de Estudios Constitucionales.

Banaszak, Bogusław. 2009. *Konstytucja Rzeczypospolitej Polskiej. Komentarz* [The Constitution of the Republic of Poland. A Commentary]. Warszawa: C.H. Beck.

Bielska-Brodziak, Agnieszka. 2008. Kłopoty z definicjami legalnymi [Difficulties with Legal Definitions]. In *System prawa a porządek prawny*, ed. O. Boguski and S. Czepita, 159–174. Szczecin: Wydawnictwo Naukowe Uniwersytetu Szczecińskiego.

Bobbio, Norberto. 1988. Reason in law. *Ratio Juris* 1:97–108.

Brożek, Bartosz, Zyzik Radosław. 2012. The theory and practice of lawmaking. A Polish perspective. In *Public law: Twenty years after. The public law after 1989 from the Polish perspective*, ed. K. Wojtyczek, 75–90. London: European Public Law Center.

Bulygin, Eugenio. 2008. What can one expect from logic in the law? (Not Everything, but More than Something: A Reply to Susan Haack). *Ratio Juris* 21:150–156.

Goetz, Klaus H., Radosław Zubek. 2005. *Stanowienie prawa w Polsce. Reguły legislacyjne a jakość ustawodawstwa* [Lawmaking in Poland. Legislative Rules and the Quality of Legislation]. Warszawa: Ernst&Young Poland.

Grabowski, Andrzej. 2013. *Juristic concept of the validity of statutory law. A critique of contemporary legal nonpositivism*. Trans. M. Kiełtyka. Heidelberg/New York/Dordrecht/London: Springer.

Gupta, Anil. 2014. Definitions. In *The Stanford encyclopedia of philosophy*, ed. E.N. Zalta. http://plato.stanford.edu/archives/spr2014/entries/definitions/. Accessed 26 Mar 2014.

Hart, H.L.A. 1961. *The concept of law*. Oxford: Clarendon Press.

Kłodawski, Maciej. 2012. Pleonazmy i analityzmy - wyrażenia redundantne pragmatycznie w języku prawnym [Pleonasms and Analytical Phrases - the Pragmatically Redundant Expressions in Legal Language]. In *Język współczesnego prawa*, ed. A. Niewiadomski, E. Sztymelska, 121–132. Warszawa: Wydawnictwo Koła Naukowego Lingua Iuris.

Kotarbińska, Janina. 1990. Definicja [Definition]. In eadem, *Z zagadnień teorii nauki i teorii języka*, 128–151. Warszawa: Państwowe Wydawnictwo Naukowe.

Lang, Wiesław. 2002. Racjonalność prawa [Rationality of Law]. In *Odwaga filozofowania. Leszkowi Nowakowi w darze*, ed. J. Brzeziński, A. Klawiter, T.A.F. Kuipers, K. Łastowski, K. Paprzycka, P. Przybysz, 273–291. Poznań: Wydawnictwo Fundacji Humaniora.

Malinowski, Andrzej, Andrzej Bałaban, Dorota Dąbek, Piotr Kędziora, Radosław Pawelec, and Ryszard Piotrowski. 2009. *Zarys metodyki pracy legislatora* [An Outline of the Methods of Legislator's Work]. Warszawa: LexisNexis.
Morawski, Lech. 2002. Wykładnia w orzecznictwie sądów. Komentarz [Interpretation in Courts' Decisions. A Commentary]. Toruń: Wydawnictwo Dom Organizatora.
Nowak, Leszek. 1969. De la rationalité du législateur comme élément de l'interpretation juridique. *Logique et Analyse* 45: 65–86.
Nowak, Leszek. 1973. *Interpretacja prawnicza. Studium z metodologii prawoznawstwa* [Legal Interpretation. A Study on the Methodology of Jurisprudence]. Warszawa: Państwowe Wydawnictwo Naukowe.
Patryas, Wojciech. 1997. *Definiowanie pojęć prawnych* [Defining Legal Concepts]. Poznań: Wydawnictwo Naukowe UAM.
Patryas, Wojciech. 2001. *Elementy logiki i legislacji* [The Elements of Logic and Legislation], 2nd ed. Poznań: Holding Edukacyjny - Paweł Pietrzyk.
Perelman, Chaïm, Lucie Olbrechts-Tyteca. 1969. *The new rhetoric. A treatise on argumentation* (trans: Wilkinson, J., Weaver, P.). Notre Dame/London: University of Notre Dame Press.
Piszko, Robert. 2002. Zasady techniki prawodawczej w procesie wykładni prawa [The Principles of Legislative Technique in the Practice of Law Interpretation]. *Ruch Prawniczy, Ekonomiczny i Socjologiczny* LXIV:23–40.
Ross, Alf. 1961. Validity and the conflict between legal positivism and natural law. *Revista Jurídica de Buenos Aires* IV:46–88.
Ross, Alf. 1968. *Directives and norms*. London: Routledge and Kegan Paul/New York: Humanities Press.
von Wright, Georg Henrik. 1963. *Norm and action. A logical enquiry*. London: Routledge and Kegan Paul.
Wierczyński, Grzegorz. 2010. *Redagowanie i ogłaszanie aktów normatywnych*. Komentarz [Editing and Promulgating the Normative Acts. A Commentary]. Warszawa: Wolters Kluwer Polska.
Wintgens, Luc J. 1999. Legisprudence: Elements for a new theory of legislation. *Associations* 3:185–209.
Wróblewski, Jerzy. 1978. Tworzenie prawa a wykładnia prawa [The Creation of Law and Legal Interpretation]. *Państwo i Prawo* 6:5–16.
Wróblewski, Jerzy. 1983. Polityka tworzenia prawa a hierarchia wartości [The Politics of Lawmaking and the Hierarchy of Values]. *Państwo i Prawo* 9:25–36.
Wróblewski, Jerzy. 1989. *Zasady tworzenia prawa* [The Principles of Lawmaking]. Warszawa: Państwowe Wydawnictwo Naukowe.
Wróblewski, Jerzy. 1990. Principles, values, and rules in legal decision-making and the dimensions of legal rationality. *Ratio Juris* 3:100–117.
Wróblewski, Jerzy. 1991. Statutory interpretation in Poland. In *Interpreting statutes. A comparative study*, ed. D.N. MacCormick and R.S. Summers, 257–309. Aldershot: Dartmouth.
Wróblewski, Jerzy. 1992. *The judicial application of law* (trans: Bańkowski, Z., MacCormick, N.). Dordrecht/Boston/London: Kluwer Academic.
Wronkowska, Sławomira. 1990. Prawodawca racjonalny jako wzór dla prawodawcy faktycznego [The Rational Legislator as a Model for the Real Lawmaker]. In *Szkice z teorii prawa i szczegółowych nauk prawnych*, ed. S. Wronkowska, M. Zieliński, 117–134. Poznań: Wydawnictwo Naukowe Uniwersytetu im. Adama Mickiewicza w Poznaniu.
Wronkowska, Sławomira. 2009. Proces prawodawczy dwóch dekad - sukcesy i niepowodzenia [The Legislative Process of the Last Two Decades - Successes and Failures]. *Ruch Prawniczy, Ekonomiczny i Socjologiczny* LXXI:111–129.
Wronkowska, Sławomira, Maciej Zieliński. 1985. O korespondencji dyrektyw redagowania i interpretowania tekstu prawnego [On the Correspondence of the Directives of the Edition and the Interpretation of Legal Texts]. *Studia Prawnicze* 3–4:301–327.
Wronkowska, Sławomira, Maciej Zieliński. 1993. *Problemy i zasady techniki redagowania tekstów prawnych* [The Problems and Principles of the Technique of Editing Legal Texts]. Warszawa: Urząd Rady Ministrów.

Wronkowska, Sławomira, Maciej Zieliński. 2004. *Komentarz do zasad techniki prawodawczej z dnia 20 czerwca 2002 r.* [Commentary to the Principles of Legislative Technique of 20 June 2002], Warszawa: Wydawnictwo Sejmowe.

Zalasiński, Tomasz. 2008. *Zasady prawidłowej legislacji w poglądach Trybunału Konstytucyjnego* [The Principles of Correct Legislation in the Views of the Constitutional Tribunal]. Warszawa: Wydawnictwo Sejmowe.

Zieliński, Maciej. 2002. *Wykładnia prawa. Zasady. Reguły. Wskazówki* [Legal Interpretation: Principles, Rules, Hints]. Warszawa: Wydawnictwo Prawnicze LexisNexis.

Ziembiński, Zygmunt. 1976. *Practical logic* (trans: Ter-Oganian, L.). Warszawa: Państwowe Wydawnictwo Naukowe/Dordrecht: D. Reidel.

Ziembiński, Zygmunt. 1985. Two concepts of rationality in legislation. *Rechtstheorie Bh.* 8:139–150.

Zirk-Sadowski, Marek. 2000. *Wprowadzenie do filozofii prawa* [Introduction to Legal Philosophy]. Kraków: Zakamycze.

Chapter 9
The Hidden Acts of Definition in Law: Statutory Definitions and Burden of Persuasion

Fabrizio Macagno and Giovanni Damele

Abstract The concept of "definition" refers both to a propositional structure, namely a type of convertible relation between the *definiens* and the *definiendum*, and a speech act that can have various definitional purposes. On the one hand, definitions can have different subject matter. For instance, it is possible to define a concept (essential definitions), the meaning of its linguistic expression (etymological definition), its possible extension (definition by enumeration), an illustration of its possible denotations (definition by example), or the operation that can be used to classify the entities falling under it (operational definition). On the other hand, definitions are the propositional content of acts aimed at producing specific effects. Definitions can impose a new meaning, or remind or inform the interlocutors of criteria of classification. However, from an argumentative perspective the acts of stipulating, reminding or informing of, or committing to a definition are not as dangerous as the implicit acts of omitting a definition and implicitly defining and redefining a concept. Sometimes crucial concepts, especially the ones concerning problematic ethical or political issues, are ill described or are left (intentionally or unintentionally) undefined. This gap can become the ground of extremely effective strategies based on tacit (re)definitions. These uses of definition can shed light on the definitional activity of the lawmakers. Statutory definitions become in this sense a limitation of the interpreters' freedom of redefining strategically a concept. For this reason, the choice of leaving a concept undefined or underdefined can be regarded as a delegation of powers to the bodies in charge of interpreting the statutes.

Keywords Definition • Redefinition • Interpretation • Argumentation schemes • Analogy • Rhetorical strategies

---

We would like to thank the Fundação para a Ciência e a Tecnologia for the research grant on Argumentation, Communication and Context (PTDC/FIL-FIL/110117/2009).

F. Macagno (✉) • G. Damele
ArgLab, IFL, Faculdade de Ciências Sociais e Humanas, Universidade Nova de Lisboa, Lisboa, Portugal
e-mail: fabrizio.macagno@fcsh.unl.pt; fabriziomacagno@hotmail.com; giovanni.damele@fcsh.unl.pt

M. Araszkiewicz, K. Płeszka (eds.), *Logic in the Theory and Practice of Lawmaking*, Legisprudence Library 2, DOI 10.1007/978-3-319-19575-9_9

9.1 Introduction

Definitions can be thought of as premises in complex patterns of reasoning (Aarnio 1977; Lindahl 2004; Moore 1980). In law they are of crucial importance, as they constitute the fundamental premise of arguments from classification (Walton, Reed and Macagno 2008), namely patterns of inference in which a legal predicate is attributed to an entity on the basis of the set of semantic features that constitutes the definition (Schiappa 2003; Zarefsky 2006, 404). Legal definitions are fundamental instruments that the lawmaker uses to try to reduce the interpretative freedom of the interpreter and forge a technical language through the re-use of terms belonging to ordinary language (Mortara Garavelli 2001, 11). Definitions can limit the interpretative discretion that constitutes the passage from a normative sentence to a legal norm (Tarello 1980, 337–339). However, in matter of legal definitions, the boundaries between the lawmaker and the interpreter are often blurred. Tarello noticed that legal definitions, inasmuch as normative sentences, need to be interpreted, namely they need to go through a process of meaning attribution (Tarello 1980, 155). Therefore, both the use of the definitions existing in legal texts and the activity of redefinition carried out by the interpreter can be considered as interpretative activities, as both the defined terms and the definitions need to be interpreted (Tarello 1980, 156). For this reason, legal definitions can fulfill their role of limiting the interpretative freedom only after, in turn, being interpreted. Such definitions are, therefore, only contingently effective: they are effective only when the terms constituting the *definiens* are less controversial than the *definiendum*.

In order to account for the different types of acts of definition and redefinition in legal interpretation, it is useful to draw a distinction between two types of definitional acts, namely the descriptive or "explicative" definitions, and the stipulative or "statutory" definitions. Both acts commit both the legislator and the people subject to the law to the definition. However, the first ones fix univocally and precisely the meaning of a potentially ambiguous or vague *definiendum* by taking it from its previous uses (Scarpelli 1985, 65). In this sense, they do not impose a new commitment; they only remind it to the addressees or specify it. Stipulative definitions introduce a new meaning of a word in order to build an artificial and unambiguous lexicon with a view to prevent potential ambiguities (Hall 1966, 15; Aarnio 1987, 57; Belvedere 1998, 88). In this sense, they create a new commitment.

Both types of definitional acts are aimed virtually at addressing and limiting two fundamental problems, ambiguity and vagueness. However, this may result in generating interpretative controversies due to the vague terms used in the definitions. Legal texts are worded in a natural language, which is clearly characterized by polysemy (different definitions related to a common core meaning) and controversial and unclear definitions. Redefinitions are used to specify one of the possible meanings that a word can have, or set the boundaries of a concept characterized by a "grey area" or borderline cases (Burgess-Jackson 1995). In this fashion, a specific, technical lexicon is produced, so that potential risks of conflicting interpretations are ideally prevented. However, the creation of a technical and unambiguous language is virtually impossible. On the one hand, in order to be understood by citizens, legal texts need to be expressed in ordinary language: "legal language is itself ordinary language, and for this reason, in a way, there is a "burden of proof" that any deviation from ordinary language usage [...] must be justified" (Aarnio 1987, 101). For this reason, the ambiguity and the vagueness of ordinary language can be only limited, not eliminated, and the absence of legal definitions of particularly vague terms (such as "torture") leaves room for the strategic uses of redefinition. On the other hand, legal language is also a technical language, as it is based also on a specific lexicon different from the ordinary one, which can lead to three risks. First, some technical terms can be introduced without being explicitly defined (see for instance the term "enemy combatant" in the US code), which can allow the interpreter to introduce *ad hoc* definitions for the purpose of justifying a classification. Second, legal definitions are texts that need to be interpreted (Tarello 1980, 155) as they are based on ordinary words, which can be interpreted in different fashions. Finally, legal definitions, can introduce ambiguity when different definitions are provided for the same *definiendum* by the legislator and the judge (the interpreter).

These areas of ambiguity and vagueness can be used strategically. The interpreter can use or introduce specific definitions to justify a classification of a case. For this reason, the vagueness of a concept becomes a strategic resource to be exploited. This practice has been called "rhetorical definition" (Lausberg 1998; Mortara Garavelli 1988), that is, a "figure of speech" based on the selection of the semantic features that can be persuasive, disregarding others that, even though equally important, are potentially self-defeating. In some cases, this definitional move can become a "persuasive definition" (Stevenson 1944). These term refers to an argumentative strategy consisting in changing the denotative meaning of an "ethical" word in order to make it possible to predicate it of an object or a state of affairs that otherwise would not be included in the extension of the term (Macagno and Walton 2008). An extremely powerful type of redefinition is the so-called implicit or pragmatically "spurious" definition (Mortara Garavelli 2001, 15–16). This type of definition, at the basis of the so-called argument by definition (Zarefsky 2006, 404), is not provided explicitly, but it is rather presupposed by the act of classifying an entity by means of a definition that is not commonly shared. In law, such definitions are presupposed by the use of a specific term with a technical meaning that cannot be derived from other legislative texts or based on previous legal interpretations or a commonly accepted legal definition (Lausberg 1981, 165). In this case, a word belonging to the ordinary language is used by the interpreter with a technical, specific meaning different from the commonly shared one. For instance, a defendant who was growing cannabis in vases can be acquitted from the accusation of having a "plantation" of cannabis as falling outside the art 26 of the Italian Consolidated Drugs Act (Cassazione Penale, XXXVII, 1997, n. 3, p. 570).

The purpose of this paper is to analyze the strategic uses of definitions, and in particular the uses of the implicit redefinitions, showing the different types and the distinct effects of these interpretative strategies.

9.2 Redefinitions and Vagueness: Omitting Definitions

In law, like in ordinary dialogical and dialectical (in the sense of adversarial) contexts, terms can be and sometimes are redefined. The speaker, in performing a redefinitional act, can advance a new meaning that conflicts with the one that is commonly shared, and for this reason he has a dialectical burden, which we can call "burden of proof" in a broad sense (see Bix 1995, 471). He has the burden of providing reasons in support of his new definition, as it is presumed not to be the accepted one. Redefinitions are presumptively not accepted. Clearly, the possibility of countering the accepted meaning lies in proving that the new definition is more acceptable, or clearer, or more appropriate than the other.

This process of justification can be easier and more effective when the commonly accepted meaning is not clearly defined, when it is controversial, or when there are borderline cases that are not covered by the shared definition. In these cases, the burden of the speaker is reduced, as the contrary definitional viewpoint is already weakly defendable. Vague (Burgess-Jackson 1995) concepts, which can be characterized by unclear, too broad, or contested definitions (Gallie 1956), allow the speaker to advance a redefinition that is much harder to attack. Clearly, this is possible when the term is not defined by law, or when the statutory definition is vague because it includes vague or undefined concepts. This relationship between legal definitions and legal redefinitions can be analysed by taking into account how potential vagueness can be exploited in the act of redefining, and how vagueness can be introduced as a specific redefinitional move, namely the act of omitting a definition.

Omissions can be considered as implicit actions, in which the agent brings about a specific effect intentionally by not performing a required action. As Thomas Aquinas put it, we can consider an omission to be decision of not doing what an agent should do when such a not doing is caused by an intrinsic voluntary cause (Thomas Aquinas, Q.2 A1, 93). For instance, the code of silence is a specific decision not to report a crime, so that the person who breached the law could not be prosecuted. In law, an omission can be generally considered as a breach of an affirmative duty to perform the omitted action (Walton 1980; Fusco 2008, 86). From a pragmatic perspective, omissions can be considered as a kind of act, in which the agent decides not to perform an action that was sufficient for the occurrence of a specific consequence at a later time (Aqvist 1974; Chisholm 1976; Walton 1980, 317). When the agent is the lawmaker and decides intentionally not to define a term whose definition is explicitly requested (for instance by super-national organizations), we can claim that this agent is performing a specific speech act, aimed at leaving open the interpretative ambiguity that results from the absence of that specific definition.[1]

The problem of the meaning of "torture" provides a clear case of omission of a definition. Before 2003, Russian criminal law contained no definition of "torture" (CAT/C/34/Add.15, 15 October 2001, art. 1 (4), p. 3) despite UN recommendations. The absence the definition of such a concept made it lawful to detain of suspects for up to 30 days, even without sufficient reasons (CAT, 28th session, 13 May 2002[2]). The police and the military in general could avoid serious criminal sentencing and only incur minor punishments for charges of "exceeding of power"[3]:

Case 1: Omission of definition – Torture

> Oleg Fedorov had been detained by two high-ranking, drunk ROVD officials on the street in Arkhangelsk. He had been interrogated by the two officials for two hours and during questioning had allegedly been severely beaten by them. Oleg Fedorov, reportedly, asked to go to the toilet and threw himself out through the window. After the incident a criminal investigation was opened against the two law enforcement officials and they were charged under Article 171(2) of the Criminal Code for "exceeding of power." In March 1996 the Department of Internal Affairs (UVD) reportedly announced publicly the dismissal of the two officers for "serious violations of the professional discipline".

The omission of this definition led to specific effects. On the one hand, according to the *nullum crimen sine lege* principle, if "torture" is not defined, there is no principle governing the application of any laws punishing this kind of behaviour. For this reason, nobody can be prosecuted for this type of crime. In this fashion, in Russia the crimes committed by police and soldiers were not prosecuted accordingly. On the other hand, the lack of a specific description of "torture" allowed the use of inhuman treatment in interrogations and a wide range of violations of humanitarian rights, as humanitarian organizations such as Amnesty International denounced.[4]

The Russian case concerning the omission of the definition of "torture" shows how the choice of not performing a required definitional act can result in a specific

[1]Clearly the strategic omission of a definition needs to be distinguished from the ordinary practice of law-making, in which the ambiguity of a sentence is needed to reach an agreement on a specific normative sentence, delegating to the interpreter the ultimate decision on the meaning. Especially when the lawmaker, which ultimately constitutes a collective agent, deals with conflicting interests or complex issues, an agreement can be reached on the abstract level of the normative sentence, without committing to the meaning thereof, i.e. to the legal norm (Sunstein 2007, 4; Tarello 1980, 365).

[2]Committee against Torture Takes up Report of the Russian Federation, CAT 28th session, 13 May 2002: http://www.reliefweb.int/rw/rwb.nsf/db900SID/ACOS-64CSAN?OpenDocument (accessed on 5th September 2011).

[3]Torture in Russia: "This man-made hell". AI Index: EUR 46/04/97. Amnesty International April 1997 (pp. 28–29). (retrieved from http://www.amnesty.org/en/library/info/EUR46/004/1997/en on 21 September 2011).

[4]Russian Federation: Denial of justice. AI Index: EUR 46/027/2002. Amnesty International October 2002 (Chap. 3). (retrieved from http://www.amnesty.org/en/library/info/EUR46/027/2002/en on 21 September 2011).

strategic and legal outcome. The absence of a definition of a concept can result in the impossibility of motivating a classification of certain behaviour as falling under such an undefined category. From a legal point of view, the decision not to define, in this sense, can correspond to the decision not to consider a crime (or certain conducts in general) as legally relevant. Omission, in this sense, is the choice of allowing the non-classification of a state of affairs.

The omission of a definition can be an instrument for opening the possibility of redefining a term. Redefinitions can be considered as dialectical strategies that are possible and effective when they are hard to reject. In particular, they are extremely effective in cases of definitional gaps, which can be used to pursue specific goals. In this sense, by omitting definitions the lawmaker can create an ambiguity that can be used strategically by the interpreter.

9.3 Introducing Ambiguity: Definitions Redefined

A crucial condition for the effectiveness of a strategic redefinition is the actual or potential vagueness of the *definiendum*, which can also be a component of another definition. In actual vagueness, the effect of the move relies on the absence of a definition, which is strategically exploited. For instance, the absence of a definition of "enemy combatant," never defined by the U.S. government (*Hamdi v. Rumsfeld*, 542 U.S. 507, 516, 2004[5]), was used to charge the defendant of a crime that would not allow him to have any rights of protection. Potential vagueness is more complex, as the speaker needs to show that the legal or accepted definition is in fact vague, by challenging and redefining one or more terms of the *definiens*. The proponent of a new definition introduces ambiguity by redefining commonly accepted but not statutorily defined words, shifting the burden of proof onto the interlocutor. Two cases are particularly illustrative of this latter tactic, the redefinition of the concepts underlying the definitions of "torture" and "targeted killing."

During the George W. Bush administration, in order to show the constitutionality of the interrogation techniques of al Qaeda operatives (relative to the U.N. *Convention Against Torture*[6] and 18 U.S.C. section 2340[7]), Jay Bybee, then Assistant U.S. Attorney General in 2002, drafted a memorandum providing his opinion on which the Department of Justice (DOJ) based its further interpretations of "torture." The crucial strategic move was the analysis of the definition provided in the US Code, which reads as follows (18 U.S.C.A. §2340(1))[8]:

[5]Retrieved from http://www.law.cornell.edu/supct/html/03-6696.ZS.html on 7 March 2014.

[6]Retrieved from http://legal.un.org/avl/ha/catcidtp/catcidtp.html on 6 March 2014.

[7]Retrieved from http://www.law.cornell.edu/uscode/text/18/2340 on 6 March 2014.

[8]Retrieved from http://www.law.cornell.edu/uscode/text/18/2340 on 6 March 2014.

Case 2: Definition – Torture

> [torture is an] act committed by a person acting under the color of law specifically intended to inflict severe physical or mental pain or suffering (other than pain or suffering incidental to lawful sanctions) upon another person within his custody or physical control.

The elements of this definition that were considered as vague were the concept of *intention* ("intended to inflict") and being severe ("severe physical or mental pain or suffering") (*Memorandum for Alberto R. Gonzales Counsel to the President* August 1, 2002, 4; hereinafter "*The Bybee Memo*"). On the one hand, "intent" was claimed to be ambiguous, as it could be interpreted as both "general intent" and "specific intent." In the first case, the defendant needed to be found guilty by showing that he possessed knowledge with respect to the actus reus of the crime. In the second case, which corresponded to the definition adopted in the memorandum, "torture" could result only if the defendant "acted with the express purpose of inflicting severe pain or suffering on a person within his custody or physical control." (*The Bybee Memo*, 3) On the other hand, the concept of "severe pain and suffering" was considered as vague, as left undefined by the statute, and was thus redefined. Its accepted dictionary meaning ("hard to sustain or endure"[9]) was narrowed and limited to one of the possible cases, namely when it can cause death. This redefinition was justified by previous uses of the term when referred to medical conditions (*The Bybee Memo*, 5–6):

Case 3: Redefinition – Severe Pain

> These statutes define an emergency condition as one "manifesting itself by acute symptoms of sufficient severity (including severe pain) such that a prudent lay person, who possesses an average knowledge of health and medicine, could reasonably expect the absence of immediate medical attention to result in placing the health of the individual . . . (i) in serious jeopardy, (ii) serious impairment to bodily functions, or (iii) serious dysfunction of any bodily organ or part." Id. §1395w-22(d)(3)(B) [. . .] These statutes suggest that "severe pain," as used in Section 2340, must rise to a similarly high level the level that would ordinarily be associated with a sufficiently serious physical condition or injury such as death, organ failure, or serious impairment of body functions in order to constitute torture.

The definition of "torture" was modified by relying on the ambiguity and potential vagueness of two of the terms used in the *definiendum*, namely "intent" and "severe pain." In particular, the absence of a statutory definition of "severe pain" led to the possibility of narrowing its meaning to one of the possible cases in which the pain is "hard to endure." In this fashion "torture" was limited to cases in which the life of the victim is seriously jeopardized, and excluding many other types of practices aimed at inflicting a type of pain that would be normally classified as "severe." The restriction of the concept of "intent" to "specific intent" narrows further the concept of torture to cases in which the torturer acts with the intent of causing the death of the victim, or the failure of his organs, or the serious impairment of his body functions.

[9]Definition taken from The Oxford English Dictionary 572 (1978). See *The Bybee Memo*, 5.

The other famous case in which the vagueness of the *definiens* is exploited for redefinitional purposes concerns the redefinition of "targeted killing," which involves the potential vagueness of some elements of the shared definition. Targeted killing is a practice adopted especially by the United States and Israel in the so-called war on terror, in which actual or alleged terrorists are killed without any due process of law. This type of behaviour is explicitly prohibited by international provisions. Under the law of armed conflict (LOAC) it is "especially forbidden [...] b) to kill or wound treacherously individuals belonging to the hostile nation or army [...] d) to declare that no quarter will be given."[10] Killing suspected terrorists without any trial or proof of guilt instead is considered as an execution,[11] which is incompatible with international law, "categorically prohibiting extra-judicial executions" (Proulx 2005, 873; Sandoz et al. 1987, 476). The prohibition on targeting noncombatant civilians is considered to be customary law.[12] Such provisions can be implemented by a shared definition. Despite the absence of a definition under international law, "targeted killing" has been defined by a UN Report as a "the intentional, premeditated and deliberate use of lethal force, by States or their agents acting under colour of law, or by an organized armed group in armed conflict, against a specific individual who is not in the physical custody of the perpetrator."[13]

Given these prohibitions, under what conditions a "targeted killing" can be considered as lawful, and when does it become an unlawful assassination? The boundaries of this kind of action have become extremely problematic since the idea of war on terror blurred the concepts of "conflict" and "combatants" (and the "participation" of non-combatants in a conflict) (Solis 2007, 133). In Israel and the United States the components of the definition of targeted killing have been carefully redefined in order to include the killing of suspected terrorists within the lawful kind of assassination (Ben-Naftali and Michaeli 2003).

A clear example of this redefinition is the Israeli case. Both in Israel and the United States, the targeted killing of individuals associated with terroristic organizations was initially justified on the basis of the right of self-defence (Solis 2007), under article 51 of the United Nations Charter (Printer 2003, 359–60; Kasher and Yadlin 2005, 45). However, the main problem in considering targeted killing as an act of self-defence has to do with the controversial concepts of "imminence" of the

---

[10]Convention (No. IV) Respecting the Laws and Customs of War on Land, with Annex of Regulations [hereafter HR IV], 18 October 1907, Annex 1, 36 Stat. 2277, TS 539 (26 January 1910), art. 23(b).

[11]Anthony Dworkin, "The Killing of Sheikh Yassin: Murder or Lawful Act of War?" Crimes of War Project, 30 March 2004, available at www.crimesofwar.org/onnews/news-yassin.html

[12]*Prosecutor v. Pavle Strugar & Others* (ICTY Case IT-01-42-AR72), Appeals Chamber decision of 22 November 2002, paras. 9–10 on interlocutory appeal. Quoted in Solis (2007, 131).

[13]Alston 2010: Report of the Special Rapporteur on extrajudicial, summary or arbitrary executions, Philip Alston Addendum study on targeted killings. http://www2.ohchr.org/english/bodies/hrcouncil/docs/14session/A.HRC.14.24.Add6.pdf

threat, and "direct participation"[14] in hostilities.[15] The 1977 Additional Protocol I[16] specifies that "civilians shall enjoy the protection afforded by this Section [General Protection against Effects of Hostilities], unless and for such time as they take a direct part in hostilities" (see Solis 2010, 202). The lawfulness of a "targeted killing" rests, ultimately, on the definition of "direct participation" in hostilities. Indeed, the "direct participation" makes the difference between "non-combatant" and "combatant" civilians. And the second ones may be lawfully targeted, since the IHL applicable to internal armed conflict (as in international armed conflict) permits the targeting of civilians who "take a direct part in hostilities." This idea was the ground of the fundamental ruling of the Israeli High Court of Justice 769/02,[17] which introduced a legal definition of targeted killing as a killing against "civilians who directly carry out a hostile act." However, this definition is vague, as there is no agreement on the kind of conduct that makes an hostile act "directly" carried out (including the problems of determining whether the membership in an organized armed group may be used as an indicator of direct participation, and the length of the participation) (Alston Targeted Killings Report §59).

The vagueness of the concepts underlying the definition left open the possibility of redefining "targeted killing," based on a more restrictive and a broader definition of "direct participation in hostilities." In the first case, direct participation in hostilities is equated with actual combat operations, requiring a "direct causal link" between the civilian conduct and "the ensuing harm for the adversary" (Melzer 2008, 335; 337), thus excluding support activities, which do not directly cause harm to the adversary. According to the broader definition, "direct participation" encompasses "all conduct that functionally corresponds to that of governmental armed forces," including "not only actual conduct of hostilities, but also activities such as planning, organizing, recruiting and assuming logistical functions" (Melzer 2008, 338). This latter definition can be strategically exploited to include civilians who do not participate in actual combat operations, but, for instance, merely develop and operate "funding channels that are crucial to acts or activities of terror" (Kasher and Yadlin 2005, 1948). The absence of a commonly accepted definition of "direct participation in hostilities" makes the definition of "targeted killing" vague and open to the interpretation of the governmental authorities.

In the United States the problem of defining (and redefining) "targeted killing" is related to establishing its lawfulness pursuant to the War Crimes Act (18 U.S.C.

[14]Deborah Sontag, "Israelis Track Down and Kill a Fatah Commander," New York Times, 10 November 2000, p. A1. Quoted in Solis (2007, 132).

[15]1977 Additional Protocol I [hereafter AP I], art. 43.2. AP I is one of two treaties that update and supplement the familiar 1949 Geneva Conventions.

[16]1977 Additional Protocol I art. 51.3. Retrieved from http://www.icrc.org/applic/ihl/ihl.nsf/Article.xsp?action=openDocument&documentId=4BEBD9920AE0AEAEC12563CD0051DC9E on 7 March 2014.

[17]HCJ 769/02, "The Public Committee against Torture in Israel et al. vs. The Government of Israel et al.".

§2441, 2006) and the Fifth Amendmentin cases in which the target is an American citizen. In the first case, a war crime is defined as a grave breach to the 3rd article of the Geneva Convention, which includes murder when the person killed (or to be killed) is taking no active part in the hostilities (*Department of Justice White Paper*, 15–16).[18] In order to justify the targeted killings in general, the U.S. Department of Justice decided to focus on the definition of "taking active part in the hostilities," which was interpreted by negation as follows: "members of such armed forces [of both the state and non-state parties to the conflict]... are considered as "taking no active part in the hostilities" only once they have disengaged from their fighting function ("have laid down their arms") or are placed hors de combat; mere suspension of combat is insufficient."[19] For this reason, operations against leaders or forces of terroristic organizations posing an "imminent threat of violent attack against the United States" cannot be considered as taking "an active part in hostilities", and, therefore, are excluded from the category of unlawful killings (*Department of Justice White Paper*, 7). This reasoning presupposes that imminent threats are considered as forms of fighting. However, the most strategic definitional move consists in providing a definition of "imminent" that could justify the killing of individuals that are only planning or are merely suspected of planning terroristic attacks against the United States. For this reason, "imminence" was redefined as follows (*Department of Justice White Paper*, 7):

Case 4: Redefinition – Imminence

> By its nature, therefore, the threat posed by al-Qa'ida and its associated forces demands a broader concept of imminence in judging when a person continually planning terror attacks presents an imminent threat, making the use of force appropriate. [...] With this understanding, a high-level official could conclude, for example, that an individual poses an "imminent threat" of violent attack against the United States where he is an operational leader of al-Qa'ida or an associated force and is personally and continually involved in planning terrorist attacks against the United States. Moreover, where the al-Qa'ida member in question has recently been involved in activities posing an imminent threat of violent attack against the United States, and there is no evidence suggesting that he has renounced or abandoned such activities, that member's involvement in al-Qa'ida's continuing terrorist campaign against the United States would support the conclusion that the member poses an imminent threat.

This definition of "imminence" allowed the classification of mere suspects as "imminent threats," making their killing lawful. This redefinition allowed the Government also to justify the apparent breach of the due process clause of the Fifth Amendment. In this case, the citizen's right to due process needs to be determined by weighing "the private interest that will be affected by the official action" against the

[18]Department of Justice. White paper. *Lawfulness of a Lethal Operation Directed Against a U.S. Citizen Who Is a Senior Operational Leader of Al-Qa'ida or An Associated Force.* Retrieved from http://msnbcmedia.msn.com/i/msnbc/sections/news/020413-DOJ-White-Paper.pdf on 20 December 2013.

[19]International Committee of the Red Cross, Interpretive Guidance on the Notion of Direct Participation in Hostilities Under International Humanitarian Law 28 (2009).

Government's asserted interest, "including the function involved and the burden that the Government would face in providing greater process" (*Hamdi v. Rumsfeld*, 529). In particular, when the targeted individual poses an imminent threat of violent attack against the United States and his capture would be infeasible, the Constitution would not require the government to provide further process (*Hamdi v. Rumsfeld*, 535). By redefining the vague and undefined concept of "imminence," the Government managed to show the lawfulness of targeted killings and justify lethal operations against American citizens without due process.

The rhetorical effectiveness of a redefinition consists in the difficulty of its being rejected. An explicit statutory definition cannot be argued against by appealing to the ordinary meaning of the *definiendum* or to other arguments. On the contrary, its absence leaves room for redefinitional moves. In the cases above, the undefined concepts of "severe pain," "direct participation," and "imminent threat" led to the possibility of redefining "torture," "murder," and "active participation," even though such redefinitions conflicted with the ordinary understanding of such terms. In these cases, the Governments found possible definitional gaps, and introduced ambiguities that did not exist.

9.4 Implicit Redefinitions

One of the most powerful acts of definition is the implicit redefinition (Macagno and Walton 2014, 142–145). The speaker, instead of proposing a new definition of a concept based on specific reasons, takes it for granted. This implicit move modifies the dialogical situation of the interlocutor, who is left with the burden of reconstructing the move, assessing the redefinition, and rebutting it. This complex mechanism can be considered as an implicit act of defining. It is a kind of definitional act, as it alters the dialectical situation by imposing to the interlocutor specific possibilities (accepting the move and the definition or rejecting it by providing contrary arguments). It is also a specific type of act, more precisely a directive, through which the speaker imposes a new definition, committing also the hearer to it without providing any reasons. However, at the same time the implicit redefinition is a non-action, as it is a presupposition, a requirement of another act performed by the speaker.

The act of taking for granted a redefinition is strictly bound to the controversial issue of presupposition. Implicit redefinitions can be analyzed as pragmatic presuppositions (Stalnaker 1970, 1998), types of directives in which the speaker displays a possible world (Stalnaker 1970, 280), which can be interpreted as a set of conditions (in case of implicit definitions, the meaning of the redefined word). Stalnaker treated this "taking a proposition for granted" as a propositional attitude, a kind of directive act (Stalnaker 2002, 701):

> Speaker presupposition is a propositional attitude of the speaker, but I and others who have emphasized the role of speaker presupposition in the explanation of linguistic phenomena have been vague and equivocal about exactly what propositional attitude it is. To presuppose

Essential Condition	Speaker (*S*) sets the presupposed proposition (*pp*) as a condition of the felicity of his speech act (*SA*); if Hearer (*H*) does not accept *pp*, *SA* will be void.
Propositional Condition	*pp* is a proposition that can be reconstructed and evaluated by *H*.
Preparatory Condition	*S* can presume that *H* can evaluate and accept *pp*.
Sincerity Condition	*S* believes that *pp*; *S* believes that *H* can evaluate and know or accept *pp*.

Fig. 9.1 Conditions of the act of presupposing

something is to take it for granted, or at least to act as if one takes it for granted, as background information – as *common ground* among the participants in the conversation.

The speaker can presuppose a shared world (or in this case a commonly known meaning), or a new one as it were part of the common ground (Stalnaker 1970, 279). In this latter case he is actually imposing some conditions. He is performing a specific implicit act (Ducrot 1972; Hopper 1981).

The implicit act of presupposing can be described according to its felicity conditions (Macagno 2012), that can be reconstructed based on the structure of an explicit act (Austin 1962, 14–15; Searle and Vanderveken 1985, 13–19; Searle and Vanderveken 2005;Holtgraves 2008, 13; Macagno and Walton 2014, 179) (Fig. 9.1).

This speech act has a direction of fit from World (of the Hearer) to Words (of the Speaker), and its purpose is to establish the conditions of the dialogue, namely the propositions that the Hearer needs to be committed to. Clearly, the Hearer needs to be in condition of reconstructing such presuppositions from the context, namely shared knowledge and dialogical situation, and the co-text, (the relevant portion of the text in which the speech act occurs) (propositional condition). For instance, the presuppositions of the sentence "I have met Bob at the library" uttered to an interlocutor that does not know Bob nor the library, could not be retrieved. The preparatory and sincerity conditions govern the acceptability of a presupposition. The Speaker can *presume* that the Hearer can accept the presuppositions. In this case the presuppositions cannot to be unacceptable by the Hearer, or known to him to be false. For instance, it is possible to presume that the interlocutor accepts that "war" means "active fighting by ground troops," but not that it refers to "peaceful diplomacy." In this sense, the presumptions bridge the gap between the speaker's and hearer's knowledge from an epistemic and argumentative perspective. The process of "thinking" (Soames 1982, 486) that the hearer accepts a presupposition can be analysed in this way as a pattern of reasoning that can be assessed. Implicit redefinitions can be conceived as the conclusion of presumptive reasoning, as the speaker presupposes a proposition based on a form of reasoning in lack of evidence. The speaker acts on the basis of rules of presumptions that are commonly accepted, such as "Speakers belonging to a specific speech community usually know the meaning of the most important words of the language used therein." For this reason, presupposing a redefinition amounts to advancing a prima facie case that the interlocutor needs to challenge and disprove (Macagno and Damele 2013).

This type of definitional act is extremely effective from a dialectical perspective. The speaker shifts the burden of supporting the new definition onto the interlocutor. The other party needs to reject the redefinition by making the new meaning explicit first, and then providing evidence that the new description of meaning is neither accepted nor acceptable. He then needs to support the commonly accepted one. This implicit move has the clear effect of inverting the dialectical roles. On the one hand, the speaker (the party introducing a new definition) does not need to provide arguments in support of the new meaning unless the interlocutor challenges it by advancing contrary arguments. On the other hand, the hearer needs to attack a definition that has never been supported by arguments, but only treated as shared. The implicit redefinition alters also the burdens of the parties. The hearer has the difficult tasks of proving that a definition is not accepted, and of defending the shared one. The speaker can act in defense, simply attacking the interlocutor's arguments.

The possibility of performing this move lies in the potential ambiguity of a concept, or rather in the possible existence of a definition different from the shared one. In this sense, the possibility of supporting a new definition by means of arguments presupposes that a new definition can be acceptable somehow (Bix 1995, 471). The interlocutor needs to be presumed to be able to accept the new meaning, which is impossible in cases in which the definition is already explicitly stated by law. In other words, it is possible to redefine implicitly a term when it is not unreasonable to attribute to it different meanings that are incompatible to the purpose of warranting the attribution of a legal predicate. Usually the implicitly redefined terms are the ones that have not been defined by law. They are the ones that have not a specific statutory definition and for this reason should be presumed to have their ordinary meaning, determined on the basis of a dictionary (Barney 2003, 9–10, and the cases cited therein). In law, the individuals are not simply presumed to know the law, but also the ordinary meaning of the words used (*McDermott Int'l, Inc. v. Wilander*, 342[20]). The problem with the "ordinary meaning" is that sometimes certain words can be polysemic, vague, or their definition controversial (Gallie 1956). Terms such as "war" can be defined in general, but they admit of borderline cases that cannot be easily determined based on a definition unless such a definition is narrowed and specified.

Implicit redefinitions are possible when they can be considered not to be simply wrong classifications, namely when they can shift the burden of proving the contrary definition. This strategy is usually not effective when the redefined concept is defined by law (the move can be easily classified as an improper or erroneous classification). In this case, the concept cannot be potentially ambiguous, nor can the speaker treat the new definition as the shared one. On the contrary, when the *definiendum* has not been statutorily defined, it is less easy for the interlocutor to reject an implicit redefinition.

[20]Retrieved from http://www.law.cornell.edu/supct/html/89-1474.ZS.html on 7 March 2014.

The reasonableness (the possibility) of an implicit redefinition needs to be distinguished from its effectiveness. As seen above, the possibility of redefining a term stems from the reasonableness of the new definition, which amounts to the possibility of being accepted, or rather of not being rejected. The effectiveness of the strategic use of a redefinition consists in the difficulty of refuting it, or at least the possibility of leading the other party to disproving it, shifting the burden of proof. The tactics of implicit redefinition are aimed at increasing the pragmatic and semantic ambiguity of the redefinitional move, making it difficult for the interlocutor to detect and reconstruct the redefinition and easier for the speaker to defend it.

9.5 Redefinitions by Classification

The simplest strategy of implicit redefinition is the so-called argument by definition (Zarefsky 1998; Schiappa 2003, 111–112; 130). Instead of stating or advancing a new definition, the speaker takes it for granted by classifying a fragment of reality, treating it as part of the interlocutors' common ground.

A clear implicit redefinition by classification is the one concerning the concept of "persecution" in *Sahi v. Gonzales* (416 F.3d 587, 589, 7th Cir. 2005).[21] Sahi was an alien member of the Ahmadi religious sect discriminated by Muslims in Pakistan. He had been beaten by orthodox Muslims, and had his property destroyed, before leaving his country. The Board of Immigration Appeals denied his application for asylum, because they classified him not as a victim of "persecution," based on the following argument (*Sahi v. Gonzales*, 416):

Case 5: Implicit redefinition – Persecution

> While this Court [namely, the immigration judge] fully recognizes that Ahmadis are discriminated against and face harassment in Pakistan because of their religious beliefs, I do not find that this fact, coupled with the general risk of random violence singles the respondent out or establishes a pattern and practice of persecution of all Ahmadis.

Instead of using the ordinary definition of "persecution" (the Board never defined this term), or advancing a new one and supporting it, the judge simply took for granted that it meant "systematic violence directed against a group." As a matter of fact, he denied the classification because it was not characterized by "a pattern and practice" and was not directed against "all Ahmadis." By means of the implicit redefinition presupposed by his classification, the judge evaded the burden of providing reasons for adopting a new interpretation of the concept. The Court of Appeals reversed the judgment, requesting the Board to provide an explicit definition.

Redefinition by classification has been the strategy at the basis of a controversial recent case between the Electronic Privacy Information Center and the Federal

[21]Retrieved from https://law.resource.org/pub/us/case/reporter/F3/416/416.F3d.587.04-2828.html on 7 March 2014.

Bureau of Investigation (*In Re: EPIC*, No. 13–58). The dispute arose from an Order in which Foreign Intelligence Surveillance Court compelled Verizon Business Network Services (of which EPIC is a customer) to produce to the National Security Agency, on an ongoing basis, all of the call detail records of Verizon customers. The crucial problem at issue was the violation of the privacy interests of all customers of the provider of communication services (*In Re: EPIC*. Jul 8 2013,[22] 18):

Case 6: Implicit redefinition – Relevant

> Specifically, the statute requires that production orders be supported by "reasonable grounds to believe that the tangible things sought are relevant to an authorized investigation. . . ." 50 U.S.C. §1861(b)(2)(A). It is simply unreasonable to conclude that all telephone records *for all Verizon customers in the United States* could be relevant to an investigation. Thus, the FISC simply "ha[d] no judicial power to do what it purport[ed] to do." *De Beers*, 325 U.S. at 217.

The FBI requested all telephone records for all Verizon customers by classifying them as "relevant to an authorized investigation." However, this classification clearly conflicts with the commonly accepted meaning of "relevant," which according to the *Merriam-Webster's Collegiate Dictionary* (2004, 1051) means "having significant and demonstrable bearing on the matter at hand" (relevant to an issue) or "affording evidence tending to prove or disprove the matter at issue or under discussion" (relevant testimony) (*In Re: EPIC*, Aug 9, 2013, 11–12[23]). In both definitions, the central characteristic is "being related to a subject in an appropriate way." The FBI, in order to classify all telephone records as relevant, used a different, implicit definition of "relevant" conflicting with the ordinary one: information that "could lead to other material that could bear on an issue in the investigation" or "facilitate the government's use of investigative tools" (*In Re: EPIC*. Oct 11, 2013, 28–29[24]). This broader definition, which potentially included everything, was made explicit and defended only after being challenged and argued against by the Petitioner. This move, however, resulted in shifting the burden of defending it. The Petitioner had to reject it, by providing evidence of a different shared meaning (dictionary definition) and an economic argument (the definition used would make the word "relevant" meaningless) (*In Re: EPIC*. Aug 9, 2013, 20–21). These arguments allowed the respondent to adopt a twofold defensive strategy, on the one hand aimed at supporting the redefinition based on the interpretation of past cases, and on the other hand directed to undermining the petitioner's argument, supporting its own

[22]Retrieved from http://epic.org/EPIC-FISC-Mandamus-Petition.pdf on 4 November 2013.

[23]Retrieved from http://www.law.indiana.edu/front/etc/section-215-amicus-8.pdf on 7 March 2014.

[24]Retrieved from https://epic.org/privacy/nsa/in-re-epic/13-58-SG-Brief.pdf on 7 March 2014.

by negation of the contrary. In particular, the economic argument was attacked by *a contrario* one, supporting the interpretation by showing that it was not excluded (*In Re: EPIC*. Oct 11, 2013, 30).

The burden of disproving a redefinition and the possibility of defending it can be increased by another strategic move, the omission of a definition. A term can be introduced without a statutory definition, thus allowing the possibility of implicitly interpreting it, namely implicitly defining it, or redefining it differently from its shared non-technical definition. One of the most famous cases concerns the concept of "enemy combatant." This term was never defined (*Hamdi v. Rumsfeld*, 516), but it was used by the Bush administration to denote a specific class of combatants, falling outside the boundaries of the Geneva Convention. The problems arose when, after the attacks on September 11, the government arrested and detained two American citizens, Hamdi and Padilla, with the charge of being "enemy combatants." The case went to court, and the problem of the implicit definition of this term came to light. Padilla was detained as an enemy combatant based on an order of President Bush (see President Bush order (June 9, 2002)[25] to hold Padilla as an enemy combatant), where the reasons for the classification were that he was "closely associated with al Qaeda," engaged in "hostile and war-like acts" including "preparation for acts of international terrorism" directed at the U.S. (June 9 Order, 2–5; *Padilla Ex Rel. Newman v. Bush*, 233 F. Supp. 2d 564, 568 S.D.N.Y. 2002[26]). Hamdi was considered as an enemy combatant because "[b]ased upon his interviews and in light of his association with the Taliban," a series of tests that determined that Hamdi met "the criteria for enemy combatants (*Hamdi v. Rumsfeld*, 513). These classifications did not provide any explicit definitions. For this reason, the implicit act forced the Court to first reconstruct a possible definition by relying on previous similar cases, the ones concerning the definition of "unlawful combatant." The interpretative controversies were solved only in 2004, when the meaning of this concept was made explicit by the Supreme Court and only then the classification could be denied (*Hamdi v. Rumsfeld*, 516). This case illustrates the force of an implicit definition. In absence of a shared or an existing definition, the burden of disproving the classification falls onto the other party, who first needs to prove a contrary definition and then, if the latter is not rejected, deny the classification. This burden can be strongly increased when the concept has never been defined and is not of common use, as in this case to the other party needs to reject a definition without relying on any alternative one.

[25]Retrived from http://www.google.pt/url?sa=t&rct=j&q=&esrc=s&source=web&cd=1&ved=0CCQQFjAA&url=http3A2F2Fnews.findlaw.com2Fcnn2Fdocs2Fterrorism2Fpadillabush60902det.pdf&ei=trsZU6CqLsm07QbNlYCQCg&usg=AFQjCNFarnYjxBWBBaupDTBu9Xtd8BNrJQ&bvm=bv.62578216,d.ZGU&cad=rja (accessed on 9 September 2011).

[26]Retrived from http://www.docstoc.com/docs/92087484/Padilla-v-Bush-233-F-Supp-2d-564-SDNY-2002 on 7 March 2014.

9.6 Redefinitions by Analogy

One of the most powerful strategies of implicit redefinition is definition by analogy. Analogy can be considered as a process of re-classification of a predicate, in which the two terms of the analogy (the Analogue and the Primary Subject) are included within a new semantic generic property (a semantic genus), which does not correspond to the original definitional characteristics of the Analogue. Analogy has three crucial dimensions: the essential difference between Analogy and Primary subject; the relevance relation; and the creation of a functional genus (Macagno and Walton 2009).

Analogy consists in the comparison between two entities or states of affairs that do not belong to the same semantic genus, namely that are essentially different (Glucksberg and Keysar 1990, 7; Macagno and Walton 2009). For instance, it would be unreasonable to draw an analogy between two kinds of apples, such as a *Golden Delicious* and a *Granny Smith*, aimed at concluding that they share essential characteristics. Rather, two species can be compared taking into account some non-essential feature, such as sweetness or taste. Analogies are extremely powerful redefinitional tools when the two terms of the comparison are essentially different (when they belong to distinct genera from a semantic point of view). For instance, an inn is essentially different from a boat, as dwellings cannot be included in the same category of vehicles. Similarly, motorhomes are essentially not vehicles, as they have not an engine and they are primarily shelters. In this sense, analogies are used when the law cannot be applied to a specific case, when the entity does not fall within the category subject to the provision of law.

Analogy is strictly bound to communicative intention. The two terms of the analogy are not regarded from the point of view of their meaning, but rather from a specific perspective, which becomes the principle of redefinition. In law this perspective or communicative intention is the application of the law, which presupposes its reconstruction through a process of interpretation. For example, in *California v. Carney* (471 U.S. 386 1985)[27] a motorhome was compared to a car for the purpose of the application of the warrant exception to the Fourth Amendment. The Fourth Amendment protects the "right of the people to be secure in their persons, houses, papers, and effects, against unreasonable searches and seizures" by requiring that searches be conducted pursuant to a warrant issued by an independent judicial officer. However, in some cases, one of which is the "automobile exception" (later included within the category of "special needs"), warrants are not necessary. The crucial problem is to establish why the exception applied to cars, by reconstructing the justificatory (or relevance) relation. According to the standard interpretation (grounded on the leading case *Carroll v. United States*, 267 U.S. 132, 1925),[28] the ground for such an exception was the mobility of the

[27]Retrieved from http://supreme.justia.com/cases/federal/us/471/386/ on 7 March 2014.

[28]Retrieved from http://supreme.justia.com/cases/federal/us/267/132/case.html on 7 March 2014.

car, which makes it impracticable to secure a warrant. The analogy between a motorhome (searched without warrant) and a car, aimed at applying the exception, was based on a reinterpretation of the purpose of the law. The "lesser degree of protection of the privacy interests" was justified based not only on the mobility of the vehicle (practicability of securing a warrant), but also on the "lower expectation of privacy" (lower privacy interests). This new relevance relation was used to construct the analogical relation.

The third dimension of analogy is the creation of a functional genus. Analogy includes both terms of comparison under a new genus, different from the originally shared, semantic one. This new generic characteristic is an *ad hoc* (Glucksberg and Keysar 1990), functional genus (Macagno and Walton 2009), namely a genus that is created for fulfilling the relevance relation. In legal analogies, the genus is created for the purpose of justifying the application of the law. For instance, by means of analogy an inn and a boat can be redefined as species of the same genus "providers of accommodation to guests reposing in them extraordinary confidence" (*Adams v. New Jersey Steamboat Co.*, 151 N.Y. 163, 1896).[29] Continuing the analysis of the automobile exception, the analogy between a car and a motorhome resulted in the abstraction of a new superordinate semantic category, "property subject to a reduced expectation of privacy." This functional genus corresponds to the abstract characteristic that at the same time can include both the terms of the comparison and justifies the application of the exception. Clearly for the purpose of the law a car (or automobile) was no longer "a self-propelled vehicle," but a specific kind of "piece of property characterized by lower expectations of privacy." For this reason, analogy implicitly redefines a concept. The structure of the redefinition by analogy can be represented as follows (see Ashley 1991, 758; Guastini 2011; Macagno 2014) (Fig. 9.2).

As shown in the table above, the predicate is redefined (Sorensen 2003) by highlighting the factors that are considered as essential for the legal qualification to apply.

The redefinition by analogy played a crucial role in the controversial cases stemming from the Foreign Intelligence Surveillance Act and the Protect America Act (In Re: Sealed, 310 f.3d 717, 2002[30]; In Re: Directives 51 F.3d 1004, FISA Ct Rev 2008[31]), involving the warrantless acquisition from communication service providers of foreign intelligence concerning third person reasonably believed to be located outside the United States. This provision, called the "foreign intelligence exception," clearly breaches the aforementioned Fourth Amendment and the need of a warrant to conduct searches. In (*In Re: Directives*, 14) the Court needed to justify the exception, which they did by reasoning by drawing an analogy with the special needs doctrine (Hirsch Ballin 2012, 501–502). As mentioned above, the exception to the warrant clause (the so-called "special needs doctrine") has been traditionally

[29]Retrieved from http://www.wneclaw.com/internet/earlyanalogycases.pdf on 7 March 2014.

[30]Retrieved from https://www.fas.org/irp/agency/doj/fisa/fiscr111802.html on 7 March 2014.

[31]Retrieved from http://www.fas.org/irp/agency/doj/fisa/fiscr082208.pdf on 7 March 2014.

Premise 1 (rule)	If *x* is *P*, the *x* has the right/is *A*.
Premise 2 (borderline)	It is not clear whether *a* (a borderline case) is *P*.
Similarity premise	*a* is similar to *b*.
Premise 3 (principle of classification)	*b* was classified as *P* because of the factors $f_1, f_2, ..., f_n$.
Redefinition premise	If *x* has the factors $f_1, f_2, ..., f_n$, the *x* is *P*.
Premise 4 (factors)	*a* has $f_1, f_2, ..., f_n$.
Conclusion	Therefore, *a* is *P*.

Fig. 9.2 Scheme from definition by analogy

justified based on special needs, "beyond the normal need for law enforcement" in cases of diminished privacy expectations"[32] (see *Vernonia School Dist.* 47J *v. Acton*, 515 U.S. 646, 653, 1995[33]). In such cases, a court may balance private and public interests to determine whether the search meets the constitutional requirement of reasonableness. The crucial problem is that surveillance with foreign intelligence purpose is primarily aimed at apprehending terrorism suspects[34] (a law-enforcement purpose). The analogy was drawn by introducing an almost new concept of "special needs," based on a redefinition of the idea of "beyond the normal need for law enforcement," and the deletion of the requirement of diminished privacy expectations. Automobile searches or drug testing inspections in schools were placed under the same functional genus of being activities with "a programmatic purpose involving some legitimate objective beyond ordinary crime control" (*In Re: Directives*, 14; *In Re: Sealed*, 745–46). In this sense, the analogy reinterpreted the purpose of the law, extending its boundaries by redefining the crucial concepts on which it is based.

In this case the analogy did not simply redefine a legal predicate, but introduced a new nameless genus created by modifying the meaning of existing concepts. The precedent cases classified as "special needs" and the new one fall within a new original category, "searches or violations of privacy with some legitimate

[32]Criminal Law. Fourth Amendment. Second Circuit Holds New York City Subway Searches Constitutional under Special Needs Doctrine. MacWade v. Kelly, 460 F.3d 260 (2d Cir. 2006). *Harvard Law Review* 120 (2), 2006, 635.

[33]Retrieved from http://www.law.cornell.edu/supct/html/94-590.ZO.html on 7 March 2014.

[34]An "agent of a foreign power" is defined in terms of criminal activity (In Re: Sealed). More specifically, they are US persons engaged in activities that "involve" or "may involve" a violation of criminal statutes of the United States (50 U.S.C. §1801(b)(2)(A)).

Premise 1 (target)	No law provides for the *x*'s that are *Q*.
Premise 2 (property)	If *x* is *P*, then *x* has the right/is *A*.
Definitional premise	*P* and *Q* belong to the same functional genus *G* characterized by properties $f_1, f_2, f_3 \ldots f_n$.
Species – Genus premise	If *x* is *G*, then *x* has the right/is *A*.
Conclusion	If *x* is *Q*, then *x* has the right/is *A*.

Fig. 9.3 Scheme from redefinition by analogy

objective beyond crime control." The structure of this (re)definitional strategy can be illustrated as follows (Macagno and Walton 2009, 173; Guastini 2011, 280–281) (Fig. 9.3).

The new genus represents a new concept, which includes the two terms of the comparison and allows the application of the legal qualification.

9.7 Redefinition by Contrary and Dichotomies

A concept can be defined or redefined by distinguishing it from its contrary, whose definition is supposed to be shared or at least not to be as such controversial. For instance, a classic case of definition "*per privantiam contrarii*" is the definition of "good" as "what is not evil" (Victorinus 1997, 23, 9–11). Definition by negation actually does not describe what the concept is; rather, it shifts the burden of providing a different and incompatible definition, and defending it, onto the interlocutor. The other party needs first to identify the dichotomy and the cause of its unacceptability; he then needs to show that it is false, and prove it. From a dialectical perspective, definitions by negation of the contrary trigger only one type of reasoning, grounded on the exclusion of the alternative within a semantic paradigm (Macagno and Walton 2011):

Disjunctive Syllogism
Either A or B.
Not B.
Therefore A.

Clearly, this type of reasoning applies to a dichotomy drawn from a specific point of view, namely the application of a legal qualification, which often results in modifying the definition of an existing concept by shifting the burden of proving the contrary onto the interlocutor. For instance, in *Adams et al. v. United States* (Case 1:90-cv-00162 2008)[35] the defendant (the Department of Health and Human Services or HHS) wanted to prove that the plaintiffs (working as investigators) were not entitled to overtime pay, as their duties were administrative, and therefore not exempt from overtime pay. The defendant advanced the following reasoning (*Adams et al. v. United States*, 9–10):

Case 7: Redefinition by dichotomy – Administrative work

> Defendant sees the production work of HHS as the sponsoring of federally-funded health care and benefit programs, not the investigation of abuses in the delivery of those programs. [...] Defendant argues that performing criminal investigations cannot be part of the production work of HHS. [...] Defendant concludes that plaintiffs were exempt administrative employees of HHS during the relevant time period.

The defendant's argument was grounded on an existing but not specifically defined dichotomy between administrative and production work. By providing a description of one of the terms of the dichotomy and defining the other by negation ("work that is not productive"), the party managed to classify investigation work as administrative, even though it did not involve managerial tasks. In this fashion, "administrative work" was implicitly redefined as work not resulting in sponsoring health care and benefit programs. The reasoning can be represented as follows (partially adapted from Macagno and Walton 2010, 251) (Fig. 9.4).

The negative definition allowed the defendant to shift the burden of providing a different definition of "administration work" and supporting a contrary classification onto the other party.

A crucial case in which the strategy of definition by dichotomy was used is the aforementioned *In Re: Sealed*, in which the problem of the limits and the consequences of collecting without a warrant private data for the purpose of obtaining foreign intelligence information arose. The crucial problems consisted in defining the type of information that the government (through the Attorney General) can collect, and how to use it (minimization procedures). The issue of defining and redefining "foreign intelligence information" hinged on a dichotomy drawn for the purpose of the Fourth Amendment. According to this provision, the individual is protected against unreasonable searches and seizures aimed at law enforcement. However, as mentioned above, the Patriot Act, Section 215[36] allowed for a specific exception: collecting evidence for the purpose of obtaining foreign intelligence information. This purpose was clearly opposed to the one protected by

[35]Retrieved from http://www.findforms.com/single-form.php/form/296181/Cross-Motion-Dispositive-District-Court-of-Federal-Claims-District-federal on 7 March 2007.

[36]USA PATRIOT Act. Pub. L. 107–56, Oct. 26, 2001. Section 215. Retrieved from http://epic.org/privacy/terrorism/hr3162.html on 7 March 2014.

Reasoning from oppositions in classification	
SHARED PREMISES	POTENTIALLY CONTROVERSIAL PREMISES
0. Either a work is administrative or it is production.	
	1. Production work is the sponsoring of federally-funded health care and benefit programs.
2. The plaintiffs' duty was criminal investigations.	
	3. Criminal investigations does not fall within "sponsoring of federally-funded health care and benefit programs".
Preliminary conclusion Therefore plaintiffs' work was not production. (from 1 and 3)	
CONCLUSION Therefore plaintiffs' work was administrative. (from prel. concl. and 0)	

Fig. 9.4 Redefinition by dichotomies

the Fourth Amendment. According to the provisions of law, warrantless electronic surveillance is allowed in specific circumstances, the most important of which is that "a significant purpose of the surveillance is to obtain foreign intelligence information" (50 USC §1804, (6)(b)). "Foreign intelligence information" is defined in its relevant part as (50 USC §1801 (e)) (emphasis added):

(1) information that relates to, and if concerning a United States person is necessary to, the ability of the United States to protect against
  (A) actual or potential attack or other grave hostile acts of a foreign power or an agent of a foreign power;
  (B) **sabotage, international terrorism**, or the international proliferation of weapons of mass destruction by a foreign power or an agent of a foreign power; or
  (C) clandestine intelligence activities by an intelligence service or network of a foreign power or by an agent of a foreign power; [. . .]

This purpose introduces an exception, which the definition of "electronic surveillance" brings to light by contrasting it with the purpose of law enforcement (50 USC §1801 (f)) (emphasis added):

Case 8: Redefinition by dichotomy – Foreign intelligence

"Electronic surveillance" means

(1) the acquisition by an electronic, mechanical, or other surveillance device of the contents of any wire or radio communication sent by or intended to be received by a particular, known United States person who is in the United States, if the contents are acquired by intentionally targeting that United States person, under circumstances in which a person has a reasonable expectation of privacy and **a warrant would be required for law enforcement purposes.**

The dichotomy between law enforcement and foreign intelligence (*In Re: Sealed*, 34[37]) implicitly specifies what "foreign intelligence" is for the purpose of the Fourth Amendment, namely a purpose that is *not* prosecution of ordinary crimes, or rather law enforcement. One of the redefinitional problems stems from the use of the collected data, as the minimisation procedures at the same time allow "the retention and dissemination of nonforeign intelligence information which is evidence of *ordinary crimes* for preventative or prosecutorial purposes" (50 U.S.C. §1801(h)(3)). In order to defend the constitutionality of the provision, the FISC Court reinterpreted the dichotomy. Instead of regarding the opposition as between crimes *related to national security* (espionage, sabotage or terrorism, see *In Re: Sealed*, 11) and the other *ordinary crimes*, the Court broadened the concept of "foreign intelligence" by contrasting it with the "*sole* purpose of criminal prosecution" " (*In Re: Sealed*, 34) (emphasis added):

Case 9: Redefinition by dichotomy – Foreign intelligence

> The better reading, it seems to us, excludes from the purpose of gaining foreign intelligence information **a sole objective of criminal prosecution**. Because, as the government points out, when it commences an electronic surveillance of a foreign agent, typically it will not have decided whether to prosecute the agent (whatever may be the subjective intent of the investigators or lawyers who initiate an investigation). So long as the government **entertains a realistic option of dealing with the agent other than through criminal prosecution**, it satisfies the significant purpose test.

This redefinition of the dichotomy modified the concept of foreign intelligence. Instead of referring to an activity including evidence of *certain* crimes (*In Re: Sealed*, 12), the term was broadened to include evidence of crimes *in general*, in addition to information concerning attacks, hostile acts, terrorism, espionage, and sabotage.

9.8 Conclusion

Rhetorical definitions (or strategic redefinitions) can be considered as argumentative strategies consisting in selecting or modifying the meaning of the *definiendum* in order to pursue a specific persuasive or dialectical goal. In law, the goal is usually to support the attribution or the non-attribution of a legal predicate to a state of affairs, leading to a consequence according to the legal norm. The purpose of this paper was to show why and how the strategic use of definition can be extremely effective in legal discourse, illustrating the various tactics of redefining a term "rhetorically." Strategic redefinitions can be considered as complex moves,

[37] *In Re: Sealed, Supplemental brief for the United States*, Case No. 02-001, Foreign Intelligence Surveillance Court, 2002.

which can be theoretically analysed by taking into account different interrelated dimensions, namely the type and the nature of the *definiendum*, the acts of definition, and the strategies or types of implicit redefinition.

The dialectical force, or effectiveness, of a redefinition consists in the effects that it produces, or rather in the difficulty of being rejected. Its force depends on the extent in which it successfully shifts the dialectical "burden of proof" onto the other party, which in this case consists in disproving the definition. For this purpose, redefinitions are aimed at selecting or altering the meaning of vague terms, or words whose definition is not shared or explicitly stated in a legal text. In this sense, also the choice of leaving a crucial term undefined (such as in the case of "torture") becomes a strategic move, a specific negative act that opens up the possibility of redefining the legal concept almost arbitrarily. The impossibility or difficulty of countering a redefinition explains also the choice of redefining the elements of a statutory definition that are taken from the ordinary use. In this sense, the redefinitional activity is aimed at introducing an ambiguity that did not exist before the definitional act, such as in the case of "imminence" or "severe pain."

The analysis of the target of rhetorical definitions and the reason thereof needs to be integrated with the investigation of the instruments used to carry out this move, and in particular the speech acts and the types of strategic redefinition. A term can be redefined through explicit and implicit speech acts, and relying on different types of redefinitional arguments, such as analogy or opposition. The most dangerous definitional acts are the implicit ones, as the interlocutor is left with the burden of reconstructing the implicit and unshared definition, and of challenging it. This act is often carried out effectively through two types of reasoning, the analogical argument and reasoning by opposition. In both cases the pattern of reasoning hides the introduction of a new semantic genus, which implicitly redefines the concepts placed under it. In this sense, the analysis of strategic redefinitions becomes essentially an investigation on the tactics used to hide a redefinition, on the hidden acts of altering the meaning of a word.

The strategies and the dangers of redefinition in interpretation can shed light on the burden, the effects, and the risks of the legislative definitional activity. Strategic redefinitions can be used when some terms are left undefined or underdefined in a legislative text, or when statutory definitions are in turn ambiguous or consisting of undefined concepts. The legislative choice of leaving terms undefined or underdefined can be considered as an instrument for reaching an incompletely theorized agreement, as Sunstein pointed out. A legislative deadlock can be avoided by agreeing upon an unspecified or underspecified text, leaving up to the interpretative bodies the burden of defining it properly. The legislator, instead of curbing or limiting the interpretative freedom setting out boundaries to the passage from the legal statement to the norms, decides to delegate his powers to the interpretative bodies. This decision, however, has the argumentative effect of reducing or even removing the burden of persuasion associated with the proposal of a redefinition. The interpreter, instead of incurring the burden of challenging and rejecting an existing definition, is allowed to advance a redefinition without fulfilling a burden of persuasion, or by meeting only a low one (deriving from one of the ordinary uses of the *definiendum*).

In this perspective, statutory definitions in legislative texts can be considered as meta-norms (Guastini 2011, 168), as they govern the interpretation of the legal statements containing the *definiendum*. In most cases, statutory definitions are impose boundaries to the interpretation of terms or phrases drawn from ordinary language. The lawmaking activity can reduce the inevitable vagueness of legal language (resulting in the interpreter's possibility of strategically redefining a term) through statutory definitions and redefinitions (Guastini 2011, 26; 56). In turn, such definitional statements, become second-order rules, governing the legal statements containing the term defined.

The relationship between strategic interpretative redefinitions and statutory (re)-definitions can be conceived in terms of burden of persuasion. A statutory definition selects some meanings of the *definiendum* and restricts its vagueness, limiting the possibility of strategically redefining it. However, every word drawn from ordinary language, including the terms used to define statutorily a term, is subject to being strategically redefined. The lawmaker's definitional activity becomes in this respect a dialectical move. The reduction of the interpretative freedom can be regarded as a move aimed at placing on to the interpreter of a higher burden of justifying a redefinition, should the latter decide to use a statutorily defined term with a different or potentially controversial meaning. The reduction of the redefinitional possibilities corresponds to a higher burden of providing arguments supporting a strategic redefinition. On the contrary, the absence or the vagueness of a definition can be conceived as a dialectical choice of allowing the interpreter to redefine a legal term without fulfilling a burden of persuasion, or fulfilling a lower one.

References

Aarnio, Aulis. 1977. *On legal reasoning*. Turku: Turun Yliopisto.

Aarnio, Aulis. 1987. *The rational as reasonable: A treatise in legal justification*. Dordrecht: Reidel.

Aqvist, Lennart. 1974. A new approach to the logical theory of actions and causality. In *Logical theory and semantics*, ed. Soren Stenlund, 73–91. Dordrecht: D. Reidel.

Ashley, Kevin. 1991. Reasoning with cases and hypotheticals in hypo. *International Journal of Man-Machine Studies* 34(6):753–796.

Austin, John. 1962. *How to do things with words*. Oxford: Clarendon.

Barney, James. 2003. In search of "Ordinary" meaning. *Journal of the Patent and Trademark Office Society* 85:101–130.

Belvedere, Andrea. 1998. I poteri semiotci del legislatore (Alice e l'art. 12 Preleggi). In *Scritti per Uberto Scarpelli*, ed. Letizia Gianformaggio e Mario Jori, 85–103. Milano: Giuffré.

Ben-Naftali, Orna, and Keren Michaeli. 2003. We must not make a scarecrow of the law: A legal analysis of the Israeli policy of targeted killings. *Cornell International Law Journal* 36:233–292.

Bix, Brian. 1995. Conceptual questions and jurisprudence. *Legal Theory* 1(4):465–479.

Burgess-Jackson, Keith. 1995. Rape and persuasive definition. *Canadian Journal of Philosophy* 25:424–425.

Chisholm, Roderick. 1976. *Person and object: A metaphysical study*. London: Routledge.

Ducrot, Oswald. 1972. *Dire et ne pas dire*. Paris: Hermann.

Fusco, Federico. 2008. Commencement of the prescription period in case of damage due to omissions. In *Essential cases on natural causation*, ed. Helmut Koziol and Barabara Stiengel, 79–93. Wien: Springer.

Gallie, Walter. 1956. Essentially contested concepts. *Proceedings of the Aristotelian Society* 56:167–198.

Glucksberg, Sam, and Boaz Keysar. 1990. Understanding metaphorical comparisons: Beyond similarity. *Psychological review* 97(1):3–18.

Guastini, Riccardo. 2011. *Interpretare e argomentare*. Milano: Giuffré.

Hall, Jerome. 1966. Analytic philosophy and jurisprudence. *Ethics* 77/1:14–28.

Hirsch Ballin, Marianne. 2012. *Anticipative criminal investigation theory and counterterrorism practice in the Netherlands and the United States*. Berlin: Springer.

Holtgraves, Thomas. 2008. *Language as social action*. Mahwah: Lawrence Erlbaum.

Hopper, Robert. 1981. How to do things without words: The taken for granted as speech action. *Communication Quarterly* 29(3):228–236.

Kasher, Asa, and Amos Yadlin. 2005. Assassination and preventive killing. *SAIS Review of International Affairs* 25(1):41–57.

Lazzaro, Giorgio. 1981. Diritto e linguaggio comune. *Rivista trimestrale di diritto e procedura civile* 1:140–181.

Lausberg, Heinrich. 1998. *Handbook of literary rhetoric: A foundation for literary study*. Leiden: Brill.

Lindahl, Lars. 2004. Deduction and justification in the law. The role of legal terms and concepts. *Ratio Juris* 17/2:182–202.

Macagno, Fabrizio. 2012. Reconstructing and assessing the conditions of meaningfulness. An argumentative approach to presupposition. In *Inside arguments: Logic and the study of argumentation*, ed. Henrique Ribeiro, 247–268. Newcastle upon Tyne: Cambridge Scholars Publishing.

Macagno, Fabrizio. 2014. Analogy and redefinition. In *Systematic approaches to argument by analogy*, ed. Henrique Ribeiro, Ch. 5. Cham: Springer.

Macagno, Fabrizio, and Giovanni Damele. 2013. The dialogical force of implicit premises: Presumptions in enthymemes. *Informal Logic* 33(3):365–393.

Macagno, Fabrizio, and Douglas Walton. 2008. Persuasive definitions: Values, meanings and implicit disagreements. *Informal Logic* 28(3):203–228.

Macagno, Fabrizio, and Douglas Walton. 2009. Argument from analogy in law, the classical tradition, and recent theories. *Philosophy and Rhetoric* 42(2):154–182.

Macagno, Fabrizio, and Douglas Walton. 2010. Dichotomies and oppositions in legal argumentation. *Ratio Juris* 23:229–257.

Macagno, Fabrizio, and Douglas Walton. 2011. Reasoning from paradigms and negative evidence. *Pragmatics and Cognition* 19(1):92–116.

Macagno, Fabrizio, and Douglas Walton. 2014. *Emotive language in argumentation*. New York: Cambridge University Press.

Melzer, Nils. 2008. *Targeted killing in international law*. Oxford: Oxford University Press.

Moore, Michael. 1980. The semantics of judging. *Southern California Law Review* 54:151–294.

Mortara Garavelli, Bice. 1988. *Manuale di retorica*. Milano: Bompiani.

Mortara Garavelli, Bice. 2001. *Le parole e la giustizia*. Torino: Einaudi.

Printer, Norman. 2003. The use of force against non-state actors under international law: An analysis of the U.S. predator strike in Yemen. *UCLA Journal of International Law and Foreign Affairs* 8:331–353.

Proulx, Vincent-Joël. 2005. If the hat fits, wear it, if the Turban fits, run for your life: Reflections on the indefinite detention and targeted killing of suspected terrorists. *Hastings Law Journal* 56(5):801–900.

Sandoz, Yves, Christophe Swinarski, and Bruno Zimmermann Sandoz. eds. 1987. *Commentary on the additional protocols of 8 June 1977*. Geneva: Martinus Nijhoff.

Scarpelli, Uberto. 1985. *Contributo alla semantica del linguaggio normativo*. Milano: Giuffré.

Schiappa, Edward. 2003. *Defining reality. Definitions and the politics of meaning*. Carbondale and Edwardsville: Southern Illinois University Press.
Searle, John, and Daniel Vanderveken. 1985. *Foundations of illocutionary logic*. Cambridge: Cambridge University Press.
Searle, John, and Daniel Vanderveken. 2005. Speech acts and illocutionary logic. In *Logic, thought and action*, ed. Daniel Vanderveken, 108–132. Dordrecht: Springer.
Soames, Scott. 1982. How presuppositions are inherited: A solution to the projection problem. *Linguistic Inquiry* 13(3):483–545.
Solis, Gary. 2007. Targeted killing and the law of armed conflict. *Naval War College Review* 60(2):127–146.
Solis, Gary 2010. *The law of armed conflict: International humanitarian law in war*. New York: Cambridge University Press.
Sorensen, Roy. 2003. Vagueness and the desiderata for definition. In *Definitions and definability: Philosophical perspectives*, ed. James Fetzer, David Shatz, and George Schlesinger, 71–109. Dordrecht: Kluwer.
Stalnaker, Robert. 1970. Pragmatics. *Synthese* 22(1–2):272–289.
Stalnaker, Robert. 2002. Common ground. *Linguistics and Philosophy* 25:701–721.
Stevenson, Charles. 1944. *Ethics and language*. New Haven: Yale University Press.
Sunstein, Cass. 2007. Incompletely theorized agreements in constitutional law. *Social Research* 74(1):1–24.
Tarello, Giovanni. 1980. *L'interpretazione della legge*. Milano: Giuffré.
Thomas, Aquinas. 2003. *On evil*. Oxford: Oxford University Press.
Victorinus, Caius Marius. 1997. *Liber de Definitionibus* (mit Einleitung, bersetzung und Kommentar von A. Pronay). Frankfurt: Peter Lang.
Walton, Douglas. 1980. Omissions and other negative actions. *Metamedicine* 1:305–324.
Walton, Douglas, Chris Reed, and Fabrizio Macagno. 2008. *Argumentation schemes*. New York: Cambridge University Press.
Zarefsky, David. 1998. Definitions. In *Argument in a time of change: Definitions, frameworks, and critiques*, ed. James Klumpp, 1–11. Annandale: National Communication Association.
Zarefsky, David. 2006. Strategic maneuvering through persuasive definitions: Implications for dialectic and rhetoric. *Argumentation* 20:399–416.

Cases cited

Adams et al. v. United States (Case 1:90-cv-00162, 2008).
Adams v. New Jersey Steamboat Co., 151 N.Y. 163, 1896.
California v. Carney, 471 U.S. 386, 1985.
Carroll v. United States, 267 U.S. 132, 1925.
Hamdi v. Rumsfeld, 542 US 507, 513, 2004.
In Re: Directives 51 F.3d 1004, FISA Ct Rev 2008.
In Re: EPIC. Supreme Court of the United States No. 13–58. Aug 9, 2013. Brief amici curiae of Professors of Information Privacy and Surveillance Law.
In Re: EPIC. Supreme Court of the United States No. 13–58. Jul 8, 2013. Petition for a writ of mandamus and prohibition, or a writ of certiorari.
In Re: EPIC. Supreme Court of the United States No. 13–58. Oct 11, 2013. Brief of respondent United States in opposition.
In Re: Sealed, 310 f.3d 717, 2002.
In Re: Sealed, Supplemental brief for the United States, Case No. 02-001, Foreign Intelligence Surveillance Court, 2002.
MacWade v. Kelly, 460 F.3d 260 (2d Cir. 2006). Harvard Law Review 120 (2), 2006: 635.
McDermott Int'l, Inc. v. Wilander, 498 U.S. 337, 1991.
Padilla Ex Rel. Newman v. Bush, 233 F. Supp. 2d 564, 568 S.D.N.Y. 2002.
Sahi v. Gonzales, 416 F.3d 587, 589, 7th Cir., 2005.
Vernonia School Dist. 47J v. Acton, 515 U.S. 646, 653, 1995.

Chapter 10
The Concept of Normative Consequence and Legislative Discourse

Michał Araszkiewicz and Krzysztof Płeszka

Abstract It is widely assumed that the normative systems in civil law countries encompass not only the norms explicitly stated in statutory texts but also the so-called normative consequences of the former norms. The concept of 'normative consequence' is to a significant extent independent of the concept of logical consequence because some, if not most, legal inference schemes are non-deductive; moreover, some valid logical inference patterns are perceived as counterintuitive by lawyers. Our research problem is to determine how the link between the wording of statutes and the eventual legal effects is established. Our thesis is that it is achieved by means of legal argumentation, and we provide an exact, semi-formal theory–the argumentation framework for legislation (AFLEG)–to represent this process. The emphasis is on the aspect of legislative discourse that concerns the anticipated application of provisions drafted by the legislator. The proposal provides a middle ground between fully formalized reconstructions of normative systems on the one hand and classical informal argumentative approaches to the subject on the other hand.

Keywords AFLEG • Argumentation schemes • Concept of law • Legal system • Legislation • Logic • Normative consequence

10.1 Introduction

The basic assumption we make in this text concerns the rationality of legislative technique. This thesis seems widely accepted because the principles of legislative technique are perceived as emanating from the theory of rational legislation. Each rational legislator should predict the possible consequences of a regulation.

The authors would like to thank all the contributors to the present volume for their work, which was an invaluable source of inspiration.

M. Araszkiewicz (✉) • K. Płeszka
Faculty of Law and Administration, Department of Legal Theory, Jagiellonian University, Kraków, Poland
e-mail: michal.araszkiewicz@uj.edu.pl; krzysztof.pleszka@uj.edu.pl

M. Araszkiewicz, K. Płeszka (eds.), *Logic in the Theory and Practice of Lawmaking*, Legisprudence Library 2, DOI 10.1007/978-3-319-19575-9_10

The research problem we address here relates to a specific sphere of legislative drafting. It is connected with the possibility, scope and manner of providing for the anticipated consequences of legislative decisions in the legislative process. Considering such consequences has been a long-standing practice. From the historical point of view, the conviction that there is a need to consider the consequences of the decisions taken in the process of law application has always been present in legal reasoning. Legal premises, such as "Fiat iustitia iustitia pereat mundus" or "Summum ius, summa iniuria", can only prove this claim. It seems, however, that legal practice is not uniform in this matter because the consideration of the consequences of the decisions taken in the process of creating and applying the law is presented in a different way. While we can pose a sensible question about the admissibility and scope of the consequences in the process of law application, posing an identical question with respect to the process of law creation, especially legislative drafting, seems trivial because of the widespread conviction that predicting the consequences of planned legislative decisions is not only admissible but also vitally important. Moreover, these consequences should be accounted for in their broadest possible scope.

In the sphere of law creation, especially legislative drafting, the means that can be utilized to determine maximally broad sets of the anticipated consequences of the planned legislative solutions become problematic. This issue is connected strictly to the definition of the concept of consequence. If we define the said concept in the broadest possible sense, treating it as a set of all social states of affairs that may be caused by the planned regulation, then the possibility of predicting the states will consist in the use of the methods of social sciences (e.g., sociology, psychology and economic sciences). These methods are applied in the so-called regulatory impact assessment, which functions in many countries. However, in this text, we do not assume this understanding of the concept of consequence and its scope.

We intend to carry out an analysis of a more fundamental issue: how to determine the set of states of affairs accepted by courts and other authorities as those that satisfy the hypotheses of the projected legal norms and thus generate legal effects. From our point of view, the determination of such sets of states of affairs is based on the referral to legal argumentation. It is the aim of this text to clarify this thesis by referring to both logical and other, less formally rigorous models of legal reasoning. Hence, we intend to present the consequences of this thesis for legislative drafting.

Legislative theory emphasises that the legal regulation of the legislative process requires solving numerous theoretical and practical problems related mostly to the systemic character of the legal order. The catalogues of these problems are usually relatively broad and comprise heterogeneous objects. From the research perspective presented in this chapter, there is no need to analyse all the issues that require settling for the purposes of the appropriate regulation of the legislative process. It is sufficient to indicate the issues that are relevant not only from the point of view of legislative theory but also from the perspective of our research purpose. We firmly believe that these issues include the choice of the concept of law and the concept of the legal system, particularly from the perspective of its open or closed nature, as well as the relation between reasoning patterns that are present in the context of law creation and law application. We intend to address all these issues in the following discussion of our investigations, beginning with examples of classical concepts of law and their stances on the scope of the legal system and the identification of its elements. These analyses are the subject of the first part of Sect. 10.2, while the second part of this section is devoted to the concept of consequence as it is understood in logic and in other theories of reasoning, with particular regard to their application in the domain of law. Section 10.3 presents a framework for the representation of normative consequences stemming from statutory provisions as they are deliberated in the legislative discourse. Section 10.4 offers examples illustrating the functioning of the framework. Section 10.4 concludes and presents recommendations for further research.

10.2 Legal System and the Notion of Consequence

10.2.1 The Scope of Legal System in Legal-Philosophical Perspective

Classical legal-philosophical conceptions quite naturally have provoked a discussion on the scope of what is known as law. It is neither our intention nor the aim of this text to analyse classical concepts of law; neither do we attempt to explain to the reader what is and what is not currently perceived as classical. The selection of concepts we have decided to review is arbitrary and original.

Our aim is to look into classical concepts in the field of legal philosophy from the perspective of the concept of law as such, particularly from the perspective of determining the scope of the legal system, that is, the need to formulate the criteria for being a part of it. As a matter of fact, the question concerning the "scope of the legal system", that is, the social norms that constitute law and therefore gain the status of a sanction of social (including state) reaction to unacceptable behaviours concerns, inter alia, has two main issues: ethical and legal. The latter is of particular interest to us. We thus ask: What rules will be applicable in the legal eligibility of behaviours (factual states)? There have been, until now, different answers to this question. The idea proposed by Opałek and Wróblewski (1969, 81–82) is an interesting attempt to formulate the typology of descriptions of the scope of the legal system. The authors distinguish four types of these descriptions, depending on the inherent features of normative texts:

1. Only general norms can be included in the system; individual norms are not included because they only occur as a result of the application of general norms.
2. The system of law includes all legal norms, irrespective of their inherent features.
3. The system of law includes only individual norms.
4. It should be assumed that there exist two distinct systems of law, one of which includes individual norms and the other general norms.

Arguments both for and against can be raised in relation to each of these ideas. It has been emphasized that many criteria for the selection of certain ideas have axiological implications. Limiting the scope of the legal system to general norms created mainly by representative entities is claimed to ensure the implementation of the accepted, democratic philosophy of the state. Relative simplicity has also been reported with respect to the determination of the system that includes only general norms because of the obligation to publish them, which reflects the abovementioned democratic philosophy of the state.

On the other hand, it has been argued that there is a lack of unity in the system that consists only of general norms. As a counter-argument for the idea of the system that includes individual norms, however, it has been indicated that considerable variability exists in the set of such norms and in the diversity of bodies competent to create them. This situation does not contribute to putting this set in order and depicting it in the form of a system. The argument on the relativity of the opposition of the creation and the application of law (which results in general and individual norms, respectively) is sometimes put forward. This argument is raised by Hans Kelsen, the originator of one of classical concepts of the legal system, which is constructed within his pure theory of law. It is an important concept insofar as it constitutes a certain point of reference for contemporary concepts of legal systems.

The distinction between the static and dynamic systems of norms is based on different constructive rules, that is, static and dynamic principles are considered in jurisprudence an indisputable achievement of Kelsen's pure theory of law:

> The norms of the order of the first type are valid on the strength of their content: because their validity can be traced back to a norm under whose content the content of the norms in question can be subsumed as the particular under the general. (...) Since all norms of an order of this type are already contained in the content of the presupposed norm, they can be deduced from it by way of a logical operation, namely a conclusion from the general to the particular. This norm, presupposed as a basic norm, supplies both the reason for the validity and the content of the norms deduced from it in a logical operation. A system of norms, whose reason for validity and content is deduced from a norm presupposed as a basic norm, is a *static norm system*. (Kelsen 1970, 195–196)

Kelsen characterises the dynamic norm system not from the perspective of the relations of the content of the norms, but from the perspective of the reasons for the validity of the norms in the system:

> Its (a norm created by an act of will) validity can (...) be based only on a presupposed norm which prescribes that one ought to behave according to the commands of the norm-creating authority or according to norms created by custom. This norm can supply only the reason for the validity, not the content of the norms based on it. These norms constitute a dynamic system norms. (Kelsen 1970, 196)

It should be emphasised that Kelsen himself treats the abovementioned types of norm systems as ideal: the static type is adequate to depict the moral system, and the dynamic type depicts the legal system. This approach allows the formulation of the thesis that in the existing norm systems, it is acceptable to combine the dynamic and static principles of the construction of the norm system:

> The static and dynamic principles may be combined in the same system if the presupposed basic norm, according to the dynamic principle, merely authorizes a norm-creating authority, and if this authority (or one authorized by it in turn) not only establishes norms by

> which other norm-creating authorities are delegated, but also norms in which the subjects are commanded to observe a certain behavior and from which further norms can be deduced, as from the general to the particular. (Kelsen 1970, 197–198)

However, although it is acceptable to combine both principles in the construction of legal norm systems, the legal system presents an essentially dynamic character. The thesis is justified from the point of view of validity: a legal norm is valid not because of its content, but because it is prescribed by another norm, and eventually by the presupposed basic norm (Kelsen 1970, 198). The rejection of the distinction between the creation and application of law is a consequence of this depiction of the relations among norms in the legal system. The creation of law constitutes its simultaneous application, for by creating certain legal norms we apply at least those that authorize a norm-creating authority to establish them. Each use of the competence to issue a legal norm provided by law is considered a creation of law.

Thus, courts and organs of public administration also create individual norms (e.g., judgements and administrative decisions) by applying general norms to resolve pending cases. In doing so, they make use of the competence vested in them by general norms. The relativity of the creation and application of law is also related to legal acts, which also result in creating individual norms. Only at the lowest level of the application of law, where merely a sanction is prescribed, do we encounter the pure application of law because no competence to create another legal norm is created. We can therefore assume that the legal system comprises general norms established in the process of the application and/creation of competence norms as well as a set of relatively scattered and to some extent structured individual norms, which occur as the consequences of the former.

Another classical concept of law, constructed by Herbert Hart, is also positivist in origin. It attributes the function performed by Kelsen's basic norm to the rule of recognition. G. Postema has emphasized that Hart's theory relies on two key notions: the social rule and the rule of recognition (Postema 2001, 269). Reference to these notions does not have the character of a definition, for it was the intention of Hart that they should constitute a characteristic pattern that provides for the explanation of the existence, functioning and structure of contemporary systems of law. The notion of the social rule proves necessary to explain the normative character of law, whereas the notion of the rule of recognition enables Hart, who perceived law as the union of primary and secondary (first-order and second-order) rules (Hart 1994, 79) in order to explain the institutional and systematic nature of law (Postema 2001, 269). G. Postema presents the main ideas of Hart's concepts in the form of 11 claims. Since not all of them are relevant from the point of view of the problems addressed herein, we present only those of some importance for the determination of the scope of the legal system and those that relate to the norms included in the legal system:

(...)

2. A legal system is made up of rules of different logical kinds, serving different functions; some imposing duties, other conferring powers.

3. These rules operate at different levels; some governing or facilitating ordinary social behavior of citizens (first-order rules), some governing (mainly) officials charged with maintaining the system of rules (second-order rules).
4. Chief among second-order rules are (a) rules of change: instituting, empowering and regulating lawmaking, (b) rules of adjudication: instituting, empowering, and regulating law-applying, and (c) rules of identification: instituting criteria of validity for the system.
5. All these rules exist, are authoritative, and constitute a unified system, by virtue of identification according to criteria defined by the rule of recognition.(...)
7. The rule of recognition of the system is not itself a valid rule of law, but is the standard of validity for all other legal rules or norms. Thus, a rule of recognition exists and is binding not as a valid rule of the system, but as a social rule, accepted and practiced by law-applying officials as a common public standard.
8. By virtue of accepting the rule of recognition, law-applying officials accept indirectly all the rules identified as valid in the system by their rule of recognition. (...)
9. Rules of law have an "open texture". The core of determinate application enables law-subjects and officials to apply them to a wide range of circumstances in a predictable ways, but they also typically have a penumbra in which their application is less determinate and open to dispute. Judges deciding cases that fall in the penumbra, are guided by law, but they make law rather than apply pre-existing law. (Postema 2001, 269–270)

The characteristics of the critical positivist theory of law explicitly demonstrate that the content of the criteria included in the rule of recognition determines the scope of the legal system and specifies the kind of principles, rules and norms, as well as their consequences, are accepted as belonging to the system.

Ronald Dworkin presents a far more complicated way of determining the scope of the legal system and the identification of its elements. Firstly, it is a commonly known fact that the critique of the criterial (conventional) concept of Hart's rule of recognition constituted the starting point of Dworkin's legal philosophy. The discussion, which was initiated in 1968 by Dworkin's article, has continued with varying intensity until the present and is known in legal philosophy as the Hart–Dworkin debate (Shapiro 2007). The debate has addressed various issues of great significance not only for legal philosophy but also because it continues among the advocates of both legal philosophers. The duration of the debate and the persuasive power of the presented arguments have also influenced both Hart and Dworkin's standpoints. Dworkin's point of view in particular has undergone major changes,[1] making it very difficult to be reconstructed. In the attempt to present only fundamental Dworkinian theses that are in the scope of our interest, we will not consider the interpretative nuances of his theory.

[1]In the contemporary analyses of the debate, and especially of Dworkin's standpoint, it is emphasized that there is the possibility of distinguishing between two versions of his legal philosophy–the early one, which is best presented in Taking Rights Seriously and the later one, which is presented in Law's Empire (Leiter 2007). However, Dworkin questions the possibility of presenting his theory in two versions (Dworkin 2006, 233).

In the above paragraphs, we indicated Dworkin's critique of the Hartian criterial rule of recognition. According to this renowned legal scholar, if the rule's only purpose is to identify legal rules and make them distinguishable from moral ones, it should be considered too simplistic. In particular, it is not the case that in every system there exists some commonly accepted social rule that allows for the indication of boundaries among legal, moral and political rules (Dworkin 1977, 59–62). For the settlement of uncomplicated cases, it is sufficient to make use of the relevant legal rule; in complex cases, however, it is imperative to refer to the legal principle. Thus, not only does the legal system include the legal rules, but it must also comprise principles and policies (Dworkin 1977, 82 ff.). The scope of the norms that are included in the system is subject to considerable extension. The critique of the criterial (conventional) concept of the rule of recognition makes Dworkin resign from the sharp distinction between the law and morality. However, the lack of criteria provokes uncertainty about the basics of adjudication, especially in the settlement of complex cases where a theoretical dispute is held with respect to legal sources. Without focusing on the character of theoretical disputes and frequency of their occurrence in the judgemental practice, one may risk the claim that the scope of the legal system seems ultimately determined in an interpretative (e.g., in accordance with legal sources) but particularly argumentative manner. The arguments that are sought to be put forward in these cases appear to have their origins in the normative social structure.

Alexy's commentary on the presented definition of law allows for specifying both the scope of the legal system and a relative identification of the normative elements that may be included therein. Alexy emphasizes that the claim to correctness is, by virtue of its definition, typical of all legal systems. Normative systems that neither lay such claims explicitly nor include them implicitly are not legal systems (Alexy 2010, 127). Moreover, the positivist legal approach is restricted in that it sets out the condition whereby only those norms that are not extremely unjust can belong to the legal system. Alexy insists that this restriction leads to the narrowing of the scope of the legal system. By contrast, the third part of the definition extends the scope by claiming that the legal system includes the procedures of its application. The extension of the scope is relatively broad:

> Everything on which an official applying the law in the open area of the law bases and/or must base a decision in order to satisfy the claim to correctness belongs to the law. So it is that principles, even when they cannot be identified as legal principles according to the validity criteria of the constitution, as well as other normative arguments justifying the decision become components of the law. (Alexy 2010, 130)

Jerzy Wróblewski, a Polish legal theorist, presents a similar approach to the scope of the legal system and criteria for identification of the elements thereof, but in contrast to Alexy's concept, his approach maintains the spirit of legal positivism. Although he has devoted many of his works to issues connected with the legal system, only one is particularly interesting from the point of view of the problems pursued herein. This work devoted to theoretical and practical problems within the legal system, which appear in the process of building the systems of legal computer science. The issue of the scope of the system and the identification of its elements constitutes one such problem (Wróblewski 1980, 7). Taking into consideration the scope and inherent qualities of the legal system, Wróblewski distinguishes two definitions that pertain to the civil law systems valid in continental Europe. It is worth noting that it is not the existing legal systems the theorist is interested in, but instead their idealisations characterised by the accepted concept of the legal source and techniques of creating and applying laws that are put into practice (Wróblewski 1980, 7). Wróblewski uses these assumptions to consider various models of legal systems.

Two clearly distinguishable types of law are statutory law which is fundamental for civil law systems, and operative law constitute the basis for his considerations. According to Wróblewski, operative law is understood as "applied and created in the decisions of state authorities which settle concrete cases" (Wróblewski 1980, 16). All the legal norms that provide the rationale for the decision of applying law constitute the paradigm of operative law in civil law systems. The principles that determine the judgement (ratio decidendi), "discovered or created in a decision" (Wróblewski 1980, 16), constitute the paradigm in common law systems. According to this approach, the character of operative law is not systemic, but instead is perceived from the point of view of a problem directed at particular cases that require settlement. Hence, operative law can be defined as law in action.

In contrast to operative law, statutory law can be demonstrated in three models differing in terms of the norms that belong to the system, thereby presenting distinct scopes of the said system (Wróblewski 1980, 10). The model that reflects the concept of the legal system in its narrowest notion recognizes only the norms "directly established by competent authorities" as belonging to the system (Wróblewski 1980, 10). Regarding the identification of the above-stated norms, the model refers to the concept of systemic validity used in positivist legal theories.[2]

The second model of the legal system, which is adequate for a broadly understood concept thereof, also refers to systemic validity. Nevertheless, the model recognizes both the established norms and the norms logically consequent upon them as included in the scope of the legal system.[3] Wróblewski emphasizes the problem of providing this formal calculus, which allows for depicting the normative discourse,

[2]The concept of systemic validity can be characterised by the following criteria:
"a rule belongs to the legal system if: (a) a rule is enacted according to the rules valid in the legal system and thus has come into force; (b) a rule has not been formally repealed ("derogated"); (c) a rule is not inconsistent with the rules valid in the legal system; (d) if a rule is inconsistent with any rule valid in the legal system then either a rule is not treated as invalid according to the rules about conflict between legal rules or a rule is interpreted in such a way as to eliminate the inconsistency in question" (Wróblewski 1980, 10). In the later version of his theory, Wróblewski introduced an additional criterion: "a rule is an acknowledged consequence of the rules valid in the legal system" (Wróblewski 1992, 77).

[3]Wróblewski claims that logical consequences should fulfil two conditions: (a) they are based on three theses of formal calculi, which are "interpreted" (in the logical meaning of this term) by the expressions occurring in the legal norms or by these norms; (b) they are claimed to be valid like the norms they derive from (Wróblewski 1980, 12).

thereby guaranteeing the transformation of valid norms into other valid norms. The calculi of alethic or deontic logics, or logics of norms, were claimed to be such calculi (Wróblewski 1980, 13).

The concept of law in its broadest notion is best reflected by the third model because the set of the norms thereby determined as belonging to the system is broader than are the sets presented in the two previous models. In this model, systemic validity is also used as the baseline for the criteria that a norm ought to fulfil in order to belong to the legal system. Here, however, not only established norms but also norms occurring as their logical consequences and their interpretative consequences comprise the set of norms that belong to the system. Interpretative directives pertaining to the interpretative paradigm accepted in a given legal culture constitute the basis for determining the normative interpretative consequences.[4]

The foregoing review of arbitrarily chosen, classical concepts of law and their respective systems demonstrates that both positivist and non-positivist concepts seek to define the scope of the legal system broadly, without placing limitations on explicitly established legal norms, but accepting various consequences thereof. Establishing those norms can take place in different ways, ranging from the procedures of law application to logical, quasi-logical and interpretative reasoning.

10.2.2 The Notion of Normative Consequence

The investigations of formal accounts of normative (i.e., legal) systems and the notion of normative consequence in particular were triggered in the second half of the twentieth century by the development of logics of norms and deontic logics. For obvious reasons, the impressive development of these formal systems cannot be reviewed here (However, the reader should consult Hilpinen and McNamara (2013) for a recent summarization of the rich state of the art and an earlier elaboration by Åqvist 1984). Generally, the research that was developed during the last several decennia and is relevant for the topic of the formalization of legal systems and the formal account of legal consequence may be typologically divided into the following streams:

(1) The development of deontic logics and normative logics as a branch of mathematical logic (a survey: Hilpinen and McNamara 2013),
(2) The application of deductive tools (classical logic and deontic logic) for reconstruction reconstructing notions such as normative system, legal norm or different patterns of legal reasoning (e.g., Alchourrón and Bulygin 1971; Royakkers 1998; Woleński 1972)

[4]Notwithstanding this, Wróblewski emphasises that for the construction of such a model it is essential to make two assumptions: "(a) there exists a limited set of interpretative directives accepted in a given system; (b) the consequences of norms built by means of these directives constitute valid norms." (Wróblewski 1980, 13–14). The second condition is trivial and fulfilled in every legal system, but the first one meets considerable obstacles caused by the heterogeneous character and the conflicting nature of the set of interpretative directives.

(3) The incidental use of the logical reconstruction of certain parts of legal system or patterns of legal reasoning in general legal theory (Alexy 1989; MacCormick 1978; Peczenik 2008; Raz 1980)
(4) The reconstruction of statutory law as a system of rules for the practical purposes of developing of legal expert systems (Bench-Capon et al. 1987; Sergot et al. 1986; Yoshino 1995, 1997)

This line of research was developed by the introduction of the elements of case-based reasoning (Ashley 1990) into the systems, which led to the emergence of the so-called hybrid systems (e.g., Rissland and Skalak 1991). Regarding recent developments, the rule-based approach has become less influential because of the emergence of research on legal ontologies (Bench-Capon and Visser 1997; Casellas 2011; Sartor et al. 2011) and the modelling of legislation based on the XML standard (Athan et al. 2013).

(5) The development of formal systems for modelling nonmonotonic or defeasible reasoning, which encompasses also defeasible deontic logic (Nute 1994; Nute 1997), which was also inspired by the research on general epistemology and artificial intelligence (Pollock 1987, 1995; Reiter 1980)
(6) The development of formal models of legal reasoning encompassing the concept of defeasibility, revisability, weighing reasons, dialogical situations and other important features of legal reasoning (see e.g., Hage 1996, 2001a, 2005; Prakken 1997; Prakken and Sartor 1996, 1998; Prakken and Vreeswijk 2002; Sartor 1992, 1995 (especially chapters 1 and 3); Sartor 2005 (especially chapters 2.2, 26 and 27); (Ferrer Beltrán and Ratti 2012 (eds.)) (a recent legal-philosophical commentary))
(7) The development of formal theories of argumentation, especially in the field of general artificial intelligence (Rahwan and Simari 2009), regarding both abstract (Dung 1995; Rahwan and Simari 2009 (e.g., the extensions discussed therein) and structured (Gordon and Walton 2006; Prakken 2010) models of argumentation
(8) The application of formal and semi-formal theories of legal argumentation for modelling different types of legally relevant argumentation, including for instance policy deliberation (e.g., Atkinson et al. 2011) or legal interpretation (Żurek 2012; Żurek and Araszkiewicz 2013)
(9) The methodological and meta-methodological investigations concerning the scope and justification of application of logical tools to legal reasoning (see e.g., the exchange between Haack (2007) and Bulygin (2008)), the controversy concerning development of special "legal" logic, particularly non-monotonic logic as opposed to classical logic (see Soeteman 2003; Hage 2001b), and so on.

The nine categories distinguished above do not exhaust the whole range of topics that are relevant to formal investigations into topics related to legislation. Moreover, these categories are also not mutually exclusive. On the contrary, many works in the literature integrate the insights in category (1) (development of mathematical systems) with those in category (4) (for the purposes of creating an intelligent system of legal knowledge and category (8) (representation of legal argumentation). However, in our opinion, the typology shown above is at least partially adequate to show the streams of research that are present in the relevant literature. This abundant research may be further ordered according to the following criteria:

(1) The degree of formalization: from mathematically correct formal theories characterized by important meta-logical features, as in category (1), to models based mainly on natural language with application of certain schemes, as in category (8));
(2) The aims: from purely theoretical ones investigations concerning formal properties of theories, as in category (1) and category (7), to purely practical ones, such as the solutions of certain problems present in legal or legislative practice, as in categories (4) and (8));
(3) The methodological character of the developed models: from purely reconstructive ones, as in category (1) to moderately reconstructive, as often in category (8), to descriptive ones, as common in category (8); this criterion is closely related to the adoption of the top-down or bottom-up approach in the development of a given model.
(4) The degree of logical orthodoxy: from systems employing only classical logic or traditional deontic logic, as in the classical works referred to in categories (2), (3) and (4), through multitudinous extensions of classical logics (the addition of new operators, logical values, and new semantics), to the development of new logical systems, particularly systems of nonmonotonic logic and extra-logical argumentation frameworks, as mainly in categories (5), (6) and (7).

Consequently, the account of the notion of the legal system and normative consequence adopted in a given formal model of law or legal reasoning will be determined by the criteria presented above, and in particular by the aims and methodological character of the developed model.

If a top-down, formal logical approach is chosen, the explication of the notion of normative consequence is quite straightforward. The normative system in question is represented in the language of the chosen, or newly developed, logical calculus. The notion of the normative consequences of this system is then identified with the notion of logical consequence, as adopted in the logical calculus. As a matter of course, we cannot discuss the (philosophy of) the concept of logical consequence here, for it is one of the central and the most interesting problems in the philosophy of logic (see the classical elaboration of Tarski 1936). Generally, logical consequence may be defined either syntactically or semantically, where the former defines logical consequence in terms of provability and the latter in terms of semantic concepts, such as valuation, satisfaction or truth (for slightly different accounts of these notions, see, for syntactic consequence, Bell and Machover 1977, 35–36; Mendelson 1977, 34; Kleene 1967, 34; for semantic consequence, Bell and Machover 1977, 71; Mendelson 1977, 71–72). In the semantic account, the role of the operation of logical consequence is the preservation of truth: if a set X is a set of true formulas, then for any α being a logical consequence of X, α also must be true.

As an example of the formalization of a normative system that makes use of the notion of logical consequence is a theory developed by Woleński (1972). We decide to present it here in detail because of the fact that it was originally published in Polish and therefore is less known by the English-speaking academy. Let us note that Woleński's work is contemporary with the seminal contribution of Alchourrón and Bulygin (1971), which has remained an important point of reference for further research on the subject.

Woleński proposed a formal (both syntactical and semantic) reconstruction of normative systems in first-order predicate logic (Woleński 1972, 45 ff.). He also defined a specific subpart of language L, referred to as the set of default obligations (Woleński 1972, 45). The set of default obligations, represented here by O_D,[5] possesses certain important features:

(1) It is consistent,
(2) It does not contain any tautologies, and
(3) Its elements are mutually independent.[6]

Woleński then defines the set of all obligations as the set of the logical consequences of the set of default obligations:

$$O =_{df} Cn\ (O_D)$$

which consequently enabled him also to define sets of prohibitions and permissions. Let us present these definitions here, again changing the original notation used in Woleński work published in Polish. Let us assume that A represents any formula belonging to the language of the assumed logic, PR represents the set of prohibitions, WP represents the set of negations of prohibitions (i.e., weak permissions), F represents the set of negations of obligations, and I represents the set of indifferent actions. We obtain the following definitions (Woleński 1972, 47):

$$A \in PR =_{df} \neg A \in O$$
$$A \in I =_{df} A \notin O \text{ and } A \notin PR$$
$$A \in WP =_{df} A \notin PR$$
$$A \in F =_{df} A \notin O$$

The semantic interpretation of these notions is as follows. Norm-giving consists in choosing from the set of all possible worlds the so-called postulated worlds, that is, worlds that realize situations described by a given set of sentences. In these postulated worlds, the sentences belonging to the set O are always true, the sentences belonging to the set PR are always false, and so on. A normative system may be equated to the set $Cn(O_D)$ (Woleński 1972, 47–48).

[5] Woleński used the symbol N_0 in this context because his work was published in Polish and the Polish word for 'obligation' (in this meaning) is 'nakaz'.

[6] These features are elements of a theory of the so-called rational norm-giver, which was very influential in Polish legal theory in the second half of the twentieth century.

Woleński draws an important analogy between normative systems (as defined above) and elementary theories in mathematics. In particular, he analogizes the set of default obligations with the set of axioms (Woleński 1972, 48–49). This enables him to define certain important metalogical concepts for normative systems, such as completeness and consistency.

This brief outline of Woleński's contribution is an example of the application of formal-logical methods for the clarification of important notions related to the concept of normative systems. Although the author was aware that this type of reconstruction was not entirely descriptively adequate (Woleński 1972, 57) he claimed that it was not a disadvantage of his proposal, for the aim of the formal theories of normative systems is to focus on selected important properties of normative systems and to provide tools for assessing the rationality of the actually existing normative systems.[7]

Woleński's referred methodological investigations may be generalized to state that any formal logical reconstruction of the concept of normative system and normative consequence is inherently limited in the sense that it is relativized to the expressiveness of the adopted logical calculus and the properties of the adopted notion of logical consequence (whether a classical logical consequence or a nonmonotonic one; see Makinson 2005). This is not a disadvantage of the logical reconstructions of these notions, for it would be unjustified to state additional demands. However, these limitations of formal logical approaches triggered research on abstract argumentation, which is neutral with respect to any accepted language of logic. In particular, Dung (1995) is the author of a seminal theory of abstract argumentation, where arguments and attack relationships between arguments remain undefined primitive concepts. This relatively simple idea enabled Dung to define the so-called semantics, that is, sets of conditions that generate extensions, that is, sets of arguments that are acceptable with respect to different intuitions (for a contemporary account of the theory, see Baroni et al. 2011). Consequently, certain arguments may be selected from an initial set of arguments without using the notion of logical consequence. A suggestion here is that because a normative system may be represented as a set of arguments (in the abstract sense), it is possible to derive sets of normative consequences (Dungian extensions) by

[7]However, at least certain inferences warranted by (classical) notion of logical consequence seem to be troubling from the point of view of descriptive adequacy as regards the actual reasoning on consequence of statutes. Let us mention the three laws of classical logic:

(a) ex falsum quidlibet: $(p \wedge \neg p) \rightarrow q$ (that is, contradiction implies an arbitrary sentence). Obviously, no lawyer would accept this kind of consequence even in case of plain and insuperable contradiction between two provisions in a statute;
(b) Attaching of an alternative: $p \rightarrow (p \vee q)$. This law lad to formulation of the famous Ross' paradox in deontic logic. Although it does not lead to actual antinomy in the normative system, this type of inference seems to be pragmatically fallacious in the context of legal discourse;
(c) Strengthening of antecedent: $(p \rightarrow q) \rightarrow ((p \wedge r) \rightarrow q)$. The critique of adequacy of this law was one of the factors that led to emergence of nonmonotonic logics applied to legal domain.

using Dungian semantics instead of a notion of logical consequence. It is possible to preserve the possibility of the use of Dungian semantics while adding structure to the notions of argument and attack (an example of such system is Prakken's ASPIC^{+} (Prakken 2010, see also Prakken 2016 in this volume); for a discussion of theory of structured argumentation see the Special Issue of the Argument and Computation Journal (Vol. 5, no. 1 2014); for an extensive (meta-)logical analysis of argumentation frameworks see Gabbay 2013). However, the family of Dungean argumentation does not exhaust the variety of existing proposals and research projects in the formal modelling of (legal) argumentation. In particular, Gordon and Walton (2006) developed the Carneades system, which is able to represent legal reasoning based on different sources (statutes and cases) and problems concerning standards of proof. It is worth noting that important mapping results have been obtained with regard to the relation of Carneades to abstract argumentation and defeasible logics. Recently, Thagard's coherence as constraint satisfaction theory (Thagard 2000) has been applied to legal reasoning (Araszkiewicz 2010, 2012; Araszkiewicz and Šavelka 2012; Šavelka 2013). This theory, inspired by research on cognitive science, enables the representation of both abstract and structured argumentation, based on different types of sources (including legislation), by means of neural network modelling.

The brief overview of the current state-of-art formal (to different degrees) research on the representation of law (legal knowledge, argumentation, statutes etc.) enables us to formulate a number of desiderata that in our opinion should be fulfilled by a theory encompassing the representation of legislation (proposals) and reasoning concerning normative consequences.

Desideratum 1. Let us recall that our main aim is to elaborate theoretically the transition from the (drafted) statutory text to the set of normative consequences that will be eventually assigned to the regulated states of affairs by judges. The text of the statutes is accepted as the input, and the determination of the set of normative consequences is generated as the output. Hence, we are of the opinion that this relation of consequence cannot be handled by means of any notion of logical consequence for the following three reasons:

(1) The operator of logical consequence (as a deductive inference) cannot add any new information to the input. Our intention is to enable the adopted normative consequence operator to add new information to the input.
(2) Many actually employed inference patterns present in legal reasoning are non-deductive inferences. The intended model of legislative discourse should be able to represent them.

Consequently, the model of legislative deliberation should encompass not only deductive but also non-deductive inferences. It should also exclude certain classical deductive inferences. Anticipating the investigations of the following section, let us refer to the set of all these relevant inferences as argumentative inferences.

Desideratum 2. The developed model should improve the precision and transparency of the structure of legislative deliberation, and it should be as descriptively adequate as possible. Hence, we do not intend to provide a full formalization of the process of legislative deliberation. We also do not aim to reconstruct any type of "complete norm" from legislation (see the discussion of this controversial concept in Sartor 1995, 143–144). On the contrary, we will focus on the analysis of the structure and content of legal provisions as they have been drafted by the legislator.

Desideratum 3. The developed model should account for the two types of normative consequences: abstract consequences (determinable based on the text of the statutes and applicable inference patterns only) and concretized consequences (stemming from the application of the projected rules to mainly hypothetical cases). The criterion of distinction between these two types of consequences is straightforward: in the former case, only the statutory terminology is used in the description of relevant states of affairs, whereas in the latter case, additional terminology is used to account for certain hypothetical case elements to determine far-reaching normative consequences of the proposed regulation. We will refer to the former type as Layer 1 and to the latter type as Layer 2 of legislative deliberation. A similar distinction was drawn in Araszkiewicz (2013) in order to distinguish two types of the so-called Extensional Statements in legal interpretation.

Desideratum 4. The developed model should be able to represent the different legal-philosophical accounts of the scope of the legal system, as discussed in the classical works quoted in the preceding subsection and the influence of these assumptions on the deliberated normative consequences.

The next section presents the outline of a framework that in our opinion satisfies the above desiderata.

10.3 An Argumentation Framework for Legislative Deliberation

10.3.1 Informal Introduction

The activity of the legislator may be characterized as either (1) choosing certain states of affairs that are in the world or (2) creating new states of affairs and (3) in both cases, assigning legal consequences to them. Because legal consequences are also states of affairs, the activity of a legislator may be rightly described as establishing links between (sets of) states of affairs. We do not intend to define the ontological concept of state of affairs here; instead, we propose to grasp this concept as the referent of a (set of) proposition(s).[8] A set of states of affairs is also a state of affairs, albeit a complex one.

This part of the activity of the legislator may be referred to as the logical layer of the legislative process because it ignores economic, social, political and other

[8]The literature on the concept of facts and / or states of affairs is too vast to be described here. For recent contributions in the field of legal theory, see Hage 2016 (in this volume).

similar consequences of legislation, and it focuses on logical relations between states of affairs and on features of linguistic expressions referring to them. This task is accomplished by enacting legal norms that are encoded in the statutory text. In continental legal culture, generally, the statutory text is perceived as the exclusive source of valid law. Therefore, it is particularly important for the legislator to draft the provisions such that the initial assumptions concerning the desired logical relations are eventually satisfied.

This chapter is not devoted to the discussion of the difference between regulative and constitutive legal rules (This issue is too vast to be described even briefly; for recent contributions to the on-going discussion, Hage 2014 and Lindahl and Reidhav 2016). It should be noted, however, that the distinctions concerning different types of legal norms should be accounted for in future elaborations of the following framework. Moreover, for the sake of simplicity, we assume that the set of states of affairs to which the legislator intends to attach legal consequences is given to him. We do not assume that the legislator is omniscient; therefore, the theory discussed below is a theory of the actual legislator, and not of an idealized, rational legislator.

Let us refer to the set of all actual and possible states of affairs as SOA_{ALL}. For obvious reasons, this set is not cognitively accessible to any human legislator. Let $SOA_{REV(REG)}$ be the set of states of affairs that are relevant (REV) with regard to the current regulation proposal (REG). For the sake of readability, we will refer to this set of SOAs simply as SOA.

The set SOA may be divided into two parts: ANT (Antecedents, the set of SOAs to which Legal Conclusions are going to be assigned) and LC (the set of SOAs referred to as Legal Conclusions). The dividing division of the set SOA into these two subsets is to a large extent conventional, and it is a result of the decision of the legislator.

Hence, the complex structure that is intended by the legislator (INT) may be tentatively described formally as the follows:

$$INT = \langle ANT_{INT}, LC_{INT}, AR_{INT} \rangle$$

where ANT_{INT} is the set of all states of affairs that are interesting for the legislator with regard to the subject of regulation and to which Legal Consequences should be attached, LC_{INT} is the set of all legal consequences that are deliberated by him, and AR_{INT} is the assignment relation, that is, a relation defined in ANT_{INT} and LC_{INT} that assigns one or more Legal Consequence to any state of affairs belonging to ANT_{INT}.

Let us emphasize that in the traditional continental legal culture (Hesselink 2001) the text of the statute should satisfy certain desiderata. In particular, it should be consistent and complete. With regard to consistency, it should not contain provisions that lead to incompatible legal consequences. With regard to completeness, it should assign legal consequences to all relevant states of affairs. The formulation of these conditions above refers to the features of a certain statute. However, it is possible to state analogous desiderata with regard to the entire legal system taken as a whole.

Taking the structure INT into account, the legislator enacts a statute. In the account presented here, this act and the practice of its application by courts and other organs lead to the emergence of a set of structures, ACT= $\langle ACT_1, \ldots, ACT_n \rangle$, each element of which is built analogously to INT:

$$ACT_i \in \mathbf{ACT} = \langle ANT_{ACTi}, LC_{ACTi}, AR_{ACTi} \rangle$$

The fact that we are considering more than one ACT structure reflects the obvious intuition that different scholars and courts may present different opinions regarding the normative content of a given regulation. In certain cases, the same statute may lead to the development of very different ACT structures, which presumably would be a symptom of poor legislative drafting, particularly the ambiguity of the normative act under deliberation.

We claim that the legislator succeeds in achieving his aims if and only if:

INT $\cong ACT_i$ such that $ACT_i \in \mathbf{ACT}$ is the dominant (the most frequent, the most widely acknowledged) ACT.

That is, when the legislator and the law-applying organs recognize the same states of affairs as relevant for the regulation in question and when they assign the legal consequences intended by the legislator to (preferably: exactly) these states of affairs, which were intended by the legislator to be assigned. Note that this ideal does not require the legislator to avoid using vague and open expressions that admit a high degree of discretion by the authorities applying the laws. However, this kind of situation should be foreseen by the legislator in a proper account of the anticipated assignment relations.

In this context, the following research question arises: Why is it so difficult for the legislator to succeed in obtaining INT $\cong$ ACT equivalence? The source of these difficulties seems threefold. First, the legislative drafter has an imperfect ability to recognize all possible potential incompatibilities and gaps that may stem from the projected statute, as well as all possible interferences of this statute with the entire legal system. This is also because of the fact that statutes are formulated in natural (informal) language, which makes it difficult to detect logical incompatibilities and instances of incompleteness. The second difficulty is related to the transition from the (abstract) Layer 1 to the (concretized) Layer 2 discussed in the preceding Section, which involves legal interpretation. As previously discussed, the results of the process of legal interpretation are not entirely foreseeable because they involve creative reasoning. Third, and most important for the aims of this chapter, the concept of normative consequence is not clear and, as discussed above, the notion of logical consequence is not very useful for the clarification of the former.

Let us analyse these problems in detail. As shown above, in his regulatory work, the legislator intends to define the set of states of affairs that are considered relevant for a given regulation, the set of legal consequences that are attached to them, and the assignment relation between them. However, that these sets are only partially made explicit in the statutory text is problematic. Let us assume for instance that according to the legislator's intention, a legal consequence LC should be attached to the state of affairs ANT. Assume that the legislator expresses the provision that should realize the state of affairs intended by him in the following manner:

If ANT, then (attach) LC.

This linguistic expression presumptively enables the law-applying organ to attach legal consequence LC to the state of affairs ANT whenever the latter is adequately presented in the course of the proceedings before this organ. However, also presumptively, the expression presented above enables the organ to apply the e contrario scheme, which, in a simplified account, authorizes the organ not to attach the legal consequence LC to a state of affairs other than ANT:

For any $K \in (ANT_{INT} \setminus ANT)$, if K, then (do not attach) LC.

According to the expression presented above, the law-applying organ should not attach the legal consequence to any state of affairs intended by the legislator to differ from ANT. Consequently, the set ANT_{INT} may be divided into two disjoint subsets: the subset $ANT_{INT\text{-}EXP}$ of the states of affairs that are explicitly mentioned in the statutory text and the subset of $ANT_{INT\text{-}IMP}$ of the states of affairs that are intended only implicitly, such as complements of the explicitly mentioned states of affairs to the entire set of intended states of affairs.

The distinction presented above presumably does not apply to the set of intended legal consequences, for in countries governed by the rule of law all legal consequences that can be applied by relevant authorities should be explicitly mentioned in the text of a normative act. However, the distinction undoubtedly applies to the assignment relation. Certainly, as in the example discussed above, the legislator explicitly expresses the assignment relation in a legal provision, such as by formulating an explicit normative conditional. However, many assignment relations may be only implicitly encoded in the statutory text, which pertains both to explicitly and implicitly expressed states of affairs. Therefore, the set AR_{INT} should be divided into two disjoint subsets analogous those distinguished with regard to the set ANT_{INT}, that is, into the subsets $AR_{INT\text{-}EXP}$ and $AR_{INT\text{-}IMP}$. Because the statutes are expressed in natural language, it is not surprising that the legislator may not detect all relevant assignment relations that are expressed implicitly in the text. Thus, it is plausible to hold that the law-applying organ may reconstruct a set AR_{ACT} that is different from AR_{INT} at least with respect to the implicit assignment relations.

So far we have focused on the first, abstract layer concerning statutory construction. The introduction of the second layer (i.e., the analysis of concrete actual or artificial examples to which the provisions should apply) further complicates the problems. The formulation of legal interpretive statements consists in establishing extensional relations between predicates expressing certain states of affairs (Araszkiewicz 2013). As a matter of course, a law-applying entity may determine the extension of a given statutory predicate in a manner that is different from that intended by the legislator. This may lead to different types of discrepancies between the structures INT and ACT.

Our investigations lead to the obvious conclusion that legislative deliberation, even if it focuses only on the logical level, is an extremely complex phenomenon. Because it is our opinion that the formal-logical approaches discussed above are generally not sufficient to grasp this complexity in its entirety, here we provide a semi-formal framework that encompasses two basic elements: (1) a formal language based on first order deontic logic (with possible extensions) and (2) an informal part encompassing a set of argument schemes. In this respect, the model presented below is analogous to the model of legal interpretation outlined in Araszkiewicz 2013.

The motivation for adopting this stance is as follows:

First, the first-order language of deontic logic (with some extensions) is a useful tool in the explication of the structure of statutory text. Although the translation from natural language to the language of first order logic is not an uncontroversial task, it is generally feasible, as shown in the literature review provided in the preceding Section. The use of formalization techniques enables us to indicate precisely the states of affairs and the legal consequences that are explicitly presented in the statutory text.

Second, we do not use the formal logical notion of consequence in order to determine the set of normative consequences. As shown in the preceding section, the use of the logical notion of consequence in formalized legal texts may lead to counterintuitive or otherwise troubling results. Nonetheless, the logical notion of consequence does not encompass many inference patterns that are considered relevant in legislative deliberation. This enables the following framework to satisfy desideratum 1.

Third, although it would be possible to formalize the legislative deliberation by mean of theories that deal with nonmonotonic reasoning (e.g., the very informative contribution of Prakken 2016), we decided not to take this stance because we are interested in showing not only the form of arguments that lead to normative consequences but also, and primarily, their content.

Fourth, the adopted method will enable us to show how the different conceptions of legal systems discussed in Sect. 10.2 above can determine different assignments of legal consequences to states of affairs relevant for the legislator (see desideratum 4 above).

Fifth, our intention is to account for the openness of the legislative deliberation process, as well as to remain close to the reality of this deliberation (see desideratum 2 above). When it is formalized in its entirety as a formal-logical theory, its consequences are determined by the rules of inference of the applied logical calculus; however, this mode of representation would, in our opinion, considerably deform the actual shape of legislative deliberation. In its logical layer, this deliberation, which encompasses the determination of normative consequences, takes the form of the exchange of legislative opinions, and it is our intention to model the development and exchange of arguments that are present in these opinions. Therefore, we intend to provide a mode of this deliberation by means of argumentation schemes theory.

The theory of argumentation schemes is currently one of the most dominant paradigms in the research on argumentation. Famously advanced by Walton (1996), argumentation schemes are now widely used in the research on legal theory (Macagno et al. 2012), AI and law research (e.g., Gordon and Walton 2009) and in general theory of argumentation (Walton et al. 2008). Argumentation schemes may be summarized as follows:

(1) They are schemes of patterns of reasoning that are present in argumentative practice. Although in reality there are many variations of any argument scheme, it is possible to distinguish one scheme from another by giving lists of their specific premises, conclusions, and so-called critical questions. For example, (Walton et al. 2008, 308 ff.) distinguish 60 basic argument schemes.
(2) Argumentation schemes are typically patterns of presumptive (non-deductive) reasoning. The emphasis is on the content of their premises and not on the formal features of the reasoning patterns.
(3) Arguments are defined as instantiations of argument schemes. Conversely, argument schemes may be referred to as argument types, whereas argument instantiations (arguments) may be referred to as argument tokens;
(4) Arguments based on argument schemes may be attacked. The typical attacks that are assigned to an argument scheme are encompassed in sets of critical questions. Although there are many conceptual schemes that are used for theoretical accounts of the attack relations between arguments, here we refer to a well-known classification of attacks (employed and formalized for instance in Prakken 2016) according to which

   - an undermining attack is an attack on the premises of an argument (i.e., by claiming that at least one of premises of the attacked argument is false or insufficiently justified),
   - an undercutting attack is an attack on the inference relation of an argument (i.e., by claiming that although the premises of an argument are well-founded, they are insufficient to support the conclusion), and
   - a rebutting attack is an attack on the conclusion of an argument.

The fact that the majority of arguments actually used in legal argumentation do not have a deductive character has been acknowledged in the literature for more than half a century (Alexy 1989; Perelman and Olbrechts-Tyteca 1958). Aleksander Peczenik devoted much of his attention to the theory of non-deductive steps in legal inference and referred to these inference patterns as jumps or transformations (e.g., Peczenik 1983, 3–10; Peczenik 1996, 300; Peczenik 2008, 96–97, 109–110). As in the case of Peczenik's jumps, it is in principle possible to transform the argument schemes into logically valid inferences, but it would necessarily involve adding controversial premises to them; moreover, it would blur the distinctive features of particular argument schemes.

For the reasons presented above, we are of the opinion that a semi-formal framework encompassing both the formalization of the text of the statute and an informal approach to the determination of the scope of their normative consequences is an optimal methodological choice with regard to building a descriptive theory of normative consequence and legislative deliberation. The next subsection offers the proposal of this framework.

10.3.2 Semi-formal Exposition

In this section, we present an outline of a semi-formal framework, to which we refer as the Argumentation Framework for Legislation (AFLEG). The purpose of AFLEG is to clarify the concept of normative consequence in a manner that is descriptively adequate and useful for the purposes of legislative practice. In particular, AFLEG is designed to deal with problems concerning potential discrepancies between the structures INT and ACT, which were discussed in the previous subsection.

The present version of AFLEG is partial. The developed portion focuses on the determination of the set of normative consequences stemming from legislative texts and other sources by means of applicable argument schemes. Certain concepts important for legislative deliberation are explicated. The details of legislative deliberation are treated informally, however.

Definition 1 (The AFLEG abstract framework). The AFLEG abstract framework is a structure ⟨AL, AR, ArgSch, CR⟩, where

(1) AL is the subject level language adopted in an instantiation of the AFLEG abstract framework.
(2) AR is the Assignment Relation defined over expressions in AL.
(3) ArgSch is a set of argument schemes, that is, structures that adopt certain expressions in (informal) meta-language as an input and different types of expressions as an output. A special type of argument schemes is assigning argument schemes, which is defined below.
(4) CR is the conflict relation defined in certain expressions of AL.

This abstract definition enables a potentially interested researcher to develop many different types of AFLEG instantiations according to her or his preferences concerning the accepted logical calculus, as well as the set of argument schemes that are acceptable in a given legal culture or in the context of accepted legal-philosophical assumptions. Here we present an instantiation of AFLEG that is in our opinion useful for the analysis of statutory law in continental legal culture. For the sake of readability, we refer to this instantiation of AFLEG abstract framework simply as AFLEG.

Definition 2 (The AFLEG subject level language (AL)). The AFLEG subject-level language (AL) encompasses the following elements:

(1) Standard first order logic symbols encompassing standard individual variables, individual constants, quantification symbols, predicates[9] and standard logical connectives,
(2) A set of standard first order logic syntactic rules concerning the formation of terms and formulas,

[9]For the sake of readability, we will not use standard formal notation of predicate symbols, but full expressions of predicates in square brackets. For instance, the sentence "There exists a cat" will not be represented by $\exists_x$ C(x), but by $\exists_x$ [cat] (x).

(3) Deontic operators:

(a) O – it is obligatory that
(b) PR – it is prohibited that
(c) PER – it is permitted that.

The version of AL used here should be understood as preliminary. It is possible to extend it to introduce additional operators, such as temporal and spatial operators, operators concerning the validity and efficacy of legal rules, and so on.

Definition 3 (Assignment Relation). The assignment relation $\langle AR \rangle \subset AL^2$ means "is being assigned with", and it may relate to certain well-formed parts of AL such that the first related element is referred to as an antecedent representation (ANTR) and the second element is referred to as legal consequence representation (LCR). The distinction between ANTR parts of AL and LCR parts of AL is relative and conventional in the sense that the same linguistic expression may play the role of ANTR in one pair of expressions connected with $\langle AR \rangle$ and the role of LCR in another pair. However, specific predicates will be typically present in expressions that play the role of LCR and not in those playing the role of ANTR. For instance, deontic operators will be typical elements of LCR expressions but not of ANTR expressions.

Definition 4 (Argument Scheme). An argument scheme is a structure (P_1, P_2, $\ldots P_n$, CON, CQ), where:

(1) P_1, P_2, $\ldots P_n$ are specific premises of a given Argument Scheme, expressed in metalanguage (natural plan language),[10] which can, however, contain certain parts expressed in AL.
(2) CON is a conclusion of an argument scheme
(3) CQ is a set of critical questions that may be used to attack the given argument scheme.

A particularly important subtype of argument schemes are assigning argument schemes, that is, such argument schemes which support or demote an assignment relation between certain ANTR_{SAT} and LCRs:

Definition 4.1 (Assigning Argument Scheme). An assigning argument scheme (AAS) is a structure (P_1, P_2, $\ldots P_n$, $\langle AR \rangle$ (ANTR_i, LCR_i), CQ), where

(1) $P_1, P_2, \ldots P_n$ are specific premises of a given AAS.
(2) $\langle AR \rangle$ (ANTR_i, LCR_i) is the conclusion of an AAS, which assigns a certain LCR to certain ANTR.
(3) CQ is a set of critical questions that may be used to attack the given argument scheme.

[10]We adopt this solution in order to avoid problems concerning the complete formalization of plain, natural language. Arguably this is not possible with the use of the first-order (deontic) language, which we adopt here as the subject level language.

Example 1 (Rule-Based Argument Scheme). The rule-based argument scheme is one of the most commonly used in legal discourse. If the legislator aims to assign certain legal consequences to a given state of affairs, presumably the simplest manner in which to realize this goal is to formulate a conditional expression in the statutory text. Let us now present the rule-based argument scheme in a slightly reformulated version, which was discussed in Araszkiewicz (2014). The present version is more suitable for legislative discourse.

Premise. There exists an expression in the statutory text that is relatively uncontroversially translatable into a conditional expression in LL of the following form: $(ANTR_1, ANTR_2, \ldots, ANTR_n) \rightarrow (LCR_1, LCR_2, \ldots LCR_n)$ (a Legal Rule).

Conclusion. $\langle AR \rangle ((ANTR_1, ANTR_2, \ldots, ANTR_n), (LCR_1, LCR_2, \ldots LCR_n))$.

Critical Questions.

CQ 1. Is the expression taken into consideration actually relatively uncontroversially translatable into a legal rule (LR)?
CQ 2. Are there any explicit exceptions to the LR?
CQ 3. Are there any other LRs in the legal system in question that would conflict with the LR in question?

As a matter of course, it also would be possible to formulate other types of critical questions to the rule-based scheme, such as those dealing with the validity or efficacy of this rule. Here, for the sake of simplicity, we do not discuss these issues, because our aim is to show the basic features of the AFLEG.

The working of a rule-based argument scheme may be represented graphically in the following figure (Fig. 10.1).

Let us now illustrate the functioning of the rule-based normative scheme using a very simple example, which is a rule encompassed in art. 415 of the Polish Civil Code,[11] according to which

> Whoever causes a damage to another person and is at fault, is obligated to compensate the damage.

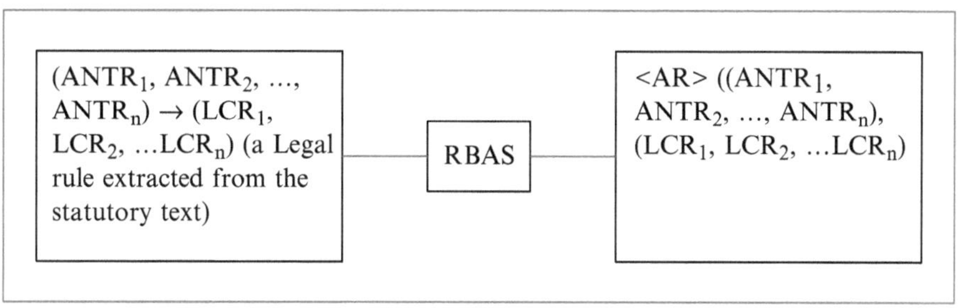

Fig. 10.1 Rule-based argument scheme

[11] *Journal of Laws* 2014.121, consolidated text as amended.

Let us instantiate the rule-based argument scheme by using the content provided by the quoted passage from the statutory text and by giving answers to critical questions:

Premise. There exists such an expression in the statutory text that is relatively uncontroversially translatable into a conditional expression in AL of the following form:

$$(\forall_{x,y} (([\text{causes\_damage}] (x,y) \wedge [\text{is\_at\_fault}] (x)) \rightarrow \text{O} ([\text{compensate}] (x,y))))$$

Conclusion. ⟨AR⟩ (([causes_damage] (x,y) ∧ [is_at_fault] (x)), O ([compensate] (x,y))

Critical Questions.

CQ 1. Is the expression taken into consideration actually relatively uncontroversially translatable into a legal rule?
Answer: Yes, the translation is actually relatively uncontroversial.

CQ 2. Are there any explicit exceptions to the LR?
Answer: No, there are no explicit exceptions in the structure of the LR in question.

CQ 3. Are there any other LRs in the legal system in question that would conflict with the LR in question?
Answer: Yes, there are many of them, such as art. 426 of the Polish Civil Code concerning the lack of civil liability of minors.

Obviously, the functioning of the RBAS in legislative discourse is modelled against the background of its use in the discourse of applying law. This is exactly the phenomenon we intend to represent in the AFLEG: by developing the INT structure, the legislator should anticipate the law-applying behaviour of competent authorities (and therefore, the exemplary ANT structures).

The rule-based argument scheme is of course only one of many argument schemes, and it is presumably one of the simplest argument schemes that may be used for establishing (presumptive) assignment relations between certain ANTRs and LCRs. In the examples given below, we propose further argument schemes that are used to establish the relevant assignment relations.

Definition 5 (Conflict Relation). The conflict relation ⟨CR⟩ is defined according to the set of expressions in AL. We hold that two expressions in AL, E_i and E_j are in conflict (⟨CR⟩ (E_i, E_j)) if they could not both be true propositions in AL, assuming standard semantics for first-order (deontic) logic.

For instance, the following pairs of LCRs would conflict with each other:

(1) "O[pays](x)" and "O[does not pay] (x)". These propositions are contrary, so they cannot be both true,
(2) "$\forall_x$ ([attorney] (x) → [lawyer] (x))" and "$\exists_x$ ([attorney] (x) ∧¬ [lawyer] (x))" – because these propositions are contradictory.

One should note that this definition does not exhaust the set of sentences that should be deemed conflicting because of the aims of the legislative process. Hence, the definition of the conflict relation should be broadened in order to encompass different types of pragmatic inconsistencies. However, the discussion of this topic is beyond the scope of the present chapter (see similar considerations in Lindahl and Reidhav 2016, in this volume).

A particularly important kind of conflict is that between LCRs. However, in order to define this conflict, certain additional stipulations are necessary. For instance, a given statute may contain both LCRs that a wrongdoer is punishable and is not punishable. However, this situation need not be problematic if these two LCRs are assigned to different ANTRs. This leads us to the following definition of a normative conflict relation.

Definition 5.1 (Normative Conflict Relation). The normative conflict relation ⟨NCR⟩ is defined according to the set of LCRs. We hold that two LCRs, LCR_i and LCR_j , are in normative conflict (⟨NCR⟩ (LCR_i, LCR_j)) if and only if

(1) There exist such $ANTR_k$ and $ANTR_l$ such that ⟨AR⟩ (($ANTR_k \cap ANTR_l$), LCR_i) and ⟨AR⟩ (($ANTR_k \cap ANTR_l$), LCR_j), and
(2) ⟨CR⟩ (LCR_i, LCR_j).

Let us now explain how the AFLEG as presented below may be used to determine the content of normative consequences of a given project of a normative act. To accomplish this aim, we introduce the notion of AFLEG theory.

Definition 6 (AFLEG Theory). AFLEG theory for a normative act project (NAP) is the structure ⟨$ANTR_{NAP}$, LCR_{NAP}, $ANTR_{SAT}$, ArgSch, $Args_{NAP}$, AR_{NAP}, NCR_{NAP}⟩, where

(1) $ANTR_{NAP}$ is the set of ANTRs expressed in the normative act project, encompassing ANTRs expressing SOA_{EXP}s as well as SOA_{IMP}s,
(2) LCR_{NAP} is the set of LCR_S expressed in the normative act project,
(3) $ANTR_{SAT}$ is the set of all ANTRs that are satisfied in the hypothetical case that is deliberated in the course of legislative discourse,
(4) ArgSch is the set of all argument schemes in AFLEG, including the Assigning argument schemes,
(5) $Args_{NAP}$ is the set of all arguments (including assigning arguments) that are applicable with regard to the normative act project, that is, instantiations of argument schemes that produce conclusions with regard to the normative act project because the premises of these Argument Schemes are satisfied,
(6) AR_{NAP} is the set of sets of LCR_{NAP}s assigned to the sets of $ANTR_{NAP}$s by means of the ⟨AR⟩,
(7) NCR_{NAP} is the set of pairs of LCRs that are in the normative conflict relation.

The semi-formal framework outlined above has several important advantages that realize the desiderata discussed in the previous section. It explicates the concept of the normative consequences of a given normative act, which are only intended in the process of legislative deliberation. They become actual when the normative act enters into force and is further applied by the relevant authorities. The set of the normative consequences of a single normative act should be identified with the set AR_{NAP}. This account of the concept of normative consequences encompasses different types of reasoning patterns that accept the statutory text as an input and eventually lead to the assignment of legal consequences to certain states of affairs. Therefore, desideratum 1 as described above is satisfied. We are also of the opinion that the AFLEG offers a reasonable balance between the precision stemming from logical reconstruction and the informal discussion enhancing descriptive adequacy of the model (desideratum 2). This will become apparent in the next section, where examples of application of the AFLEG will be presented. The AFLEG framework is able to represent both abstract Layer 1 (where only normative consequences drawn are based on statutory expressions) and concretized Layer 2 (where additional information, such as that representing states of affairs in hypothetical cases, is introduced). Thus, desideratum 3 is satisfied. The framework offers the possibility of the legal-philosophical analysis of legislative argumentation when the set of applicable Argument Schemes is deliberated. Arguably, a non-positivist would accept more types of argument schemes than a legal positivist would (The latter focuses on argument schemes based on authoritative sources, and the former also adopts argument schemes appealing to morality, unwritten principles, etc.). This topic will be discussed later in the concluding part of the chapter.

Additionally, the AFLEG enables us to define certain important concepts that are used in actual legislative deliberation. The concept of normative conflict was discussed above. Let us now present how the so-called genuine legal gap and axiological legal gap may be defined in the AFLEG.

Definition 7 (Genuine Legal Gap). There is a genuine legal gap in a normative act project (GLG_{NAP}) if and only if there exists $ANTR_i \in ANTR_{NAP}$ such that there does not exist $LCR_j \in LCR_{NAP}$ such that ⟨AR⟩ ($ANTR_i$, LCR_j), according to any argument $\in Arg_{NAP}$.

The definition presented above encompasses an intuition according to which there exists a state of affairs that is relevant for the scope of a given normative act. However, no acceptable legal argument exists that would assign any legal consequence to this state of affairs.

Definition 8 (Axiological Legal Gap). There is an axiological legal gap in a normative act project (ALG_{NAP}) if for a certain $ANTR_i \in ANTR_{NAP}$ there exists argument $\in Arg_{NAP}$ that is based on evaluative premises and assigns no LCR to $ANTR_i$, and at the same time, there exists at least one Arg $\in Arg_{NAP}$ that is not based on evaluative premises and that assigns a LCR $\in LCR_{NAP}$ to $ANTR_i$.

The explication presented above shows that axiological gaps are not a threat to the assignment of legal consequences to any relevant state of affairs that should be regulated by a given normative act. Definitions 7 and 8 also precisely show the differences between genuine and axiological legal gaps.

Similarly, AFLEG is able to provide definitions of apparent and genuine normative inconsistency.

Definition 9 (Apparent Normative Inconsistency). There is an apparent normative inconsistency (ANI) in the normative act project if

(1) For some LCR_i, $LCR_j \in LCR_{NAP}$, presumptively ⟨NCR⟩ (LCR_i, LCR_j), but at the same time
(2) Assuming that $ANTR_k$, $ANTR_l \in ANTR_{NAP}$ at least of the premises of an argument $ARG_x \in Arg_{NAP}$ supporting the assignment relation ⟨AR⟩ (($ANTR_k \cap ANTR_l$), LCR_i) or assignment relation ⟨AR⟩ (($ANTR_k \cap ANTR_l$), LCR_j) is false or at least questionable, or
(3) There is a proposition in the AFLEG theory for NAP that renders the premises of ARG_x insufficient to support either the assignment relation ⟨AR⟩ (($ANTR_k \cap ANTR_l$), LCR_i) or assignment relation ⟨AR⟩ (($ANTR_k \cap ANTR_l$), LCR_j), or both, even if the premises of ARG_x are not questionable, or
(4) There is an argument $ARG_y \in Arg_{NAP}$ that is stronger (more persuasive) than ARG_x that supports the negation of the conclusions of ARG_x, or
(5) The proposition ⟨NCR⟩ (LCR_i, LCR_j) is at least questionable or simply false, or
(6) There exists such $Arg_z \in Arg_{NAP}$ that is stronger (more persuasive) that ARG_x and supports the following assignment relation ⟨AR⟩ (($ANTR_k$ $ANTR_l$), LCR_i) and assignment relation ⟨AR⟩ (($ANTR_k$ $ANTR_l$), LCR_j).

The definition of ANI presented above encompasses important reasoning patterns that are used to eliminate apparent inconsistencies from the projects of normative acts and from the normative acts in force. Point (2) above represents an undermining attack, which aims to show that the argument supporting the thesis that some state of affairs is assigned two different incompatible legal consequences is based on wrong premises. Point (3) questions the presumptive justificatory force of this argument (undercutting attack). Point (4) represents an attack on the conclusion, which shows that at least one of the different legal consequences is not assigned to the state of affairs in question: the successful uses of *lex superior* and *lex posterior* collision rules are examples of this phenomenon. Point (5) represents calling the conflicting character of legal consequences into question. Finally, point (6) represents the functioning of the *lex specialis collision rule*, leading to the statement that one of the apparently colliding rules is an exception to another one. Note that in the present version of the AFLEG framework, we do not formalize attack relations that may relate different arguments to each other.

Definition 10 (Genuine Normative Inconsistency). There is genuine normative inconsistency (GNI) in the normative act project if

(1) For some LCR_i, $LCR_j \in LCR_{NAP}$, presumptively ⟨NCR⟩ (LCR_i, LCR_j) and
(2) LCR_i and LCR_j do not create ANI.

The considerations presented above enable us to define the notions of consistency and completeness of normative act projects.

Definition 11 (Consistent Normative Act Project). A normative act project is consistent if and only if $GNI_{NAP} = \varnothing$.

Otherwise, it is inconsistent. Note that AFLEG enables us to count the number of inconsistencies in a NAP.

Definition 12 (Complete Normative Act Project). A normative act project is complete if and only if $GLG_{NAP} = \varnothing$.

Until this point, we have shown that the AFLEG, in addition to satisfaction of the desiderata outlined in the previous section, is able to represent persuasively important concepts that are related to the theory of the legal system and the assessment of legislative proposals with regard to their logical features. However, the AFLEG is primarily designed to represent the discussion of the normative consequence of legislative proposals in actual legislative discourse. The next section provides a brief discussion of two exemplary cases.

10.3.3 Discussion of Cases

In this section, we present AFLEG representations of two actual examples taken from the Polish legislative practice. The aim of this section is to present the expressive power of the AFLEG framework, as well as to justify the descriptive adequacy of the proposed account of the concept of normative consequence. Although the discussed examples are relatively simple, they require a complex representation in AFLEG. Consequently, these examples may be viewed as illustrations of the complexity of actual legislative processes and the need to elaborate frameworks that would improve the transparency and precision of the process of legislative discourse.

In the presented account, the structure of legislative discourse encompasses the following phases:

(1) The formalization of the legal provision in question and mining of relevant SOA representations (encompassing both ANTRs and LCRs),
(2) The development of an AFLEG theory encompassing application of relevant Argumentation Schemes and determination of the normative consequences (that is, the set of elements related with AR),
(3) The development of alternative AFLEG theories stemming from the addition of certain SOA representations (in particular, extra-statutory predicates related to hypothetical situations concerning the application of legal rules) and certain new arguments,
(4) The comparison of the generated AFLEG theories with respect to a set of criteria (e.g., with respect to values that should be realized by a given rule or statute).

The present version of the AFLEG is able to represent phases 1–3 in a semi-formal manner, whereas phase 4 (assessment and comparison of AFLEG theories) is represented informally.

The first example is taken from the area of tax law (Value Added Tax law reform), and the second one is taken from the domain of civil law (Consumer Rights Act project).

Case 1. The example is from the amendment to the Value-Added Tax Act, which was adopted by the Polish Parliament on 7 December 2012. The bill to Parliament on amendments to the Value-Added Tax Act (hereafter the VAT Project) was submitted to the House of Representatives (the Sejm) on 16 October 2012, primarily with the view to implement two Council Directives:

(1) Directive 2010/45/EU of 13 July amending Directive 2006/112/EC on the common system of value added tax as regards the rules on invoicing and
(2) Directive 2008/8/EC of 12 February 2008 amending Directive 2006/112/EC regarding the place of supply of services (in the scope in which the Directive was not implemented until the bill was submitted).

Apart from the abovementioned purpose, the bill aimed at adapting provisions to the judgements of the European Court of Justice and the rulings of administrative courts, adapting binding provisions to the rules and institutions provided for in Directive 2006/112/EC more accurately, and removing inconsistencies between the provisions and the rules of the European Union. In particular, the VAT Project provided for the amendment of the key provision of the Act, which regulates the right to reduce the tax due by the amount of input tax.

The original text of this provision was extensive, comprising two pages at the moment of its first adoption in 2004. Currently, however, it is a three-page document. Because the provision was edited in such a way, we have to introduce the appropriate changes in order to make the text ready for its formalization. The changes do not influence the nature of argumentation in any way because they concern referrals and scope disambiguations that are irrelevant from our point of view.

The key part of the text, which expresses the fundamental constructive institution of the value-added tax namely the right to deduction of input tax, is binding with the preserved original wording until today and reads as follows:

> Art. 86(1) To the extent to which the purchased goods and services are used for the purposes of taxed transactions, a taxpayer (...) is entitled to reduce the tax due by the amount of input tax (...).

With the exception of the first paragraph, the text has been amended several times over the years. The regulation that is relevant from the perspective of our example has been included in the second paragraph[12]:

[12] Because of the numerous legislative changes, in the example we use the text from 2011, that is, its wording from before the introduction of the VAT Project. It should be emphasized, however, that this particular institution has been construed and applied exactly in this way since the analysed regulation came into force.

2. The following constitute the amount of input tax: (...)
4) the amount of tax due by virtue of: (...)
c) intra-community acquisition of goods;

The legislative issue we consider in the presented example concerns the determination of the moment upon which there arises a right to reduce the tax due. This issue was governed by Art. 86(10)(2):

10. The right to reduce the amount of tax due arises: (...)
2) in the events referred to in paragraph 2(4) – in the period in which the tax due became chargeable for the purchaser or recipient of the services with respect to provided services, where the recipient of the services is a taxpayer, on intra-community acquisitions of goods or on the supply of goods, where the purchaser is a taxpayer;

It is necessary to simplify this Act by the omission of irrelevant expressions. This allows for the following presentation of the original wording of the Act:

10. The right to reduce the amount of tax due arises: (...)
2) in the events referred to in paragraph 2(4) - in the period in which the tax became chargeable (...) on intra-community acquisitions of goods;

Let us present the rule quoted above in a formalized manner. For the sake of readability, we substitute the referring clause ("in paragraph 2(4)") by the referred content ("by virtue of intra community acquisition of goods"). Furthermore, because of the fact that statutory predicates used in the provision are quite extensive, we propose the following shortened conventions:

- instead of [the_ amount_of_due_by_virtue_of_intra-community_acquisition_of_goods] we will write [the_amount_of_due];
- instead of [the_right_to_reduce_the_amount_of_tax_due] we will write [the_right_to_reduce], and
- instead of [the_period_in_which_became_chargeable_on_intra-community_acquisition_of_goods] we will write [chargeable].

(VAT art. 86.10.2) $(([\text{tax}](x) \wedge ([\text{the\_amount\_of\_due}](x) \rightarrow [\text{input}](x)) \wedge [\text{the\_right\_to\_reduce}](y)) \rightarrow ([\text{chargeable}](x) \rightarrow [\text{arises}](y))$

Let us repeat that with respect to the intra-community acquisition of goods, the right to reduce the tax due has been construed and applied in this way since the day the Tax Act came into force. It is possible to state the hypothesis that in the case of this provision, the INT structure was equal to at least the majority of ANT structures generated in the process of the application of law. Indeed, the AFLEG theory representing the normative consequences of the legal rule in question is quite straightforward.

(VAT 86.10.2) AFLEG theory.

(1) $\text{ANTR}_{(\text{VAT})} = \langle[\text{tax}](x), ([\text{the\_amount\_of\_due}](x) \rightarrow [\text{input}](x)), [\text{the\_right\_to\_reduce}](y), [\text{chargeable}](x)\rangle$
(2) $\text{LCR}_{(\text{VAT})} = \langle[\text{arises}](y)\rangle$
(3) $\text{ANTR}_{\text{SAT}} = ([\text{tax}](x), [\text{the\_amount\_of\_due}](x), [\text{the\_right\_to\_reduce}](y), [\text{chargeable}](x))$

(4) ArgSch = ⟨RBAS⟩
(5) $\text{Args}_{(\text{VAT})}$ = ⟨instantiation of RBAS⟩[13]
(6) $\text{AR}_{(\text{VAT})}$ = ⟨AR⟩ (([tax](x), ([the_amount_of_due](x) → [input](x)), [the_right_to_reduce](y), [chargeable] (x)), [arises](y))
(7) $\text{NCR}_{(\text{VAT})} = \varnothing$

In consequence, the former version of the legal rule in question provided for the following assignment of normative consequences: if the tax becomes chargeable on intra-community acquisition of goods, then the right to reduction of tax due arises. This enabled the taxpayers involved in the intra-community acquisition of goods transactions to reduce the tax due (and in consequence not to carry its burden) without any additional conditions.

The VAT Project introduced to the Parliament included the following proposal of changing the moment upon which the right to reduce the amount of the tax arises:

Art. 86:

2. The following constitute the amount of input tax: (...)
4) the amount of tax due by virtue of: (...)
c) intra-community acquisitions of goods, (...) determined pursuant to the received invoice issued in accordance with the provisions of the Directive 2006/112/CE, evidencing the supply of goods which constitutes the intra-community acquisition of goods for a taxpayer.

Without taking into consideration repetitions and other legislative lapses, this definition had understandable consequences in the determination of the moment upon which the tax becomes chargeable, which was reflected in Art. 1(41) of the VAT Project:

> Paragraph 10 is as follows:
> 10. The right to reduce the amount of tax due by the amount of input tax arises in the period in which the tax becomes chargeable with respect to the goods and services purchased domestically or imported by a taxpayer. In the event referred to in paragraph 2(1)(a) and (4)(c), the above-mentioned right arises not earlier than in the period in which a taxpayer received an invoice or a custom document, (...).

Let us present a formalized version of the rule in question stemming from the VAT project:

(VAT art. 86.10.2)*[14] (([tax](x) ∧ ([the_amount_of_due](x) → [input](x)) ∧ [the_right_to_reduce](y) ∧ [taxpayer](z)) → (([chargeable](x) ∧ (received_an_invoice)(z)) → [arises](y))

It is not difficult to state that the VAT Project introduced an additional condition for the right of reduction to arise: it may arise no earlier than the period of receiving of an invoice (or a custom document) by a taxpayer. Let us present two AFLEG

[13]We do not represent it here for the sake of conciseness and due to the fact that the instantiation of RBAS is obvious in this theory.

[14]The asterisk (*) indicates that this version of the provision is taken from a draft of a statute and not from the valid law.

theories based on this new provision, one of which encompasses a situation in which the taxpayer received an invoice and the second one in which this state of affairs is not present.

(VAT 86.10.2)* AFLEG theory (IR[15]).

(1) ANTR(VAT) = ⟨ [tax](*x*), ([the_amount_of_due](*x*) → [input](*x*)), [the_right_to_reduce](*y*), [chargeable](*x*), [taxpayer](*z*), [received_an_invoice](*z*)⟩
(2) LCR(VAT) = ⟨[arises](*y*)⟩
(3) ANTRSAT = ⟨[tax](*x*), [the_amount_of_due](*x*), [the_right_to_reduce](*y*), [chargeable](*x*), [taxpayer](*z*), [received_an_invoice](*z*)⟩
(4) ArgSch = ⟨RBAS⟩
(5) Args(VAT) = ⟨instantiation of RBAS⟩
(6) AR(VAT) = ⟨AR⟩ (([tax](*x*), ([the_amount_of_due](*x*) → [input](*x*)), [the_right_to_reduce](*y*), [chargeable](*x*), [taxpayer](*z*), [received_an_invoice](*z*)), [arises](*y*))
(7) NCR(VAT) = ∅.

In the theory presented above, all conditions of the rule (VAT art. 86.10.2)*–hence, the assignment of normative consequence to the contemplated set of states of affairs–is possible.

(VAT 86.10.2)* AFLEG theory (INR[16]).

(1) ANTR(VAT) = ⟨[tax](*x*), ([the_amount_of_due](*x*) → [input](*x*)), [the_right_to_reduce](*y*), [chargeable](*x*), [taxpayer](*z*), [received_an_invoice](*z*)⟩
(2) LCR(VAT) = ⟨[arises](*y*)⟩
(3) ANTRSAT = ⟨[tax](*x*), [the_amount_of_due](*x*), [the_right_to_reduce](*y*), [chargeable](*x*), [taxpayer](*z*)⟩
(4) ArgSch = ⟨RBAS⟩
(5) Args(VAT) = ∅
(6) AR(VAT) = ∅
(7) NCR(VAT) = ∅.

In the theory presented above it is not possible to instantiate the RBAS because one of the conditions of the rule in question is not satisfied (i.e., the invoice has not been received by the taxpayer). Hence, the right to reduction does not emerge. This result has been assessed as troubling in the course of legislative proceedings.

In order to make the reasoning more explicit, let us introduce a new argument scheme, that is, the *E Contrario* argument scheme (ECAS), to the theory. The structure of the ECAS is as follows:

[15]Invoice received.

[16]Invoice not received.

E Contrario Argument Scheme.

Premise 1. There exists such an expression in the statutory text that is relatively uncontroversially translatable into a conditional expression in LL of the following form: $(\mathrm{ANTR}_1, \mathrm{ANTR}_2, \ldots, \mathrm{ANTR}_n) \rightarrow (\mathrm{LCR}_1, \mathrm{LCR}_2, \ldots \mathrm{LCR}_n)$ (a Legal Rule).

Premise 2. At least one of the expressions $\mathrm{ANTR}_i \notin \mathrm{ANTR}_{SAT}$.

Conclusion. $\langle \mathrm{AR} \rangle ((\mathrm{ANTR}_{SAT}), \neg (\mathrm{LCR}_1, \mathrm{LCR}_2, \ldots \mathrm{LCR}_n))$.

We omit a set of critical questions for this argument scheme because it is not necessary for the remainder of the analysis. Let us now present an extended version of the AFLEG theory for the deliberated provision, which encompasses the ECAS instantiation:

(VAT 86.10.2)* AFLEG extended theory (INR).

(1) $\mathrm{ANTR}_{(VAT)} = \langle[\mathrm{tax}](x), ([\mathrm{the\_amount\_of\_due}](x) \rightarrow [\mathrm{input}](x)), [\mathrm{the\_right\_to\_reduce}](y), [\mathrm{chargeable}](x), [\mathrm{taxpayer}](z), [\mathrm{received\_an\_invoice}](z)\rangle$
(2) $\mathrm{LCR}_{(VAT)} = \langle[\mathrm{arises}](y)\rangle$
(3) $\mathrm{ANTR}_{SAT} = \langle[\mathrm{tax}](x), [\mathrm{the\_amount\_of\_due}](x), [\mathrm{the\_right\_to\_reduce}](y), [\mathrm{chargeable}](x), [\mathrm{taxpayer}](z)\rangle$
(4) $\mathrm{ArgSch} = \langle \mathrm{RBAS}, \mathrm{ECAS}\rangle$
(5) $\mathrm{Args}_{(VAT)} = \langle$instantiation of ECAS$\rangle$
(6) $\mathrm{AR}_{(VAT)} = \langle \mathrm{AR}\rangle ([\mathrm{tax}](x), [\mathrm{the\_amount\_of\_due}](x), [\mathrm{the\_right\_to\_reduce}](y), [\mathrm{chargeable}]\ (x), [\mathrm{taxpayer}](z)), \neg\ [\mathrm{arises}](y))$
(7) $\mathrm{NCR}_{(VAT)} = \varnothing$.

We can easily see that the *e contrario* argument enables us to derive a conclusion according to which the legal consequence (the right does not arise) is attached to the deliberated hypothetically factual situation.

In the course of the legislative process, several opinions concerning the proposed solutions were presented. One opinion, prepared by a tax advisor from Ernst and Young[17] (Pokrop 2012), contained arguments pertaining to the abovementioned proposed legislative solutions. The arguments presented in the opinion indicated certain sets of states of affairs (consequences), which, according to the author of the opinion, were not desirable from several points of view: economic, praxeological, the wording of the text, definitional compatibility with the text of the VAT directives and so on. The critique of the definition formulated in Art. 86(2)(4)(c) of the VAT Project is the starting point of the argumentation. The critical argument concerns the inconsistency between the definition in the proposed act and the definition contained in Art. 168(c) of Directive 2006/112/CE, which is implemented by this Vat Act itself:

> Such a definition is not provided for by Art.168(c) of the Vat Directive, which doubtlessly indicates that in the case of IC acquisition of goods, the amount of already paid tax due constitutes input tax (Pokrop 2012, 3).

[17]This is an entity registered as conducting professional lobbying activities.

The consequences indicated in the arguments had the character of anticipated empirical consequences, that is, states of affairs that were likely to happen in reality, and that were perceived as undesirable states. The consequences were presented in the analysed opinion in the form of the following catalogue of undesirable states of affairs with regard to taxpayers:

1) a negative influence on financial transactions (additional cost of financing VAT);
2) in many cases the necessity to pay interest for the delay;
3) increase of burden and administrative costs connected with the necessity of multiple corrections of VAT declarations and filing motions on setting off additional payment against tax arrears to settle the tax due from IC acquisition of goods, for which the invoice was received with delay;
4) increase of administrative costs because of the necessity of adapting financial and book-keeping systems to the new regulations (including the necessity of monitoring the issuance of invoices evidencing IC acquisition of goods) (Pokrop 2012, 4).

The author of the opinion emphasised that the increase of burden and administrative costs indicated in point (2) of the catalogue will affect not only the financial and book-keeping departments of taxpayers, but also accounting departments of revenue offices (Pokrop 2012, 6). Because these arguments do not belong to the logical layer of legislative deliberation, we will not focus on them in the elaboration of the example.

However, in addition to the arguments pertaining to the consequences characterized by the anticipated and empirically identifiable sets of states of affairs, the opinion also refers to the argument expressing a normative consequence based on the infringement of the principle of VAT neutrality. The preamble of the Directive and Art. 1(2) of the VAT Directive 2006/112/CE are perceived as the sources of the said principle.[18] The principle expresses the right to deduct the input tax from the tax due in the previous turnover phases:

> Neutrality in the case of taxpayers performing tax transactions is mainly reflected in the possibility of reducing the tax due upon sale by the input tax upon purchase and the possibility of obtaining a return of the surplus of input tax over tax due (Bącal et al. 2009, 6).

---

[18] Art.1 (...)
2. The principle of the common system of VAT entails the application to goods and services of a general tax on consumption exactly proportional to the price of the goods and services; however, many transactions take place in the production and distribution process before the stage at which the tax is charged.

On each transaction, VAT, calculated on the price of the goods or services at the rate applicable to such goods or services, shall be chargeable after deduction of the amount of VAT borne directly by the various cost components.

The common system of VAT shall be applied up to and including the retail trade stage.

And the points from the preamble:

"(30) In order to preserve neutrality of VAT, the rates applied by Member States should be such as to enable, as a general rule, deduction of the VAT applied at the preceding stage.

(34) However, such a reduction in the VAT rate is not without risk for the smooth functioning of the internal market and for tax neutrality. (...)" (Council Directive 2006/112/EC of 28 November 2006 on the common system of value added tax, Official Journal of the European Union L 347/1).

The right to deduction constitutes the fundamental construction of the VAT tax and distinguishes it from other turnover taxes. The content of the neutrality principle was shaped mainly by the case-law of the ECJ:

> It is also apparent from case-law that measures to prevent tax evasion or avoidance may not, in principle, derogate from the basis for charging VAT except within the limits strictly necessary for achieving that specific aim. They must have as little effect as possible on the objectives and principles of the VAT Directive and may not therefore be used in such a way that they would have the effect of undermining VAT neutrality, which is a fundamental principle of the common system of VAT established by the relevant European Union legislation (see, to that effect, Case C-330/95 Goldsmiths [1997] ECR I-3801, paragraph 21; Case C566/07 Stadeco [2009] ECR I5295, paragraph 39 and the case-law cited: and Case C489/09 Vandoorne [2011] ECR I225, paragraph 27). (Judgment of the Court from 26 January 2012, Case C-588/10 Kraft Foods Polska, paragraph 28)).

The argument formulated in the analysed legislative opinion referring to the normative consequence as to the infringement of the principle of VAT neutrality reads as follows:

> (...) the possibility of deducting the VAT input tax is not a taxpayer's privilege but constitutes their fundamental and basic right, resulting from the very construction of the VAT tax. Making deduction of the VAT tax in the case of IC acquisition of goods dependent on receiving the invoice may mean that in some cases (e.g. when the invoice got lost or the supplier did not issue the invoice, despite the obligation to do so, etc.) the tax due will have to be paid and the right to deduction will never arise. (Pokrop 2012, 7).

The argumentation presented above enables us to reconstruct an additional rule, based on the mentioned principle of neutrality and accounting for a set of conditions present in the original version of the provision as sufficient for the realization of the right. This rule would have the same content as the original formulation of art. 86.10.2 of the Vat Act.

(VAT 86.10.2)* AFLEG extended theory (INR, neutrality principle).

(1) $ANTR_{(VAT)} = \langle$[tax](x), ([the_amount_of_due](x) → [input](x)), [the_right_to_reduce](y), [chargeable](x), [taxpayer](z), [received_an_invoice](z)$\rangle$
$ANTR_{(VAT]} = \langle$ [tax](x), ([the_amount_of_due](x) → [input](x)), [the_right_to_reduce](y), [chargeable](x)$\rangle$

(2) $LCR_{(VAT)} = \langle$[arises](y)$\rangle$

(3) $ANTR_{SAT} = \langle$[tax](x), [the_amount_of_due](x), [the_right_to_reduce](y), [chargeable](x), [taxpayer](z)$\rangle$

(4) ArgSch = ⟨RBAS, ECAS⟩

(5) $Args_{(VAT)} = \langle$instantiation RBAS, instantiation of ECAS$\rangle$

(6) $AR_{(VAT)} = \langle AR\rangle$([tax]($x$), [the_amount_of_due]($x$), [the_right_to_reduce](y), [chargeable] (x), [taxpayer](z)), ¬ [arises](y))
$AR_{(VAT)} = \langle AR\rangle$([tax]($x$), [the_amount_of_due]($x$), [the_right_to_reduce](y), [chargeable] (x), [taxpayer](z)), [arises](y))

(7) $NCR_{(VAT)} = \langle NCR\rangle$ ([arises](y), ¬ [arises] (y))

The presented AFLEG theory proves that the proposed legislative solution is inadmissible form the point of view of the realization of the neutrality principle.

The deliberated version of the relevant provisions of the VAT Project lead to direct inconsistency with the neutrality principle. Therefore, the author of the opinion petitions for striking the new formulation of Art. 86(2)(4)(c) and Art. 86(10) off the bill and, consequently, keeping in force the existing legislative solution.

In the present version of the AFLEG, we do not formalize the attack relation between different arguments and the procedure for resolution of normative inconsistencies. However, the framework is able to represent precisely the inconsistency stemming from the proposed formulation of legal rules in the context of relevant legal principles.

Case 2. This example is taken from the domain of consumer protection law. On 17 January 2014, a project of the Consumer Rights Act (hereafter: the CRA Project) was submitted to the Polish House of Representatives. The projected statute was intended to implement the Directive on Consumer Rights (2011/83/EC) and contained new provisions, as well as modificatory provisions related to the Polish Civil Code. In particular, the CRA Project proposed the following new formulation of art. 560 § 1 of the PCC:

> If the sold item is defective, the seller may demand a reduction of price or may withdraw from the agreement, unless the seller, promptly and without undue inconvenience to the buyer, replaces the defective item or removes the defect.

The quoted provision may be represented in the AL in the following manner (we use certain shortenings of the statutory expressions for the sake of readability):

(PCC 560 §1) ([seller](x) $\wedge$ [buyer](y)) $\rightarrow$ (([defective_item](z) $\wedge$ ($\neg$ [replaces](x, z) $\vee$ [removes_the_defect_from](x, z))) $\rightarrow$ ([authorized_to_demand_reduction_of_price_from](x,y) $\vee$ ([authorized_to_withdraw from_the_agreement](y)))

For the sake of further analysis, the "unless" clause contained in the statutory text is not relevant. Let us therefore present a simpler version of the rule in question:

(PCC 560 § 1)* ([seller](x) $\wedge$ [buyer](y) $\wedge$ [sells_a_defective_item](x,y)) $\rightarrow$ ([authorized_to_demand_reduction_of_price_from](x,y) $\vee$ ([authorized_to_withdraw from_the_agreement](y))

Let us now present a simple AFLEG theory connected with the (560 § 1)* legal rule. The elements of this theory should be represented in the following manner:

(560 § 1)* AFLEG theory.

(1) $\text{ANTR}_{(\text{PCC})}$ = ⟨[seller](x), [buyer](y), [sells_a_defective_item](x,y)⟩
(2) $\text{LCR}_{(\text{PCC})}$ = ⟨ [authorized_to_demand_reduction_of_price_from](x,y), [authorized_to_withdraw from_the_agreement](y)⟩
(3) ANTR_{SAT} = ⟨ [seller](x), [buyer](y), [sells_a_defective_item](x,y)⟩
(4) ArgSch = ⟨RBAS⟩
(5) $\text{Args}_{(\text{PCC})}$ = ⟨ instantiation of RBAS⟩[19]

[19] Again, we do not represent the instantiation of RBAS due to its straightforwardness.

(6) $AR_{(PCC)}$ = ⟨ AR⟩ ([seller](x) ∧ [buyer](y) ∧ [sells_a_defective_item](x,y)), ([authorized_to_demand_reduction_of_price_from](x,y) ∨ ([authorized_to_withdraw from_the_agreement](y))
(7) $NCR_{(PCC)} = \varnothing$.

Because the AFLEG theory presented above represents the normative consequences of one rule derived from one argument, it is not surprising that it is relatively uncontroversial (in particular, no conflicting propositions may be detected here). However, it is contestable whether all applicable argument schemes have been applied to the reconstructed rule in question.

An official legislative opinion concerning the CRA Project was submitted (Lanckoroński 2014), which contained much criticism concerning certain solutions proposed in the project. In particular, the formulation of the new art. 560 § 1 of the PCC was criticized. Lanckoroński rightly observed that the formulation "may demand a reduction of price" should be classified as the so-called claim right, that is, the kind of right that authorizes person X to demand a certain kind of behaviour from another person Y. However, if person Y does not intend to comply with the demand, person X has to sue the person Y and win a litigation in order to obtain the desired legal consequence. This pattern of reasoning may be referred to as the claim right argument scheme, and it can be constructed as follows:

Claim Right Argument Scheme (CRAS)

Premise 1. If a statutory expression S grants person X the right to demand a certain kind of behaviour Z from person Y, then person X has the claim that person Y behaves in a manner
Premise 2. If person X demands a claim to be fulfilled by person Y, the content of the claim is realized only if person Y agrees to fulfil a claim or if a court acknowledges the claim of person X is
Premise 3. A statutory expression S (EXPRESSION) grants person X the right to demand a certain kind of behaviour Z from person Y.
Premise 4. Person X demands a claim to be fulfilled by person Y.
Premise 5. If person Y does not agree to fulfil a claim and person X does not win a lawsuit against person Y, the content of a claim is not realized.
Premise 6.(¬) [agrees_to_fulfil_a_claim](y) or [wins_a_lawsuit](x,y)

Conclusion. ⟨AR⟩ ([authorized_to [CLAIM]](x,y), [realized_[CLAIM]](x,y)).

The structure of the argument scheme presented above is more complicated than the structure of the RBAS discussed in the previous section. In particular, the conclusion of the argument scheme is alternative: person X's claim is realized or not realized, depending on the satisfaction or non-satisfaction of Premises 6 and 7 of the argument scheme (in the context of Premise 5). Note that the word CLAIM in the conclusion is a variable under which the content of a concrete claim should be substituted.

Let us now present an extended AFLEG theory concerning the possible application of the deliberated legal rule to a situation in which the buyer actually demands the price be reduced. Note that this extended theory involves Layer 2, which was discussed in Sect. 10.2, because additional predicates not extracted from the statutory text are used here. Here, following Lanckoroński (2014) and the jurisprudence of the Polish Supreme Court, we analyse the normative consequences of a demand for reduction in price by the buyer where the seller disagrees to reduce the price and the buyer has not won the litigation yet (e.g., because he has not filed a lawsuit). However, this extension enables us to determine precisely the scope of normative consequences of the rule in question.

(PCC 560 § 1)* AFLEG extended theory.

(1) $ANTR_{(PCC)}$ = ⟨[seller](*x*), [buyer](*y*), [sells_a_defective_item](*x*,*y*), [demands_reduction_of_price](*x*), ¬ ([agrees_to_fulfill_a_claim](*y*)), [wins_a_lawsuit](*y*,*x*) ⟩
(2) $LCR_{(PCC)}$ = ⟨[authorized_to_demand_reduction_of_price_from](*x*,*y*), [authorized_to_withdraw from_the_agreement](*y*)]
(3) $ANTR_{SAT}$ = ⟨[seller](*x*), [buyer](*y*), [sells_a_defective_item](*x*,*y*), [demands_reduction_of_price](*x*), ¬ ([agrees_to_fulfill_a_claim](*y*))⟩
(4) ArgSch = ⟨RBAS, CRAS⟩
(5) $Args_{(PCC)}$ = ⟨instantiation of RBAS⟩
(6) $AR_{(PCC)}$ = ⟨AR⟩ ([seller](*x*) ∧ [buyer](*y*) ∧ [sells_a_defective_item](*x*,*y*)), ([authorized_to_demand_reduction_of_price_from](*x*,*y*) ∨ ([authorized_to_withdraw_from_the_agreement](*y*))
(7) $NCR_{(PCC\ 560\ \S\ 1)^*} = \varnothing$.

The theory presented above shows the consequences of application of the rule in question to a case in which the buyer demands a reduction in the price, yet the seller does not agree with the demand, and the judgment of the court has not been obtained. The application of RBAS to the legal rule in question produces an alternative to LCRs. However, CRAS cannot be instantiated because neither of its conditions is fulfilled (Moreover, we know that the seller explicitly disagrees to reduce the price, so the buyer is forced to win the litigation in order to realize his or her claim.)

According to Lanckoroński (2014, 22–24), this result is troubling because the Consumer Rights Act should contain a regulation that is more advantageous from the perspective of the buyer. In his opinion, the right to the reduction in the price should have the structure of a potestative right and not of a claim. Unlike a claim, a potestative right may be realized by the authorized person based on the statement by this person. The agreement of another party or a court order is not necessary to bring about the legal consequences desired by the authorized person.

Consequently, the author of the opinion proposes another formulation of the rule in question, which could be represented as follows:

(560 § 1)** ([seller] (*x*) ∧ [buyer](*y*) ∧ [sells_a_defective_item](*x*,*y*)) → ([authorized_to_reduce_the_price](*x*) ∨ ([authorized_to_withdraw from_the_agreement](*y*))

The apparently minor change in the formulation of the rule leads to entirely different normative consequences. Because the right to reduce the price is no longer a claim but a potestative right, it is not possible to apply the CRAS to the rule in question. Instead, another argument scheme, that is, a potestative right argument scheme (PRAS), should be applied to determine the set of normative consequences.

Potestative Right Argument Scheme (PRAS).

Premise 1. If a statutory expression S grants person X the right to issue a statement aiming at obtaining certain legal consequences LC, then person X has a potestative right regarding the realization of the legal effect (EFFECT).
Premise 2. If person X has a potestative right regarding the realization of legal effect, then if person X issues a statement (STATEMENT), then the legal effect (EFFECT) is realized.
Premise 3. A statutory expression S (EXPRESSION) grants person X a potestative right regarding the realization of legal consequences LC.
Premise 4. Person X issues a statement (STATEMENT).

Conclusion. $\langle AR \rangle$([authorized_to [STATEMENT]](x), [realized_[EFFECT]](x)).

The application of PRAS to the case in which the buyer issues a statement of reduction in price is much more straightforward than the application of CRAS in the case of a claim is. This is encompassed by the following AFLEG theory in determining the normative consequences of the rule (560 § 1)**.

(PCC 560 § 1) AFLEG extended theory.**

(1) $ANTR_{(PCC)}$ = ⟨[seller](x), [buyer](y), [sells_a_defective_item](x,y), [states_that_the_price_is_reduced] (y)⟩
(2) $LCR_{(PCC)}$ = ⟨[authorized_to_reduce_the_price](y), [authorized_to_withdraw_from_the_agreement](y)⟩
(3) $ANTR_{SAT}$ = ⟨[seller](x), [buyer](y), [sells_a_defective_item](x,y), [states_that_the_price_is_reduced](y)⟩
(4) ArgSch = ⟨RBAS, CRAS, PRAS⟩
(5) $Args_{(PCC)}$ = ⟨instantiation of RBAS, instantiation of PRAS⟩
(6) $AR_{(PCC)}$ = ⟨AR⟩ ([seller](x) $\wedge$ [buyer](y) $\wedge$ [sells_a_defective_item](x,y)), ([authorized_to_reduce_the_price](y) $\vee$ ([authorized_to_withdraw from_the_agreement](y));
⟨AR⟩ ([authorized_to_reduce_the_price](y), [effectively_reduces_price](y))
(7) $NCR_{(PCC)} = \varnothing$.

According to the version of art. 560 § 1 of the PCC proposed by the legislative opinion, the right to the reduction of a price is a potestative right. Note that although CRAS is included in the theory, it cannot be instantiated because the new formulation of the rule does not give grounds for the reconstruction of a claim.

The (560 § 1)** AFLEG theory should be assessed higher than the (560 § 1)* AFLEG theory is with respect to the protection of the position of the buyer.

Therefore, the (560 § 1)** rule should be assessed as better than (560 § 1)* with respect to this criterion. Interestingly, the legislator accepted this argumentation, and the version of the relevant provision in the Consumer Rights Act[20] accounts for the right to the reduction of the price of the defective sold item as a potestative right.

The two examples presented above show both the advantages and the limits of the present version of the AFLEG with regard to the determination of the set of normative consequences of a given normative act project, as well as the structure of legislative deliberation. With respect to the advantages, we would like to emphasize the possibility of modelling the phenomenon of normative inconsistencies, as well as the application of potentially unlimited number of different argument schemes. For the sake of descriptive adequacy, these argument schemes should be reconstructed from actual legislative materials. The limitation of the present version of the AFLEG is the lack of the systematic treatment of the phenomenon of attack between arguments and the remaining elements of legislative deliberation. These subjects were treated informally in the discussed examples. Moreover, the first-order language formalization of the legal provisions is sometimes controversial, especially in cases of complicated examples, such as Example 1 discussed above. However, one should note that the choice of a particular AL is a matter of convention. Furthermore, other formal languages can be chosen to represent the content of normative acts.

10.4 Conclusions

The following conclusions can be drawn from the analyses and investigations presented in this chapter:

1. The concept of normative consequence (in the sense that is relevant for the analysis of actual legal systems and legislative proceedings) may be characterized descriptively in an adequate manner as the assignment of certain (sets of) states of affairs (referred to as legal consequences) to other states of affairs. This assignment may be well-captured in a semi-formal argumentation framework. The AFLEG presented in this chapter is an example of this framework, although obviously it is not the only way to reconstruct the concept of normative consequence. Indeed, we managed to show that the concept of normative consequence is relative to the assumptions (e.g., concerning the aim and the method used to develop of a given model) adopted by the researcher. However, our opinion is that the proposed semi-formal argumentation framework should be assessed as particularly favourably because of its descriptive adequacy.

2. The different types of normative consequences discussed in the literature (e.g., logical, argumentative, and interpretative consequences) should be subsumed under

[20]The Consumer Rights Act of 30 May 2014, Journal of Laws 2014, 827.

a broad category of consequences stemming from the application of arguments based on argument schemes. This approach models well the phenomenon of the defeasibility of legal reasoning and enables the researcher to focus on not only the form of arguments and statements present in legislative discourse but also their content. However, nothing prevents one from fully formalizing the semi-formal argumentation framework as either an abstract argumentation framework (by treating arguments as indivisible wholes) or a structured argumentation framework, based on classical or non-classical logics. (However, this would require much effort related to the formalization of natural language expressions, which is problematic with regard to the well-structured statutory text and even more demanding with regard to the mining of arguments from legislative materials.)

We are sceptical about the possibility of the descriptively adequate reconstruction of a normative system as a theory formalized in a logical calculus and closed under an operation of a classically construed logical consequence.

3. The main idea of the AFLEG framework is as follows. The work of the legislator may be characterized as the creation of a theory encompassing the statutory text as an input and the generation of a set of assignment relations between certain states of affairs as an output. The transition between these two tasks is made possible by arguments that are based on argumentation schemes). The legislator attempts to anticipate the structure and content of the analogous theories that presumably will be developed by the law-applying authorities.

4. It is apparent that the existing research on the logical analysis of legal systems and legal argumentation does not have strong connections with the legal-philosophical work concerning the scope of the concept of law and of the legal system. The AFLEG framework enables the researcher to establish such links, by analysing the source of states of affairs and arguments that are present in AFLEG theories related to deliberated statutory text projects.

We are of the opinion that the presented framework can be assessed as an efficient tool for the analysis of the content of the projects of normative acts, as well as of the legislative discourse. However, it also should be stressed that the present version of the framework is partial. The part related to the determination of the content of analysed provisions and of their normative consequences is developed. However, the part comprising the relations between different arguments, establishing preference relations between them, and assessing of AFLEG theories from the point of view of relevant values needs elaboration.

In addition to the need to develop the "discursive" part of the AFLEG, several further points are fruitful perspectives of further research. In particular, first, an attempt should be made to apply a much richer language to represent the structure of statutory provisions. This task should be accomplished in connection with the research on legal ontologies, theories of normative positions (Sergot 2013), and the research on temporal aspects of functioning of the legal system. Second, a systematic study concerning the types of argument schemes used in legislative discourse should be conducted.

References

Alchourrón, Carlos, and Eugenio Bulygin. 1971. *Normative systems*. Wien/New York: Springer.

Alexy, Robert. 1989. *A theory of legal argumentation: The theory of rational discourse as a theory of legal justification*. Trans. R. Adler and N. MacCormick. Oxford: Clarendon Press. 1st German ed. 1978.

Alexy, Robert. 2010. *The argument from injustice: A reply to legal positivism*. Trans. B. Litschewski-Paulson and S.L. Paulson. Oxford: Oxford University Press.

Araszkiewicz, Michał. 2010. Balancing of legal principles and constraint satisfaction. In *Legal knowledge and information systems. JURIX: The twenty-third annual conference*. Frontiers in artificial intelligence and applications, vol. 223, ed. R. Winkels, 7–16. Amsterdam: IOS Press.

Araszkiewicz, Michał. 2012. Coherence-based account of the doctrine of consistent interpretation. In *AI approaches to the complexity of legal systems. Models and ethical challenges for legal systems, legal language and legal ontologies, argumentation and software agents*, ed. M. Palmirani, U. Pagallo, P. Casanovas, and G. Sartor, 33–47. Berlin/New York: Springer.

Araszkiewicz, Michał. 2013. Towards systematic research on statutory interpretation in AL and law. In *Legal knowledge and information systems. JURIX: The twenty-sixth annual conference*. Frontiers in artificial intelligence and applications, vol. 259, ed. K. Ashley, 15–24. Amsterdam: IOS Press.

Araszkiewicz, Michał. 2014. Legal rules: Defeasible or indefeasible? In *Problems of rules, normativity and rule-following*, ed. M. Araszkiewicz, P. Bana, T. Gizbert-Studnicki, and K. Płeszka. Dordrecht: Springer.

Araszkiewicz, Michał, and Jaromír Šavelka. 2012. Refined coherence as constraint satisfaction framework for representing judicial reasoning. In *Legal knowledge and information systems. JURIX: The twenty-fifth annual conference*. Frontiers in artificial intelligence and applications, vol. 250, ed. B. Schäfer, 1–20. Amsterdam: IOS Press.

Ashley, Kevin. 1990. *Modeling legal argument: Reasoning with cases and hypotheticals*. Cambridge: MIT Press.

Athan, Tara, Boley Harold, Governatori Guido, Palmirani Monica, Paschke Aadrian, and Wyner Adam. 2012. OASIS LegalRuleML. In *International conference on artificial intelligence and law, ICAIL '13, Rome*, 3–12. New York: ACM.

Atkinson, Katie, Trevor Bench-Capon, Dan Cartwright, and Adam Wyner. 2011. Semantic models for policy deliberation. In *The 13th international conference on artificial intelligence and law, proceedings of the conference*, Pittsburgh, 81–90. New York: ACM.

Åqvist, Lennart. 1984. Deontic logic. In *Handbook of philosophical logic*. Volume II: Extensions of classical logic, ed. D. Gabbay and F. Guenthner, 605–714. Dordrecht/Boston/Lancaster: D. Reidel.

Bącal, Adam, Dagmara Dominik, Małgorzata Militz, and Piotr Ogiński. 2009. Zasady dotyczące podatku od towarów i usług (The Principles Concerning the Value Added Tax). Przegląd Podatkowy 11(223).

Baroni, Pietro, Martin Caminada, and Massimiliano Giacomin. 2011. An introduction to argumentation semantics. *Knowledge Engineering Review* 26(4):365–410.

Bell, John, and Moshé Machover, 1977. *A course in mathematical logic*. Amsterdam/New York/Oxford: North Holland Publishing Company.

Bench-Capon, Trevor, and Pepijn R.S. Visser. 1997. Ontologies in legal information systems: The need for explicit specifications of domain conceptualisations. In *Proceedings of the sixth international conference on artificial intelligence and law ICAIL '97*, Melbourne, 132–141. New York: ACM.

Bench-Capon, Trevor, G.O. Robinson, Tom Routen, and Marek J. Sergot. 1987. Logic programming for large scale applications in law: A formalisation of supplementary benefit legislation. In *Proceedings of the first international conference on artificial intelligence and law*, ICAIL '87, Boston. 190–198. New York: ACM.

Bulygin, Eugenio. 2008. What can one expect from logic in the law? (Not everything, but more than something: A reply to Susan Haack). *Ratio Juris* 21(1):150–156.
Casellas, Núria. 2011. *Legal ontology engineering. Methodologies, modelling trends and the ontology of professional judicial knowledge.* Dordrecht/Heidelberg/London/New York: Springer.
Dung, Phan Minh. 1995. On the acceptability of arguments and its fundamental role in nonmonotonic reasoning, logic programming and n-person games. *Artificial Intelligence* 77(2):321–358.
Dworkin, Ronald. 1977. *Taking rights seriously*. Cambridge: Harvard University Press.
Dworkin, Ronald. 2006. *Justice in robes*. Cambridge/London: The Belknap Press of Harvard University Press.
Ferrer Beltrán, Jordi, and Giovanni Battista Ratti. eds. 2012. *The logic of legal requirements: essays on defeasibilism.* Oxford: Oxford University Press.
Gabbay, Dov. 2013. *Meta-logical investigations in argumentation networks*. London: College Publications.
Gordon, Thomas, and Douglas Walton. 2006. The Carneades argumentation framework – using presumptions and exceptions to model critical questions. In *Proceedings of the first international conference on computational models of argument (COMMA 06)*, Liverpool, ed. P.E. Dunne, 195–207.
Gordon, Thomas, and Douglas Walton. 2009. Legal reasoning with argumentation schemes. In *Proceedings of the 10th international conference on artificial intelligence and law, ICAIL 2009*, 137–146. New York: ACM.
Haack, Susan. 2007. On logic in the law: "Something, but not all". *Ratio Juris* 20(1):1–31.
Hage, Jaap. 1996. A theory of legal reasoning and a logic to match. *Artificial Intelligence and Law* 4(3–4):199–273.
Hage, Jaap. 2001a. Formalizing legal coherence. In *Proceedings of the eighth international conference on artificial intelligence and law, ICAIL 2001*, St. Louis, 22–31. New York: ACM.
Hage, Jaap. 2001b. Legal logic, its existence, nature and use. In *Pluralism and law*, ed. A. Soeteman, 347–374. Dordrecht: Kluwer Academic.
Hage, Jaap. 2005. *Studies in legal logic*. Berlin: Springer.
Hage, Jaap. 2014. Separating rules from normativity. In *Problems of normativity, rules and rule-following*. Law and philosophy library series, ed. M. Araszkiewicz, P. Banaś, T. Gizbert-Studnicki, and K. Płeszka. Cham/Heidelberg/New York/Dordrecht/London: Springer.
Hage, Jaap. 2016. The (onto)logical structure of law: A conceptual toolkit for legislators. In *Logic in the theory and practice of lawmaking*, ed. M. Araszkiewicz, K. Płeszka. Cham: Springer.
Hart, Herbert L.A. 1994. *The concept of law*, 2nd ed. Oxford: Oxford University Press.
Hesselink, Martijn. 2001. *The new European legal culture*. Denventer: Kluwer Academic.
Hilpinen, Risto, and Paul McNamara. 2013. Deontic logic: A historical survey and introduction. In *Handbook of deontic logic and normative systems*, ed. D. Gabbay, J. Horty, X. Parent, R. van der Meyden, and L. van der Torre, 3–136. London: College Publications.
Kelsen, Hans. 1970. *The pure theory of law*. Berkeley: University of California Press.
Kleene, Stephen Cole. 1967. *Mathematical logic*. Mineola/New York: Dover Publications.
Lanckoroński, Bogusław. 2014. Ekspertyza dotycząca projektu ustawy o prawach konsumenta [Expert opinion concerning the Project of Consumer Rights Act]. http://orka.sejm.gov.pl/rexdomk7.nsf/Opdodr?OpenPage&nr=2076. Accessed 5 Aug 2014.
Leiter, Brian. 2007. Explaining theoretical disagreement. *The University of Chicago Law Review* 76:1215–1250.
Lindahl, Lars, and David Reidhav. 2016. Conflict of legal norms: Definition and varieties. In *Logic in the theory and practice of lawmaking*, ed. M. Araszkiewicz and K. Płeszka. Cham: Springer.
Macagno, Fabrizio, Douglas Walton, and Giovanni Sartor. 2012. Argumentation schemes for statutory interpretation. In *International conference on alternative methods of argumentation in law*, Brno, 25 Oct 2012, ed. M. Araszkiewicz, M. Myška, T. Smejkálova, J. Šavelka, and M. Škop, 63–75. Brno: Masarykova University.
MacCormick, Neil. 1978. *Legal reasoning and legal theory*. Oxford: Clarendon Press. Reprinted in 2003.

Makinson, David. 2005. *Bridges from classical to nonmonotonic logic*. London: College Publications.

Mendelson, Eliot. 1977. *Introduction to mathematical Logic*, 4th ed. New York: Chapman & Hall.

Nute, Donald. 1994. Defeasible logic. In *Handbook of logic in artificial intelligence and logic programming*, ed. D. Gabbay, C. Hogger, and J. Robinson, 353–396. Oxford: Clarendon Press.

Nute, Donald. ed. 1997. *Defeasible deontic logic*. Synthese library. Dordrecht: Kluwer Academic Publishers.

Opałek, Kazimierz, and Jerzy Wróblewski. 1969. Zagadnienia teorii prawa [Issues in Legal Theory]. PWN: Warszawa.

Peczenik, Aleksander. 1983. *The basis of legal justification*. Lund: A. Peczenik.

Peczenik, Aleksander. 1996. Jumps and logic in the law: What one can expect from logical models of legal argumentation? *Artificial Intelligence and Law* 4:297–329.

Peczenik, Aleksander. 2008. *On law and reason*, 2nd ed. Dordrecht: Springer.

Perelman, Chaïm, and Lucie Olbrechts-Tyteca. 1958. Traité de l'argumentation: La nouvelle rhétorique. Paris: Presses Universitaires de France.

Pokrop, Dorota. 2012. Propozycja rozwiązań prawnych [A proposal of legal solutions]. http://orka.sejm.gov.pl/opinie7.nsf/opdodr?OpenPage&nr=805. Accessed 6 Aug 2014.

Pollock, John. 1987. Defeasible reasoning. *Cognitive Science* 11:481–518.

Pollock, John. 1995. *Cognitive carpentry: A blueprint for how to build a person*. Cambridge: MIT Press.

Postema, Gerald, 2001. *Legal philosophy in the twentieth century: The common law world*. A treatise of legal philosophy and general jurisprudence, vol. 11, ed. E. Pattaro. Dordrecht/Heidelberg/London/New York: Springer.

Prakken, Henry. 1997. *Logical tools for modelling legal argument: A study of defeasible reasoning in law*. Dordrecht/Boston/London: Kluwer Academic.

Prakken, Henry. 2010. An abstract framework for argumentation with structured arguments. *Argument & Computation* 1(2):93–124.

Prakken, Henry. 2016. Formalizing debates about law-making proposals as practical reasoning. In *Logic in the theory and practice of lawmaking*, ed. M. Araszkiewicz and K. Płeszka. Cham: Springer.

Prakken, Henry, and Giovanni Sartor. 1996. A dialectical model of assessing conflicting arguments in legal reasoning. *Artificial Intelligence and Law* 4(3–4):331–368.

Prakken, Henry, and Giovanni Sartor. 1998. Modelling reasoning with precedents in a formal dialogue game. *Artificial Intelligence and Law* 6(2–4):231–287.

Prakken, Henry, and Gerard Vreeswijk. 2002. Logics for defeasible argumentation. In *Handbook of philosophical logic*, vol. 4, 2nd ed., ed. Dov Gabbay and Franz Guenthner, 219–318. Dodrecht/Boston/London: Kluwer Academic.

Rahwan, Iyad, and Guillermo R. Simari. eds. 2009. *Argumentation in artificial intelligence*. Dordrecht/Heidelberg/London/New York: Springer.

Raz, Joseph. 1980. *The concept of a legal system: An introduction to the theory of the legal system*. Oxford: Oxford University Press.

Reiter, R. 1980. A logic for default reasoning. *Artificial Intelligence* 13(1–2):81–132.

Rissland, Edwina, and David B. Skalak. 1991. CABARET: Rule interpretation in a hybrid architecture. *International Journal of Man-Machine Studies* 34(6):839–887.

Royakkers, Lambèr M.M. 1998. *Extending deontic logic for the formalisation of legal rules*. Dordrecht: Springer.

Sartor, Giovanni. 1992. Normative conflicts in legal reasoning. *Artificial Intelligence and Law* 1(2–3):209–235.

Sartor, Giovanni. 1995. Defeasibility in legal reasoning. In *Informatics and the foundations of legal reasoning*, ed. Z. Bankowski, I. White, and U. Hahn, 119–137. Dordrecht: Kluwer Academic.

Sartor, Giovanni. 2005. *Legal reasoning. A cognitive approach to law*. A treatise of legal philosophy and general jurisprudence, vol. 5. Dordrecht: Springer.

Sartor, Giovanni, Pompeu Casanovas, Maria Angela Biasotti, and Meritxell Fernández-Barrera. eds. 2011. *Approaches to legal ontologies: Theories, domains, methodologies*. Dordrecht/Heidelberg/London/New York: Springer.

Šavelka, Jaromír. 2013. Coherence as constraint satisfaction: Judicial reasoning support mechanism. In *Coherence: Insights from philosophy, jurisprudence and artificial intelligence*, ed. M. Araszkiewicz and J. Šavelka, 203–216. Dordrecht/Heidelberg/New York/London: Springer.

Sergot, Marek. 2013. Normative positions. In *Handbook of deontic logic and normative systems*, ed. D. Gabbay, J. Horty, X. Parent, R. van der Meyden, and L. van der Torre, 353–406. London: College Publications.

Sergot, Marek, Fariba Sadri, Robert A. Kowalski, Frank Kriwaczek, Peter Hammond, and H.T. Cory. 1986. The British nationality act as a logic program. *Communications ACM* 29(5):370–386.

Shapiro, Scott, 2007. The "Hart–Dworkin Debate": A short guide for the perplexed. In *Ronald Dworkin*, ed. A. Ripstein, 22–55. Cambridge: Cambridge University Press.

Soeteman, Arend. 2003. Legal logic? Or can we do without? *Artificial Intelligence and Law* 11(2–3):197–210.

Tarski, Alfred. 1936. On the concept of logical consequence. In *Logic, semantics, metamathematics*, ed. A. Tarski, 409–420. Trans. J.H. Woodger. Oxford: Clarendon Press.

Thagard, Paul. 2000. *Coherence in thought and action*. Cambridge: MIT Press.

Walton, Douglas. 1996. *Argumentation schemes for presumptive reasoning*. New York/London: Routledge.

Walton, Douglas, Chris Reed, and Fabrizio Macagno. 2008. *Argumentation schemes*. Cambridge: Cambridge University Press.

Woleński, Jan. 1972. *Logiczne problemy wykładni prawa [Logical problems of legal interpretation]*. Kraków: Uniwersytet Jagielloński.

Wróblewski, Jerzy. 1980. Pojęcie systemu prawa a informatyka prawnicza [The concept of legal system and legal informatics]. Studia Prawno-Ekonomiczne XXV.

Wróblewski, Jerzy. 1992. *Judicial application of law*, ed. Zenon Bankowski and Neil MacCormick. Dordrecht/Boston/London: Kluwer Academic.

Yoshino, Hajime. 1995. The systematization of legal meta-inference. In *Proceedings of the fifth international conference on artificial intelligence and law, ICAIL '95*, College Park, Maryland, 266–275. New York: ACM.

Yoshino, Hajime. 1997. On the logical foundations of compound predicate formulae for legal knowledge representation. *Artificial Intelligence and Law* 5(1–2):77–96.

Żurek, Tomasz. 2012. Modelling of a fortiori reasoning. *Expert Systems and Applications* 39(12):10772–10779.

Żurek, Tomasz and Michał Araszkiewicz. 2013. Modeling teleological interpretation. In *International conference on artificial intelligence and law, ICAIL '13*, Rome, 160–168. New York: ACM.

Sartor, Giovanni, Pompeu Casanovas, Maria Angela Biasiotti, and Meritxell Fernández-Barrera, eds. 2011. *Approaches to legal ontologies: Theories, domains, methodologies*. Dordrecht/Heidelberg/London/New York: Springer.

Šavelka, Jaromír. 2013. Coherence as constraint satisfaction: Judicial reasoning support mechanism. In *Coherence: Insights from philosophy, jurisprudence and artificial intelligence*, ed. M. Araszkiewicz and J. Šavelka, 203–216. Dordrecht/Heidelberg/New York/London: Springer.

Sergot, Marek. 2013. Normative positions. In *Handbook of deontic logic and normative systems*, ed. D. Gabbay, J. Horty, X. Parent, R. van der Meyden, and L. van der Torre, 353–406. London: College Publications.

Sergot, Marek, Fariba Sadri, Robert A. Kowalski, Frank Kriwaczek, Peter Hammond, and H.T. Cory. 1986. The British nationality act as a logic program. *Communications of the ACM* 29(5): 370–386.

[illegible]

Part II
... to the Practice of Lawmaking

Chapter 11
Formalising Debates About Law-Making Proposals as Practical Reasoning

Henry Prakken

Abstract In this paper the *ASPIC*$^+$ framework for argumentation-based inference is used for formally reconstructing two legal debates about law-making proposals: an opinion of a legal scholar on a Dutch legislative proposal and a US common-law judicial decision on whether an existing common law rule should be followed or distinguished. Both debates are formalised as practical reasoning, with versions of the argument schemes from good and bad consequences. These case studies aim to contribute to an understanding of the logical structure of debates about law-making proposals. Another aim of the case studies is to provide new benchmark examples for comparing alternative formal frameworks for modelling argumentation. In particular, this paper aims to illustrate the usefulness of two features of *ASPIC*$^+$: its distinction between deductive and defeasible inference rules and its ability to express arbitrary preference orderings on arguments.

Keywords Law making debates • Practical reasoning • Argumentation • Formalisation • Argument schemes

11.1 Introduction

Modern approaches to legal logic account for the fact that legal reasoning is not only about *constructing* arguments but also about *attacking* and *comparing* them. This is partly since legal reasoning often takes place in adversarial contexts (the court room, parliament). But even an individual legal reasoner (judge, solicitor, politician or politically interested citizen) often considers reasons for and against claims or proposals. Modern logic provides tools for formalising such argumentative

H. Prakken (✉)
Department of Information and Computing Sciences, Utrecht University, Utrecht, Netherlands

Faculty of Law, University of Groningen, Groningen, Netherlands
e-mail: h.prakken@uu.nl

M. Araszkiewicz, K. Płeszka (eds.), *Logic in the Theory and Practice of Lawmaking*, Legisprudence Library 2, DOI 10.1007/978-3-319-19575-9_11

reasoning. This paper[1] aims to provide an illustration of the usefulness of these tools, in the form of two case studies of how law-making debates can be formalised in an argumentation logic. In the first case study an opinion of a legal scholar on a Dutch legislative proposal is formalised, while in the second case study a judicial decision in the US common law of contract is reconstructed. Both case studies employ the *ASPIC*$^+$ framework for argumentation (Modgil and Prakken 2013; Prakken 2010), which currently is one of the main logical frameworks for argumentation in the field of artificial intelligence (AI). The *ASPIC*$^+$ framework has been applied earlier in a realistic case study in Prakken (2012b); in that paper the main arguments were not about law making proposals but about interpreting and applying legal concepts.

Both case studies concern law-making debates, one about a proposal for legislation in a civil law jurisdiction and the other in the context of common law precedent. While thus the legal context is different in the case studies, it will turn out that the reasoning forms are quite similar and are instances of what philosophers call practical reasoning, that is, reasoning about what to do. In particular, in both cases use is made of so-called argument schemes of good and bad consequences of decisions for action. Recently, these schemes have received much attention in the AI (& Law) literature. In this paper they will be formalised as proposed in Bench-Capon and Prakken (2010) and Bench-Capon et al. (2011). Unlike other formulations of these schemes, these formulations do not refer to *single* but to *sets* of consequences of actions, thus allowing for aggregation of reasons for and against proposals. The present paper's main advance over Bench-Capon and Prakken (2010) and Bench-Capon et al. (2011) is that it models an actual example of a legal argument in its full detail instead of modelling a simplified example that is more loosely based on actual textual material.

Another aim of the two case studies in this paper is to provide new benchmark examples for comparing alternative formal frameworks for modelling argumentation. In both general AI and AI & law several formal frameworks for argumentation-based inference have been proposed, such as assumption-based argumentation (Bondarenko et al. 1997), classical argumentation (Besnard and Hunter 2008), Carneades (Gordon et al. 2007) and *ASPIC*$^+$. This raises the question which framework is best suited for formalising natural, in particular legal arguments. The present paper aims to contribute to this discussion. While case studies cannot decide which framework is the best, they help in providing evidence and formulating benchmark examples. Compared to assumption-based and classical argumentation, the main distinguishing features of *ASPIC*$^+$ are an explicit distinction between deductive and defeasible inference rules and an explicit preference ordering on arguments. Accordingly, one aim of the present case studies is to illustrate the usefulness of these features.

[1]This paper is an extended and revised version of Prakken (2012a). The use of recursive labellings in *ASPIC*$^+$ is new, Sect. 11.6 is new, and the text of the other sections has been extended.

This paper is organised as follows. First in Sect. 11.2 the idea of logical argumentation systems is introduced, after which in Sect. 11.3 the $ASPIC^+$ framework is reviewed. Then in Sect. 11.4 the Dutch legal opinion is presented, which is reconstructed in $ASPIC^+$ in Sect. 11.5. In Sect. 11.6 the Monge case from US common contract law is presented and formalised. The paper concludes in Sect. 11.7.

11.2 Introduction to Logical Argumentation Systems

Logical research in AI & Law has recognised from the start that legal reasoning is defeasible and that therefore some form of nonmonotonic logic is needed to formalise legal argument, that is, a logic that allows that valid conclusions can be invalidated by further information. While in the early days of AI & Law nonmonotonic logic of several kinds were used, such as Reason-Based Logic of Hage (1997) and Verheij (1996), nowadays argumentation-based logics are the most commonly used. Such systems formalise defeasible reasoning as the construction and comparison of arguments for and against certain conclusions. An argument only warrants its conclusion if firstly, it is properly constructed and, secondly, it can be defended against counterarguments. Thus argumentation logics define three things: how arguments can be constructed, how they can be attacked by counterarguments and how they can be defended against such attacks. In general, three kinds of *attack* are distinguished: arguing for a contradictory conclusion, arguing that an inference rule has an exception, or denying a premise. An argument A is then said to *defeat* an argument B if A attacks B and is not weaker than B. The relative strength between arguments is determined with any standard that is appropriate to the problem at hand and may itself be the subject of argumentation. Note that if two arguments attack each other and are equally strong or their relative strength cannot be determined, then they defeat each other. The defeasibility of arguments arises from the fact that new information may give rise to new counterarguments that defeat the original argument.

To determine which arguments are acceptable, it does not suffice to determine the defeat relations between two arguments that attack each other. We must also look at how arguments can be *defended* by other arguments. Suppose we have three arguments A, B and C such that B strictly defeats A and C strictly defeats B. Then C defends A against B so, since C is not defeated by any argument, both A and C (and their conclusions) are acceptable while B is not acceptable. However, we can easily imagine more complex examples where our intuitions fall short. For instance, another argument D could be constructed such that C and D defeat each other, then an argument E could be constructed that defeats D but is defeated by A, and so on: which arguments can now be accepted and which should be rejected? Here we cannot rely on intuitions but need a precise formal definition. Such a definition should dialectically assess all constructible arguments in terms of three classes (three and not two since some conflicts cannot be resolved). Intuitively, the *justified arguments* are those that survive all conflicts with their attackers and so can be accepted, the *overruled arguments* are those that are defeated by a justified argument and so must be rejected; and the *defensible arguments* are those that are involved in conflicts that cannot be resolved. Furthermore, a *statement is justified* if it has a justified argument, it is *overruled* if all arguments for it are overruled, and it is *defensible* if it has a defensible argument but no justified arguments. In terms more familiar to lawyers, if a claim is justified, then a rational adjudicator is convinced that the claim is true, if it is overruled, such an adjudicator is convinced that the claim is false, while if it is defensible, s/he is neither convinced that it is true nor that it is false.

11.3 The *ASPIC*$^+$ Framework

In this section we review the *ASPIC*$^+$ framework of Prakken (2010) and Modgil and Prakken (2013). It defines arguments as inference trees formed by applying strict or defeasible inference rules to premises formulated in some logical language. Informally, if an inference rule's antecedents are accepted, then if the rule is strict, its consequent must be accepted *no matter what*, while if the rule is defeasible, its consequent must be accepted *if there are no good reasons not to accept it*. Arguments can be attacked on their (non-axiom) premises and on their applications of defeasible inference rules. Some attacks succeed as *defeats*, which is partly determined by preferences. The acceptability status of arguments is then defined by checking whether an argument can be defended against all its defeaters.

ASPIC$^+$ is not a system but a framework for specifying systems. It defines the notion of an abstract *argumentation system* as a structure consisting of a logical language $\mathscr{L}$ closed under negation, a set $\mathscr{R}$ consisting of two subsets $\mathscr{R}_s$ and $\mathscr{R}_d$ of strict and defeasible inference rules, and a naming convention n in $\mathscr{L}$ for defeasible rules in order to talk about the applicability of defeasible rules in $\mathscr{L}$. Thus, informally, $n(r)$ is a well-formed formula in $\mathscr{L}$ which says that rule $r \in \mathscr{R}$ is applicable. (As is usual, the inference rules in $\mathscr{R}$ are defined *over* the language $\mathscr{L}$ and are not elements *in* the language.)

ASPIC$^+$ does not commit to a particular logical language or to particular sets of inference rules. For $\mathscr{L}$ any logical language can be chosen, such as the language of propositional logic, first-order predicate logic or deontic logic. *ASPIC*$^+$'s inference rules can be used in two ways: they could encode domain-specific information (such as commonsense generalisations or legal rules) but they could also express general laws of reasoning. When used in the latter way, the strict rules over $\mathscr{L}$ can be based on the semantic interpretation of $\mathscr{L}$ by saying that $\mathscr{R}_s$ contains all inference rules that are semantically valid over $\mathscr{L}$ (according to the chosen semantics). So, for example, if $\mathscr{L}$ is chosen to be the language of standard propositional logic, then $\mathscr{R}_s$ can be chosen to consist of all semantically valid inferences in standard propositional logic (whether such an inference is valid can be tested with, for example, the truth-table method).

The defeasible inference rules $\mathscr{R}_d$ cannot be based on the semantic interpretation of $\mathscr{L}$, since they go beyond the meaning of the logical constants in $\mathscr{L}$. Consider, for example, defeasible modus ponens: 'if P then usually Q' and P do not together deductively imply Q, since we could have an unusual case of P. In other words, defeasible inference rules are deductively invalid. They can instead be based on insights from epistemology or argumentation theory. For example, $\mathscr{R}_d$ could be filled with presumptive argument schemes in the sense of Walton (1996) and Walton et al. (2008). The critical questions of these schemes are then pointers to counterarguments.

In *ASPIC*$^+$ argumentation systems are applied to knowledge bases to generate arguments and counterarguments. Combining these with an argument ordering results in so-called argumentation theories.

Definition 1 (Argumentation systems). An *argumentation system* is a triple $AS = (\mathscr{L}, \mathscr{R}, n)$ where:

- $\mathscr{L}$ is a logical language with a unary negation symbol ($\neg$).
- $\mathscr{R}_s$ and $\mathscr{R}_d$ are two disjoint sets of strict ($\mathscr{R}_s$) and defeasible ($\mathscr{R}_d$) inference rules of the form $\varphi_1, \ldots, \varphi_n \rightarrow \varphi$ and $\varphi_1, \ldots, \varphi_n \Rightarrow \varphi$ respectively (where φ_i, φ are meta-variables ranging over well-formed formulas in $\mathscr{L}$).
- n is a naming convention for defeasible rules, which to each rule r in $\mathscr{R}_d$ assigns a well-formed formula φ from $\mathscr{L}$ (written as $n(r) = \varphi$).

We write $\psi = -\varphi$ just in case $\psi = \neg\varphi$ or $\varphi = \neg\psi$.

Definition 2 (Knowledge bases). A *knowledge base* in an $AS = (\mathscr{L}, \mathscr{R}, n)$ is a set $\mathscr{K} \subseteq \mathscr{L}$ consisting of two disjoint subsets $\mathscr{K}_n$ (the *axioms*) and $\mathscr{K}_p$ (the *ordinary premises*).

Intuitively, the axioms are certain knowledge and thus cannot be attacked, whereas the ordinary premises are uncertain and thus can be attacked.

Arguments can be constructed step-by-step from knowledge bases by chaining inference rules into trees. Arguments thus contain subarguments, which are the structures that support intermediate conclusions (plus the argument itself and its premises as limiting cases). In what follows, for a given argument A the function `Prem` returns all its premises, `Conc` returns its conclusion, `TopRule` returns the final rule applied in the argument, `Sub` returns all its sub-arguments and `ImmSub` returns all its immediate sub-arguments, i.e., the subarguments to which conclusions the argument's top rule was applied.

Definition 3 (Arguments). An *argument* A on the basis of a knowledge base KB in an argumentation system $(\mathscr{L}, \mathscr{R}, n)$ is:

1. φ if $\varphi \in \mathscr{K}$ with:
   `Prem`$(A) = \{\varphi\}$;
   `Conc`$(A) = \varphi$;
   `TopRule`(A) = undefined;
   `Sub`$(A) = \{\varphi\}$;
   `ImmSub`$(A) = \emptyset$.

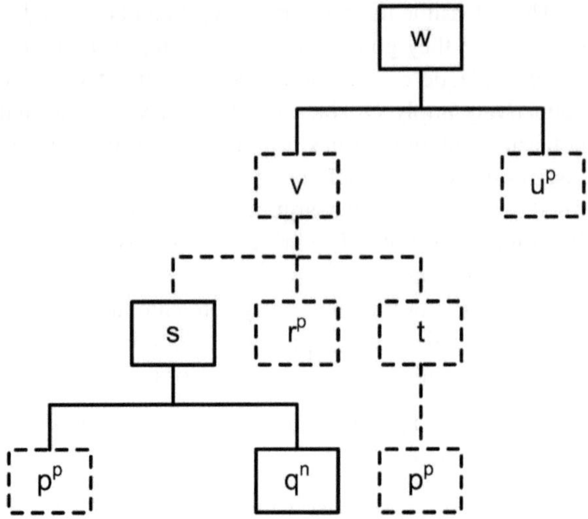

Fig. 11.1 An argument

2. $A_1, \ldots A_n \rightarrow/\Rightarrow \psi$ if $A_1, \ldots, A_n$ are arguments such that there exists a strict/defeasible rule $\texttt{Conc}(A_1), \ldots, \texttt{Conc}(A_n) \rightarrow/\Rightarrow \psi$ in $\mathcal{R}_s/\mathcal{R}_d$, with
   $\texttt{Prem}(A) = \texttt{Prem}(A_1) \cup \ldots \cup \texttt{Prem}(A_n)$;
   $\texttt{Conc}(A) = \psi$;
   $\texttt{TopRule}(A) = \texttt{Conc}(A_1), \ldots, \texttt{Conc}(A_n) \rightarrow/\Rightarrow \psi$;
   $\texttt{Sub}(A) = \texttt{Sub}(A_1) \cup \ldots \cup \texttt{Sub}(A_n) \cup \{A\}$;
   $\texttt{ImmSub}(A) = \{A_1, \ldots, A_n\}$.

Example 1. Consider a knowledge base in an argumentation system with

$\mathcal{R}_s = \{p, q \rightarrow s;\ u, v \rightarrow w\}$; $\mathcal{R}_d = \{p \Rightarrow t;\ s, r, t \Rightarrow v\}$

$\mathcal{K}_n = \{q\}$; $\mathcal{K}_p = \{p, u, r\}$

An argument for w is displayed in Fig. 11.1. The type of a premise is indicated with a superscript and defeasible inferences and attackable premises and conclusions are displayed with dotted lines.

Formally the argument and its subarguments are written as follows:

A_1: p	A_5: $A_1 \Rightarrow t$
A_2: q	A_6: $A_1, A_2 \rightarrow s$
A_3: r	A_7: $A_5, A_3, A_6 \Rightarrow v$
A_4: u	A_8: $A_7, A_4 \rightarrow w$

We have that

$\texttt{Prem}(A_8) =$	$\{p, q, r, u\}$
$\texttt{Conc}(A_8) =$	w
$\texttt{Sub}(A_8) =$	$\{A_1, A_2, A_3, A_4, A_5, A_6, A_7, A_8\}$
$\texttt{ImmSub}(A_8) =$	$\{A_4, A_7\}$
$\texttt{DefRules}(A_8) =$	$\{p \Rightarrow t;\ s, r, t \Rightarrow v\}$
$\texttt{TopRule}(A_8) =$	$u, v \rightarrow w$

Arguments can be attacked in three ways: on their premises (undermining attack), on their conclusion (rebutting attack) or on an inference step (undercutting attack). The latter two are only possible on applications of defeasible inference rules.

Definition 4 (Attack). *A attacks B* iff *A undercuts*, *rebuts* or *undermines B*, where:

- *A undercuts* argument B (on B') iff $\texttt{Conc}(A) = -n(r)$ for some $B' \in \texttt{Sub}(B)$ such that B''s top rule r is defeasible.
- *A rebuts* argument B (on B') iff $\texttt{Conc}(A) = -\varphi$ for some $B' \in \texttt{Sub}(B)$ of the form $B''_1, \ldots, B''_n \Rightarrow \varphi$.
- Argument *A undermines B* (on B') iff $\texttt{Conc}(A) = -\varphi$ for some $B' = \varphi$, $\varphi \notin \mathcal{K}_n$.

The argument in Example 1 can be undermined on any premise except on q, it can be rebutted by arguments with a conclusion $\neg t$ or $\neg v$ and it can be undercut by arguments with a conclusion $\neg r_1$ and $\neg r_2$, assuming that $n(p \Rightarrow t) = r_1$ and $n(s, r, t \Rightarrow v) = r_2$.

Argumentation systems plus knowledge bases form argumentation theories, which induce structured argumentation frameworks.

Definition 5 (Structured Argumentation Frameworks). Let *AT* be an *argumentation theory* (*AS*, *KB*). A *structured argumentation framework* (SAF) defined by *AT*, is a triple $\langle \mathcal{A}, \mathcal{C}, \preceq \rangle$ where $\mathcal{A}$ is the set of all finite arguments constructed from *KB* in *AS*, $\preceq$ is an ordering on $\mathcal{A}$, and $(X, Y) \in \mathcal{C}$ iff X attacks Y.

The notion of *defeat* can then be defined by using the argument ordering to check which attacks succeed as defeats. Assumptions could be made on the properties of $\preceq$ (such as that it is transitive) but the definition of defeat does not rely on any assumption. In fact, undercutting attacks succeed as *defeats* independently of preferences over arguments, since they express exceptions to defeasible inference rules. By contrast, rebutting and undermining attacks succeed only if the attacked argument is not stronger than the attacking argument. ($A \prec B$ is defined as usual as $A \preceq B$ and $B \npreceq A$.)

Definition 6 (Defeat). *A defeats B* iff:

- A undercuts B; or
- A rebuts/undermines B on B' and $A \nprec B'$.

A strictly defeats B iff *A* defeats *B* and *B* does not defeat *A*

The success of rebutting and undermining attacks thus involves comparing the conflicting arguments at the points where they conflict. The definition of successful undermining exploits the fact that an argument premise is also a subargument.

The final task is to define how the arguments of an argumentation theory can be evaluated in the context of all arguments in the theory and their defeat relations. The following definition of recursive argument labellings, originally proposed by

Pollock (1995), achieves this.[2] It uses the notion of an *immediate* subargument of an argument. This notion was in Definition 3 defined as ImmSub(A), that is, as those arguments that provide the antecedents of the top rule of argument A. Note that arguments taken from $\mathcal{K}$ thus have no immediate subarguments.

The definition of recursive argument labellings uses the notion of direct defeat. That an argument A *directly defeats* an argument B means that A rebuts, undercuts or undermines B on B (and $A \not\prec B$ in case A rebuts or undermines B).

Definition 7 (Recursive argument labellings). For any structured argumentation framework $SAF = \langle \mathcal{A}, \mathcal{C}, \preceq \rangle$, a *p-labelling* of SAF is a pair of sets (In, Out) (where both In and Out are subsets of $\mathcal{A}$) such that $In \cap Out = \emptyset$ and for all arguments A in $\mathcal{A}$ it holds that:

1. argument A is labelled *in* iff:

   a. all arguments in $\mathcal{A}$ that directly defeat A are labelled *out*; and
   b. all immediate subarguments of A are labelled *in*; and

2. argument A is labelled *out* iff:

   a. A is directly defeated by an argument in $\mathcal{A}$ that is labelled *in*; or
   b. An immediate subargument of A is labelled *out*.

This definition implies that an argument is *out* if at least one of its subarguments is *out*. Note also that according to this definition not all arguments have to be labelled. For example, if the argumentation theory contains just two arguments A and B, which defeat each other, then $(\emptyset, \emptyset)$ is a well-defined labelling. Moreover, in general the set of all arguments can be labelled in more than one way that satisfies this definition. For instance, in our example two further well-defined labellings are respectively, a labelling in which A is *in* while B is *out* and a labelling in which B is *in* while A is *out*. To further select from these well-defined labellings, several labelling policies are possible, which correspond to different so-called semantics for argument evaluation (cf. Caminada 2006). We discuss two of them. *Grounded semantics* minimises the set of all arguments that are labelled *in*. So in our example, only $(\emptyset, \emptyset)$ is a grounded labelling. *Preferred semantics* instead maximises the set of arguments that are labelled *in*. So in our example the two labellings that label one argument *in* and the other *out* are the two preferred labellings. It is known that the grounded labelling is always unique (since if an argument can both be labelled *in* and labelled *out*, it leaves the argument unlabelled), while preferred semantics allows for alternative labellings (since if an argument can both be labelled *in* and

[2] In previous publications on $ASPIC^+$ arguments were instead evaluated by generating a so-called abstract argumentation framework from an argumentation theory and evaluating arguments with any of the abstract semantics of Dung (1995). While this is theoretically fine, in Prakken (2013) I argued that Pollock's (1995) recursive labellings support a more natural explanation of argument evaluation. I also proved that the two ways to evaluate arguments always yield the same outcome, so that logically their differences do not matter.

labelled *out*, it alternatively explores both choices). In this paper preferred semantics will be used, since it allows for identifying alternative coherent positions.

Finally, in preferred semantics an argument is *justified* if it is labelled *in* in all labellings, it is *overruled* if it is labelled *out* in all labellings, and it is *defensible* if it is neither justified nor overruled. Furthermore, a statement is *justified* if it is the conclusion of a justified argument, while it is *defensible* if it is not justified but the conclusion of a defensible argument, and *overruled* if it is defeated by a justified argument.

11.4 An Example of Natural Argument

The following text is a summary of an opinion by Nico Kwakman of the Faculty of Law, University of Groningen, The Netherlands.[3] The topic is whether the legislative proposal by the Dutch government to impose mandatory minimum sentences for serious crimes is a good idea.

> Despite strong criticism from the Council of State (Raad van State, RvS), the Cabinet is going to continue to introduce mandatory minimum sentences for serious offences. Dr Nico Kwakman, criminal justice expert at the University of Groningen, is critical of the bill, but can also understand the reasoning behind it. The effectiveness of the bill is doubtful, but the symbolic impact is large. The cabinet is sending out a strong signal and it has every right to do so.
>
> The Netherlands Bar Association, the Council of State, the Netherlands Association for the Judiciary, they are all advising the cabinet not to introduce the bill. However, the cabinet is ignoring their advice and continuing on with its plans. Criminals who commit a serious crime for the second time within ten years must be given a minimum sentence of at least half of the maximum sentence allocated to that offence, says the Cabinet. The bill has been drawn up under great pressure from the PVV party.
>
> **Not effective**
>
> Regarding content, the bill raises a lot of question marks, explains Kwakman. Heavy sentences do not reduce the chances of recidivism, academic research has revealed. Nor has it ever been demonstrated that heavy sentences lead to a reduction in the crime figures. Kwakman: 'It is very important for a judge to be able to tailor a punishment to the individual offender. That increases the chances of a successful return to society. In the future, judges will have much less room for such tailoring.'
>
> **Call from the public**
>
> The Cabinet says that the new bill is meeting the call from the public for heavier sentences. This is despite the fact that international comparisons show that crime in the Netherlands is already heavily punished. Kwakman: 'Dutch judges are definitely not softies, as is often claimed. Even without politics ordering them to, in the past few years they have become much stricter in reaction to what is going on in society. This bill, completely unnecessarily, will force them to go even further'.

---

[3] Published at http://www.rug.nl/news-and-events/people-perspectives/opinie/2012/06nicokwakman?lang=en on 29 February 2012.

Symbolic impact

Kwakman does have a certain amount of sympathy for the Cabinet's reasoning. 'The effectiveness of the bill is doubtful, but criminal law revolves around more than effectiveness alone. It will also have a significant symbolic impact. The Cabinet is probably mainly interested in the symbolism, in underlining norms. The Cabinet is sending out a strong signal and it has every right to do so as the democratically elected legislator. Anyone who doesn't agree should vote for a different party the next time.'

French kissing is rape

Judges currently have a lot of freedom when setting sentences but that will be significantly less in the future. Kwakman: 'A forced French kiss is a graphic example. It officially counts as rape, but judges impose relatively mild sentences for it. Soon judges will be forced to impose half of the maximum punishment for rape on someone who is guilty of a forced French kiss for the second time. Only in extremely exceptional cases can that sentence be changed.'

Taking a stand

And that is where the dangers of the new bill lurk, thinks Kwakman. Judges who don't think the mandatory sentence is suitable will look for ways to get around the bill. These could include not assuming so quickly that punishable offences have been proven, interpreting the bill in a very wide way on their own initiative, or by thinking up emergency constructions. Kwakman: 'In this way judges will be taking on more and more of the legislative and law formation tasks, and that is a real shame. The legislature and the judiciary should complement each other. This bill will force people to take a stand and the relationship between legislator and judge will harden.'

11.5 A Formal Reconstruction in *ASPIC*$^+$

I next model the example of the previous section in the *ASPIC*$^+$ framework, leaving the logical language formally undefined and instead using streamlined natural language for expressing the premises and conclusions of the arguments. Argument schemes are modelled as defeasible inference rules. The case is reconstructed in terms of argument schemes from good and bad consequences recently proposed by Bench-Capon et al. (2011) and some other schemes. Contrary to the usual formulations of schemes from consequences (e.g. Atkinson and Bench-Capon 2007; Walton et al. 2008), they do not refer to single but to *sets of* good or bad consequences.[4] Thus argumentation can be modelled as collecting and then weighing all good and bad consequences of alternative action proposals. An early application of this idea in Reason-Based logic was proposed by Hage (2004). Current work generally respects Hage's insights but formalises them in the context of an argumentation logic.

[4] As usual, inference rules with free variables are schemes for all their ground instances.

Argument scheme from good consequences

Action A results in C_1

...

Action A results in C_n

C_1 is good

...

C_n is good

Therefore (presumably), action A is good.

Argument scheme from bad consequences

Action A results in C_1

...

Action A results in C_m

C_1 is bad

...

C_m is bad

Therefore (presumably), action A is bad.

These schemes have four critical questions:

1. Does A result in $C_1, \ldots, C_n/C_m$?
2. Is $C_1, \ldots, C_n/C_m$ really good/bad?
3. Does A also result in something which is bad (good)?
4. Is there another way to realise C_n/C_m?

In $ASPIC^+$ these questions are pointers to counterarguments. Questions 1 and point to undermines, question 3 to rebuttals and question 4 to undercutters. Note that if there is more than one good (bad) consequence of a given action, then the scheme of good (bad) consequences can be instantiated several times, namely for each combination of one or more of these consequences. This makes it possible to model a kind of accrual, or aggregation of reasons for or against an action proposal.

My reconstruction of Kwakman's opinion is visualised in Fig. 11.2. In this figure, solid lines stand for applications of inference rules (with their antecedents below and their consequent above). A solid line that branches out toward below indicates an inference rule applied to multiple antecedents. The three dotted lines indicate direct attack relations. The four boxes with thick borders are the 'final' conclusions of the four largest arguments. Finally, the grey colourings of some nodes will be explained later.

All arguments in my reconstruction either instantiate one of these schemes or attack one of their premises, using another argument scheme, which I now informally specify: (all inferences in Fig. 11.2 are labelled with the name of the inference rule that they apply):

- GCi and BCi stand for, respectively, the i'th application of the scheme from good, respectively, bad consequences.

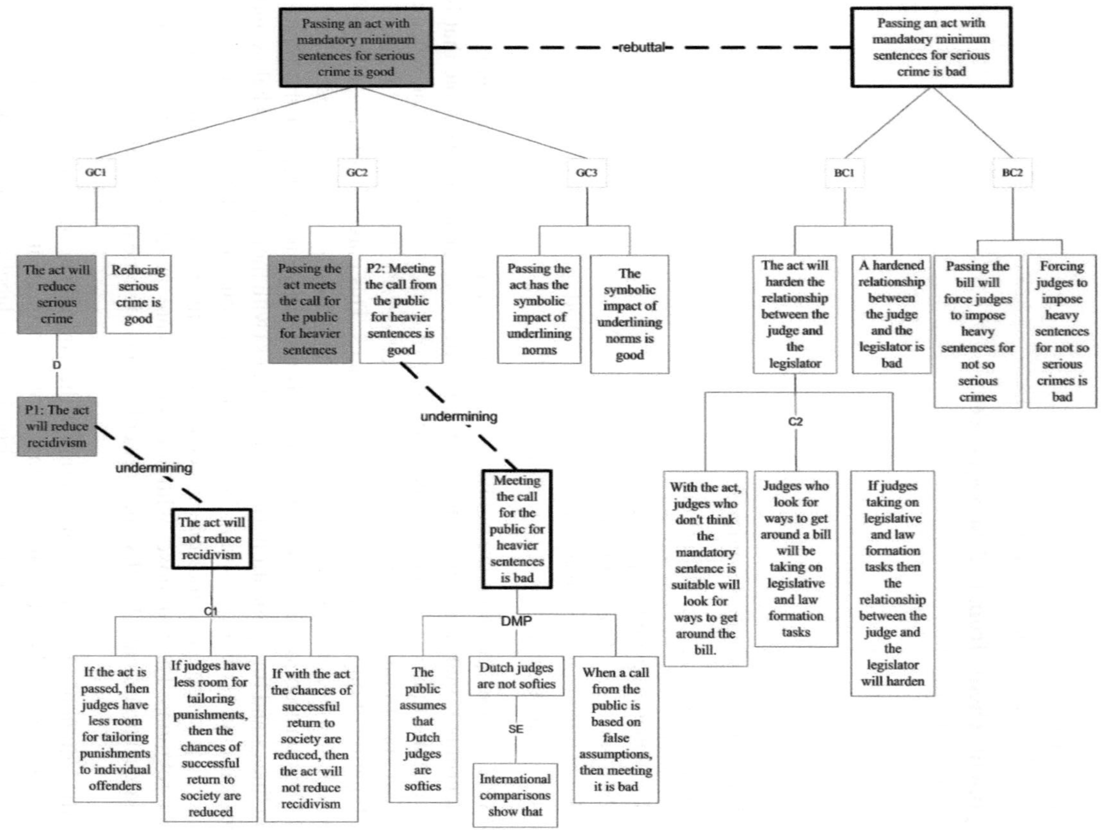

Fig. 11.2 The reconstruction

- D stands for the application of a definition in a deductive inference:

  P (categorically/presumably) causes Q
  Q is by definition a case of R
  ———
  Therefore (strictly), P (categorically/presumably) causes R

- C1 and C2 stand for two applications of causal chaining:

  P_1 (categorically/presumably) causes P_2
  P_2 (categorically/presumably) causes ...
  ... (categorically/presumably) causes P_n
  ———
  Therefore (strictly/presumably), P_1 causes P_n

  This inference rule is strict or defeasible depending on whether the causal relations are assumed to be categorical or presumptive.

- DMP stands for defeasible modus ponens:

  If P_1 and ... and P_n then usually/typically/normally Q
  P_1 and ... and P_n
  ———
  Therefore (presumably) Q

- SE is shorthand for a 'scientific evidence' scheme:

  Scientific evidence shows that P
  ———
  Therefore (presumably) P

The links in Fig. 11.2 to the final two conclusions require some explanation. If there is a set S of reasons why action A is good, then the scheme from good consequences can be instantiated for any nonempty subset of S. This is informally visualised by introducing a name on the support links for any of these reasons. This summarises all possible instances of the scheme from good consequences. Thus in the example there are seven such instances, one combining GC1, GC2 and GC3 (denoted below by GC_{123}), three with any combination of two reasons (denoted below by $GC_{12}, GC_{13}, GC_{23}$) and three applying any individual reason (denoted below by G_1, G_2 and G_3). Likewise, there are three instances of the scheme from bad consequences, two applying an individual reason for a bad consequence (BC_1 and BC_2) and one combining these reasons (BC_{12}). Below we will see that this complicates the identification of the various preferred labellings.

The argumentation system and knowledge base corresponding to Fig. 11.2 can be summarised as follows:

- $\mathscr{L}$ is a first-order predicate-logic language (here informally presented), where for ease of notation 'Action A is good' and 'Action A is bad' are regarded as negating each other.
- R_s contains at least the D rule mentioned above, and it contains the C rule if the causal relations in the example to which it is applied are regarded as categorical. Furthermore, it contains all deductively valid propositional and first-order predicate-logic inferences.
- R_d consists of the argument schemes from good and bad consequences, the C rule if not included in $\mathscr{R}_s$, and the SE and DMP rules.

- $\mathscr{K}_n$ is empty, while $\mathscr{K}_p$ consists of the leafs of the four argument trees (where their conclusions are regarded as their roots). $\mathscr{K}$ thus consists of 18 ordinary premises.

The argumentation theory induced by this argumentation system and this knowledge base is as follows:

- $\mathscr{A}$ consists of quite a number of arguments:
  - all 18 premises;
  - two applications of the C rule: C_1 and C_2;
  - one application of the DMP rule: *DMP*;
  - one application of the D rule: *D*;
  - seven applications of the GC scheme: $GC_1, GC_2, GC_3, GC_{12}, GC_{13}, GC_{23}, GC_{123}$;
  - three applications of the BC scheme: BC_1, BC_2, BC_{12}.

  So in total the reconstruction contains 29 arguments. Note that all 11 non-premise arguments contain other arguments from $\mathscr{A}$ as their subarguments.
- The attack relations are more in number than the three shown in Fig. 11.2:
  - Any argument applying GC rebuts any argument applying BC and vice versa;
  - C_1 undermines the premise argument P_1 = 'The act will reduce recidivism' and all arguments using it, that is, the arguments $D, GC_1, GC_{12}, GC_{13}, GC_{123}$;
  - The premise argument P_1 in turn rebuts argument C_1;
  - *DMP* undermines the premise argument P_2 = 'Meeting the call for the public for heavier sentences is good' and all arguments using it, that is, $GC_2, GC_{12}, GC_{23}, GC_{123}$;
  - The premise argument P_2 in turn rebuts argument *DMP*.
- Various argument orderings can be assumed, resulting in different defeat relations. Note that the argument ordering is only applied to 'direct' attacks, namely, to the attacks between C_1 and P_1, between C_2 and P_2, and between all applications of the GC scheme and all applications of the BC scheme.

Let us now for simplicity assume that the argument ordering counts reasons for and against an action, and moreover that, for whatever reason, $P_1 \prec C_1$ while $DMP \approx P_2$.[5]

What are now the preferred labellings? To determine them, we must take into account that Fig. 11.2 in fact summarises seven applications of the scheme from good consequences and three applications of the scheme from bad consequences. So strictly speaking the conclusion that passing the act is good should be multiplied seven times in Fig. 11.2 and the conclusion that passing the act is bad should be tripled. This would clutter the graph and make it poorly understandable. Fortunately, we can simplify our analysis as follows. Note first that GC_1 is always *out* since its

[5]For a way to model debates about the argument ordering see e.g. Modgil and Prakken (2010).

subargument P_1 is directly defeated by C_1, which has no defeaters and is therefore always *in*. So P_1 is always *out*. But then D is always *out* since it has an immediate subargument that is *out* and so for the same reason GC_1 is always *out*. By the same line of reasoning GC_{12}, GC_{13} and GC_{123} are also always *out* since they have a subargument (P_1) that is always *out*. Furthermore, note that argument GC_{23} is stronger in the argument ordering than both GC_2 and GC_3, since the argument ordering counts the number of good and bad consequences. Moreover, GC_{23} has no attackers that do not also attack either GC_2 or GC_3, so we can safely ignore GC_2 and GC_3. We can therefore safely assume in Fig. 11.2 that the statement that passing the act is good is the conclusion of GC_{23}. For similar reasons we can safely assume in Fig. 11.2 that the statement that passing the act is bad is the conclusion of BC_{12}.

Now there are two conflicts between equally strong arguments in Fig. 11.2 that induce alternative preferred labellings (recall that if an argument can be both labelled *in* and labelled *out*, preferred semantics always explores both options). Consider first the conflict between *DMP* and P_2. We can make *DMP* *in* if we make P_2 *out*, since all subarguments of *DMP* are *in* since they have no defeater. But then GC_{23} has a subargument that is *out* so GC_{23} is also *out*. Then BC_{12} is *in* since, firstly, its only defeater is *out* and, second, all its subarguments are *in* since none of them has a defeater. The resulting labelling is displayed in Fig. 11.2, in which grey boxes are conclusions of arguments that are *out* while white boxes are conclusions of arguments that are *in* (so in this labelling there are no unlabelled arguments).

Alternatively, we can make P_1 *in* and *DMP* *out*. Then we have to consider the conflict between GC_{23} and BC_{12}. For both of them it now holds that all their subarguments are *in*. So we have two options: make GC_{23} *in* and BC_{12} *out* or vice versa. For reasons of space we display only the first of these labellings, in Fig. 11.3. The alternative labelling can be visualised by just switching the labels of GC_{23} and BC_{12}.

In sum, there are both labellings where GC_{23} is *in* and BC_{12} is *out* and labellings where GC_{23} is *out* and BC_{12} is *in*. Therefore, both the conclusion that passing the act is good and the conclusion that passing it is bad are defensible. To make the conclusion that passing the act is good justified, one should either argue that *DMP* is strictly preferred over P_2 or argue that for some reason the two good consequences 2 and 3 together outweigh the two bad consequences 1 and 2.

11.6 Law Making Debates in Case Law: The Olga Monge Case

Above I illustrated how legislative debates can be reconstructed as practical reasoning. In this section I illustrate that the same is sometimes possible for common-law judicial decisions about whether to follow or to distinguish a common-law rule. I illustrate this with an American common law of contract case, the *Olga Monge v. Beebe Rubber Company* case, decided by the Supreme Court of New Hampshire (USA), February 28, 1974. In brief, the facts were that Olga Monge, according to

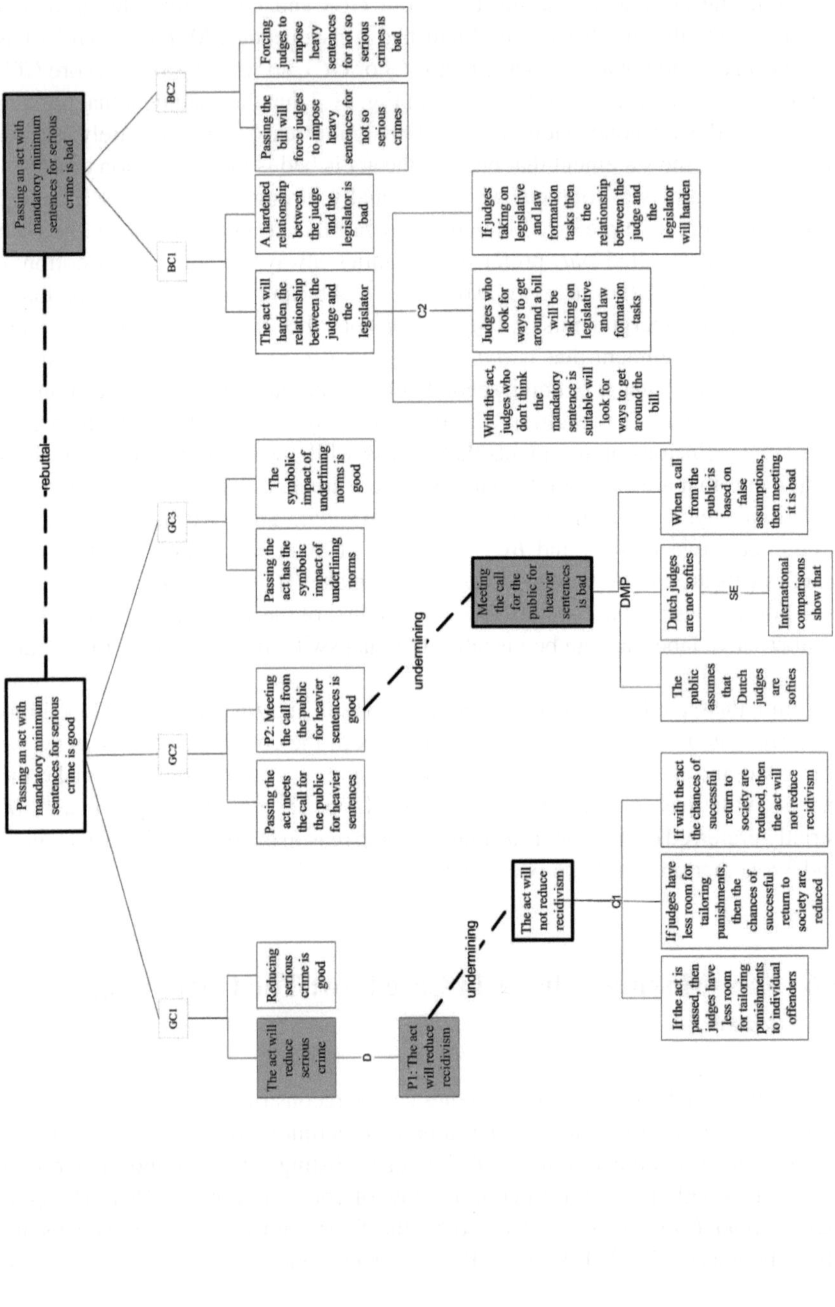

Fig. 11.3 The first preferred labelling

the court "a virtuous mother of three", was employed at will (that is, for an indefinite period of time) by Beebe Rubber Company. The relevant common law rule at that time said that every employment contract that specifies no duration is terminable at will by either party, which means that the employee can be fired for any reason or no reason at all. At some point, Olga Monge was fired for no reason by her foreman. Olga claimed that this was since she had refused to go out with him and she claimed breach of contract, arguing that the common law rule does not apply if the employee was fired in bad faith, malice, or retaliation. The court accepted that she was fired was that reason and was then faced with the problem whether to follow the old rule and decide that there was no breach of contract, or to distinguish the rule into a new rule by adding an exception in case the employee was fired in bad faith, malice, or retaliation, in order to decide that there was breach of contract. Here it is relevant that according to one common law theory of precedential constraint, courts can distinguish an old rule by adding an extra condition as long as the new rule still gives the same outcome in all precedent cases as the old rule. See Horty (2011) and Horty and Bench-Capon (2012) for a discussion and formalisation of this theory.

The court decided to distinguish the old rule, on the following grounds:

> In all employment contracts, whether at will or for a definite term, the employer's interest in running his business as he sees fit must be balanced against the interest of the employee in maintaining his employment, and the public's interest in maintaining a proper balance between the two.
> (...)
> We hold that a termination by the employer of a contract of employment at will which is motivated by bad faith or malice or based on retaliation is not in the best interest of the economic system or the public good and constitutes a breach of the employment contract.

I now reconstruct this reasoning as practical reasoning with the argument scheme from good consequences. The two alternative decisions are to follow the old rule or to distinguish it into the new rule by adding a condition 'unless the employee was fired in bad faith, malice, or retaliation'. In my interpretation the court stated as a good consequence of following the old rule that the employer's interest in running his business as he sees fit are protected while it stated a good consequence of distinguishing it promotes the interest of the economic system and the public good. We then have two instances of the argument scheme from good consequences for conflicting decisions. The conclusion of both of these arguments is then combined with an argument that applies the adopted rule. The resulting reconstruction is visualised in Fig. 11.4. For space limitations we leave implicit that if Olga Monge could (could not) be fired for no reason, then firing her for no reason was not (was) breach of contract.

Two arguments in this reconstruction apply the argument scheme from a single good consequence GC1. One argument applies the causal chaining scheme C. Two arguments apply the classical modus ponens inference rule MP. Finally, the two top rules of the rebutting arguments for whether Olga Monge could be fired for no reason apply defeasible modus ponens on the Old, respectively, the New Rule (where the second application of defeasible modus ponens is in fact applied to the 'only if' part of the New Rule).

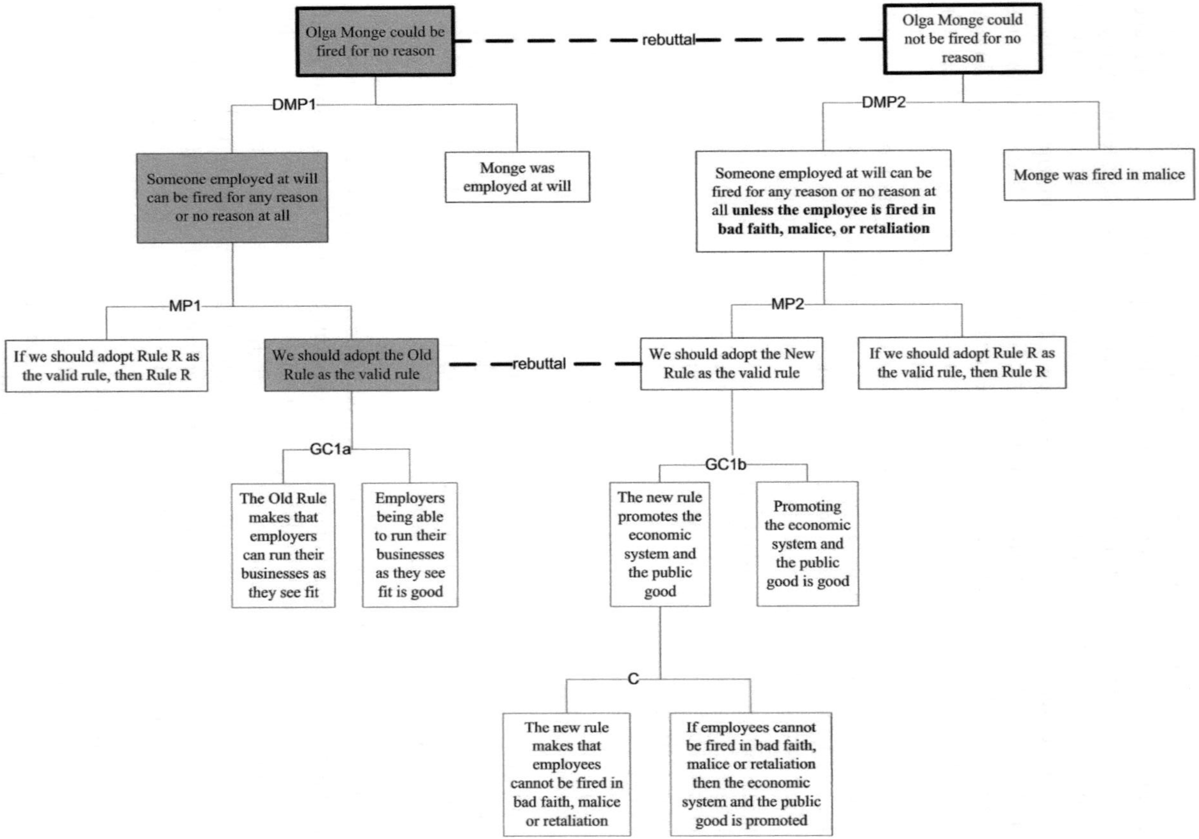

Fig. 11.4 The preferred labelling

The $ASPIC^+$ argumentation system and knowledge base corresponding to Fig. 11.4 can be summarised as follows:

- $\mathscr{L}$ is as above a first-order predicate-logic language (here informally presented), where for ease of notation 'We should adopt the Old Rule as the valid rule' and 'We should adopt the New Rule as the valid rule' are regarded as negating each other. Furthermore, we assume that $\mathscr{L}$ has a defeasible connective for representing legal rules.
- R_s contains all deductively valid propositional and first-order predicate-logic inferences.
- R_d consists of defeasible modus ponens for legal rules, the two argument schemes from good and bad consequences and the C rule.
- $\mathscr{K}_n$ is empty, while $\mathscr{K}_p$ consists of the leafs of the two argument trees (where their conclusions are regarded as their roots). $\mathscr{K}$ thus consists of eight ordinary premises.

The $ASPIC^+$ argumentation theory induced by this argumentation theory is as follows:

- $\mathscr{A}$ consists of the following arguments:
  - all eight premises;
  - one application of the C rule: C;
  - two applications of the modus ponens rule: MP_1 and MP_2;
  - two applications of the GC scheme: GC_{1a} and GC_{1b};
  - two applications of defeasible modus ponens on legal rules: DMP_1 and DMP_2.

  So in total the reconstruction contains 15 arguments.
- The attack relations are again more in number than the two shown in Fig. 11.4:
  - Arguments DMP_1 and DMP_2 directly rebut each other.
  - Arguments GC_{1a} and GC_{1b} directly rebut each other. Therefore, GC_{1a} also indirectly rebuts arguments MP_2 and DMP_2, namely on GC_{1b}. Likewise, GC_{1b} indirectly rebuts arguments MP_1 and DMP_1, namely on GC_{1a}.
- As for the argument ordering, in my interpretation the court found for Olga Monge on the grounds that the good consequences of adopting the New Rule outweigh the good consequences of adopting the Old Rule. On this interpretation it must be assumed that $GC_{1a} \prec GC_{1b}$, so that GC_{1b} strictly defeats GC_{1a}. Then the argument ordering between the other arguments is irrelevant for the outcome.

It is now easy to see that there is just one preferred labelling (actually displayed in Fig. 11.4). To start with, argument GC_{1b} must be labelled *in* since it has no defeaters (since $GC_{1a} \prec GC_{1b}$). Then GC_{1a} must be labelled *out* since it is directly defeated by an argument that is *in*, namely, GC_{1b}. Then MP_1 is *out* since it has an immediate subargument that is *out*, so DMP_1 is *out* for the same reason. But then DMP_2 must be labelled *in* since its only direct defeater is labelled *out* and none of its subarguments is defeated, so all its immediate subarguments are *in*. In sum, the conclusion that

Olga Monge could not be fired for no reason (and so that firing her for no reason was breach of contract) is justified.

11.7 Conclusions

In this paper the *ASPIC*$^+$ framework for argumentation-based inference was used for formally reconstructing two legal debates about law-making proposals: an opinion of a legal scholar on a Dutch legislative proposal and a US common-law judicial decision on whether an existing common law rule should be followed or distinguished. Both debates were formalised as practical reasoning, that is, as reasoning about what to do. Versions of the argument schemes from good and bad consequences of decisions turned out to be useful in formally reconstructing the debates. This paper has thereby hopefully contributed to clarifying the logical structure of debates about law-making proposals.

Another aim of the case studies was to provide new benchmark examples for comparing alternative formal frameworks for modelling argumentation. Accordingly, an obvious topic for future research is to formalise the same examples in such alternative frameworks and to compare the resulting formalisations with the ones given in this paper.

References

Atkinson, Katie, and Trevor Bench-Capon. 2007. Practical reasoning as presumptive argumentation using action based alternating transition systems. *Artificial Intelligence* 171:855–874.

Bench-Capon, Trevor, and Henry Prakken. 2010. A lightweight formal model of two–phase democratic deliberation. In *Legal knowledge and information systems. JURIX 2010: The twenty–third annual conference*, ed. R. Winkels, 27–36. Amsterdam etc.: IOS.

Bench-Capon, Trevor, Henry Prakken, and Wietske Visser. 2011. Argument schemes for two–phase democratic deliberation. In *Proceedings of the thirteenth international conference on artificial intelligence and law*, 21–30. New York: ACM Press.

Besnard, Philippe, and Anthony Hunter. 2008. *Elements of argumentation*. Cambridge: MIT Press.

Bondarenko, Andrey, Phan Minh Dung, Robert Kowalski, and Francesca Toni. 1997. An abstract, argumentation–theoretic approach to default reasoning. *Artificial Intelligence* 93:63–101.

Caminada, Martin. 2006. On the issue of reinstatement in argumentation. In *Proceedings of the 11th european conference on logics in artificial intelligence (JELIA 2006)*, Number 4160 in springer lecture notes in AI, 111–123. Berlin: Springer.

Dung, Phan MInh. 1995. On the acceptability of arguments and its fundamental role in non–monotonic reasoning, logic programming, and n–person games. *Artificial Intelligence* 77:321–357.

Gordon, Thomas, Henry Prakken, and Douglas Walton. 2007. The Carneades model of argument and burden of proof. *Artificial Intelligence* 171:875–896.

Hage, Jaap. 1997. *Reasoning with rules. An essay on legal reasoning and its underlying logic*, Law and philosophy library. Dordrecht/Boston/London: Kluwer Academic.

Hage, Jaap. 2004. Comparing alternatives in the law. Legal applications of qualitative comparative reasoning. *Artificial Intelligence and Law* 12:181–225.

Horty, John. 2011. Rules and reasons in the theory of precedent. *Legal Theory* 17:1–33.

Horty, John, and T. Bench-Capon, 2012. A factor-based definition of precedential constraint. *Artificial Intelligence and Law* 20:181–214.

Modgil, Sanjay, and Henry Prakken 2010. Reasoning about preferences in structured extended argumentation frameworks. In *Computational models of argument. Proceedings of COMMA 2010*, ed. P. Baroni, F. Cerutti, M. Giacomin, and G. Simari, 347–358. Amsterdam etc.: IOS Press.

Modgil, Sanjay, and Henry Prakken. 2013. A general account of argumentation with preferences. *Artificial Intelligence* 195:361–397.

Pollock, John 1995. *Cognitive Carpentry. A blueprint for how to build a person*. Cambridge: MIT Press.

Prakken, Henry 2010. An abstract framework for argumentation with structured arguments. *Argument and Computation* 1:93–124.

Prakken, Henry 2012a. Formalising a legal opinion on a legislative proposal in the ASPIC$^+$ framework. In *Legal knowledge and information systems. JURIX 2012: The twenty-fifth annual conference*, ed. B. Schafer, 119–128. Amsterdam etc.: IOS Press.

Prakken, Henry 2012b. Reconstructing Popov v. Hayashi in a framework for argumentation with structured arguments and Dungean semantics. *Artificial Intelligence and Law* 20:57–82.

Prakken, Henry 2013. Relating ways to instantiate abstract argumentation frameworks. In *From knowledge representation to argumentation in AI, law and policy making. A Festschrift in honour of Trevor Bench-Capon on the occasion of his 60th birthday*, ed. K. Atkinson, H. Prakken, and A. Wyner, 167–189. London: College Publications.

Verheij, Bart 1996. Rules, reasons, arguments: Formal studies of argumentation and defeat. Doctoral diss., University of Maastricht.

Walton, Douglas. 1996. *Argumentation schemes for presumptive reasoning*. Mahwah: Lawrence Erlbaum Associates.

Walton, Douglas, Christopher Reed, and Fabrizio Macagno. 2008. *Argumentation schemes*. Cambridge: Cambridge University Press.

Chapter 12
Logics for Legal Dynamics

Guido Governatori and Antonino Rotolo

Abstract Legal dynamics is an important aspect of legal reasoning that inspired the area of belief revision. While formal models of belief revision have been thoroughly examined, the formalisation of legal dynamics has been mostly neglected. In this contribution we propose Temporal Defeasible Logic to model legal dynamics. We build such a logic in steps starting from basic defeasible logic, and we show how to use it to model different forms of modifications such as derogations, textual modifications, abrogation and annulment.

Keywords Norm change • Legal dynamics • Defeasible logic • Temporal reasoning • Theory revision

12.1 Introduction

One peculiar feature of the law is that it necessarily takes the form of a dynamic normative system (Hart 1994; Kelsen 1991). Despite the importance of norm-change mechanisms, the logical investigation of legal dynamics was for long time underdeveloped. However, research is rapidly evolving and recent contributions exist.

In the 1980s a promising research effort was devoted by Alchourrón, Gärdenfors and Makinson (1985) to develop a logical model (AGM) for also modeling norm change. As is well-known, the AGM framework distinguishes three types of change operation over theories. Contraction is an operation that removes a specified sentence ϕ from a given theory Γ (a logically closed set of sentences) in such a way that Γ is set aside in favor of another theory Γ^-_ϕ which is a subset of Γ not containing ϕ. Expansion operation adds a given sentence ϕ to Γ so that the resulting

G. Governatori (✉)
NICTA and Queensland University of Technology, Brisbane, QLD, Australia
e-mail: guido.governatori@nicta.com.au

A. Rotolo
CIRSFID and Department of Legal Studies, University of Bologna, Bologna, Italy
e-mail: antonino.rotolo@unibo.it

M. Araszkiewicz, K. Płeszka (eds.), *Logic in the Theory and Practice of Lawmaking*, Legisprudence Library 2, DOI 10.1007/978-3-319-19575-9_12

theory Γ_ϕ^+ is the smallest logically closed set that contains both Γ and ϕ. Revision operation adds ϕ to Γ but it is ensured that the resulting theory Γ_ϕ^* be consistent. Alchourrón, Gärdenfors and Makinson argued that, when Γ is a code of legal norms, contraction corresponds to norm derogation (norm removal) and revision to norm amendment.

AGM framework has the advantage of being very abstract but works with theories consisting of simple logical assertions. For this reason, it is perhaps suitable to capture the dynamics of obligations and permissions, not of legal norms. In fact, it is essential to distinguish norms from obligations and permissions (Boella et al. 2009; Governatori and Rotolo 2010): the latter ones are just possible effects of the application of norms and their dynamics do not necessarily require to remove or revise norms, but correspond in most cases to instances of the notion of *norm defeasibility* (Governatori and Rotolo 2010). Very recently, some research has been carried out to reframe AGM ideas within rule-based logical systems, which take this distinction into account (Rotolo 2010; Stolpe 2010). However, also these attempts suffer from some drawbacks, as they fail to handle the following aspects of legal norm change:

1. the law usually regulate its own changes by setting specific norms whose peculiar objective is to change the system by stating what and how other existing norms should be modified;
2. since legal modifications are derived from these peculiar norms, they can be in conflict and so are defeasible;
3. legal norms are qualified by temporal properties, such as the time when the norm comes into existence and belongs to the legal system, the time when the norm is in force, the time when the norm produces legal effects, and the time when the normative effects hold.

Hence, legal dynamics can be hardly modelled without considering defeasibility and temporal reasoning. Some works (see, in particular, Governatori and Rotolo 2010) have attempted to address these research issues. All norms are qualified by the above mentioned different temporal parameters and the modifying norms are represented as defeasible meta-rules, i.e., rules where the conclusions are temporalised rules.

This work reports on this research line and shows how suitable temporal extensions of Defeasible Logic can do a good job in faithfully modelling interesting aspects of legal dynamics.

The layout of the chapter is as follows. In the next section we are going to provide an introduction to Defeasible Logic and to show how to use it for modelling legal knowledge and legal reasoning. In particular in Sect. 12.2.1 we present Basic Defeasible Logic; then in Sect. 12.2.2 we introduce Deontic operators: this allows us to distinguish between constitutive and prescriptive rules and to speak about deontic effects. The next step is to extend the logic obtained so far with time (Sect. 12.2.3). The final logic we describe is the extension with meta-rules rules about rules meant to captures norms about norms, which are essential to model norm dynamics. Section 12.3 first introduces the types of changes we examine in this contribution (Sect. 12.3), and then in Sects. 12.3.2 and 12.3.3 we discuss how textual modifications and derogations are handled by the logic, and to conclude with repeal type modifications (abrogation and annulment, Sects. 12.3.5 and 12.3.7); in Sect. 12.3.6 we also shortly analyse the challenges posed to logical systems by retroactive modifications. Section 12.4 offers a short overview of alternative approaches.

12.2 Logic for Norms

In this section we are going to illustrate and provide the foundations of our logical framework.

Our choice of logic to represent norms falls on Defeasible Logic (Nute 1994). Defeasible Logic is a simple, flexible, extensible non-monotonic formalism.

12.2.1 Basic Defeasible Logic

Knowledge in Defeasible logic is structured in three components:

- A set of facts (corresponding to indisputable statements represented as literals, where a literal is either an atomic proposition or its negation).
- A set of rules. A rule establishes a connection between a set of premises and a conclusion. In particular, for reasoning with norms, it is reasonable to assume that a rule provides the formal representation of a norm. Accordingly, the premises encode the conditions under which the norm is applicable, and the conclusion is the normative effect of the norm.
- A preference relation over the rules. The preference relation just gives the relative strength of rules. It is used in contexts where two rules with opposite conclusions fire simultaneously, and determines that one rule overrides the other in that particular context.

Formally, the knowledge in the logic is organised in Defeasible Theories, where a Defeasible Theory D is a structure

$$(F, R, \prec) \tag{12.1}$$

where F is the set of facts, R is the set of rules, and $\prec$ is a binary relation over the set of rules, i.e., $\prec \subseteq R \times R$.[1]

[1]Defeasible Logic does not impose any property for $\prec$. However, in many application is useful to assume that the transitive closure to be acyclic to prevent situations where, at the same time a rule overrules another rule and it is overridden by it.

As we have alluded to above, a rule is formally a binary relation between, a set premises and a conclusion. Thus if Lit is the set of literals, the set Rule of all rules is:

$$\text{Rule} \subseteq 2^{\text{Lit}} \times \text{Lit}. \tag{12.2}$$

Accordingly, a rule is an expression with the following form[2]:

$$r\colon a_1, \ldots, a_n \hookrightarrow c \tag{12.3}$$

where r is a unique label identifying the rule. Given that a rule is a relation, we can ask what is the strength of the link between the premises and the conclusion. We can distinguish three different strengths: (i) given the premises the conclusion always holds, (ii) given the premises the conclusion holds sometimes, and (iii) given the premises the opposite of the conclusions does not hold. Therefore, to capture theses types Defeasible Logic is equipped with three types of rules: *strict rules*, *defeasible rules* and *defeaters*. We will use $\rightarrow$, $\Rightarrow$ and $\leadsto$ instead of $\hookrightarrow$ to represent, respectively, strict rules, defeasible rules and defeaters. We will continue to use $\hookrightarrow$ for a rule when the strength is either not known or irrelevant.

Given a rule like rule r in (12.3) we use the following notation to refer to the various elements of the rule. $A(r)$ denotes the *antecedent* or *premises* of the rule, in this case, $\{a_1, \ldots, a_n\}$, and $C(r)$ denotes the *conclusion* or *consequent*, that is, c. From time to time we use *head* and *body* of a rule to refer, respectively, to the consequent and to the antecedent of the rule.

Strict rules are rules in the classic sense: whenever the premises are indisputable so is the conclusion. Strict rules can be used to model legal definitions that do not admit exceptions, for example the definition of minor: " 'minor' means any person under the age of eighteen years". This definition can be represented as

$$age(x) < 18yrs \rightarrow minor(x). \tag{12.4}$$

Defeasible Rules are rules such that the conclusions normally or typically follows from the premises, unless there are evidence or reasons to the contrary.

Defeaters are rules that do not support directly the derivation of a conclusion, but that can be used to prevent a conclusion.

Finally, for the *superiority relation*, given two rules r and s, we use $r \prec s$ to indicate that rule r defeats rule s; in other terms, if the two rules are in conflict with each other and they are both applicable, then r prevails over s, and we derive only the conclusion of r.

---

[2]More correctly, we should use $r\colon \{a_1, \ldots, a_n\} \hookrightarrow c$. However, to improve readability, we drop the set notation for the antecedent of rule.

Example 1. We illustrate defeasible rules and defeaters with the help of the definition of complaint from the Australian Telecommunication Consumer Protections Code 2012 TCP-C268_2012 May 2012 (TCPC).

> **Complaint** means an expression of dissatisfaction made to a Supplier in relation to its Telecommunications Products or the complaints handling process itself, where a response or Resolution is explicitly or implicitly expected by the Consumer.
> An initial call to a provider to request a service or information or to request support is not necessarily a Complaint. An initial call to report a fault or service difficulty is not a Complaint. However, if a Customer advises that they want this initial call treated as a Complaint, the Supplier will also treat this initial call as a Complaint.
> If a Supplier is uncertain, a Supplier must ask a Customer if they wish to make a Complaint and must rely on the Customer's response.

Here is a (simplified) formal representation:

$$tcpc_1\colon ExpressionDissatisfaction \Rightarrow Complaint$$

$$tcpc_2\colon InformationCall \Rightarrow \neg Complaint$$

$$tcpc_3\colon ProblemCall, FirstCall \leadsto Complaint$$

$$tcpc_4\colon AdviseComplaint \Rightarrow Complaint$$

where $tcpc_2 \prec tcpc_1$ and $tcpc_4 \prec tcpc_2$.

The first rule $tcpc_1$ sets the basic conditions for something to be a complaint. On the other hand, rule $tcpc_2$ provides an exception to the first rule, and rule $tcpc_4$ is an exception to the exception provided by rule $tcpc_2$. Finally, $tcpc_3$ does not alone warrant the call to be a complaint (though, it does not preclude the possibility that the call turns out to be a complaint; hence the use of a defeater to capture this case).

Defeasible Logic is a constructive logic. This means that at the heart of it we have its proof theory, and for every conclusion we draw from a defeasible theory we can provide a proof for it, giving the steps used to reach the conclusion, and at the same time, providing a (formal) explanation or justification of the conclusion. Furthermore, the logic distinguishes *positive* and *negative* conclusion, and the strength of a conclusion. This is achieved by labelling each step in a derivation with a proof tag. As usual a derivation is a (finite) sequence of formulas, each obtained from the previous ones using inference conditions.

Let D be a Defeasible Theory. The following are the proof tags we consider for basic Defeasible Logic:

- $+\Delta$ if a literal p is tagged by $+\Delta$, then this means that p is provable using only the facts and strict rules in a defeasible theory. We also say that p is *definitely provable* from D.
- $-\Delta$ if a literal p is tagged by $-\Delta$, then this means that p is refuted using only the facts and strict rules in a defeasible theory. In other terms, it indicates that the literal p cannot be proved from D using only facts and strict rules. We also say that p is *definitely refuted* from D.

$+\partial$ if a literal p is tagged by $+\partial$, then this means that p is *defeasibly provable* from D.

$-\partial$ if a literal p is tagged by $-\partial$, then this means that p is *defeasibly refutable* from D.

Some more notation is needed before explaining how tagged conclusions can be asserted. Given a set of rules R, we use R_x to indicate particular subsets of rules: R_s for strict rules, R_d for defeasible rules, R_{sd} for strict or defeasible rules, R_{dft} for defeaters; finally $R[q]$ denotes the rules in R whose conclusion is q.

There are two ways to prove $+\Delta p$ at the n-th step of a derivation: the first is that p is one of the facts of the theory. The second case is when we have a strict rule r for p and all elements in the antecedent of r have been definitely proved at previous steps of the derivation.

For $-\Delta p$ we have to argue that there is no possible way to derive p using facts and strict rules. Accordingly, p must not be one of the facts of the theory, and second for every rule in $R_s[p]$ (all strict rules which are able to conclude p) the rule cannot be applied, meaning that at least one of the elements in the antecedent of the rule has already refuted (definitely refuted). The base case is where the literal to be refuted is not a fact and there are no strict rules having the literal as their head.

Defeasible derivations have a three phases argumentation-like structure.[3] To show that $+\partial p$ is provable at step n of a derivation we have to[4]:

1. give an argument for p;
2. consider all counterarguments for p; and
3. rebut each counterargument by either:

    a. showing that the counterargument is not valid;
    b. providing a valid argument for p defeating the counterargument.

In this context, in the first phase, an argument is simply a strict or defeasible rule for the conclusion we want to prove, where all the elements are at least defeasibly provable. In the second phase we consider all rules for the opposite or complement of the conclusion to be proved. Here, an argument (counterargument) is not valid if the argument is not supported.[5] Here "supported" means that all the elements of the body are at least defeasibly provable.

[3]The relationships between Defeasible Logic and argumentation are, in fact, deeper than the similarity of the argumentation like proof theory. Governatori et al. (2004) prove characterisation theorems for defeasible logic variants and Dung style argumentation semantics (Dung 1995). In addition Governatori (2011) proved that the Carneades argumentation framework (Gordon et al. 2007), widely discussed in the AI and Law literature, turns out to be just a syntactic variant of Defeasible Logic.

[4]Here we concentrate on proper defeasible derivations. In addition we notice that defeasible derivations inherit from definite derivations, thus we can assert $+\partial p$ if we have already established $+\Delta p$.

[5]It is possible to give different definitions of support to obtain variants of the logic tailored for various intuitions of non-monotonic reasoning. Billington et al. (2010) show how to modify the notion of support to obtain variants capturing such intuitions, for example by weakening the

Finally to defeasibly refute a literal, we have to show that either, the opposite is at least defeasible provable, or show that an exhaustive search for a constructive proof for the literal fails (i.e., there are rules for such a conclusion or all rules are either 'invalid' argument or they are not stronger than valid arguments for the opposite).

Example 2. Consider again the set of rules encoding the TCPC 2012 definition of complaint given in Example 1. Assume to have a situation where there is an initial call from a customer who is dissatisfied with some aspects of the service received so far where she asks for some information about the service. In this case rules $tcpc_1$ and $tcpc_2$ are both applicable (we assume that the facts of the case include the union of the premises of the two rules, but *AdviseComplaint* is not a fact). Here, $tcpc_2$ defeats $tcpc_1$, and $tcpc_4$ cannot be used. Hence, we can conclude $-\partial AdviseComplaint$ and consequently $+\partial\neg Complaint$ and $-\partial Complaint$. However, if the customer stated that she wanted to complain for the service, then the fact *AdviseComplaint* would appears in the facts. Therefore we can conclude $+\partial AdviseComplaint$, making then rule $tcpc_4$ applicable, and we can reverse the conclusions, namely: $+\partial Complaint$ and $-\partial\neg Complaint$.

While the Defeasible Logic we outlined in this section and its variants are able to model different features of legal reasoning (e.g., burden of proof (Governatori and Sartor 2010) and proof standards (Governatori 2011) covering and extending the proof standards discussed in Gordon et al. (2007)), we believe that a few important characteristics of legal reasoning are missing. First we do not address the temporal dimension of norms (and, obviously, this is of paramount importance to model norm dynamics), and second, we do not handle the normative character of norms: norms specify what are the obligations, prohibitions and permissions in force and what are the conditions under which they are in force. In the next sections we are going to extend Defeasible Logic with (1) deontic operators, to capture the normative nature of norms and (2) time, to model the temporal dimensions used in reasoning with norms.

12.2.2 Defeasible Deontic Logic

Norms in a normative system can have (among others, but typically) the following functions:

1. to define the terms and concepts used in the normative system, and
2. to prescribe the behaviours the subjects of the normative system are meant to comply with.

requirements for a rule to be supported: instead of being defeasibly provable a rule is supported if it is possible to build a reasoning chain from the facts ignoring rules for the complements.

The distinction just introduced is that of *constitutive* rules and *prescriptive rules.* The "mode" of the behaviours prescribed by the prescriptive rules is determined by deontic modalities (e.g., obligation, prohibition, permission). The Defeasible Logic presented in the previous section accounts for constitutive rules. To model prescriptive rules we have (i) to extend the language with deontic operators (ii) to use again the idea that rules are just binary relations and add a dimension, that is the *mode*, in the classification of rules. Hence rules can be classified according to their strength as well as their mode.

In this contribution we concentrate on the following deontic operators: O, P and F, respectively for obligation, permission and prohibition. In the language of Defeasible Deontic Logic the set of literals Lit is partitioned in *plain literals* and *deontic literals*. A plain literal is a literal in the sense of basic defeasible logic, while a deontic literal is obtained by placing a plain literal in the scope of a deontic operator or a negated deontic operator. Accordingly, expressions like $\mathsf{O}l$, $\neg\mathsf{P}l$ and $\mathsf{F}\neg l$ are deontic literals, where l is plain literal.

In Defeasible Deontic Logic rules are defined with the following signature

$$\text{Rule: } 2^{\text{Lit}} \times \text{PlainLit} \tag{12.5}$$

where PlainLit is the set of all plain literals. This means that the antecedent of a rule can contain both plain and deontic literal, but in any case the conclusion is plain literal. Thus the question is if the conclusions of rules are plain literals, where do we get deontic literals? The answer is that we have two different modes of for the rules. The first mode is that of constitutive rule, where the conclusion is an assertion with the same mode as it appears in the rule (i.e., as an institutional fact); the second mode is that of prescriptive rule, where the conclusion is asserted with a deontic mode (where the deontic mode corresponds to one of the deontic operators). Accordingly, a Defeasible Deontic Theory is a structure

$$(F, R_C, R_{\mathsf{O}}, \prec) \tag{12.6}$$

where R_C is a set of constitutive rules, and R_{O} is a set of prescriptive rules. Constitutive rules behaves as the rules in Basic Defeasible Logic, and we continue to use $\hookrightarrow$ to denote the arrow of a constitutive rule. $\hookrightarrow_{\mathsf{O}}$ for the arrow of a prescriptive rule.

The main idea is that given the constitutive defeasible rule

$$a_1, \ldots, a_n \Rightarrow_C b \tag{12.7}$$

we can assert b, given $a_1, \ldots, a_n$, thus the behaviour of constitutive rule is just the normal behaviour of rules we examined in the previous section. For prescriptive rules the behaviour is a different. From the rule

$$a_1, \ldots, a_n \Rightarrow_{\mathsf{O}} b \tag{12.8}$$

we conclude $\mathsf{O}b$ when we have $a_1, \ldots, a_n$. Thus we conclude the obligation of the consequent of the rule, namely that b is obligatory, i.e., $\mathsf{O}b$, not just the consequent of the rule, i.e., b.[6]

The reasoning mechanism is essentially the same as that of basic defeasible presented in Sect. 12.2.1. The first difference is that an argument can only be attacked by an argument of the same type. Thus if we have an argument consisting of a constitutive rule for p, a counterargument should be a constitutive rule for $\sim p$. The same applies for prescriptive rule. An exception to this is when we have a constitutive rule for p such that all its premises are provable as obligations. In this case the constitutive rule behaves like a prescriptive rule, and can be use as a counterargument for a prescriptive rule for $\sim p$, or the other way around.

Consider, for example, the following two rules

$$r_1\colon a_1, a_2 \Rightarrow_C b \tag{12.9}$$

$$r_2\colon c \Rightarrow_{\mathsf{O}} \neg b. \tag{12.10}$$

The idea expressed by r_1 is that, in a particular normative system, the combination of a_1 and a_2 is recognised as the institutional fact b, while r_2 prohibits b given c. Suppose now that a_1 and a_2 are both obligatory. Under these conditions it is admissible to assert that b is obligatory as well. Accordingly r_1 can be used to conclude $\mathsf{O}b$ instead of simply b. This means that the conclusions of r_1 and r_2 are conflicting: thus r_1, when its premises are asserted as obligation, can be used to counter an argument (e.g., r_2) forbidding b (making $\neg b$ obligatory, or $\mathsf{O}\neg b$).

The second difference is that now the proof tags are labelled with either C, e.g., $+\partial_C p$, (for constitutive conclusions) or with O, e.g., $-\partial_{\mathsf{O}} q$ (for prescriptive conclusions). Accordingly, when we are able to derive $+\partial_{\mathsf{O}} p$ we can say that $\mathsf{O}p$ is (defeasibly) provable.

This feature poses the question of how we model the other deontic operators (i.e., permission and prohibition). As customary in Deontic Logic, we assume the following principles governing the interactions of the deontic operators.[7]

$$\mathsf{O}{\sim}l \equiv \mathsf{F}l \tag{12.11}$$

$$\mathsf{O}l \wedge \mathsf{O}{\sim}l \rightarrow \bot \tag{12.12}$$

$$\mathsf{O}l \wedge \mathsf{P}{\sim}l \rightarrow \bot \tag{12.13}$$

[6]As explained elsewhere (Governatori and Rotolo 2010), we do not add a deontic operator in the consequent of rules (i.e., $a_1, \ldots, a_n \Rightarrow \mathsf{O}b$), but we rather differentiate the mode of conclusions by distinguishing diverse rule types. This choice has a technical motivation: (a) it considerably makes simpler and more compact the proof theory; (b) it allows us to characterise a specific logical consequence relation for O. However, another version of the logic (much more cumbersome) can be adopted where deontic rules have the form $a_1, \ldots, a_n \Rightarrow \mathsf{O}b$ without affecting our treatment of legal dynamics.

[7]In the three formulas below $\rightarrow$ is the material implication of classical logic.

Principle (12.11) provides the equivalence of a prohibition with a negative obligation (i.e., obligation not). The second and the third are rationality postulates stipulating that it is not possible to have that something and its opposite are at the same time obligatory (12.12) and that a normative system makes something obligatory and its opposite is permitted (12.13). Equation (12.11) gives us the immediate answer on how prohibition is modeled. A rule giving a prohibition can be modelled just as a prescriptive rule for a negated literal. This means that to conclude $\mathsf{F}p$ we have to derive $+\partial_{\mathsf{O}}\neg p$, in other terms that $\neg p$ is (defeasibly) provable as an obligation.

Example 3. Section 40 of the Australian Road Rules (ARR)[8]

Making a U–turn at an intersection with traffic lights
A driver must not make a U–turn at an intersection with traffic lights unless there is a U–turn permitted sign at the intersection.

The prohibition of making U-turns at traffic lights can be encoded by the following rule:

$$arr_{40a}\colon \mathit{AtTrafficLigths} \Rightarrow_{\mathsf{O}} \neg \mathit{Uturn}.$$

In a situation where *AtTrafficLights* is given we derive $+\partial_{\mathsf{O}}\neg \mathit{Uturn}$ which corresponds to $\mathsf{F}\mathit{Uturn}$.

The pending issue is how to model permissions. Two types of permissions have been discussed in literature following von Wright (1963), Alchourrón and Bulygin (1984) and Soeteman (1989): (i) weak permission, meaning that there is no obligation to the contrary; and (ii) strong permission, a permission explicitly derogates an obligation to the contrary. In this case we have an exception. For both types of permission we have that the obligation to the contrary does not hold. Defeasible Deontic Logic is capable to handle the two types of permission is a single shot if we establish that $\mathsf{P}p$ is captured by $-\partial_{\mathsf{O}}{\sim}p$. The meaning of $-\partial_{\mathsf{O}}p$ is that p is refuted as obligation, or that it is not possible to prove p as an obligation; hence it means that we cannot establish that p is obligatory, thus there is no obligation contrary to ${\sim}p$.

The final aspect we address is how to model strong permissions. Remember that strong permissions are meant to be exceptions. Exceptions in Defeasible Logic can be easily captured by rules for the opposite plus a superiority relation. Accordingly, this could be modelled by

$$arr_{40e}\colon \mathit{UturnPermittedSign} \Rightarrow_{\mathsf{O}} \mathit{Uturn}.$$

[8]This norm makes use of "must not", to see that "must not" is understood as prohibition in legal documents see, the Australian National Consumer Credit Protection Act 2009, Section 29, whose heading is "Prohibition on engaging in credit activities without a licence", recites "(1) A person must not engage in a credit activity if the person does not hold a licence authorising the person to engage in the credit activity".

and $arr_{40e} \prec arr_{40a}$. We use a prescriptive defeasible rule for obligation to block the prohibition to U-turn. But, since arr_{49e} prevails over arr_{49a}, we derive that U-turn is obligatory, i.e., $+\partial_{\mathsf{O}} Uturn$.

Thus, when permissions derogate to prohibitions (or obligations), there are good reasons to argue that defeaters for O are suitable to express an idea of strong permission.[9] Explicit rules such as $r: a \leadsto_{\mathsf{O}} q$ state that a is a specific reason for blocking the derivation of $\mathsf{O}\neg q$ (but not for proving $\mathsf{O}q$), i.e., this rule does not support any conclusion, but states that $\neg q$ is deontically undesirable. Accordingly, we can rewrite the derogating rule as

$$arr_{40e}\colon UturnPermittedSign \leadsto_{\mathsf{O}} Uturn.$$

In this case, given *UturnPermittedSign* we derive $-\partial_{\mathsf{O}}\neg Uturn$.

For an in-depth presentation of Defeasible Deontic Logic, its properties and a detailed analysis of how to use it to model obligations and permissions (and several ways to do it) we refer the reader to Governatori et al. (2013a).

12.2.3 Defeasible Deontic Logic with Time

The extension of Defeasible Logic with deontic operators makes the the logic more expressive and more capable of representing aspects of legal reasoning insofar as it allows us to consider the important distinction between constitutive rules and prescriptive rules, and to differentiate among normative effects. However, a key element is still missing: time. Very often norms have temporal parameters and Deontic Defeasible Logic is not able to reason about them. In this section we are going to extend the logic with temporal parameters. In particular we are going to *temporalise* the logic. This means that we attach a temporal parameter to the atomic elements of the logic, i.e., to the atomic propositions. For the logic we assume a discrete totally ordered set of instants of time $\mathcal{T} = \{t_0, t_1, t_2, \dots\}$. Based on this we can introduce the notion of *temporalised literals*. Thus if l is a plain literal, i.e., $l \in$ PlainLit, and $t \in \mathcal{T}$ then l^t is a temporalised literals. The intuitive interpretation of l^t is that l is true (or holds) at time t. We use TempLit to denote the set of temporalised literals. Deontic literals are now obtained from temporalised literals using the same conditions as in Sect. 12.2.2; thus a deontic literal is an expression like $\mathsf{O}l^t$, where its natural reading is that l is obligatory at time t, or that the obligation of l is in force at time t. Finally, given a time instant t and $y \in \{pers, tran\}$ (for *persistent* and *transient*) we call the combination of (t, y) *duration specification*, and literals labelled with a duration specification duration literals. A duration literal has the form $l^{(t,y)}$. We denote the set of duration literals DurLit. The set of literals

[9]The idea of using defeaters to introduce permissions was introduced by Governatori et al. (2005b).

is now composed by the set of temporalised literals and the set of deontic literals, namely Lit = DeonLit ∪ TempLit. The signature of rules is now

$$\text{Rule}: 2^{\text{Lit}} \times \text{DurLit} \tag{12.14}$$

this means that a rule has the following form

$$r: a_1^{t_1}, \ldots, a_n^{t_n} \hookrightarrow_X c^{(t,y)} \tag{12.15}$$

where $X \in \{C, \mathsf{O}\}$, specifying whether the rules is a constitutive or a prescriptive one, and $y \in \{tran, pers\}$ indicating whether the conclusion of the rule is either *transient* or *persistent*.

The idea behind the distinction between a transient and persistent conclusion is whether the conclusion is guaranteed to hold for a single instant or it continues to hold until it is terminated. This is particular relevant for prescriptive rules, since their conclusions are obligations (or, in general deontic effects), and obligations, once triggered, remain in force until they are complied with, violated, or explicitly terminated. Accordingly we can use the duration specification $(t, tran)$ to indicate that on obligation is in force at a specific time t, and must be fulfilled at that time, while the duration specification $(t, pers)$ establishes that an obligation enters in force at time t.

The inference mechanism extends that of Defeasible Deontic Logic taking into account the temporal and durations specification. To assert that p holds at time t we have two ways:

1. Give an argument for p at time t'[10];
2. Evaluate all counterarguments against it. Here, we have a few cases:
   a. If the duration specification of p is $(t, tran)$ $(t' = t)$, then, the counterargument must be for the same time t given that p is ensured to hold only for t.
   b. If the duration specification of p is $(t', pers)$, then t' can precede t and we can 'carry' over the conclusion from previous times. In this case, the counterarguments we have to consider are all rules whose conclusion has a duration specification (t'', z) such that $t' \leq t'' \leq t$.
3. Rebut the counterarguments. This is the same as the corresponding step of basic defeasible logic, the only thing to pay attention to is that when we rebut with a stronger argument, the stronger argument should have t'' in the duration specification of the conclusion.

The general idea of the conditions outline above is that, as we have already alluded to, it is possible to assert that something holds at time t, because it did hold at time

[10] We equate arguments with rules, thus this is the same as saying that there is (defeasible) rule such that all the elements in its antecedent are provable and the conclusion is $p^{(t',y)}$.

t', $t' < t$, by persistence, but there must be no reasons to terminate it. Thus new information defeats previous one.

The following example illustrates the intuitions we just described

Example 4. Section 8.2.1.a of the Australian Telecommunications Consumers Protection Code 2012 (TCPC 2012).

> A Supplier must take the following actions to enable this outcome:
>
> (a) **Demonstrate fairness, courtesy, objectivity and efficiency:** Suppliers must demonstrate, fairness and courtesy, objectivity, and efficiency by:
>
> (i) Acknowledging a Complaint:
>
> A. immediately where the Complaint is made in person or by telephone;
> B. within 2 Working Days of receipt where the Complaint is made by email; . . . .

The normative fragment above can be represented by the following set of rules[11]:

$$tcpc_1\text{:}Complaint^t, inPerson^t \Rightarrow_{\mathsf{O}} Acknowledge^{(t,tran)}$$

$$tcpc_2\text{:}Complaint^t \Rightarrow_{\mathsf{O}} Acknowledge^{(t,pers)}$$

$$tcpc_3\text{:}Complaint^t \rightsquigarrow_{\mathsf{O}} \neg Acknowledge^{(t+2d,tran)}$$

Rule $tcpc_1$ covers the case of a complaint made in person of by phone. Given that the complaint must be acknowledged immediately, we can use the duration specification $(t, tran)$, where t is the time when the complaint is received. The *tran* specification implies that the obligation to acknowledge the complain is in force only at t and not acknowledging at t results in a violation. For the case regulated by paragraph B, we use two rules. The first $tcpc_2$ is to initiate the obligation (at the same time t when the complaint is received), while $tcpc_3$ gives the deadline by when the content of the obligation must be fulfilled. Notice that we use a defeater to terminate the obligation. When we have a complaint at time t rule $tcpc_2$ is triggered and we can conclude that there is the obligation to acknowledge the complaint, i.e., $+\partial_{\mathsf{O}} Acknowledge^t$. This obligation persists until it is terminated. To terminate it we need a rule for the opposite, namely a rule for $\neg Acknowledge^{t'}$, $t' > t$. If the rule for the termination were a strict or defeasible rule then from t' we would have the prohibition of acknowledging the complaint from time t'; formally $+\partial_{\mathsf{O}} \neg Acknowledge^{t'}$. On the other hand, a defeater cannot be used to derive a positive conclusion. The defeater allows us to conclude that from t' onwards, we cannot derive the obligation of *Acknowledge*, formally $-\partial_{\mathsf{O}} Acknowledge^{t'}$.

[11]In the following formalisation, we have used $t + 2d$ to indicate the time when a complaint has been received, represented by the variable t, plus 2 days. We formalism we propose is neutral about the representation of time and the granularity used in such a representation. All we need is a representation of time isomorphic to the set of natural numbers. Moreover, the time variables in the rules have to be instantiated with the specific time values.

Suppose we have a complaint by email on day 10. From this we can derive $+\partial_{O}Acknowledge^{10}$ from rule $tcpc_2$. By persistence we have that $+\partial_{O}Acknowledge^{11}$. On day 12 the effect of rule $tcpc_3$ kicks in, and we have $-\partial_{O}Acknowledge^{12}$.

For thorough presentations of temporal defeasible logic, its properties and application to modelling obligation with time and deadlines we refer the reader to Governatori et al. (2005b, 2007a), and Governatori and Rotolo (2013).

12.2.4 From Rules to Meta-rules

The temporal Defeasible Logic just presented allows us to reasons about the times specified inside norms, but it is not able to capture the lifecycle of norms. To obviate this problem Governatori and Rotolo (2010) propose to consider a legal system as a time-series of its versions, where each version is obtained from previous versions by some norm changes, e.g., norms entering in the legal system, modification of existing norms, repeals of existing norms, ... This means that we can represent a legal system LS as a sequence

$$LS(t_1), LS(t_2), \ldots, LS(t_j) \tag{12.16}$$

where each $LS(t_i)$ is the snapshot of the rules (norms) in the legal system at time t_i. Graphically it can be represented by the picture in Fig. 12.1

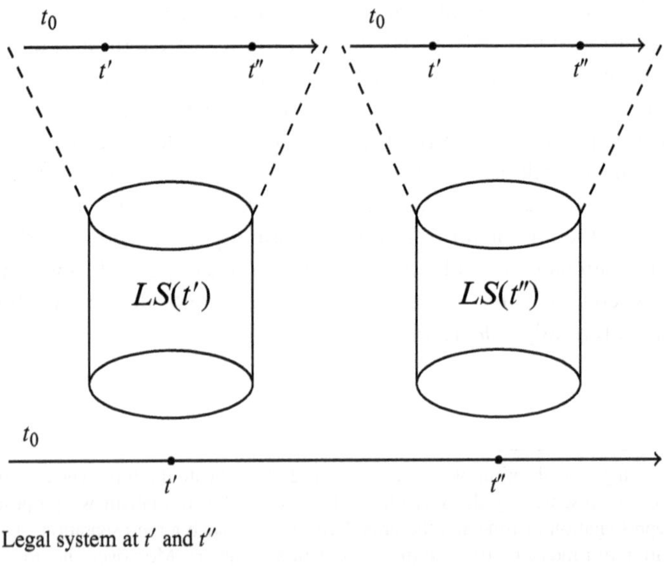

Fig. 12.1 Legal system at t' and t''

A *rule* is a relation between a set of premises (conditions of applicability of the rule) and a conclusion. In this paper the admissible conclusions are either literals or rules themselves; in addition the conclusions and the premises will be qualified with the time when they hold. We consider two classes of rules: *meta-rules* and *proper rules*. Meta-rules describe the inference mechanism of the institution on which norms are formalised and can be used to establish conditions for the creation and modification of other rules or norms, while proper rules correspond to norms in a normative system. In what follows we will use Rule to denote the set of rules, and MetaRules for the set of meta-rules, i.e., rules whose consequent is a rule.

A *temporalised rule* is either an expression $(r\colon \bot)^{(t,x)}$ (the void rule) or $(r\colon \emptyset)^{(t,x)}$ (the empty rule) or $(r\colon A \hookrightarrow_X B)^{(t,x)}$, where r is a rule label, A is a (possibly empty) set of temporalised literals, $X \in \{C, \mathsf{O}\}$, B is a duration literal, $t \in \mathcal{T}$ and $x \in \{tran, pers\}$.

For a transient duration literal $l^{(t,x)}@(t', tran)$ the reading is that the validity of l at t is specific to the legal system corresponding to repository associated to t', while $l^{(t,x)}@(t', pers)$ indicates that the validity of l at t is preserved when we move to legal systems after the legal system identified by t'. An expression $r^{(t,tran)}$ sets the value of r at time t and just at that time, while $r^{(t,pers)}$ sets the values of r for all times instants after t (t included).

The meaning of a temporalised rule $(r\colon A \hookrightarrow B)^{(t,x)}$ is that the rule is effective (i.e., it can produce a conclusion) from time t if $x = pers$ or at time t if $x = tran$. Notice that we have introduced two special rule contents: the *void* rule and the *empty* rule. In both case these rules have an "empty" content, this means that they cannot produce any (legal) effect. The difference between these two rules is that the void rule $(r\colon \bot)^{(t,x)}$ means that the rule "exists" at time t but it is not able to produce any conclusion, while for the empty rule $(r\colon \emptyset)^{(t,x)}$ the intuition is that the rule does not exist at that time. As we shall see in the rest of this contribution, they are needed for technical reasons to distinguish different types of repeals, specifically annulment and abrogation.

We have to consider two temporal dimensions for norms in a normative system. The first dimension is when the norm is in force in a normative system, and the second is when the norm exists in the normative system from a certain viewpoint. So far temporalised rules capture only one dimension, the time of force. Intuitively, the temporal viewpoint represents the temporal version of a legal system LS at a certain time t ($LS(t)$). In this way, we can capture cases where, for example, a legal rule exists in that version $LS(t)$ of the system but can be temporarily ineffective (i.e., it cannot produce effects holding at t) or when a legal rule has been enacted but is not yet in force. To cover this other dimension (the temporal viewpoint) we introduce the notion of temporalised rule with viewpoint. A *temporalised rule with viewpoint* is an expression

$$(r\colon A \hookrightarrow_X B)^{(t,x)}@(t', y), \tag{12.17}$$

where $(r\colon A \hookrightarrow_X B)^{(t,x)}$ is a temporalised rule, $t' \in \mathcal{T}$ and $y \in \{tran, pers\}$.

The meaning of (12.17) is that rule r enters in the legal system at time t', and according to the legal system the rule begins to produce legal effects from time t. In other terms t' is the time when a norm (or more frequently a code containing the norm) is enacted, and t is the commencement date for the norm. This means that the *viewpoint* (t', y) specifies the time when or from when the norm $(r: A \hookrightarrow_X B)^{(t,x)}$ must be considered valid in a given legal system.

Finally, we introduce meta-rules, that is, rules where the conclusion is not a simple duration literal but a temporalised rule. Thus a *meta-rule* is an expression

$$(s: A \hookrightarrow (r: B \hookrightarrow_X C)^{(t',x)})@(t, y), \tag{12.18}$$

where $(r: B \hookrightarrow_X C)^{(t',x)}$ is a temporalised rule, $r \neq s$, $t \in \mathscr{T}$ and $y \in \{tran, pers\}$. Notice that meta-rules carry only the viewpoint time (the validity time) but not the "in force" time. The intuition behind this is that meta-rules yield the conditions to modify a legal system. Thus they specify what rules (norms) are in a normative system, at what time the rules are valid, and the content of the rules. Accordingly, these rules must have an indication when they have been inserted in a normative system, but then they are universal (i.e., apply to all instants) within a particular instance of a normative system.

Example 5. Clause 1.5 (Commencement date) of TCTP 2012 recites:

> Except as provided in this clause 1.5, this Code will commence on the day of registration with the ACMA.
> [...]
> The obligations under clause 4.1.2 will not commence until that date which is 6 months after the date of registration of this Code with the ACMA.

TCPC 2012 was registered with ACMA on 1 September 2012. Accordingly, we can rewrite $tcpc_2$ above as

$$(tcpc_2: Complaint^t \Rightarrow_O Acknowledge^{(t,pers)})^{(1\ \text{Sep}\ 2012, pers)} @(1\ \text{Sep}\ 2012, pers)$$

Notice that in this case the time attached to the rule and the time of the viewpoint are the same. This indicates, following the textual provision, that all clauses in Section 8.2 become effective at the time the Code is enacted.

Similarly, the template for rules formalising clause 4.1.2 is[12]:

$$(tcpc_{4.1.2}: a_1^{t_1}, \ldots, a_n^{t_n} \hookrightarrow_O c^{(t,x)})^{(1\ \text{Mar}\ 2013, pers)} @(1\ \text{Sep}\ 2012, pers)$$

However, in this case, the two timestamps are different $(1\ \text{Sep}\ 2012, pers)$ is the viewpoint which indicates when the Code is registered with ACMA, at which time it

[12]There are many subclauses of clause 4.1.2 and it is well outside the scope of this work to formalise them. Hence, we limit ourselves to formalise a template that has to be instantiated with the appropriate content. In any case, all rules will have the same duration specifications.

begins its legal validity, and the rules encoding clause 4.1.2 are all effective from the date given in the duration specification attached to the rules, i.e., $(1\text{ Mar }2013, \mathit{pers})$.

Every temporalised rule is identified by its rule label and its time. Formally we can express this relationship by establishing that every rule label r is a function

$$r\colon \mathcal{T} \mapsto \text{Rule}. \tag{12.19}$$

Thus a temporalised rule r^t returns the value/content of the rule 'r' at time t. This construction allows us to uniquely identify rules by their labels,[13] and to replace rules by their labels when rules occur inside other rules. In addition there is no risk that a rule includes its label in itself.

Example 6. Let us see how the idea we have just introduced can be use to model the Australian Act No. 22 of 2012 (Superannuation Guarantee (Administration) Amendment Act 2012) registered on 2 April 2012 that defines a schedule for the gradual increase of the percentage of superannuation from 9 % to 12 % over 7 years.

(2) The charge percentage for a quarter in a year described in column 1 of an item of the table is the number specified in column 2 of the item.

Charge percentage (unless reduced under section 22 or 23)		
Item	**Column 1** **Year**	**Column 2** **Charge percentage**
1	Year starting on 1 July 2013	9.25
2	Year starting on 1 July 2014	9.5
3	Year starting on 1 July 2015	10
4	Year starting on 1 July 2016	10.5
5	Year starting on 1 July 2017	11
6	Year starting on 1 July 2018	11.5
7	Year starting on or after 1 July 2019	12

The schedule can be represented as follows:

$$gsc\colon (Salary^t, \neg Theshold^t \Rightarrow_{\mathsf{O}} Contribution \geq 9.25\,\%^{(t,tran)})^{(1\text{ Jul }2013,pers)} \tag{12.20}$$

$$gsc\colon (Salary^t, \neg Threshold^t \Rightarrow_{\mathsf{O}} Contribution \geq 9.5\,\%^{(t,tran)})^{(1\text{ Jul }2014,pers)} \tag{12.21}$$

$$\dots$$

$$gsc\colon (Salary^t, \neg Threshold^t \Rightarrow_{\mathsf{O}} Contribution \geq 12\,\%^{(t,tran)})^{(1\text{ Jul }2019,pers)} \tag{12.22}$$

[13]We do not need to impose that the function is injective: while each label should have only one content at any given time, we may have that different labels (rules) have the same content.

Let us examine the meaning of the above expressions. The general idea is that when an employer pays an instalment of the salary of an employee, that employer has to contribute (at least) the percentage of salary in the schedule for the part of the salary less than the maximum salary guaranteed superannuation contribution threshold to the employee superannuation. In other terms the (temporalised) rule *gsc* specifies how to compute the employer contribution. From 1 July 2013 to 30 June 2014 the recipe to compute the contribution is given by the rule in (12.20). Then from 1 July 2014 (12.21) is superseded by the rule in (12.21), which can be used until 30 June 2015, and which will be replaced by the rule for the 2015–2016 fiscal year, and so on until we reach 1 July 2019 when the rule in (12.22) is used. This shows that the expressions in (12.20)–(12.22) are different temporal manifestations of the same rule, the rule whose label/name is *gsc*.

In the same way a temporalised rule is a function from $\mathscr{T}$ to Rule, we will understand a temporalised rule with viewpoint as a function with the following signature:

$$\mathscr{T} \mapsto (\mathscr{T} \mapsto \text{Rule}). \tag{12.23}$$

As we have seen above a legal system LS is a sequence of versions $LS(t_0), LS(t_1), \ldots$. The temporal dimension of viewpoint corresponds to a version while the temporal dimension temporalising a rule corresponds to the time-line inside a version. Thus the meaning of an expression $r^{t_v} @ t_r$ is that we take the value of the temporalised rule r^{t_v} in $LS(t_r)$. Accordingly, a version of LS is just a repository (set) of norms (implemented as temporal functions). Accordingly, given a rule r, the expression $r^t @ t'$ gives the value of the rule (set of premises and conclusion of the rule) at time t in the repository t'.

Remark 1. The content of a void rule, e.g., $(r\colon \bot)^t @ t'$ is $\bot$, while for the empty rule the value is the empty set. This means that the void rule has a value for the combination of the temporal parameters, while for the empty rule, the content of the rule does not exist for the given temporal parameters. Another way to look at the difference between the empty rule and the void rule is to consider that a rule is a relationship between a set of premises and a conclusion. For the void rule this relationship is between the empty set of premises and the empty conclusion; thus the rule exists but it does not produce any conclusion. For the empty rule, the relationship is empty, thus there is no rule. Alternatively, we can think of the function corresponding to temporalised rules as a partial function, and the empty rule identifies instants when the rule is not defined.

We will often identify rules with their labels, and, when unnecessary, we will drop the labels of rules inside meta-rules. Similarly, to simplify the presentation and when possible, we will only include the specification whether an element is persistent or transient only for the elements for which it is relevant for the discussion at hand.

Example 7. Let us use the Superannuation Guarantee (Administration) Amendment Act 2012 again to illustrate the intuition behind the notion of temporalised rule with viewpoint. The Act amends the Superannuation Guarantee (Administration) Act 1992 of 22 December 1992 where the compulsory superannuation contribution was introduced and initially fixed to 3 % with predefined steppings to reach 9 % after 10 years. Accordingly, we can represent *gsc* as follows:

$$gsc\colon (Salary^t, \neg Theshold^t \Rightarrow_O \\ Contribution \geq 3\,\%^{(t,tran)})^{(1\text{ Jul }1994,pers)}@(22\text{ Dec }1992, pers) \tag{12.24}$$

$$\dots$$

$$gsc\colon (Salary^t, \neg Theshold^t \Rightarrow_O \\ Contribution \geq 9\,\%^{(t,tran)})^{(1\text{ Jul }2002,pers)}@(22\text{ Dec }1992, pers) \tag{12.25}$$

$$gsc\colon (Salary^t, \neg Theshold^t \Rightarrow_O \\ Contribution \geq 9.25\,\%^{(t,tran)})^{(1\text{ Jul }2013,pers)}@(2\text{ Apr }2012, pers) \tag{12.26}$$

$$gsc\colon (Salary^t, \neg Theshold^t \Rightarrow_O \\ Contribution \geq 9.5\,\%^{(t,tran)})^{(1\text{ Jul }2014,pers)}@(2\text{ Apr }2012, pers) \tag{12.27}$$

$$\dots$$

$$gsc\colon (Salary^t, \neg Theshold^t \Rightarrow_O \\ Contribution \geq 12\,\%^{(t,tran)})^{(1\text{ Jul }2019,pers)}@(2\text{ Apr }2012, pers) \tag{12.28}$$

The instances of the rule in (12.24)–(12.25) correspond to the schedule enacted in 1992 and effective from 1 July 1994. The instances in (12.26)–(12.28) implement the schedule, valid from 2 April 2012, amending the 1992 Act, and effective from 1 July 2013. The idea that a temporalised rule with viewpoint is a function with the signature given in (12.23) is as follows: take a date, let us say 1 January 1993; based on the value of the date, we can retrieve all instances of the rule *gsc* as determined by the Act valid at that time. For the date at hand this gives us

$$gsc@(1\text{ Jan }1992) = \left\{gsc^{(1\text{ Jul }1994,pers)}, \dots, gsc^{(1\text{ Jul }2002,pers)}\right\}.$$

In other terms the function corresponding to the rule returns the set of instances of the rule in (12.24)–(12.25). Now we can ask what is the percentage of the compulsory employer contribution at a particular time. For the sake of the example we consider two dates: 1 February 1993 and 1 October 2010. Let us consider the first one:

$$gsc^{(1\text{ Feb }1993)}@(1\text{ Jan }1992) = \bot.$$

In this case we get the void rule. The rule exists in the legal system, but it is not in force at that time, this is different from having $\emptyset$, i.e., the empty rule, meaning that there is no rule, see Remark 1 above.

When we consider the second date, we get:

$$gsc^{(1\text{ Oct }2010)}@(1\text{ Jan }1992) = \mathit{Salary}^t, \neg \mathit{Threshold}^t \Rightarrow_O \mathit{Contribution} \geq 9\,\%^{(t,tran)}$$

specifying that eligible employers are entitled to a minimum compulsory superannuation contribution of 9 % of their salary.

Meta-rules describe the inference mechanism of the institution on which norms are formalised and can be used to establish conditions for the creation and modification of other rules or norms, while proper rules correspond to norms in a normative system. Thus a temporalised rule r^t gives the 'content' of the rule 'r' at time t; in legal terms it tells us that norm r is in force at time t. The expression

$$(p^{t_p}, q^{t_q} \Rightarrow (p^{t_p} \Rightarrow_O s^{(t_s,pers)})^{(t_r,pers)})@(t, tran) \tag{12.29}$$

means that, for the repository at t, if p is true at time t_p and q at time t_q, then $p^{t_p} \Rightarrow_O s^{(t_s,pers)}$ is in force from time t_r onwards.

Example 8. Clause 1.5 of TCPC 2012 (see Example 5 above) is itself a norm. Its effect is to determine when the other norms/clauses in the Code are effective. Thus an alternative is to use meta-rules to model the conditions specified by it. Accordingly,

$$tcpc_{1.5/tcpc_2}\colon (\Rightarrow$$
$$(tcpc_2\colon \mathit{Complaint}^t \Rightarrow_O \mathit{Acknowledge}^{(t,pers)})^{(1\text{ Sep }2012,pers)})@(1\text{ Sep }2012, pers)$$
$$tcpc_{1.5/tcpc_{4.1.2}}\colon (\Rightarrow$$
$$(tcpc_{4.1.2}\colon a_1^{t_1}, \ldots, a_n^{t_n} \hookrightarrow_O c^{(t,x)})^{(1\text{ Mar }2013,pers)})@(1\text{ Sep }2012, pers)$$

Rule $tcpc_{1.5/tcpc_2}$ specifies that the norm encoded by rule $tcpc_2$ commences its efficacy at the same time when the code is registered; while rule $tcpc_{1.5/tcpc_{4.1.2}}$ establishes that the provisions in section 4.1.2 (and the corresponding rules) are effective from 1 March 2013.

A legal system is represented by a temporalised defeasible theory, called *normative theory*, i.e., a structure

$$(F, R, R^{\text{meta}}, \prec) \tag{12.30}$$

where F is a finite set of facts (i.e., fully temporalised literals), R is a finite set of prescriptive and constitutive rules, R^{meta} is a finite set of meta rules, and $\prec$, the superiority relation over rules is formally defined as $\mathcal{T} \mapsto (\mathcal{T} \mapsto \text{Rule} \times \text{Rule})$.

accounting that we can have different instances of the superiority relation depending on the legal systems (external time) and the time when the rules involved in the superiority are evaluated.[14]

In the current logic a conclusion has a form like: $+\partial t@t'\ p^{t_p}$, meaning that the conclusion that p holds at time t_p is derivable at time t using the information included in the version of the legal system at time t'.

The inference mechanism with meta-rules is essentially an extension of that of temporal defeasible logic, but it involves more steps. Rules are no longer just given, but they can be derived from meta-rules. Thus to prove $+\partial t@t' p^{t_p}$ the first thing to do is to see if it is possible to derive a rule r having p^{t_p} as its head. But we have to derive such rule at the appropriate time. Here, we want to remember that a rule is a function from time (validity time or version of a legal system) to time (when a rule is in force in a version of a legal system) to the content of the rule (relationship between a set of premises and a conclusion). The basic intuition is that a rule corresponds to a norm, and there could be several modifications of a norm, thus deriving a rule means to derive one of such modifications. As we shall see in the next section a meta-rule (or more generally a set of meta-rules) can be used to encode a modification of a norm. In general it is possible to have multiple (conflicting) modifications of a norm. Accordingly, to derive a rule, we have to check that there are no conflicting modifications[15] or the conflicting modifications are weaker than the current modification. The final consideration is that in this case we have two temporal dimensions, and the persistence applies to both. Thus we can have persistence inside a legal system, thus we can conclude $+\partial t''@t'\ p^{t_p}$ from $+\partial t@t'\ p^{t_p}$, where $t < t''$ as well as persistence over versions, thus $+\partial t@t''\ p^{t_p}$ from $+\partial t@t'\ p^{t_p}$, where $t' < t''$.

12.3 Modelling Legal Changes

12.3.1 Types of Legal Change

Norm changes in the law can be explicit or implicit (Governatori and Rotolo 2010; Governatori et al. 2005a, 2007b):

Explicit: The law introduces norms whose peculiar objective is to change the system by specifying what and how other existing norms should be modified;

Implicit: the legal system is revised by introducing new norms which are not specifically meant to modify previous norms, but which change in fact the system

---

[14]For instance, if we have $s \prec^{2007}_{Monday} r$ and $r \prec^{2007}_{Tuesday} s$, it means that, according to the regulation in force in 2007, on Mondays rule s is stronger than rule r, but on Tuesdays r is stronger than s.

[15]Two meta-rules are conflicting, when the two meta-rules have the same rule as their head, but with a different content.

because they are incompatible with such existing norms and prevail over them. (The new norms prevail because, for example, have a higher ranking status in the hierarchy of the legal sources or because have been subsequently enacted.)

While investigating implicit changes is interesting, when we deal with explicit modifications we can more easily classify a large number of modification types. In general, we have different types of modifying norms, as their effects (the resulting modifications) may concern, for example, the text of legal provisions, their scope, or their time of force, efficacy, or applicability, or their own existence or validity (Governatori et al. 2005a, 2007b; Guastini 1998).

In our analysis derogation is an example of scope change: a norm n supporting a conclusion p and holding at the national level may be derogated by a norm n' supporting a different conclusion p' within a regional context. Hence, derogation corresponds to introducing one or more exceptions to n.[16]

Temporal changes impact on the target norm in regard to its date of force (the time when the norm is formally binding and "usable"), date of effectiveness (when the norm in fact produces its legal effects) or date of application (when conditions of norm applicability hold): the time of force is meant standardly to indicate when the norm is formally valid in a legal system, the time of effectiveness is when the effects of a norm hold (a norm in force since yesterday can generate obligations that hold from tomorrow onwards), the time of application is when the applicability condition of a norm hold (a norm in force since yesterday is made applicable by conditions occurring today and thus generates for this reason obligations that will hold from tomorrow onwards). An example of change impacting on time of force is when a norm n is originally in force in 2007 but a modification postpones n to 2008.

Substitution is an example of textual modification, as it generically replaces some textual components of a provision with other components. For instance, some of its applicability conditions are replaced by other conditions.

Finally, we have modifications on norm validity and existence, such as abrogation and annulment. For instance, an annulment is usually seen as a kind of repeal (in several system being typically made through the judgment of constitutional courts), as it makes a norm invalid and removes it from the legal system. As we will see, its peculiar effect applies *ex tunc*: annulled norms are prevented to produce all their legal effects, independently of when they are obtained.

[16]In this way, we detach from the terminology adopted in several legal systems and accepted, e.g., by Alchourrón and Makinson (1981, 1982) and Alchourrón and Bulygin (1981). Indeed, since we clearly distinguish the dynamics of obligations and permissions from the ones of legal norms, we can identify various reasons for undoing legal effects by manipulating the same set of legal norms: when legal effects are undone via adding exceptions, we will have derogations, when they are undone via norm removal we will have annulments or abrogations, etc. See below and, for further references, cf. Governatori et al. (2005a) and Stolpe (2010).

12.3.2 Modifications of Scope: Derogation

Derogations are modifications of norm scope. A fictional example from the Italian constitution (enacted in 1948) is the following:

Example 9 (Derogation).

> [**Target of the modification**] Article 3 (1) All citizens have equal social status and are equal before the law, without regard to their sex, race, language, religion, political opinions, and personal or social conditions.
>
> [**Modification enacted in 2014 and effective in 2015**] In derogation to the provisions set out in Article 3, paragraph 1, of the Constitution, the citizens who are resident in Bologna may have different social status, but this modification will be effective only in 2015, when Italy will be no longer in EU.

From the logical point of view, derogation can be simply modeled by adding exceptions, in particular defeaters. Using meta-rules, Example 9 can be captured as follows.[17]

Example 10 (Derogation (continued)). Let $D = (F, R, R^{meta}, \prec)$ be a normative theory such that

$$Art.\ 3\colon (Citizen^x \Rightarrow_{\mathsf{O}} Equal\_status^x)^{(1948,pers)}@(1948,tran) \in R$$

Example 9 is modeled by stating that R^{meta} includes the following meta-rule

$$derog_{Art.\,3}\colon (\sim EU^x \Rightarrow$$
$$(r'\colon Citizen^x, Resident\_Bologna^x \rightsquigarrow_{\mathsf{O}} \sim Equal\_status^x)^{(2015,pers)})@(2014,pers)$$

and that $\prec$ is as follows (where $t \geq 2015$)[18]:

$$\{s \prec^{2014}_{2015} r'\colon s \in R[Equal\_status^x] \text{ and } A(s) \cap \partial^-(D) \neq \emptyset\} \in \prec$$

$$\{mr \prec^{2014}_{2015} derog_{Art.\,3}\colon mr \in R^{meta}[\sim r^t] \text{ and } A(mr) \cap \partial^-(D) \neq \emptyset\} \in \prec$$

Notice that the above conditions on $\prec$ ensures that this operation minimises the impact of the added meta-rule and the related defeater. In fact, the operation works on art. 3 (and any other similar provision) only when any conflicting meta-rule and art. 3 are applicable.

---

[17] In the remainder of the paper, when temporal parameters are not essential we will not specify them and will just add a superscript x.

[18] Recall that, for any rule s, $A(s)$ denotes the set of antecedents of s, while $\partial^-(D)$ stands for the set of negative conclusions of the theory D. i.e., the literals occurring in conclusions of the form $-\partial$.

12.3.3 Textual Modifications: Substitution

Consider a textual modification such as substitution, which typically replaces some textual components of a provision with other textual components. Another fictional (but this time reasonable!) example from the Italian constitution is the following:

Example 11 (Substitution).

> [**Target of the modification**] Article 3 (1) All citizens have equal social status and are equal before the law, without regard to their sex, race, language, religion, political opinions, and personal or social conditions.
>
> [**Modification enacted and effective in 2014**] In the Article 3, paragraph 1 of the Italian constitution the expression "citizens" is replaced with "human beings".

This can be represented by the normative theory $D = (F, R, R^{meta}, \prec)$ such that

$$Art.\ 3\colon (Citizen^{x} \Rightarrow_{\mathsf{O}} Equal\_status^{x})^{(1948,pers)}\,@\,(1948, tran) \in R,$$

the substitution is modelled by the following meta-rule in R^{meta}

$$sub_{Art.\,3}\colon (\Rightarrow (Art.\ 3\colon Human\_being^{x} \Rightarrow_{\mathsf{O}} Equal\_status^{x})^{(2014,pers)})\,@\,(2014, pers)$$

and $\prec$ is as follows (where $t \geq 2014$):

$$\{s \prec^{2014}_{2014} Art.\ 3^{2014}\colon s \in R[Equal\_status^{x}] \text{ and } A(s) \cap \partial^{-}(D) \neq \emptyset\} \in \prec$$
$$\{sub_{Art.\,3} \prec^{2014}_{2014} Art.\ 3^{2013}\} \in \prec$$
$$\{mr \prec^{2014}_{t} sub^{2014}_{Art.\,3}, mr \in R^{meta}[\sim Art.\ 3^{2014}] \text{ and } A(mr) \cap \partial^{-}(D) \neq \emptyset\} \in \prec .$$

12.3.4 Temporal Modifications

Temporal modifications are performed by meta-rules that change norms in regard to their time of force, efficacy, or applicability. Consider this example:

Example 12 (Temporal modification).

> [**Target of the modification**] Legislative Act n. 124, 23 July 2008.
> [...]
> Art. 8. This legislative act is in force since the date of publication of the *Gazzetta Ufficiale* [23 August 2008]
>
> [**Modification enacted and effective at 1 August 2008**] Legislative Act n. 124, 23 July 2008 is in force since 1 January 2009.

Example 12 is reconstructed as follows.

Example 13 (Temporal modification (continued)). For the sake of simplicity, assume that the content of Legislative Act n. 124 is $a_1^x, \dots a_n^x \Rightarrow_O b^x$. Hence, we have that R^{meta} contains the following meta-rule modeling the enactment of Legislative Act n. 124;

$$mr: (\Rightarrow (L.\ 124 : a_1^x, \dots a_n^x \Rightarrow_O b^x)^{(23\text{ Aug }2008, pers)})@(23\text{ Jul }2008, pers).$$

The modification at hand is expressed by having in R^{meta} other two meta-rules mr' and mr'' such that

$$temp'_{L.\ 124}: (\rightsquigarrow \sim(L.\ 124{:}\ a_1^x, \dots a_n^x \Rightarrow_O b^x)^{(23\text{ Aug }2008, pers)})@(1\text{ Aug }2008, pers)$$

$$temp''_{L.\ 124}: (\Rightarrow (L.\ 124{:}\ a_1^x, \dots a_n^x \Rightarrow_O b^x)^{(1\text{ Jan }2009, pers)})@(1\text{ Aug }2008, pers)$$

such that $(temp'_{L.\ 124} \prec^{23\text{ Aug }2008}_{1\text{ Aug }2008} mr) \in \prec$.

12.3.5 Modifications on Norm Validity and Existence: Annulment vs. Abrogation

The expression *repeal* is sometimes used to generically denote the operation of norm withdrawal. However, at least two forms of withdrawal are possible: annulment and abrogation.

An *annulment* makes the target norm invalid and removes it from the legal system. Its peculiar effect applies *ex tunc*: annulled norms are prevented to produce all their legal effects, independently of when they are obtained. Annulments typically operate when the grounds (another norm) for annulling are hierarchically higher in the legal system than the target norm which is annulled: consider when a legislative provision is annulled (typically by the Constitutional Court) because it violates the constitution.

An *abrogation* works differently; the main point is usually that abrogations operate *ex nunc* and so do not cancel the effects that were obtained from the target norm before the modification. If so, it seems that abrogations cannot operate retroactively. In fact, if a norm n_1 is abrogated in 2012, its effects are no longer obtained after then. But, if a case should be decided at time 2013 but the facts of the case are dated 2011, n_1, if applicable, will anyway produce its effects because the facts held in 2011, when n_1 was still in force (and abrogations are not retroactive). Accordingly, n_1 is still in the legal system, even though is no longer in force after 2012. Abrogations typically operate when the grounds (another norm) for abrogating is placed at the same level in the hierarchy of legal sources of the target norm which is abrogated: consider when a legislative provision is abrogated by a subsequent legislative act.

Consider this case:

Example 14 (Abrogation vs Annulment).

> [**Target of the modification**] Legislative Act n. 124, 23 July 2008
> Art. 1. With the exception of the cases mentioned under the Articles 90 and 96 of the Constitution, criminal proceedings against the President of the Republic, the President of the Senate, the President of the House of Representatives, and the Prime Minister, are suspended for the entire duration of tenure. [...]

In case of abrogation, we could have that the legislator enacts the following provision:

> [**Abrogation enacted and effective at 1 January 2011**] Legislative Act n. 124, 23 July 2008 is abrogated.

In case of (judicial) annulment, we would rather have

> [**Annulment enacted and effective at 1 January 2011**] On account of Art. 3 of the Constitution [...] the Constitutional Court hereby declares the constitutional illegitimacy of Art. 1 of the Act n. 124, 23 July 2008.

As we have recalled, the difference between the two cases is that the annulment has retroactive effects. In particular, let us focus on the following provisions from the Italian penal code:

> Art. 157 Italian Penal Code – Terms of statute-barred penal provisions.
> When the the terms for statute-barred penal effects expire, the corresponding crime is canceled [...]
> Art. 158 Italian Penal Code – Effectiveness of the terms of statute-barred penal provisions
> The effectiveness of terms of statute-barred penal provisions begins starting from the time when the crime was committed.
> Art. 159 Italian Penal Code – Suspension of time limits for statute-barred penal effects.
> The terms for statute-barred penal effects [...] are suspended whenever the criminal proceedings are suspended under any legislative provisions [...]

Consider a hypothetical case where the Italian Prime Minister is accused in 2007 of accepting bribes at the beginning of 2006. Clearly, if Legislative Act n. 124 is abrogated in 2011, since abrogation has no retroactive effects, art. 159 of Italian Penal Code applied from 2008 to 2011, and so the counting of terms has been suspended between these two years. Hence, from the perspective of 2011 (immediately after the abrogation) the relevant time passed is 2 years and 6 months (2006, 2007, and until July 2008). Instead, if the act is annulled in 2011, more time has passed from the perspective of 2011, because it is as if the Legislative Act n. 124 were never enacted: from 2006 until 2011.

As we can see, modeling retroactive legal modifications is far from obvious. The logical model proposed in Governatori and Rotolo (2010) and recalled in Sect. 12.2.3 offers a solution. In the next section we will illustrate the intuition and apply to the above example of annulment and abrogation.

12.3.6 *Intermezzo: Temporal Dynamics and Retroactivity*

As we have previously argued, if $t_0, t_1, \ldots, t_j$ are points in time, the dynamics of a legal system LS can be captured by a time-series $LS(t_0), LS(t_1), \ldots, LS(t_j)$ of its versions. Each version of LS is like a norm repository: the passage from one repository to another is effected by legal modifications or simply by temporal persistence. This model is suitable for modeling complex modifications such as retroactive changes, i.e., changes that affect the legal system with respect to legal effects which were also obtained before the legal change was done.

The dynamics of norm change and retroactivity need to fully make use of the time-line within each version of LS (the time-line placed on top of each repository in Fig. 12.2). Clearly, retroactivity does not imply that we can really change the past: this is "physically" impossible. Rather, we need to set a mechanism through which we are able to reason on the legal system from the viewpoint of its current version but *as if* it were revised in the past: when we change some $LS(i)$ retroactively, this does not mean that we modify some $LS(k)$, $k < i$, but that we move back from the perspective of $LS(i)$. Hence, we can "travel" to the past along this inner time-line, i.e., from the viewpoint of the current version of LS where we modify norms.

Figure 12.2 shows a case where the legal system LS and its norm r persist from time t' to time t'' and can have effects immediately from t'. Now, the figure represents the situation where r is retroactively repealed at t'' by stating that the modification applies from t_a (which is between t' and t'') onwards. The difference between abrogation and annulment is illustrated with some details in Fig. 12.3a, b.

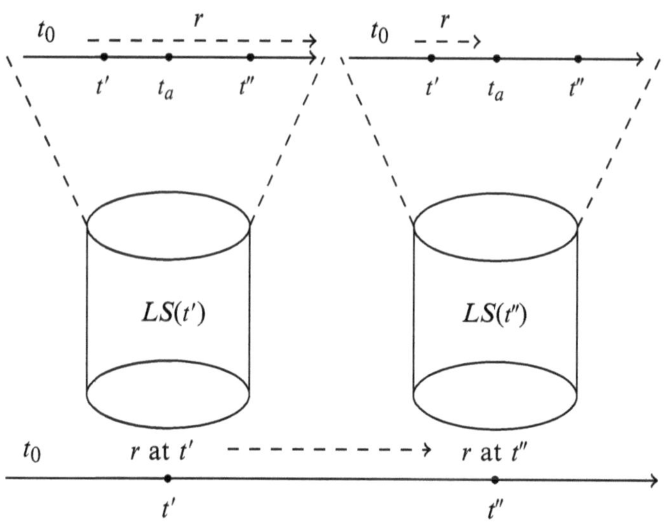

Fig. 12.2 Legal system at t' and t''

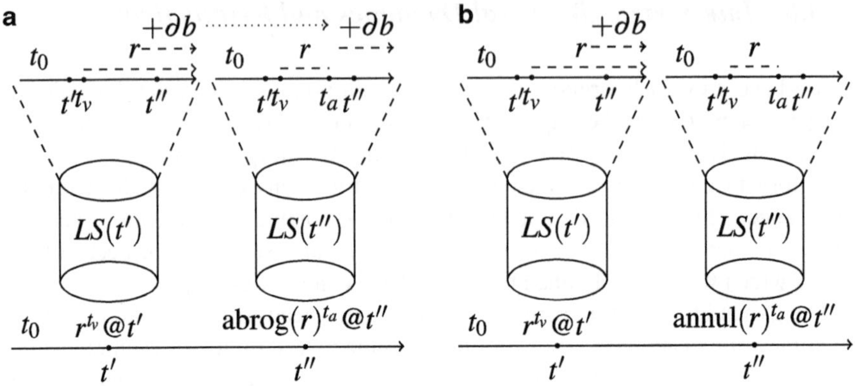

Abrogation. In $LS(t')$ rule r produces a persistent effect b. Literal b carries over by persistence to $LS(t'')$ even if r is no longer in force.

Annulment. In $LS(t')$ rule r is applied and produces a persistent effect b. Since r is annulled in $LS(t'')$, b must be undone as well.

Fig. 12.3 Abrogation and annulment

The reader should bear in mind that the "real" time-line is the one from $LS(t')$ and $LS(t'')$, which is represented by the temporal arrow below the repositories. As we can easily notice, the two cases of annulment and abrogation are quite similar except in regard to the behaviour of the literal b, i.e., the legal effect of the norm r. Indeed, the nature of this retroactive annulment is that it is performed at t'' (with respect to the past time t_a) and this operation removes b since t_a without any additional legislative or administrative act. This is the reason why b does not appear in $LS(t'')$ and is not propagated there from $LS(t')$. On the contrary, an abrogation at t_a does not block the propagation of b from one repository to the subsequent one.

12.3.7 Modifications on Norm Validity and Existence: Annulment vs. Abrogation (Continued)

On account of our previous considerations, the cases in Example 14 can be reconstructed as follows.

Example 15 (Abrogation vs Annulment (continued)). First of all, for the sake of simplicity let us

- only consider the case of Prime Minister (Legislative Act n. 124 mentions other institutional roles),
- assume that the dates of enactment and effectiveness coincide and are generically 2008,

- the duration of tenure covers a time span from 2008 to 2012,

and formalize the corresponding fragment of art. 1 of Legislative Act n. 124 (23 July 2008) as follows:

$$L.\ 124\colon (Crime^{x}, Tenure^{x+y} \Rightarrow_{\mathsf{O}} Suspended^{(x+y,tran)})^{(2008,pers)})@(2008, pers)$$

The duration of tenure spanning from 2008 to 2012 is represented as follows:

$$r1\colon (Elected^{2008} \Rightarrow_{\mathsf{O}} Tenure^{(2008,pers)})^{(2008,pers)})@(2008, pers)$$

$$r2\colon (Elected^{2008} \rightsquigarrow_{\mathsf{O}} \neg Tenure^{2012})^{(2008,pers)})@(2008, pers)$$

Arts. 157–159 of the Italian Penal Code state the following:

$$Art.\ 157\colon (Crime^{x}, Terms^{x+y} \Rightarrow_{\mathsf{O}} CrimeCancelled^{(x+y,pers)})^{(z,pers)})@(z, pers)$$

$$Art.\ 158\colon (Crime^{x} \Rightarrow_{\mathsf{O}} Terms^{(x,pers)})^{(z,pers)})@(z, pers)$$

$$Art.\ 159\colon (Crime^{x}, Suspended^{x+y} \Rightarrow_{\mathsf{O}} \neg Terms^{(x+y,tran)})^{(z,pers)})@(z, pers)$$

As proposed by Governatori and Rotolo (2010), the distinction between abrogation and annulment requires to distinguish between *void* rules and *empty* rules. The content of a void rule, e.g., $(r\colon \bot)^{t}@t'$ is $\bot$, while for the empty rule the value is the empty set. This means that the void rule has value for the combination of the temporal parameters, while for the empty rule, the content of the rule does not exist for the given temporal parameters.

Given a rule $(r\colon A \Rightarrow b^{t_b})^{t_r}@t$, the abrogation of r at t_a in repository t' is basically obtained by having in the theory the following meta-rule

$$(abr_r\colon \Rightarrow (r\colon \bot)^{(t_a,pers)})@(t', pers) \tag{12.31}$$

where $t' > t$. The abrogation simply terminates the applicability of the rule. More precisely this operation sets the rule to the void rule. The rule is not removed from the system, but it has now a form where no longer can produce effects. In the case of the Legislative Act n. 124 (23 July 2008) we would have

$$(abr_{L.\ 124}\colon \Rightarrow (L.\ 124\colon \bot)^{(2011,pers)})@(2011, pers)$$

Hence, we can derive, for example

- $+\partial_{\mathsf{O}} x@x\ Suspended^{x}$, $2008 \leq x \leq 2010$;
- $-\partial_{\mathsf{O}} x@x\ Terms^{x}$, $2008 \leq x \leq 2010$;
- $-\partial_{\mathsf{O}} 2011@2011\ Suspended^{2011}$;
- $+\partial_{\mathsf{O}} 2011@2011\ Terms^{2011}$.

This is in contrast to what we do for annulment where the rule to be annulled is set to the empty rule. This essentially amounts to removing the rule from the repository. From the time of the annulment the rule has no longer any value. All past effects are thus blocked as well.

The definition of a modification function for annulment depends on the underlying variants of the logic, in particular whether conclusions persist across repositories. Minimally, the operation requires the introduction of a meta-rule setting the rule r to be annulled to $\emptyset$, with the time when the rule is annulled and the time when the meta-rule is inserted in the legal system:

$$(annul_r\colon \Rightarrow (r\colon \emptyset)^{(t_a, pers)})@(t', pers) \tag{12.32}$$

Hence,

$$(annul_{L.\ 124}\colon \Rightarrow (L.\ 124\colon \emptyset)^{(2008, pers)})@(2011, pers)$$

If we assume that conclusions persist over repositories we need some additional technical machinery to block pasts effects from previous repositories. In this case, since *L.* 124 is modeled as a transient rule, we have basically to add a defeater like the following[19]:

$$((annul_{ef}\colon \leadsto_{\mathsf{O}} \neg Suspended^{2008})^{(2008, pers)})@(2011, pers)$$

Hence, we now have, for example

- $-\partial_{\mathsf{O}} x@2011\ Suspended^x$, $2008 \le x$;
- $+\partial_{\mathsf{O}} x@2011\ Terms^x$, $2008 \le x$.

12.4 State of the Art

Alchourrón and Makinson were the first to logically study the changes of a legal code (Alchourrón and Bulygin 1981; Alchourrón and Makinson 1981, 1982). The addition of a new norm n causes an enlargement of the code, consisting of the new norm plus all the regulations that can be derived from n. Alchourrón and Makinson distinguish two other types of change. When the new norm is incoherent with the existing ones, we have an *amendment* of the code: in order to coherently add the new regulation, we need to reject those norms that conflict with n. Finally, *derogation* is the elimination of a norm n together with whatever part of the legal code that implies n.[20]

[19]The general procedure to block conclusions when conclusions persist over repositories can be very complex: for all details, see Governatori and Rotolo (2010).

[20]Hence, derogation was not meant by Alchourrón and Makinson as a process of adding exceptions. On this point, see above footnote 16.

Alchourrón, Gärdenfors and Makinson (1985) inspired by the works above proposed the so called AGM framework for belief revision. This area proved to a very fertile one and the phenomenon of revision of logical theories has been thoroughly investigated. It is then natural to ask if belief revision offers a satisfactory framework for the problem of norm revision. Some of the AGM axioms seem to be rational requirements in a legal context, whereas they have been criticized when imposed on belief change operators. An example is the *success* postulate, requiring that a new input must always be accepted in the belief set. It is reasonable to impose such a requirement when we wish to enforce a new norm or obligation. However, it gives rise to irrational behaviors when imposed to a belief set, as observed in Gabbay et al. (2003).

The AGM operation of contraction is perhaps the most controversial one, due to some postulates such as recovery (Governatori and Rotolo 2010; Wheeler and Alberti 2011), and to elusive nature of legal changes such as derogations and repeals, which are all meant to contract legal effects but in remarkably different ways (Governatori and Rotolo 2010). Standard AGM framework is of little help here: it has the advantage of being very abstract – it works with theories consisting of simple logical assertions – but precisely for this reason it is more suitable to capture the dynamics of obligations and permissions than the one of legal norms. In fact, it is hard in AGM to represent how the same set of legal effects can be contracted in many different ways, depending on how norms are changed. For this reason, previous works (Governatori and Rotolo 2010; Governatori et al. 2005a, 2007b) proposed to combine a rule-based system like Defeasible Logic with some forms of temporal reasoning.

Difficulties behind AGM have been considered and some research has been carried out to reframe AGM ideas within reasonably richer rule-based logical systems able to capture the distinction between norms and legal effects (Rotolo 2010; Stolpe 2010). However, these attempts suffer from some drawbacks: they fail to handle reasoning on deontic effects and are based on a very simple representation of legal systems.

Another limit of standard AGM framework is that it is very abstract and so it is hard to model the distinction between norm change and the change of normative effects (such as obligation change). This difficulty has been addressed in logical frameworks combining AGM ideas with richer rule-based logical systems, such as standard or Defeasible Logic (Governatori et al. 2013b; Rotolo 2010) or Input/Output Logic (Boella et al. 2009; Stolpe 2010). Wheeler and Alberti (2011) suggested a different route, i.e., employing in the law existing techniques – such as iterated belief change, two-dimensional belief change, belief bases, and weakened contraction – that can obviate problems identified in Governatori and Rotolo (2010) for standard AGM.

12.5 Summary

This work reports on research on extensions of Defeasible Logic to faithfully model aspects of legal dynamics. In particular, different temporal variants of the logic capture different temporal and deontic aspects of the norm-modification process. These variants increase the expressive power of the logic and it allows us to also represent meta-rules describing norm-modifications by referring to a variety of possible time-lines through which conclusions, rules and derivations can persist over time. We identified several temporal constraints that permit to allow for, or block, persistence with respect to specific time-lines. We described some issues related to norm modifications and versioning and we illustrated the techniques with some relevant modifications such as annulment, abrogation, substitution and derogation. In particular, we illustrated the problem of how legal effects of ex-tunc modifications, such as annulment, can be blocked after the modification applied. The idea we suggested is to block persistence of derivations across repositories. In other words, the conclusions of the annulled rule will only be derived in the repository in which the modification does not occur. The proposed methodology illustrates the possibilities of the formalism and we intend to apply it to the logical analysis of a larger corpus of norm-modifications.

Our contribution is a research on theory and practice of lawmaking.

From the theoretical viewpoint, our logical framework offers indeed a formal model for grasping several subtleties of legislative and judicial mechanisms behind norm change and the dynamics of legal systems. In particular, our work is the first attempt to logically reconstruct retroactive legal modifications.

From the practical viewpoint, our work is expected to provide new methods in order to develop automated tools for legal consolidation. Indeed, the need to obtain updated legal corpora is crucial for lawyers, practitioners, and law-makers: collections of digital legal documents managed within information systems open the way to the automation of legal consolidation so that users can access the updated version of legal provisions. However, some risks may occur in developing efficient tools for legal consolidation, such as (i) the collapse of the temporal dimensions of force, efficacy and applicability into a flat model, so the modifications are applied to the legal documents in a wrong time sequence; (ii) failing to have a global view of legal systems; (iii) failing to deal with conditional modifications, i.e., modifications that apply upon the occurrence of certain pre-conditions (something that we can easily handle in our model using meta-rules); (iv) the inability of being proactive, in the sense that we do not detect modifications that have not been factored into consolidation. As a remedy to these potential drawbacks, our logic offers robust and flexible conceptual and computational methods for managing the process whereby the legal provisions in a normative system get consolidated.

Acknowledgements NICTA is funded by the Australian Government through the Department of Communications and the Australian Research Council through the ICT Centre of Excellence Program.

References

Alchourrón, Carlos E., and Eugenio Bulygin. 1981. The expressive conception of norms. *In New studies in deontic logic*, ed. Risto Hilpinen, 95–125. Dordrecht: D. Reidel.

Alchourrón, C., and E. Bulygin. 1984. *Permission and permissive norms*. Berlin: Duncker & Humblot.

Alchourrón, C., and P. Gärdenfors. 1985. On the logic of theory change: Partial meet. *Journal of Symbolic Logic* 50:510–530.

Alchourrón, C., and D. Makinson. 1981. Hierarchies of regulations and their logic. In *New studies in deontic logic*, ed. R. Hilpinen, 125–148. Boston: D. Reidel.

Alchourrón, C., and D. Makinson. 1982. The logic of theory change: Contraction functions and their associated revision functions. *Theoria* 48:14–37.

Billington, D., G. Antoniou, G. Governatori, and M. Maher. 2010. An inclusion theorem for defeasible logic. *ACM Transactions in Computational Logic* 12(1):6.

Boella, G. G. Pigozzi, and L. van der Torre. 2009. A normative framework for norm change. In *8th international joint conference on autonomous agents and multiagent systems (AAMAS 2009)*, 169–176. Richland: IFAAMAS.

Dung, P. (1995). On the acceptability of arguments and its fundamental. *Artificial Intelligence* 77(2):321–358.

Gabbay, D., G. Pigozzi, J. Woods, and D. Walton. 2003. Controlled revision – An algorithmic approach for belief revision. *Journal of Logic and Computation* 13(1):3–22.

Gordon, T., H. Prakken. 2007. The Carneades model of argument and burden of proof. *Artificial Intelligence* 171(10–11):875–896.

Governatori, G. (2011). On the relationship between Carneades and defeasible logic. In *The 13th international conference on artificial intelligence and law (ICAIL 2011)*, ed. K. Ashley, 31–40. New York: ACM Press.

Governatori, G., and A. Rotolo. 2010. Changing legal systems: Legal abrogations and annulments in defeasible logic. *The Logic Journal of IGPL* 18(1):157–194.

Governatori, Guido, and Antonino Rotolo. 2013. Computing temporal defeasible logic. In *7th international symposium on theory, practice, and applications of rules on the web (RuleML 2013)*, ed. Leora Morgenstern, Petros S. Stefaneas, François Lévy, Adam Wyner, and Adrian Paschke. LNCS, vol. 8035, 114-128. Heidelberg: Springer.

Governatori, Guido, and Giovanni Sartor. 2010. Burdens of proof in monological argumentation. In *The twenty-third annual conference on legal knowledge and information systems (Jurix 2010)*, ed. Radboud Winkels, vol.223, 57–66. Amsterdam: IOS Press. doi:http://dx.doi.org/10.3233/978-1-60750-682-9-57.

Governatori, G., M. Maher, D. Billington, and G. Antoniou. 2004. Argumentation semantics for defeasible logics. *Journal of Logic and Computation* 14(5):675–702.

Governatori, Guido, Monica Palmirani, Régis Riveret, Antonino Rotolo, and Giovanni Sartor. 2005a. Norm modifications in defeasible logic. In *The eighteenth annual conference on legal knowledge and information systems (Jurix 2005)*, ed. Marie-Francine Moens and Peter Spyns, 13–22. Amsterdam: IOS Press.

Governatori, Guido, Antonino Rotolo, and Giovanni Sartor. 2005b. Temporalised normative positions in defeasible logic. In *The 10th international conference on artificial intelligence and law (ICAIL 2005)*, ed. Anne Gardner, 25–34. New York: ACM.

Governatori, G., J. Hulstijn, R. Riveret, and A. Rotolo. 2007a. Characterising deadlines in temporal modal defeasible. In *20th Australian joint conference on artificial intelligence*, ed. M. Orgun, and J. Thornton, 486–496. Berlin: Springer.

Governatori, Guido, Antonino Rotolo, Régis Riveret, Monica Palmirani, and Giovanni Sartor. 2007. Variants of temporal defeasible logic for modelling norm modifications. In *The 11th international conference on artificial intelligence and law (ICAIL 2007)*, ed. Radboud Winkels, 155–159. New York: ACM. doi:10.1145/1276318.1276347.

Governatori, G., F. Olivieri, A. Rotolo, and S. Scannapieco. 2013a. Computing strong and weak permissions in defeasible. *Journal of Philosophical Logic* 42(6):799–829.

Governatori, G., A. Rotolo, F. Olivieri, and S. Scannapieco. 2013b. Legal contractions: A logical analysis. In *The 14th international conference on artificial intelligence and law (ICAIL 2013)*, ed. B. Verheij, 63–72. New York: ACM Press.

Guastini, Riccardo. 1998. *Teoria e dogmatica delle fonti.* Milan: Giuffré.

Hart, H.L.A. 1994. *The concept of law*. Oxford: Clarendon.

Kelsen, Hans. 1991. *General theory of norms*. Oxford: Clarendon.

Nute, Donald. 1994. Defeasible logic. In *Handbook of logic in artificial intelligence and logic programmingI,* ed. Gabbay, Dov M., Hogger, Christopher John, and John Alan Robinson, vol.3, 353-395. Oxford: Oxford University Press.

Rotolo, A. (2010). Retroactive legal changes and revision theory in defeasible logic. In *Proceedings of the 10th international conference on deontic logic in computer science (DEON 2010)*, ed. Governatori, G., and G. Sartor, 116–131. Berlin/New York: Springer.

Soeteman, A. (1989). *Logic in law*. Dodrecht: Kluwer.

Stolpe, A. (2010). Norm-system revision: Theory and application. *Artificial Intelligence and Law* 18(3):247–283.

von Wright, Georg Henrik. 1963. *Norm and action: A logical inquiry*. London: Routledge and Kegan Paul.

Wheeler, G., and M. Alberti. 2011. NO revision and NO contraction. *Minds and Machines* 21(3):411–430.

Chapter 13
Representing the Logic of Statutory Rules in the United States

Vern R. Walker, Bernadette C. Lopez, Matthew T. Rutchik, and Julie L. Agris

Abstract This chapter presents one method of representing the logical structure of systems of legal rules, as they are established by statute in the United States. The chapter uses default logic and "rule trees" to reflect the dynamic and pragmatic context in which legal rules are used, as well as the interplay among legal rules, policy objectives and evidence. Rule trees also capture such important sub–structures as relevant–factor rules and legal presumptions. They are also operational structures available for software computation or for exchange in digital form, and help legal practitioners organize evidence and arguments. Examples throughout are drawn from the statute governing the Vaccine Injury Compensation Program (VICP), which provides compensation to persons who have sustained vaccine–related injuries. Although the examples are from this particular statute, the default–logic framework is applicable to any other statute in the United States and to those in many other jurisdictions.

Keywords Legal rules • Default logic • Rule systems • Governmental decision-making • Evidence assessment

13.1 Introduction

In the United States as elsewhere, statutes contain the basic legal rules established by the legislative branch of government. This chapter focuses on the dynamic and pragmatic aspects of such legal rules, and of the systems of legal rules that statutes create. One challenge for logical analysis is to represent systems of rules in such

---

V.R. Walker (✉) • B.C. Lopez • M.T. Rutchik
Research Laboratory for Law, Logic & Technology, Maurice A. Deane School of Law, Hofstra University, New York, NY, USA
e-mail: Vern.R.Walker@Hofstra.edu

J.L. Agris
Hofstra North Shore–LIJ School of Medicine, Hofstra University, New York, NY, USA

Research Laboratory for Law, Logic & Technology, Maurice A. Deane School of Law, Hofstra University, New York, NY, USA

M. Araszkiewicz, K. Płeszka (eds.), *Logic in the Theory and Practice of Lawmaking*, Legisprudence Library 2, DOI 10.1007/978-3-319-19575-9_13

a way that the dynamic processes by which they are created and which they create in turn are reflected in the analysis. Similarly, the representation should reflect the pragmatic nature of rule systems – being used to orchestrate decision processes in real time, with limited resources and limited information. To the extent that a logical representation succeeds in reflecting this dynamic and pragmatic context, it is also likely to be practical – that is, of everyday use to participants in legal proceedings. In this chapter, we describe the core structure of such a logical representation.

13.2 The Rule of Law, Processes, and Systems of Rules

The rule of law requires governmental action (and sometimes inaction) to be justifiable (MacCormick 2005, 12–16; Walker 2007b, 1687–93). In the United States, a primary goal in enacting any statute is to control the use of governmental power by setting up complex processes that constrain the discretion of governmental actors when they take actions. For example, statutes may prescribe procedural and substantive conditions under which an administrative agency is authorized or required to issue legislative rules, or they may prescribe conditions under which a court is required to order compensation for a plaintiff. As a result, statutes create or presume decision–making processes for types of governmental action. Broad types of governmental action (such as legislating, enforcing, or adjudicating) are typically processes made up of numerous constituent actions. For example, issuing a valid legislative rule might involve official publication of notice, taking testimony at a hearing, and official publication of the agency's reasoning. Issuing a valid judicial judgment ordering compensation might involve serving notice on a defendant, filing and deciding motions, and conducting a trial. A primary goal of many statutes is to prescribe conditions for lawfully conducting a process leading to an ultimate governmental action.

Different participants often play different roles with regard to distinct logical components of the decision process. For example, in the process of legislative rule-making, various actors, such as agency officials, the potentially affected members of the public, and the courts, may all play different roles. Parties and intervenors, witnesses, judges and juries may all play different roles in the process of judicial adjudication. With respect to each decision or action within a process, a statute may state not only the substantive conditions under which the governmental action (or inaction) is required, permitted, or prohibited, but also the process conditions (both procedural and evidentiary) for making the decision lawfully. This section of the chapter discusses three logical components of such processes, and then describes a formal system for representing systems of legal rules applicable to decisions about those components.

As an example of the U.S. statute, this chapter will use the National Childhood Vaccine Injury Act of 1986 ("Vaccine Act"), which sets up the Vaccine Injury

Compensation Program (VICP).[1] The VICP is a hybrid administrative–judicial system in the United States that provides compensation to persons who have sustained vaccine–related injuries (Walker 2009; Walker et al. 2013).[2] Petitioners seeking compensation file claims in the Court of Federal Claims. If the Secretary of the Department of Health and Human Services (HHS) contests a claim, a special master within the Court of Federal Claims decides whether it is meritorious. Contested VICP cases often involve complex issues of fact about causation – e.g., whether the vaccine played a causal role in bringing about the injury. Such factual adjudication by special masters requires taking into account medical, scientific, and other expert evidence, along with the non–expert evidence, and the decisions of special masters include "findings of fact and conclusions of law."[3] These decisions are subject to review by the Court of Federal Claims, whose judgments are in turn appealable to the Court of Appeals for the Federal Circuit.[4] This statute provides illustrations of the logical structure that we describe in this chapter.

13.2.1 Logical Components Within Governmental Decision–Making Processes

Statutorily created processes leading to governmental action typically involve three major types of logical components: policy objectives, legal rules, and evidence (Walker et al. 2013). Instances of these major components play roles in different types of decisions or actions. For example, policy objectives can be adopted by governmental actors, used to justify or argue against governmental actions, and promoted or undermined by such actions; legal rules are established, modified, and applied; evidence is admitted into the record of a proceeding or excluded from the record, and is used to warrant findings of fact. In general terms, policy objectives help to justify adopting or modifying legal rules, and help guide the application of those rules in particular cases, in accordance with the evidence.

Distinguishing these types of logical components allows the structuring of complex processes for making decisions, in which different participants perform different tasks with respect to different decisions or actions. For example, the major governmental decision makers in the VICP include the United States Congress, the Secretary of HHS, the Supreme Court of the United States, the United States Court of Appeals for the Federal Circuit, the United States Court of Federal Claims, and special masters attached to the Court of Federal Claims. These participants have

[1] 42 U.S.C. § 300aa–10(a) (2011).

[2] Compensation awards are paid out of the Vaccine Injury Compensation Trust Fund, which is funded by an excise tax on each dose of covered vaccine. See 26 U.S.C. § 9510 (2012), and 42 U.S.C. § 300aa–15(i)(2) (2011).

[3] 42 U.S.C. § 300aa–12(d) (2011).

[4] 42 U.S.C. § 300aa–12(f) (2011).

different roles to play with respect to different decisions regarding the different types of logical components. For example, Congress established the fundamental policy objectives for the VICP, and the statutory legal rules that are fundamental to the claims process in the VICP, while administrative agencies can create certain additional types of rules, and reviewing courts interpret and elaborate all of those rules. Special masters function as factfinders by assessing the evidence in particular cases and making findings of fact; the Court of Federal Claims provides a first level of review of those findings; and the Court of Appeals and the Supreme Court provide appellate review. The actions of each decision maker are governed by systems of legal rules, some of which are constitutional in origin, but far more are statutory.

Having different participants perform different actions with respect to different logical components within a single process means that different institutions can have the particular structures and competences needed to perform the particular tasks assigned. For example, the political nature of Congress is optimal for negotiating and striking the trade–offs needed in balancing competing policy objectives; the experience of appellate court judges is best fitted for interpreting statutory language, formulating legal rules, and combining those rules into complete and consistent systems; and the experience of special masters in deciding a high number of vaccine cases prepares them for assessing the credibility of the expert witnesses who appear in such cases. Distinctions such as that between "issues of law" (to be decided de novo by reviewing courts) and "issues of fact" (to be judicially reviewed under a deferential standard) are made in rules designed to ensure that particular institutions with particular competences play suitable roles, and do not encroach upon the decisional role of another institution. Moreover, institutions with different structures, competences and missions can collectively provide a process that has internal "checks and balances" among the different participants. For example, reviewing courts can ensure that special masters understand and correctly apply the legal rules, while special masters can ensure that the evidence in each particular case receives individual treatment under those rules.

Policy Objectives. Within the framework of principles established by the United States Constitution (such as due process and equal protection),[5] Congress adopts particular policy objectives for any particular statutory program, and participants within the decision–making processes established for that program are expected to pursue those policies when implementing the program. The structure of the process ensures that only certain participants have policy–making authority outright, while other participants can implement and balance policies when performing other decision–making tasks. For example, Congress established the fundamental policy objectives specific to the VICP, including increasing the supply of vaccine manufacturers and decreasing the cost of vaccines,[6] as well as promoting the use of vaccines and providing an effective and efficient compensation system for those injured by vaccines (Binski 2011, 693–94, 705–09; Meyers 2011, 794; Grey

[5] U.S. Constitution, Amendment 14.

[6] H.R. Rep. 99–908, 1986 U.S.C.C.A.N. 6344, 6345–46 (26 September 1986).

2011, 355–66; Currier 2009, 232–36). Various participants are responsible for implementing these Congressional objectives in their activities, for example: the Secretary of HHS as the party respondent in the adjudication of particular claims, the reviewing courts in interpreting statutory provisions, and the special masters when they issue findings of fact and conclusions of law in particular cases. The Secretary and the appellate courts can also implement policies that are more generic than the VICP, such as administrative efficiency. Moreover, the adjudication processes all share the same "epistemic policy": to produce determinations of fact that (1) are as accurate as possible and (2) are warranted by the legally available evidence (Walker 2003).

Legal rules. Legal rules are essential means for achieving the rule of law, because they make the justification of governmental action more transparent, as well as help ensure that similar cases are decided similarly (Walker 2007a, 1690–96; 2007b, 198–207). For example, in the vaccine compensation process, legal rules play a central role in deciding whether the vaccination played a causal role in bringing about the person's injury or death. Congress created the core causation rules in the statute (discussed in Sect. 13.3 below), the Secretary can add to those rules by amending the Vaccine Injury Table, and the appellate courts add more explicit rules when they decide cases. Decisions by the Court of Federal Claims do not create legal rules binding on other decisions of the same court on other claims,[7] nor do decisions by special masters create rules binding on other special masters.[8] Thus, the process ensures that the governmental institutions that have rule–creating authority have the experience and competence to create rules that appropriately balance competing epistemic and non–epistemic policies. As discussed in Sects. 13.3 and 13.4 below, legal rules are either substantive or process rules, with the latter category including both procedural rules and evidentiary rules.

Evidence. As Sect. 13.2.2 discusses, legal rules determine what issues of fact are relevant to any particular decision–making process, by identifying the situations that will satisfy the rule requirements. One or more participants in a process will be responsible for assessing the evidence and deciding whether or not the rule conditions have been met. In vaccine compensation cases, for example, the special master assesses the probative value of the evidence and makes "findings of fact and conclusions of law" concerning causation.[9] The Court of Federal Claims may set aside those findings of fact only if they are "arbitrary, capricious, an abuse of

---

[7] West Coast General Corp. v. Dalton, 39 F.3d 312, 315 (Fed. Cir. 1994) ("Court of Federal Claims decisions, while persuasive, do not set binding precedent for separate and distinct cases in that court."); Ains, Inc. v. United States, 365 F.3d 1333, 1336 n. 1 (Fed. Cir. 2004) ("CFC [Court of Federal Claims] holdings, like those of federal district courts, are instructive but not precedential, and do not bind future court rulings.").

[8] Graves v. Secretary of the Department of Health and Human Services, 101 Fed. Cl. 310, 332 (Fed. Cl. 2011) ("Special masters are not bound by decisions of other special masters.").

[9] 42 U.S.C. § 300aa–12(d)(3)(A)(i) (2011).

discretion, or otherwise not in accordance with law."[10] If the Court of Federal Claims does set aside a special master's finding of fact, then the Court may either "issue its own findings of fact" or "remand the petition to the special master for further action in accordance with the court's direction."[11] In keeping with the general rule that appellate courts decide de novo only issues of law, not issues of fact, the standard of review in the Court of Appeals for the Federal Circuit is that the Court "uphold[s] the Special Master's findings of fact unless they are arbitrary or capricious."[12]

13.2.2 Representing Action–Oriented Systems of Legal Rules

The logic used to represent legal rules must allow for the dynamic and pragmatic nature of rule–based legal reasoning. Legal reasoning is "pragmatic" in at least three senses. First, the ultimate subject matter of such reasoning is decision–making leading to governmental action. The ultimate focus on whether or not to engage in some action gives the rule–based reasoning a pragmatic focus. Second, legal decision–making occurs in real time, uses limited resources, and is usually based on incomplete information – it is decision–making under uncertainty (Kahneman et al. 1982; Morgan and Henrion 1990). Thus, rule–based legal reasoning is constrained by pragmatic circumstances. Third, legal reasoning balances the "epistemic objective" of law against the applicable "non–epistemic objectives" (Walker 2003, 132). The epistemic objective is to produce determinations of fact that (1) are as accurate as possible and (2) are warranted by the legally available evidence. Weighed against this epistemic objective are numerous non–epistemic objectives – for example, procedural fairness, administrative efficiency, or adequate vaccine production. One function of a system of legal rules is to strike the appropriate balance between the epistemic objective and the applicable non–epistemic objectives. Given these three dimensions in which legal reasoning must be pragmatic, it is no surprise that the logic of legal reasoning generally goes well beyond deductive logic, and incorporates abductive logic (Josephson and Josephson 1996) and nonmonotonic logic (Brewka et al. 1997; Kyburg and Teng 2001, 117–51; Levi 1996, 120–59; Prakken 1997, 67–100), as well as scientific reasoning, decision theory, risk analysis, risk–benefit analysis, and other methodologies that can adequately capture rule–based and policy–based reasoning.

The topic of this chapter, however, is representing the logic of *statutory rules*, which is in many ways more straightforward than representing the logic of either evidence assessment or policy–based reasoning. Evidence assessment is the process

[10] 42 U.S.C. § 300aa–12(e)(2)(B) (2011); Stotts v. Secretary of the Department of Health and Human Services, 23 Cl. Ct. 352, 358–62 (Ct. Cl. 1991).

[11] 42 U.S.C. § 300aa–12(e)(2)(B)–(C) (2011).

[12] Carson *ex rel.* Carson v. Secretary of Health and Human Services, 727 F.3d 1365, 1368 (Fed. Cir. 2013).

of reasoning from the evidence in the legal record of a proceeding to findings about whether the governing rule conditions are satisfied in a particular case. Evidence assessment might well require nonmonotonic logic and scientific reasoning. Policy–based reasoning is the process of determining whether a particular rule or factual finding is prudent or justifiable, when measured against the applicable policy objectives. Policy–based reasoning often requires decision theory, risk analysis, and risk–benefit analysis. By contrast, the representation of statutory legal rules generally requires only default logic, of the kind discussed next.

By "default logic," we mean the logic of default reasoning. Default reasoning employs presumptive inference rules and the available evidence to warrant default or provisional conclusions, which are subject to revision on the basis of defeating evidence – and default logic formalizes such reasoning (Brachman and Levesque 2004, 205–33; Kyburg and Teng 2001, 121–34; Brewka et al. 1997, 40–51; Poole 1988; Reiter 1980). Default logic has a presumptive or *prima facie* quality that is well suited for representing legal reasoning – whether reasoning within the system of legal rules itself, or evidence assessment applying those rules to particular cases, or policy–based reasoning about legal rules or findings. In the case of a system of legal rules, the default quality shows up primarily in two ways. First, the rule system may formally contain explicit "defeaters" – propositions that act to defeat an otherwise valid line of reasoning or support (Pollock 1990, 79; Brewka et al. 1997, 2–3, 16; Prakken et al. 2003, 32, 37–38; Prakken and Sartor 2004, 120–24; Prakken and Sartor 1997, 3; Walker 2007a, 199–204, 213–15). In law, such explicit defeaters are found in the form of exceptions to a rule or as an affirmative defense to a claim. Second, the rule system itself is generally open to revision – for example, by interpreting or defining a legal phrase in an existing rule (thereby creating a new rule) or by creating an exception to an existing rule. We will see examples of all of these variations in the rules governing the VICP.

First, however, we will sketch the semantic elements of a formal representation of a legal rule, and of a system of legal rules. A single legal rule is a conditional proposition, such as "if *p*, then *q*," with a single *q* as the conclusion and one or more propositions as the condition(s) (Brewer 1996, 972). Whenever multiple conditions are present, they are connected to the conclusion by one of three logical connectives:

"AND" (the conclusion is true if, but only if, all connected conditions are true);

"OR" (the conclusion is true if, but only if, at least one of the connected conditions is true); or

"RULE FACTORS" (the listed conditions are relevant in determining whether the conclusion is true, but the rule specifies no algorithm or formula for assigning a truth–value to the conclusion as a function of the truth–values of those conditions).

Graphical depictions of these three possibilities are shown in Fig. 13.1 below.

Every proposition in a rule has one of three truth–values: "true"/"undecided"/ "false." The conclusion is dependent for its truth–value upon the truth–values of its rule conditions. This three–valued logic captures the dynamic nature of legal proof. For example, when any particular vaccine–compensation proceeding begins, all propositions in the rule tree are "undecided." The parties might stipulate some propositions as true or false, with the remainder being contested issues. The parties

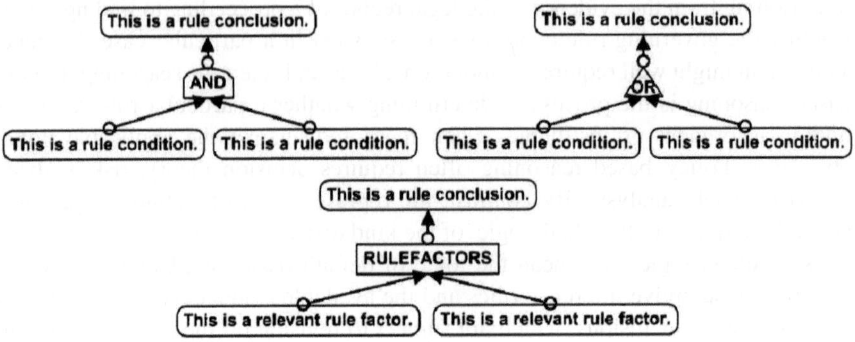

Fig. 13.1 Graphic representation of rule forms with logical connectives AND, OR, and RULE FACTORS

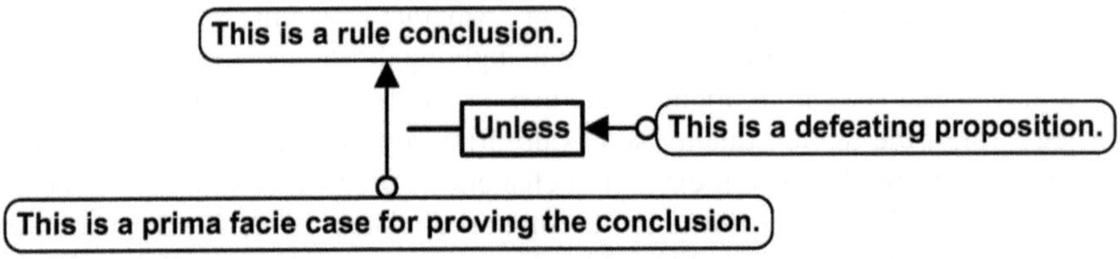

Fig. 13.2 Graphic representation of rule form with logical connective UNLESS

then produce evidence on those contested issues and try to persuade the special master (as factfinder) to make favorable findings of fact on the contested rule conditions. When the factfinder makes findings of fact about a rule's conditions, the rule's logical connective determines the truth–value of the conclusion (with the exception of the RULE FACTORS connective, as noted above). Expressed generally, a legal rule identifies the propositions that are relevant to proving the rule's conclusion, and may determine a truth–functional logical connective for multiple conditions, but a particular proceeding to apply that rule begins with the decision maker being neutral on whether the conditions for applying the rule are satisfied or not.

When a rule states an exception or an affirmative defense, the condition is a defeating proposition for the conclusion, and the logical connective is "UNLESS." UNLESS has the meaning of "but not if": if the defeating condition is true, then the conclusion is false, even if the main *prima facie* conditions for establishing that conclusion are true. The rule conditions that would determine the truth–value of the conclusion in the absence of a defeater constitute the *prima facie* case for the conclusion. Thus, a true defeater trumps or overrides the *prima facie* proof, by dictating that the conclusion must be false. A defeater relation can be depicted graphically as in Fig. 13.2 above.

Of course, representing particular statutory provisions might warrant the use of additional or different logical connectives (e.g., exclusive OR) or logical operators (e.g., negations), but several considerations advise caution. "Occam's razor" or the principle of parsimony cautions against adding connectives unnecessarily, especially those not readily intuitive to humans. Using unnecessary and unintuitive distinctions in representing statutory text is likely to increase the cost of the resources needed to extract the logical structure (e.g., the time needed to resolve alternative logical representations, or the computation needed to automatically extract that structure) and to increase the risk of error (inaccuracy in representing the logic of statutory provisions). Moreover, in a many–valued logic system, even seemingly simple logical concepts such as negation may result in numerous logical operators (Gottwald 2001, 84–88). In addition, there is always a decision to be made about what meaning to represent in logical form and what to leave for linguistic annotation or treatment. For example, so far in our work representing the logic of particular statutes, we have needed to use only the basic, three–valued connectives AND, OR, RULE FACTORS, and UNLESS, and we have left the representation of concepts like negation and quantification for semantic annotation and rules, rather than trying to represent them using logical formalism.

Legal rules can be chained together, with a condition of one rule becoming a conclusion of another rule. A *system* of legal rules is represented as an inverted rule tree, the top or "root" node of the tree being the ultimate conclusion to be proved, and each level of each branch extending downward from the top node stating the logical conditions for proving the immediately higher proposition. Inferences proceed upward, from the conditions of one rule to its conclusion, which in turn helps (with any sibling propositions on the same level) to determine the truth–value of its conclusion in the next higher level of the tree. The top conclusion of the rule tree is the ultimate issue to be proved in order for the governmental action to be justified – for example, in the case of claims under the VICP, that "the petitioner is entitled to compensation under the National Vaccine Injury Compensation Program." Thus, a single rule tree can represent the complete set of process and substantive conditions that must be satisfied before a governmental decision or action can be lawful. Moreover, a rule tree provides the logical form for representing the systems of legal rules that statutes create.[13] The next section will present a portion of the rule tree governing the VICP.

[13]We present here only the semantic elements and a graphical depiction of the logic of a rule tree, for it is straightforward to represent the same information in various symbolic forms. For example, a system of rules can be represented as conditional propositions nested within the conditions of other conditional propositions, with an entire rule tree represented as a single complex conditional. (Note, however, that if the conditional contains a RULE FACTORS connective somewhere within it, it will not be entirely truth–functional.) In addition, the propositions forming a rule tree can be represented as nested elements in an XML file, for data exchange over the Internet.

13.3 Substantive Rules: Limiting the Field of Governmental Action

This section uses the rule system governing compensation decisions in the VICP to illustrate substantive rules and how they limit the field within which governmental actors can lawfully take action. The VICP examples also illustrate how the use of rule trees to represent the logical structure of a system of substantive rules can provide a very practical method of organizing evidence and applying these rules.

A critical substantive issue in many contested VICP cases is "causation": whether the vaccination played a causal role in bringing about the injury or death as alleged by the petitioner. A VICP decision is fair and efficient only if the vaccination did in fact cause the injury (Walker et al. 2013, 193). It would be inefficient to use money raised by the vaccine taxes and targeted for vaccine–related injuries to pay for injuries that are unrelated to vaccines. On the other hand, it would be unfair not to pay compensation if the vaccine did in fact causally contribute to the injury, and as a result people might under–utilize vaccines. Congress sought to balance its multiple policy objectives by providing two alternative sets of rules for proving that a vaccine caused an injury: rules for "on–Table causation" (or merely "Table causation") and rules for "off–Table causation."

The first of these two alternative sets of rules governs proving Table causation or causation in "Table cases." The statute established an initial Vaccine Injury Table (Table) and conferred authority on the Secretary of HHS to update and maintain the Table through administrative rulemaking (Meyers 2011, 799).[14] The Table lists (a) covered vaccines, (b) recognized adverse reactions that might result from the administration of particular vaccines, and (c) recognized time periods in which the first symptom or manifestation of onset must occur after vaccine administration.[15] A petitioner seeking to prove causation in a Table case has the burden of proving (1) that the injury was "set forth in the Vaccine Injury Table in association with the vaccine" and (2) that "the first symptom or manifestation of the onset or of the significant aggravation" of the injury "occurred within the time period after vaccine administration set forth in the Table."[16] Proving these two conditions to be true triggers a statutory presumption of causation.[17] As we discuss below, this presumption is rebutted if the injury was in fact due to factors unrelated to the administration of the vaccine. A portion of the rule tree representing this presumption is shown in Fig. 13.3.

---

[14] 42 U.S.C. § 300aa–14 (2011); 42 C.F.R. 100.3 (2011).

[15] 42 U.S.C. § 300aa–14 (2011).

[16] 42 U.S.C. § 300aa–11(c)(1)(C)(i) (2011).

[17] Shalala v. Whitecotton, 514 U.S. 268, 270 (1995); Grant v. Secretary of the Department of Health and Human Services, 956 F.2d 1144, 1147 (Fed. Cir. 1992); Althen v. Secretary of Health and Human Services, 418 F.3d 1274, 1278 (Fed. Cir. 2005).

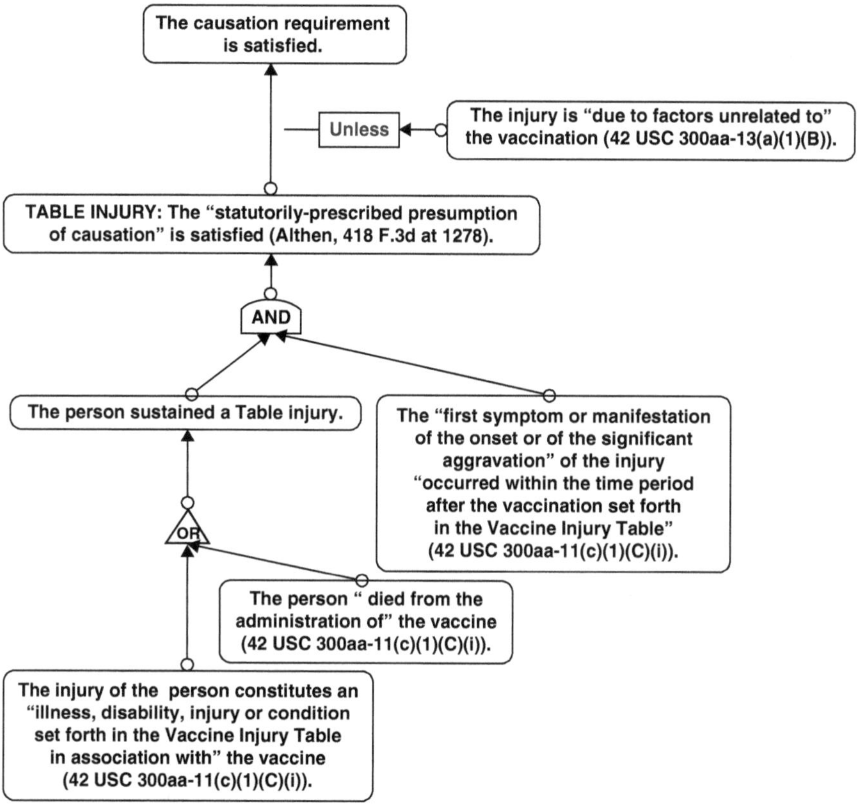

Fig. 13.3 Partial rule tree for vaccine decisions, showing the statutory presumption of causation and the defeating proposition (Figure 13.3 was originally published online in the journal Law, Probability and Risk (May 26, 2014): Vern R. Walker, "Representing the use of rule-based presumptions in legal decision documents," p. 13. Vern R. Walker is the creator and copyright holder)

The second set of rules governs proving "causation in fact" in "off–Table" or "non–Table" cases.[18] This method of proof is available when the petitioner cannot prove one or both of the propositions needed to trigger the statutory presumption of causation.[19] In such a case, in order to receive compensation, the petitioner must prove that the injury "was caused by" the vaccination.[20] Because the statute is

[18]Shyface v. Secretary of Health and Human Services, 165 F.3d 1344, 1350–51 (Fed. Cir. 1999); *Althen*, 418 F.3d at 1278; Pafford v. Secretary of Health and Human Services, 451 F.3d 1352, 1355 (Fed. Cir. 2006).

[19]42 U.S.C. § 300aa–11(c)(1)(C)(ii) (2011).

[20]Id.

silent as to the meaning of the phrase "was caused by,"[21] the Court of Appeals for the Federal Circuit interpreted the meaning, by elaborating sub–rules for proving this statutory requirement. In 2005, the Court in *Althen v. Secretary of Health and Human Services*, 418 F.3d 1274, 1278 (Fed. Cir. 2005), stated that in off–Table cases the petitioner's

> burden is to show by preponderant evidence that the vaccination brought about her injury by providing: (1) a medical theory causally connecting the vaccination and the injury; (2) a logical sequence of cause and effect showing that the vaccination was the reason for the injury; and (3) a showing of a proximate temporal relationship between vaccination and injury.

In interpreting the meaning of the statutory phrase and in elaborating the rules for causation in off–Table cases, the Court was guided by its earlier determination that "[n]ational uniformity in administration" was implicit in Congress' purpose with the Vaccine Act, and by its prior holding that a "uniform approach, one which implements the statutory purpose, is that of the Restatement (Second) of Torts."[22] If a claimant succeeds in making a *prima facie* showing of causation in an off–Table case, her proof may still be rebutted if the injury was in fact "due to factors unrelated to the administration of the vaccine." (Walker et al. 2013, 194) The portion of the rule tree representing these three Althen conditions or "prongs" is shown in Fig. 13.4.

The Federal Circuit elaborated on the first *Althen* prong (that "a medical theory causally connect[s] the vaccination and the injury"[23]) by explaining that it means that the vaccine "can cause" the injury.[24] In other words, the first prong has been explained in terms of "general causation": whether a medical theory has been advanced by the petitioner that causally links the type of vaccine involved in the particular case to the type of injury alleged. For this reason, as proof under the first *Althen* prong, a petitioner normally produces a medical expert who testifies about a medical theory, supported by medical or scientific evidence and explanation.

The Federal Circuit elaborated on the second *Althen* prong (that "a logical sequence of cause and effect show[s] that the vaccination was the reason for the injury") by explaining that the petitioner must show that the vaccine was a "but–for" cause of or "the reason for the injury."[25] Often, this might involve showing that the stages of progression (and symptoms, signs, and test results) expected to occur under the medical theory in *Althen* prong 1 did in fact occur in the petitioner's case. And *Althen* prong 3 (that there was "a proximate temporal relationship between the vaccination and the injury") is merely a specific instance of actually observing in

[21] *Shyface*, 165 F.3d at 1350–51 ("the statute does not elaborate on the requirement of causation in the proof of a non–Table case").

[22] Id. at 1351–52.

[23] *Althen*, 418 F.3d at 1278. This substantive condition derived from *Grant*, 956 F.2d at 1148; see *Shyface*, 165 F.3d at 1353.

[24] Capizzano v. Secretary of Health and Human Services, 440 F.3d 1317, 1326 (Fed. Cir. 2006).

[25] *Pafford*, 451 F.3d at 1357.

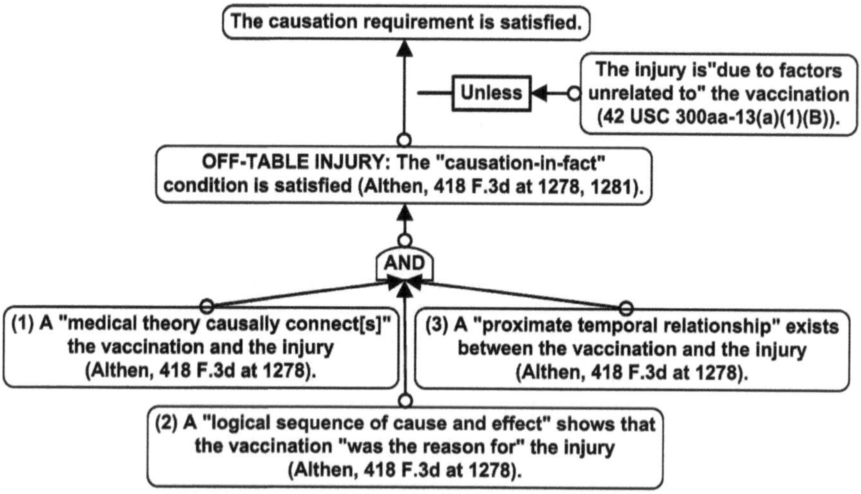

Fig. 13.4 Partial rule tree for vaccine decisions, showing the *Althen prima facie* case on causation and the defeating proposition (Figure 13.4 was adapted from a graphic originally published online in the journal Law, Probability and Risk (May 26, 2014): Vern R. Walker, "Representing the use of rule-based presumptions in legal decision documents," p. 14. Vern R. Walker is the creator and copyright holder)

fact what the medical theory leads us to expect. Thus, *Althen's* second and third conditions apply the general causal theory of the first condition to the evidence in the specific case.

Finally, for all cases, the statute requires a finding that "that there is not a preponderance of the evidence that the illness, disability, injury, condition, or death described in the petition is due to factors unrelated to the administration of the vaccine described in the petition."[26] Although the statute did not place the burden of proving this issue on any particular party, the courts have reasonably placed it on the government, thereby interpreting the statute as establishing a defense available to the Secretary of HHS.[27] Moreover, given its placement in the statute, this defense applies to Table as well as off–Table cases.[28] We discuss additional aspects of this defense in Sects. 13.4.2.2 and 13.4.2.3 below.

[26]42 U.S.C. § 300aa–13(a)(1)(B) (2011).

[27]*See* Knudsen v. Secretary of Health and Human Services, 35 F.3d 543, 547 (Fed.Cir. 1994); *Althen*, 418 F.3d at 1278.

[28]*See* 42 U.S.C. § 300aa–13(a)(1)(B) (2011); *see Grant*, 956 F.2d at 1149–50.

13.4 Process Rules: Channeling Governmental Discretion

While substantive rules identify the relevant issues to be proved in a legal process, such as causation, process rules govern the operation of the process itself. Aside from this distinction between what is to be proved and the process of proving it, however, substantive and process rules share the same logical form as conditional propositions. This means that we can also use rule trees to represent process rules and systems of process rules. Moreover, from a logical perspective, there is an advantage to not needing to draw a formal distinction between substantive and process rules, in avoiding the resulting vagueness of borderline cases. Finally, a balancing of divergent policy objectives can be used to justify adopting process rules, just as they can justify adopting substantive rules.

Combining substantive and process rules into a single system is logically straightforward in situations where a statute prescribes both substantive and process conditions for a governmental decision or action. For example, the court might be required to give a defendant due notice of the proceedings, the judge might be required to decide all motions made by parties, and to give correct instructions to the jury. In such situations, we can generally integrate the substantive and process rules merely by joining them as conjuncts of the same rule tree (Walker 2007a, 232–33).

It is important to keep in mind, however, that an entire rule tree (often containing conjunctions of both substantive and process branches) is ultimately rooted in a single conclusion that warrants some governmental action. Different types of actions will normally be governed by different rule trees. For example, the substantive rules of causation are constituents of the rule tree governing entitlement to compensation under the VICP, and they are necessary conditions for warranting a judicial judgment ordering compensation from the VICP Fund. During the proof process leading to such a conclusion, however, there may be numerous other decisions that the presiding special master must make – for example, deciding a motion about the admissibility of certain evidence into the legal record of the proceeding. That decision or action to exclude evidence might be governed by its own set of rules, represented by another rule tree, containing substantive and process rules from the statute that set up the VICP, or from another statute, or from the rules of the court, or from elsewhere. Also, from a practical standpoint, it makes sense to represent such rules separately from the rules governing entitlement decisions, because the same rules on evidence admissibility may be applicable to different decision processes involving different governmental decisions or actions. We should not confuse two distinct points: while we can formally conjoin substantive and process rules into a single tree when appropriate, distinct decisions or actions within the same legal process often require different rule trees representing different sets of rules.

The following two sub-sections distinguish and discuss two types of process rules: procedural rules and evidentiary rules.

13.4.1 Procedural Process Rules

Procedural rules govern the dynamics of legal processes by authorizing or requiring decisions that are warranted only at specified periods of time or under specific circumstances. Examples from civil proceedings in federal court are: a defendant may move to dismiss for lack of jurisdiction on the basis of the pleadings[29]; a motion for summary judgment may be filed "at any time until 30 days after the close of all discovery"[30]; and motions for directed verdict or for judgment as a matter of law are decided after evidence has been produced at trial (Hazard et al. 2011, §§ 11.19, 11.21).[31] From a logical perspective, the dynamics and timing of a legal process are controlled by the content of the applicable process rules. Rule trees governing such process decisions may themselves also contain substantive conditions to be satisfied – for example, in order for summary judgment to be valid it must be true that "there is no genuine dispute as to any material fact and the movant is entitled to judgment as a matter of law."[32]

The jurisdiction of a federal court provides examples of procedural conditions – such as diversity jurisdiction,[33] general federal–question jurisdiction,[34] and admiralty jurisdiction (Hazard et al. 2011, §§ 2.3–2.8).[35] The statute establishing the VICP confers jurisdiction on the Court of Federal Claims and the special masters over proceedings to determine whether a petitioner is entitled to compensation under the Program.[36] Petitioners are barred from filing their action in both the Court of Federal Claims and in state court concurrently.[37] Further, the statute gives jurisdiction to the Court of Federal Claims to review a special master's decision, and to: (A) uphold the findings and conclusions of the special master and sustain the special master's decision; (B) "set aside any findings of fact or conclusion of law of the special master found to be arbitrary, capricious, an abuse of discretion, or otherwise not in accordance with law and issue its own findings of fact and conclusions of law"; or (C) remand the petition to the special master for further action.[38] Another statute grants the Court of Appeals for the Federal Circuit exclusive jurisdiction over an appeal from a final decision of the Court of Federal

[29]Federal Rule of Civil Procedure 12(b) (2013).

[30]Federal Rule of Civil Procedure 56(b) (2013).

[31]*See* Federal Rule of Civil Procedure 50(a) (2013).

[32]Federal Rule of Civil Procedure 56(a) (2013).

[33]28 U.S.C. § 1332 (2012).

[34]28 U.S.C. § 1331 (2012) (authorizing actions "arising under the Constitution, laws, or treaties of the United States").

[35]28 U.S.C. § 1333 (2012).

[36]42 U.S.C. § 300aa–12 (2011).

[37]42 U.S.C. §§ 300aa–11(a)(2)–(3), 300aa–16(c) (2011).

[38]42 U.S.C. § 300aa–12(e)(2)(A)–(C) (2011).

Claims.[39] After the action is completed in the Court of Federal Claims, petitioners may file a civil action in state or federal court against the vaccine administrator or manufacturer on claims not preempted by the Vaccine Act (Meyers 2011, 787).[40]

Another example of a procedural process rule governing the VICP is the statute of limitations. In the case of vaccine–related injury other than death, petitioner is barred from filing a petition for compensation under the Program more than 36 months "after the date of the occurrence of the first symptom or manifestation of onset or of the significant aggravation of such injury."[41] If this rule presents a contested factual issue in a particular case, then a factfinding process might be needed to decide whether the statute of limitations has been satisfied.[42]

Finally, an important class of procedural rules are those assigning a "burden of production" – also called a "burden of going forward with the evidence" (Hazard et al. 2011, §§ 11.12, 11.25). Such a rule imposes upon some particular party, with respect to some particular issue, the burden of developing evidence and introducing it into the legal record in the case. For example, in VICP cases, the burden is on the petitioner to produce evidence on all of the required elements of the petition.[43] If the party with the burden of production fails to produce the minimum amount or quality of evidence that is deemed "legally sufficient," then that party should lose on that issue "as a matter of law" (Hazard et al. 2011, § 11.15). The totality of evidence in the record that is relevant to a particular issue is "legally sufficient" if a factfinder could make reasonable inferences from that evidence to a conclusion or finding on that issue in favor of that party. The presiding judge (as distinct from the factfinder) decides whether a party has satisfied its burden of production, and therefore whether the factfinder should be allowed to assess the evidence and reach a finding (Hazard et al. 2011, §§ 11.15, 11.19).

For VICP cases, the Federal Circuit has developed a number of sufficiency–of–evidence rules, establishing that certain types of evidence are insufficient or sufficient as a matter of law to support a legal finding (Walker 2009, 33). For example, when proving causation–in–fact in off–Table vaccine cases, a temporal association between vaccination and the onset of injury is, by itself, insufficient evidence of causation; nor is it sufficient to establish a mere similarity between a petitioner's injury and an injury listed on the Vaccine Injury Table.[44] As an example of a rule establishing legally sufficient evidence, the Court has held that "causation [in fact] can be found in vaccine cases based on epidemiological evidence and the

[39] 28 U.S.C. § 1295(3) (2012).

[40] *See* 42 U.S.C. § 300aa–22 (2011).

[41] 42 U.S.C. § 300aa–16(a)(2) (2011).

[42] *See, e.g.*, Cipollone v. Liggett Group, Inc., 893 F.2d 541, 579 (3rd Cir. 1990), *aff'd in part and rev'd in part on other grounds*, 499 U.S. 935 (1991) (holding that the district court's grant of summary judgment against the defendants on their statute of limitations defense was inappropriate and that the issue would need to be tried).

[43] *See* 42 U.S.C. § 300aa–11(c) (2011).

[44] *Grant*, 956 F.2d at 1148.

clinical picture regarding the particular child without detailed medical and scientific exposition on the biological mechanisms."[45] Because sufficiency–of–evidence rules establish what counts as sufficient or insufficient evidence as a matter of law, they give reviewing courts the means to set aside findings of fact, without deference to the factfinder. Such rules govern the procedural aspect of the legal process, because rulings of insufficient evidence in response to a motion can curtail the proceeding either before or during trial. Rules such as those in the examples above furnish a means of resolving the substantive issues raised by those motions (e.g., summary judgment's requirement that there be "no genuine issue as to any material fact"). These rules also form a natural point of departure for exploring evidentiary process rules, because they establish a floor of evidence (however porous) necessary for the evidence assessment process, which is discussed in the next sub–section.[46]

13.4.2 Evidentiary Process Rules

Evidentiary process rules are rules that help to structure the assessment of the evidence in a particular case, and the inferential process from evidence to conclusions or findings (Walker 2007a, 237–41). Examples are rules about what type of evidence is relevant or irrelevant to which issues; rules about admissibility of evidence, either excluding some proffered evidence from the case altogether, or admitting particular items of evidence because they are relevant to some issue in the case[47]; rules about the standard of proof for the factfinder to use in making findings of fact (Hazard et al. 2011, §§ 11.5, 11.14; Walker 1996, 1075–78, 1097–1120); and rules allocating the burden of persuasion to particular parties on particular issues, which determine which party loses if the totality of relevant evidence is in equipoise on the proof threshold established by the standard of proof (Hazard et al. 2011, § 11.13). All of these rules constrain the factfinder's discretion in assessing the probative value of the evidence and in making findings, and they allow the presiding legal authority to oversee the factfinding process. The following sub–sections discuss several major categories of evidentiary rules, providing examples from the VICP.

---

[45]Knudsen v. Secretary of Health and Human Services, 35 F.3d 543, 549 (Fed. Cir. 1994).

[46]Indeed, by emphasizing the substantive conditions of sufficiency–of–evidence rules, a good argument can be made for considering them as evidentiary process rules instead of procedural process rules.

[47]E.g., Federal Rule of Evidence 407 (2013) (excluding evidence of subsequent "measures . . . taken that would have made an earlier injury or harm less likely to occur" to prove negligence or a defect in a product, but not requiring exclusion of such evidence when it is offered "for another purpose, such as . . . proving . . . the feasibility of precautionary measures").

13.4.2.1 Relevant–Factor Rules

Some rules constrain the discretion of the factfinder by defining "relevant" evidence and prescribing some applications of that definition. Federal Rule of Evidence 401 defines evidence as being "relevant" if "it has any tendency to make a fact [of consequence in determining the action] more or less probable than it would be without the evidence." Other rules, which we call "relevant–factor rules," are rules that prescribe which factual issues or evidence ("factors") the factfinder either must (compulsory) or may (permissive) consider in making a finding on a particular type of issue. The statute establishing the VICP, for example, establishes the issues that must be proved in order to obtain compensation, by specifying the required contents of a petition and requiring the petitioner to demonstrate those matters by a preponderance of the evidence.[48] The statute then directs that a special master

> ... shall consider, in addition to all other relevant medical and scientific evidence contained in the record –
>
> (A) any diagnosis, conclusion, medical judgment, or autopsy or coroner's report which is contained in the record regarding the nature, causation, and aggravation of the petitioner's illness, disability, injury, condition, or death, and
> (B) the results of any diagnostic or evaluative test which are contained in the record and the summaries and conclusions.[49]

Thus, the statute sets the basic rules for what evidence is relevant in deciding whether to order compensation.

Of course, when establishing the necessary elements of a petitioner's *prima facie* case, the statutory rules do more than merely specify that those elements are relevant: the statute also mandates that proof of *all* of the elements is a necessary condition for compensation. The rule tree therefore represents the connection of those elements to the ultimate conclusion using the stronger logical connective AND, instead of the weaker connective RULE FACTORS. By contrast, a mere listing of relevant factors (as in the quotation above, stating what a special master "shall consider") is represented using the RULE FACTORS connective discussed in Sect. 13.2. Although a relevant–factor rule might specify which types of evidence a factfinder must or may consider in reaching a conclusion on a particular issue, or which types of evidence a factfinder is not allowed to consider, it sometimes provides no guidance on how the factfinder should combine, weigh, or prioritize those factors. Such rules ensure that certain types of evidence are or are not taken into account, without prescribing any formula for reaching a conclusion (in the way that the connectives AND and OR do prescribe formulas). Nevertheless, a finding may be set aside as "arbitrary and capricious" if the factfinder fails to take into account a required factor, or does take into account an irrelevant factor, or fails

---

[48] 42 U.S.C. § 300aa–13(a)(1)(A) (2011).

[49] 42 U.S.C. § 300aa–13(b)(1) (2011). The Federal Circuit has also provided examples of permissive relevant factors, and has emphasized the probative value of some evidence such as medical opinions of treating physicians. *See Capizzano*, 440 F.3d at 1326.

to adequately explain the factfinder's reasoning to the conclusion in light of the factor.[50]

13.4.2.2 Rules on the Standard of Proof and the Burden of Persuasion

The standard of proof applicable in VICP cases, as in U.S. civil litigation generally, is the preponderance–of–evidence standard (Hazard et al. 2011, § 11.5).[51] The rule under this standard is that the factfinder must make a finding in the direction in which the "greater weight of the evidence" or its "convincing force" points (i.e., either for or against the proposition to be proved) (Walker 1996, 1076; Hazard et al. 2011, § 11.14). In order to make a finding, the factfinder must determine that the proposition is "more probably true than false" (Walker 1996, 1076).

Moreover, just as there generally are legal rules that assign to some party, for any particular issue, a burden of production, there are also rules that assign to some party, for any particular issue, a "burden of persuasion." If the standard of proof is by a preponderance, and the factfinder determines that the weight of the evidence on that issue is in equipoise, then the party who bears the burden of persuasion must lose on that issue (Hazard et al. 2011, §§ 11.13, 11.14; Mueller and Kirkpatrick 2003, 101–09; Wright et al. 2013, § 5122).

Rules regarding the standard of proof and the burden of persuasion provide guidance to factfinders in assessing the evidence, and also constrain their discretion in drawing inferences. For example, Congress had as one policy objective that the VICP should be a program "in which close calls regarding causation are [to be] resolved in favor of injured claimants."[52] Some special masters have interpreted this as meaning that "50% and a feather" warrants a finding in the petitioner's favor,[53] and the Federal Circuit has upheld findings made under this understanding.[54] The Federal Circuit has also recognized that "the purpose of the Vaccine Act's preponderance standard is to allow the finding of causation in a field bereft of complete and direct proof of how vaccines affect the human body."[55] Thus, the Congressional policy objectives behind the VICP can influence how the special

---

[50] *See* Citizens to Preserve Overton Park, Inc. v. Volpe, 401 U.S. 402, 416 (1971); Motor Vehicle Mfr. Assoc. v. State Farm Mutual Automobile Ins. Co., 463 U.S. 29, 43 (1983).

[51] 42 U.S.C. § 300aa–13(a)(1)(A) (2011).

[52] *Althen*, 418 F.3d at 1280.

[53] *E.g.*, Colon v. Secretary of Health and Human Services, 2007 U.S. Claims LEXIS 13, at *47 (2007) (stating that "[u]nder the Vaccine Act, a petitioner is not required to prove his case by medical certainty but only by a preponderance of the evidence, which this Court has described as 50% and a feather").

[54] See *Pafford*, 451 F.3d at 1360 (upholding the decision of the special master, with the dissent stating that although "the Special Master 'painstakingly looked for the feather in Petitioners argument that would tip the scales' as to causation in fact," the special master did not find such additional evidence).

[55] *Althen*, 418 F.3d at 1280.

masters assess causation evidence, and how the reviewing courts apply rules about the legal sufficiency of the evidence.

One interesting feature of the VICP statute involving the burden of persuasion (and the burden of production) is the requirement, discussed in Sect. 13.3, that compensation may not be awarded if the alleged injury or the death "is due to factors unrelated to the administration of the vaccine."[56] The statute does not, however, explicitly assign the burden of persuasion or production on this issue to any particular party – that is, it does not prescribe which party must bring forward legally sufficient evidence for a finding in its favor on this issue, or which party will lose if the weight of the evidence produced is in equipoise.[57] The courts, however, have interpreted the statute as creating this as a defense, and have imposed upon the government, as the respondent in vaccine cases, the burden of production and persuasion. The U.S. Supreme Court has stated that "[t]he Secretary of Health and Human Services may rebut a prima facie case by proving that the injury or death was in fact caused by 'factors unrelated to the administration of the vaccine.' ... If the Secretary fails to rebut, the claimant is entitled to compensation."[58] As the Federal Circuit has explicitly held for Table cases:

> In a "table" case, the petitioner has an initial burden to prove an injury listed in the Vaccine Injury Table within the prescribed time period .... Upon satisfying this initial burden, the petitioner earns a presumption of causation. At that point, the burden shifts to the respondent to prove that a factor unrelated to the vaccination actually caused the illness, disability, injury, or condition.[59]

It has similarly held that in off–Table cases, "[s]o long as the petitioner has satisfied all three prongs of the *Althen* test, she bears no burden to rule out possible alternative causes," but the government can defeat this showing with "factors unrelated to the administration of the vaccine."[60] In short, "if a petitioner has ... obtained the benefit of a presumption, and the government cannot prove actual alternative causation for whatever reason, then the petitioner is entitled to compensation."[61] Moreover, this allocation of burdens follows a typical pattern for U.S. courts, of placing the burden of proving a *prima facie* basis for governmental action on the proponent of that action (in a VICP case, the petitioner seeking compensation), while placing the burden of introducing and proving an alternative, defeating proposition on the opponent of the action – often, an alternative exception made less than probable

[56] 42 U.S.C. § 300aa–13(a)(1)(B) (2011).

[57] *See id.*

[58] *Whitecotton*, 514 U.S. at 270–271.

[59] *Pafford*, 451 F.3d at 1355.

[60] De Bazan v. Secretary of Health and Human Services, 539 F.3d 1347, 1352–54 (Fed. Cir. 2008). For example, the Court said in the *De Bazan* case that "the government may defeat a petitioner's claim with a theory of viral infection, and [by proving] that the viral infection 'in the particular case [was] ... principally responsible for *causing* the petitioner's illness, disability, injury, condition, or death.'" *Id.* at 1353–54.

[61] *Knudsen*, 35 F.3d at 547.

once the *prima facie* case has been proved. This pattern may also be captured in legal rules in the form of a presumption, whose logical form is the topic of the next sub–section.

13.4.2.3 Presumptions

As illustrated above, a statute will occasionally use legal rules to structure the process of evidence assessment into a form called a "legal presumption," or simply "presumption." This sub–section discusses the rule–tree representation of such a legal presumption.[62]

In order to understand the various forms of legal presumptions, it is necessary to define three categories for classifying the probative value of the totality of evidence relevant to any particular issue of fact in a case. First, the evidence might be so inadequate as to be *legally insufficient as a matter of law* – that is, it fails to satisfy the legal rules governing the party's burden of production (Hazard et al. 2011, § 11.19). Second, the evidence might be legally sufficient and a reasonable factfinder could decide the issue for or against the party with the burden of persuasion. In this situation, involving what we call "*sufficient but inconclusive evidence*," the factfinder must assess the evidence and make findings of fact. Third, the evidence might be so compelling that any reasonable factfinder would decide in favor of one party, so that it is not necessary to actually give the issue to the factfinder to decide. Courts generally say that they can decide issues supported by such evidence "as a matter of law," without involving the factfinder. We call this "*conclusive evidence*" (Wright et al. 2013, § 5122).

These three categories of probative evidence lead to a range of theories of presumptions in U.S. law, within which there are two principal theories. These two theories build on the same logical form of presumption, which is: "if **p**, then **q**, unless not–**q**." This can be interpreted as: "if **p** is proven to be true, then **q** is presumed to be true by default (based solely upon **p** as evidence), unless not–**q** is in fact proven to be true (based on other evidence, in spite of **p**)." The antecedent **p** is often called the "basic fact"; the consequent **q** is the "presumed fact"; and we call the negation not–**q** the "defeater proposition" for the presumption. A rule stating a presumption requires an inference from **p** to **q** unless the evidence in a particular case shows that the inference is unwarranted. While this pattern of default reasoning is ubiquitous in common–sense, technical and scientific reasoning, and is therefore also found in evidence assessment in legal proceedings, statutes also occasionally enshrine such presumptions into legal rules.

[62]Vern R. Walker first presented many of the ideas discussed in this sub–section in a paper entitled "Representing the Use of Rule–Based Presumptions in Legal Decision Documents," at the Workshop on "Formal Argument and Evidential Inference," during the Fourteenth International Conference on Artificial Intelligence and Law (ICAIL 2013), held in Rome, Italy, on June 14, 2013.

As discussed above, the VICP statute provides a clear example. The statute requires that compensation be paid to a petitioner if the factfinder makes two findings: (A) that the petitioner has demonstrated by a preponderance of the evidence that the required allegations in the petition (including causation) are true, and (B) that "there is not a preponderance of the evidence" in the legal record that the injury "is due to factors unrelated to" the vaccination.[63] The statute places the burden of persuasion (and by implication the burden of production) with respect to (A) on the petitioner, but is silent as to which party bears a burden of production or persuasion with respect to (B). Using the logical form of a presumption, and focusing on the causation requirement, the "basic fact" **p** is the *prima facie* proof that the vaccination caused the injury (either by satisfying the Table requirements or by proving the three *Althen* prongs), the "presumed fact" **q** is that the vaccination caused the injury, and the "defeater proposition" not–**q** is that in fact the particular injury was due (entirely) to factors unrelated to the vaccination. Figure 13.3 depicts the statutory presumption of Table causation, including the *prima facie* conditions for triggering this presumption.

The two competing theories of presumption add to this formal representation the concepts of burden of production and burden of persuasion. Under the first, more traditional theory, a legal presumption shifts to the opponent *only* the burden of production with respect to the negation of the presumed fact (the defeater proposition): "if the proponent of **q** proves **p** to be true, then **q** is presumed to be true, unless the opponent *has produced sufficient evidence* for a reasonable factfinder to find not–**q**." Under this interpretation, the presumption itself "disappears" from the case (plays no further inferential role) once the presiding judge decides that the party opposing the presumption has produced sufficient evidence of not–**q**. Once the presumption disappears, the factfinder has the discretion to choose between **q** and not–**q** solely on the basis of the relevant evidence in the legal record of the case. The legal theorists Thayer and Wigmore espoused this theory of legal presumptions (Giannelli 2009, 58–59; Wright et al. 2013, § 5122.1).

The theory at the other extreme is that the presumption continues to play an inferential role in a case even after the opponent produces sufficient evidence of not–**q**, and the presumption also places upon the opponent a burden of *persuasion* with respect to not–**q**. Formally, "if the proponent of **q** proves **p** to be true, then **q** is presumed to be true, unless the opponent *proves* not–**q** to be true." In cases where the evidence of not–**q** is conclusive, the judge may find not–**q** to be true "as a matter of law." This interpretation is normally identified with the theorists Morgan and McCormick, as a "reform view" that considered the traditional view to give too little inferential effect to presumptions (Mueller and Kirkpatrick 2003, 111; Wright et al. 2013, § 5122.1).

In the case of the VICP statute, the courts have regularly referred to the Table method of proving causation as a "statutorily–prescribed presumption."[64] Moreover,

[63] 42 U.S.C. § 300aa–13(a)(1) (2011).

[64] E.g., *Althen*, 418 F.3d at 1278.

proving the basic facts of this statutory presumption of causation shifts both a burden of production and a burden of persuasion to the government with respect to the defeating proposition. If there is insufficient evidence in the record to support a finding that the injury was due to factors unrelated to the vaccination, then compensation must be awarded.[65] In addition, if there is sufficient but inconclusive evidence in the record that not–**q** is true, and the factfinder does not find this defeating proposition to be true, then compensation must be awarded.[66] Thus, the statute prescribes a strong presumption, of the type favored by Morgan. This presumption is triggered by the petitioner's proving, by a preponderance of the evidence, that the basic facts are true, which in turn requires the factfinder to infer that the presumed fact is true, unless *the government proves* by a preponderance of the evidence that the defeater proposition is true – and if the government proves not–**q**, then the factfinder must conclude that the presumed fact **q** is false.

13.5 Conclusion

This chapter has presented a formal method for representing the logic of statutory rules in the United States. This method extracts from statutes the legal rules that govern types of governmental decisions and actions, thus reflecting the dynamic and pragmatic conception of law that is common in the U.S. Moreover, the chapter discussed how policy objectives and evidence form an essential context for understanding how legal rules are justified and applied. The formal structure of a rule tree, with the ultimate issue to be decided at the top, allows us to represent in a single structure an entire system containing the process and substantive rules that govern a particular type of action. Within the rule tree, we can use sub–structures such as truth–functional connectives, relevant–factor rules, and presumptions to capture particular patterns of reasoning.

But rule trees are not merely theoretical structures. They are useful for abstracting the logical essence of statutes and forming it into an operational structure, which can provide the basis for software computation and for exchange of legal knowledge in digital form. Rule trees are also of practical use to attorneys and judges, because they identify all issues that are relevant to a particular decision or action, they omit all issues that are irrelevant, and they provide a practical framework for organizing both evidence and arguments in a legal case. Viewed in this way, statutory rules are not a static set of definitions, but rather a core mechanism that can be used to generate organized, fair and efficient legal processes.

Finally, this method of representing the logic of statutory rules suggests some guidelines for effective drafting of legislation. It would be helpful to judges and attorneys if legislative drafters would anticipate the pragmatic use of statutes,

[65] See § 300aa–13(a)(1)(B) (2011).

[66] Id.

and prior evaluation of a draft statute from this pragmatic perspective would also provide a useful check on the adequacy of statutory provisions. For example, it would be helpful to list in advance those governmental actions that the statute requires, authorizes, or prohibits, and to examine the processes leading to those actions, to ensure that competent actors play suitable roles. In addition, the rules governing each action in each process should be representable in a rule tree, and should be evaluated for adequacy. The roles of judges and other policy–appliers should also be evaluated, as well as the roles involved in evidence assessment. The foreseeable actions of all of these actors should be suitably governed by a variety of logical devices, including substantive, procedural and evidentiary rules and legal presumptions. Conducting the kind of logical evaluation proposed in this chapter should lead to clearer statutory drafting, and to more satisfactory statutory oversight of those actors and actions upon which successful implementation depends.

Acknowledgements We gratefully acknowledge the generous support of the Maurice A. Deane School of Law for this research by the Research Laboratory for Law, Logic and Technology.

References

Binski, Laura A. 2011. Balancing policy tensions of the vaccine act in light of the omnibus autism proceeding: Are petitioners getting a fair shot at compensation? *Hofstra Law Review* 39:683–721.

Brachman, Ronald J., and Hector J. Levesque. 2004. *Knowledge representation and reasoning*. Amsterdam: Elsevier.

Brewer, Scott. 1996. Exemplary reasoning: Semantics, pragmatics, and the rational force of legal argument by analogy. *Harvard Law Review* 109:923–1028.

Brewka, Gerhard, Jürgen Dix, and Kurt Konolige. 1997. *Nonmonotonic reasoning: An overview*. Stanford: CSLI Publications.

Currier, James B. 2009. Too sick, too soon?: The causation burden under the national vaccine injury compensation program following De Bazan v. secretary of health & human services. *Federal Circuit Bar Journal* 19:229–252.

Giannelli, Paul C. 2009. *Understanding evidence*, 3rd ed. New Providence: LexisNexis, Matthew Bender & Co.

Gottwald, Siegfried. 2001. *A treatise on many-valued logics*. Baldock: Research Studies Press.

Grey, Betsy J. 2011. The plague of causation in the national childhood vaccine injury act. *Harvard Journal on Legislation* 48:343–414.

Hazard, Geoffrey C., Jr., John Leubsdorf, and Debra Lyn Bassett. 2011. *Civil procedure*, 6th ed. New York: Foundation Press.

Josephson, John R., and Susan G. Josephson, eds. 1996. *Abductive inference: Computation, philosophy, technology*. Cambridge: Cambridge University Press.

Kahneman, David, Paul Slovic, and Amos Tversky, eds. 1982. *Judgment under uncertainty: Heuristics and biases*. Cambridge: Cambridge University Press.

Kyburg, Henry E., Jr., and Choh Man Teng. 2001. *Uncertain inference*. Cambridge: Cambridge University Press.

Levi, Isaac. 1996. *For the sake of argument: Ramsey test conditionals, inductive inference, and nonmonotonic reasoning*. Cambridge: Cambridge University Press.

MacCormick, Neil. 2005. *Rhetoric and the rule of law: A theory of legal reasoning*. Oxford: Oxford University Press.

Meyers, Peter H. 2011. Fixing the flaws in the federal vaccine injury compensation program. *Administrative Law Review* 63:785–851.
Morgan, M. Granger, and Max Henrion. 1990. *Uncertainty: A guide to dealing with uncertainty in quantitative risk and policy analysis*. Cambridge: Cambridge University Press.
Mueller, Christopher B., and Laird C. Kirkpatrick. 2003. *Evidence*, 3rd ed. New York: Aspen Publishers.
Pollock, John L. 1990. *Nomic probability and the foundations of induction*. New York/Oxford: Oxford University Press.
Poole, David. 1988. A logical framework for default reasoning. *Artificial Intelligence* 36:27–47.
Prakken, Henry. 1997. *Logical tools for modelling legal argument: A study of defeasible reasoning in law*. Dordrecht/Boston/London: Kluwer.
Prakken, Henry, and Giovanni Sartor. 1997. Reasoning with precedents in a dialogue game. In *Proceedings of the sixth international conference on artificial intelligence and law (ICAIL 1997)*, Melbourne, 1–9.
Prakken, Henry, and Giovanni Sartor. 2004. The three faces of defeasibility in the law. *Ratio Juris* 17(1):118–139.
Prakken, Henry, Chris Reed, and Douglas Walton. 2003. Argumentation schemes and generalizations in reasoning about evidence. In *Proceedings of the ninth international conference on artificial intelligence and law (ICAIL 2003)*, Edinburgh, 32–41.
Reiter, Raymund. 1980. A logic for default reasoning. *Artificial Intelligence* 13:81–132.
Walker, Vern R. 1996. Preponderance, probability and warranted factfinding. *Brooklyn Law Review* 62:1075–1136.
Walker, Vern R. 2003. Epistemic and non–epistemic aspects of the factfinding process in law. *American Philosophical Association Newsletter on Law and Philosophy* 3(1):132–136.
Walker, Vern R. 2007a. A default–logic paradigm for legal fact–finding. *Jurimetrics* 47:193–243.
Walker, Vern R. 2007b. Discovering the logic of legal reasoning. *Hofstra Law Review* 35:1687–1707.
Walker, Vern R. 2009. Designing factfinding for cross–border healthcare. *Opinio Juris in Comparatione* 3, paper n. 1, 1–40.
Walker, Vern R., Chan Hee Park, Philip H. Hwang, Arthur John, Evgeny I. Krasnov, and Keith Langlais. 2013. A process approach to inferences of causation: Empirical research from vaccine cases in the USA. *Law, Probability and Risk* 12(3–4):189–205.
Wright, Charles Alan, Kenneth W. Graham, Jr., Victor James Gold, and Michael H. Graham. 2013. *Federal practice & procedure, federal rules of evidence*, vol. 21B, 2nd ed. Westlaw, Thomson Reuters. http://www.westlaw.com.

Chapter 14
Modern Logic as a Tool for Remedying Ambiguities in Legal Documents and Analyzing the Structure of Legal Documents' Contained Definitions

Layman E. Allen and Leon J. Lysaght

Abstract There are three forms of indeterminacy in legal documents (statutes, constitutions, regulations, contracts, briefs, forms and other): (1) ambiguity, (2) scope of reference, and (3) vagueness. The first two, ambiguity and scope of reference indeterminacies, can be avoided – and should be. The third, vagueness, is inevitable, but its scope can be managed. For example, "giving notice" can be required in 24 hours, 30 days, one year or in a timely fashion. The solution of the drafters, for example, of the Uniform Commercial Code (of the United States) was "seasonable notice". So, sometimes deliberate vagueness is the course of wisdom and preferred choice.

The First Amendment of the United States Constitution and Article 9-608 of the Uniform Commercial Code contain various ambiguities and indefiniteness in scope of reference that are analyzed here in detail along with our proposed resolutions.

Keywords Ambiguity • Logical terms (and, or, and various forms of if-then) • Modern logics • Scope of reference • Vagueness

14.1 Introduction

The "scope of reference" indeterminacy usually occurs in the words surrounding occurrences of the words "and", "or", and other such terms. A classic example

L.E. Allen (✉)
Professor of Law and Senior Research Scientist, University of Michigan (emeritus), Ann Arbor, MI, USA

Scholar, University of Detroit Mercy Law School, Detroit, MI, USA
e-mail: laymanal@umich.edu

L.J. Lysaght
Associate Professor of Law, University of Detroit Mercy Law School, Detroit, MI, USA
e-mail: lysaghtl@udmercy.edu; lysaghtl@aol.com

M. Araszkiewicz, K. Płeszka (eds.), *Logic in the Theory and Practice of Lawmaking*, Legisprudence Library 2, DOI 10.1007/978-3-319-19575-9_14

occurred a 1955 case in the California Supreme Court on the California pimping statute which stated: "Any male person ... who solicits or receives compensation for soliciting for her, is guilty of pimping, a felony ..." The California Supreme Court (California v. Smith, 44 Cal.2d 77 (1955)) upheld the decision of the lower court that the defendant had not violated the statute since Smith had not solicited compensation for soliciting for her even though he had solicited for her. Thus, the Court interpreted the ambiguous statute as being directed only at "soliciting compensation for soliciting for her" and "receiving compensation for soliciting for her", and not at mere soliciting for her alone. Such scope ambiguities can usually be avoided by the mere repetition of a few words.

The really troublesome indeterminacy, and the one that is addressed here, is the one that involves ambiguity, which appears on every page of virtually every legal document produced. Surprisingly, the problem of pervasive ambiguity in all legal documents is virtually ignored in legal literature. Similarly ignored in legal writings are the extraordinary developments that have occurred in the field of logic in the late Nineteenth and Twentieth Centuries. The only logic that receives virtually any mention in legal literature in the United States is that ancient primitive one of Aristotle – as though it is the only one of relevance, and then it is largely dismissed as inadequate for legal purposes. Eight of the logics of the most recent two centuries are used in constructing the Legal-Relations* language, an elaboration of the powerful Hohfeldian system of legal analysis and an extraordinarily powerful tool for detecting and remediating the numerous ambiguities appearing in legal documents. Some of the Legal Relations language and Hohfeld's Fundamental Legal Conceptions are used in the analysis here (Hohfeld 1917).

* Defined Terms in the Legal-Relations language are signaled by capitalizing and underlining their initial letters. The full 80-Term Legal-Relations language is available online at http://law.alf-learning.org. (Terms that are underlined and bold-faced terms are hyper-links to definitions of or further information about those terms in versions of this article where hyper-links are permitted.)

In the last quarter of the Twentieth Century researchers in the field of artificial intelligence combined with researchers in law around the world to form the International Association of Artificial Intelligence and Law and sponsor a bi-annual conference called the International Conference of Artificial Intelligence and Law at various sites in Europe, North America, Australia, and Asia. Pointedly at its meeting in Rome when the group was selecting the name of the organization, it rejected as the name of the new organization "International Association of Artificial Intelligence *and Logic* and Law" in favor the shorter version selected. Much, if not most, of the logical work published in the proceedings of the bi-annual conferences of ICAIL deal with efforts that involve a branch of knowledge called "Non-monotonic Logic". As described in the Stanford Encyclopedia of Philosophy "The term "non-monotonic logic" covers a family of formal frameworks devised to capture and represent *defeasible inference*, i.e., that kind of inference of everyday life in which persons draw conclusions tentatively, reserving the right to retract them in the light of further information. Such inferences are called "non-monotonic" because the set of conclusions warranted on the basis of a given knowledge base, given as a set of premises, does not increase (in fact, it can shrink) with the size of the knowledge base itself. This is in contrast to standard logical frameworks (e.g., classical first-order) logic, whose inferences, being deductively valid, can never be "undone" by new information."

The Legal-Relations language used in this article is based entirely upon monotonic logics. It will be used in remediating detected ambiguities as exemplified in two important areas in American law: The First Amendment of the United States Constitution and Article 9-608 of the Uniform Commercial Code, which has been adopted in varying degrees in all 50 states of the United States.

14.2 The First Amendment of the United States Constitution

The 45-word sentence that constitutes the First Amendment of the United States Constitution is perhaps the most remarkable example of inadvertent ambiguity ever constructed. It contains eleven ambiguities that give rise to either 3,317,760 or 49,766,400 alternative interpretations* – just which number depends upon how the final ambiguity with respect to the occurrence of the word "and" is resolved. It reads as follows: (with the superscripted numerals indicating the ambiguities that will be discussed below)

> Congress **shall make no**[1] law **respecting**[2 & 3] an **establishment of religion**[4], **or**[5] prohibiting the free exercise thereof: **or**[6] abridging the freedom of speech, **or**[7] of the press; **or**[8] the **right**[9] of the people **peaceably**[10] to assemble, **and**[11] to petition to government for a redress of grievances.

The Terms involving the ambiguities are bold-faced and enumerated.

The Term "shall make no" involves a dual semantic-logical ambiguity, while the four occurrences of "or" and the single occurrence of "and" involve logical and scope of reference ambiguities, the occurrences of "respecting" and "right" involve semantic ambiguities, and the occurrences of "respecting", "abridging" and "peaceably" involve syntactic scope-of-reference ambiguities. The eleven ambiguities in the First Amendment will be presented here in the form of eleven multiple-choice questions with possible responses labeled by capital letters. Thus, a reader's interpretation of the First Amendment by his or her resolution of the eleven (or twelve) ambiguities can be indicated be an eleven-letter string of letters such as: ACBB AACB BJB. Alternatively, the resolution could be a twelve-letter string, if the answer to the eleventh ambiguity is A, such as: ACBB AACB BJAB. If readers keep track of their answers to the ambiguity questions, they can compare them with the authors" suggestions which are provided at the end of the presentation of the eleven (or twelve) ambiguities.

Your Interpretation: 1 2 3 4 5 6 7 8 9A1 9A2 9B 10 11

Ambiguity 1

"Congress shall make no law respecting an establishment of religion ..." Which of the following is the most appropriate interpretation of the semantic meaning of "shall make no"?

A. Congress **lacks Power** to make law respecting an establishment of religion ..., i.e., **has a Disability to make** such law.

B. 1. Congress **has Power** to make law respecting an establishment of religion ... **And**
   2. Congress **has a Duty** to persons with an **Interest* Not** to exercise that **Power**.
      * Persons who have
      (a) a **Right** that Congress **Not** exercise its **Power** to make such a law, along with
      (b) a **Power** to enforce that **Right** along with
      (c) a **Privilege** to exercise that **Power**, all three of the above of which have an **Immunity** from being terminated by anyone.

C. 1. Congress **has Power to make** law respecting an establishment of religion ... **And**
   2. Congress is **Forbidden** to exercise that **Power**.

Ambiguity 2

Which of the following is the most appropriate interpretation of the syntactic scope of reference of the word "respecting"?

There are four alternative interpretations of the scope of reference of "respecting" to be considered in terms of which of the four following phrases it refers to: (1) an establishment of religion, (2) prohibiting the free exercise thereof, (3) abridging the freedom of speech, or of the press, and (4) the right of the people peaceably to assemble.

A. The word "respecting" refers only to (1) an establishment of religion.
B. The word "respecting" refers only to (1) an establishment of religion, and (2) prohibiting the free exercise thereof.
C. The word "respecting" refers only to (1) an establishment of religion, (2) prohibiting the free exercise thereof, and (3) abridging the freedom of speech.
D. The word "respecting" refers to all four (1) an establishment of religion, (2) prohibiting the free exercise thereof, (3) abridging the freedom of speech and (4) the right of the people peaceably to assemble.

Ambiguity 3

Which is the most appropriate interpretation of the semantic meaning of the word "respecting"?

A. Congress shall make no law *giving* respect *to* an establishment of religion.
B. Congress shall make no law *with* respect to an establishment of religion.
C. Congress shall make no law *giving respect to* an establishment of religion, AND Congress shall make no law with respect to an establishment of religion.

Ambiguity 4
Which is the most appropriate interpretation of the semantic meaning of the phrase "an establishment of religion"?

A. Congress shall make no law respecting a religious establishment (an institution).
B. Congress shall make no law respecting the establishing of a religion.
C. Congress shall make no law respecting a religious establishment (an institution), AND Congress shall make no law respecting the establishing of a religion.

In interpreting the four occurrences of "or" in Ambiguities 5, 6, 7 and 8 use the following abbreviations for "or". [A. **Or**$_c$ conjunction B. **Or**$_d$ inclusive disjunction C. **Or**$_s$ logical sum D. **Or**$_x$ exclusive disjunction].

> Congress **shall make no**[1] law **respecting**[23] an **establishment of religion**[4], **or**[5] prohibiting the free exercise thereof: **or**[6] abridging the freedom of speech, **or**[7] of the press; **or**[8] the **right**[9] of the people **peaceably**[10] to assemble, **and**[11] to petition to government for a redress of grievances.

Ambiguity 5
Congress shall make no law respecting an establishment of religion, **or**[5] prohibiting the free exercise thereof....

A. **Or**$_c$ conjunction B. **Or**$_d$ inclusive disjunction C. **Or**$_s$ logical sum D. **Or**$_x$ exclusive disjunction

Ambiguity 6
Congress shall make no law prohibiting the free exercise of religion: **or**[6] abridging the freedom

A. **Or**$_c$ conjunction B. **Or**$_d$ inclusive disjunction C. **Or**$_s$ logical sum D. **Or**$_x$ exclusive disjunction

Ambiguity 7
Congress shall make no law abridging the freedom of speech, **or**[7] of the press....

A. **Or**$_c$ conjunction B. **Or**$_d$ inclusive disjunction C. **Or**$_s$ logical sum D. **Or**x exclusive disjunction

Ambiguity 8
Congress shall make no law abridging the freedom of the press; **or**[8] the right of the people peaceably to assemble....

A. **Or**$_c$ conjunction B. **Or**$_d$ inclusive disjunction C. **Or**$_s$ logical sum D. **Or**$_x$ exclusive disjunction

Because there is a somewhat complex relationship between Ambiguity 9 and Ambiguity 11, which requires a resolution of Ambiguity 11 before knowing how to proceed with resolving Ambiguity 9, Ambiguities 10 and 11 are being presented before Ambiguity 9. However your answers to Ambiguities 10 and 11 should be recorded in the slots for Ambiguities 10 and 11, the two slots after the slot for Ambiguity 9 of the word "right".

Ambiguity 10

Which is the most appropriate syntactic scope of reference of the word "peaceably" in the First Amendment?

A. The word "peaceably" refers only to the phrase "to assemble".
B. The word "peaceably" refers both to the phrase "to assemble" and to the phrase "to petition…"

Ambiguity 11

Which is the most appropriate logical interpretation of the word "and", which involves a syntactic scope of reference aspect in, "Congress shall make no law …respecting …the right of the people peaceably to assemble, **and** to petition to government for a redress of grievances"?

A. $\underline{\textbf{And}}_c$ conjunction B. $\underline{\textbf{And}}_p$ logical product C. $\underline{\textbf{And}}_d$ disjunction
D. $\underline{\textbf{And}}_x$ exclusive disjunction

It is your answer to this eleventh ambiguity that determines whether there are 3,317,760 or 49,766,400 different interpretations of the First Amendment as indicated in the tabulation below.

Questions: 1 2 3 4 5 6 7 8 9A1 9A1 9B 10 11
Alternatives: 3×4×3×3×4×4×4×4× _ × _ × 15 × 2 × 4 = 3,317,760 Interpretations
Alternatives: 3×4×3×3×4×4×4×4×15 ×15×2×4 = 49,766,400 Interpretations

Furthermore, the eleventh is the only one of the eleven ambiguities that has been expressly ruled on by the United States Supreme Court. We shall see in later discussion here that the status of that ruling has been more intricate than is customary.

The ambiguity of the word "right", which is Ambiguity 9, is by any measure the most complicated ambiguity of all. Its ambiguity was recognized at the outset of the Twentieth Century by Wesley N. Hohfeld in his seminal pair of articles in 23 Yale Law Journal on Fundamental Legal Conceptions in 1917. Hohfeld used eight terms to specify his Fundamental Legal Conceptions, not by definitions, but by setting them forth in tables – correlative and opposite relationships between the eight terms. He erroneously claimed that these eight Fundamental Legal Conceptions could represent all legal states of affairs and all changes from one legal state to another. The Legal Relations language, on the other hand, accomplishes this and considerably more.

Fundamental Legal Conceptions

Jural Opposites: right no-right privilege duty power disability immunity liability
Jural Correlatives: right duty privilege no-right power liability immunity disability

Hohfeld pointed out and gave examples in judicial opinions and other legal literature of the ambiguity of "right" being used to indicate four different of his Fundamental Legal Conceptions, namely: immunity, power, privilege and right (itself). Hohfeld's advice about clarifying usage of the term has been vigorously ignored in an astonishing preponderance of legal literature throughout the Twentieth Century and down to this day. Furthermore, the word "right" is more ambiguous than just the four alternatives that Hohfeld mentioned. The word "right" is sometimes used to indicate the eleven other various combinations of those four. It will be helpful to set forth the full pattern of the fifteen alternative references of the word "right" in its legal sense in the Legal-Relations language Terms.

A. Immunity	E. Immunity-Power	K. Immunity-Power-Privilege	O. Immunity-Power-Privilege-Right
B. Power	F. Immunity-Privilege	L. Immunity-Power-Right	
C. Privilege	G. Immunity-Right	M. Immunity-Privilege-Right	
D. Right	H. Power-Privilege	N. Power-Privilege-Right	
	I. Power-Right		
	J. Privilege-Right		

For example with respect to the O alternative: The combined **Power** of the people to successfully sue if others interfere with their efforts to peaceably to assemble and the **Immunity** of the people peaceably to assemble without successful suit by others to prevent their assembling and the **Privilege** of the people with respect to others to bring suit against those who interfere with their efforts to peaceably assemble and the **Right** of the people with respect to others peaceably to assemble.

Hence, there are the preceding fifteen alternative choices for the interpretation of "right" in the First Amendment. The eight Terms of Hohfeld's Fundamental Legal Conceptions are more precisely defined in the Legal-Relations language **And**$_c$* are used in specifying the fifteen alternative interpretations of the word "right" as it appears in the legal literature. The eight Hohfeldiian Fundamental Legal Conceptions set forth in his tables of correlatives and opposites are more precisely defined in the Legal-Relations language as used in specifying the fifteen alternative interpretations of the word "right" as it appears in the legal literature.

* A defined "**And**$_c$" in the Legal-Relations language indicates its use as a conjunction rather than as a logical product or otherwise.

In the Legal-Relations language the four basic deontic (D) Legal-Relations are:
Right(a,b,s): Person-a has a Right that Person-b see to it that state-of-affairs-s is so.
Duty(b,a,s): Person-b has a Duty to Person-a to see to it that state-of-affairs-s is so.
Privilege(b.a.s): Person-b has a Privilege with respect to Person-a to see to it that state-of-affairs-s is so.
No-right(a,b,s): Person-a has a No-right that Person-b see to it that state-of-affairs-s is so.

There are two second-level Legal-Relations: Conditional-Deontic (CD) and Power-Deontic (PD). For example: Conditional-Duty(b,a,s) and Power(c, Duty(b,a,s) i.e., Power of Person-c to create Duty(b,a,s). There are four third -level Legal-Relations: Conditional-Conditional Deontic (CCD), Conditional Conditional- Power-Deontic (CPD), Power-Conditional-Deontic (PCD) and Power-Power-Deontic PPD). It continues to expand in this fashion: eight at 4th level, 16 at 5th level, 32 at 6th level, 64 at 7th level to the many-infinite at the infinite-th level. Needless to say, the Legal-Relations Language is an extraordinarily rich language.

It can express precisely a multi-infinite number of different Legal-Relations, only a very small fraction of which are necessary to comprehensively describe all Legal-Relations in every legal system on earth:

(1) every existing legal state of affairs between every set of two legal persons,
(2) every change in every existing legal state of affairs to another legal state,
(3) every legal argument, And_c
(4) every legal rule.

For a more complete description of the 80-Term Legal-Relations language, the defined Terms of which are signaled by underlined and capitalized initial letters, see online: The Legal-Relations Language at: http://law.alf-learning.org. There, the unusual inventiveness of the Hohfeldian Fundamental Legal Conceptions and the extraordinary richness of the Legal Relations language are set forth in more extensive detail.

Ambiguity 9
Which is the most appropriate interpretation of the semantic legal meaning of the word "right"? The appropriate response to this question is going to depend heavily upon the response given to Ambiguity 11 above with respect to the word "and". If you chose Alternative A to Ambiguity 11, that the word "and" expressed the conjunction of the two complete sentences, one of which contains "to assemble …" and the other of which contains "to petition …", then you should both: (1) choose from among the 15 alternatives in Set A, and (2) also choose from among the 15 alternatives in Set B. However, if you chose Alternative B that the word "and" expressed the logical product of the combination of "to assemble …" with, "to petition …", then you should choose from among the 15 alternatives in Set A below only. Hence, choose from either of the following, but not both:

(1) For choosing Alternative A to Question 11, select (1) both (a) from the 15 alternatives in Set A and also (b) from the 15 alternatives in Set B.
(2) For choosing Alternative B to Question 11, select from the 15 alternatives in Set B alone below.

Set A Choose from these 15 alternatives, whether you chose Alternative A or Alternative B to Question 11.
Congress shall make no law abridging …

A. the **Immunity** of the people peaceably to assemble without successful suit by others that they refrain from assembling.
B. the **Power** of the people to successfully sue if others interfere with their efforts peaceably to assemble.
C. the **Privilege** of the people with respect to others peaceably to assemble.
D. the **Right** of the people with respect to others peaceably to assemble.
E. 1. the **Immunity** of the people peaceably to assemble without successful suit by others to prevent their assembling, $\textbf{And}_c$
   2. the **Power** of the people to successfully sue if others interfere with their efforts peaceably to assemble.

F. 1. the **Immunity** of the people peaceably to assemble without successful suit by others to prevent their assembling, **And**$_c$

2. the **Privilege** of the people with respect to others peaceably to assemble without successful suit by others to prevent their assembling.

G. 1. the **Immunity** of the people peaceably to assemble without successful suit by others to prevent their assembling, **And**$_c$

2. the **Right** of the people with respect to others peaceably to assemble without interference by others to prevent their assembling.

H. 1. the **Power** of the people successfully to sue those who interfere with their efforts peaceably to assemble, **And**$_c$

2. the **Privilege** of the people with respect to others to bring suit against those who interfere with their efforts to peaceably assemble.

I. 1. the **Power** of the people successfully to sue those who interfere with their efforts peaceably to assemble, **And**$_c$

2. the **Right** of the people with respect to others peaceably to assemble without interference by others to prevent their assembling.

J. 1. the **Privilege** of the people to bring suit against those who interfere with their efforts to peaceably assemble, **And**$_c$

2. the **Right** of the people with respect to others peaceably to assemble without interference by others to prevent their assembling.

K. 1. the **Immunity** of the people peaceably to assemble without successful suit by others to prevent their assembling, **And**$_c$

2. the **Power** of the people to successfully sue if others interfere with their efforts peaceably to assemble, **And**$_c$

3. the **Privilege** of the people with respect to others to bring suit against those who interfere with their efforts to peaceably assemble.

L. 1. the **Immunity** of the people peaceably to assemble without successful suit by others to prevent their assembling, **And**$_c$

2. the **Power** of the people to successfully sue if others interfere with their efforts peaceably to assemble, **And**$_c$

3. the **Right** of the people with respect to others peaceably to assemble without interference by others to prevent their assembling.

M. 1. the **Immunity** of the people peaceably to assemble without successful suit by others to prevent their assembling, **And**$_c$

2. the **Privilege** of the people with respect to others to bring suit against those who interfere with their efforts to peaceably, **And**$_c$

3. the **Right** of the people with respect to others peaceably to assemble without interference by others to prevent their assembling.

N. 1. the **Power** of the people to successfully sue if others interfere with their efforts peaceably to assemble, **And**$_c$

2. the **Privilege** of the people with respect to others to bring suit against those who interfere with their efforts to peaceably assemble, **AND**$_c$

3. the **Right** of the people with respect to others peaceably to assemble without interference by others to prevent their assembling.

O. 1. the **Immunity** of the people peaceably to assemble without successful suit by others to prevent their assembling, **And**$_c$

2. the **Power** of the people to successfully sue if others interfere with their efforts peaceably to assemble, **And**$_c$

3. the **Privilege** of the people with respect to others to bring suit against those who interfere with their efforts to peaceably assemble, **AND**$_c$

4. the **Right** of the people with respect to others peaceably to assemble without interference by others to prevent their assembling.

Set B Choose from these 15 alternatives only if you chose Alternative A to Question 11.

Congress shall make no law abridging . . .

A. the **Immunity** of the people peaceably to assemble without successful suit by others to refrain from assembling, and to petition to government for a redress of grievances.

B. the **Power** of the people to successfully sue if others interfere with their efforts peaceably to assemble, and to petition to government for a redress of grievances.

C. the **Privilege** of the people with respect to others peaceably to assemble, and to petition to government for a redress of grievances.

D. the **Right** of the people with respect to others peaceably to assemble, and to petition to government for a redress of grievances.

E. 1. the **Immunity** of the people peaceably to assemble . . . **And**$_c$

2. the **Power** of the people to successfully sue . . . .

F. 1. the **Immunity** of the people peaceably to assemble . . . , **And**$_c$

2. the **Privilege** of the people with respect to others peaceably to assemble . . . .

G. 1. the **Immunity** of the people peaceably to assemble . . . , **And**$_c$

2. the **Right** of the people with respect to others peaceably to assemble . . . .

H. 1. the **Power** of the people successfully to sue those who interfere with their efforts peaceably to assemble and to petition to government for a redress of grievances, **And**$_c$

2. the **Privilege** of the people with respect to others to bring suit against those who interfere with their efforts to peaceably assemble and to petition to government for a redress of grievances.

I. 1. the **Power** of the people successfully to sue those who interfere with their efforts peaceably to assemble and to petition to government for a redress of grievances, **And**$_c$

2. the **Right** of the people with respect to others peaceably to assemble and to petition to government for a redress of grievances without interference by others to prevent their assembling and petitioning.

J. 1. the **Privilege** of the people to bring suit against those who interfere with their efforts to peaceably assemble and to petition to government for a redress of grievances, **And**$_c$

2. the **Right** of the people with respect to others peaceably to assemble and to petition to government for a redress of grievances without interference by others to prevent their assembling and petitioning.

K. 1. the **Immunity** of the people peaceably to assemble without successful suit by others to prevent their assembling, and to petition to government for a redress of grievances, **And**$_c$
2. the **Power** of the people to successfully sue if others interfere with their efforts peaceably to assemble and to petition to government for a redress of grievances, **And**$_c$
3. the **Privilege** of the people with respect to others to bring suit against those who interfere with their efforts to peaceably assemble and to petition to government for a redress of grievances.

L. 1. the **Immunity** of the people peaceably to assemble without successful suit by others to prevent their assembling, and to petition to government for a redress of grievances, **And**$_c$
2. the **Power** of the people to successfully sue if others interfere with their efforts peaceably to assemble and to petition to government for a redress of grievances, **And**$_c$
3. the **Right** of the people with respect to others peaceably to assemble and to petition to government for a redress of grievances without interference by others to prevent their assembling and petitioning.

M. 1. the **Immunity** of the people peaceably to assemble without successful suit by others to prevent their assembling, and to petition to government for a redress of grievances, **And**$_c$
2. the **Privilege** of the people with respect to others to bring suit against those who interfere with their efforts to peaceably assemble and to petition to government for a redress of grievances, **And**$_c$
3. the **Right** of the people with respect to others peaceably to assemble and to petition to government for a redress of grievances without interference by others to prevent their assembling and petitioning.

N. 1. the **Power** of the people to successfully sue if others interfere with their efforts peaceably to assemble and to petition to government for a redress of grievances, **And**$_c$
2. the **Privilege** of the people with respect to others to bring suit against those who interfere with their efforts to peaceably assemble and to petition to government for a redress of grievances, **And**$_c$
3. the **Right** of the people with respect to others peaceably to assemble and to petition to government for a redress of grievances without interference by others to prevent their assembling and petitioning.

O. 1. the **Immunity** of the people peaceably to assemble without successful suit by others to prevent their assembling, and to petition to government for a redress of grievances, **And**$_c$
2. the **Power** of the people to successfully sue if others interfere with their efforts peaceably to assemble and to petition to government for a redress of grievances, **And**$_c$
3. the **Privilege** of the people with respect to others to bring suit against those who interfere with their efforts to peaceably assemble and to petition to government for a redress of grievances, **And**$_c$

4. the **Right** of the people with respect to others peaceably to assemble and to petition to government for a redress of grievances without interference by others to prevent their assembling and petitioning.

Ambiguity 11 Remember to report this one from above after Ambiguity 8 in the correct order here.

Summary of Your Interpretation

Ambiguity	1	2	3	4	5	6	7	8	9A	9B	10	11
Your Choice	_	_	_	_	_	_	_	_	__	__	__	__

Our interpretation of the First Amendment in NORMALIZED FORM and its corresponding ARROW DIAGRAM is expressed in the following Fig. 14.1:

There is a pair of interesting matters made apparent by the ARROW DIAGRAMATIC representation of the First Amendment. First, expressing it in such form emphasizes that there are 21 alternative ways to reach the conclusion about the

IF

univ_con 1. all other relevant conditions are fulfilled for the application of the first Amendment of the United States Constitution,

THEN

Ambiguity # IF

A— 2 A) Congress makes a law in which the word "respecting" refers only to (1) an establishment of religion, and (2) prohibiting the free exercise thereof, **OR**

B— 3 B) Congress makes a law *giving respect to* an establishment of religion, **OR** Congress makes a law *with* respect to an establishment of religion, **OR**

C— 4 C) Congress makes a law respecting a religious establishment (an institution), **OR** Congress makes a law respecting the establishing of a religion, **OR**

D— 5 D) Congress makes a law respecting an establishment of religion, **Or**$_d$ prohibiting the free exercise thereof … **OR**

E— 6 E) Congress makes a law prohibiting the free exercise of religion, **OR**

F— 7 F) Congress makes a law abridging the freedom of speech, **Or**$_d$ of the press … **OR**

* The "**Or**$_d$" expresses the disjunction of two complete sentences also.

G— 8 G) Congress makes a law abridging the right of the people peaceably to assemble, **OR**

H— 9A H) 1) Congress makes a law abridging the **Immunity** of the people to assemble without successful suit by others to prevent their assembling, **OR**

2) Congress makes a law abridging the **Power** of the people to successfully sue if others interfere with their efforts peaceably to assemble, **OR**

3) Congress makes a law abridging the **Privilege** of the people with respect to others to bring suit against those who interfere with their efforts to peaceably assemble, **OR**

4) Congress makes a law abridging the **Right** of the people with respect to others peaceably to assemble without interference by others to prevent their assembling, **OR**

Fig. 14.1 ARROW DIAGRAM: Authors First Amendment Interpretation BDCC AAAA DDBA

I — 9B I) 1) Congress makes a law abridging the **Immunity** of the people peaceably to assemble without successful suit by others to prevent their assembling, and to petition to government for a redress of grievances, **OR**

2) Congress makes a law abridging the **Power** of the people to successfully sue if others interfere with their efforts peaceably to assemble and to petition to government for a redress of grievances, **OR**

3) Congress makes a law abridging the **Privilege** of the people with respect to others to bring suit against those who interfere with their efforts to peaceably assemble and to petition to government for a redress of grievances, **OR**

4. Congress makes a law abridging the **Right** of the people with respect to others peaceably to assemble and to petition to government for a redress of grievances without interference by others to prevent their assembling and petitioning, **OR**

J — 10 J) Congress makes a law ... abridging the right of the people peaceably to assemble, **OR**

K — 11 K) Congress makes a law ... respecting ... the right of the people peaceably to petition to government for a redress of grievances

▼ THEN

L L) Congress **has a Duty** to persons with an **Interest*** **Not** to exercise that **Power.**

* Persons who have
(1) a **Right** that Congress Not exercise its **Power** to make such a law, along with
(2) a **Power** to enforce that **Right** along with
(3) a **Privilege** to exercise that **Power**,
all three of the above of which have an **Immunity** from being terminated by anyone.

(Alternative C is also true as the conclusion, but not as fully correct as Alternative B.)

► BO BUT-OTHERWISE,

Not M) IT-IS-NOT-SO-THAT the First Amendment applies.

Fig. 14.1 (continued)

Duty of Congress to persons with an Interest Not to exercise 21 different types of Power. The second interesting characteristic of expressing the First Amendment in *conditional* ARROW DIAGRAMATIC form above is that each of the four occurrences of the word "or" are interpreted as expressing *inclusive disjunction*, whereas the interpretation of each of the four occurrences of "or" in the original text of the First Amendment expressed as a *universally negated assertion* are appropriately interpreted as expressing *conjunction*.

The first case in the United States Supreme Court to include comment on the interpretation of "and" in the First Amendment was United States v. Cruickshank, 92 U.S. 542 (1875). Chief Justice Waite, in dicta to the decision made in the case, indicated in effect a view that the "and" in the First Amendment was most appropriately interpreted as indicating a logical product (B), rather than as indicating a conjunction (A). The case involved the largest massacre of black Americans that has ever occurred in the United States, and its dicta was repeatedly quoted in Supreme Court Opinions for eighty years until Justice Harlan pointed out in a dissenting opinion in United States v. Guest, 383 U.S. 745 (1966) that Justice Waite's observations were mere dicta. Thereafter the citing of the Cruikshank case for the narrower *logical product* interpretation fell off virtually completely, and the "and" has become viewed as indicating *conjunction*.

14.3 Uniform Commercial Code Article 9-608

Turning now to the Uniform Commercial Code (UCC), most of which has been enacted in the 50 states of the United States governing business affairs in those states, the ambiguities in a provision from Article 9 that deals with the financing of commercial business, namely Article 9-608, will be examined in minute detail. This section addresses ambiguities found in the version of the UCC enacted in New York. Similar versions have been enacted all 50 states of the United States. The ambiguities found in Article 9-608 examined here are typical of those found throughout the UCC.

The nineteen bold underlined terms in Article 9-608 below are defined terms in the UCC, and their definitions can be found at the end of this section. In hyper-linked versions of this article you can access the definitions in a Word document by simultaneously pressing "Ctrl": and left-clicking on the defined Term. Then you can return to where the defined Term occurred in the document by pressing simultaneously "Alt" and "←". One of the extreme complexities of the use of defined Terms in the UCC is that typically embedded in the definitions will be further defined Terms. For example the defined Term "**collateral**" used in Article 9-608 contains ten defined Terms, nine of which are new ones not occurring in the nineteen defined Terms of Article 9-608. Those nine new defined Terms will, in turn, contain further new defined Terms at the next level. This process of defined Terms contained within defined Terms typically continues at least five levels deep so that the number of defined Terms that needs to be understood to understand a section of the UCC will usually be more than a hundred of the total the 502 different defined Terms used in the UCC. This complex definitional practice, combined with the presence of a multitude of Definition_Q Terms (which will be discussed later) makes the UCC extremely difficult to fully understand.

§9-608. Application of Proceeds of Collection or Enforcement; Liability for Deficiency and Right to Surplus (Remember, bold underlined terms are defined terms, and there are definitions of them at the end of the article.)

(a) **Application of proceeds, surplus, and deficiency if obligation secured.** If a **security interest_1** or **agricultural lien** secures payment or performance of an obligation, the following rules apply:

(1) A **secured party** shall apply or pay over for application the **cash proceeds** of collection or enforcement under Section 9-607 in the following **order_Q** to:
  (A) the reasonable expenses of collection and enforcement and, to the extent provided for by **agreement_1** and not prohibited by law, reasonable attorney's fees and legal expenses incurred by the **secured party**;
  (B) the satisfaction of obligations secured by the **security interest_1** or **agricultural lien** under which the collection or enforcement is made; and
  (C) the satisfaction of obligations secured by any subordinate **security interest_1** in or other **lien_Q** on the **collateral** subject to the **security interest_1** or **agricultural lien** under which the collection or enforcement is made if the **secured party** receives an **authenticate**d demand for **proceeds** before distribution of the **proceeds** is completed.

(2) If **request**ed by a **secured party**, a **holder** of a subordinate **security interest_1** or other **lien_Q** shall furnish reasonable proof of the interest or **lien_Q** within a reasonable time. Unless the **holder** complies, the **secured party** need not comply with the **holder**'s demand under paragraph (1) (C).

(3) A **secured party** need not apply or pay over for application **noncash proceeds** of collection and enforcement under Section 9-607 unless the failure to do so would be commercially unreasonable. A **secured party** that applies or pays over for application **noncash proceeds** shall do so in a commercially reasonable manner.

(4) A **secured party** shall **account** to and pay a **debtor** for any surplus, and the **obligor** is liable for any deficiency.

(b) **No surplus or deficiency in sales of certain rights to payment.** If the underlying transaction is a **sale** of **account**s, **chattel paper**, **payment intangible**s, or **promissory note**s, the **debtor** is not entitled to any surplus, and the **obligor** is not liable for any deficiency.

The above is a rendition of Article 9-608 as it appears in the UCC with the one modification that each defined term is identified by being underlined. Readers need to be aware that provisions of the UCC are extremely heavily laced with defined terms in a somewhat haphazard fashion without any indication when such a term occurs that it is a defined term. In the next rendition of Article 9-608 here the 33 potential ambiguities are identified by being **bold faced** and *italicized and enumerated.*

§9-608. Application of Proceeds of Collection or Enforcement; Liability for Deficiency and Right to Surplus

(a) **Application of proceeds, surplus, and deficiency if obligation secured.**
If?A1 a security interest ***or***?A2 **agricultural lien** secures payment ***or***?A3 performance of an obligation, the following rules apply:

(1) A **secured party** *shall*?A4 apply *or*?A5 pay over for application the **cash proceeds** of collection *or*?A6 enforcement under Section 9-607 in the following order to:

(A) the reasonable expenses of collection *and*?A7 enforcement *and*?A8, to the extent provided for by agreement *and*? A9 not prohibited by law, reasonable attorney's fees *and*?A10 legal expenses incurred by the **secured party**;

(B) the satisfaction of obligations secured by the security interest *or*?A11 **agricultural lien** under which the collection *or*?A12 enforcement is made; *and*?A13

(C) the satisfaction of obligations secured by any subordinate security interest in *or*?A14 other lien on the **collateral** subject to the security interest *or*?A15 **agricultural lien** under which the collection *or*?A16 enforcement is made *if*?A17 the **secured party** receives an **authenticate**d demand for **proceeds** before distribution of the **proceeds** is completed.

(2) *If*?A18 **request**ed by a **secured party**, a **holder** of a subordinate security interest *or*?A19 other lien *shall*?A20 furnish reasonable proof of the interest *or*?A21 lien within a reasonable time. *Unless*?A22 the **holder** complies, the **secured party** need not comply with the **holder**'s demand under paragraph (1)(C).

(3) A **secured party** need not apply *or*?A23 pay over for application **noncash proceeds** of collection *and*?A24 enforcement under Section 9-607 *unless*?A25 the failure to do so would be commercially unreasonable. A **secured party** that applies *or*?A26 pays over for application **noncash proceeds** *shall*?A27 do so in a commercially reasonable manner.

(4) A **secured party** *shall*?A28 **account** to *and*?A29 pay a **debtor** for any surplus, *and*?A30 the **obligor** is liable for any deficiency.

(b) No surplus or deficiency in sales of certain rights to payment.
If?A 31 the underlying transaction is a **sale** of **account**s, **chattel paper**, **payment intangible**s, *or*?A32 **promissory note**s, the **debtor** is not entitled to any surplus, *and*?A33 the **obligor** is not liable for any deficiency.

Potential Ambiguities [In **bold face** and *italicized* type above]

If	or	or	shall	or	or	and	and	and	and	or	or	and	or	or	or	if	If	or	shall
1	2	3	4	5	6	7	8	9	10	11	12	13	14	15	16	17	18	19	20

or	Unless	or	and	unless	or	shall	shall	and	and	If	or	and
21	22	23	24	25	26	27	28	29	30	31	32	33

With our interpretation of the appropriate resolution of the 33 ambiguities, Article 9-608 can be presented in a NORMALIZED FORM of conditional statements using the following resolutions of the various ambiguities:

or? [**OR**$_c$ conjunction, **OR**$_d$ inclusive disjunction, **OR**$_s$ logical sum], **OR**$_x$ [exclusive disjunction,];

and,? [**And**$_c$ conjunction, **And**$_d$ inclusive disjunction], **And**$_x$ exclusive disjunction,

And$_P$ [logical product];
(*if*?, ***unless***?) [IF ... THEN... (conditional), IF-AND-ONLY-IF... THEN... (bi-conditional)];
shall? (have an **Obligation** to, have an **Obligatory-Power** to).

(a) Application of proceeds, surplus, and deficiency if obligation secured.

IF-AND-ONLY-IF A1 (A1, A2, ... A33 indicate the ambiguities resolved.)

1. a security interest **Or**$_x$A2 **agricultural lien** secures payment **Or**$_x$A3 performance of an obligation,

THEN

2. the following rules apply:
   A. **secured party** has an Obligatory-**Power** toA4 apply **Or**$_x$A5 pay over for application the **cash proceeds** of collection **Or**$_x$A6 enforcement under Section 9-607 in the following order to:
      1. the reasonable expenses of collection **And**$_c$A7 enforcement **And**$_c$A8 to the extent provided for by agreement **And**$_p$A9 not prohibited by law, reasonable attorney's fees **And**$_c$A10 legal expenses incurred by the **secured party**,
      2. the satisfaction of obligations secured by the security interest **Or**$_x$A11 **agricultural lien** under which the collection **Or**$_c$A12 enforcement is made, **And**$_c$A13
      3. **IF-AND-ONLY-IF** A17
         a. the **secured party** receives an **authenticate**d demand for **proceeds** before distribution of the **proceeds** is completed,

         THEN

         b. the satisfaction of obligations secured by any subordinate security interest in **Or**$_x$A14 other lien on the **collateral** subject to the security interest **Or**$_x$A15 **agricultural lien** under which the collection **Or**$_c$A16 enforcement is made, **AND**
   B. 1. **IF-AND-ONLY-IF** A18
      it is **request**ed by a **secured party**,

      THEN

         a. a **holder** of a subordinate security interest **Or**$_x$A19 other lien **has an Obligatory-Power to**A20 furnish reasonable proof of the interest **Or**$_x$A21 lien within a reasonable time, **AND**
      2. **IF-AND-ONLY-IF** A22
         a. IT-IS-NOT-SO-THAT the **holder** does comply,

         THEN

         b. the **secured party** need not comply with the **holder**'s demand under section 2A3 above, **AND**
   C. 1. **IF-AND-ONLY-IF**A25
         a. IT-IS-NOT-SO-THAT the failure to do so would be commercially unreasonable,

         THEN

         b. a **secured party** need not apply **Or**$_c$A23 pay over for application **noncash proceeds** of collection **And**$_c$A24 enforcement under Section 9-607, **AND**

c. A **secured party** that applies **Or**$_c$A26 pays over for application **noncash proceeds** has an **Obligatory-Power to**?A27 do so in a commercially reasonable manner, **AND**

D. a **secured party has an Obligatory-Power to**A28 **account** to **And**$_c$A29 pay a **debtor** for any surplus, **And**A30 the **obligor** is liable for any deficiency.

(b) No surplus or deficiency in sales of certain rights to payment.

IF-AND-ONLY-IF A31

1. the underlying transaction is a **sale** of **accounts**, **chattel paper**, **payment intangibles**, **Or**$_x$A32 **promissory notes**, **THEN**
2. the **debtor** is not entitled to any surplus, **And**A33 the **obligor** is not liable for any deficiency.

The above rendition of Article 9-608 – with the ambiguity markers, A1 ... A33, removed – is an interpretation of Article 9-608 resolving the 33 ambiguities identified. The 33 ambiguities give rise to $(4^{2304})x2$ * alternative interpretations as indicated below.
*Of the seven online scientific calculators that we tried to use to evaluate this number, three gave the response "infinity", two gave the response "overflow" and two gave the response "error". The hand calculation indicates 144,115,188,075,855,872 alternative interpretations, i.e. 144 quadrillion plus.
1 2 3 4 5 6 7 8 9 10 11 12 13 14 15 16 17 18 19 20 21 22 23 24 25 26 27 28 29 30 31 32 33

2×4×4×2×4×4×4×4×4× 4 ×4 × 4× 4 ×4× 4 × 4× 2 ×2 × 4× 2 ×4 ×2 × 4× 4× 2× 4× 2× 2 × 4× 4 × 4 × 4 × 4 = $(4^{2304}) \times 2$ = 144 quadrillion plus

This interpretation of Article 9-608 can be represented by an ARROW DIAGRAM accompanied by its corresponding representation in NORMALIZED FORM and its corresponding ARROW DIAGRAM in the following Fig. 14.2.

This analysis of Article 9-608 of the Uniform Commercial Code in detecting and remediating its extraordinarily numerous and troublesome ambiguities is a demonstration of the usefulness of modern logics for a Twentieth Century practicing attorney's analytic tool-kit. It will hopefully be a provocative stimulus for practicing attorneys to undertake the task of learning more about the powerful new logics that have been developed in the late Eighteenth and Nineteenth Centuries. Those included in defining the Legal-Relations language include sentential logic, predicate logic, class logic, alethic logic, deontic logic, time logic, action logic and capacitive logic. It should be clear by now that Aristotle did not cover the whole universe of logic.

IF-AND-ONLY-IF univ_con
1. all other relevant conditions are fulfilled for the application of Article 9-608 of the Uniform Commercial Code,

THEN

(a) Application of proceeds, surplus, and deficiency if obligation secured.

Ambiguity # S# of sentence

2A 1 2. **IF-AND-ONLY-IF**
2 S1 A. a security interest **Or**$_x$A2 **agricultural lien** secures payment
3 **Or**$_x$A3 performance of an obligation,
THEN
2B: S2 B. the following rules apply:
4 S3 1. A **secured party has an Obligatory-Power to**A4 apply
5 **Or**$_x$A5 pay over for application the **cash proceeds** of
6 collection **Or**$_x$A6 enforcement under Section 9-607 in the following order to:
7 a. the reasonable expenses of collection **And**$_c$A7
8 enforcement **And**$_c$A8 to the extent provided for by
9 agreement **And**$_D$A9 not prohibited by law, attorney's
10 fees **And**$_c$A10 legal expenses incurred by the **secured party**,
b. the satisfaction of obligations secured by the security
11 interest **Or**$_x$A11 **agricultural lien** under which the
12 & 13 collection **Or**$_c$A12 enforcement is made **And**$_c$A13
17 c. **IF-AND-ONLY-IF**A17
1 S4 1. the **secured party** receives an **authenticated** demand for **proceeds** before distribution of the

Fig. 14.2 UCC Article 9-608: Normalized Version of Our Interpretation

Definitions of Defined Terms in New York Uniform Commercial Code Article 9-608

"**Account**", except as used in "account for", means a **right_1** to payment of a **monetary obligation_Q**, ("Q" indicates "Questionable".) whether or not earned by performance, (i) for property that has been or is to be sold, **lease**d, licensed, assigned, or otherwise disposed of, (ii) for services rundered or to be rundered, (iii) for a policy of insurance **issue_Q**d or to be **issue_Q**d, (iv) for a secondary obligation incurred or to be incurred, (v) for energy provided or to be provided, (vi) for the use or hire of a vessel under a charter or other **contract_1**, (vii) arising out of the use of a credit or charge card or information contained on or for use with the card, or (viii) as winnings in a lottery or other game of chance operated or sponsored by a **State**, **governmental unit** of a **State**, or **person_1** licensed or authorized to operate the game by a **State** or **governmental unit** of a **State**. The **term_1** includes **health-care-insurance receivable**s. The **term_1** does not include (i) **rights_1** to payment evidenced by **chattel paper** or an **instrument**,

proceeds is completed,
THEN
2 S5 2. the satisfaction of obligations secured by any
14 subordinate security interest_1 in **Or_x**A14 other
lien_O on the **collateral** subject to the security
15 interest in **Or_x**A15 **agricultural lien** under which
16 the collection **Or_c**A16 enforcement is made, **AND**
2 18 2. a. **IF-AND-ONLY-IF**A18
1 S6 1. [it is] **requested** by a **secured party**,
S7 **THEN**
2 19 2. a **holder** of a subordinate security interest **Or_x**A19
20 other lien **has an Obligatory-Power to**A20 furnish
21 reasonable proof of the interest **Or_x**A21 lien within
a reasonable time, **AND**
22 b. **IF-AND-ONLY-IF**A22
1 S8 1. IT-IS-NOT-SO-THAT the **holder** does comply,
THEN
2 S9 2. the **secured party** need not comply with the
holder's demand under section 2A3
above, **AND**
3 25 3. A. **IF-AND-ONLY-IF**A25
1 S10 1. IT-IS-NOT-SO-THAT the failure to do so
would be commercially unreasonable,
THEN
2 23 S11 2. a **secured party** need not apply **Or_c**A23
pay over for application **noncash proceeds**
of collection enforcement under Section
9-607, **AND**
26 S12 B. a **secured party** that applies **Or_c**A26 pays over
application **noncash proceeds has an**
27 **Obligatory-Power to**?A27 do so in a
commercially reasonable manner, **AND**
28 S13 4. a **secured party has an Obligatory-Power to**
29 **account** to **And_c**A29 pay a **debtor** for any surplus,
30 **And_c**A30 the **obligor** is liable for any deficiency.

(b) No surplus or deficiency in sales of certain rights to payment.

31 3. **IF-AND-ONLY-IF**A31
S14 A. the underlying transaction is a **sale** of **accounts**,
32 **chattel paper**, **payment intangibles**, **Or_x**A32
promissory notes,
33 S15 B. the **debtor** is not entitled to any surplus, **And_c**A33
the **obligor** is not liable for any deficiency.

Fig. 14.2 (continued)

(ii) **commercial tort claims**, (iii) **Deposit accounts**, (iv) **investment property**, (v) letter-of-credit rights or letters of credit, or (vi) **rights_1** to payment for **money_1** or funds advanced or sold, other than **rights_1** arising out of the use of a credit or charge card or information contained on or for use with the card. **agricultural lien**

"**Agreement_1**" means the bargain of the parties in fact as found in their language or by implication from other circumstances including course of dealing or usage of trade or course of performance as provided in this Act (Sections **1-205** and 2-208). Whether an **agreement_1** has legal consequences is determined by the provisions of this Act, if applicable; otherwise by the law of **contract_1**s (Section 1-103). (Compare " **Contract_1**".)

"**Agricultural lien**" means an interest, other than a **security interest_1**, in **farm products**:

(A) which secures payment or performance of an obligation for:
  (i) **goods** or services furnished in connection with a **debtor**'s **farming operation**; or
  (ii) rent on real property **lease**d by a **debtor** in connection with its **farming operation**; and

(B) which is created by statute in favor of a **person_1** that:
  (i) in the ordinary course of its business furnished **goods** or services to a **debtor** in connection with a **debtor**'s **farming operation**; or
  (ii) **lease**d real property to a **debtor** in connection with the **debtor**'s **farming operation**; and

(C) whose effectiveness does not depend on the **person_1**'s possession of the personal property.

"**Authenticate**" means:

(A) to sign; or

(B) to **execute_Q** or otherwise adopt a symbol, or encrypt or similarly process a **record** in whole or in part, with the present intent of the authenticating **person_1** to identify the **person_1** and adopt or **accept_Q** a **record**.

"**Cash proceeds**" means **proceeds** that are **money_1**, **check**s, **deposit accounts**, or the like **chattel paper**.

"**Chattel paper**" means a **record** or **record**s that evidence both a **monetary obligation** and a **security interest_1** in specific **goods**, a **security interest_1** in specific **goods** and **software** used in the **goods**, a **security interest_1** in specific **goods** and license of **software** used in the **goods**, a **lease** of specific **goods**, or a **lease** of specific **goods** and license of **software** used in the **goods**. In this paragraph, "**monetary obligation**" means a **monetary obligation** secured by the **goods** or owed under a **lease** of the **goods** and includes a **monetary obligation** , with respect to **software** used in the **goods**. The **term_1** does not include

(i) charters or other **contract_1**s involving the use or hire of a vessel or

(ii) **record**s that evidence a **right_1** to payment arising out of the use of a credit or charge card or information contained on or for use with the card. If a transaction is evidenced by **record**s that include an **instrument** or series of **instrument**s, the group of **record**s taken together constitutes **chattel paper**.

"**Collateral**" means the property subject to a **security interest_1** or **agricultural lien**. The **term_1** includes:
(A) **proceeds** to which a **security interest_1** attaches;
(B) **accounts**, **chattel paper**, **payment intangibles**, and **promissory notes** that have been sold; and
(C) **goods** that are the subject of a **consignment**.

"**Debtor**" means:
(A) a **person_1** having an interest, other than a **security interest_1** or other **lien_Q**, in the **collateral**, whether or not the **person_1** is an **obligor**;
(B) a **seller_Q** of **accounts**, **chattel paper**, **payment intangibles**, or **promissory notes**; or
(C) a **consignee**.

"**Holder_1**" means a **person_1** who is in possession of a document of title or an **instrument_Q** or an investment **certificated security_Q** drawn, **issue_Q**d or indorsed to him or to his **order_Q** or to **bearer** or in blank.

"**Lien_Q**" means "**Lien**" that may be questionable. ("Q" indicates "Questionable".) It indicates that the appropriate definition may be either of those immediately below.
(a) "**Lien_2A**" means a charge against or interest in **goods_2A** to secure payment of a debt or performance of an obligation, but the **term_1** does not include a **security interest_1**.
(b) "**Lien_Q**" (**Lien** that may be the above **Lien_2A** or some other kind of a **Lien** entirely perhaps).

"**Noncash proceeds**" means **proceeds** other than **cash proceeds**.

"**Obligor**" means a **person_1** that, with respect to an obligation secured by a **security interest_1** in or an **agricultural lien** on the **collateral**, (i) owes payment or other performance of the obligation, (ii) has provided property other than the **collateral** to secure payment or other performance of the obligation, or (iii) is otherwise accountable in whole or in part for payment or other performance of the obligation. The **term_1** does not include **issuers** or **nominated persons** under a **letter of credit**.

"**Order_Q**" means an **Order** that may be Questionable. ("Q" indicates "Questionable".) It indicates that the appropriate definition may be either of those immediately below.
(a) An "**order_3**" is a direction to pay and must be more than an authorization or **request**. It must identify the **person_1** to pay with reasonable certainty. It may be addressed to one or more such **person_1**s jointly or in the alternative but not in succession.
(b) "**Order_Q**" (an **Order** that may be the above **order_3** or some other kind of **Order** entirely perhaps).

"**Payment intangible**" means a **general intangible** under which the **account debtor**'s principal obligation is a **monetary obligation_Q**.

"**Proceeds**", except as used in Section **9-609** (b), means the following property:

(A) Whatever is acquired upon the **sale**, **lease**, license, exchange, or other disposition of **collateral**;
(B) whatever is collected on, or distributed on **account** of, **collateral**;
(C) **rights_1** arising out of **collateral**;
(D) to the extent of the **value_1** of **collateral**, claims arising out of the loss, nonconformity, or interference with the use of, defects or infringement of **rights_1** in, or damage to, the **collateral**; or
(E) to the extent of the **value_1** of **collateral** and to the extent payable to the **debtor** or the **secured party**, insurance payable by reason of the loss or nonconformity of, defects or infringement of **rights_1** in, or damage to, the **collateral**.

"**Promissory note**" means an **instrument** that evidences a **promise_Q** to pay a **monetary obligation_Q**, does not evidence an **order_Q** to pay, and does not contain an acknowledgment by a **bank** that the **bank** has received for deposit a sum of **money_1** or funds.
A "**Sale**" consists in the passing of title from the **seller_2** to the **buyer_2** for a price (Section **2-401**).

"**Secured party**" means:

(A) a **person_1** in whose favor a **security interest_1** is created or provided for under a **security agreement**, whether or not any obligation to be secured is outstanding;
(B) a **person_1** that holds an **agricultural lien**;
(C) a **consignor**;
(D) a **person_1** to which **account**s, **chattel paper**, **payment intangible**s, or **promissory note**s have been sold;
(E) a trustee, indenture trustee, agent, **collateral** agent, or other **representative_1** in whose favor a **security interest_1** or **agricultural lien** is created or provided for; or
(F) a **person_1** that holds a **security interest_1** arising under Section **2-401**, **2-505**, **2-711** (3), **2A-508** (5), **4-210**, or **5-118**.

"**Security interest_1**" means an interest in personal property or **fixtures_Q** which secures payment or performance of an obligation. The **term_1** also includes any interest of a **consignor_Q** and a **buyer_Q** of **account**s, **chattel paper**, a **payment intangible**, or a **promissory note_Q** in a transaction that is subject to Article 9. The special property interest of a buyer_Q of **goods_Q** on **identification_Q** of those **goods_Q** to a **contract for sale_Q** under Section 2-401 is not a "**security interest_1**", but a **buyer_Q** may also acquire a "**security interest_1**" by complying with Article 9. Except as otherwise provided in Section 2-505, the **right_1** of a **seller_Q** or **lessor_Q** of **goods_Q** under Article 2 or 2A to retain or acquire possession of the **goods_Q** is not a "**security interest_1**", but a **seller_Q** or **lessor_Q** may also acquire a "**security interest_1**" by complying with Article 9. The retention or reservation of title by a **seller_Q** of **goods_Q** notwithstanding shipment or **delivery_1** to the **buyer_Q** (Section **2-401**) is limited in effect to a reservation of a "**security interest_1**".

(a) Whether a transaction creates a **lease_Q** or **security interest_1** is determined by the facts of each case; however, a transaction creates a **security interest_1** if the consideration the **lessee_Q** is to pay the **lessor_Q** for the **right_1** to possession and use of the **goods_Q** is an obligation for the **term_1** of the **lease_Q** not subject to termination_Q by the **lessee_Q**, and:
   (i) the original **term_1** of the **lease_Q** is equal to or greater than the remaining economic life of the **goods_Q**,
   (ii) the **lessee_Q** is bound to renew the **lease_Q** for the remaining economic life of the **goods_Q** or is bound to become the owner of the **goods_Q**,
   (iii) the **lessee_Q** has an option to renew the **lease_Q** for the remaining economic life of the
   goods_Q for no additional consideration or nominal additional consideration upon compliance with the **lease_Q agreement_1**, or
   (iv) the **lessee_Q** has an option to become the owner of the **goods_Q** for no additional consideration or nominal additional consideration upon compliance with the **lease_Q agreement_1**.

(b) A transaction does not create a **security interest_1** merely because it provides that:
   (i) the **present value_1** of the consideration the **lessee_Q** is obligated to pay the **lessor_Q** for the **right_1** to possession and use of the **goods_Q** is substantially equal to or is greater than the fair market **value_1** of the **goods_Q** at the time the **lease_Q** is entered into,
   (ii) the assumes risk of loss of the **goods_Q**, or agrees to pay taxes, insurance, filing, recording, or registration fees, or service or maintenance costs with respect to the **goods_Q**,
   (iii) the **lessee_Q** has an option to renew the **lease_Q** or to become the owner of the **goods_Q**,
   (iv) the **lessee_Q** has an option to renew the **lease_Q** for a fixed rent that is equal to or greater than the **reasonably predictable_1** fair market rent for the use of the **goods_Q** for the **term_1** of the renewal at the time the option is to be performed, or
   (v) the **lessee_Q** has an option to become the owner of the **goods_Q** for a fixed price that is equal to or greater than the **reasonably predictable_1** fair market **value_1** of the **goods_Q** at the time the option is to be performed.

(c) For purposes of this subsection (37):
   (i) Additional consideration is not nominal if (A) when the option to renew the **lease_Q** is granted to the **lessee_Q** the rent is **State**d to be the fair market rent for the use of the for the **term_1** of the **lessee_Q**'s **reasonably predictable_1** cost of performing under the **lease_Q agreement_1** if the option is not exercised;
   (ii) "**Reasonably predictable_1**" and

"**remaining economic life of the goods_1**" are to be determined with reference to the facts and circumstances at the time the transaction is entered into; and

(iii) "**Present value_1**" means the amount as of a date certain of one or more sums payable in the future, discounted to the date certain. The discount is determined by the interest rate specified by the parties if the rate is not manifestly unreasonable at the time the transaction is entered into; otherwise, the discount is determined by a commercially reasonable rate that takes into **account** the facts and circumstances of each case at the time the transaction was entered into.

These nineteen defined Terms from Article 9-608 are a representative sample of the 502 defined Terms in the Uniform Commercial Code as a whole, each itself typically laden with additional defined Terms. Each Article of the UCC contains its own set of defined Terms. In addition, there are a set of definitions in Article 1 that apply in subsequent Articles, if the Article 1 defined Term is not defined in that subsequent Article, but nevertheless occurs there. A numeral preceded by an underline after a defined term indicates the Article in which that term is defined. Thus, "**agreement_1**" indicates that "agreement" is defined in Article 1. Definitions such as "**Collateral**" without any subsequent numeral are Article 9 definitions. However, a defined term followed by "_Q" indicates a serious confusion in the definitional practices of the drafters of the UCC. For example, " **promise_Q**" in the definition of "**Promissory note**s" indicates the "promise" is not defined in either Article 9 or Article 1, but that it is defined in one or more other Articles of the UCC. Presumably, an interpreter is free to employ any of those definitions as appropriate in Article 9. For example, the term "acceptance" is not defined in either Article 1 or in Article 9, but it is defined in Articles 2, 2A, 3, 4, 4A, and 5. Which, if any or more than one, of those six definitions of "acceptance" is the appropriate one for the many occurrences of "acceptance" in Article 9 is an interesting question?

It would seem that a code with 502 definitions can be read more intelligently – perhaps only intelligently – in a hyper-texted version connecting the defined terms to their definitions for easy reference and back and forth.

Reference

Hohfeld, Wesley E. 1917. Fundamental legal conceptions as applied in judicial reasoning. *Yale Law Journal* 26:710.

Chapter 15
From the Language of Legislation to Executable Logic Programs

Adam Wyner

Abstract Starting in the 1980s with the British Nationality Act 1981, there have been efforts to represent legislation as executable logic programs. With such programs, the objective is to draw inferences given base facts, test alternative scenarios, check the representation (and law) for consistency, serve the legislation as web-pages on the internet, and electronically transmit the law. Early work was entirely manual. More recently, tools that use controlled natural language have been applied. Generally, such tools require that the language of the legislation is manually scoped and revised to suit a controlled language (a fixed subset of the vocabulary and grammar of the natural language), which constrains the applicability of the tools and filters out information. More recently, well-developed, large scale parsers with related logical representations have been applied to legislation, overcoming manual preprocessing. On the other hand, it requires significant post-processing analysis to check the output. In this paper, we discuss the background, state-of-the-art, problems, and future directions in the translation of natural language legislation to a formal, logical representation.

Keywords Legislation • Language • Logic programs

15.1 Introduction

One of the "classic" ambitions of artificial intelligence and law has been to formalise and implement legislation as a logic program which, given base facts, draws inferences (Bench-Capon et al. 1987; Sergot 1988; Sergot et al. 1986). It could also be used to test alternative scenarios, check the representation (and law) for consistency, serve the legislation as web-pages on the internet, and electronically transmit the law. In outline, the process identifies the relevant portions and language of the legislation, paraphrases (if need be), and formalises it in an executable logic such as Prolog. Since this early work, commercial products have become

A. Wyner (✉)
University of Aberdeen, Aberdeen, UK
e-mail: azwyner@abdn.ac.uk

M. Araszkiewicz, K. Płeszka (eds.), *Logic in the Theory and Practice of Lawmaking*, Legisprudence Library 2, DOI 10.1007/978-3-319-19575-9_15

available which support aspects of this process. For example, http://www.oracle.com/industries/government/pdfs/oracle-haley-enterprise-public-sector-ds.pdf, Oracle Policy Management (OPM) takes statements of rules expressed in natural language and provides for semi-automatic translation to a logic; it has been applied to the examples discussed in Sergot et al. (1986).[1] OPM provides large scale, web-based tools to governments around the world, serving fragments of legislation concerning tax law, benefits, and similar to the public: an individual is asked for specific information (e.g. age, living arrangements, income) and to answer statements; given the input, the individual is given a determination such as whether she is eligible for a benefit and for how much. However, proprietary products restrict their exposure, use, and development. On the other hand, open systems for *natural language processing* such as *controlled natural language* (CNL) tools, e.g. Fuchs et al. (2008) and Wyner et al. (2010a), or wide-coverage parsers with semantic representation, e.g. Bos et al. (2004) and Wyner et al. (2012), provide opportunities to investigate, apply, and develop tools to formalise and model legislation.

In this chapter, we draw together a discussion from previously published work that reviews and comments on computational tools to translate the language of legislation to executable logic programs, giving example fragments. These studies have been small scale feasibility studies to exercise the tools, examine results, highlight issues, and set agendas for future work. There is progress, yet we are far from simply inputting legislation to some tool and automatically receiving an executable version. Given this, the use of the chapter is as an overview of what has been done to this point as well as a reference to relevant work.

The structure of the paper is as follows. In Sect. 15.2, we outline some of the early work. In Sect. 15.3, we discuss extraction of information from legislation using text analytic tools. In Sect. 15.4, we consider how a controlled natural language tool can apply in a simple instance. And in Sect. 15.5, we look at the results of a more sophisticated approach. Each has advantages and disadvantages. In Sect. 15.6, we mention some current trends that may take us further along the path of natural language analysis of the law. And the paper concludes in Sect. 15.7.

15.2 Legislation and Formalisation: Early Days

One of the early ambitions and achievements of artificial intelligence and law was to formalise legislation as a logic program.[2] It outlines the legislation, the task the representation supports, and problems in creating the representation. It was part of the effort to develop expert systems and executable representations of knowledge in general and legal knowledge (Hammond 1983; Leith 1982; Stamper 1980). Several

---

[1]Disclosure: Oracle Office Rules are a product of Oracle and are based on products from Haley (formerly RuleBurst, formerly SoftLaw); the author was a research partner on a project which involved Haley, and he received a training certificate in the application of the technology.

[2]Much of this section previously appears as a subsection in Wyner (2012).

large scale projects were carried out (Bench-Capon et al. 1987, 1993; Sergot 1988; Sergot et al. 1986). The method, executed manually, was to take the source legal text, identify the relevant textual portions, decompose and paraphrase them as necessary, and then formalise the language in an executable logic such as Prolog, creating an *expert system*. From this formalisation, ground facts may be provided to the system which are then used to reason, for example, to provide determinations (from facts to inferences), explanations (from inferences to their proofs), or as compliance monitors (checking that procedures are adhered to).

Among the exercises were translations of the *British Nationality Act 1981* (BNA)[3] and the *Supplementary Benefit 1985* (SB). The first clause of the BNA is:

> 1.-(1) A person born in the United Kingdom after commencement shall be a British citizen if at the time of birth his father or mother is (a) a British citizen; or (b) settled in the United Kingdom.

The objective is to translate such statements to Prolog, which implements *Definite Horn Clauses* (DHC), where each rule has one conclusion A and zero or more conjoined conditions B_i, where A and B_i are predicates of or relations between variables:

$$\text{A if } B_1 \text{ and } B_2 \text{ and} \ldots B_n$$

There are several differences between DHCs and *material implication* of the form $(B \rightarrow A)$, for example: in material implications, the conclusion can be arbitrarily complex, e.g. with conjunctions and negations, while in DHCs, the conclusion must be a literal; material implication has a semantically equivalent form $(\neg A \rightarrow \neg B)$, which is not allowed in DHCs. Given DHCs, we can forward chain to conclusions that are inferred; given conclusions, we can backwards chain to identify what must hold to infer the conclusion. The constraints on the expression of statements in Prolog is rather loose: the statements of the clauses are predicates applied to terms and combined using conjunction and negation; any string of characters is treated as a predicate or a term; lower case text represents constants and upper case variables. *High-level* concepts were defined in terms of lower level concepts, and eventually grounded in facts in a database or supplied by the user; in other words complex predicates were created that could be decomposed in terms of simpler rules, e.g. *after_commencement*. This is a fragment of the program reported in Bench-Capon et al. (1993):

```
uk_citizen(X, section_1, Date) :-
    born_in(X,uk),
    born_on(X,Date),
    after_commencement(Date),
    parent_of(Parent,X),
    citizen_or_settled_in(Parent,uk).
after_commencement(date(D,M,Y)) :-
```

[3] http://www.legislation.gov.uk/ukpga/1981/61/contents

```
        commencement_date(date(A,B,C)),
        after(date(D,M,Y),date(A,B,C)).
    after(date(D1,M1,Y1),date(D2,M2,Y2)) :-
        Y1 > Y2.
    citizen_or_settled_in(Parent,uk) :-
        uk_citizen(Parent, Section, Date).
```

The BNA study was a rather constrained, focused, feasibility study of a self-contained article of law that led to a reasonably sized application. The study with SB was intended to see what would happen with a large piece of legislation that had been revised and that interacted with other laws. It was funded by the government of the United Kingdom to create artificial intelligence software that supported the application of legislation by government offices, in this case, the Department of Health and Social Services (DHSS), which was a large, complex, organisation tasked with applying social legislation. The SB itself is an extensive piece of legislation (600 pages) including definitions; asides from the legislation, there were auxiliary documents such as a guidance manual. In the end, 90 percent of the legislation was coded over a period of two months, though unsupervised and not evaluated.

In Bench-Capon et al. (1993), requirements for users of the legislation are distinguished, e.g. clerks who apply the law need different information, solicitors who advise on how the law is likely to be applied, and individuals or organisations that want to comply with the law. Rather than creating different representations of the same legislation, which would lead not only to redundancy, but possible inconsistency and unclarity, it was proposed to create a logical, executable formalisation of the legislation that could be used as a core across requirements and upon which additional functionalities could be built. For example, it may be useful to provide determinations (from facts to inferences), explanations (from inferences to their proofs), or as compliance monitors (checking that procedures are adhered to). Thus, to maintain a link between the source legislation and the code, the legislation itself is the basis of the translation to logic programming. This was in contrast to Hammond (1983) that did not translate the legislation itself, but created an expert system, such as how a clerk might apply the legislation.

As with the BNA, the approach was to code directly, starting top-down, based on a reading of the legislation, and without a specific methodology or discipline. High-level concepts were defined in terms of lower level concepts, and eventually grounded in facts in a database or supplied by the user. This rule-based approach contrasts with Stamper (1980), which has a preliminary analysis of legislation in terms of entities and relationships, what we would currently refer to as *ontological analysis*. Nor was there an intermediate representation, e.g. a 'structured English' form of the legislation (what we might now refer to as a controlled language Wyner et al. 2010a), which would have clarified the analysis and supported verification.

For example, we have a *Conditions of Entitlement* Regulation 6(b):

> [a claimant is not required to be available for employment if] "...he is regularly and substantially engaged in caring for a severely disabled person...."

In a programming logic-like format, we have something along the following lines:

X is-not-required-to-be-available-for-employment *if*
  X is-regularly-and-substantially-engaged-in-caring-for-a-severely-disabled-person.

X is-regularly-and-substantially-engaged-in-caring-for-a-severely-disabled-person *if*
  X is-regularly-and-substantially-engaged-in-caring-for **Y**,
  Y is-severely-disabled.

15.2.1 Issues

While these are significant developments, their overall contributions are limited. First, the methodology of analysis remains largely that of trial and error: the source text is analysed manually, scoped, and paraphrased (perhaps in a restricted or controlled natural language). There may (or may not be) some limited automated support of a parser and semantic interpreter.[4] In these ways, translation is costly. Second, as small scale exercises or proprietary products, the systems are restricted in exposure, use, and development. More generally, the tools cannot be extended or developed to cover other linguistic phenomena as and where they appear relevant.

In the course of such analyses, some general issues were identified such as the following, which is not an exhaustive list.

First, what predicates should the formalisation represent as basic and what as complex? The guiding principle for BNA and SB was to decompose as little as possible. Yet, this could constrain reuse.

Second, how should dependencies between portions of text be treated? In other words, one portion of text may refer to another portion of text. Such relationships have to be coordinated, which is problematic and raises the issue of what is being represented. In practice, reference to clauses were incorporated into complex predicates, though there could be long chains of such references. For SB, it was proposed to create a database of the structure of the legislation, which would be maintained and used for reference.

Third, how should negation and exception be treated? Rules allow negative conditions (exceptions) such as *X if Y unless Z*, where unless Z is the negated condition. This requires extended Extended Horn clause logic, which allows some

[4] A parser gives a grammatical analysis, identifying the nouns, verbs, and so on of a sentence as well as the grammatical relations such as subject and object of the verb. A semantic interpreter provides a translation of the sentence into a logic, e.g. "Some man is happy" is translated to $\exists x$ [man(x) & happy(x)].

or all of the conditions to be negated. It is also possible that legal statements require negative conclusions, which Extended Horn clause logic does not allow. For exception clauses, *negation as failure* seems to be sufficient; under the *closed world assumption, anything which is not known or not provable is assumed to be false*: not[Q] holds when all ways of showing Q fail. The problem is that the closed world assumption may not be realistic for legislation since it may be that we cannot find all ways of showing something is false; that is, there may be some way to show it holds, but this is not part of the legislation or of the program. Other interpretations of negation, default reasoning, or nonmonotonic reasoning may be needed.

Fourth, how do entitlements or definitions relate to temporal spans, so the temporality of events and properties of individuals must be addressed. Objects and relationships change in time through the influence of events that occur in the world. For example, an individual's entitlement may change over time. In addition, there are idiosyncratic definitions in the legislation for temporal periods, e.g. what counts as a continuous temporal period may include breaks, or retrospective rules, e.g. as in receiving a benefit as the result of appealing a decision. Some capability for temporal reasoning is required.

Fifth, how is implicit or background information to be represented, for legal statements presume information that is not explicitly presented? For example, an accountant keeps financial books and does calculations, though this need not be stated explicitly in a piece of legislation restricting the conduct of accountants. Fifth, legislation may be written with complex patterns of conjunction, disjunction, and negation. It is left to the analyst to provide an unambiguous paraphrase of the intended interpretation.

Sixth, many concepts appear 'open textured' so cannot be captured directly by fixed rules. For example, a prohibition against vehicles in a park may apply to gas-powered cars, but not to baby buggies.

Seventh, Prolog employs Horn clauses, which is a fragment of First Order Logic (FOL). In general, this may be too restrictive, for natural language can represent concepts that are not straightforwardly represented in FOL terms, e.g. modals, generics, second order quantifiers.

Eighth, legislation is often expressed with sentences of a high degree of syntactic complexity. While manual analysis may (with difficulty) manage to translate expressions, there are few tools to support the translation.

Nineth, legislation may include vague expressions, e.g. *being of good character*, *having a reasonable excuse*, and *having sufficient knowledge of English*. Vagueness may be resolved by deferring to the user who answers a question (rather than automating it) or by giving some rule by which the vague term can be made more determined. It is not up to the analyst or logic to eliminate what the vagueness inherent in our conceptualisation of the world and social relations. Similarly, imprecise and ambiguous expressions are given to the analyst to resolve.

Tenth, counterfactuals appear in legislation, where a counterfactual is contrary to the fact. The solution was to present all the alternative circumstances which the counterfactual was intended to cover.

15.2.2 Oracle Policy Management

Since this early work, some commerical products have become available which support aspects of this process and serve the resultant expert systems to users on the web (Dayal et al. 1993; Dayal and Johnson 2000; Johnson and Mead 1991). In particular, with http://www.oracle.com/industries/government/pdfs/oracle-haley-enterprise-public-sector-ds.pdf, Oracle Policy Management (OPM), analysts scope, interprete, and normalise the source legislation, composing rules that are expressed in a derivative natural language, yet which can be automatically parsed and translated into a logic. An inference engine can be applied to grounded statements, providing determinations; there is a web-interface to serve the system statements to users. Explanatory notes, document access, and alternative evaluations are auxiliary capabilities. It has been applied to the examples discussed in Sergot et al. (1986) and many other acts; it is in widespread use by government agencies in the United Kingdom and United States, e.g. for tax calculation and citizen benefits.

While OPM can address many of the issues pointed out above, it requires a labour intensive translation of the source text to the normalised language of OPM. Thus, its applicability is limited.

15.3 Text Annotation of Regulations

An intermediate position between manually and fully translation from source text to executable program is an approach that provides some automated support to identify textually relevant material using *text analytic tools*.[5] Such tool can be developed to identify and extract rules from legislation and regulations, in particular, conditional and deontic rules, specifying the antecedents, consequences, agents, themes, actions, and exceptions. In this section, we give brief overview of this approach.

15.3.1 Materials, Initial Analysis, and Model

For source materials, we have selected a passage from the US Code of Federal Regulations, US Food and Drug Administration, Department of Health and Human Services regulation for blood banks on testing requirements for communicable disease agents in human blood, Title 21 part 610 section 40.[6] This is a four page document of 1,777 words. Despite its size, the document offers much to consider as a starting point.

[5]This section is based on Wyner and Peters (2011).

[6]See in general: http://www.gpoaccess.gov/cfr/index.html The citation to the regulation is 21CFR610.40. Search for regulations in https://www.accessdata.fda.gov/scripts/cdrh/cfdocs/cfcfr/cfrsearch.cfm

For an initial analysis, we applied the Stanford Parser to the source document in order to identify the linguistic characterisations of the target elements. The Stanford Parser (version 1.6.8) is a robust, well-developed, well-maintained parser for English. It uses a Probabilistic Context-Free Grammar which was trained on the Penn Treebank; the Penn Treebank is a corpus of manually parsed newspaper articles; the parser performs well on newspaper articles. However, when we submitted our source document to the Stanford Parser (as a GATE plugin), it failed to parse. The source was then divided into subportions, creating a small corpus of documents, until all the subportions were successfully parsed. The parser outputs a range of syntactic parses, sequences of words that form a grammatical phrase, as well as dependency information, relationships between phrases such as *subject* of a sentence, *object* of a preposition, and so on. The parser generates a number of alternative parses that can be investigated for grammatical information.

We identify three causes why the parser failed, which is tied to the underlying source material used to train the parser, and in particular, to structural differences between our regulatory materials and newspaper articles. We found that regulatory texts have the following. First, there are *long, complex sentences* of several coordinated clauses or subordinate clauses. Such clauses may have several alternative parses. Second, lists are used, which use list punctuation, including enumerations, colons, etc. Such punctuation confounds tokenisation and sentence splitting, which are essential, initial processes. Third, references are used that contain a mix of punctuation and alpha-numeric characters that confound tokenisation and sentence splitting.

These elements alone may contribute to long parse times or failures to parse. The observations indicate that *for parsers to work successfully on legal materials, specialised preprocessors and training corpora must be developed.*

For parsed documents, we find a range of additional issues, where regulatory texts: contain embedded exception clauses; contain active and passive sentences; and have ambiguities from alternative parses of noun phrase and prepositional phrase.

Despite these issues, we find a range of constituents of interest: clauses for exceptions, deontic concepts, main verbs, negation, subjects and direct objects, and the structures of conditional sentences.

To focus our analysis on rule extraction, we identified: agent and theme, which are semantic roles that must be associated with noun phrases in grammatical (subject or object) roles in the sentence. These are used to account for active-passive alternations and identify the individual's relationship to the deontic concept; deontic modals such as "must" and verbs such as "obligated"; main verbs; exception clauses, e.g. "unless the citizen is a minor", which may appear in lists; and conditional sentences which have antecedents and consequences, where antecedents may appear in lists.

15.3.2 Method, Modules and Sample Output

We have used GATE, which is an open-source framework for language engineering applications (Cunningham et al. 2002; Wyner and Peters 2010a). The interface enables linguists and text engineers to develop and apply a variety of natural language processing tools to a corpus. We followed a methodology outlined in Wyner and Peters (2010a,b), which decomposes the larger problem into subtasks and structures a range of derivative data for analysis.

The GATE platform (Cunningham et al. 2002) enables template-based extraction on the basis of heuristic pattern-based grammars as well as a pipeline of standard natural language processing components such as tokenisation, sentence splitting, part of speech tagging, morphological analysis (lemmatisation), verb and noun phrase chunking, and a parser (Jurafsky and Martin 2008). In this study, we used the Stanford Parser Using information from these components, we have created targeted annotation modules for elements of our model; these modules are expressed in the gazetteer lists and Java Annotation Patterns Engine (JAPE) rules, where gazetteer lists are lists of strings that the tool looks up and annotates, while JAPE rules match patterns in the annotated text, then add additional annotations.

For our purposes here, we present the results of applying our GATE modules to our textual material.

Conditional sentences are those which contain the conditional marker *if*; they appear in alternative forms e.g. *If Bill is happy, Jill is happy*; *If Bill is happy, then Jill is happy*; *Jill is happy, if Bill is happy*; *Jill is happy if: (a) Bill is happy; and (b) Bill and Jill are together.* Additional rules are required to handle other contexts (e.g. with *then* and lists). They contain antecedents (that can be lists) and consequents. See Fig. 15.1 (GATE produces coloured output, so the black and white figure is only indicative).

For deontic rules, we identify the deontic operator, the main verb, the semantic roles that noun phrases play, and any exceptions. For the deontic concepts, we have a gazetteer for each basic deontic concept, e.g. *Obligation*, *Prohibition*, and *Permission*, where each is a list of terms that synonymously express that concept; for *Obligation*, we have *must*, *obligate*, *obligation*; tokens in the text are lemmatised and matched against the gazetteers. The Stanford Parser annotates the main verb *Verb*.

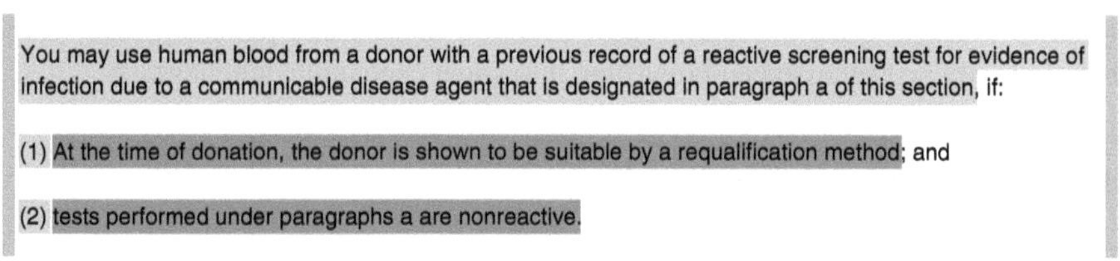

Fig. 15.1 Conditional with list antecedent

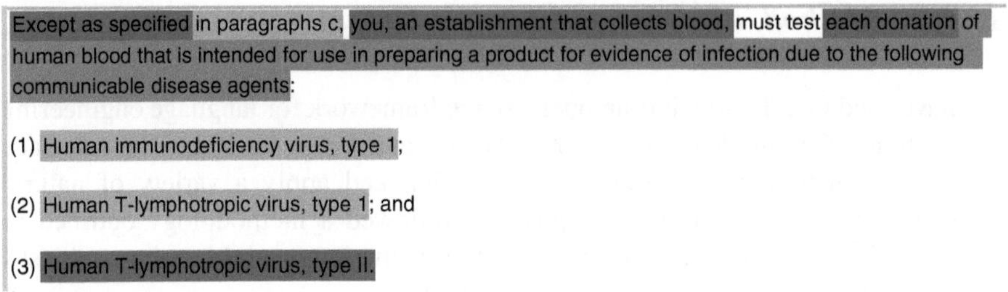
Except as specified in paragraphs c, you, an establishment that collects blood, must test each donation of human blood that is intended for use in preparing a product for evidence of infection due to the following communicable disease agents:

(1) Human immunodeficiency virus, type 1;

(2) Human T-lymphotropic virus, type 1; and

(3) Human T-lymphotropic virus, type II.

Fig. 15.2 Deontic rule with exception clause and list

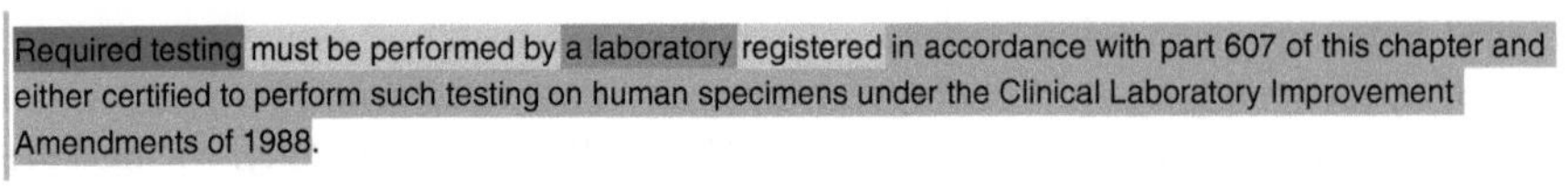
Required testing must be performed by a laboratory registered in accordance with part 607 of this chapter and either certified to perform such testing on human specimens under the Clinical Laboratory Improvement Amendments of 1988.

Fig. 15.3 Deontic rule with passive

In Fig. 15.2, we present a deontic rule, where the annotations in order are: an exception clause *Except as specified in paragraph c*; an agent *you, an establishment that collects blood* in subject position (the sentence is active), the modal operator *must*, the main verb *test*, the theme *each donation of human blood....agents* in object position, and a list of elements (1)–(3). In Fig. 15.3, we have a passive deontic rule.

A linguistically interesting module is the mapping of thematic roles to syntactic position given alternative syntactic patterns (*diathesis alternations*) such as the *active-passive alternation*: in the active sentence, *You must label each donation*, the agent of the action *you* is found in the subject position and the theme *each donation* is in the object position; in the corresponding passive sentence, *Each donation must be labelled by you*, the theme is in the subject position, while the agent is in a *by-phrase* or is implicit. For deontic notions, it is essential to identify the agent of the action, not simply the subject of the sentence, as the bearer of the obligation. To associate grammatical roles (subject and object) with thematic roles (agent and theme), we use grammatical information from the Stanford Parser (passive annotation and dependency information) along with information on thematic roles derived from VerbNet (Kipper et al. 2008; Wyner and Peters 2010a).

In Wyner and Peters (2011), we discuss results of our processing and a range of issues that arise. For our purposes here, the point is that we can use text analytic tools to aid in the identification and extraction of rule components, which may subsequently be processed and rewritten into some executable language.

15.4 Attempto Controlled English

To this point, we have considered manual translation of legislation to an executable and text analytic identification and extraction of relevant textual portions. In this section, we discuss *Attempto Controlled English* (ACE) tool, which constrains the linguistic expressions to controlled natural language (Wyner et al. 2010a); this facilitates automatic parsing and translation into Prolog.[7] Given some of the complexities already observed about legislative and regulatory language, we consider a simplified and constrained context and resource – policy making discussions.

15.4.1 Sample Policy Discussion

In Wyner and van Engers (2010) and Wyner et al. (2010b), a sample policy discussion is created concerning recycling and taxation that addresses the question *Should people be paid to recycle?*. While the original analysis considered argumentation, more sentences, and more complex sentences, for our purposes here we can consider a small sample of statements and their syntactic and semantic analysis in ACE.

The statements were:

(1) Every household creates some garbage.
(2) Every household should pay some tax for the household's garbage.
(3) No household should pay some tax for the household's garbage.

In the next section, we discuss the syntactic and semantic analysis of the input sentences.

15.4.2 Overview of Attempto Controlled English

To facilitate the processing of sentences, we use a well-developed controlled natural language system – Attempto Controlled English (ACE).[8] Our objective is to give enough of an overview of ACE to understand its capabilities and to make sense of the semantic representations in following sections. A controlled language has a specified vocabulary and a restricted range of grammatical constructions so as to provide a consistent linguistic expression, which can then be used to formally represent knowledge. The vocabulary and grammatical constructions are a subset of a natural language (e.g. English) so that sentences written and read in the controlled language appear as normal sentences, allowing the user to read and write English sentences, but to translate them into a formal representation. ACE provides a range of support tools to input statements, represent them in different forms, and process them further such as for reasoning, information extraction, or information interchange using XML. To use ACE, the user has to have some familiarity with the vocabulary, grammar, and interpretation rules.

---

[7]This section is based on Wyner and van Engers (2010) and Wyner et al. (2010b).

[8]http://attempto.ifi.uzh.ch/site/description/

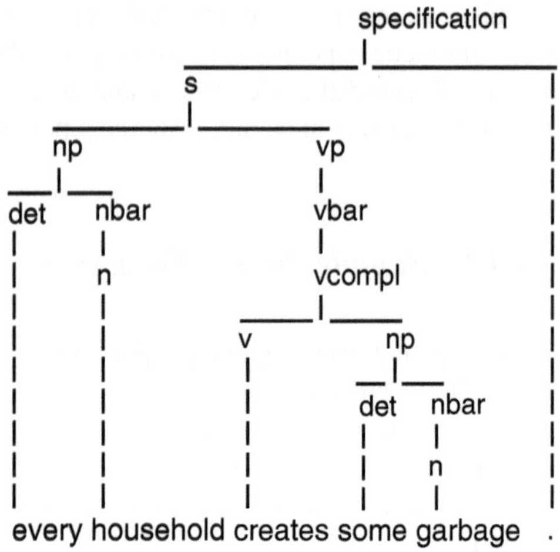

Fig. 15.4 Syntactic structure of *Every household creates some garbage*

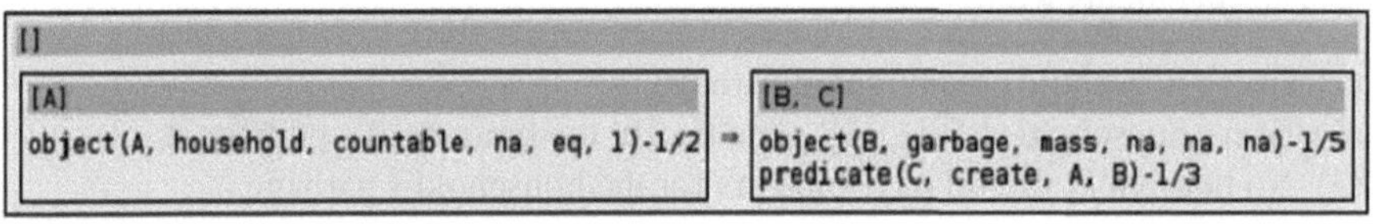

Fig. 15.5 Semantic structure of *Every household creates some garbage*

Consider a simple sentence such as "Every household creates some garbage." A user enters in the sentence to an ACE interface such as the online web server; different representations can be requested such as a syntactic phrase structure tree or semantic representation such as given in Fig. 15.4. In the semantic representation, we use a *Discourse Representation Structure* (DRS see Kamp and Reyle 1993 and Asher 1993), which is a variant of first order logic and supports the semantic representation of aspects of discourse such as pronominal anaphora. In Fig. 15.5, discourse referents (objects) A, B, and C are introduced (some of the details of the representation are discussed further below). With respect to these objects, A is indicated to be the object *household*, B is the object *garbage*, and C is an eventive object "creating" that holds between the household and the garbage. The sentence "Every household creates some garbage." is interpreted as a conditional rule. The DRS in Fig. 15.5 is equivalent to the first order expression $\forall x[[household'(x)] \rightarrow \exists y[garbage'(y) \wedge create'(x,y)]]$, where the box to the left of the conditional symbol => is understood to have a universal quantifier with scope over the antecedent and consequent, while the box to the right of => is understood to have an existential quantifier. Objects in the box on the right are the same as those introduced in the box on the left. Within a box, the statements are interpreted as conjuncts. As a first order logical representation, a DRS can be used for reasoning.

ACE supports a large lexicon, a range of grammatical constructions, and correlated semantic interpretations: negation on nouns or verbs, conjunction, disjunction, conditionals, quantifiers, adjectives, relative clauses, discourse anaphora, modals ("necessity", "possibility", "permission", and "recommendation"), possessives, prepositional phrases, verbs with three arguments, and verbs with subordinate clauses.[9]

ACE checks that the sentences input to the system satisfy the constraints of the syntax and semantics of the language, thus the user is only able to input grammatically acceptable and semantically interpretable sentences in building the knowledge base. For instance, every common noun (e.g. household, dog, etc) must appear in a noun phrase with a quantifier (e.g. a, some, every, at least two, etc); a transitive verb must appear with a direct object; adjectives which modify nouns must precede the noun. While there are a range of such constraints, most of them are familiar from English grammar or from guidelines to good English expository style. Other constraints may be less familiar such as anaphoric reference is to the most recent noun phrase (in *A dog chased another dog. It was black and white.*, the pronoun "it" is linked to the second dog.), definite noun phrases must be introduced by an indefinite noun as in a discourse *A dog walked in. The dog lay down.*, differences of interpretation of prepositions *of* and *for*, and verbs which take more than two arguments (e.g. *give*).

15.4.3 Discussion of Paraphrases

While ACE is fairly straightforward, there are many ways to formulate a sentence that might intuitively seem synonymous, but which yield unintended interpretations in ACE, or alternatively are unacceptable to ACE (see Wyner et al. 2010b for further discussion).

For instance, a sentence such as *Every householder should pay some tax for the garbage which the householder throws away* is has changes from *householder* to *household* to give a more general statement, eliminating *throws away* (a complex verb), and making the relative clause a possessive. Alternatives such as *Every householder should pay tax for garbage which the householder throws away.* or *Every householder should pay some tax for all of the garbage which the householder throws away.* are unacceptable in ACE. An alternative sentence *Every household should pay some tax for its garbage.* is grammatically well-formed, but it yields the unintended interpretation in ACE of *Every household should pay some tax for the tax's garbage.*; while speakers use pragmatics to determine the antecedent of pronouns, ACE uses the most recent pronoun. Replacing the possessive pronoun

[9] We discuss several of these later. However, while most of ACE is first order, the modals ("must", "can", "should", and "may") and verbs which take a sentential complement (e.g. "say") are not semantically interpretable.

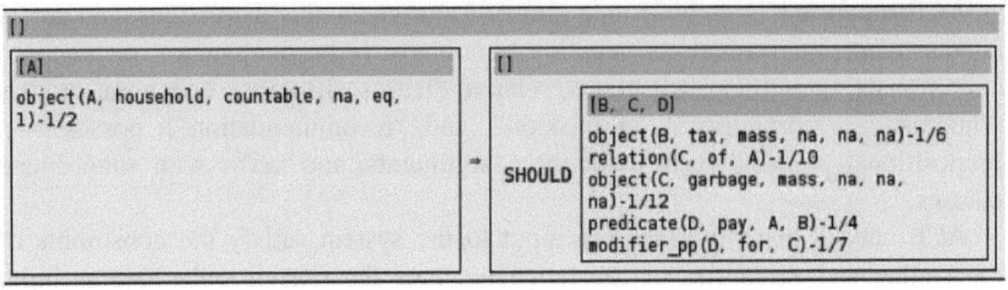

Fig. 15.6 Every household should pay some tax for the household's garbage

with a possessive noun clarifies the meaning. Finally, the subject noun phrase *every household* would appear outside the scope of the modal *should*, indicating what should hold for each household (distributively) rather than what should hold for all the households together (collectively) (Fig. 15.6).

15.4.4 Guidelines

From observations across a range of sentences, we developed some auxiliary guidelines for sentence construction. Broadly speaking, while all of our initial sentences are grammatical and have the intended interpretation to a native English speaker, not all of them are also grammatical and have the intended interpretation in ACE (cf. Shiffman et al. 2010 for similar issue about the composition of clinical guidelines). There may be constructions and interpretive rules that English speakers have which ACE does not yet have. Thus, our objective was to find a way to present the intended interpretation in a syntactic expression that accommodates ACE. Given practice, this is not difficult. Indeed, on may claim that the exercise demonstrates not only the functionality of ACE, but the value in explicit formulation of the sentences which made explicit information that otherwise might have been implicit in the sentences. We outline the issues by way of highlighting what must be considered in making use of ACE.

- Simplify the lexicon and syntax where possible.
- Use simple morphological forms rather than complex forms:
  - Gerunds – verbs as nouns, e.g. *Recycling is good.*
  - Participles – verbs as adjectives, e.g. *Recycled garbage is good*
  - Complex noun morphology – tax versus taxation.
- Noun-noun combinations are not available in ACE such as *garbage dump* unless they are hyphenated as *garbage-dump* and appear in the lexicon; rewrite such combinations as a relative clause *a dump which is for some garbage.*

- Use determiners on nouns – *some, a, every* – and follow the constraint on the definite determiner *the* in a countable noun phrase. For mass noun phrases, this constraint does not apply.
- Use common nouns that have a mass interpretation such as *garbage* with a determiner as in *the garbage* or possessive *the household's garbage*.
- Use possessive nouns rather than pronouns. Pronouns refer to the most recent noun and can give an unintended interpretation.
- Observe the interpretations that arise with different propositions *of, for, on*, etc, particularly with respect to verbs that take two or more arguments such as *give, pay*, and others. Where the arguments of verbs may appear in different syntactic orders – *diathesis alternations* as in the passive or in *Bill gave a present to Jill* versus *Bill gave Jill a present* – follow the canonical word order (active and using the prepositional phrase).
- Make implicit knowledge explicit and state all relevant participants.
- Where ACE finds some word or phrase unacceptable, seek an alternative synonymous word or phrase. While ACE can accept new lexical items, we have chosen to keep to the lexicon ACE provides.
- Consider the syntax and interpretation of quantifiers, modals, and negation.

15.4.5 Logical Issues

Assuming a set of sentences that are well-formed according to ACE and that have the intended semantic representation, we can turn to consider semantic issues such as consistency, query, and inference.

One of the tools allied with ACE is the first-order Reasoning in ACE (RACE) inference engine. ACE sentences can be input to RACE, which can be tested for consistency and queried; inferences can be drawn from the sentences, that is, theorems can be proven). However, as a first-order reasoner, RACE cannot reason with modal operators such as *should* or verbs which take sentential complements such as *say*; to reason with these expressions requires a modal logic, which has not been implemented with ACE.[10] To side step these issues, statements with *should* ((1), (2), (6), and (15)) are revised as generic statements with the simple, present tense; the verb *say* is removed from (9), making the subordinate clause a main clause and leaving the speaker implicit. Neither of these moves substantively impact on our analysis since it is common for statements of law to be expressed in terms of generics rather than with modal operators (de Maat and Winkels 2008), generics have modal interpretations (Pelletier and Carlson 1995), and one might claim that every statement has an implicit speech act and speaker (Horn and Ward 2004). However, these issues remain to be explored further.

[10]Automated reasoning with modal logic is under active development. See http://www.cs.man.ac.uk/~schmidt/tools/ on various tools and related literature.

Given the revised sentences, we can input a set of ACE sentences into RACE. For example, we can input the set of sentences below:

> Every household pays some tax for the household's garbage. Every household which pays some tax for the household's garbage increases an amount of the household's garbage which the household recycles. If a household increases an amount of the household's garbage which the household recycles then the household benefits the household's society. Every household which recycles the household's garbage reduces a need of a new dump which is for the garbage. Every household which reduces a need of a new dump benefits the household's society. A household pays some tax for the household's garbage.

RACE reports that these are consistent. We can query and prove theorems:

(1) Is a household which recycles the household's garbage a household which benefits the household's society?
(2) There is a household which benefits the household's society.
(3) Every household benefits the household's society.

The query (1) returns the answer *true*, (2) is proven with respect to the statements, and (3) cannot be proven. Other sets of sentences can similarly be consistent, be queried, and be used to prove theorems.

In this section, we have discussed another approach to mediating the relationship between natural language and executable programs. The strength of ACE is the application of a controlled language, which simplifies, constrains, and clarifies the range of possible expressions. On the other hand, the limited expressivity is not sufficient for the semantic representation of the language of legislation and regulation. For this, we turn to a more flexible, but also more problematic, tool.

15.5 C&C/Boxer

In this section, we outline results on information extraction, automated parsing, and formal semantic representation of a corpus of legal text using an open source tool, C&C/Boxer (Bos 2008), that parses and semantically represents text.[11] We find that legal language can be processed, but that particular issues arise about identifying the correct relevant elements as well as parsing. Thus, prior to submitting formalised legal expressions to deduction engines, we must develop higher quality extraction tools and also check that the formal representations correspond to the intended semantic interpretation.

15.5.1 Method

In this section, we describe the tool and materials that we use in our study. We use the Groningen Meaning Bank (GMB), which uses C&C/Boxer, a tool that parses

[11]This section is based on Wyner et al. (2012).

and semantically represents text. The GMB (Basile et al. 2012) is a freely available, online corpus of English texts that have been automatically parsed and given an associated semantic representation using the C&C/Boxer tool. GMB comprises thousands of public domain documents.

C&C/Boxer consists of a combinatory categorial grammar (CCG) parser (Bos 2008) and Boxer, a tool that provides semantic representations in Discourse Representation Structures (DRSs) of Discourse Representation Theory (DRT) (Kamp and Reyle 1993). DRT was developed to provide semantic representations for discourses, including pronominal anaphora and discourse relations. The parser was trained and developed on the Penn Treebank, a newswire corpus: the CCG parser shows a high coverage for texts in the corpus, is robust and fast, and is therefore suitable for producing approximations to gold-standard annotations. It must be emphasised that there are consequences to the choice of training corpus since constructions common to one corpus may not be found in some other corpus with the consequence that the parser fails on those constructions found in the latter corpus. The pipeline consists of the usual steps (e.g. token and sentence detection) plus tagging with CCG categories, parsing with the categories, then boxing to give a semantic analysis.

For the purposes of this presentation, a categorial grammar specifies typed categories of lexical items along with their mode of combination. NP stands for *noun phrase*, S stands for *sentence*, NP\S is a function that takes NPs on the left as input and outputs Ss. For example, a verb such as *runs* has the category of NP\S, and a noun such as *Bill* has a category of NP; combining something of NP category on the left of something of NP\S category on the right yields a category of type S, which is a sentence. Along with the syntactic parse, a formal semantic translation expressed in the λ-calculus is provided,[12] where the semantic derivation follows the structure of the syntactic parse.

To give an impression of the analysis, we illustrate the automatic output of the tool with a very simple example below, which has the FOL expression (with some grammatical information), the syntactic analysis in Fig. 15.7,[13] and the DRS Fig. 15.8:

- Cameron is a British citizen.
- ∃ A:(per1cameron(A) ∧ ∃ B:∃ C:(a1british(C) ∧ (nam1citizen(C) ∧ A=C)))

In providing the FOL expression, universal quantifiers and conditionals are replaced with their equivalents using existential quantifiers, negation, and conjunction. C&C/Boxer also outputs a Prolog representation of the FOL expressions that are suitable for FOL theorem provers, e.g. *vampire*.

[12]With the λ-calculus, one can specify parts and the way the parts functionally and systematically combine.

[13]The figure is not intended to be legible, but only to give a sense of how the analysis proceeds by layers that combine simple units to more complex units. Given the scale, the image is either too hard to read or too big to present.

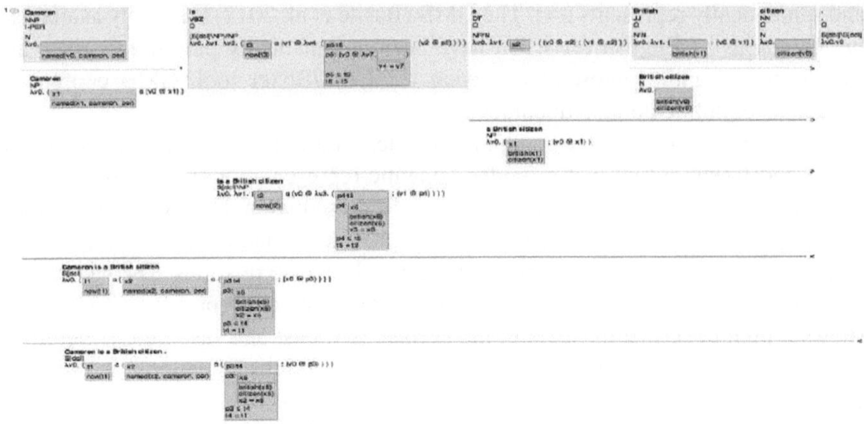

Fig. 15.7 Parse of *Cameron is a British citizen*

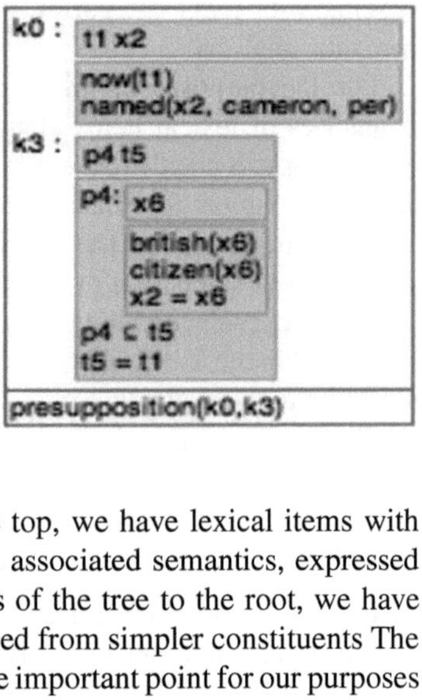

Fig. 15.8 DRS of *Cameron is a British citizen*

In Fig. 15.7, we have a derivation tree. At the top, we have lexical items with their assigned categorial grammar categories and associated semantics, expressed in the λ-calculus. Descending down the branches of the tree to the root, we have complex syntactic and semantic constituents formed from simpler constituents The root of the tree reduces to the DRS of Fig. 15.8. The important point for our purposes is that C&C/Boxer provides a syntactic and semantic analysis automatically. The correctness can be adjudicated on the GMB website, then committed to the gold standard corpus.[14]

Turning to the DRS in Fig. 15.8, we give some flavour of the significance of the representation (Lascarides and Asher 2007). There is a k box notation, k0 and k2, where each box represents a knowledge base or Discourse Unit of FOL expressions, where a top sub-box represents discourse referents and a lower sub-box the FOL

[14]A gold standard corpus is a corpus that is intended to be *correct* by consensus of the annotators of the texts.

predications. The boxes can be related, e.g. presuppostion(k0,k2), which means that k2 presupposes the objects and time of k0. In the example, it is presupposed in k0 that there is a named entity relation between a variable *x1*, the string *cameron*, and the type *person*. This content is used to resolve k2. The second k box, k2, contains a proposition variable *p* and its propositional content, which introduces a discourse referent x4, some predications on x4, and an identification of discourse referents.

Syntactic and semantic derivations can be given for longer, more complex sentences and discourse continuations. For instance, later we provide examples of DRSs for conditional sentences. Such complex sentences and discourses must be carefully checked that the derivation is correct and, more importantly, that the semantic output corresponds to semantic intuitions for an interpretation of the meanings of the sentences. Thus, our key objective is to use the tools to analyse, curate, and committed statements to a gold standard corpus.

Asides from complex sentences or discourse continuations, as we've noted, it is widely understood that FOL is not sufficient to represent the semantics of natural language expressions. For instance, *generalised quantifiers*, *quantification of properties*, *modification of modifiers*, *genericity*, *comparatives*, *intensional operators*, and *pragmatics* all seem to go beyond FOL.[15] While there are all these significant issues, we can, nonetheless, make useful progress on the analysis of the expressions. The advantage of our approach is that we have a transparent, systematic, and grounded means to curate the corpus.

15.5.2 Example

In this section, we report an analysis of a sentence in C&C/Boxer, looking particularly at the analysis of conditionals. One particularly interesting aspect that the analysis makes explicit are *discontinuous clauses*, where some interjection appears, particularly a what we may call a *defeasibility clause*, where we have marked up the clauses. We give the example of a statement from the *British Nationality Act 1981*, then manually provided parse.

> If an application is made to register as a British citizen a person who is a British overseas territories citizen, the Secretary of State may, if he thinks fit, cause the person to be so registered.[16]

> If <Antecedent-1> an application is made to register as a British citizen a person who is a British overseas territories citizen </Antecedent-1>, <Consequent-1> the Secretary of State may, </Consequent-1> if <Antecedent-2> he thinks fit, </Antecedent-2> cause <Consequent-1> the person to be so registered </Consequent-1>.

[15]For these various constructions, it is useful to look at introductory textbooks (Chierchia and McConnell-Ginet 2000).

[16]The commas around the interjection are relevant to parsing, so added to the source text.

We see that the consequent, Consequent-1, is discontinuous in the sense that there is an additional antecedent, Antecedent-2, that intervenes. There are issues of semantic representation. First, what is the semantic representation in terms of the antecedent and consequents? Two possibilities are (using the tags to abbreviate the clauses):

<Antecedent-1> → [<Antecedent-2> → <Consequent-1>]
[<Antecedent-1> ∧ <Antecedent-2>] → <Consequent-1>]

While these are semantically equivalent in Propositional Logic, the discourse structure may play a role. Moreover, the second issue is that <Antecedent-2> introduces a generic defeasible clause; that is, there are unspecified contexts where the rule may or may not apply, which is left to the discretion of the Secretary of State. In fact, this sort of phrase, *if he thinks fit* occurs frequently in the source document. Notably, while defeasible clauses might be presented as exception clauses, which could appear here as 'unless he thinks otherwise', in this data we have a positive expression of the defeasible hedge.

These two points raise issues for the parser and semantic representation, in particular, how to parse the discontinuous constituent, how to assign the interjection the right semantic representation, and finally, how to semantically represent the generic defeasible clause. We see how C&C/Boxer represents these issues in the following.

Turning to C&C/Boxer, we discuss the sentence introduced above.

The DRS in Fig. 15.9 must be manually analysed in order to ensure that it represents the intuitive semantics of the source sentence as various individuals and predicates are introduced across the representation. While the sentence is parsed and given a semantic representation and there are parts that are acceptable and correct, there are other portions of the representation that are either unclear or incorrect. Thus, in parsing and semantically representing a legal text such as our sample, further work is required, which is what the legal-GMB corpus and GMB tool are to support. We briefly outline some aspects of the representation, leaving aside temporal structure in particular.

The top box, k0, that is presupposed with respect to the lower box, k5, introduces a time, three discourse referents, and four predications – *now*, *male*, *secretary*, and *state*. The bottom k5 box introduces a conditional with an embedded conditional, following the first logical analysis above. In the first antecedent, various discourse referents and predications are introduced. We paraphrase the result, using discourse referents to link to the representation:

First Antecedent

1. A *person* (x9) is identified as a *british overseas citizen* (see x14 in P10).
2. A *making* event (e7) has an *application* (x6) as *Theme*.
3. A *registering* event (e12) has the *application* (x6) as *Agent* and x9 as *Theme*.
4. The *registering* event (e12) is in the *as* relation with a *british citizen* (x13), which is distinct from x14.

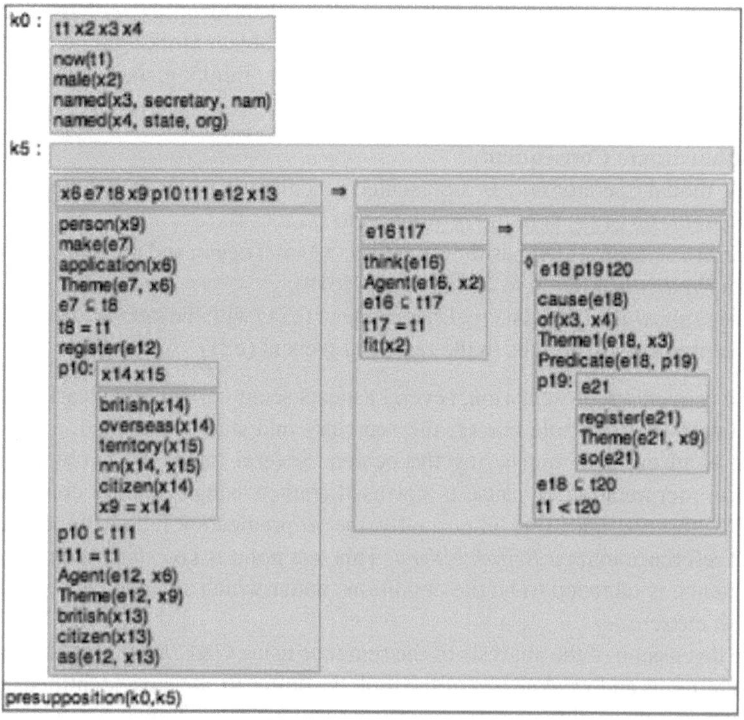

Fig. 15.9 DRS of discontinuous constituent example

This captures some interesting issues – the difference between different forms of predication, e.g. *as a British Citizen* and *is a British Citizen*, while leaving their exact interpretation aside. The proposition (p10) correctly predicates being a British overseas territory citizen of the person (x9) who wants to be a British citizen. There are two events – a making event and a registering event, where the theme of making (the application) is the agent of registering; this captures accurately the link between the passive and the subject of the infinitive. However, it makes an abstract noun the agent of registering, which is a conceptual ambiguity of the text. The agent of making is left unspecified, as it is in the source, though conceptually there ought to be one.

Turning to the antecedent of the consequent, we it has two parts – an antecedent and a consequent:

Subordinate Antecedent

1. A *thinking* event (e12) has x2, the *male*, as *Agent* and *proposition* (p17) as *Theme*.
2. The *male* (x2) is *fit*.

This antecedent captures that someone (who is later identified with the Secretary of State) thinks, though it leaves the propositional object of thought unspecified. It also introduces the happy (incorrect) concept that by thinking, were it but so.

Finally, we have the final consequent box.

Subordinate Consequent

1. The modal operator *may* is represented as a diamond over the whole box.
2. The *secretary* (x3) is in the *of* relation to *state* (x4)
3. A *causing* event (e18) has the *secretary* (x3) as *Theme*; and the *causing* event is in a *Predicate* relation to a *proposition* (p19).
4. The *proposition* (p19) is a *registering* event (e21) with the *person* (x9) as *Theme*.
5. The predicate *so* applies to the *registering* event (e21).

As a semantic representation, several aspects seem correct and clear: the modal has scope over the whole clause; the secretary and state are related; and what is caused is an event of registering the person. Several things are problematic: the agentive interpretation of cause is not used (rather using a *middle* construction); the *of* is obscure; and, very importantly, the *so* predication fails to function as an elliptic reference to *as a British citizen*. This last point is key since the meaning of the sentence is intended to be the conditions under which someone is registered as a British citizen.

The discussion of the analysis of the sentence using C&C/Boxer highlights some of the strengths and weaknesses of the tool. By doing so, we have identified specific issues for future development, among them thematic role alignment and ellipsis.

15.5.3 Inference

As with ACE, we can consider inferences in C&C/Box from the FOL (DRS) Prolog representations that are output by C&C/Boxer. In keeping with the Recognising Textual Entailment tasks (RTE) (Dagan et al. 2009), the *Nutcracker* inference engine supplied with C&C/Boxer requires explicit statement of a *Theory* (T) from which the inference engine proves that an explicit *Hypothesis* (H) follows. Tools in the RTE tasks typically also identify contradiction. To succeed, tools in the RTE tasks are provided with development and testing corpora, where the development corpus is a gold standard for entailment and contradiction relations between textual portions. Having trained on the development corpus, the tool is then applied to the testing corpus, and performance is measured. Thus a specific development task for inference in the legal domain is to provide development and training corpora with respect to entailment and contradiction based on material from the BNA1. For instance, we would have a pair such as follows, where T does intuitively imply H; we would have similar pairs were T does not intuitively imply H or T is contradictory with H.

- T: A person born in the United Kingdom shall be a British Citizen if at the time of his birth his father is a British citizen. Mary Woods was born on 20 February 1968. Her father was a UK citizen then.
- H: Mary Woods is a British Citizen.

In principle, we ought to be able to carry out the task of evaluating the capabilities of inferences using C&C/Boxer on a set of legal sentences. However, this has as prerequisite a suitable *training* corpus of legal sentences that can be accurately and acceptably parsed and semantically represented in C&C/Boxer. Yet we do not, so we are not in a position to evaluate its performance.

In this section, we have discussed using C&C/Boxer to parse and semantically represent statements from legislation. It is, as we can see, a very articulate tool, but in the absence of a suitable gold standard training corpus, we cannot yet evaluate its capabilities to support inference in legislation.

15.6 Other Formal Approaches

To this point, we have reviewed several ways to process and formalise legislative text into some machine-executable form, considering manual, text analytic, controlled language processing, and wide-scale parsing and semantic representation.

Recently, other approaches have emerged that would provide alternative formal targets than logic programming.

One approach is to provide a legal ontology in OWL such as Wyner and Hoekstra (2012), though this is for case reasoning and not legislation. An ontology is a formal knowledge representation of the entities, properties, and relations in some domain (Noy and McGuinness 2000). Given an ontology, one can test it for consistency and draw inferences. It might be feasible to construct an ontology for legislation and regulation, but this has not, to our knowledge, been done. Such an ontology could only represent FOL compatible aspects of the domain, given the constraints of OWL; thus the non-FOL aspects that are claimed for the legal domain, which are substantial, would not be covered. An alternative is a knowledge representation language, e.g. Legal Knowledge Interchange Format (LKIF) (Hoekstra et al. 2009), which includes some non-monotonic aspects.

Another approach is to formalise legislative structure and rules in an XML compatible format. Prominent examples ares *Akoma Ntoso* and the *the National Archives of the United Kingdom.*[17] XML schemes are provided to annotate a large range of primarily *structural* aspects of legislative and regulatory documents. However, the contentful aspects, e.g. rules and fine-grained textual information, are largely outside the scope of the schemes.

[17] Respectively, http://www.akomantoso.org/ and https://www.tso.co.uk/our-expertise/case-studies/national-archives-wwwlegislationgovuk

Finally, LegalRuleML is an XML language to mark up the rules and related auxiliary elements found in legislative and regulatory texts (Athan et al. 2013a,b). It is related to RuleML, so identifies the rule structure of antecedents and conclusions. It is a rich language, allocating elements for roles, temporal information, and defeasibility, in regard of which it is unusual amongst the various formal languages.

While OWL ontologies and XML schemes make richer structures to target translations, they all require manual annotation. Thus, the initial bottleneck – passing from natural language semi or fully automatically – remains.

15.7 Conclusion

In this chapter, we have considered a range of approaches to the translation of the natural language of legislation to executable logic programs (or other machine readable formats). While none of the approaches have succeeded beyond pilot projects or required large manual investment, they have made it clear what *subproblems* that can be more or less straightforwardly addressed and what needs further work. In our view, there has been substantial progress to understanding and addressing these problems and issues, taking an incremental and decompositional approach.

The purpose of formalisation is to make explicit and transparent, to what extent possible, the structure and meaning of the material being formalised. Taking the text step to make the formalisation operational is to make use of the formalisation. Thus, the formalisation and operationalisation is intended not only to make greater use of the law, e.g. to query, to give access, to function in websites, to reformat, and so on, but to help in gaining a greater understanding of the structure and meaning of the law itself; and in particular, to address such broad questions such as *what is a law such that individuals abide or violate it?*

References

Asher, N. 1993. *Reference to abstract objects in discourse*. Dordrecht/Boston: Kluwer Academic.

Athan, Tara, Harold Boley, Guido Governatori, Monica Palmirani, Adrian Paschke, and Adam Wyner. 2013a. Legalruleml: From metamodel to use cases – (a tutorial). In *RuleML*, Volume 8035 of lecture notes in computer science, ed. L. Morgenstern, P.S. Stefaneas, F. Lévy, A. Wyner, and A. Paschke, 13–18. Springer: Heidelberg.

Athan, Tara, Harold Boley, Guido Governatori, Monica Palmirani, Adrian Pasckhe, and Adam Wyner. 2013b. OASIS LegalRuleML. In Proceedings of 14th international conference on artificial intelligence and law, ICAIL 2013, 3–12. Rome: ACM.

Basile, Valerio, Johan Bos, Kilian Evang, and Noortje Venhuizen. 2012. A platform for collaborative semantic annotation. In *Proceedings of the demonstrations at the 13th conference of the European chapter of the association for computational linguistics (EACL)*, Avignon, 92–96.

Bench-Capon, Trevor, G.O. Robinson, Tom Routen, and Marek J. Sergot. 1987. Logic programming for large scale applications in law: A formalisation of supplementary benefit legislation. In *International conference on artificial intelligence and law*, Boston, 190–198.

Bench-Capon, Trevor, Frans Coenen, and Paul Orton. 1993. Argument based explanation of the british nationality act as a logic program. *Information and Communications Technology Law* 2:53–66.

Bos, Johan. 2008. Wide-coverage semantic analysis with boxer. In *Semantics in text processing. STEP 2008 conference proceedings, research in computational semantics*, ed. J. Bos and R. Delmonte, 277–286. College Publications.

Bos, Johan, Stephen Clark, Mark Steedman, James Curran, and Julia Hockenmaier. 2004. Wide–coverage semantic representations from a CCG parser. In *Proceedings of the 20th international conference on computational linguistics (COLING 04)*, 1240–1246. Morristown: Association for Computational Linguistics.

Chierchia, Gennaro, and Sally McConnell-Ginet. 2000. *Meaning and grammar: An introduction to semantics*. Cambridge: MIT.

Cunningham, Hamish, Diana Maynard, Kalina Bontcheva, and Valentin Tablan. 2002. GATE: A framework and graphical development environment for robust NLP tools and applications. In *Proceedings of the 40th anniversary meeting of the association for computational linguistics (ACL02)*, Philadelphia, 168–175.

Dagan, Ido, Bill Dolan, Bernardo Magnini, and Dan Roth. 2009. Recognizing textual entailment: Rational, evaluation and approaches. *Natural Language Engineering* 15(4). pp. i–xvii.

Dayal, Surendra, Michael Harmer, Peter Johnson, and David Mead. 1993. Beyond knowledge representation: Commercial uses for legal knowledge bases. In *Proceedings of the 4th international conference on artificial intelligence and law, ICAIL 93*, 167–174. New York: ACM.

Dayal, Surendra, and Peter Johnson. 2000. A web-based revolution in Australian public administration. *Journal of Information, Law, and Technology*, 1. http://www2.warwick.ac.uk/fac/soc/law/elj/jilt/2000_1/austlii/dayal/

de Maat, Emile, and Radboud Winkels. 2008. Automatic classification of sentences in dutch laws. In *Legal knowledge and information systems. Jurix 2008: The 21st annual conference, frontiers in artificial intelligence and applications*, 207–216. IOS Press: Amsterdam.

Fuchs, Norbert E., Kaarel Kaljurand, and Tobias Kuhn. 2008. Attempto controlled english for knowledge representation. In *Reasoning web*, Volume 5224 of lecture notes in computer science, ed. C. Baroglio, P.A. Bonatti, J. Maluszynski, M. Marchiori, A. Polleres, and S. Schaffert, 104–124. Berlin/Heidelberg: Springer.

Hammond, Peter. 1983. Representation of DHSS Regulations as a Logic Program. Department of Computing: Research report DoC.

Hoekstra, Rinke, Joost Breuker, Marcello Di Bello, and Alexander Boer. 2009. LKIF core: Principled ontology development for the legal domain. In *Law, ontologies and the semantic web*, Volume 188 of frontiers in artificial intelligence and applications, ed. J. Breuker, P. Casanovas, M.C.A. Klein, and E. Francesconi, 21–52. Amsterdam: IOS Press.

Horn, Laurence, and Gregory Ward. eds. 2004. *Handbook of pragmatics*. Malden: Blackwell.

Johnson, Peter, and David Mead. 1991. Legislative knowledge base systems for public administration: Some practical issues. In *ICAIL*, Oxford, 108–117.

Jurafsky, Daniel, and James H. Martin. 2008. *Speech and language processing*, Prentice hall series in artificial intelligence, 2nd ed. Prentice Hall, Upper Saddle River: N.J.

Kamp, Hans, and Uwe Reyle. 1993. *From discourse to logic: Introduction to model-theoretic semantics of natural language: Formal logic and discourse representation theory*. Springer, Dordrecht.

Kipper, Karin, Anna Korhonen, Neville Ryant, and Martha Palmer. 2008. A large-scale classification of english verbs. *Language Resources and Evaluation* 42(1):21–40.

Lascarides, Alex, and Nicholas Asher. 2007. Segmented discourse representation theory: Dynamic semantics with discourse structure. In *Computing meaning: Volume 3*, ed. H. Bunt and R. Muskens, 87–124. Kluwer Academic, Dordrecht.

Leith, Philip. 1982. ELI: An expert legislative consultant. In *Proceedings of the IEE conference on man/machine systems UMIST*, Number 212. Conference Publication. London: IEE Conference Publication.
Noy, N., and D. McGuinness. 2000. Ontology development 101: A guide to creating your first ontology. Technical report, Stanford University.
Pelletier, Francis, and Gregory Carlson. 1995. *The generic book*. Chicago: The University of Chicago Press: Chicago.
Sergot, Marek. 1988. Representing legislation as logic programs. In *Machine intelligence*, volume 11: 209–260. Oxford: Oxford University Press.
Sergot, Marek, Fariba Sadri, Robert A. Kowalski, Frank Kriwaczek, Peter Hammond, and H.T. Cory. 1986. The British Nationality Act as a logic program. *Communications of the ACM* 29(5):370–386.
Shiffman, Richard N., George Michel, Michael Krauthammer, Norbert E. Fuchs, Kaarel Kaljurand, and Tobias Kuhn. 2010. Writing clinical practice guidelines in controlled natural language. In *Proceedings of the 2009 conference on controlled natural language, CNL09*, 265–280. Berlin/Heidelberg: Springer.
Stamper, Ronald. 1980. LEGOL: Modelling legal rules by computer. In *Computer science and law*, 45–71. Cambridge: Cambridge University Press.
Wyner, Adam. 2012. Commentary on–Trevor Bench-Capon, Gwen Robinson, Tom Routen, and Marek Sergot. Logic programming for large scale applications in law: a formalisation of supplementary benefit legislation. *Artificial Intelligence and Law* 20(3):9–10
Wyner, Adam, and Rinke Hoekstra. 2012. A legal case OWL ontology with an instantiation of Popov v. Hayashi. *Artificial Intelligence and Law* 20(1):83–107.
Wyner, Adam, and Wim Peters. 2010a. Lexical semantics and expert legal knowledge towards the identification of legal case factors. In *Proceedings of legal knowledge and information systems (JURIX 2010)*, ed. R. Winkels, 127–136. Amsterdam: IOS Press.
Wyner, Adam, and Wim Peters. 2010b. Towards annotating and extracting textual legal case factors. In *Proceedings of the language resources and evaluation conference workshop on semantic processing of legal texts (SPLeT 2010)*, 36–45. Valletta: ELRA.
Wyner, Adam, and Wim Peters. 2011. On rule extraction from regulations. In *Legal knowledge and information systems – JURIX 2011: The twenty-fourth annual conference*, ed. K. Atkinson, 113–122. Amsterdam: IOS Press.
Wyner, Adam, and Tom M. van Engers. 2010. A framework for enriched, controlled on-line discussion forums for e-government policy-making. In *Electronic government and electronic participation*, ed. J.-L. Chappelet, O. Glassey, M. Janssen, A. Macintosh, J. Scholl, E. Tambouris, and M. Wimmer, 357–364. Linz: Trauner Verlag.
Wyner, Adam, Krasimir Angelov, Guntis Barzdins, Danica Damljanovic, Brian Davis, Norbert E. Fuchs, Stefan Hfler, Ken Jones, Kaarel Kaljurand, and Tobias Kuhn. 2010a. On controlled natural languages: Properties and prospects. In *Proceedings of the 2009 conference on controlled natural language, CNL09*, 281–289. Berlin/Heidelberg: Springer.
Wyner, Adam, Johan Bos, Valerio Basile, and Paulo Quaresma. 2012. An empirical approach to the semantic representation of law. In *Proceedings of 25th international conference on legal knowledge and information systems (JURIX 2012)*, 177–180. Amsterdam: IOS Press.
Wyner, Adam, Tom M. van Engers, and Kiavash Bahreini. 2010b. From policy-making statements to first-order logic. In *EGOVIS*, Volume 6267 of lecture notes in computer science, ed. K.N. Andersen, E. Francesconi, Å. Grönlund, and T.M. van Engers, 47–61. Berlin/Heidelberg: Springer.

Chapter 16
A Rule–Based Graphical Decision Charting Approach to Legal Knowledge Based System

Nitin B. Bilgi

Abstract Rule based systems have been around for quite some time now without breaking into mainstream computing. These systems represent the rules in the form of simple if–then blocks and collections of facts and are controlled by an inference engine. In this research work a rule is represented in form of decision chart. Using this graphical decision chart approach a legal expert system/knowledge based system, with specific reference to the transfer of property act, within the Indian legal system which is often in demand is developed. The VisiRule software made available by Logic Programming Associates is used in the development of this expert system. VisiRule is a decision charting tool, in which the rules are defined by a combination of graphical shapes and pieces of text, and produces rules.

Keywords Transfer of property act • Knowledge based system, expert system • Rule based system • VisiRule

16.1 Preliminary Remarks

As Edward Shortliffe, the creator of MYCIN, often called the inventor of expert system, observed more than 20 years ago, doctors will not use an expert system, no matter how good the advice it gives, unless it saves them time (Shortliffe and Duda 1983). The author feels that same is also true of lawyers. The building of legal expert systems, most of the time is for the specific users. The choice of a specific type of user influence the way the expert system is built in law. It is possible to create expert systems in law directed towards the general population also. These expert systems in law can be a vehicle for spreading legal knowledge monopolized by legal experts, among common man. Hence the author of this research work decided

N.B. Bilgi (✉)
Department of Computer Science & Engineering, Maratha Mandal Engineering College, Belgaum, Karnataka, India
e-mail: nbbbgm@rediffmail.com

M. Araszkiewicz, K. Płeszka (eds.), *Logic in the Theory and Practice of Lawmaking*, Legisprudence Library 2, DOI 10.1007/978-3-319-19575-9_16

to build **TPA–EXPERT (Transfer of Property Act–Expert System)** (Bilgi et al. 2010). The objective of this research work is to apply AI to Law, and also in order to propagate legal knowledge among common man. The author has made the choice of specific law of Indian legal domain (Transfer of Property Act) which is frequently sought after by a common man. The author has selected a legal domain in which a consensus among lawyers exists as the rules are very specific. Though the work is not directed at experts but still this work will help them in making fast productive decisions.

The outline of the research is that author initially introduces the domain of expert systems in AI and law and related them to theory and practice of legislation. The subsequent section deals with the literature review, legal aspects in Indian law and related terminologies, research methodology adopted, brief introduction to rule based systems, sample modules developed and finally the conclusion.

16.1.1 Expert Systems in Law

The work on legal expert system began in the US with James Sprowl in late 1970s. 10 years later (1989) there was an international conference edited by Marino with contributions from all over the world. Generally the expert systems in law are built for lawyers by the researchers in computer domain. The rules are collected from the lawyers which are standpoint of the formalized legal knowledge. Expert systems in law are now in use on a regular basis as well as on experimental basis in many broad administration of justice of the Indian courts (Bilgi et al. 2008). The research work on expert systems in law, over the last three decades (1980–2009) has been pioneered by L.T. McCarty, A. Gardner, A.A. Martino, J.C. Smith, G.S. Deedman, J.A. Sprowl, R. Susskind, T. Bench–Capon, H. Praken, T.F. Gordon, J. Vanthienen to name a few.

The author of this research work developed a prototype of an expert system (Bilgi and Kulkarni 2008a) in **TPA** directed towards non–lawyers in order to create awareness in their land dealings. The author has selected the specific domain of Transfer of Property Act 1882 of Indian legal domain for three main reasons. Firstly, everyone is faced with a land/housing problem at least once in their life time. Transfer of Property Act is a legal domain which affects people in their day–to–day life over the buying and selling of property. Indian property–law which is substantially codified is contained in different enactments dating from about the year 1882 till this date, with no less than 1 Lac cases per year (Bilgi et al. 2010). We hypothesized that more accessible legal knowledge about Transfer of Property Act which would help people settle case conflicts in a more positive way than any tribunal could. Finally, legal expertise was more accessible to the author of this research work (Gour 1987).

16.1.2 Relation of Rules with Theory and Practice of Legislation

Leading legal theorist Ronald Dworkin rejects the old fashioned view that the law is just a set of rules that can be applied to any situation. Instead, Dworkin theorises that "lawyers ... make use of standards that do not function as rules, but operate differently as principles and policies".[1] The interpretation of any law must take into account those standards. The three operative parts can be summarized: (i) Rules are "applicable in an all–or–nothing fashion".[2] They may have exceptions but these need to be stated, and are often found in legislation. (ii) A policy is "a standard that sets out a goal to be reached"[3] and may be used to justify political and judicial decisions. (iii) A principle is "a standard to be observed... because it is a requirement of justice or fairness or some other dimension of morality".[4] Dworkin contends that policy should be left to the politicians. In his leading work, Taking Rights Seriously, he suggests that the courts should take note of the established doctrine of legislative supremacy (that is, Parliament having the ultimate right to pass legislation). As such, courts should pay "qualified deference to the acts of legislature."[5]

16.2 Domain Requirement

Expert systems are used in many different subject domains. One of the domains that pose both difficult problems and interesting challenges is case law research. The lawyer wants authority for his point of view. He wants a viable argument that will support his claim from a binding case if he can get it, from a persuasive one if he cannot. Failing that, he will take any helpful argument he can find. He may even want some configuration of facts and legal concepts which, although it does not constitute an argument in itself, will help him to construct one. The following description of a lawyer"s search shows the usual cognitive phenomenon.

> No lawyer ever thought out the case of a client in terms of the syllogism. He begins with a conclusion he intends to reach, favourable to his client of course, and then analyzes the facts of the situation to find material out of which to construct a favourable statement of facts, to "form" a minor premise. At the same time he goes over recorded cases to find rules of law employed in cases which can be presented as similar, rules which will substantiate a

[1] Available at http://epublications.bond.edu.au/cgi/viewcontent.cgi?article=1135&context=nle

[2] Available at http://epublications.bond.edu.au/cgi/viewcontent.cgi?article=1135&context=nle

[3] Available at http://epublications.bond.edu.au/cgi/viewcontent.cgi?article=1135&context=nle

[4] Available at http://epublications.bond.edu.au/cgi/viewcontent.cgi?article=1135&context=nle

[5] Available at http://epublications.bond.edu.au/cgi/viewcontent.cgi?article=1135&context=nle

> certain way of looking at and interpreting the facts. And as his acquaintance with rules of law judged applicable widens, he probably alters perspective and emphasis in selection of the facts which are to form his evidential data. And as he learns more of the facts of the case he may modify his selection of rules of law upon which he bases his case (Dewey 1927).

In order to construct his argument, the lawyer will need to navigate among legal concepts with their related facts; and he will need to make associations among selected legal concepts. Finding information in law cases is challenging. Each case is unique. Patterns of literary similarity are not common among cases. There are many writers, and many styles. There are no generally accepted conventions as to how decisions ought to be constructed. The reasoning is diffuse, dense, and original. The language used in cases is formal and technical. However, the vocabulary is derived from everyday language. There are very few legal expert systems for non–lawyers. The researcher of this work has chosen non–experts as users. As stated earlier, the author wanted to investigate the feasibility of propagating legal knowledge to the general population through new technological means. Hence the author felt that a legal expert system would be a good means of giving people safe and accurate information about buying and selling of property.

16.3 A Literature Study

The author during the literature study has observed that during the 1990s, there was a special trend of using the term **"Knowledge–Based Systems"** for not only computer applications implementing Artificial Intelligence concepts, but also organizational systems that paid a special attention to knowledge acquisition, storage and retrieval (Bilgi and Kulkarni 2008b). In order to know of the previous research done in this direction, the author examined several studies dedicated to the topic or to broader topics including references to KBSs. Most of studies dealt with broader topics with references to KBSs. Subsequent paragraphs the author discusses some of related works in field of knowledge based systems.

Andrew Stranieri et al. claims that the evaluation strategies to assess the effectiveness of Legal Knowledge Based Systems enable strengths and limitations of systems to be accurately articulated. This facilitates efforts in the research community to develop systems and also promotes the adoption of research prototypes in the commercial world (Stranieri and Zeleznikow 1999).

Bench–Capon discusses the potential for providing knowledge based support for the task of formulating policy, and determining what legislation is required to implement the policy. The author also discuss of previous work in this area, certain major obstacles are identified, chief among these is the need to match what the KBS can do with the way in which policy makers conceptualize and perform their task (Bench–Capon 1994).

Groendijk (1992) claims that in most contemporary Legal Knowledge Based Systems, conclusions are reached by applying rules to case descriptions. A case description usually consists of a limited set of facts. In human judicial problem solving, the application of legal rules is not based on the facts directly, but on a structured interpretation of these raw data. Author propose, a neural method to create structured data interpretations is advocated and a method to integrate these networks with a rule based system is presented (Groendijk 1992).

Hage (1992) Argue the thesis that the rules of law are best viewed as rules for dialogues rather than as rules constituting institutional facts. Starting from this view, a dialogical model of legal reasoning is developed. The adoption by AI researchers specializing in law of new AI techniques, such as case based reasoning, neural networks, fuzzy logic, deontic logics and non–monotonic logics may move closer to achieving an automation of legal reasoning (Hage et al. 1992).

Michael Aikenhead claims that Computers have long been utilized in the legal environment. The main use of computers however, has merely been to automate office tasks. More exciting is the prospect of using artificial intelligence (AI) technology to create computers that can emulate the substantive legal jobs performed by lawyers to create computers that can autonomously reason with the law to determine legal solutions. Such attempts have not been successful. Modeling the law and emulating the processes of legal reasoning have proved to be more complex and subtle than originally envisaged (Aikenhead 1995).

16.4 Background

In this section the author discuss the conceptual background of Indian legal systems and the process adopted are discussed. The Indian legal systems and western legal systems have certain difference. Hence the author discusses the finer details of transfer of property law and processes Indian legal system.

Property law is the area of law that governs the various forms of ownership and tenancy in real property (land as distinct from personal or movable possessions) and in personal property, within the common law legal system. In the civil law system, there is a division between movable and immovable property. Movable property roughly corresponds to personal property, while immovable property corresponds to real estate or real property, and the associated rights and obligations thereon. The concept, idea or philosophy of property underlies all property law. In some jurisdictions, historically all property was owned by the monarch and it devolved through feudal land tenure or other feudal systems of loyalty and fealty. Though the Napoleonic code was among the first government acts of modern times to introduce the notion of absolute ownership into statute, protection of personal property rights was present in medieval Islamic law and jurisprudence, and in more feudalist forms in the common law courts of medieval and early modern England.[6]

[6]Available at http://en.wikipedia.org/wiki/Property-law

16.4.1 Legal Aspects and Related Terminologies

A property, movable or immovable, is transferred from one person to another under various different situations and circumstances and for different values. By its very existence, society mandates interaction, exchange or transfer. The transfer may be a gift, an inheritance or an asset acquired by paying full value. When a movable property is transferred *inter–vivos* (between two living persons), Sales of Goods Act, 1930 comes into play (Gour 1987). When an immovable property is transferred from dead person to living person(s), the Transfer of Property Act, 1882 (Gour 1987) comes into play. In case, the property is transferred from a dead person to a living person(s), the law applied will be the law of succession. Should a person die without leaving a will (*intestate*), the law of intestate succession is applicable and in cases where a person dies leaving a will, the law of testamentary succession is applicable. In India, the personal laws governed the transfer of property assisted by orders of courts under civil procedure code before the transfer of property act, 1882 came into existence. Transfer of movable goods was regulated to an extent by the Indian contract act, 1872. For transfer of immovable property, the Anglo–Indian courts often turned to principles of justice, equity and good conscience as it prevailed in England at the time. This rarely did any good due to the vast differences in customs and society of the two countries. The rapidly growing commerce and infrastructure in the late nineteenth century lead to more conflicts even in business. Thus, an immediate need was felt for a clear and pragmatic law regarding property and transfers suited to India and its peculiar problems as well as to take care of the potential economic problems. The task of drafting such legislation fell upon the First Law Commission and was later referred to the Second Law Commission (Gour 1987).

The term "property" can be defined as "as any entity which can be owned". Thus, right of ownership may be exercised by a person against a property. A person is any "entity" which has rights and duties under law. A "person" may be a natural person (a human being) or an artificial person (such as a company, a corporation, etc.). Ownership is a right by which the property belongs to the owner to the exclusion of all others. In fact, it is a collection of rights which the owner has against the property owned by him. Right of possession and enjoyment, right of alienation, right of destruction, etc. are some of the rights which an owner can exercise against his property, subject to the laws of the land and rights of others. "Title" is the evidence of ownership, and a title deed is a document that shows how and when a person became the owner of a property.

Transfer of property means transfer of some or all of the rights of owner in respect of a property to some other person. If the transfer is of all the rights of the owner, the transfer is a complete transfer of property else it is a partial transfer of property. "*Sale*", "*exchange*" and "*gift*" are complete transfers of property, while "*lease*" and "*mortgage*" are examples of partial transfers of property. Once the owner transfers his property by way of a complete transfer, he ceases to be the owner and the *transferee* becomes the owner.

The "*transferor*" loses his right of transfer and the "transferee" gets the right of transfer. In case of partial transfer of property, the transferor continues to be the owner and hence, retains the right to transfer the property, subject to the rights of the transferee. For example, if the landlord sells the property leased by him to a tenant, the purchaser will purchase the property subject to that lease. So also in case of mortgage the purchaser will purchase the property subject to the mortgage. In other words, the transferee always gets the same rights and obligations of the transferor in respect of the property transferred to him. Such obligations subject to which the property is transferable are called the "*encumbrance*" over the property. A transferee has to see that the transferor has the authority to transfer the property, and that there are no encumbrances attached to the property.

Under sec. 17 of the Indian Registration Act, a deed witnessing transfer of an immovable property must be compulsorily registered; otherwise it cannot be admitted in evidence. Therefore, if the transferor has received a property under an unregistered transfer deed, it will be impossible to prove that he had title to the property. Therefore, the transferee will not be able to prove that he has received a good title from the transferor whose title itself cannot be proved. Hence, registration of the deed under which the transferor has received the property is one of the most important aspects to be verified (Gour 1987).

Sale, exchange, gift, lease, mortgage are transfers "*inter vivos*", i.e., transfers by one or more living persons to one or more other living persons. If the owner of a property does not transfer his property to any other person during his life time, the property devolves upon his successors after his death, by way of succession. Succession may be "*testamentary succession*" or "*intestate succession*". If the deceased owner of the property leaves behind him a valid will and expresses his desire to give that property some person after his death, the property devolves upon that other person, called the "*legatee*", by way of testamentary succession. If the deceased does not leave behind him a valid will the property devolves upon his heirs by way of intestate succession. So also even if the deceased has left behind him a valid will, but has not provided for devolution of a particular property in that will, the property not covered by the will devolve upon his legal heirs. This is called "partial intestacy". In case of a will a "probate" is to be obtained to prove the genuineness of the will. Once a probate is granted by a competent court, it is conclusive proof of the fact that the will is genuine. Therefore, one can purchase the property from the legatee to whom it is gifted by the deceased. In case of intestate succession, one of the heirs may obtain "letters of administration" from a competent court. He is called the "*administrator*" of the estate of the deceased and is competent to transfer the properties of the deceased. However, now obtaining probate or letter of administration is not compulsory. In lieu of them one may obtain a succession certificate from a competent court.

Once it is proved that the transferee has the title to the property, it is also necessary to verify whether the person from whom he has obtained the property had a clear and marketable title to the property. If he did not have one, then the transferor cannot have one, as already seen above. In such a case the true owner may file a suit for setting aside the transfer and the transferee will be deprived of the property. Though he may file a suit for recovery of the money he has paid to the transferor, it will be an unnecessary trouble which may be avoided by taking a little care. It is to be noted here that though the original owner can file a suit for setting aside the transfer, he can do so within 12 years from the date of transfer of his property by a third party. Therefore, if the transferor has purchased the property more than 13 years ago, suit against him will be time barred, and no special precaution is necessary. Otherwise, the suit will be well within limitation prescribed by the limitation act, and the flow of title of the property will have to be traced for the last 13 years by looking into the Record of Rights maintained by the *revenue authorities*.

The transferee in case of a transfer intervivos, and a legatee or legal heir in case of succession is having title to the property. Now once the title to the property is established, it is necessary to examine whether the property is free of encumbrances. For that purpose one has to obtain a "*Nil Encumbrance Certificate*" from the sub–registrars office within whose jurisdiction the property or any part of it is situated. If there is encumbrance on the property, such a certificate will not be issued.

Further, if the transferor has not paid the taxes in respect of the property to the respective public authorities, the government will have a charge over the property, and the money may be recovered by forfeiture or by attachment and sale of the property even in the hands of the transferee. Therefore, it is imperative to verify that the transferor does not have any tax dues, by looking into the up–to–date tax paid receipts. This is, in short, the procedure for verifying the title to the property to be purchased, and of verifying that it is free from encumbrances.

16.4.2 Issues Involved in Tracing the Title of Immovable Property

Indian Property–Law which is substantially codified is contained in different enactments dating from about the year 1882 till this date. These enactments deal with and provide for making of contract and its validly; void and voidable agreements; performance, breach, frustration and enforcement of contract; contracts that are specifically enforceable and contracts for the breach of which damages only is the remedy; rectification, recession and cancellation of contracts; declaratory reliefs and the reliefs of *perpetual and mandatory injunctions* in respect of the rights in and or pertaining to any property (Gour 1987).

Transfer and conveyance in terms of *sale, lease, sub–lease, mortgage, gift and exchange* etc. of movable and immovable properties; Essential features and contents of all such transactions including the requisite covenants, terms and conditions to be incorporated in the documentation pertaining to such transfers and conveyance etc; Testate and intestate succession applicable to the various *religious denominations*; Law of making and revoking of wills and codicils, capacity of individuals to make wills; rules of interpretation of the testamentary documents; grant of letters of representation such as probate, letters of administration and succession certificate etc. pertaining to the property and credits of the deceased and the administration of the estate pursuant thereto.

Total/partial partition of the properties *intellectual property law* i.e. the law dealing with copyrights, patents, designs, trademarks, passing of and the law pertaining to the information technology; Stamp duties payable in respect of the diverse property transactions; modality for computation and quantification of such duties; adjudication, payment and recovery of stamp duty; Compulsory and optional registration of documents in respect of the property transactions; consequences arising from non–registration of the transactions with the registering authorities.

Procedural and adjective laws providing remedies for the enforcement of legal rights, establishment of different forums and their jurisdiction, provision for the payment of court fees, etc. and the rules of conducting trials, leading evidence thereat and the execution of *decrees, orders and awards* passed by the various courts, tribunals arbitrators and the other duly empowered authorities.

16.4.3 Process to Trace Title of Property

Tracing the flow of title is the most important part of the investigation of title. Thorough knowledge of the various aspects of law especially civil law is a must for this. Law relating to minors and the legally disabled, law of succession, both inter vivos and intestate; Different land tenures prevalent in the locality; Special Statutes like the *Karnataka State Land Reforms Act (Karnataka is one state in Indian Union),*[7] *The Schedule Tribes Act*, The Land Assignment Act the modes of obtaining title through decrees of court etc are to be thoroughly known to the Investigator in order to make a proper tracing of title. Some of the issues related to tracing of title of property, which should be known and understood are explained in the subsequent paragraphs (Gour 1987).

Transactions in immovable property are carried out by parties in properties containing the elements: *original owner, intermediary owners, promoter, developer, contractor, investor, marketing agency, prospective buyer, lending institutions, association of owners. The nature of properties: land, houses, flats/apartments, infrastructure, special amenities and facilities. The nature of rights: ownership, possession, leasehold rights, rights under a mortgage, easement, license, lien.*

Properties attract the following taxation: *service tax (on services in contracts), VAT* (on transfer of goods in contracts), income tax on income and capital gains, tax exemptions and deductions under special schemes for housing, economic zones etc.[8]

The various modes by means of which any person can acquire any type of right, title and interest in an immovable property: *direct purchase/transfer, gift/settlement,*

[7] Available at http://dpal.kar.nic.in/10\%20of\%201962\%20\%28E\%29.pdf

[8] All India Taxes (A Ready Referencer) CA Alok Kr Agarwal & CA Shailendra Mishra.

will/probate/succession certificate, intestate succession and inheritance, partition, release, family settlement, reunion, family arrangement, partition among co–owners, property as a capital contribution in a firm, distribution of assets in a firm on reconstitution and on the dissolution of a firm, private trust, amalgamation, merger, de–merger and liquidation of companies, rights and interests held through shares in companies, cooperative society etc, adverse possession, awards in arbitration proceedings, orders and decrees of courts of law and other statutory authorities including *lok adalats*. By operation of various provisions of *personal laws relating to Hindus, Mohammedans, Christians, Sikhs, Parsis, Jews etc.. By operation of law under laws relating to other persons and legal entities including cooperative societies, other societies including mutual benefit societies and other Association of Persons, BDA sites(Block Development Authority), Land acquisition, Urban Land (Ceiling and Regulation) Act, 1976 (now repealed). By grants given or orders passed by Governments and statutory authorities. By a Conciliation Order passed under section 19(v) (i) and (ii) read with Section 21 of the Legal Services Authority Act, 1977. Such an order can be passed by a High Court Judge and other competent authorities by which rights and interests between contending parties can be settled and established (Gour 1987).*

16.5 Research Methodology Adopted

Identifying the knowledge used in decision making or problem solving is the most crucial component of an expert system design. In our case, the task of acquiring the knowledge used in decision making in the process of evaluation of proposal of sub–domain say Transfer of property law involves extensive survey of literature available and close interaction in the form of interviews and questionnaires, with eminent practicing advocates and academicians in teaching law. The phases that are involved in the design of the expert system are depicted Fig. 16.1 (Desai and Kulkarni 2000).

The procedure used for the development of the prototype was followed for the development of the comprehensive development of rule based expert system. Literature survey of different software available for the development of the expert system and continued interaction and discussions with the advocates and professors in law schools helped in framing the rules in computer readable format.

16.5.1 Literature Survey of Different Software Available for the Development of the Expert System

The literature survey of the software for implementation was carried out. In the development of the prototype the author had used the software's such as expert

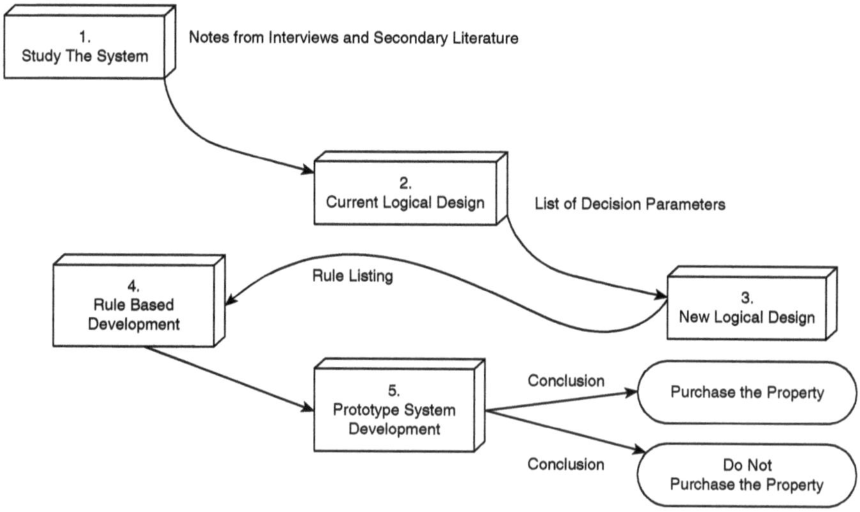

Fig. 16.1 System development cycle (Desai and Kulkarni 2000)

system builder 3.0 and CLIPS. These are basically an expert system shells which are used in the development of the expert systems. The author has evaluated other software which is open source such as CLIPS.[9]

16.5.2 C Language Integrated Production System (CLIPS)

A CLIPS is an expert system tool developed by the Software Technology Branch (STB) at the NASA/Lyndon B. Johnson Space Centre. It was released in 1986 for the first time and has undergone continual refinement and improvement ever since. The detailed information of CLIPS is available at the official CLIPS web page.

CLIPS is a tool that is designed to make the development of software to model human expertise easier. Apart from being used as a stand–alone tool, CLIPS can also be called from a procedural language, or CLIPS can call procedural code itself. It has been designed for integration with other languages such as C, C++, and Ada. A CLIP represents (human) knowledge in three ways: (i) rules for experience–based, heuristic knowledge, (ii) deffunctions and generic functions for procedural knowledge, (iii) OO programming, also for procedural knowledge. The CLIPS language looks a lot like LISP. Commands are written between "(" and ")" characters and it uses similar features like atoms, numbers, strings and lists. Adding 7 and 5 would be done by typing: "(+ 7 5)" at the command line. CLIPS will then

[9] Available at http://clipsrules.sourceforge.net/WhatIsCLIPS.html

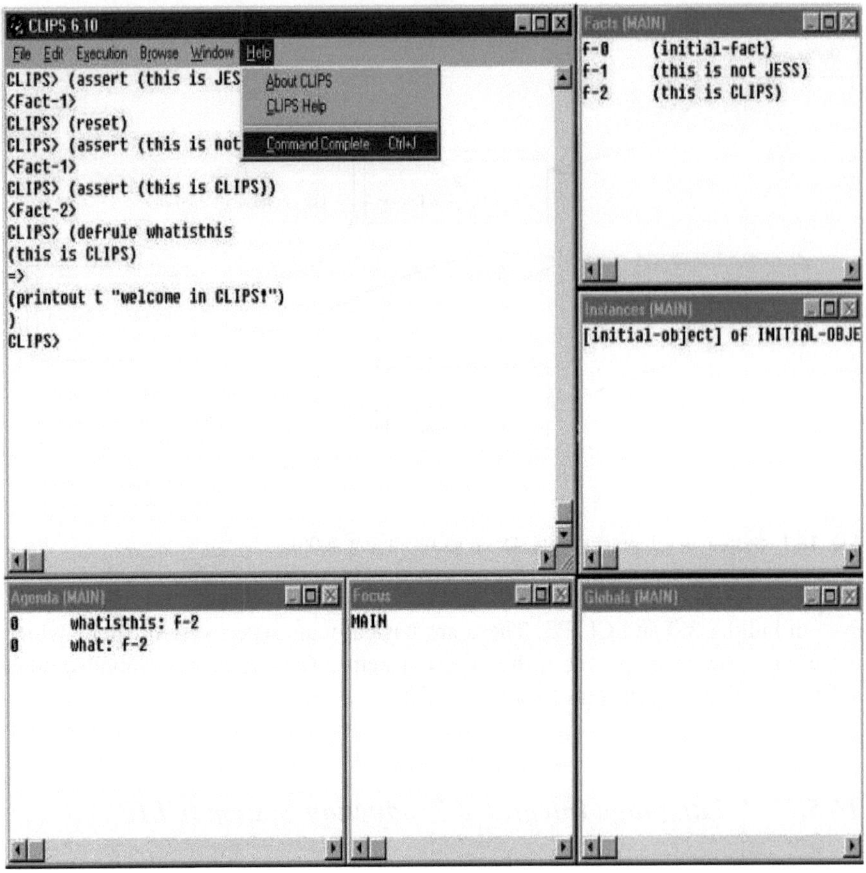

Fig. 16.2 Snapshot of CLIPS WINDOW

respond with 12. Section 16.5.3 illustrates a simple example is as shown in Fig. 16.2 with snapshot of CLIPS Window and the code. The CLIPS shell provides the basic elements of an expert system: a fact–list, and instance–list: this is global memory for data, a knowledge–base: which contains all the rules, an inference engine: for controlling the execution of rules.

Facts are data that usually designate relations or information like: (is–animal duck) or (animals duck horse cow chicken) or (this is a test). Rules can be applied on these facts in the form of IF–THEN rules. These rules are special because they "fire" only once. Variables and wildcards can be used in the rules, functions can be defined to manage the rules. The subsequent section shows how these facts and rules can be implemented. The researcher also had other choices of ES shells, such as JESS, which is based on CLIPS. JESS was originally a clone of essential core of CLIPS, but has begun to acquire a Java influenced flavour of its own.

16.5.3 An Example Application

A SAMPLE Code:

```
CLIPS > (assert (light green)) ;this is how to create a
fact
CLIPS > (defrule go ; this is how to create a rule
(light green) ; if light is green
→ ; then
(printout t 'go' crlf)) ; print 'go'
CLIPS > (defrule stop
(light red)
→
(printout t 'stop' crlf))
CLIPS > (defrule red
(light red)
→
(retract *) ; retract all facts
(assert (light green))) ; and assert the (light green) fact
CLIPS> (defrule green
(light green)
→
(retract *)
(assert (light red)))
(run)
CLIPS > stop
Go
Stop
Go
Stop
```

The author has used a VISIRULE, a graphical tool which developed by Logic Programming Associates ltd (Langley and Spenser 2007). The tool helps to draw a decision chart and execute in situ. The main constructs are nodes which act as questions. Visirule generates a code in form flex rules that can be executed and viewed and can be exported to other applications.

16.5.4 Continued Interaction and Discussions with the Advocates and Professors in Law Schools

As a part of research work the author did an extensive work in interacting with proponents of the law. The practicing advocates in High Court and Supreme Court of India were contacted and a series of discussion and the interviews were held with them. The discussions mainly centered transfer of property and the intricacies involved in them. The practicing advocates gave their interpretation of the transfer of property act and gave the practical side and theoretical side. They also explained the how the rules are formed.

The broad outlines of the rules which need to be framed were noted. The discussions and the interviews with the academicians who are teaching law and transfer of property act were held. The views and interpretation of transfer of property act from the point of view of academician was also understood. These interviews were of great help in framing of the rules.

16.5.5 Conceptualizing the Rules in Required Format

After interaction and discussion broad outlines of the rules of the transfer of property act of Indian legal domain were understood. The next step was to convert the rules in computer readable format or as the software chosen for the implementation of rules. The rules were framed as per statues of books of law and in the language which is understandable for a common man in to a rule based system.

16.6 Rule Based System

A rule–based system is a system that uses "rules" derive "conclusions" from "premises." A rule has the form

$$\frac{\text{IF condition}}{\text{THEN action}}$$

A rule–based system is a model that can be used to solve many AI problems. As with any AI technique, rule–based systems have limitations and strengths. This model is good for problems where the knowledge can be represented by a small number of if–then rules. If the number of rules is too large, it can slow down the performance of the system. To create a rule–based system for a given problem, we must have (or create) the following: A set of facts to represent the initial working memory. This should be anything relevant to the beginning state of the system, a set of rules. This should encompass any and all actions that should be taken within the scope of a problem, but nothing irrelevant. The number of rules in the system can affect its performance, so you don't want any that aren't needed. A condition that determines that a solution has been found or that none exists. This is necessary to terminate some rule–based systems that find themselves in infinite loops otherwise.[10]

A rule–based system works by applying the rules that are applicable to the current state of the system. At the beginning, the "working memory" consists of the description of the initial state of the system. It then finds all the rules that are applicable to this state. If there is only one rule applicable, then there are no conflicts. If there is more than one, the rules that are applicable are called the

[10]Available at http://ai-depot.com/Tutorial/RuleBased.html

"Conflict Set". Which rule in the conflict set will be selected to apply (or which rule fires?) is dependent on the "Conflict Resolution Strategy." When a rule fires, the actions specified by the then–part of the rule are carried out. This causes a change in the state of the problem – reflected as changes in the working memory. Some common strategies for conflict resolution are: first applicable: If the rules are in a specified order, firing the first applicable one allows control over the order in which rules fire. This is the simplest strategy and has a potential for a large problem: that of an infinite loop on the same rule. If the working memory remains the same, as does the rule–base, then the conditions of the first rule have not changed and it will fire again and again. To solve this, it is a common practice to suspend a fired rule and prevent it from re–firing until the data in working memory, that satisfied the rule's conditions, has changed. Random: though it doesn't provide the predictability or control of the first–applicable strategy, it does have its advantages. For one thing, its unpredictability is an advantage in some circumstances (such as games for example). A random strategy simply chooses a single random rule to fire from the conflict set. Another possibility for a random strategy is a fuzzy rule–based system in which each of the rules has a probability such that some rules are more likely to fire than others. Most Specific: this strategy is based on the number of conditions of the rules. From the conflict set, the rule with the most conditions is chosen. This is based on the assumption that if it has the most conditions then it has the most relevance to the existing data. Least Recently Used: each of the rules is accompanied by a time or step stamp, which marks the last time it was used. This maximizes the number of individual rules that are fired at least once. If all rules are needed for the solution of a given problem, this is a perfect strategy. "Best" rule: for this to work, each rule is given a "weight," which specifies how much it should be considered over the alternatives. The rule with the most preferable outcomes is chosen based on this weight. An expert system is a rule–based system that captures the knowledge of human experts in their field and uses it to solve difficult problems.[11]

16.6.1 Architecture of a Rule–Based System

A typical rule–based system contains: an inference engine, pattern–matcher: this is used to determine which rules fire (construct the conflict set), Agenda: the rules in the conflict set can be placed in some order this is called the agenda. Execution Engine: the process that actually applies the rules. A rule base: also called the "knowledge base", a working memory: also called the fact base. An expert system contains: inference engine, knowledge base, working memory, rule–base editor: a system that lets the developer add/delete/modify rules, an explanation generator, and a user interface: a GUI or a natural language interface for the user. An expert–system shell has all the above components, except the problem–specific knowledge base. A developer uses the shell to build the expert system. The typical expert system can be represented in diagrammatical form (Fig. 16.3):

[11] Available at http://ai-depot.com/Tutorial/RuleBased.html

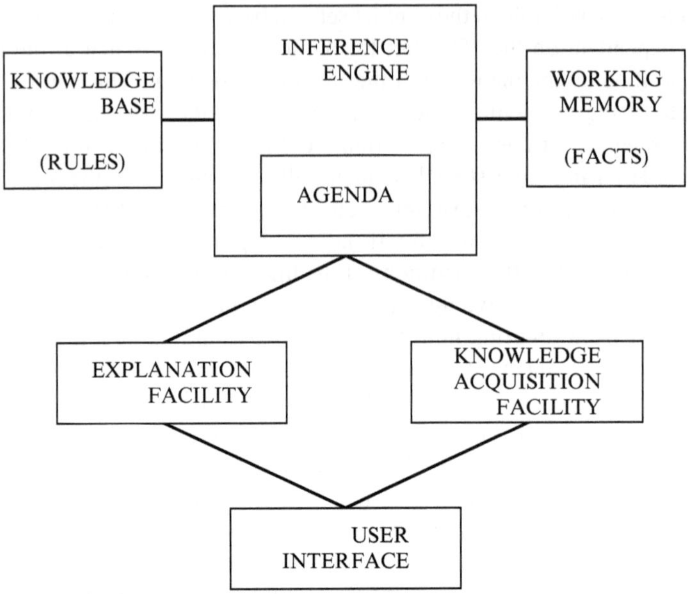

Fig. 16.3 System development cycle

16.6.2 Developing Rule–Based Systems

In the development of rule based systems the points which need to considered are Knowledge Engineering: The first step in the development. Collect the knowledge from which the rules will be derived. Prepare questionnaires for the human experts. Derive rules based on the answers. Knowledge can be obtained from books, the Internet, etc. Knowledge Engineers do this. The second step is structuring the data: developing the expert system is like any other major software task. Selecting the right data structures is important. The third step is writing the rules. Fourth step is interface building: expert systems may have to get their data from databases, or read them off from instruments interfaces connect them to sources of data. Lastly testing: tests to check intermediate results; tests to check the whole system. Testing should be automated.

16.6.3 Approach Adopted in Research Work

In the development of rules based system we used the intelligent flowcharting approach. VisiRule is a tool for creating decision support software purely by drawing flowcharts. The end result is Flex or Prolog code which is automatically generated, compiled and ready to run, but which can also be copied and used in a separate program. Not only can VisiRule be used by people with minimal programming skills. VisiRule also enhances productivity by considerably reducing the time it takes to produce a decision support system. VisiRule is an intelligent

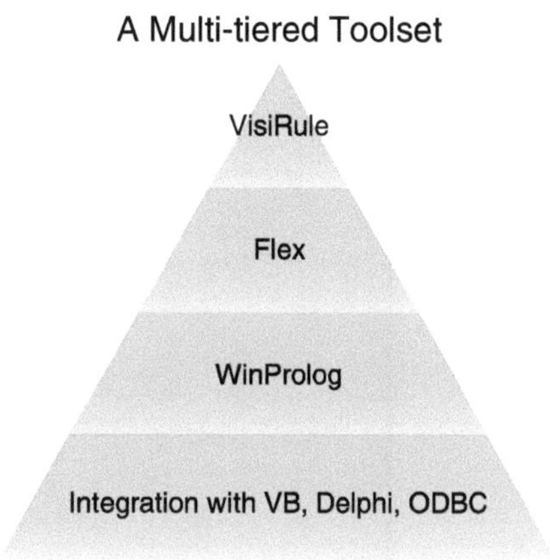

Fig. 16.4 VisiRule architecture

flowcharting tool in two senses. Firstly, it is used to create knowledge–based systems and, secondly, it intelligently guides the construction process by constraining what you can and can't do on the basis of the semantic content of the emerging program. VisiRule provides the automatic construction of menu dialogues from questions. These are populated by items inferred from expression boxes throughout the flowchart tree which have a path to the question. VisiRule also offers: a wide variety of question types including single and multiple choice, numeric and integer entry, text and set entry. A powerful expression handling logic statement boxes for computable answers which are not decided by questioning the user. Code boxes for procedural code and external functions, modularity allowing multiple charts to define one executable program. In particular we can build decision trees, classifiers and diagnostic systems of arbitrary complexity using these simple tools (Langley and Spenser 2007) (Fig. 16.4).

16.6.4 Simple Chart in Visirule

The simplest VisiRule charts consist of a start box, one or more question boxes, some expression boxes and some end boxes which are the conclusions drawn from the answers to the questions (Fig. 16.5).

16.7 Development of Prototype and Study Carried Out with Visirule

The author of this study carried out the development of the prototype in Clips (CLIPS explained in previous section). The development of the prototype was done and proper verification and validation by the Legal experts was carried out. The extensive developmental study of the modules conceived was studied and VisiRule software was selected for the development purpose. For the purpose of study an

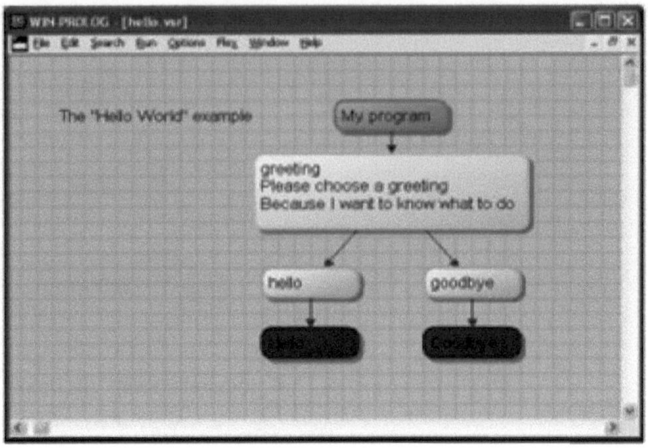

Fig. 16.5 Simple chart in VisiRule

example flowchart of rules which can be used in the development of one of the module is mentioned in the subsequent part. As space is constraint the author have considered including only one of module.

Following are the some examples of rules which are used in the development of the prototype using the flowchart given subsequently (Fig. 16.6)

```
RULE 1:
if (the subject is acquisition of property)
then
property is acquired by transfer
else
property is acquired by succession
```

```
RULE 2:
if (the property is acquired by transfer)
and if (transfer deed is available)
then
the transfer deed is registered
else
the transfer deed is unregistered
```

16.7.1 The Framing of Rules Using the Legal Knowledge and Incorporation in Visirule

The rules in the Visirule are in for nodes which are represented as nodes. The various nodes type which are used in visirule are question nodes, expression nodes, statement boxes, code boxes, start and end nodes. A sample application using the rules is framed and is illustrated below (Fig. 16.7).

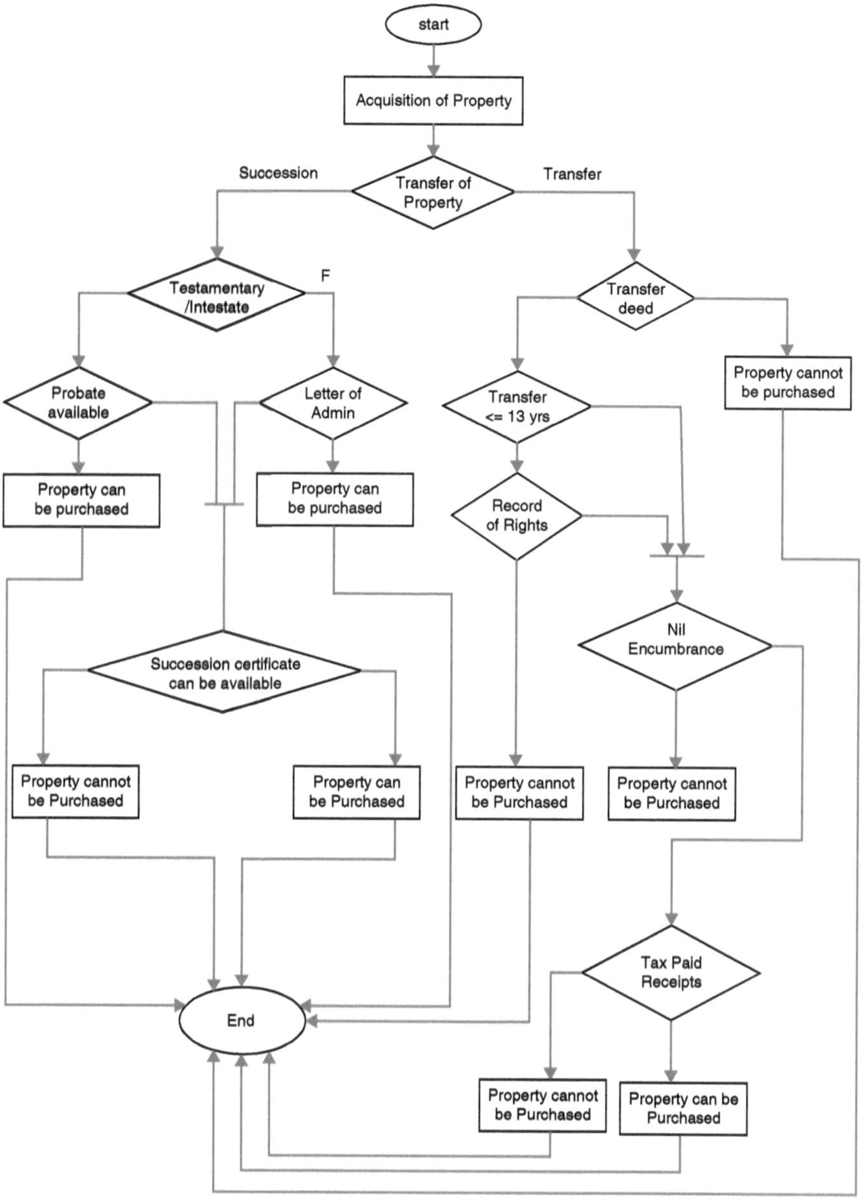

Fig. 16.6 Flowchart of sample module

16.7.2 A Sample Application Developed in Visirule

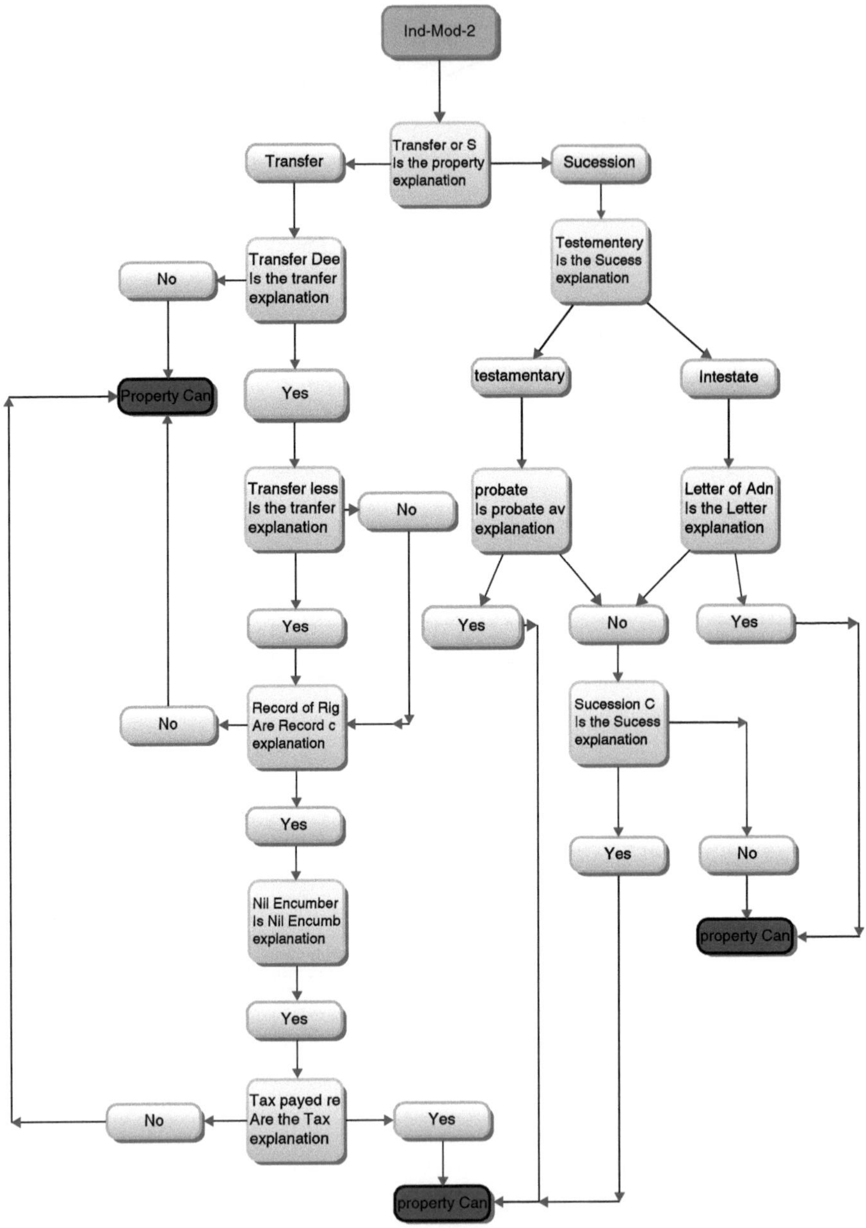

Fig. 16.7 Sample module – 1 developed in Visirule

16.7.3 Visirule Implementation of the Module–2

Another module of the Transfer of Property Act is also developed and is used for the reference only (Fig. 16.8).

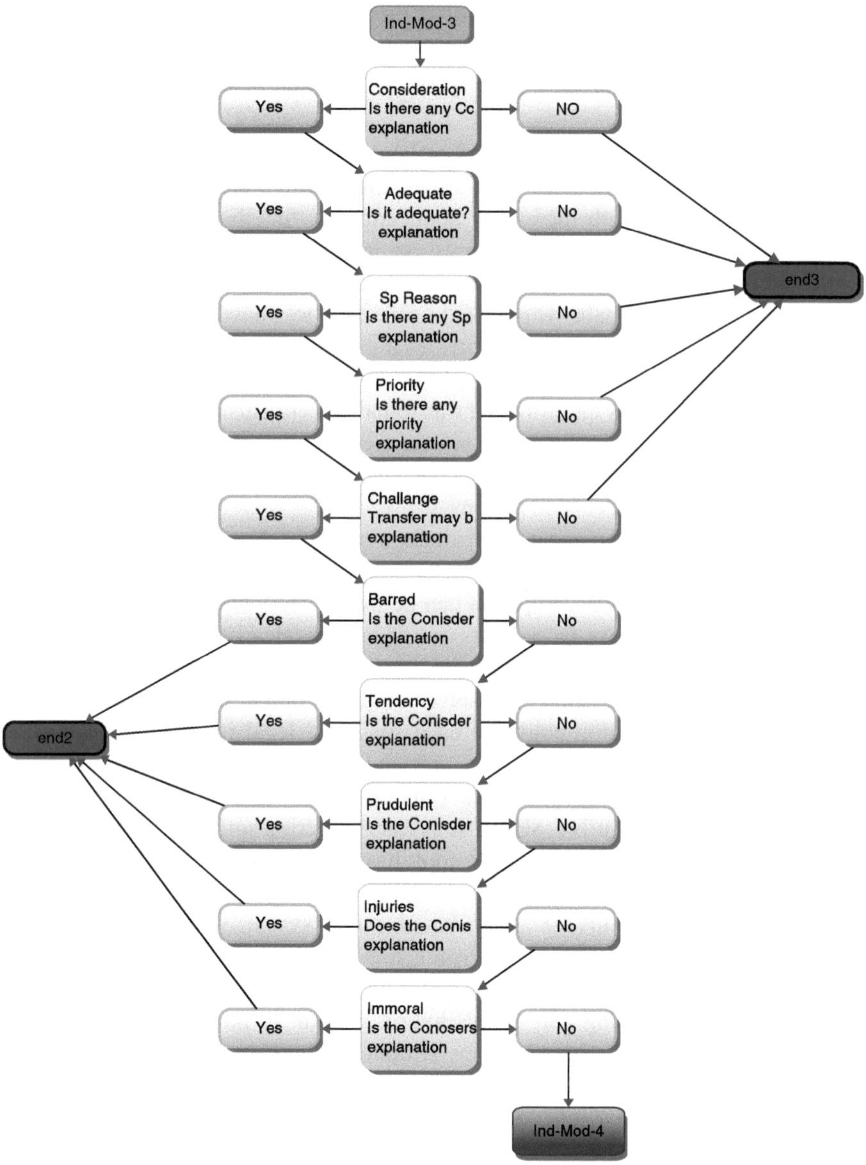

Fig. 16.8 Sample module – 2 developed in Visirule

16.8 Conclusion

In the introduction, a view was expressed with a hope that the work in this thesis could be a step towards a general purpose development of composite knowledge–based system for Indian legal domain with specific reference to transfer of property act. The author will also suggest some future research directions.

The aim of this research has been to develop knowledge–based system based upon a realistic approach to the Indian legal systems with specific reference to transfer of property act.

To conclude, the use of computers in law has moved from simple automated search and office management programs to informative programs and finally to diagnostic programs with increasing application of "intelligent" algorithms over time. The research work has developed an integrated knowledge–based system which incorporates the rule–based and case–based reasoning for transfer of property act of Indian legal domain with specific reference to transfer of property act by using VisiRule and Java. VisiRule provides a graphical decision charting logic for representing rules, which makes the application development easy. The performance of the system is tested by case study. It was found that conclusions of domain experts and conclusion arrived by the expert system were similar. Hence, this work can be of great help to both the non–law–literates and also for experts in the field of law for productive and fast decision making.

Programs display increasing sophistication not only due to improved computer speed and memory but also due to software development. The question facing researchers is not whether computers can be used effectively in legal research but how to best use them. As far as tasks go, computers clearly are already useful in teaching and research as well as in legal practice. As far as software technologies go, neural networks may show themselves to be useful, but they have not yet. The computer language Prolog could be used for some legal inferencing (deductive inferencing for example) but has an unfriendly interface. Further, WIN–Prolog from Logic Programming Associates London has many tools such VISIRULE, CHIMERA, INTELLIGENT SERVER is very effective software in development of expert systems. The VISIRULE tool has been used to develop the rule–based expert systems. The rule–based expert systems are a proven technology. To combine the flexibility of a rule based expert system with the forward and backward chaining capabilities of Prolog may be the best future – and indeed the JAVA NET BEANS system does allow that, which has been used to develop the Case–based reasoning part in this hybrid system. In all events, the future of automated hybrid legal expert systems is both challenging and bright. Hopefully these programs illustrate some of the problems and possibilities of this fascinating field.

References

Aikenhead, Michael. 1995. Legal knowledge based systems: Some observations on the future. First Published Web Journal of Current Legal Issues in association with Blackstone Press Ltd [1995] 2 Web JCLI.

Bench–Capon, Trevor. 1994. Support for policy makers: Prospects for knowledge based systems. In *Legal knowledge based systems: Information technology and law*. ISBN:90 5458 031.

Bilgi, Nitin, and R.V. Kulkarni. 2008a. Knowledge based system prototype application for transfer of property law in indian judicial system. *International Journal of Intelligent Information Processing*, 137–144. ISSN NO:0973–3892.

Bilgi, Nitin, and R.V. Kulkarni. 2008b. A investigative survey of application of knowledge based system In legal domain. *International Journal of Information Technology and Knowledge Management*, 517–525. ISSN NO:0973–4414.

Bilgi, Nitin, R.V. Kulkarni, and R.R. Kulkarni. 2008. E–Governance applications in legal knowledge–based systems in India: A perspective. In *National conference on E–Governance and its application*, Dayanand Sagar College Bangalore, 27 and 28 Nov 2008.

Bilgi, Nitin, R.V. Kulkarni, and Clive Spenser. 2010. An expert system using a decision logic charting approach for Indian legal domain with specific reference to transfer of property act. *Computer Science Journals (CSC Journals) International Journal of Artificial Intelligence and Expert systems(IJAE)*, 32–39. ISSN NO(Online):2180–124X.

Desai, B.L., and R.V. Kulkarni. 2000. Rule based expert system for SST term–loan evaluation for banks and financial institutions. *Vivek AI Quarterly Publication*. 13(4), 3–14

Dewey, John. 1927. Logical method and the law. [1] Ithaca, NY: Cornell, 1927. MacGUIGAN (editor) (1966), 548–552.

Gour, Hari S. 1987. *Transfer of property act*, 9th ed. Law Publishers. Allahabad: India.

Groendijk, Cees. 1992. Neural Schemata in automated judicial problem solving. In *Legal knowledge based systems. JURIX 92: Information Technology and Law*. The Foundation for Legal Knowledge Systems, pp. 147–158, 1994 ISBN:90 5458 031.

Hage, Jaap C., Georges P.J. Span, and Arno R. Lodder. 1992. A dialogical model of legal reasoning. In *Legal knowledge based systems JURIX 92: Information Technology and Law*, 113–122, 994. The Foundation for Legal Knowledge Systems. ISBN:90 5458 031 3.

Langley, Charles and Clive Spenser. VisiRule Tutorial. Copyright (c) 2007 Logic Programming Associates Ltd. All Rights Reserved.

Shortliffe, Edward H., and Richard O. Duda. 1983. Expert systems research. *Science Digest* 220(4594), 261–267

Stranieri, Andrew, and John Zeleznikow. 1999. The evaluation of legal knowledge based systems. In *International conference on artificial intelligence and law proceedings of the 7th international conference on artificial intelligence and law*, Oslo, 18–24, Norway Year of Publication: 1999. ISBN:1–58113–165–8.

Chapter 17
Logic Oriented Methods for Structuring in the Context of Lawmaking

Vytautas Čyras and Friedrich Lachmayer

Abstract A distinction between legislative texts and legal texts lies in open formulations. Legislative texts allow alternative formulations. In contrast, the wording of a valid legal text is fixed. The sole variation of a legal text is its interpretation. At a decision-making point in a legislative process the interpretation is basically open. However, it can be pushed in a certain direction with the help of additional materials, such as parliamentary reports. With the transition from a text culture to a machine culture, the language changes, too. The language of the machine culture is the formal logic that is adequate for the machine, but not in the same way for people in their everyday language usage. In the mainstream of greater rationalisation, logic is increasingly used in legislation, especially allowing only correct interpretations. However, logic is not the only instrument which can be used to shape and improve legislative rationality. In the neighbourhood of logic there are further methods which can find application in structuring legislative texts. We propose to supplement legislative documents ex ante with explicit logic-oriented information which is relevant to ontologies, thesauruses and taxonomies. This information in a form of a mini-thesaurus can already be used in ex ante legislative procedure, and should not be added only in the ex post analysis of legal documentation. The proposed method can be assigned to structural visualisation. In the end, the paper examines variations of structural legal visualisation (SLV) – dynamic SLV and static SLV. Their specific feature is the visualisation of the legal meaning.

Keywords Drafting • Ex ante and ex post analysis • Legal informatics • Selective application of logic • Structural legal visualisation

V. Čyras (✉)
Faculty of Mathematics and Informatics, Vilnius University, Vilnius, Lithuania
e-mail: vytautas.cyras@mif.vu.lt

F. Lachmayer
Faculty of Law, University of Innsbruck, Innsbruck, Austria
e-mail: friedrich.lachmayer@uibk.ac.at

M. Araszkiewicz, K. Płeszka (eds.), *Logic in the Theory and Practice of Lawmaking*, Legisprudence Library 2, DOI 10.1007/978-3-319-19575-9_17

17.1 Introduction

The subject matter of logic and lawmaking as investigated in this article concerns three themes:

Theme 1 – Three layers of a discourse
Theme 2 – Logic for the professional quality of the text
Theme 3 – Importance of the medium-level abstraction in law

Each theme is discussed further in a separate section, after which we discuss selective application of logic. We think that in legal practice it is barely possible to translate an entire legal text in a logical notation, but it is possible to do so with a passage. Next, we discuss how logic expands legal interpretation. Then structural legal visualisation is investigated and conclusions are summed up.

17.2 Theme 1: Three Layers

The first theme comprises three layers:

1. *Political conflict*
2. *Argument*. The actors are political players from the political conflict above
3. *Meta-level: logic and rhetoric*

We further describe each layer below.

17.2.1 Political Conflict

Political actors perform speech acts (usually in a parliamentary discourse) that are directed against each other. Here the goal is to universalise partial opinions, taking over in a draft and, finally, in legislation. The purpose is to achieve a compromise, to answer how to do the agreed, and to make capable of being used and understand by all.

Political discourse is a struggle of opinions. Its model comprises adversarial political actors. Each actor has adversarial goals. The actors compete to achieve a draft (Fig. 17.1).

The adversarial actors can also be called parties. They are not necessarily political parties and they number two in the simplest case.

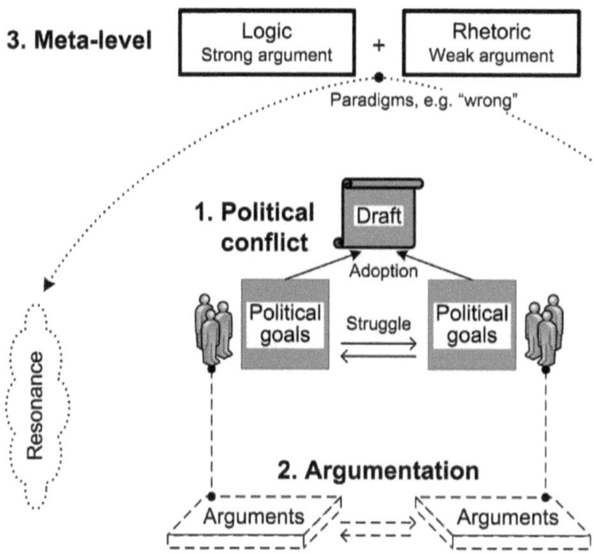

Fig. 17.1 A conceptualisation of three layers of the subject matter. *Dotted arrows* show the use of logic and rhetoric on the meta-level and *dashed arrows* show argumentation

17.2.2 Argumentation

This is supplementary information which comes up with replies to the opinions. Argument's goal is acceptance, which is generally achieved by response. Argumentation strengthens political opinions and produces resonance, a bigger response from the public. Argumentation is shown with dashed arrows in Fig. 17.1.

17.2.3 Logic and Rhetoric

This forms a meta-level to the two paradigms above. Mostly it concerns rhetoric that determines the victory of political opinions. There is also logic as a meta-level of discourse, but it is an alternative and not dominant in the parliamentary debate. A decision in the parliament does not result due to the logical arguments. Yet they are not to be underestimated, at least not point-wise.

The importance of rhetoric is also emphasised by Fritjof Haft (2009), who is also a godfather of legal informatics; this can be illustrated with Fiedler et al. (1988). The notion of *Normfall* (in German) is introduced in Haft (2010); we would also say normal case to stress the opposite of an extreme, boundary case. *Normfalls*, which are assigned to politics, are taken into the law.

The question is about paradigms on the meta-level of logic and rhetoric. There are various paradigms. Some patterns are formed with all-round words such as "always," "from now on," "henceforth," "that is not true," "wrong." The use of the paradigms is shown with dotted arrows in Fig. 17.1. To sum up, logical arguments can be used; however, logic is not central.

17.3 Theme 2: Logic for the Professional Quality of the Text

Logic in legislative texts is usually relevant for the professional quality of the texts. On the other hand, rhetoric is mostly important for the evolution of parliamentary discourse. Logic plays a small role here. Parliamentary discourse is determined by the will (in other words, free will, volition, intentions of the parties) and not rationality. The conflict of the wills is at the forefront. The parliamentary discourse is influenced by opinions and is brought to an end by the struggle of opinions.

Thus rhetoric determines parliamentary events in many parts. Speech acts during discourses in the parliament are political speech acts. A legislative draft is also a political act rather than a legal act. This is shown in Fig. 17.2.

Logic is important for professional legists (drafters of laws). Jurists in government departments are responsible for the professional quality of the texts. Professional drafters use logic to make texts correct and logically consistent. However, this is a serving, ministering function of logic. The drafters are also capable of intensifying the logic which was used in a parliamentary discourse.

Politicians are the dominant actors in a parliamentary discourse. The drafters, however, formulate their wills correctly and hence play a serving role. Thus the function of rhetoric dominates over the function of logic.

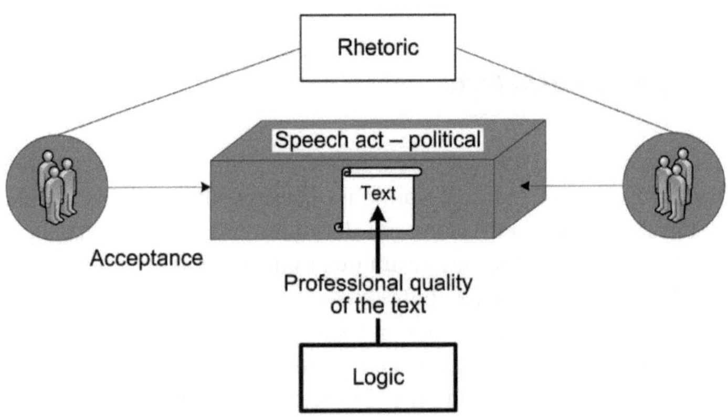

Fig. 17.2 Logic is important for the professional quality of legislative texts

17.4 Theme 3: Middle-Level Abstraction

We first introduce three layers of abstraction in the legislative domain (Fig. 17.3):

- *formal abstraction* (in other words, high-level abstraction);
- *middle-level abstraction* (in other words, interpretative abstraction). We focus on it in this article as we hold that it contains more potential for legal informatics;
- *substantive abstraction* (low-level abstraction).

Each abstraction layer is discussed further separately. We conclude that middle-level abstraction is more important in the context of logic and legislation.

17.4.1 Formal Abstraction

Formal abstraction is not as dynamic as middle-level and substantive abstraction. Once found, it stays that way. As examples, the following works can be mentioned: Ilmar Tammelo's notation for the legal domain (1978), Jerzy Wróblewski's analytical theory of law (1992), Ota Weinberger's legal logic (1989), etc. Different sorts of formal logic, such as propositional logic, predicate logic, deontic logic, etc., are used here. These include, to mention just a few, studies in legal logic by Jaap Hage (2005), modeling legal argument by Henry Prakken and Marek Sergot (1996), Henry Prakken (1997), input/output logics by David Makinson (2000), legal reasoning by Giovanni Sartor (2007), and visualising normative systems by Silvano Colombo Tosatto (2012).

The logic of political will. Attempts to formalise the logic of willing (including political will) can be assigned to this level of abstraction. A formalisation of moral

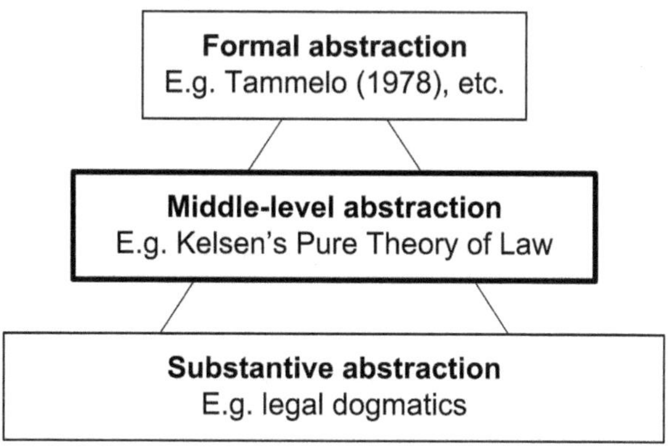

Fig. 17.3 Three levels of abstraction

will was proposed by Ernst Mally (1926).[1] Mally's deontic logic was an attempt to axiomatise strivings. This is connected with intentionality, i.e., intending something. Mally's formalisation constitutes a preliminary phase of legal logic.

The logic of wishes (*utinam*), which is explored by Kazimierz Opałek (1986), is similar. His formalisation with the operator *Utinam(A)* ("may it …") exceeds the logic of willing and leads to a whole theory of directives and norms (Opałek 1986, 54–60). In this work, the analysis of a will *Will(A)* leads to the analysis of a norm *Norm(A)*. This demonstrates a pathway from unconscious (political) willings to conscious norms. The logic of political will is a scientific concept and its formalisation, in preliminary phases, makes sense. We think that such formalisation could contribute further to the development of software that is capable of planning political wills in social domains.

17.4.2 Middle-Level Abstraction

Within middle-level abstraction, Hans Kelsen's *Pure Theory of Law* (1967) is a relevant example. Here we find a mixture of formal structuring and material closeness. This is the area of scientific progress. This level is more elastic than other two. We find this level more creative, at least for legal informatics and our investigation. On the one hand, there is enough potential for abstraction in this layer; on the other, the substantive matters are not forgotten. It should be noted that the content of concrete norms is not examined in this layer.

An example of formalisation on this level of abstraction, though in chemistry, is a chemical formula notation such as H_2O. Practice shows that reasoning with such formulas is very effective, although this notation is primarily concerned with the structure and has little to do with logic. The following are examples of structural notation: relational representations such as causation $B \rightarrow^{causal} A$ and teleology $A \rightarrow^{telos} B$, and a model of legal norms such as $Norm(A \rightarrow B)$. Here a rule of the general form *If [state of affairs] then [legal consequence]* serves as a simple model of norms. Such representation of norms is used in computer science and legal expert systems; see, e.g., Jones et al. (1993) and Oberle et al. (2012) etc.

Creativity with ontologies in the legislative domain can also be assigned to this layer. For example, the formalisation of the norm graph concept is the starting phase in the approach of Oberle et al. (2012) to engineering compliant software. Here a norm graph consists of legal concepts (nodes) and links between them. Creativity is required to build the norm graph. Norm graph formalisation is conducted by a legal expert and starts from extracting the required legal vocabulary. The vocabulary

[1] http://plato.stanford.edu/entries/mally-deontic/,http://plato.stanford.edu/entries/mally/. Accessed 20 April 2014.

forms the basis of a legal lexicon which complements extracted terms by additional information. In turn, the lexicon serves as a basis for creating the computational model which consists of classes and relations.

In the development above we see a transformation of a vocabulary (or ontology) into a computational model. We hold that there is a difference between a computational model (a database schema) and an ontology. A computational model follows the *closed world assumption*. This means that what is not currently known to be true, is assumed false. In other words, what is not in the model is not in the world. An ontology follows the *open world assumption*, which means that what is not currently known to be true is simply unknown.[2]

The main components of ontologies (shared vocabularies) are terms that are connected with links such as synonymy, near synonymy, antonymy, hyponymy,[3] hypernymy etc. (Peters et al. 2007); see also a definition of an ontology in computer science.[4] In contrast, the main components of computational models are entities (things) and the relationships that can exist among them.

17.4.3 Substantive Abstraction

Substantive disciplines, such as legal theory and legal dogmatics (*Rechtsdogmatik*, no exact translation in the terminology of common law; legal science) describe the object in principle with words. However, these disciplines are not really of interest here, because abstraction is too concrete and it is difficult to raise it to an upper layer. The content of concrete norms is examined in this layer and hence contrasts with the two upper layers.

It is difficult to invent on the top, i.e., on the formal abstraction layer. For the same reason, we also do not focus on substantive abstraction. For instance, once an article in a law consists of a complete list of variations one can barely add more. However, we hold that creativity can be demonstrated on the medium abstraction layer. Formalising the interpretations of facts can be assigned to the medium abstraction. An example is ontologies; see above. We aim at structuring the legislative domain; namely, the big picture of the structure. In this layer, new formal notations could still be introduced, and they are not too far away from the substantive contents. This is in contrast to certain people who work on a low level and can interpret legal texts, but find it difficult to grasp the whole structure correctly.

---

[2]http://en.wikipedia.org/wiki/Open-world-assumption. Accessed 20 April 2014.

[3]A hyponym is a word or phrase whose semantic field is included within that of another word, its hypernym. For example, there is the hyponymic relationship between red and colour. http://en.wikipedia.org/wiki/Hyponymy-and-hypernymy. Accessed 20 April 2014.

[4]http://en.wikipedia.org/wiki/Ontology(informationscience). Accessed 20 April 2014.

17.5 Only Selective Application of Logic

A legal act comprises a *legal text*, which is Element 1 in our consideration (Fig. 17.4). Legal texts are usually long and composed of structural parts such as sections, articles, paragraphs, etc., and are structured according to documentary rules.

In a *legal text*, there is a *text passage* (*Textstelle*) which can be translated in a notation of formal logic. This text passage is Element 2. In legal practice, it is barely feasible to expect to reproduce (translate, transform) the entire lengthy text into a logical notation. A text passage can expand through several paragraphs and need not necessarily be a sentence. A legal norm is usually not formulated in one sentence and can expand through several places. For example, a norm's element, such as a condition, a subject, an obligatory action, or a provision, can be structured differently. The thesis that a universal model for reconstructing norms from legal text is possible can be rejected; see, e.g., Wróblewski (1992).

Legal texts are not structured in the units of norms. In other words, a legal norm is neither a structural element of a legal text nor of a legal document. A norm is a product of interpretation. This is conducted by legal sciences, courts and the judicature. Probably, a legal norm is closer to what Kelsen called "legal sentence" (*Rechtssatz*). However, norms are linguistically formulated and jurists are linguistically-oriented. For example, this can be observed in a speech of a judge. A legal provision may be collected from several places.

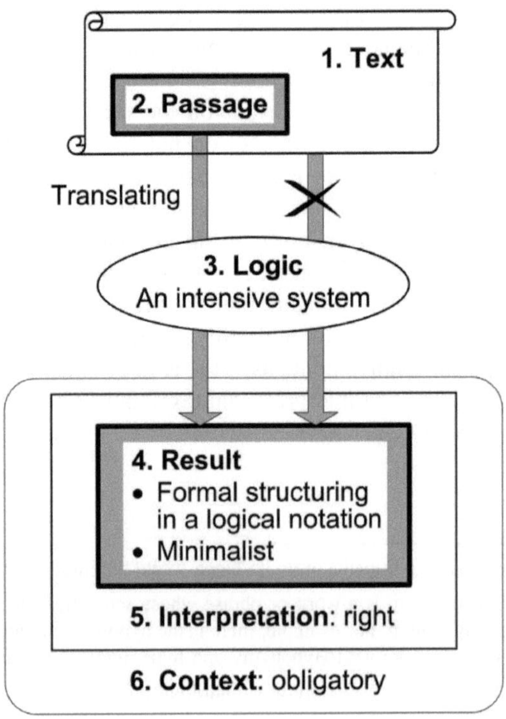

Fig. 17.4 Selective application of logic. In legal practice, it is barely possible to translate the whole text in a logical notation, but possible to do so with a passage

Element 3 is logic, which is used to translate a *passage* into a logical notation. Element 4 is the result of the translation, i.e., a product. Hence the product is a formal structuring of the text passage, whereas Element 3 is a system of logic.

Translation has been attempted by many researchers. For example, Ilmar Tammelo (1978) used Polish prefix notation that comprises a deontic modality. Jürgen Rödig (1980) employed predicate logic and inference rules. Hajime Yoshino used a Prolog-like notation in his Logical Jurisprudence (2011). Less of formal notations have been used by Ota Weinberger (1989). Up to now a success was translating only small passages such as a separate phrase, a provision, or a sentence.

The idea is that the translation is minimalist. Again, we hold that it is barely possible (at least at present) to reproduce the whole legal text in a logical notation. However, this is possible with smaller text passages. This thesis is backed by the cited research and numerous attempts to represent the meaning of a (legal) text using artificial intelligence; for a critique see, e.g., Philip Leith (2010). We would mention difficulties first in representing the whole interconnectedness of norms and, second the open texture problem, which occurs while interpreting legal concepts.

The principle of selective application of logic is also true in legislation. Logic is not enough for an entire legal text such as a statute and allows only selective application. Only important passages can be represented in a logical notation. In legislation, hence, logic can be applied intensively but selectively. Here "intensively" means providing less open texture, a higher degree shift from an open world to a closed world, or from loose to more strict interpretation.

One problem is the application of logic to reproduce the whole text. The selective application of logic can be compared with a scalpel. You cannot use a scalpel to chop as you would an axe. Logic is a precise tool and its limitations should be considered in legislation. It is meaningful to single out key sentences and to investigate them selectively: what interpretations do they allow? What consequences will they lead to? This is a targeted application of logic by legists. Such a checking of legislative drafts would be limited to selective analysis of key passages.

17.6 Logic Expands Interpretation

Logic is important in creating an interpretative space. This interpretation (see Element 5 in Fig. 17.4) is a correct one. Thus the system of logic contributes to eliminating wrong interpretations. Therefore the interpretation is interesting and various consequences follow from it. Of course, other factors such as different values can be considered in the creation of space for interpretation.

Next, the context is expanded through logic. Consequences are right (correct logically) and obligatory. In the case that the behaviour of a subject is expressed with deontic modalities such as obligation O(A) and prohibition F(B), the subject is clearly obligated to perform an action A and to refrain from B.

In legislation, both effects are important: the rightness of interpretation and the obligation of actions to pursue consequences. Hence, logic emerges as an instrument

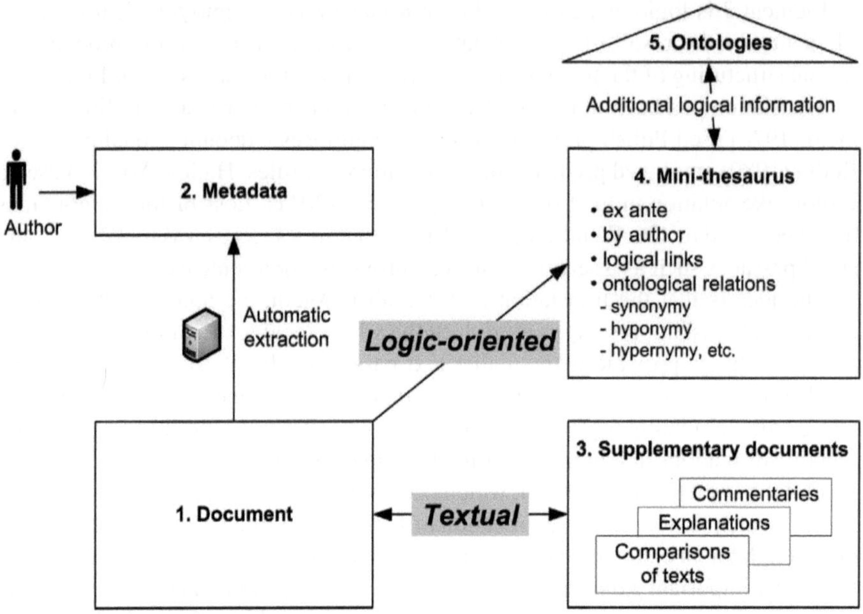

Fig. 17.5 Supplementary logical information to a document, a legislative draft

to achieve both. Obligatory consequences lead us to the roots of examining the deontic field; see, e.g., Wesley Hohfeld et al. (1920) and Georg von Wright (1951).

Proposal: supplementary logic-oriented information. Our proposal is to supplement a legislative document with additional logic-oriented information (Fig. 17.5) such as a mini-thesaurus. This would be prepared ex ante (contrary to ex post documentalistic information which is added to legislative documents) by an author or an authority in a legislative process. A mini-thesaurus would contain links and ontological relations such as synonymy, hyponymy, hypernymy, etc. This is contrary to traditional metadata that is textual.

In a traditional legislative process, a legislative draft is supplemented with textual documents such as commentaries, explanations, comparisons of texts, abstracts, etc. Our proposal is to activate logic-oriented ontology-relevant thinking and to add linking in the form of a mini-thesaurus with various links. A relevant research was conducted in the LOIS project where the five ontological relations have been identified; see Peters et al. (2007) and Schweighofer and Liebwald (2007).

Part of metadata is prepared by an author or authorities such as ministries and part is extracted from a document automatically. However, even more supplementary metadata could be extracted automatically (or semi-automatically); see, e.g., Le et al. (2013) and Yoshida et al. (2013).

To sum up, the novelty of the proposal is to supplement legislative documents with explicit logic-oriented structural information which is relevant to ontologies, thesauruses and taxonomies. The purpose is neither supplementing the document with additional metadata automatically nor advancing general legal ontologies.

The proposed above appears in a pre-logical area, needs not strict semantics, and is intended for transforming into a logical notation. This can be called *structural visualisation*. Similarly as legislation is not yet law, so the proposed method is not yet a formal logic, but probably is in a perimeter to logic. The area of the legislation is more diffuse and more open than the range of applicable law. Therefore, other methods are also adequate. It may be that in the future 30 years more formal methods will be used than possible today. But now in a kind of transition phase, it is first necessary to leave the bank of the purely textual and go to an intermediate medium, and this may be well found in the area of structural visualisation.

Structural visualisation is relevant to legislative drafting as it can bring transparency to complex structures. This is important in formulating political wills and their public assessment in the sense of e-participation. This is also relevant to the idea of supplementary mini-thesaurus. Therefore structural visualisation is examined further in more detail.

17.7 Structural Legal Visualisation

On the middle-level abstraction layer there are (semi)formal representations of legal texts and legal norms. On the one hand there are formal notations, which go beyond the textual ones; on the other hand, there are visual representations that also occur in competition with the text. In the structural visualisations in turn two different types can be distinguished: first, the visualisations formed according to strict formal rules; second, the more intuitive pictures which can detect situations better.

We propose logic-oriented visualisation method that makes the complexity of regulations visible in a sequence of layers. We call the method *structural legal visualisation* (SLV). Examples further show the need of such visualisation in the legislative domain. SLV is about a sequence of images in time for a human to understand the meaning of legal contents. Thus SLV has links to both information visualisation (Card 2008; Spence 2001) and knowledge visualisation (Eppler and Burkhard 2006), but has differences from each of them (see further). SLV applies primarily to logical pictures (*logische Bilder*); see Röhl and Ulbrich (2007).

With the regard to the visualisation object – a dynamic (film or slide presentation) or a static one (e.g. a diagram, scheme, picture, mindmap, etc.) – SLV can be divided into the following major variations (i.e. build-ups of the resulting diagram):

1. *Dynamic SLV.* A dynamic object is viewed; the object changes. The development in time is important.
2. *Static SLV.* A static object is viewed; the object does not change in time. This variation can be divided into two sub-variations:

(a) *Incremental SLV.* The process of adding items is important. The object's presentation grows quantitatively. Graphical items are supposed to have links to the reference area and legal effect description.
(b) *Alternating focuses SLV.* The process of changing the viewer's focus is important. The user moves between broad overviews and detailed views.

3. Other techniques. Probably other types of SLV make sense? For example, you could also take a picture and just wander around with the focus.

The emphasis for the present study is on the first two variations above. In the dynamic SLV it is about building images along a time axis. The outcome is a series of different images in time. This variation can be compared with film demonstration.

In the static SLV it is about building images within a systematic map, but the individual elements are only highlighted sequentially. This is because the whole object is too complicated and visualising at once would be too much.

On legal visualisation in general. Klaus Röhl and Stefan Ulbrich (2007) provide a detailed study of visualisation in law and motivate it. The lack of pictures in jurisprudence becomes a learning obstacle (ibid., 15–17). A starting position is "Law is text" and therefore law is always textual for jurists. Hence there are reasons for jurists' reluctance of visualisations. Pictures bring a risk of drawbacks, such as redundancy, a low level of abstraction, trivialisation, emotions (ibid., 18–25, 100–102). However the use of logical pictures can bring advantages. Metaphors and symbols can be employed to represent norms and hence pictorial two-dimensional representations emerge (ibid., 42–62). An ancient example is the frontispiece of the book Leviathan by Thomas Hobbes.[5] To summarise, the combination of words "law and visualisations" contains a kind of a paradoxical contradiction.

Besides pictorial visualisations, logical diagrammatical visualisations including info-graphics are widely used to represent legal content such as argumentation graphs, story-telling, legal workflow, etc. (Kahlig 2008).

There are also quite different approaches to visualisation, for instance, through semiotics. The classical philosophy of law, however, as approximately represented by Arthur Kaufmann (see Lachmayer 2005), has provided a methodological introduction to visualisation with the thought pattern of *tertium comparationis*. Especially in the European Union with its many official languages, a visualisation, which appears as a *tertium*, can form a mental bridge between different languages.

The sequence of images within SLV corresponds to a narrative (in other words, a story). The addressant (narrator, storyteller, speaker, sender) tells the addressee (listener, recipient) a description of events. A form is a sequence of written or spoken words, or a sequence of (moving) pictures. Further we observe two variations: first sequential SLV then dynamic SLV.

[5]http://en.wikipedia.org/wiki/Leviathan (book). Accessed 20 April 2014.

17.8 Dynamic SLV

An example of the dynamic SLV is as follows. Suppose visualising different roles of a person in the different stages of criminal proceedings: (a) suspect in the pre-trial stage, (b) defendant (accused) in the judicial stage, and (c) convict in the punishment stage (Fig. 17.6).

In this paper we are interested primarily in dynamic SLV who's object is a scheme. In addition to this, there is also dynamic SLV with moving pictures that are implemented in films.

Film visualisation. For example, films within the Tele-Jura project[6] have been created for legal education. Film visualisations serve for situational visualisation. A good example is "Menzi-Muck timber case – the Film!".[7] This four-minute film takes a familiar case (BGE 129 III 181 ff.). In this 2002 decision, the Swiss Federal Court defined criteria to distinguish between favour (*Gefälligkeit*), gratuitous contract (*unentgeltlicher Auftrag*), negotiorum gestio (*Geschäftsführung ohne Auftrag*) and the claim to compensation by a person who gave voluntary help to another (*Schadenersatzanspruch der unentgeltlich helfenden Person*). The film shows and explains the decision tree, which is employed by the visualised judge to make the judgment. To explain the law, clear graphic style descriptions are employed. This trend can be assigned to multisensory law as called by Colette Brunschwig (2014).

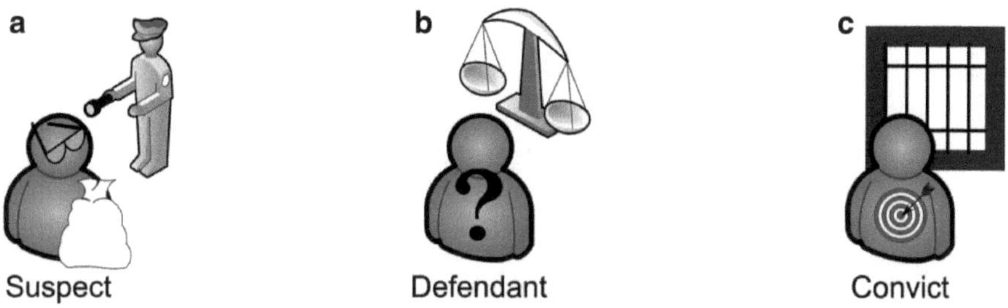

Fig. 17.6 A sample dynamic SLV

[6] Tele-Jura is a project by Radosław Czupryniak, Matthias Frohn, Peter Reineke and Stephan Trebeß. Films run parallel to a course by Matthias Frohn at the Institute of International Private Law of the Free University of Berlin, see http://www.telejura.de/. Accessed 20 April 2014.

[7] http://www.youtube.com/watch?v=KI7zeuayum4. Accessed 20 April 2014. See also the comment by lawyer Arnold Rusch, http://www.arnoldrusch.ch/pdf/130311-menzimuck.pdf. The case concerned the claim for damages suffered by the person who gratuitously helps another.

17.9 Static SLV

We see a need to divide static SLV into two sub-variations: (a) incremental SLV and (b) alternate focuses SLV.

17.9.1 Incremental SLV

In this sub-variation, diagram elements are added sequentially and in the end the view becomes enriched quantitatively and complex. Figures 17.1, 17.4, and 17.5 could serve as examples when each numbered element would be added to the view incrementally. Static SLV can be related with a focus + context technique in information visualisation. [8] Following is a simple reference model for visualisation (Card 2008, 536), originally in Card et al. (1999):

Raw Data → Data Tables → Visual Structures → Views

Each added image may be graphically very simple, e.g. a rectangular box, but semantically difficult to understand, because it represents a complex (legal) concept. A figure might supplement a text and a presentation that typically is dominated by voice explanation. However, the picture format is not so rich to show animation, because printed text provides less visual effects than a slide tool.

17.9.2 Alternate Focuses SLV

In alternate focuses SLV, single elements are added and others are taken away, so the number of picture elements per view remains manageable. Again, Figs. 17.1, 17.4, and 17.5 could serve as examples, but when each numbered element magnified and viewed from a different focus.

This visualisation consists of a series of views each showing a perspective from a different focus. Here different methods of information visualisation can be applied including focus + context. They emerge in the presentation problem, where different methods of scrolling, context map and image magnification (zooming) are used. Spence (2001, 116) identifies "the problem created by the need to have context information beneficially co-existing with detail of the focus of attention."

[8] [C]onsider visualizations in which the machine is no longer passive, but its mappings from Visual Structure to View are altered by the computer according to the its model of the user's degree of interest. . . .Focus+context views are based on several premises: First, the user needs both overview (context) and detail information (focus) during information access, and providing these in separate screens or separate displays is likely to cost more in user time. Second, information needed in the overview may be different from the needed in the detail. . . . Third, these two types of information can be combined within a single dynamic display, much as human vision uses a two-level focus and context strategy. (Card 2008, 536)

Related methods of visualisation. Advanced visualisation tools and computer graphics systems can allow more visualisation techniques than slide preparation systems which do not allow much interactivity. It is worth noting focus + context presentation techniques which might extend SLV variations: bifocal or fisheye display, distortion in both X- and Y-dimensions, suppression of irrelevant data, selecting focuses concurrently, Z-thru mapping, A Really Useful Map employing distortion and suppression, Magic Lense etc. (Spence 2001, ch. 7). These techniques enable the user to discern information of interest. For example, multiple layers can be viewed from different focuses and with different transparency of each layer. To summarise, the motivation is to provide balance of local detail and global context.

SLV might gain from the riffling technique Rapid Serial Visual Presentation (RSVP, Spence 2001, 127) and zooming and panning.[9] A commonality is that all these techniques produce a series of images in time. However, a difference in SLV is as follows. The teller (the sender of images) is active and the listener (recipient) is passive. In information visualisation, the viewer is active and interactively controls the computer that produces images. In other words, in SLV the teller presents his scenario and the listener simply listens.

Static SLV with accumulation has a commonality with information visualisation notion semantic zoom (Spence 2001, 132–133). Both techniques concern parts and the whole but in the opposite directions. Static SLV goes from a part to the whole scheme, whereas semantic zoom goes from the whole to a detail. Semantic zoom can be observed in air traffic control systems.

17.10 Specifics of SLV: Visualising legal Meanings

In visualisations in the legislative domain our attention is attracted by the following two specific features. Firstly, legal visualisation is characterised by specific raw data. It can be not limited to a specific norm or law and covers legal sources, legal doctrine, legal science, and other elements.

Secondly, the object of visualisation is a legal meaning. This differentiates legal visualisation from data visualisation and information visualisation. In the latter, computer-supported interactive visual representations are important. However, this is not a case in legal visualisation. In the comprehension of law, communicating the meaning of law to the human user is of primary importance. In this sense legal visualisation is related to knowledge visualisation. The visual structure is a diagram that represents the meaning. Here diagrams serve well as legal norm visualisations (*Rechtsnormbilder*, Röhl and Ulbrich 2007, 109–111).

[9] Panning is the smooth movement of a viewing frame over a two-dimensional image of a greater size. (Spence 2001, 130)

The meaning of law is not easy to grasp for laymen. Hence, the visualisation of legal meaning is distinct from information visualisations, such as a presentation of goods and services to potential customers, who wish searching for a particular item. Three functions of instructive pictures can be distinguished (Röhl and Ulbrich 2007, 91):

1. pointing function (e.g. an anatomy atlas)
2. situational function ("A picture is worth a thousand words")
3. construction (structure, design) function. The picture helps a viewer to build a mental model in her mind.

Our personal experience shows the importance of the latter two functions in the visualisation of legal meaning. The semantics conveyed by a visualisation, i.e. the meaning of the representation, is also addressed by Fill (2009) in a chapter which is devoted to the analysis of visualisations.[10]

Knowledge explication is a primary aim of legal visualisation in our approach. Here we refer to Fill (2009, 172) who holds that "the goal of *knowledge explication* ... is to explicate knowledge that resides in the heads and minds of people and express it by a visualisation" and lists four basic aims of visualisations: *knowledge explication*, knowledge transfer, knowledge creation, and knowledge application. A subsequent aim, the knowledge transfer, can be achieved by the following tasks: Diverge, Converge, Organise, Elaborate, Abstract, Evaluate, and Build Consensus (Fill 2009, 173–174).

To summarise, the goal of comprehending the meaning of law is distinguished from searching for items or information.

17.11 Related Works on Visualisation

Information visualisation and knowledge visualisation are distinguished.

17.11.1 Information Visualisation

While investigating SLV, the purpose of visualization has to be agreed. Here we can refer to *information visualisation* that can be defined as "the use of computer-supported, interactive, visual representations of abstract data in order to amplify

[10]Visualisation semantics are therefore related to questions such as *What may a user associate with the resulting graphical representation?* or *Is the intended meaning of the visualisation correctly transferred to the user or would another type of representation better fit?* (Fill 2009, 163).

cognition" (Card et al. 1999). Hence, amplifying cognition is the purpose of information visualisation (Card 2008, 515). Speaking about terminology, information visualisation is distinguished from scientific visualisation, which is applied to scientific data and is typically physically based. Both belong to the broader field of *data graphics*, "which is the use of abstract, nonrepresentational visual representation to amplify cognition. Data graphics, in turn, is part of *information design*, which concerns itself with external representations for amplifying cognition." (Card 2008, 515)

We find diagrammatical representations in the legislative domain relevant with Hans-Georg Fill's work (2009). He positions his work in the area of fundamental research of business informatics, observes the fields which are related to the term "visualisation," and surveys and surveys existing visualisations approaches. In the context of business informatics, Fill classifies the related fields have been classified into three categories (Fill 2009, 25–26):

1. Application level
    - Knowledge Visualisation
    - Enterprise Modeling
2. Conceptual Level
    - Graph Theory and Graph Drawing
    - Descriptive Statistics
    - Information Visualisation
3. Implementation Level
    - Computer Graphics

Visualisations in business informatics concern primarily business frameworks and business processes. The variety of their elements is very big (Fill 2009, ch. 3). A shared goal is to communicate business information.

Fill's survey of visualisations in business informatics may serve as a template to perform a survey of visualisation methods in the legislative domain. An interested reader can be referred to Röhl and Ulbrich (2007). The latter book is however written in a different manner than Fill's survey which is devoted to people in business informatics or computer science.

17.11.2 Knowledge Visualisation (KV)

Studies in visual cognition lead to a conclusion that visualisation dramatically increases our ability to think and communicate. Eppler and Burkhard (2006) link knowledge visualisation with knowledge management and list numerous benefits of visual representations. Hence, a longstanding objective is knowledge management.[11]

KV is differentiated from other approaches, such as information visualisation or visual communication.[12] Information visualisation typically helps in human-computer interaction while knowledge visualisation primarily is used in communication among individuals (ibid., 552). A knowledge visualisation framework is comprised of three perspectives which answer three key questions with regard to visualising knowledge (ibid., 553):

1. Knowledge type (What? What type of knowledge is visualised (object)?)
2. Visualisation goal (Why? Why should that knowledge be visualised (purpose)?)
3. Visualisation format (How? How can the knowledge be represented (method)?)

The visualisation format perspective structures the visualisation formats into six main groups: (1) heuristic sketches, (2) conceptual diagrams, (3) visual metaphors, (4) knowledge animations, (5) knowledge maps, and (6) domain structures. The conceptual diagrams are important from the view of knowledge representation. Eppler and Burkhard (2006, 554) list 18 types of frequently used conceptual diagrams, such as process, flowchart, etc.

17.12 Conclusions

Three issues emerge while exploring the relationship between logic and lawmaking: political conflict, argument and logic and rhetoric. Logical arguments can be used; however, rhetoric determines parliamentary events. Logic is important for legists who make texts logically consistent. This is a serving function of logic.

Both legislative texts and legal texts differ from a common narrative text in the reference range. They restrict narrative space and contain more executive space that is constituted with a normative language. Logic is used for rationalisation, especially since it is able to harden the texts allowing only correct interpretations.

We hold that the creativity in using logic in law can be demonstrated on the middle-level of abstraction. On this level, the usage of formal notations is still not too far away from the substantive contents of law.

---

[11]Knowledge visualisation is defined as a field that "examines the use of visual representations to improve the creation and transfer of knowledge between at least two people. Knowledge visualisation thus designates all graphic means that can be used to construct and convey complex insights". (Eppler and Burkhard 2006, 55)

[12]Information visualisation aims to explore large amounts of abstract (often numeric) data to derive new insights or simply make the stored data more accessible. Knowledge visualisation, in contrast, facilitates the transfer and creation of knowledge among people by giving them richer means of expressing what they know. (Eppler and Burkhard 2006, 551)

Logic is important as an opening door to legal interpretation. The right interpretation is made explicit and incorrect variations are eliminated. Translating a law into logic contributes to following the consequences of the law. Consequences, which are implicit in a law, can be made explicit in a logical notation. Thus logic brings quantity. Computers can also be employed here.

Acknowledgements V. Čyras was supported by the project "Theoretical and engineering aspects of e-service technology development and application in high-performance computing platforms" (No. VP1-3.1-ŠMM-08-K-01-010) funded by the European Social Fund.

References

Brunschwig, Colette R. 2014. On visual law: Visual legal communication practices and their scholarly exploration. In *Symbol and magic of law: Liber amicorum Friedrich Lachmayer (Zeichen und Zauber des Rechts)*, ed. E. Schweighofer, M. Handstanger, H. Hoffmann, F. Kummer, E. Primosch, G. Schefbeck, and G. Withalm, 899–933. Bern: Editions Weblaw. http://ssrn.com/abstract=2405378. Accessed 15 June 2015.

Card, Stuart. 2008. Information visualisation. In *The human-computer interaction handbook: Fundamentals, evolving technologies, and emerging applications*, ed. Andrew Sears, and Julie A. Jacko, 2nd ed. New York: Lawrence Erlbaum Associates/Taylor & Francis Group.

Card, Stuart K., Jock D. Mackinlay, and Ben Shneiderman. 1999. *Information visualization: Using vision to think.* San Francisco: Morgan Kaufmann.

Eppler, Martin J., and Remo Burkhard. 2006. Knowledge visualization. In *Encyclopedia of knowledge management*, ed. David G. Schwartz, 551–560. Hershey: Idea Group Reference.

Fiedler, Herbert, Fritjof Haft, and Roland Traunmüller, ed. 1988. *Expert systems in law – Impacts on legal theory and computer law*. Series Neue Methoden im Recht, vol. 4. Tübingen: Attempto.

Fill, Hans-Georg. 2009. *Visualisation for semantic information systems*. Wiesbaden: Gabler.

Haft, Fritjof. 2009. *Legal rhetoric (Juristische Rhetorik)*, 8th ed. Freiburg (Breisgau)/München: Alber.

Haft, Fritjof. 2010. *Normal-case book (Das Normfall-Buch: IT-gestütztes Strukturdenken und Informationsmanagement)*, 4th ed. München: Normfall-GmbH.

Hage, Jaap. 2005. *Studies in legal logic*. Law and philosophy library, vol. 70. Dordrecht: Springer.

Hohfeld, Wesley Newcomb, and Walter Wheeler Cook. 1920. *Fundamental legal conceptions as applied in judicial reasoning and other legal essays*. New Haven: Yale University Press.

Jones, Andrew J.I., and Marek Sergot. 1993. On the characterization of law and computer systems: The normative systems perspective. In *Deontic logic in computer science: Normative system specification*, ed. John-Jules Ch. Meyer and Roel J. Wieringa, 275–307. Chichester: Wiley.

Kahlig, Wolfgang. 2008. *Modeling law in e-government: Case examples for legistic (Rechtsmodellierung im e-Government: Fallbeispiele zur Legistik)*. Saarbrücken: VDM Verlag Dr. Müller.

Kelsen, Hans. 1967. *Pure theory of law*, 2nd ed. Trans. M. Knight. Berkeley: University of California Press.

Lachmayer, Friedrich. 2005. Tertium comparationis in law. Variations on a theme of Arthur Kaufmann (Das tertium comparationis im Recht. Variationen zu einem Thema von Arthur Kaufmann). In: *Responsible law – The philosophy of law of Arthur Kaufmann (Verantwortetes Recht – die Rechtsphilosophie Arthur Kaufmanns)*, Archiv für Rechts- und Sozialphilosophie, ed. Ulfrid Neumann, Winfried Hassemer, and Ulrich Schroth. ARSP, vol. 100, 67–77. Wiesbaden: Franz Steiner Verlag.

Leith, Philip. 2010. The rise and fall of the legal expert system. *European Journal of Law and Technology* 1(1). http://ejlt.org//article/view/14/1. Accessed 20 Apr 2014.

Le, Tho Thi Ngoc, Minh Le Nguyen, and Akira Shimazu. 2013. Unsupervised keyword extraction for Japanese legal documents. In *Legal knowledge and information systems, JURIX 2013: The twenty-sixth annual conference*, ed. K. D. Ashley, 97–106. Amsterdam: IOS Press.

Makinson, David, and Leendert van der Torre. 2000. Input/output logics. *Journal of Philosophical Logic* 29(4):383–408. doi:10.1023/A:1004748624537.

Mally, Ernst. 1926. The basic laws of ought: Elements of the logic of willing (Grundgesetze des Sollens: Elemente der Logic des Willens). Graz: Leuschner & Lubensky. Reprinted in *Ernst Mally, Logische Schriften: Grosses Logikfragment – Grundgesetze des Sollens*, ed. Karl Wolf and Paul Weingartner, 227–324. Dordrecht: Reidel. 1971.

Oberle, Daniel, Felix Drefs, Richard Wacker, Christian Baumann, and Oliver Raabe. 2012. Engineering compliant software: Advising developers by automating legal reasoning. *SCRIPTed* 9(3):280–313. doi:10.2966/scrip.090312.280 [interactive]. http://script-ed.org/wp-content/uploads/2011/12/oberle.pdf. Accessed 20 April 2014.

Opałek, Kazimierz. 1986. *A theory of directives and norms (Theorie der Direktiven und der Normen)*. Vienna: Springer.

Peters, Wim, Maria-Teresa Sagri, and Daniela Tiscornia. 2007. The structuring of legal knowledge in LOIS. *Artificial Intelligence and Law* 15(2):117–135.

Prakken, Henry. 1997. *Logical tools for modelling legal argument: A study of defeasible reasoning in law*. Dordrecht: Kluwer Academic.

Prakken, Henry, and Marek Sergot. 1996. Contrary-to-duty obligations. *Studia Logica* 57(1):91–115. doi:10.1007/BF00370671.

Rödig, Jürgen. 1980. *Writings on legal logic (Schriften zur juristischen Logik)*, ed. Elmar Bund, Burkhard Schmiedel, and Gerda Thieler-Mevissen. Berlin/Heidelberg: Springer.

Röhl, Klaus F., and Stefan Ulbrich. 2007. *Law graphically: Visualisation in the education of jurists (Recht anschaulich. Visualisierung in der Juristenausbildung)*. Edition medienpraxis, vol. 3. Köln: Halem.

Sartor, Giovanni. 2007. *Legal reasoning: A cognitive approach to the law*. A treatise of legal philosophy and general jurisprudence, vol. 5. Heidelberg: Springer.

Schweighofer, Erich, and Doris Liebwald. 2007. Advanced lexical ontologies and hybrid knowledge based systems: First steps to a dynamic legal electronic commentary. *Artificial Intelligence and Law*, 15(2):103–115.

Spence, Robert. 2001. *Information visualization*. Harlow, England: Addison-Wesley.

Tammelo, Ilmar. 1978. *Modern logic in the service of law*. Wien/New York: Springer.

Tosatto, Silvano Colombo, Guido Boella, Leendert van der Torre, and Serena Villata. 2012. Visualising normative systems: An abstract approach. In *Proceedings of the deontic logic in computer science – 11th international conference, DEON 2012* Bergen, 16–18 July 2012, LNCS, vol. 7393, ed. T. Ågotnes, J. Broersen, D. Elgesem, 16–30. Springer. doi:0.1007/978-3-642-31570-1-2.

von Wright, Georg Henrik. 1951. Deontic logic. *Mind, New Series* 60(237):1–15.

Weinberger, Ota. 1989. *Legal logic (Rechtslogik)*. Berlin: Duncker & Humblot.

Wróblewski, Jerzy. 1992. *The judicial application of law*, ed. Zenon Bankowski and Neil MacCormick. Dordrecht: Kluwer Academic.

Yoshida, Yutaka, Kozo Honda, Yuichi Sei, Hiroyuki Nakagawa, Yasuyuki Tahara, and Akihiko Ohsuga. 2013. Towards semi-automatic identification of functional requirements in legal texts for public administration. In *Legal knowledge and information systems, JURIX 2013: The twenty-sixth annual conference*, ed. K. D. Ashley, 175–184. Amsterdam: IOS Press.

Yoshino, Hajime. 2011. The systematization of law in terms of the validity. In *Proceedings of the 13th international conference on artificial intelligence and law (ICAIL '11)*, 121–125. New York: ACM.

Chapter 18
Creating CoReO, the Computer Assisted Copyright Reform Observatory

Ermo Täks, Addi Rull, Anni Säär, and Burkhard Schäfer

Abstract The paper proposes an approach to AI assisted law reform, that tries to align research in Artificial Intelligence and Law with the jurisprudential philosophy of Luc Wintgens. Taking a holistic, system-oriented view, we propose a visualisation based link analysis that allows lawmakers to identify those parts of the legal system where the smallest amount of change has the largest effect.

Keywords Link analysis • Natural language processing • Law reform • Copyright law

18.1 Introduction

This paper proposes a new approach for artificial intelligence (AI) support for legislative drafting. Using link analysis and computer assisted visualisation tools, it creates an "observatory" for the way in which a suggested law reform will affect the wider legal system. In particular, we will use the example of copyright law to demonstrate the not just the practical usefulness of a computer assisted "Copyright Reform Observatory", but also how such an approach can be understood as implementing a specific theoretical perspective of the legislative process. We argue

We are grateful for the support by the RCUK funded CREATE network www.create.ac.uk, and in particular for the contribution our research assistant, Laurence Diver, provided for the research and editing of this paper.

E. Täks (✉) • A. Rull
Tallinn Technical University, Tallin, Estonia
e-mail: ermotaks@gmail.com; addi.rull@ttu.ee

A. Säär
Estonian Human Rights Centre, Tallin, Estonia
e-mail: anni.saar@humanrights.ee; anni.saar@hotmail.com

B. Schäfer
University of Edinburgh, Edinburgh, UK
e-mail: B.schafer@ed.ac.uk

M. Araszkiewicz, K. Płeszka (eds.), *Logic in the Theory and Practice of Lawmaking*, Legisprudence Library 2, DOI 10.1007/978-3-319-19575-9_18

that just as traditional legal expert systems that aim to assist judges or litigators need to be grounded in an appropriate jurisprudential theory, so does the development of expert systems that assist legislators. But while jurisprudential theories of legal reasoning are readily available and widely used in the development of legal expert system for the application of law, the same hasn't happened yet in the field of AI assisted law creation. One reason for this is the relative scarcity of jurisprudential (as opposed to politological) theories of law making. In the first part of the paper, we introduce a suitable candidate for a theoretically grounded approach to AI supported legislative drafting, Luc Wintgen's "legisprudence". Possibly somewhat counterintuitively, it takes a "sceptical" position towards legislation, in the sense that it imposes a stringent burden of proof on legislative proposals, favouring as a default a state of "freedom", the absence of laws, over regulation – unless the proposes regulation can be justified on its merits. As a consequence, our system too will not (just) assist in the creation of new laws, but rather help to minimise the need for the creation of new laws. Increase in the quantity of legislation and the speed of legislative reform create considerable compliance costs for businesses. Being intrinsically disruptive, they also create problems for law firms and legal counsel, for example in the form of training costs. In the second part, we demonstrate using as test case copyright law how methods from computer linguistics, link analysis and graph visualisation theory can be brought together to render some core features of Wintgen's legisprudential theory computational.

One reason to allocate a burden of proof on proposals for law reform is that it is intrinsically disruptive and costly. Our proposed system takes both an inward and outward facing perspective to facilitate the management of this type of disruptive change and to minimise the costs associated with it.

From the inward facing perspective, the system addresses the legislator. Here its aim is to assist the identification of "minimally disruptive" legislative changes. This can mean achieving a significant degree of substantive legal reform by changing a small number of "core" laws only (the aim of a major reform project). By modelling and identifying the interdependence between legal provisions across the legal system, our approach identifies those laws that are so highly connected with other provisions that a direct change of one legal provision indirectly affects as high a number of other provisions as possible. Conversely, some law reform projects intend only a minimal change to address a specific problem. In this case our system assist the legislators by identifying suitable candidates for reform that are only minimally interlinked with the rest of the legal system. In both cases we take our inspiration from link analysis, in particular the analysis of criminal networks and the way in which it informs the work of the police – sometimes intentionally disrupting the entire system by removing core players (e.g. the head of an organisation), sometimes keeping the network intact but reducing its dangerousness by targeting more isolated members who nonetheless pose high risks (the "henchmen").

From the outward perspective, the system assists lawyers as addressees of legislation to predict the impact a proposed law reform is likely to have on their business and clients. It should be able for example to estimate how many legacy contracts or licenses will require revision in light of a legislative change, or to identify and triage training needs. In both cases the aim is to reduce the costs of litigation by reducing the costs that are created by disruptive legislative activity.

Assisting legislative drafting has become a major research interest within the field of AI and law (see for example Voermans et al. 1997; Breuker et al. 2000; Hafner and Lauritsen 2007; Hoekstra et al. 2003; Winkels and Den Haan 1995; Palmirani 2010; Voermans et al. 2012). Over the same period legisprudence – the jurisprudential analysis of legislation – has also risen to prominence. The term "legisprudence" was coined in 1950 (Cohen 1949–1950) and has experienced a recent revival with the 2003 publication of the Proceedings of the Fourth Benelux-Scandinavian Symposium on Legal Theory, under the title "Legisprudence: A New Theoretical Approach to Legislation". In 2007 Luc J. Wintgens founded the journal Legisprudence, published by Hart. In 2008, Boston University School of Law held a symposium on legislation, the proceedings of which were published in the *Boston University Law Review* in 2009. By that time use of the term "legisprudence" had become a matter of course, most notably in the "Editors" Note on "Legisprudence", (2009) 89 *B.U. L. Rev.* 331 which notes that "[l]egisprudence has a short history, but a long tradition."

AI approaches to legislative drafting and legisprudence share ostensibly the same goal – applying theory to improve the legislative process. Despite this convergence of interests, there has so far been little systematic recognition of legisprudence research in AI and law. We argue that this is not by chance; there is a real (if non-obvious) tension between the approaches favoured by researchers in AI and Law and the positions advocated by some of the most influential legisprudence researchers, in particular the work of Luc Wintgens and Jeremy Waldron. In response, we propose a somewhat different way in which artificial intelligence can support not just the legislature but also law firms as "consumers" of legislation. By taking the notion of a legal *system* as our starting point, we conceive of law as similar to a social network, with different parts "communicating" with others to varying degrees. By matching and re-engineering these "channels of communication", we can transpose other concepts from social network analysis to enable legal reform that is informed by legisprudential analysis. By perceiving law as a "communication network", we express in the language of the semantic web a more traditional understanding of the concept of legal system, described by Örücü (1987) in her treaty on comparative law as

> By a legal system is meant a body of law systematically unfolding, between the parts of which there is coherence and consistency. A legal system, composed of legal norms, rules, principles and concepts, has running through it a connecting thread. It has its own vocabulary used to express concepts; its rules are arranged into categories; it has techniques for expressing rules and interpreting them; it is linked to a view of the social order itself, which determines the way in which law is applied, and shapes the very function of law in that society

Using a definition of legal system that has been shown to work in the context of comparative law has several advantages for our project. Very often, legal change is driven by external forces and the way in which legal systems interact with each other. In copyright law in particular, law reform is often driven by international harmonization projects such as the Berne Convention for the Protection of Literary and Artistic Works or the EU Copyright Directive.[1] Being able to model eventually not just the law of one country, but its interaction with other legal systems from a comparative perspective is therefore important. At the same time, several of the features that the definition identified as constitutive for a legal system will find their direct representation in our approach, and we will in particular represent the idea of a "specific vocabulary", the "arrangement of rules in categories" and the "coherence and consistency between parts".

18.2 The Inherent Tension Between AI and Legisprudence

In this section, we explain in more detail where we see the inherent tension between AI approaches to legislation on the one hand, and legisprudence on the other. The information technology revolution has often been called a second industrial revolution (Forester 1985). As with the industrial revolution of the nineteenth century, this mainly implies the promise of producing goods or services faster, cheaper, and in greater quantities, thus satisfying the growing market. "More, faster and cheaper" are also promises of the ICT revolution (see for example Becchetti et al. 2013; Swierczek et al. 2005). For AI and law, this is particularly visible when systems are designed to increase access to justice: if courts were able to resolve disputes faster and cheaper, people currently excluded from justice could have their cases heard. This in turn would result in more judicial decisions being made (see for example Berman and Hafner 1989; Staudt 2008), and with this the need for better information retrieval tools arises. But are "laws" the type of entity where "more" *ceteris paribus* equals "better"? As we discuss in more detail below, there are reasons to distrust this idea. One need not share Thoreau's anarchism to see some truth in his dictum that "the government is best which governs least" (Thoreau 1849, 1). Legislation, as an exercise of sovereign power, is also always inevitably an exercise in violence – justified violence in many cases, but not necessarily something one should cherish as an end in itself.[2] The deeper philosophical issues that an increase in "legislative productivity" can raise were highlighted in Lon Fuller's influential book *The Morality of Law* (Fuller 1969). There, Fuller develops the parable of the inept lawmaker King Rex who, despite his best intentions, fails to actually create law. On his 8th attempt, he increases the efficiency of his lawmaking to new heights, changing (and maybe even in a sense "improving") laws on a daily

[1]Directive 2001/29/EC of the European Parliament and of the Council of 22 May 2001 on the harmonisation of certain aspects of copyright and related rights in the information society.

[2]We follow in this the highly influential analysis by Robert Cover, laid out first in his 1986 essay "Violence and the Word". For further details and discussion on the notion of law as inherently an exercise in (justified) violence the reader is referred to the papers in Brady and Garver (1991), Sarat and Kearns (1992), and Sarat (2001).

basis. But even if the laws were objectively improvements and of good quality, the sheer speed of reform made their actual implementation impossible, and thus they missed their function of "subject[ing] human conduct to the governance of rules" since the citizens could not any longer determine what the operative rules were.[3] While this seems a farfetched example, typical for philosophical analysis but far removed from the reality of law, some anecdotal experience indicates that contemporary lawmakers can encounter similar problems. During the BSE (Bovine spongiform encephalopathy) crisis in the UK, the government issued "statutory instruments" almost daily to adjust the relevant laws as new medical evidence and data became available. At least one judge was compelled to seek the research support of academics because he had decided cases on the basis of rules that had been quickly superseded, the newer regulations not having been promulgated quickly enough to enable application in the courtroom.[4]

By contrast, a slow and cumbersome legislative drafting process encourages the stability that the application of law requires. It also helps to avoid undue public pressure after particularly high profile tragedies or scandals. Emotionally charged atmospheres, of the type often seen in the aftermath of for example a high profile crime, are not necessarily an environment where rational deliberation about law can take place; "hard cases" often result in bad law (Brazier 1997). If complexity of procedure means the legislative process inevitably includes certain delays, this can create a distance between an event and the legal response which allows for a more sober analysis of which course of action is most appropriate.

So far our discussion has focused on the question of speed. Our tentative conclusion is that the use of computers to increase the speed of law-making has advantages and disadvantages. However, speed of production is only one indicator of productivity. Another diagnostic criterion is reduction in cost – producing the same amount of a product, but at a lower price. Translated into a legislative setting, this could be achieved by, for example, reducing the number of people involved in the legislative drafting process, or by supplying the expertise required to draft the substance of the regulation at a lower cost. Yet another option is to increase the range of products that are produced, while keeping the costs and the rate of production constant. To address the question of whether these methods of increasing productivity are unequivocally beneficial where the product is law, we need to reflect further on what we mean by a "good" process of law-making. This is the main concern of any theory of legisprudence, so it is to that field that we turn for help, looking in particular at the legisprudential theory of Luc Wintgens described in his

[3]Fuller considered the relative stability of law an aspect of its "inner morality". Herbert Hart, famously, disagreed, calling it a mere functional requirement of efficacy (Hart 1957). For our purposepurposes, the precise classification is irrelevant,; what matters is that rapid change in the law is a problem for the legal order.

[4]Scott Wortely, in personal communication. Wortely was one of the Strathclyde academics who started to compile and annotate the rapidly changing rules. A description of the background to the problem can be found in Aitken (1997), which also illustrates the speed with which rules were created and repealed at that time.

2006 paper *Legisprudence as a New Theory of Legislation*. In this paper, Wintgens argues that any theory of legisprudence as a rational theory of legislation has to start with "a reflection on the organisation of political space since Modernity", and thereby with a reflection on freedom (Wintgens 2006, 2). Wintgens pursues a twofold strategy. The first part of his paper is a critical account of traditional jurisprudential theories. The second is to overcome the historical limitations that made a "jurisprudence of law making" all but impossible, and to give a systematic account of the parameters for such a theory.

In the historical section, his main criticism is directed at Hobbes and Rousseau, but they are only used as a stand-in for all contemporaneous attempts to develop a theory of law and the state that is "scientific" in the Descartian sense. For Descartes, true jurisprudential statements, just like any other true statement of practical philosophy, must secure their certainty by being derived from first principles that have the same clarity and distinctiveness as the famous *cogito ergo sum*. From such a certain foundation, reality can be "built up" in a rational way. As a corollary, everything that is not amenable to logical or empirical proof is not rational and hence also not scientifically sound, true knowledge.

Here we encounter a problem that also has implications for the project of AI assisted law-making. The values and preferences of individuals are not capable of logical or empirical proof; from the Descartian perspective sketched out above they are not rational and hence not a subject of true knowledge. Hobbes, Rousseau and the other contract theorists resolve this issue by basing their theory of the law on the concept of the social contract.

Just as the *cogito* in theoretical epistemology forces its truth on us, reflection about ourselves and the use of our rational capacities leads to the inevitable conclusion that entering into the social contract is preferable to staying in the state of nature. This is particularly clear in Rousseau: it is the unfolding of reason itself that leads to the "true principles of public law". The truth of the premise, that is the social contract, logically leads to the truth of propositions based on it, that is laws. This, as Wintgens argues (2006, 3), leads in turn to legalism, the pattern of legal thinking that was dominant from the seventeenth to the mid-twentieth century. In legalism, normative behaviour is reduced to rule-following (Shklar 1964, 1), with the source of such rules becoming irrelevant (Bankowski 1993): law is "just there" (Wintgens 2006, 4ff).

Once legalism is established as a necessary consequence of modern theories of law and the state, Wintgens lists four further characteristics of the legal system thus conceived: firstly, if the construction of laws results in true normative propositions (because they can be derived from the social contract) those propositions must be, according to the Cartesian tradition, timeless.

Secondly, and most importantly for our purposes, since laws *are* true, there can be no scientific discussion about their content. To quote Wintgens (2006, 4):

> This entails that the disputable nature of values, goals and ends is concealed. Any rule is true which means that the value, goal or end is morally correct. On this view, laws are considered instruments for their realisation without any need to be chosen. This characteristic of legalism can be called concealed instrumentalism.

Thirdly, once the social contract is concluded, any normative proposition of the sovereign *ipso facto* trumps any other normative statement. Since the law of the state describes what is right or wrong, the subjective moral intuitions of the subject become irrelevant. Fourthly, "legal knowledge" or study of the law is the knowledge of true legal propositions. Consequently, the legal system is a closed set of logically connected propositions. A science of law is thus possible, provided it restricts itself to the analysis of law as already provided by the sovereign.

Why does this matter for a research project in AI and Law, or more precisely, AI and Law-making? "Strong legalism" of the type Wintgens describes as the dominant paradigm of (secular) legal science provides an obvious foundation for legal AI, understood as a formal model of legal reasoning. But at the same time, it renders any attempt of theoretically informed *legal* AI in the service of law-making impossible, or so we argue. If law is nothing but a closed set of logically connected propositions, possibly closed under deduction, then legal expert systems are as easily designed as early proponents of this idea thought they would be – an inference engine and a list of true propositions are all that is required. But by the same token, and for the same reason, a legal expert system that assists law-making is a contradiction in terms. Legalism excludes any form of theorizing about legislation. Quoting Wintgens again (2006, 5):

> Legislation is a matter of politics, and politics is a matter of choice. Choices are disputable, so a theory that would take them to be the object of knowledge is condemned to failure from the very beginning.

Knowledge of the rules is both necessary and sufficient in order to know what we ought to do. Rules fully describe all rights and duties. The first stage in building a legal expert system is knowledge acquisition (Boose 1989). In legal AI, as in AI in general, this will typically involve an evaluative aspect – what is the best practice in a given domain that the system can, or should, model (O'Leary 1998)? But, as we have seen, in the tradition of political philosophy of Hobbes or Rousseau, there cannot be such a thing as "knowledge" of a good legislative process, let alone one that can be modeled through rules. For if there were such a thing, the legislator as a sovereign actor within political space would be bound by rules, and if he were, he would not be a sovereign. Judges, by contrast, *can* be bound by rules, which quite naturally results in the reduction of jurisprudence to the theory of the application of rules by judges.

Following this line of reasoning further, since law-making is now excluded from the domain of legal theory, there can be no theoretically-informed computational modeling of law-making. There can of course be other ways to assist a lawmaker through IT support, but the best we can hope for are generic approaches that would benefit the running of any organization, such as document management and information retrieval. These are not genuinely legal AI approaches, however. If we want a broader notion of legal theory that can be applied to legislative drafting, we therefore have to go beyond the tradition of classical liberal philosophy of the state. We will see below how Wintgens develops such a model that we deem particularly suitable for our purpose, but of course, other avenues to overcome the stranglehold of Hobbes and Rousseau are possible. For us, Wintgens historical analysis is nonetheless helpful and relevant, because in the history of AI and law, we often encounter a belief in strong legalism of the type just described. The earliest rule-based expert systems, such as TAXMAN (McCarty 1980) or Sergot's influential formalization of the British Nationality Act (Sergot et al. 1986), most clearly mirrored a conception of law as closed sets of propositions under deduction. While subsequent approaches enriched and refined this model substantially, the main focus remained on attempting to find those rules that mirror most accurately the judicial application of the law at a given moment in time. By contrast, the recent interest in the legislative process is often more "content neutral", in the sense that the process is treated simply as a generic complex administrative task rather than as something *sui generis*. A result is that discussions around the legislative process are much less likely to be aligned to specific debates in jurisprudence the way in which this is not uncommon in legal expert system design.

18.3 Resolving the Tension: Artificial Intelligence and the Principles of Legisprudence

Legal AI that tries to improve the legislative process therefore faces several challenges: if understood merely as generic IT system design applied to the legislative process, it may be capable of increasing the speed, or reduce the costs, of law-making. But even from a purely utilitarian perspective, simply improving the speed or reducing the cost of the legislative process might be a mixed blessing. Time delays provide legislators with a necessary distance from highly-charged and emotional events, while high costs incentivise them to legislate only as a last resort. Removing or reducing either obstacle may result in even more "juridification" of the social world (Teubner 1987), where more rules and regulations create burdens on the norm recipient with potentially little benefit to society (Blichner and Molander 2008).

If we are more ambitious in our aims and seek to develop AI approaches that are built upon specifically *legal* knowledge to assist in better or more varied outputs of the "product" (law), then we face the problems discussed above: if legalism is true, there cannot possibly be the type of knowledge in rule form that could underpin such an endeavor. Indeed, there could not be any legal theory, *qua* legal theory, that could provide a theoretical underpinning.

Wintgens though offers us more than a mere critique of legalism in the tradition of Rousseau or Hobbes. He also proposes "weak legalism", and with that an option to incorporate a theory of law-making under the umbrella of legal theory that stays true to modernity's understanding of law and the legal process.

In this alternative model of "weak legalism", freedom is asserted as a general principle of the legal order, and a prior goal that all laws have ultimately to serve. This creates a justificatory pressure on the social contract and the laws that it generates. Citizens, upon entering the contract, do not give a general and irrevocable authority to legislate on their behalf to the sovereign. Rather, in every instance, and for every external limitation of freedom through law, values such as life and safety have to be balanced against the loss of freedom. Whereas in the Hobbesian model the formation of the social contract results in a general and a priori trade-off of freedom, citizens in the weak legalism retain, in principle, their moral capacity to act on their conceptions of freedom. Once freedom is established as the governing principle of legal order, external limitation of freedom must be justified in every case. For Wintgens, the theory of legisprudence is about what constitutes such justifications, and their evaluation. The duty of justification is precisely what legisprudence is about. As a rational theory of legislation, it provides general – and hence rule-based – principles that allow us to create legal orders which maximize freedom through justifiable trade-offs (Wintgens 2006, 8–10).

If the way in which we justify trade-offs is through abstract and general principles, then these principles in turn can be formally represented – and with that we have the type of knowledge that lends itself to AI tools, which can then in turn be used to assist the process of justification. Wintgens suggests four principles in particular. We will try to show how his informal discussion can be translated into the language of computer science, and in particular into the language of "requirement engineering". Requirement engineering is understood as the process of "soliciting, structuring and formulating software requirements" and so "a systematic way of producing system models" (Sommerville and Kotonya 1998, 139). We will briefly discuss each of the four principles defined by Wintgens and indicate some of the conclusions we can draw from them which have a bearing on the design of our software.

The four principles that any AI-enabled legisprudential drafting aid should model are:

1. The Principle of Alternativity (PA)
2. The Principle of Normative Density (PND)
3. The Principle of Temporality (PT), and
4. The Principle of Coherence (PC).

The Principle of Alternativity (PA)

The Principle of Alternativity (Wintgens 2006, 10) is the most abstract of the four principles and to a degree encapsulates and summarizes the preceding discussion. It establishes as a baseline that where social interactions work without external guidance through laws, there is no legitimate role for legislation. Legislation is to be used only to correct failing social interactions.

In the theory of Internet governance, Lawrence Lessig (1996) popularized the four regulatory modalities of legislation, the market, social norms and architecture. For Lessig, these are in principle equally valid ways of guiding behavior, though different situations may make one or other of them the more efficient means of doing so. Since legisprudence concerns itself exclusively with regulation by law, however, its underlying assumption is that social practices are self-regulating. Citizens create meaning through their interactions and in doing so refer to rules that are embedded in social practice. Unlike Lessig, this creates in Wintgens' model an asymmetry between formal laws as a method of regulation by the sovereign, and other forms of regulation. Citing Hunyadi with approval, his model assumes also that the existence of these rules becomes visible in the case of conflict (Hunyadi 1995). In conclusion therefore, PA claims that the sovereign can only intervene if he can show that (i) there are societal conflicts, and (ii) other modes of social interaction fail to resolve them. Only in such circumstances is external limitation of freedom preferable to internal limitation.

From the perspective of *legal* AI for legislative drafting, PA poses a number of challenges and opportunities. Challenging is in particular condition (ii), to establish that no alternative to legislation is available. To determine this in practice requires a comparative evaluation of legal and non-legal modes of regulation, and therefore points with necessity beyond legal knowledge and its formal modeling. There has been considerable recent interest in "evidence based policy formulation", and the type of questions that evidence based policy making raises would also be the target of a computational model of PA. As a knowledge intensive task, IT based support seems *prima facie* possible, but the knowledge that would be modeled is not legal knowledge, but based on economic, psychological and organizational data. Examples of this type of knowledge in the field of copyright reform, the main application of this paper, can be found in, for example, Towse (2011) or Kretschmer and Towse (2013).

Slightly more accessible to a purely legal analysis is condition (i), determining that there is a social conflict in the first place. We could, for example, take the number of cases litigated under a law as a proxy for the fact that there is a social conflict to be resolved. A simple link analysis system that connects statutes to cases could then give us an indication of whether a specific legal provision "earns its keep" by being used to resolve a large number of litigated disputes. There are, however, problems with this assumption. The most obvious limitation is that it assumes that there is already a law in place whose usage can be measured. It fails in those situations where we contemplate enacting an entirely new piece of legislation. Furthermore, a law might be so efficient, for instance when its deterrent effect is particularly strong, that no further litigation arises once it is enacted. Finally, a law that does not impute a sanction, and is formulated in a particularly precise way, is also unlikely to create litigation. An example might be a rule that limits tort claims to within 5 years after an accident has occurred. Apart from possible constitutional challenges, it is unlikely that a norm like this will create a significant amount of case law. Conversely, a large amount of litigation on a specific legal provision can well be a sign that it is badly drafted, not a sign that there is a considerable underlying social problem in need of regulation.

The Principle of Normative Density (PND)

The PND states that rules which impose sanctions need special justification, and the more severe the sanction, the greater the pressure for justification and legitimation (Wintgens 2006, 11–13). The "principle of proportionality in European

Union law, according to which the individual should not have his freedom of action limited beyond the degree necessary in the public interest" [5] is a concrete expression of this idea. The intuitive reason for this rule is the "double impact" of sanctions on the concept of freedom. For example, a norm that sanctions a certain behavior X with a prison sentence first reduces freedom by limiting the right of citizens to choose behavior X and then, in the case of rule violation, reduces this freedom even further by restricting the individual's ability to act according to his or her preferences in a significant way. In practical terms this means that, everything else being equal and PA being fulfilled, a law that does not impose a sanction (but creates, for example, an agency charged with assisting citizens in following a norm, or creates a new power that helps them resolve conflict amongst themselves) is preferable over one that imposes a sanction on the citizen.

Wintgens argues that the range of possible legal consequences comes with a variable degree of normative density, with sanctions representing the maximum possible impact on citizens (Wintgens 2006, 12). Norms that create only information duties and thus enable informed consent could, by contrast, be considered as a minimum density rule. We agree that this is an important first step to quantify the burden of proof on the legislator when legitimizing a specific proposed norm. However, we also argue that it should be properly understood in the context of law as a complex system. "Density" then means not just the legal impact of one particular rule, but should be understood as the totality of possible legal sanctions that attach to a certain real life activity. This means it is possible in principle that the density of regulation within a given sphere of life is extraordinary high, even if none of the individual rules carries a sanction. The sheer quantity of norms that apply to this sphere of human activity sees to it. In some cases, this regulatory density can be so high that a trade-off against a smaller number of sanction-carrying norms can, on balance, increase freedom (as an example, one could imagine in a medical setting a highly burdensome regime requiring the reporting of even the most minor deviations from "best practice standards", compared with a norm that imposes prison for medical malpractice, but only in those narrow cases where serious harm was actually caused). Wintgens does not refer explicitly to the totality of rules when discussing legal density, and one could read his proposal as if normative density is a property of individual rules. We think however that our understanding of the rule of density as the totality of rules regulating a specific social fact is in line with Wintgen's own emphasis on the systematic character of law which will be discussed further below. Understood this way, normative density acquires a quantitative dimension that makes it particularly amenable for computational modeling.

The Principle of Temporality (PT)

PT emphasises the temporal dimension of laws (Wintgens 2006, 13–15). As argued above, one problem with strong legalism was the notion that the laws of man

[5] Advocate General in *Internationale Handelsgesellschaft mbH v Einfuhr- und Vorratsstelle für Getreide und Futtermittel.* [1970] ECR 1125 Case 11/70.

and the laws of nature share an atemporal quality. Once our theory of gravity is justified by overwhelming empirical evidence, we only revisit it under exceptional circumstances. If we extend this idea to the realm of human laws, we create a strong presumption that existing laws, as at least approximations of the "best" possible legal solution, remain valid until proven otherwise. In the same way in which therefore laws of nature do not normally carry temporal indices ("the theory of gravity, as valid from…to…), legal norms too are typically drafted without temporal indices, especially they do not normally display "valid until" provisions. PT takes the opposite approach. Laws are created by human beings in reaction to perceived conflicts. What might constitute a reasonable tradeoff between conflict settlement and freedom in one specific context and time may be an unnecessary intrusion into our ability to live according to our own conception of the good life in another. In the field of technology regulation for example, it can be sensible to restrict or prohibit initially the use of a new and untested technology, or to impose special liability or duty-of-care regimes. A classic example are "red flag" laws, named after the Locomotive Act that mandated that trains with more than 2 vehicles should have a man with a red flag walking at least 55 m ahead of each vehicle, to enforce a speed limit and warn horse riders.[6] Although this was a reasonable precaution while the technology was new, it soon became obsolete as people developed appropriate patterns of behaviour when encountering a locomotive. PT stresses the historical character of rules and their justifications. In legislative practice, it points towards the use of "sunset clauses" as a drafting default, requiring the legislator periodically to revisit the justification and efficiency of a law (see for example Davis 1981; Finn 2009; and more critically Kysar 2011). In AI terms, it indicates the need to revise and update the system regularly, incorporating mechanisms such as non-monotonic logic. Wintgens (2006, 15) notes that "[t]his process of justification should include the consciousness that external limitations must be kept in track with changing circumstances. Obsolete legislation or external limitations that are eroded by desuetude are no longer legitimated. They are to be withdrawn, changed or qualified in view of the PA and the PN". While we agree in principle, it should be noted that change, even justified change, comes with costs attached to it. We introduced above the example of King Rex, and his failure to legislate properly when his law reform agenda became too fast to be implemented. We will come back to this point when outlining the business model for CoReO, and note here only that as a regulatory aspiration, PT faces costs that may be reducible through the use of technology.

The Principle of Coherence (PC)

The final principle Wintgens proposes is the notion that justification of legislation needs to look at the legal system as a whole (Wintgens 2006, 15–21). According to him, a legal system is "a complex and dynamic set of intertwined propositions"

[6]https://www.direct.gov.uk/prod-consum-dg/groups/dg-digitalassets/@dg/@en/@motor/documents/digitalasset/dg-180212.pdf

(Wintgens 2006, 15) so that any change in one part of the system may affect it as a whole. The exponential growth of the number of laws threatens this systemic character, as the degree of complexity, and with that the number of complicated inter-systemic interactions, becomes difficult to control. Wintgens theory of coherence is rather complex. For our purposes, the main point of importance however is the notion that on the one hand, it is not sufficient to justify a proposed new law in isolation, we always also need to look at the way the new law will affect, through its interaction with other norms, the system as a whole. On the other hand, steady growth in legislation has increased exponentially the number of norms that are linked with each other, through explicit cross-referencing or by using identical expressions. Complexity, so Wintgens, lead to complication (Wintgens 2006, 15). As a result, even for an expert, let alone for laypeople, it has become impossible to know all the possible interactions and linkages of a law that connects it with other pieces of legislation.

18.4 Turning Legisprudence into AI Specifications

From the above discussion, we can now consider what an AI system that assists a legisprudential analysis of law-making of the type that Wintgens proposes should look like. Here, and in the example in the technical part below, we use copyright reform for illustration purposes. Copyright law is a suitable test case for a variety of reasons:

First, it has been an area of persistent legislative activity over an extended period of time. From the Statute of Anne in 1710 to the present day, every generation seems to have amended, modified or extended their copyright provisions. This is a tendency that is largely independent of jurisdiction, and even in common law countries, much of the dynamic of reform has been driven by legislative intervention and not just by the courts. The result has been a complex legislative framework dominated by general rules and a plethora of increasingly fine-tuned exceptions.

Second, despite this, it is a field of law where there is strong evidence that underlying social conflicts remains unresolved (the "broken copyright" meme, see for example Kretschmer 2008; Tehranian 2007; Samuelson 2013).

Third, law reform therefore remains on the agenda for the foreseeable future, as evidenced by the Hargreaves report in the UK (Hargeraves 2011) or the discussion on the "third batch" of copyright reform in Germany (Beger 2010; see also Party 2012 for the US).

Fourth, it is an area where alternatives to legislation are discussed prominently, for example regulation through markets or, famously, through computational architecture such as Digital Rights Management (DRM) systems (Lessig 1999). This makes it a good case study for PA.

Finally, pressure for law reform frequently originates outside national jurisdictions, for instance through the Berne Convention for the Protection of Literary and Artistic Works or, within the EU, the Directive 2001/29/EC ("Copyright Directive") from 2001. Monitoring foreign and international law can create particular burdens on law firms and increase costs of litigation.

We can now look at a specific legislative reform proposal, namely the suggestion that the UK follow the lead of the US and establish a copyright law if an otherwise protected work is used for the purposes of parody (see for example Deazley 2010; Mendis and Kretschmer 2013). In an ideal world, an AI system for legislative support that embodies the jurisprudential principles discussed above would help to evaluate the proposed reform against those four principles, and on this basis determine which possible route would maximize freedom while minimizing social conflict. We can immediately see why this would be an overly ambitious task that goes well beyond the capacities of any current or near-future AI system.

We can first ask if creating a new exception even requires an evaluation against the Principle of Alternativity the way it was introduced above? Would it increase or decrease normative density? Neither question has a straightforward answer that could be tackled computationally. On the syntactic level, the creation of a new regulation increases the total volume of legislative text. This might be a threshold which triggers our evaluation process. But since the new norm is an exception to an existing rule, merely counting words in statutes could be misleading. It might be more appropriate to treat a new exception as a revocation of a law rather than a new enactment. Presumably, though Wintgens does not say so explicitly, mere revocation of laws that impose sanctions on citizens does not require the same type of justification that enacting a new law does, even if in the legal system in question, amending laws or revoking them formally involves enacting a separate piece of legislation. The same ambiguity can be found if we drill down a bit further and look at the semantic content of the norm. In one reading, a possible sanction for an action is removed through the suggested reform. Where previously I might have faced civil litigation and damages, or even criminal prosecution for copyright theft, I am now free to do so. From the perspective of both PA and PND, this seems *prima facie* to be a net gain in freedom. Analyzing the problem like this, however, hides some important political and philosophical choices. It treats copyright as a mere regulatory system that tries to enhance market efficiency. Another way to frame the problem could be from the perspective of the creators. If we think of copyright as a natural law that precedes the social contract, then the new exemption not only interferes with a right, it potentially creates a regime of sanctions. As an artist, if I now act against the person who uses my work for parody, by for example withholding money owed to him or by pulping his offending works, I can in turn be subjected to both civil and criminal litigation and sanctions. On this reading, PA and PND are highly relevant. Which of these two conceptions of copyright is "the better one" or prevails is a substantive question of policy, not something that can be mechanically deduced from first principles through a process of computation by a machine.

We conclude from this discussion that while we cannot hope to give a computational reading of the full semantic content of PA, PND, PC and PT, we can nonetheless assist the legislative process by identifying suitable proxies for each of them. Ideally, they should be amenable to a quantitative treatment and be based on syntactic categories, rather than involving qualitative reasoning about word meaning. We already indicated one very crude way in which PA could be translated into such a computational format. On the most basic level, we could count individual sections of a law, and rate the justificatory burden relative to the amount of additional (or reduced) regulatory instruments that they create. A more refined version could distinguish between direct rules and exceptions to rules. Although more refined, this approach would still be tied to the syntax of the law. It would also only capture rules with punitive sanctions or those which create powers or privileges. The added value of such a computation-friendly evaluation would be slim for all but the most complex pieces of law reform, and would tell legislators mainly things they already (should) know.[7] If we approach the problem mainly from the perspective of PC, however, another option becomes available for us. This means we start with law as a complex system that, at the point of legislation, is "always already there" and of such a complexity that its interaction with a new piece of proposed legislation cannot any longer be immediately seen. We can then model these possible interactions through a link analysis, which can tell us something about the impact the new law will have on PA, PN and PC. It could warn us for example that what was intended as a small, technical change to one specific piece of law creates the danger to "percolate" through the entire legal system, because this law is interconnected with other regulations in specific ways. Conversely, this can help us to identify the spot in a legal system where a change causes the greatest effect. Sometimes we may want to enact a substantial reform of the entire legal system. Ideally this is done by enacting as few new laws as possible (because this reduces the cost of retraining lawyers, and the cost to the legislative process). Alternatively, sometimes legislators may want to enact only a minimal reform and are concerned that interfering with the system could have unforeseen consequences. In our example, after the empirical data has been collected we might conclude that the problems experienced by users of copyrighted material are only a side effect of the more general malaise of a country's property regime. In this case, introducing a single law that creates a "social acceptability" exemption covering all forms of property – from real estate to movables to intangible property – would achieve the maximum desired change with the minimum of legislative effort. Conversely, we might find that this type of dispute is typical for text-based works only, and therefore a new, general exception for all types of copyrighted work is not necessary. In this case, the least disruptive reform has to ensure that no other parts of the legal system are accidentally affected, for example by introducing a new definition for a term that is also used elsewhere.

This type of cognitive operation is similar to that carried out by a police officer who contemplates how to deal with a criminal network. In some cases, it might

[7]Exceptions to this could be particularly complex and complicated pieces of legislation, such as the Patient Protection and Affordable Care Act in the US, which had not been read by most of the politicians who voted for or against it. Here, even a syntactic parsing exercise that tells the decision maker how many new duties, privileges, exceptions etcetera are created might result in better informed judgments.

be best to "take out" a highly-level member, in the hope that the organisation will disintegrate quickly as a result. In other situations, arresting people at the periphery may be preferable, to prevent the main target from being alerted to the fact that s/he is subject to an investigation, to minimise social harm, or to prevent succession conflicts and inter-gang wars breaking out. Computerised link analysis and visualization tools have been shown to play an assistive role in this task (see for example Hutchins and Benham-Hutchins 2010; Schwartz and Rouselle 2009; Xu and Chen 2005).

The idea of modelling the legal system as an interconnected graph like structure is by no means new, though the application suggested here, that is utilizing them for more strategic law reform, may well be. Typically, such models base their approach on explicit references and citations (see for example Bommarito and Katz 2010; Boulet et al. 2011; Kim 2013). For our purposes, while this approach can and should play an important role for the type of system we envisage, it provides a limited picture only. Firstly, these models map only those connections which the legislator is aware of and decided to make explicit. But as our discussion of Wintgens showed above, the complexity of the legal system is partly due to its growing organically in the absence of strategic planning. The legal system, as Wintgens argued, is not merely complex, it is also complicated (Wintgens 2006, 15). These complications are the result of unintentional, unplanned interaction between the constituent parts of the legal system, which gives particular prominence to PC as an aspect of a rational theory of legisprudence. Secondly, what we are interested in is not (just) the explicit correlation between statutes, which follow the internal logic of the law and its administrative and historical subdivisions. Rather, following the analysis of PA and PND above, our concern is the regulatory density of "spheres of life", the factual substratum to which the law applies. Creators of artistic works face external legal constraints that overlap and combine into a multitude of heterogeneous legal issues, from copyright to employment law to contract law to criminal law. The law divides and separates artificially issues that, from the perspective of the norm recipient, are phenomenologically one set of external factors that limit their freedom. It is unlikely, and from the internal organizational logic of the law, indeed undesirable to connect all the relevant laws to one another through explicit references and citations. If, however, we want to determine if there are alternative ways available to regulate a certain real life problem, we cannot limit ourselves to the "obvious", explicit connections between laws. Rather, we have to discover existing but implicit pathways between regulations that can impact on the same set of factual circumstances. Our approach therefore maps graphically those connections between laws that are not (just) the result of explicit citations, but also those that are the result of the semantic features of the natural language expressions that the legislator chose to frame the law.

18.5 Technical Implementation

As discussed above, legal systems evolve incrementally over time. Even in post-revolutionary legal orders, law reform rarely starts with a blank slate. Rather, we are inevitably confronted with a complex set of pre-existing interacting norms. This insight from legisprudence motivates our approach of "reverse engineering". Rather than building a legal system from scratch – the way strong legalism uses the social contract model – we take the existence of complex legal systems that are at least partially opaque as a given. With "opaque" we mean that legal systems have a degree of complexity that makes it impossible to "see" at one glance how every individual part of the system influences and is influenced by all other parts. This in turn means that we cannot any longer establish simple causal links between individual laws and the outcome of legal disputes, the law becomes a "black box". When in software engineering, we encounter a system that is impenetrable in this sense, we normally try to reverse engineer it. Reverse engineering is the process of developing a set of specifications for a complex hardware system by an orderly examination of specimens of that system. Following Chikofsky and Cross (1990), it is a process of analysing a system or a complex object to (1) identify the system's components and their interrelationships, and (2) to create representations of the system in another form or at a higher level of abstraction.

At this stage legislation is viewed as consisting of individual particles, norms, which are grouped based on similarity and combined together in the form of legal texts. These structural units do carry certain semantic meanings; different norms within paragraphs, for example, are usually grouped together in order to regulate one specific legal response to a perceived societal need. A norm typically contains two parts, the description of the state of affairs that is regulated, and the legal consequence that is triggered if that state is met. From the perspective of the legal system, these consequences are a main organizational feature. For example, we group together all those norms with a prison sentence in the consequent (the "then" part) of a rule together under the label "criminal law". As indicated above, however, for our purposes the clause in the antecedent of the norm (the "if" part) is at least as important to identify structural connections between norms. Thus, in our view, a rule that decrees a punishment for an artist who libels a person in his work, and a norm that enables an artist to recover monetary payment for his work, are connected even if they come from entirely different legal fields. Computational linguistics allows us to implement this idea by analyzing the degree of similarity that the antecedents of the two norms display. The greater the similarity, the higher is the likelihood that the two norms regulate the same type of event. The clause is the smallest linguistic structural unit found able to carry the meaning of one norm. It is the natural container able to represent the full meaning of the norm by itself and therefore chosen to be the basic unit of legislation structure analysis.

The clause is by definition a group of words containing a subject and predicate, and functions as a member of a complex or compound sentence (Clause). The subject is a noun and the predicate is a verb (Definition: Subject, Predicate). To

Table 18.1 Two way table representing the content of the norm (Täks et al. 2013)

Noun/verb	Has
Everyone	1
Right	1
Liberty	1
Security	1
Person	1

simplify, and in order to estimate the most meaningful, information-rich elements of the norm – the so-called "data carriers" – we can focus on these two types of words. Our experiments have shown that by picking out only these two types of words it is possible to capture 60–80 % of the norm content embedded in clauses (Täks et al. 2011, 93–102). As an example we take a norm from the Estonian Constitution: "§20. Everyone has the right to liberty and security of person."[8] With a use of suitable text analysis software it is possible to automatically estimate the beginning and the end of the clause, the types of words used (nouns, verbs, numerals, conjunctions), and to count the frequency of noun and verb pairs, as shown in Table 18.1.

Such an approach allows us to extract and visualize the norm content. Linkage between words can be presented as a graph; relative importance of the link can be illustrated with help of connection "weights", which in the current case reflect the frequency of use of these words within the clause. Computationally this means the formation of two-way tables, consisting of nouns (in rows) and verbs (in columns) with the frequency of found word pairs the evaluative criterion. Verb and noun concordance two-way table representation can be used to capture a concentrated content of the single norm but also for the set of closely related norms or groups of norms, represented in text as a paragraphs, chapters, legal acts or even entire legislation.

Further scaling of this method toward larger sets of captured norms will bring us to more sizeable cross tables and graphs. An example of norms extracted from the Parliament Election Act of Estonia is shown in Table 18.2.

The number of words in this graph reached almost 600, and the number of links was 1081. To make it easier to read the results, it is possible to filter out the most dense, fully-connected network of keywords to create a "skeleton" of the legal act (Fig. 18.1). The graph edges represent the words and the size of edges show the degree of connection – how many different words it connects. Arcs show connections between words and the line thickness shows how many times this pair of words appeared in one clause (max. 34 times).

Extracting selected words from the text and preserving their connections for further analysis allows capturing the norm content in the range of 60–80 %. The text analyses of approximately 400 Estonian legal acts and showed that nouns and verbs account for an average content of 60 % (approx. $\frac{1}{4}$ are verbs and $\frac{3}{4}$ are nouns).

[8]The Constitution of the Republic of Estonia RT 1992, 26, 349; RT I, 27.04.2011, 2, §20.

Table 18.2 The two-way table, showing the concordance of nouns and verbs within clauses (Täks et al. 2013)

Nouns/verbs	Be/is	Submit	Carry/enter	Do	Write up	Give	Keep	Become	Organize	Think
Electoral commission	21	2	2	16	0	4	9	6	4	0
Elector	34	3	5	0	9	10	3	9	0	0
List	6	3	25	10	8	0	2	3	0	0
Appeal	4	20	0	0	0	0	0	0	0	0
Person	9	11	14	3	4	4	5	0	0	0
Day	10	0	5	8	0	0	0	2	1	27
Party	10	8	12	0	0	4	0	2	0	0
Division committee	3	4	0	4	0	0	0	0	0	0
Member	4	7	7	0	0	14	4	0	0	0
Candidate	4	1	0	1	0	2	2	2	0	0
Voter	12	1	2	1	3	4	1	2	0	0
Independent candidate	0	9	2	1	5	8	0	0	0	0
Vote	8	0	0	1	0	0	2	0	24	0
Envelope	0	0	0	0	0	0	0	0	0	0
Decision	5	0	0	10	0	0	0	0	0	0
Time	0	0	4	4	0	3	0	1	0	0
Family member	15	0	0	1	0	3	13	0	0	0

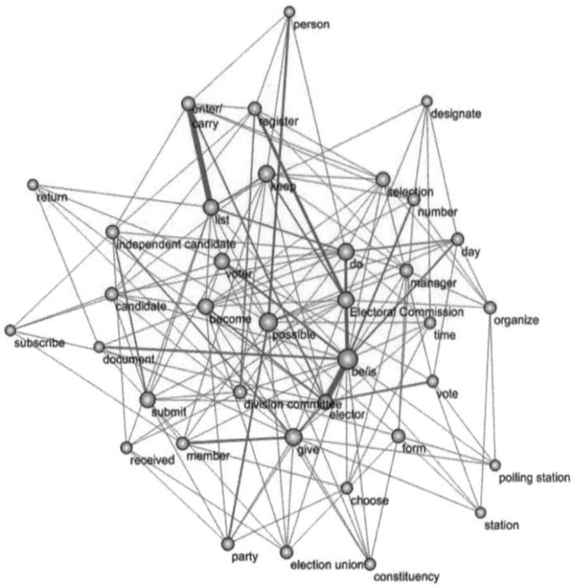

Fig. 18.1 Graph derived from verbs and nouns concordance in the clause

The percentage may vary for each individual act, but the average 60 % is achieved by excluding all unnecessary data that consists of numbers, symbols, conjunctions, adjectives, etc. Additionally, efficiency is achieved by transforming nouns and verbs into their basic forms. The Estonian language is one of the most difficult languages with its fourteen different cases, meaning that each noun can be written in fourteen different ways. Using the basic form of a noun enables to delimit it to one. The method enables to reduce the search base quantitatively more than 50 %, yet, at the same time to maintain the qualitative information carried by norms up to 80 %. The method relies on the postulate that nouns and verbs alone convey most of the valuable information contained in norms, enabling an automated analyses of legal texts in a novel way. The two-way table forms a layer above the actual legal texts, reflecting the content of it at a very high level of abstraction, is machine readable and computable with help of different mathematical methods (data mining, graph computations by machines). This presentation of information is (1) scalable – it can consolidate the norm, a subdivision, a chapter, a legal act or whole legislation; (2) computable – with help of formal tools (data mining, graph theory etc.) it can be easily analysed by computers; (3) visual – it can be presented visually for human users and deliver a high-level overview about the content of the legal document; (4) information enriched – the picture communicates the most frequent keywords in the legal artefact (as in a "word cloud") and provides information about connections between different words and characterises.

The visual representation of legal text as graphs also makes it possible to perform similarity measurements. Thus it is possible to find the use of the same noun and verb combinations (the "legal clause") within different legal instruments, and thus to perform a quantitative analysis of the legal text by applying graph theory and graph mining ideas and methods. Evaluating the similarity of two graphs is commonly referred to as graph matching, which aims to find a correspondence between the nodes and edges of two graphs that satisfies pre-defined constraints. In other words, similar substructures in one graph are mapped to similar structures in the other graph and extent of the result can be measured (Aggarwal and Wang 2010, 219).

18.5.1 A Test Using Estonian Legislation

The test is based on the doctoral dissertation by Ermo Täks, who has been working on methods of text analyses that can be used for systematization of legal norms (Täks et al. 2013). In order to fit graph matching results for specific legislation analysis techniques and perform act to act similarity measurements, an experimental fitness function was generated. The function estimated the result in three stages: how many shared verbs were found, how many shared nouns connected to specific verbs, and the frequency with which each pair was used. The general weight is a sum of shared verbs account for 45 %, shared nouns connected to specific verbs 45 %, and concordance frequency 10 %.

The particular calculation weights chosen above are still under investigation in order to tune the measurement method, but the results gained thus far already allow us to arrive at some reasonably justified conclusions.

To test the method of normative system structural analysis, we selected 386 Estonian legal acts which were randomly chosen; each legal act was compared to every other legal act (148996 comparisons).

As a result a similarity table was created, consisting of 386 rows and 386 columns. Some interesting general characteristics appeared. On average the instruments shared around 1/3 textual content (with exceptions – for example, in 167 cases (0.22 %) the compared instruments did not share any content). According to these results it can be said that there is a general overlapping between legal provisions.

In 20 cases, the similarity was measured at 80 % or higher. A control of the two most similar legal acts (Estonian Parliament Election Act and European Parliament Election Act) showed a remarkable similarity of texts including up to some parts exactly copied from one another (Fig. 18.2).

In order to present a complex connected system, it has been useful to use extreme representation principles. For our case study of Estonian legislation we applied the principle of the maximal similarity spanning tree, which has been successfully used to graph biological systems (Võhandu 1961).[9] To use this principle for our task, a

[9] Leo Võhandu was given a task to categorise living beings of nature by their characteristics. There are many different caharacteristics, for instance, giving a birth or laying eggs; flying or living in water, etc. He made a cross table with kinds of beings and their characteristics. If a being had a described characteristic, then it was marked as "1" and if a characteristic did not exist, then it was marked as "0". Such tables are hard for the human eye to process. Võhandu came up with a

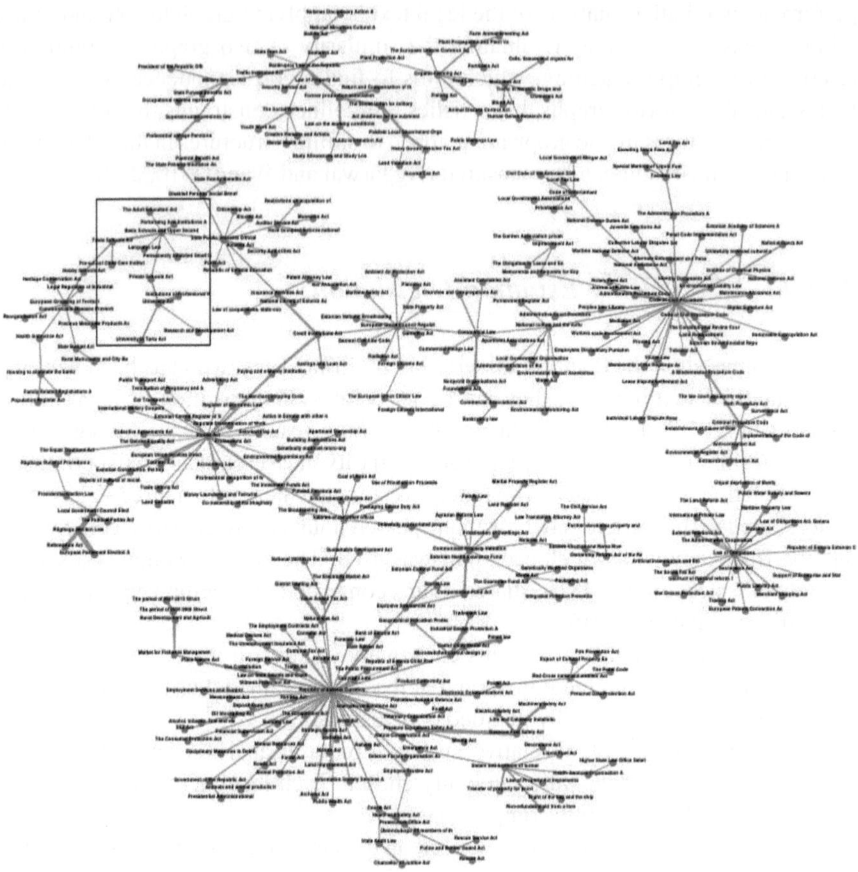

Fig. 18.2 Similarity structure of Estonian legislation, where each legal provision is connected to its most similar provision

similarity matrix of legal provisions, the maximally connected path was computed. In Fig. 18.2 every legal provision is connected to its most similar provision. The zoomed rectangular area of this graph is shown in Fig. 18.3.

To match the clauses more precisely to each other and test the ability of the method for finding exact matches between legal sources originating from different locations.

methodology how connections can be visualized by creating a maximum connectivity tree so that concentrated information spots can be visually captured.

Fig. 18.3 Extracted part of similarity structure

18.5.2 Methodological Refinement

In order to perform direct subgraph to subgraph comparisons and measure their similarity, we used the method described in the previous section and adjusted it according to the task. The developed method focused on norms (graph elements), originating from the clauses that are specific for the legal act, and compared these to each other graph element originating from other legal acts to pinpoint the related norms within different texts and to evaluate their similarity. The experimental fitness function described above was adjusted, and the concordance frequency was left out: the function estimated the result in two stages – how many shared verbs were found, and how many shared nouns connected to specific verbs.[10] The general similarity is a sum of shared verbs that account for 50 % and shared nouns connected to specific verbs that account for 50 %.

Two Acts (the Copyright Law[11] Act and Law of Obligations Act[12]) were chosen in order to test the refined method. This choice was motived by legal doctrinal research into copyright law reform. Kretschmer et al. (2010) had shown surprising and sometimes problematic dependencies between contract law and copyright law, and our approach could be one way to not only test these findings on a more abstract level for Estonian law, but also to utilize them strategically for law reform proposals. Summary characteristics of the legal acts can be found in Table 18.3.

[10]The method described earlier enables to determine similarity between different legal acts as whole, whereas now we were interested in establishing connections between legal norms of different legal acts. The similarity of legal acts as whole was discussed in Täks et al. (2011).

[11]Copyright Act RT 1992, 49, 615; RT I, 28.12.2011, 1 (hereinafter Copyright Act).

[12]Law of Obligations Act RT I 2001, 81, 487; RT I, 05.04.2013, 1 (hereinafter Law of Obligations Act).

Table 18.3 Short characteristics of Copyright Law and Law of Obligations

Legal act	Clauses	Words
The Copyright Law	818	13676
Law of Obligations	5767	93770

Table 18.4 Example of analysed legal text after indexing, estimating the type and stemming the words

Clause ID	Word ID	Words	Type	Basic form of word
97696	1231627	1	N	1
97696	1231628	kindlustusandja	S	kindlustusandja
97696	1231629	vabaneb	V	vabanema
97696	1231630	täitmise	S	täitmine
97696	1231631	kohustuseste	S	kohustus
97696	1231632	kui	J	kui
97696	1231633	kindlustusvõtja	S	kindlustusvõtja
97696	1231634	kindlustatud	V	kindlustama
97696	1231635	või	J	või
97696	1231636	soodustatud	A	soodustatud
97696	1231637	isik	S	isik
97696	1231638	põhjustas	V	põhjustam
97696	1231639	kindlustusjuhtumi	S	kindlustusjuhtum
97696	1231640	toimumise	S	toimumine
97696	1231641	tahtlikult	D	tahtlikult

Table 18.5 Example of entry from the list of elementary graphs

Clause ID	Verb ID	Basic form of verb	Noun ID	Basic form of noun
§	2636	97696	97696	§
1231629	vabanema	1231628	kindlustusandja	1231629
1231634	kindlustama	1231630	täitmine	1231634
1231638	põhjustama	1231631	kohustus	1231638
		1231633	kindlustusvõtja	
		1231637	isik	
		1231639	kindlustusjuhtum	
		1231640	toimumine	

After indexing, estimating the type and stemming the words found within legal case clause (see Table 18.4), the second stage involved separating keywords from the clauses and creating a list of elementary graphs (groups of norm specific nouns and words) together with identification information to relate them back to the legal act; (see Table 18.5). A similarity measurement according to the fitness function was performed in order to get actual similarity measurement results (see Table 18.6).

There were 32,600 cases found where the similarity between two sub graphs was higher or equal to 30 %; those were grouped based on similarity, and passed over to legal scientists to evaluate the value of the findings and usability of the results.

Table 18.6 Example of table of gained similarity measurement results

Legal act	Clause ID	Compared legal act	Law of Obligations	Law of Obligations	Law of Obligations
The Copyright Law	59894	Compared legal act clause ID	97697	97759	97836
		Similarity, %	100	35	87.5

18.5.3 Legal Analysis

All 79 links that gave a 100 % similarity were analysed. The purpose of the analyses was to understand whether the method links content which is related by some common features; or concepts that have a meaning in a legal discipline. Examples are discussed below.

Sample 1

Paragraph 14 of the Copyright Act regulates the author's right to remuneration.[13] The right to be paid for the use of author's work when author's economic rights are exercised is one of the main principles of copyright law. It is generally understood that whenever a work is used for business purposes either directly or indirectly, the author or a rightsholder should be compensated.[14] A recording reproduced and sold is a form of direct business, but listening to the radio or watching TV in a hotel room is a value-adding element incorporated into the price of the room which therefore influences the booking of rooms indirectly. Copyright law may provide exceptions as to when it is not necessary to pay for the use of a work. Generally, when a person uses a work for private purposes, for example reproducing a CD for the purpose of sharing it with family or close friends, it is not necessary to compensate the author. Exceptions derogating from the rule to pay are to be interpreted narrowly.[15] The rule to pay the author is a fundamental principle in Copyright Law.

Subsection 3 of § 14 provides that it is prohibited to use a work before agreement is made between the author, or the collective management organisation representing authors, and the user of the work. That agreement should specify the amount of remuneration and the procedure for collection and payment.[16] This subsection was linked to the second sentence "[a]ny agreement which derogates therefrom is void",

[13]Copyright Act, § 14.

[14]See e.g. C-162/10 Phonographic Performance (Ireland) limited v. Ireland; C-306/05 Sociedad General de Autores y Editores de Espana (SGAE) versus Rafael Hoteles SA.

[15]Exceptions have to conform to the three-step-test. Article 9 of the Berne Convention for the Protection of Literary and Artistic Works of 9 September 1886. Paris Act of 24 July 1971, as amended on 28 September 1979. WIPO, Geneva; § 17 of the Copyright Act.

[16] Copyright Act § 14 (3).

found in §452(1), §490(2), §677(3) and §846 of the Law of Obligations Act.[17] As an example, §452(1) of the Law of Obligations Act provides that an insurer is not obliged to perform if the insured person intentionally caused the occurrence of the insured event.[18] This is followed by the clause "Any agreement which derogates therefrom is void".[19] This is one of the fundamental principles of insurance law. The derogation is not possible because it would lead to a conflict of norms. If the derogation were possible, it would mean that the insured person would be compensated for the commission of crime, because the intentionally caused event constitutes insurance fraud.[20] The possibility of the conflict between the Law of Obligations Act and the Penal Law Act is excluded by the imperative norm stating that it is not possible to make an agreement contrary to this principle.

Similarly, if the work is used without permission of the author it can be a criminal act under the Penal Law Act.[21] It is imperative that the agreement has to be reached.

Sample 2

Copyright law regulates the ownership of copyright-protected works created under an employer-employee relationship. If the employment contract is silent on the transfer of the author's economic rights, then the general principle presumes that it transfers to the employer. This follows from the idea that the investor is entitled to the fruits of his or her investment. The purpose of this rule is to provide legal certainty, because copyright is not covered in most employment contracts. Yet, an employer and employee are always free contractually to regulate the transfer of copyright differently from the default principle. Similarly, the producer becomes the owner of the author's economic rights in an audio-visual work because the transfer of rights is presumed by law. The transfer of rights is often a practicality necessary for the investor to be able to manage the business related to the work. §14(6) of the Copyright Act regulates the author's right to remuneration after the transfer of economic rights has been agreed by contract or presumed by law.[22] According to

---

[17]Law of Obligations Act, §§452 (1); 490 (2); 677 (3); 846.

[18]Ibid. §452 (1).

[19]Ibid.

[20]Penal Code RT I 2001,61,364; RT I 29.12.2011,1, §212."§212. Insurance fraud(1) A person who intentionally brings about an insured event or causes a misconception of the occurrence of an insured event with the intention to receive an insurance indemnity from the insurer shall be punished by a pecuniary punishment or up to 5 years imprisonment.(2) The same act, if committed by a legal person, is punishable by a pecuniary punishment."

[21]Ibid. §223. "§223. Unlawful direction of works or objects of related rights towards public (1) Unlawful public performance, showing, transmission, re-transmission or making available to the public or a work or an object of related rights for commercial purposes is punishable by a pecuniary punishment or up to one year of imprisonment. (2) The same act, if performed by using a pirated copy, is punishable by a pecuniary punishment or up to 3 years imprisonment. (3) An act provided for in subsection (1) or (2) of this section, if committed by a legal person, is punishable by a pecuniary punishment. (4) The court shall confiscate the object which was the direct object of the offence provided for in subsection (2) of this section."

[22]Copyright Act §14 (6).

this subsection, although the producer of the audio-visual work may become the sole owner of the economic rights, the author still retains the right to equitable remuneration. The producer has the sole right to decide about the reproduction, adaptation and publication of the work, but if proceeds are made as a result of these decisions then the author is entitled to receive the equitable share. The same applies in relation to rental of phonograms, under § 14(7) of the Copyright Act.

Both subsections provide that "[a]n agreement to waive the right to obtain equitable remuneration is void".[23] These subsections were connected to the provisions of §452(1), §490(2), §672, §677(3) and §846 of the Law of Obligations Act by the sentence "Any agreement which derogates therefrom is void".[24]

Sample 3

Furthermore, according to §67(1) of the Copyright Act "[a] performer has the exclusive right to use and to authorise or prohibit the use of the performance of a work and to obtain, for such use, remuneration agreed upon by the parties except in the cases prescribed by this Act and an agreement between the parties".[25] This subsection was linked to the provisions of §452(1), §490(2), §677(3), and §846 of the Law of Obligations Act by the sentence "Any agreement which derogates therefrom is void".[26] It is imperative that agreement be reached on how exclusive rights are used and remunerated under Copyright law, because the breach of these principles is criminalised.

Sample 4

§32(1) of the Copyright Act provides that the author shall enjoy copyright in works created under an employment contract or while in public service, but the economic rights shall be transferred to the employer unless otherwise agreed by contract.[27] This subsection is linked to §8(2) of the Law of Obligations, which provides that "[a] contract is binding on parties".[28] Although the norm is dispositional, the presumption of transfer of economic rights prescribed in copyright law is an important exception, because it is not evident that on the basis of general principles of contract law parties should transfer rights automatically without any communication of the intent to do so. *Pacta sunt servanda* is the moral imperative in contract law, but as a norm it is dispositional, in the sense that parties are free to decide upon conditions of withdrawal from a contract. Both principles allow derogations provided that parties describe the transfer of the author's economic rights in a contract differently from the default rule of copyright law.

---

[23]Ibid.

[24]Law of Obligations Act, §§452 (1); 490 (2); 672; 677 (3); 846.

[25]Copyright Act, §67 (1).

[26]Law of Obligations Act, §§452 (1); 490 (2); 677 (3); 846.

[27]Copyright Act, §32 (1).

[28]Law of Obligations Act, §8 (2).

The experiment has thus given us preliminary results, which must be further analysed. The extent to which this method identifies all imperative norms contained in the Copyright Act and the Law of Obligations Act is an open question, because it only analyses links of 100 % similarity, and there is no research material indicating the number of imperative norms contained in those Acts. No definite result, which could only be calculated, based on such a comparison, can therefore at this point be stated. It can be said that 82.3 % of the 79 links that rendered 100 % similarity have a connection that has a legally significant meaning, according to the legal analysis.

18.6 Conclusion and Future Work

What have we achieved so far? We began our study by identifying a need: To mirror the success of AI applications for legal reasoning and the application of law, the development of AI approaches for legal drafting and the creation of law also ought to be grounded in a sound philosophical analysis of this activity. But while there are plenty of jurisprudential theories of legal reasoning, law making has attracted comparatively little interest by legal (as opposed to political) theorist. Luc Wintgens' "legisprudence" explained not only how this "blind spot" of legal theory was the inevitable consequence of a conception of law that gained prominence in eighteenth century Europe, but also how this limitation can be overcome. His proposal develops a number of parameters, tests in the form of general rules, that any proposed piece of legislation should pass as a bare minimum condition for "good" legislation.

In the next step, we discussed how Wintgens' parameters could be translated into a computational format. Much of their substantive content cannot currently be captured and requires human judgment. Nonetheless, it is possible to render some knowledge intensive sub-tasks into an algorithmic format, which then in turn can assist the human decision maker. The greatest amount of "added value" of a computational version of Wintgens' legisprudence addresses one of the main problems of modern legal systems: the considerable growth in the quantity of laws is causing an even greater increase in the complexity of legal systems. The reason for this, so we argued with Wintgens, is the systemic nature of laws. A legal system is not just a set of individual and isolated rules. Rather, individual rules are best understood as "component parts", little machines or sub-routines that have to work together with other parts of the legal system to complete their task. Sometimes, the interdependence of individual legal provisions and acts is known by the legislator and a conscious design feature. In this case, we often find explicit cross-references between individual acts. However, the organic growth of legal systems, and the limits of legal language (such as the limited vocabulary that inevitably means that very different laws will have to use identical terms), means that in addition to these explicit and intended connections, laws will also have a multitude of possible connections to other pieces of legislation. While these often remain dormant, they can in principle be used one day by a lawyer for an argument by analogy. The interpretative trope of the "unity of the legal system"[29] enables the use of the interpretation of a term in one piece of legislation as a heuristic device to determine its meaning in another context. The speed and quantity of growth in legislation, coupled with the implicit and indirect nature of these links, makes it difficult or even impossible for a human to anticipate all the ways in which the legal system as a whole might change as a result of new legislation.

We used methods from natural language processing, information retrieval and visualization to make these unintended and implicit links as visible as the explicit cross references between laws. Using copyright law as an example, the links revealed by this method suggest that it is possible to pinpoint imperative norms and some core principles important to the Estonian Copyright Law and Law of Obligations Acts which are not "obvious" or linked through explicit citations. As a proof of concept the analysis fulfills the tasks that we set ourselves in the introduction. It allows the legislator to identify "hidden" connections between laws.

The result is what we called a "Copyright Law Reform Observatory". It allows lawmakers and law users to predict, how suggested changes to the law will affect the entire system at various levels of granularity – zooming in on copyright law, zooming out to see the network of intellectual property in general, or taking an even wider look, at private law or the entire legal system. Different reform proposals can be added to the system, and their respective impact compared. This can assist lawmakers in several different ways. The degree of connection between laws is a proxy of what Wintgens' termed normative density. Making the hidden connections visible can thus work as a heuristic to reduce PA and identify non-obvious alternatives for legislative reform that may be less intrusive on citizens" freedom. For example, by creating enabling norms in contract law, we may be able to avoid sanction-introducing norms in copyright law, thus maximizing individual freedom while achieving the same economic objective. Second, it allows to balance the amount of new legislation against the intended change in the legal system. Norms that are particularly well connected to the rest of the legal system are candidates for reform when a larger field of law is deemed to be "broken" and not resolving societal conflicts in the desirable way. Changing these norms carries comparatively lower costs for the legislative process, while effecting maximal change for the entire legal system, the equivalent we argued of removing the head of a criminal gang. Norms at the periphery, with only a limited number of connections, are in contrast candidates for reform when very specific are technical problems need to be resolved. In this case, changing laws that impact on the wider system are unnecessarily disruptive and as a result create unnecessary legal uncertainty, and with that costs for the justice system and the economy.

Once a suitable law as a target for reform has been identified, different formulations of the suggested replacement can be added to the database. Depending on the vocabulary tha was used, each of them will create its own new set of connections.

[29]In particular in continental legal systems such as German law explicitly recognized as a method of interpretation. See e.g. Rüthers and Fischer (2010), at 147a.

Taking Wintgens' Principle of Coherence as a starting point and placing the notion of a legal system at the heart of our analysis, the resulting graphs can alert the legislator to unforeseen consequences of legislative reform, for example if a change in definition in one part of the system can also impact on word meaning in an apparently unrelated part. This helps to maintain overall coherence and helps to identify possibly unwanted consequences.

Conversely, practicing lawyers can use CoREO to estimate just how much their business will be affected by a proposed law reform It provides an "at a glance" view of dependency pathways and the ways in which a specific reform can impact on the legal system as a whole. One benefit is to identify training needs. The other is to help with the management of legacy contracts. This functionality is of particular importance for inhouse lawyers, for instance in the creative industries. It flags up indirect changes in the legal system that may require to revisit or reword contracts that were drafted before the law reform was put into place. By triaging the likely impact that a proposed change will have – focusing on those laws where the path to the specific reform under consideration is shortest first, a cost efficient process of revision can be implemented.

In the future, apart from evaluating larger segments of Estonian regulation, we hope to combine this method with citation analysis tools to see in greater detail how explicit and implicit interconnection between norms can be data mined to assist the legislative process, and to bring our proxies closer to the semantic content of Wintgens' four principles of rational legisprudence. Secondly we hope to incorporate also case law. Especially cases where the court sanctioned analogous argumentation impact on the way in which legal provisions are linked with each other. While our system at present models all possible links, a different form of visualization, for instance through color coding, could be devised to highly those pathways that in an argument by analogy have already received legal recognition. Finally, the Principle of Temporality should become focus of further research. CoReO at present depicts a static snapshot of a legal system. By incorporating explicitly a time dimension, it should be possible to visualize in a dynamic display how the various linkages in a legal system change over time, and in this way affect the topology of the legal order. The result, we hope, will be a practical computational tool that assists both legislators and the subjects of legislation, while being at the same time deeply rooted in jurisprudential analysis.

References

Aggarwal, Charu C., and Haixun Wang. 2010. *Managing and mining graph data*, vol. 40. New York: Springer.

Aitken, Gary. 1997. The law of BSE. *Journal of the Law Society of Scotland* 42:17–20.

Bankowski, Zenon. 1993. Don't think about it legalism and legality. *Rechtstheorie. Beiheft* 15: 27–45.

Becchetti, Leonardo, David Andres, Londono Bedoya, and Luigi Paganetto. 2003. ICT investment, productivity and efficiency: Evidence at firm level using a stochastic frontier approach. *Journal of Productivity Analysis* 20(2):143–167.

Beger, Gabriele. 2010. Open Access und die dritte Reform des Urheberrechts in der Informationsgesellschaft. *PIK-Praxis der Informationsverarbeitung und Kommunikation* 33(3):185–186.

Berman, Donald H., and Carol Hafner. 1989. The potential of artificial intelligence to help solve the crisis in our legal system. *Communications of the ACM* 32(8):928–938.

Blichner, Lars Chr, and Anders Molander. 2008. Mapping juridification. *European Law Journal* 14(1):36–54.

Bommarito II, Michael J., and Daniel M. Katz. 2010. A mathematical approach to the study of the united states code. *Physica A: Statistical Mechanics and Its Applications* 389(19): 4195–4200.

Boose, John H. 1989. A survey of knowledge acquisition techniques and tools. *Knowledge Acquisition* 1(1):3–37.

Boulet, Romain, Pierre Mazzega, and Daniéle Bourcier. 2011. A network approach to the French system of legal codes–part I: Analysis of a dense network. *Artificial Intelligence and Law* 19(4):333–355.

Brady, James B., and Newton Garver, ed. 1991. *Justice, law, and violence*. Philadelphia: Temple University Press.

Brazier, Margaret. 1997. Hard cases make bad law? *Journal of Medical Ethics* 23(6):341–343.

Breuker, Joost, Emil Petkov, and Radboud Winkels. 2000. Drafting and validating regulations: The inevitable use of intelligent tools. In *Artificial intelligence: Methodology, systems, and applications*, 21–33. Heidelberg: Springer.

Chikofsky, Elliot J., and James H. Cross. 1990. Reverse engineering and design recovery: A taxonomy. *IEEE Software* 7(1):13–17.

Cohen, Julius. 1949–1950. Towards realism in legisprudence. *The Yale Law Journal* 59:886–897.

Cover, Robert. M. 1986. Violence and the word. *Yale Law Journal* 95:1601–1629.

Davis, Lewis Anthony. 1981. Review procedures and public accountability in sunset legislation: An analysis and proposal for reform. *Administrative Law Review* 33(4):393–413.

Deazley, Ronan. 2010. Copyright and parody: Taking backward the Gowers review?. *The Modern Law Review* 73(5):785–807.

Finn, John E. 2009. Sunset clauses and democratic deliberation: Assessing the significance of sunset provisions in antiterrorism legislation. *Columbia Journal of Transnational Law* 48:442.

Forester, Tom, ed. 1985. *The information technology revolution*. Cambridge: MIT Press.

Fuller, Lon L. 1969. *The morality of law*. Yale: Yale University Press.

Hafner, Carole D., and Marc Lauritsen. 2007. Extending the power of automated legal drafting technology. In *Proceedings of the 2007 conference on legal knowledge and information systems: JURIX 2007: The twentieth annual conference*, 59–68. Amsterdam: IOS Press.

Hargeraves, Ian. 2011. Digital opportunity: A review of intellectual property and growth. Available at http://www.ipo.gov.uk/ipreview-finalreport.pdf.

Hart, Herbert L.A. 1957. Positivism and the separation of law and morals. *Harvard Law Review* 71:615–621.

Hoekstra, Rinke, Alexander Boer, Radboud Winkels, and Tom M. van Engers. 2003. Knowledge management for legislative drafting in an international setting. In *Legal knowledge and information systems: Jurix 2003: The sixteenth annual conference*, 91–100. Amsterdam: IOS Press.

Hunyadi, Mark. 1995. *La vertu du conflit. Pour une morale de la médiation*. Paris: Cerf.

Hutchins, Christopher E., and Marge Benham-Hutchins. 2010. Hiding in plain sight: Criminal network analysis. *Computational and Mathematical Organization Theory* 16(1):89–111.

Kim, Rakhyun E. 2013. The emergent network structure of the multilateral environmental agreement system. *Global Environmental Change* 23(5):980–991.

Kretschmer, Martin. 2008. Creativity stifled? A joint academic statement on the proposed copyright term extension for sound recordings. *European Intellectual Property Review* 30(9): 341–374.

Kretschmer, Martin, and Ruth Towse, ed. 2013. *What constitutes evidence for copyright policy? Digital proceedings of ESRC symposium.* www.copyrightevidence.org/create/esrc-evidence-symposium.

Kretschmer, Martin., Estelle Derclaye, Marcella Favale, and Richard Watt. 2010. The relationship between copyright and contract law: A review commissioned by the UK strategic advisory board for intellectual property policy (SABIP) (172pp). Available at: http://www.ipo.gov.uk/ipresearch.

Kysar, Rebecca. 2011. Lasting legislation. *University of Pennsylvania Law Review* 159:101.

Lessig, Lawrence. 1996. The zones of cyberspace. *Stanford Law Review* 48(5):1403–1411.

Lessig, Lawrence. 1999. *Code and other laws of cyberspace*. New York: Basic Books.

McCarty, L. Thorne. 1980. The TAXMAN project: Towards a cognitive theory of legal argument. In *Computer science and law: An advanced course*, ed. B. Nesbit, 23-43. Cambridge: Cambridge University Press.

Mendis, Dinousha, and Martin Kretschmer. 2013. The treatment of parodies under copyright law in seven jurisdictions: A comparative review of the underlying principles. Intellectual property office available at http://www.ipo.gov.uk/ipresearch-parody-report2-150313.pdf.

O'Leary, Daniel E. 1998. Enterprise knowledge management. *Computer* 31(3):54–61.

Örücü, Esin. 1987. An exercise on the internal logic of legal systems. *Legal Studies* 7(3): 310–318.

Palmirani, Monica. 2010. Legislative change management with Akoma-Ntoso. In *Legislative XML for the Semantic Web*, 101–130. Dordrecht: Springer Netherlands.

Patry, William. 2012. *How to fix copyright*. Oxford: Oxford University Press.

Rüthers, Bernd, and Christian Fischer. 2010. *Rechtstheorie: Begriff, Geltung und Anwendung des Rechts*. München: Beck.

Samuelson, Pamela. 2013. Is copyright reform possible? *Harvard Law Review* 126:740–779.

Sarat, Austin, ed. 2001. *Law, violence, and the possibility of justice*. Princeton: Princeton University Press.

Sarat, Austin, and Thomas R. Kearns, ed. 1992. *Law's violence*. Ann Arbor: University of Michigan Press.

Schwartz, Daniel M., and Tony D.A. Rouselle. 2009. Using social network analysis to target criminal networks. *Trends in Organized Crime* 12(2):188–207.

Sergot, Marek J., et al. 1986. The British nationality act as a logic program. *Communications of the ACM* 29(5):370–386.

Shklar, Judith N. 1964. *Legalism: Law, morals, and political trials*. Cambridge, MA: Harvard University Press.

Sommerville, Ian, and Gerald Kotonya. 1998. *Requirements engineering: Processes and techniques*. Hoboken: Wiley.

Staudt, Ronald W. 2008. All the wild possibilities: Technology that attacks barriers to access to justice. *Loyola of Los Angeles Law Review* 42:1117–1146.

Swierczek, Fredric William, Pritam K. Shrestha, and Clemens Bechter. 2005. Information technology, productivity and profitability in Asia-Pacific Banks. *Journal of Global Information Technology Management* 8(1):6–26.

Täks, Ermo, et al. 2011. An experiment to find the deep structure of Estonian legislation. In *Legal knowledge and information systems: Jurix 2011*, ed. Katie M. Atkinson, 93–102. Amsterdam/New York: IOS Press.

Täks, Ermo, Rein Kuusik, and Katrin Merike Nyman-Metcalf. 2013. *An automated legal content capture and visualisation method*. Tallinn: Tallinn University Press.

Tehranian, John. 2007. Infringement nation: Copyright reform and the law/norm gap. *Utah Law Review* 3:537–550.

Teubner, Gunther. 1987. Concepts, aspects, limits, solutions. In *Juridification of social spheres: A comparative analysis of labour corporate government: Trust and social welfare law*, ed. Gunther Teubner, 3–48. New York: de Gruyter.

Thoreau, Henry D. 1849. (republished 2012). *Civil disobedience and other essays*. Mineola: Courier Dover.

Towse, Ruth. 2011. What we know, what we don't know and what policy-makers would like us to know about the economics of copyright. *Review of Economic Research on Copyright Issues* 8:101–120.

Voermans, Wim, Luuk Matthijssen, and Egon Verharen. 1997. Legimatics in Europe: The LEDA-project. *New Review of Applied Expert Systems* 3:155–167.

Voermans, Wim J.M., Remco Van Wijk, and Welmoed Fokkema. 2012. Free the legislative process of its paper chains: IT-inspired redesign of the legislative procedure. In *Public administration in the information age: Revisited*, ed. I.Th.M. Snellen, M. Thaens, and Van De Donk, 237–251. Amsterdam: IOS Press.

Võhandu, Leo. K. 1961. Analysis of biological systems with many variables. In *III conference of mathematical methods in biology*, 19–22. Leningrad: Leningrad University Press.

Winkels, Radboud, and Nienke Den Haan. 1995. Automated legislative drafting: Generating paraphrases of legislation. In *Proceedings of the 5th international conference on artificial intelligence and law*, 112–118. New York: ACM.

Wintgens, Luc J. 2006. Legisprudence as a new theory of legislation. *Ratio Juris* 19(1):1–25.

Xu, Jennifer J., and Hsinchun Chen. 2005. CrimeNet explorer: A framework for criminal network knowledge discovery. *ACM Transactions on Information Systems (TOIS)* 23(2):201–226.

Chapter 19
Legal Knowledge Modeling for Managing Legislation in the Semantic Web

Enrico Francesconi

Abstract Regulation quality and accessibility are essential requirements to guarantee a transparent policy making framework, thus promoting democracy, certainty of rights and participation of citizens in the decision-making process. In particular European Union policies about eGovernment call for high level Information and Communication Technologies (ICT) solutions for promoting a more transparent, participatory and accountable decision-making process. Legal knowledge modeling can represent a pre-condition for meeting such requirements; at the same time the Semantic Web can provide the background of principles and tools allowing the implementation of advanced legislative drafting processes in mono and multilingual domains, as well as retrieval and reasoning services on legislation. This paper will investigate such issues according to semantic and logic profiles of legal texts, as well as possible technical implementations of such services.

Keywords eGovernment • Legal knowledge modeling • Semantic Web • Legal drafting • Legal information retrieval

19.1 Introduction

Over the past decades the EU has developed a sophisticated regulatory environment as essential pre-condition to support the economic growth, stimulate competitiveness in business, facilitate social development, as well as to guarantee democracy. Regulation quality and accessibility in the EU multilingual environment, as well as a transparent decision and policy making framework, are essential requirements for achieving these objectives.

Such policies have been outlined and promoted by the European Commission in specific guidelines for EU eGovernment policies, in particular in the Action

E. Francesconi (✉)
ITTIG-CNR (Institute of Legal Information Theory and Techniques of the National Research Council of Italy), Florence, Italy
e-mail: enrico.francesconi@publications.europa.eu; francesconi@ittig.cnr.it

M. Araszkiewicz, K. Płeszka (eds.), *Logic in the Theory and Practice of Lawmaking*, Legisprudence Library 2, DOI 10.1007/978-3-319-19575-9_19

Plan 2006–2011 (COM(2006) 173 final) based on the Manchester Declaration,[1] renewed in the subsequent Action Plan 2011–2015 (COM(2010) 743 final), based on the Malmö Declaration.[2] Both plans share a main common objective: providing citizens and businesses with eGovernment transparent services designed around users' needs, as well as promoting the democratic participation of citizens in the decision-making process.

On the other hand, the need of regulation quality has been specifically addressed in the so-called "better regulation" key-documents of the European Commission.

At first the Mandelkern Report on Better Regulation (2001) identified the main requirements for a successful better regulation programme in the simplicity, clarity and accessibility of EU provisions, in the consultation of interested parties by EU and national policymakers, as well as in the implementation of regulatory impact assessment policies, allowing that decisions are taken with clear knowledge of the evidence.

In 2010, with the communication on "Smart Regulation in the European Union" (COM(2010) 543 final), the EU Commission aimed to "close the cycle" from better to smart regulation. Such communication presents the measures to improve the whole policy cycle: from the design to implementation, enforcement, evaluation and revision of a piece of legislation. Moreover, it stresses the shared responsibility of EU institutions and Member States in promoting quality and accessibility in regulation, as well as the need of opening EU policy making to stakeholders.

In 2012, with the communication on EU Regulatory Fitness, the EU Commission has outlined the "Regulatory fitness and performance programme" (REFIT) (COM(2012 746 final) to achieve a "simple, clear, stable and predictable regulatory framework for businesses, workers and citizens". Such programme firstly aims to review EU regulation, in particular to detect regulatory burdens, gaps and inefficiencies; to identify opportunities for simplification; to enable the Commission to propose that Council and Parliament revise or repeal legislation where appropriate. The aim of the REFIT programme is to simplify EU laws and making them clearer and easier to understand, thus reducing possible regulatory burden related to how EU legislation is implemented at the national and sub-national level. This can be achieved by deploying different tools in Smart Regulation policy for impact assessment and evaluation of EU regulatory measures, as well as by promoting the consultation of citizens and stakeholders in the policy cycle.

The development of such eGovernment tools were promoted by the EU Commission since 2006 within the eParticipation initiative[3] aimed at developing and using Information and Communication Technologies in the legislative decision-making processes. The aim of such initiative was to foster the quality of the legislative

[1]24 November 2005, Manchester, UK. http://www.epractice.eu/en/library/281737 (Retrieved on 7 June 2014).

[2]http://ec.europa.eu/digital-agenda/sites/digital-agenda/files/ministerial-declaration-on-egovernment-malmo.pdf (Retrieved on 7 June 2014).

[3]https://ec.europa.eu/digital-agenda/en/eparticipation (Retrieved on 7 June 2014).

production, to enhance accessibility and alignment of legislation at European level, as well as to promote awareness and democratic participation of citizens to the legislative process.

This paper will describe some projects developed within the eParticipation framework and will propose an integrated solution aligned with the more recent policies of better and smart regulation, able to approach all the phases of the EU multilingual law-making process (proposal, drafting, debate), as well as foster a wider, more informed and collaborative participation in the law-making debate, reconnecting citizens and decision-makers in the democratic game.

19.2 Background

Within the eParticipation initiative several projects have been launched with the aim to promote transparency of the law making procedures.

The DALOS project[4] aimed at ensuring that legal drafters and decision-makers have control over the legal language at national and European level, by providing law-makers with linguistic and knowledge management tools, in a multi language domain, to be used in the legislative processes (Francesconi et al. 2010). In the DALOS project the lexical complexity of European law is faced by an ontological approach, by which it is possible to characterize the conceptual meaning of lexical units,[5] as well as to provide a detailed description of the semantic properties of the related concepts and their relationships. Within the SEAL project, on the other hand, some editors for legislative drafting and amending have been fine-tuned and tested. These editors included MetaVex (developed by the Leibniz Center for Law of the University of Amsterdam (van de Ven et al. 2007)), xmLegesEditor[6] (developed by ITTIG-CNR (Agnoloni et al. 2007)), and NormaEditor (developed by CIRSFID, Univ. of Bologna (Palmirani and Benigni 2007)). Such editors implement national XML[7] standards that are compliant with CEN MetaLex, the European legislative XML standard defined as a CEN recommendation (Boer et al. 2009). Implementing specific XML standards means that, by using such editors, the users are guided to produce legal documents with a well-defined structure, which is described by specific national XML schema representing the content organization of a particular typology of documents. xmLegesEditor has also implemented the semantic resources created in DALOS for supporting multilingual legislative drafting: the drafters in fact have the possibility to browse the DALOS ontological structure, in order to choose a specific concept to be used in a new text, having

[4]http://www.dalosproject.eu

[5]The notion of conceptual meaning of a lexical unit derives from linguistic semantics and represents the specification of the meaning of a term (simple or complex because represented by one or more words, respectively) by its belonging to a synset (class of synonyms) or ontology class.

[6]http://www.xmleges.org

[7]XML (eXtensible Markup Language) is a standard syntax to describe contents.

support to select the term (simple or complex) expressing such concept in different languages. Moreover, in SEAL a prototype of a legislative content management and workflow system has been developed as well, which aims to complete the functionalities of the DALOS drafting environment. In particular functions for managing the amendments of a new bill under debate are provided.

The outcomes of both DALOS and SEAL projects have been tested by both Italian and Dutch Parliaments, as well as by legal drafters at the Catalan Parliament as regards the Spanish case. DALOS focused on enhancing the quality of legislative texts in a multilingual environment, while SEAL supported the process of legal drafting and workflow, but did not have multi-language support. The developed services and semantic solutions were tested to assess the production of EU regulation as well as the legislative workflow support. In particular the projects were able to simplify the EU regulatory environment, as well as to rationalise the transposition of Community legislation into national laws, assessed by legal experts and citizens. As regards the services provided by the two projects (multilingual semantic tools provided by DALOS and legislation amending facilities and workflow management provided by SEAL) users perceived the new tools as a good step forward to guarantee a higher quality level in the production of legislative texts, especially when they are the results of the transposition of the European legislation. Tests revealed good results in the amendment support as well, since such service has actually been implemented on xmLegesEditor within the SEAL project, and it was the matter of the SEAL test, jointly carried on. In Table 19.1 the overall results of the DALOS-SEAL joint test, regarding about 25 users, are reported.

As regards the test of the projects outcomes carried out by citizens, two aspects were validated, namely increase in comprehension and increase in retrieval. A test was realised in order to assess the benefits that the joint DALOS and SEAL solutions might have produced, by describing documents using CEN Metalex compliant standards, as well using the DALOS ontological resource to provide multilingual tagging and retrieval facilities. An increase of the retrieval performances were obtained by querying CEN Metalex XML versions of documents, tagged with the DALOS ontology rather than the plain text ones. Such retrieval performances enhancement was deemed as a good index of better content comprehension as well, since such enhancement is an index of how users are able to better express their information needs by using the available semantic tools in relation to the document contents.

Table 19.1 Average ratings of the DALOS-SEAL joint test

	Very good (%)	Good (%)	Same (%)	Poor (%)	Very poor (%)	N/A (%)	Total (%)
Drafting	46.40	43.15	7.30	2.25	0.00	0.90	100.00
Amending	35.30	53.90	7.50	2.20	0.00	1.10	100.00
Assessing	36.95	51.05	9.80	1.45	0.00	0.70	100.00
Implementing	71.65	28.35	0.00	0.00	0.00	0.00	100.00
Overall rating	47.57	44.12	6.15	1.48	0.00	0.69	100.00

19.3 An Integrated Solution for Multilingual Law-Making

Stemming from DALOS and SEAL strictly interrelated projects of the eParticipation preparatory action, an integrated solution can be foreseen, aimed to improve the quality of the law-making process (proposal, formation, debate, approval of new bills) in a multilingual environment, as well as to promote a direct participation of citizens in the democratic game, by providing effective and collaborative tools for law-making stakeholders, enhancing transparency and accessibility of the decision-making process.

In this respect the solution here proposed provides a multilingual legislative drafting environment able to harmonize legal concepts at EU level, improve clarity and accessibility of legislative texts, facilitate transposition of EU regulation into national laws, implement detailed semantic annotations of legislative texts (specifying links, concepts, functions of provisions, etc.), at a very early stage of the drafting process.

Moreover, a collaborative platform is foreseen for stimulating the interaction of all stakeholders in the decision making through the semantic information embedded in, or associated with, legislation. For example citizens will be able to selectively retrieve bills, visualise semantically related text fragments, enrich them with comments, make proposals for changes, and express specific ratings (Fig. 19.1). The envisaged solution represents a step forward in managing the legislative process and, potentially, can give a dramatic contribution to citizens enhancing their deep understanding of the European regulatory system in a multilingual environment. In particular it can represent an important opportunity for the EU to build a stronger

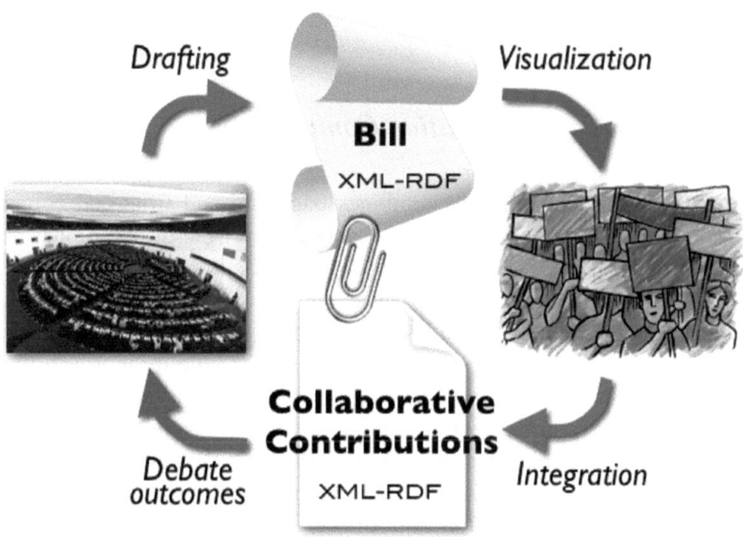

Fig. 19.1 The scenario

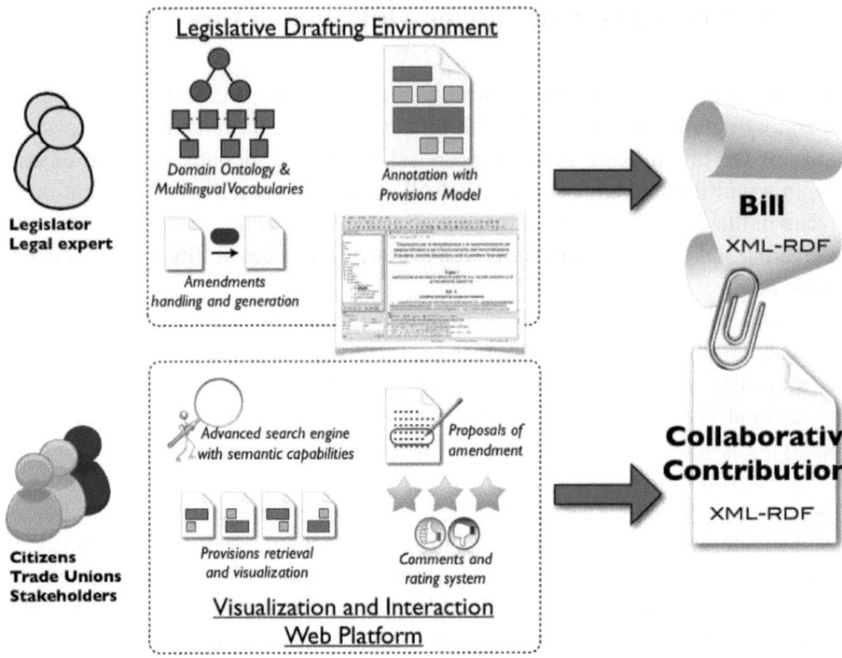

Fig. 19.2 The components of the integrated law-making environment

relationship between citizens and public institutions by empowering citizens to take a more active role in public services and to improve their participation in EU policy and decision-making processes.

19.3.1 The Integrated Solution Components

The proposed integrated solution combines back-end and front-end components with respect to the legislative production, able to cover the different phases of the legislative process, as well as to involve the different actors of the democratic game: decision-makers, legal drafters and citizens.

The back-end components include (Fig. 19.2):

First, a multilingual linguistic-ontological resource able to approach the complexity of European law during the legislative drafting phase, so to avoid terminological inconsistencies in EU legislation and misalignments in the transposition of EU Directives into national laws, as well as to classify new bills.

Second, a semantic model for EU legislation, able to provide content oriented annotation of provisions (Biagioli and Grossi 2008), classifying them according to provision types (as for example: Definition, Duty, Right, Prohibition, Sanction, Competence, etc., as well as Insertion, Substitution, Repeal), and provision attributes, namely the roles of the entities which a provision type applies to (for example the Bearer of a Duty), in conjunction to the multilingual linguistic-ontological resource, previously mentioned, able to provide a language independent characterization, as well as their lexicalizations in a multilanguage environment, of such entities.

Third, a legislative drafting environment allowing law-makers to draft new bills and to manage the structure and the semantics in a standardized format and in a multilingual environment at the very early stage of the European and national legislative processes.

The front-end component will include (Fig. 19.2):

A collaborative platform (basically a content management systems, endowed with indexing and search facilities) allowing both law-makers and citizens, according to a proper authorization scheme, to: access legislation during the law-making process by using the same semantic and cross-language facilities used during the drafting phase; obtain intuitive, effective and focused views on pieces of legislation, selected according to structural and semantic point of views; provide comments, suggestions, modifications and rating on legislation fragments.

As for the provisions semantic annotation, a provisions types and attributes model (Biagioli and Grossi 2008) can be used to qualify legislative text fragments. For example, the following text fragment:

> The supplier shall communicate to the consumer all the contractual terms and conditions and the information referred to in Article 3(1) and Article 4 on paper or on another durable medium available and accessible to the consumer in good time before the consumer is bound by any distance contract or offer.

besides being considered as a formal partition (a paragraph) of the related EU directive, can also be viewed as a semantic component (a provision) and qualified as a Duty, whose attributes, expressed as parameters in a functional notation:

hasDutyBearer = "Supplier"
hasDutyObject = "Contractual terms and conditions . . . "
hasDutyAction = "Communication"
hasDutyCounterpart = "Consumer"

Provisions, in this context, are semantic objects which a legislative text is made of; they are usually represented by legislative text paragraphs or sentences.

Such semantics can be used to implement advanced access and reasoning services to legislation in terms of provisions (for example to retrieve all the Duties of the Supplier, as well as the Rights where the Supplier is Counterpart which are actually Duties of the Supplier himself) (Francesconi 2014).

19.3.2 The Envisaged Usage of the Service

The back-end solution can be used by legislative drafting offices to approach the complexity of the law-making, and in particular of the legislative drafting process.

The back-end solution will be able to produce structured and semantically annotated legislative documents in semantic Web native formats at a very early stage of the document management and workflow. To this aim a legislative editor (for example an integrated solution from the editor developed and tested within DALOS and SEAL projects) can be conceived: the editor will provide all the necessary facilities to approach the drafting process (new bill proposal, debate, changes, approval) exploiting the potentialities of Semantic Web standards, as defined for the legal domain within the previously mentioned projects, as well as in the CEN Metalex pan-European initiative, without the need for the users to know the technical details of the document standards actually used. With this service the drafters are guided to draft a new bill according to the structural (organization of a legislative text in terms of articles and paragraphs) and semantic (medatata) requirements, without specific knowledge of the technical aspects of such specifications. For example such tools will prohibit the inclusion of an article in another one, while they allow the inclusion of a paragraph in an article.

The front-end solution gives the possibility of a growing interaction between lawmakers, legal drafters and citizens. If and when required, the discussion on new bills can start as soon as a first draft becomes available, allowing an early involvement of the stakeholders, or discussions between drafters, which will also help to identify possible problems on a new bill at an early stage. These discussions can also contribute to expand the knowledge base around the legal documents and, under an appropriate authorization scheme, upgrading the multilingual domain ontology.

The envisaged service will allow the implementation of an increased amount of enhanced services for citizens, like providing intuitive views and access to documents under debate, in order to improve their interaction within the decision-making process. Participants in the discussion will be able to attach notes to textual sections. Clear distinction of the target text will be possible due to the structured format in which a text is natively[8] drafted. To further facilitate the discussion, these notes can be classified as to their role in the discussion. Users can select a document section along with a subset of notes so that they can view only notes related to the issue at hand.

To further support the discussion on the proposed changes to legislation, the collaborative platform services will allow the selection of documents being discussed. This will help discussion amongst participants to determine the impact of the new text. A viewer will be used to present documents, their semantic annotations and the relations with other documents; moreover it will provide services to select related documents in two different ways. First of all, all documents referring to a section that is changed are selected, because they can potentially be affected by that change. These references are stored in standardized format and can be retrieved from the stored data. The second method is through the combination of a domain ontology and the semantic model of provisions. The ontology is able to tag specific terms and it can be used to select documents dealing with specific topics; similarly

[8]Use of XML standard during the drafting phase.

the ontology provides contents to the attributes of specific provisions, therefore all the provisions regulating a specific scenario can be retrieved. For example it will be possible to retrieve all the provisions related to the consumer in the consumer law, as well as all the rights of the consumer itself.

As a possible service to such a system, an innovative semantic search strategy could be envisaged for the Pre-lex[9] system, by enabling the retrieval of all documentation related to legislation in progress grouped around specific legal issues, thus monitoring the evolution of the decision-making. This function can therefore provide an additional semantic retrieval service for both legislators and citizens, able to give monitoring facilities for the law-making process, thus promoting an active participation to it of all the stakeholders.

19.4 Objectives of the Proposed Solution

The envisaged solution represents a step forward in the legislative process management and in related stakeholders involvement. It can give an important opportunity for the European Union to reconstruct the relationship between citizens and public institutions by empowering citizens to take a more active role in public services and in public decision-making.

By incorporating the results of two strictly interrelated projects of the eParticipation preparatory action, as DALOS and SEAL, as well as including a collaborative platform for stakeholders interaction, the whole solution is aimed to tackle all the phases of the law-making process (proposal, drafting phase and debate), fostering the involvements of decision-makers, legal drafters, citizens.

The solution will result in an improvement of quality and accessibility of legislative texts in a multilingual environment, from the structure, the semantic and the linguistic point of view. The harmonization of legal concepts provided by the use of the multilingual linguistic-ontological resource, in particular, can be effectively used:

first, to facilitate the transfer into national laws of concepts and related terminology used in the European legislation;

second, as a source of a rich and consistent multilingual indexing of EU legislation.

The integrated solution will also contribute to the transparency of the law-making process, allowing public sector organisations to give regularly updated information on the decision-making, promoting citizens' awareness in the EU democratic mechanisms.

Moreover, it will help public institutions to provide public, easily accessible, focused views on legislation for citizens, as well as make it easy for citizens to refer

[9]http://ec.europa.eu/prelex/apcnet.cfm?CL=en (Retrieved on 7 June 2014).

to, comment on and link to particular legislation fragments, which can be selected in a semantic advanced modalities, irrespective to language and legal barriers.

Finally the envisage solution can provide feedback mechanisms for citizens, who can submit comments, suggestions, change proposals, either without having access to other comments, or having the possibility afterwards to see (and comment on) feedback and suggestions of other stakeholders, and, if necessary, change their comments as well as comment, vote and rate the others.

19.5 Innovative Aspects and Added Values for the Users

The proposed system can provide innovative services to different categories of law-making process stakeholders.

Legal drafters will have more control over the multilingual complexity of EU law, keeping coherence among different linguistic versions of the same text, as well as be facilitated in the process of coherent transposition of EU Directives into national law.

Moreover, they will be given the possibility of providing and managing a detailed legal semantic description of legislative text fragments according to a provisions model at a very early stage of the legal drafting process: text partitions can be organized according to their content, affinities etc., properly located within the document according to the preferences of the drafter and specific presentation styles. For instance, according to a common criterion followed in the European directives, at least, the Definitions are grouped in a single partition, at the beginning of the document. Another typical criterion is the aggregation of Duty, Procedure and Derogation, related to a specific action. Since a provision detailed description of a legislative text is linked to formal partitions (paragraphs) or sub-partitions (sentences), their coherent semantic aggregation will be obtained. The final result is the improvement of legislative texts quality, in terms of organization, readability and accessibility in a multilingual environment.

A detailed semantic description of legal texts according to a provision model can pave the way to the implementation of advanced services of legal texts search, retrieval and visualization in favour of law-making process stakeholders and citizens.

The use of a multilingual ontology provides a common semantic infrastructure for search and retrieval by subject matters as well as by full texts, irrespective to the language: this allows to harmonize semantic search modalities beyond language barriers. Similarly, a detailed semantic description of legislative texts can provide legal experts, as well as laymen, with advanced access facilities of different levels of complexity, able to query new bills according to specific concepts or from a more legal oriented perspective given by provisions annotation, bridging the gap between decision-makers, legal drafters and laymen, as far as legal knowledge awareness is concerned.

Relevant impacts can be obtained on national transposition laws, which usually lack multilingual parallel texts. In fact, using a multilingual ontology for drafting a transposition law, texts will natively inherit multilingual semantic annotations, thus providing citizens with cross-language search facilities.

Moreover, the front-end service gives multilingual facilities able to support the construction of simple queries able to retrieve all the provisions related to a particular category of citizens, as well as more complex queries able to retrieve, for example, all the duties pertaining to a specific bearer in relation to a specific action, thus providing a focused view (document tree as well as graphs sketching text relations) on legislative text fragments. Similarly, citizens can attach comments and provide possible changes on such text fragments. All of these benefits are possible on the basis of the early stage detailed semantic annotation of legislative texts.

19.6 Target Outcomes and Expected Impact

The envisage services are firstly addressed to enable transparent decision and policy making by providing support at the legislative drafting level for politicians and decision-makers. In fact, the described solution provides an XML native legislative drafting environment[10] able to produce new bills in standardized format and to provide semantic annotation at the very early stage of the law-making process. The integrated use of a multilingual linguistic-ontological resource within the legislative drafting process will facilitate law-makers' work as well as simplify and harmonize legal language and concepts at national and European levels. The implementation of detailed provision semantics and multilingual controlled terminology through the ontological approach is able to improve quality and readability of legislative texts, thus contributing to the "certainty of the law".

The improvement in legislative texts accessibility will pave the way to enhance the direct participation of citizens and civil society in the decision-making process, as well as to improve the access to relevant content. Comments and changes can be given to the legislation under debate, according to a proper authorization scheme, thus enabling citizens to interact with decision-makers in real time and with concrete contributions.

By providing users with advanced search, retrieval and visualization facilities, based on the same detailed semantic and multilingual linguistic-ontological resources annotation tools used for drafting, citizens can effectively retrieve the iure condendo, thus having the possibility to be better involved and have more instruments to participate in the process of proposal, formation and approval of a new bill.

[10]A textual drafting tool with which user can manage and produce documents according to a specific XML format.

Today, search engines for legal information retrieval in fact usually do not include legal knowledge into their search strategies. Current strategies include keyword and metadata search facilities, but usually do not address keyword semantics, which would allow, for instance, conceptual query expansion, better matching user information needs. In other words, there is no semantic relationship between information needs of the user and the information content of documents apart from text pattern matching. Often, query formulation by either legal practitioners or laymen users is only an imperfect description of an information need (Matthijssen 1999). The architecture of the proposed multilingual linguistic-ontological resource as well as the detailed, provision-oriented semantic annotation implemented for the bills under construction and debate ensure the possibility to capture specific stakeholders information needs, in relation to the differences between legal concepts, as expressed in different languages and legal systems.

Finally, the proposed solution is targeted to provide ICT solutions of high level maturity for promoting a more transparent, participatory and accountable decision-making process, by exploiting open standards for legal documents representation, based on XML techniques, thus making information more accessible for stakeholders and ready to be exploited by a wide number of services. The use of Web 2.0 collaborative and participatory technologies are, in fact, able to foster the democratic participation of citizens in the democratic game, thus building "Communities of Interests" among loosely connected citizens, as well as promoting citizens' capacity to participate in EU policy and decision-making through wide scale collaboration across the EU.

References

Agnoloni, Tommaso, Enrico Francesconi, and Pierluigi Spinosa. 2007. xmLegesEditor: An OpenSource visual XML editor for supporting legal national standards. In *Proceedings of the V legislative XML workshop*, 239–251. Florence: European Press Academic Publishing.

Biagioli, Carlo, and Grossi Davide. 2008. Formal aspects of legislative meta-drafting. In *Proceedings of the JURIX conference: Legal knowledge and information systems*, Florence, 192–201.

Boer, Alexander, Rinke Hoekstra, Emile de Maat, Erik Hupkes, Fabio Vitali, and Monica Palmirani. 2009. CEN workshop agreement open XML interchange format for legal and legislative resources, CEN/ISSS Workshop Metalex.

Francesconi, Enrico. 2014. A description logic framework for advanced accessing and reasoning over normative provisions. *International Journal on Artificial Intelligence and Law*. doi:10.1007/s10506-014-9158-2. Springer.

Francesconi, Enrico, Simonetta Montemagni, Wim Peters, and Daniela Tiscornia. 2010. Integrating a bottom-up and top down methodology for building semantic resources for a multilingual legal domain. In *Semantic processing of legal texts. Where the language of law meets the law of language*, LNCS-LNAI, vol. 6036, ed. E. Francesconi, S. Montemagni, W. Peters, and D. Tiscornia, 95–121. Berlin/New York: Springer.

Matthijssen, Luuk. 1999. Interfacing between lawyers and computers: An architecture for knowledge-based interfaces to legal databases. Kluwer Law International. ISBN 90-411-1181-6.

Palmirani, Monica, and Francesca Benigni. 2007. Norma-system: A legal information system for managing time. In *Proceedings of the V legislative XML workshop*, 205–223. Florence: European Press Academic Publishing.

van de Ven, Saskia, Rinke Hoekstra, Radboud Winkels, Emile de Maat, and Ádám Kollar. 2007. Metavex: Regulation drafting meets the semantic web. In *Computable models of the law. Languages, dialogues, games, ontologies*, Lecture notes in computer science, vol. 4884. Heidelberg/Berlin: Springer.

Additional Sources

European Commission, The European eGovernment Action Plan 2011–2015. Harnessing ICT to promote smart, sustainable & innovative Government COM(2010) 743 final.

Mandelkern group on better regulation. Final report, technical report, European Commission, 13 November 2001.

European Commission, Smart Regulation in the European Union, COM(2010) 543 final.

European Commission, EU Regulatory Fitness, COM(2012) 746 final.

European Commission, i2010 eGovernment Action Plan: Accelerating eGovernment in Europe for the Benefit of All, COM 2006/173.

Chapter 20
Computer-Aided Legislation Based on Immune-Like Processing of Legal Texts

Tomasz Pełech-Pilichowski and Wojciech Cyrul

Abstract The article analyses the possibility of applying immune-like processing of legal texts in the legislative process. It also discusses the required format for recording legal information and the relationships between the formats for recording legal information and the methods used to analyse it. On this ground we argue that the formal analysis of a legal text must extend beyond its logical consistency. This is so due to the fact that the quality of legislation depends not only on the lack of internal contradictions within a legal text but also on the number of requirements a legal text has to meet. Legislation should not only be consistent but also coherent, uniform and comprehensible. This requires, inter alia, consistent terminology, a lack of redundancy, appropriate references and compliance with the requirements set forth in the principles of legislation. In order to achieve the above-mentioned aims legislators are beginning to apply new tools to complement traditional approaches. As a consequence, legal drafting is nowadays aided by various information and communication technologies usually based on classic editing tools and algorithms for text processing. However, due to deficiencies in already existing solutions it is important to consider using novel, adaptive and specially dedicated algorithms, which would allow for similarity analyses of legal texts and in particular would detect patterns, relationships or coincidences in their content and structure. Such algorithms can be based on computational intelligence, and more specifically on artificial immune systems. As a consequence, the article will discuss both the scope of application and the capacity of tools based upon the idea of natural immune systems as means of increasing the quality of legislation.

Keywords Legal text processing • Legislation • Artificial immune systems • Artificial intelligence

T. Pełech-Pilichowski (✉)
AGH University of Science and Technology, Kraków, Poland
e-mail: tomek@agh.edu.pl

W. Cyrul
Jagiellonian University in Kraków, Kraków, Poland
e-mail: wojciech.cyrul@uj.edu.pl; cyrulwojciech@hotmail.com

M. Araszkiewicz, K. Płeszka (eds.), *Logic in the Theory and Practice of Lawmaking*, Legisprudence Library 2, DOI 10.1007/978-3-319-19575-9_20

20.1 Introduction

The role of ICT technologies in the legislative process is growing rapidly. Today legislative processes are already supported in many respects by diverse types of software tools, such as, e.g., dedicated text editors supporting the xml markup of legal documents, document management systems, websites for web-based legislative consultations, databases for storing or managing marked-up documents, converters automating the conversion of legal documents stored in different standards or derived from different legal systems, web platforms for managing legislative workflow, and name resolvers enabling access to official sources of law stored in digital form or search engines and publication systems.[1] Therefore, we should be aware that the features of these tools directly or indirectly affects the quality of legislation process and its outcome.

Existing Information and communication technologies (ICTs) provide legislators with many useful services, such as text formatting tools, basic syntactic search engines, collaboration tools, language translators, thesauruses, simple mechanisms for validating legal language etc.[2] However, despite all their advantages, ICT tools and techniques used in the legislation process can support them only to a limited extent. The main reasons for this are the absence of a universal standard for managing legislation, the peculiarities of local laws and technological limitations.

The task of globally standardizing and unifying methods, algorithms, file formats etc. used in legislative practices is limited by the particularities of national legal systems and features of established ICT standards. Consequently, mainly national or possibly transnational standards governing the informatization and computation of legal and other normative documents have been developed and implemented.[3] Although local ITC solutions for legislation are usually based on universal standards, such as Extensible Markup Language (XML)[4] and XML Schema[5] (XML Schema Definition, XSD), they still vary significantly, as the needs of national legislators and the legal context in which they operate differ from one another. Therefore, there is no one common structured standard (or, thus, file format) for legal documents and other normative acts, there are no universal and efficient legislative editors, and finally there are no universal and reliable search tools dedicated to legal information retrieval that would ensure an efficient semantic

---

[1] Cyrul et al. (2014).

[2] Sartor et al. (2011).

[3] Francesconi (2011).

[4] XML documents contain mark-ups which encode a description of the document's storage layout and logical structure. XML makes it possible to impose constraints on the storage layout and logical structure. See: W3C Recommendation, February 10, 1998. http://www.w3.org/TR/1998/REC-xml-19980210. Accessed 16 December 2013.

[5] Language for expressing constraints about XML documents. For example, it can be used to provide a list of elements and attributes in a vocabulary or to place restrictions on when elements and attributes can appear. See: http://www.w3.org/standards/xml/schema. Accessed 16 December 12.

search in a legal database. Moreover, taking into account the steadily increasing number of legal documents stored in digital form, all these factors reduce the probability of obtaining unequivocal and valid search results.

In order to limit the scope of legal information crisis in many states tools have been developed that fit mainly local needs. For example, in Europe several national standards for legislation management have been devised and implemented, in particular Austrian eLaw,[6] Danish LexDania.[7] Dutch MetaLex[8] and SDU BWB,[9] English Crown CML Schema for legislation,[10] Italian NormeinRete[11] and Swiss CHLexML.[12] Similar developments have occurred in other regions of the world. Mention might be made here in particular of the Tasmanian EnAct[13] and the Australian AGLS standards.[14] However, important attempts have also been made to create transnational legislative standards. The best example is the Akoma-Ntoso standard for African Parliaments, which provides a framework for local solutions ensuring semantic interoperability for exchanged information and technical interoperability of related applications and interfaces.[15] To some extent a similar role can be played by Formex, a standard proposed for specifying the formats to be used for exchanging data between the Publication Office of the European Union and its contractors.[16]

As was mentioned above, the applicability of particular ICT tools for legislative purposes is also limited by the restrictions of existing technical standards. For example, traditional text editors based on word processors like Microsoft Word or Open Office do not provide a semantic search, advanced categorization of legal documents, validation mechanisms, identification of inconsistencies or time dependencies adequate for different legal systems. Moreover, the available standards usually do not ensure the interoperability of systems and applications functioning in the legal domain. Therefore, dedicated legislative editors have been developed[17]

[6]See more http://www.digitales.oesterreich.gv.at/site/6565/default.aspx. Accessed 6.05.2014.

[7]See more https://www.ministerialtidende.dk/Forms/L0500.aspx?page=5. Accessed 6.05.2014.

[8]See more http://www.metalex.nl/, http://www.metalex.eu/. Accessed 6.05.2014.

[9]See more http://www.estrellaproject.org/doc/D3.1-General-XML-formats-For-Legal-Sources.pdf. Accessed 6.05.2014.

[10]See more http://webarchive.nationalarchives.gov.uk/20100225080346/opsi.gov.uk/legislation/schema/. Accessed 6.05.2014.

[11]See more http://www.ittig.cnr.it/Ricerca/UnitaEng.php?Id=40. Accessed 6.05.2014.

[12]See more http://www.svri.ch/de/pdf/CHLexMLReference1.0.pdf. Accessed 6.05.2014.

[13]See more http://www.thelaw.tas.gov.au/about/enact.w3p. Accessed 6.05.2014.

[14]See more http://www.agls.gov.au/. Accessed 6.05.2014.

[15]See more in Palmirani and Vitali (2011).

[16]See: http://formex.publications.europa.eu/index.html. Accessed 16 December 2013.

[17]For example, Legalis (http://www.legalis.pl/wydarzenia/dokument/rewolucja-w-legislacji/), EDAP (http://mac.bip.gov.pl/elektroniczna-forma-aktow-prawnych/elektroniczna-forma-aktow-prawnych.html), xmLeges (http://www.xmleges.org/eng/), DALOS (http://www.dalosproject.eu/). Accessed 6.05.2014.

that ensure the correct application of national standards and metadata, automate or facilitate the manual mark-up of legal documents or enable automatic consolidation of various versions of documents etc.

Computer-based legal research systems are used for storing, processing, systematizing, presenting and retrieving information.[18] They are widely based on database management systems (equipped with indexing engines) containing a relatively complex and organized collection of legal documents, a specified interface and a syntactic search capability. Such electronic databases are helpful not only in legal practice but also during the legislation process as they offer additional functionalities such as hyperlinks, references, court opinions or commentaries. Nevertheless, legal retrieval systems are slow when processing complex queries and most of them do not allow for semantic searches. With regard to the legislation process, they are useful only as a relatively reliable and comprehensive source of state or local laws. However, the growing importance of transnational regulations, globalization of legislative processes and the globalization of legal market requires implementing algorithmic solutions, which are capable of identifying similarities between documents and detecting any possible irregularities in highly complex systems. This entails interdisciplinary research aimed at developing new paradigms and methods of informatizing legal information as well as exploring new computer solutions (ICT) for computer-aided legislation. In particular, it requires designing new algorithms for similarity-based analyses of text-based content. Algorithms evaluated for data analysis purposes can be adapted to identify incorrect, abnormal data (outliers) or anomalies,[19] incorrect patterns and irregularities.[20] From the perspective of text (document) processing, such algorithms can be based on similarity analysis between analyzed objects (words, sentences, paragraphs, chapters etc.), such as in the field of data mining and many scientific fields (Ashby and Perrin 1988). Inversely rated measures of similarity or distance can be employed for this purpose.[21]

Implementing such algorithms in computer-based legal research systems can be very beneficial, especially as a means of increasing the accuracy of findings, limiting the number of outcomes, and ranking them according to both syntactic and semantic criteria. It can also advance the quality and reliability of searches. New solutions, in particular artificial immune systems, can improve the detection of inconsistencies between the drafts of new legal acts and valid legal texts collected in the system, as well as provide new ways of making comparison and referencing. Such solutions can also improve the evaluation of legal provisions or texts drafted by legislators and can help decision-makers control or supervise the actions of their subordinates.

[18] As described by Cyrul et al. (2014).

[19] Note that text or numerical values entered by the user can not conform to expected constraints, patterns, data types (including data entered instead of numeric, incorrect values/grammatical form).

[20] Analysed data can be incompatible with the expected pattern, schema, template, law, code etc.

[21] A large distance indicates little similarity.

20.2 On the Possibilities of Increasing the Quality of Legislation with Immune-Like Text Processing

20.2.1 Artificial Immune Systems

Artificial immune systems (AIS) are a relatively new form of engineering (Wolfram 1986) when a problem does not require specifying the behaviour of each component of the studied system. They may be defined as adaptive systems based on the general rules of the natural immune system[22] (Somayaji et al. 1998; Pełech and Duda 2005; Wierzchoń 2001). Artificial immune systems are usually presented as systems of cells and lymphocytes responsible for the analysis of cells and related responses of the system to detected changes (pathogens). They are capable of learning and memorizing so as to process data and solve problems.

This computational intelligence paradigm first and foremost deals with the following nature-inspired mechanisms: the theory of clonal selection[23] and affinity maturation,[24] somatic hyper mutation (SHM),[25] negative selection,[26] first and second immune response and adaptive immune memory.[27]

---

[22]The natural immune system protects bodies from pathogens (infectious agents). Antigens make it possible to identify invading agents by the immune cells and molecules to provoke an immune response. In general, two types of cells are considered: lymphocytes T (called as T-lymphocytes, T-cells) and B (B-lymphocytes, B-cells), which are constantly produced by the human body. When T-cells are used to identify a new kind of pathogen through binding, the primary immune response is trigged. A number of antibodies (cells of type B) are produced to eliminate an antigen from the body and keep this knowledge in the immune memory. Immune memory makes it possible to perform secondary immune response when a similar antigen is encountered again (Timmis et al. 2004; Somayaji et al. 1998; Pełech and Duda 2005).

[23]Clonal selection mechanism makes it possible to adapt the system by producing a number of antigens in response to a pathogen. Activated lymphocytes are widely cloned and modified to match with and adapt to the pathogen. They are then evaluated and selected to leave a population of well-adapted lymphocytes in the system.

[24]The efficiency of pathogen detection increases in tandem with the increasing frequency with which the same antigen is encountered in time (i.a. a number of clonal selections are triggered).

[25]Somatic hyper mutation (SHM) allows for the diversification of lymphocytes to detect (recognize) unknown cells (objects, structures) by producing a number of diversified structures. As a result, well-matched antibodies are generated and the immune system is adapted. To maintain the diversity of detectors genetic operators are employed, including mutation (typically, a change in selected value(s)) and crossover (a new detector is produced through its combination with another detector).

[26]During the maturation process, self-reactive lymphocytes are removed from the system. Thus, the process of nonself detection is based on the recognition of unknown or untypical cells/object/structures.

[27]When a pathogen is encountered for the first time, the first immune response is triggered and the pathogen is removed (mutation and clonal selection are performed). The system retains information on the detection scheme in the immune memory used during subsequent recognitions of the pathogen. This memory is adaptive (the current activities of the system cells are retained; efficient

AISs are a family of still relative new, naturally inspired learning algorithms (Tang and Velmuri 2005). The application of an immune paradigm to numerical or text data processing allows for a binary classification of analyzed objects. They have been developed to detect and destroy viruses following the emergence of computer viruses and are used in antivirus detection processes (Karakose 2013) and they have been successfully applied to many application areas (de Castro et al. 2002; Tang and Velmuri 2005) such as virus detection systems (Forrest et al. 1994), intrusion detection systems (Glickman et al. 2005), SPAM filtering (Mahmoud and Mahfouz 2012), anomaly/fault detection (Gonzalez et al. 2002), image and pattern recognition, data mining and prediction (Hunt and Cooke 1996), adaptive control (Timmis et al. 2000) and many others. It should be noted that artificial immune systems can be used for text-processing-purposes, among other things, to perform SPAM filtering (Mahmoud and Mahfouz 2012), grammar checking (Kumar and Shivashankar 2007), keyword extraction (Romero and Nino 2007), sentiment mining (Samsudin et al. 2012) and document clustering (Tang and Velmuri 2005) tasks.

The idea of artificial immune systems is based on formulating a research problem in a category of immune-like data processing where data are to be defined as cell structures (selfs/nonselfs), and detectors (detection algorithms) are well designed. With this aim in mind, both a schema and rules for the use of the immune memory need to be specified.

In such an approach, the available data should be represented as cells. Depending on the processing conditions, the aim of the analysis, the fixed accuracy of the obtained results, and the sensitivity of the system, self-cells (selfs) should represent, for example, correct data, consistent data or acceptable calculation results. Nonself-cells (nonselfs) - taking their inspiration from pathogens – should represent incorrect or inconsistent data, unknown structures or incorrect results. Information (texts, numbers) is to be encoded as numbers and/or texts (including related attributes), in a way that would ensure differentiation between cells (selfs and nonselfs).[28] It is recommended that information be stored using a fixed schema (structure), the same for all cells.[29] An incorrect cell schema (structure) can result in a loss of information, imprecise distinction between selfs and nonselfs or difficulties in cell analysis, hence the efficiency of the processing results obtained by the immune-inspired system. Considering the fixed structure of selfs and nonselfs, in the next step of the system design the main function of the lymphocytes (T and B cells) is used

schema are strengthened). Note that the accuracy of detection and the possibility of rapid removal from the system is also due to affinity maturation and thus clonal selection.

[28] A cell which represents information on a book can be encoded as text and numerical data on *inter alia* the author(s), title, major form (novel, poem etc.), genre (tragedy, comedy, epic, lyric etc.), technique (prose, poetry), physical format (paper, electronic, hardcover), International Standard Book Number (ISBN), release date, publisher, indexes in catalogues (databases). In such a case, each book should be encoded with the same encoding schema. Self-cells can represent, for example, the correct information on a book.

[29] To retain information on text-based content as a cell, it is important to encode both text component and related attributes.

as inspiration to create mechanisms responsible for nonself detection[30] (T-cells) and certain actions/activities (performed by B-cells).[31] Typically, for computation purposes and external requirements, it is the evaluation of detectors inspired by T-cells that is mostly investigated.

The mechanism of cell recognition by T-lymphocytes is particularly interesting and promising for data processing purposes. From the perspective of text (document) processing, algorithms inspired by T-cells can be based on similarity analysis between analyzed objects. In this view, a new analyzed object (a cell; for example, text-based content) can be compared to others of the same type that are correct (previously validated) to indicate a degree of similarity in terms of content, consistency or structure. Such a comparison should be performed by a specified detector[32] (lymphocyte) or a set of detectors adjusted to identify different features, attributes or relations.

A fundamental component of such detectors is a detection algorithm adjusted to the nature of the problem (a detection task). According to the clonal selection principle, somatic hypermutation and affinity maturation, such algorithms should be adaptable. Changes in behavior can be achieved by fixing the parameters of the algorithms.[33] The detector shape (its structure) should include changeable attributes (encoded as text and/or number data), which specify the application of the detector and the expected results of its activation.

An AIS may be used at different degrees of detail (inspiration) where immune-like mechanisms are defined, simplified or omitted. Depending on the field of application, the purposes and completeness of the analysis, certain immune-like mechanisms should be used. In certain situations only a negative selection can be utilized while in other cases an immune paradigm can be used in a complex way to include adaptive immune memory, distinguish between lymphocyte types etc. By referring to the computer legislation support, an AIS approach can be used to identify incorrect texts entered by the legislator (for example, incorrect references or definitions) supported by algorithmic mechanism inspired by somatic hypermutation and clonal selection. In this case, each system cell (word, provision etc.) should be analyzed to identify as a self (a text that is correct) or a non-self by exploring the available data set. On the other hand, the SHM, clonal selection and immune memory (thus, affinity maturation) can be used to enable complex analysis of a large number of legal texts when composing a particular text in real time. An immune memory can store information on a class of detection algorithms suitable for the pathogen, the system's response (marking of words, suggesting changes, indicating related normative acts etc.).

---

[30]More precisely: recognition of cells other than self-cells.

[31]For example, improve an analysed text, remove incorrect words, tagging.

[32]Detectors can be adjusted to analyse content, consistency or structure.

[33]A typical parameter of an adaptive algorithm is window width. For example, the same algorithm can be used to analyse one sentence (a narrow window width) and a whole paragraph (a wide width).

The adaptability of immune-like processing is mainly a result of two important processes: somatic hypermutation of lymphocytes and clonal selection.[34] These processes make it possible to achieve a diverse representation of input data thereby recognizing various pathogen shapes. Furthermore, immune algorithms are very flexible and are resistant to system changes.

In practice, an artificial immune system can be treated as a specific, parallel[35] and distributed[36] adaptive[37] system with partially decentralized supervised mechanisms[38] (Dasgupta 2006). Flexibility ensures resistance to relatively minor system disturbances. Individual components are not vital (critical) to the overall system but the same components, when aggregated, have complex properties (which correspond with the agent-systems-idea) (Wierzchoń 2001). AIS can be used to design hybrid algorithms, which combine together selected immune-like methods (natural-inspired mechanisms) and other approaches (for example, a training data generator for neural networks (Schadwinkel and Dilger 2006)).

20.2.2 Application of Artificial Immune Systems for Legislation Purposes

Information and communication technologies adapted to support legislation typically focus on the use of syntactic search tools and (dedicated) text editors to produce legal documents (containing legal provisions and other types of legally relevant information) in a specific file format or schema.[39] Furthermore, document versioning, collaboration tools and supplementary services can provide valuable support for the legislator's work. However – as was mentioned above (see Sect. 20.1) – the great complexity of legal systems implies the need to implement new algorithmic solutions so as to capture similarities between legal documents (the system's objects) and to detect any possible irregularities. Such identification may be oriented towards an analysis of a texts (legal provisions or other types of editorial units of legal text), meaning, grammatical or logical structure, inconsistencies, time or hierarchical dependencies etc. Features of algorithms based on immune-like data processing (including adaptability, distributed detection, negative selection and clonal selection mechanisms) suggest that it is worth examining the feasibility of an immune paradigm for legal text processing.

---

[34]To achieve this result cells and detectors are adapted. This can be done in a genetic way.

[35]Parallel systems can compute many computational tasks simultaneously.

[36]Computations can be distributed on different tasks.

[37]Adaptive systems are based on algorithms which can adapt to new data (information) received, processing conditions etc.

[38]An artificial immune system may consist of subsystems (modules) based on supervised learning algorithms aimed at producing the inferred function on the basis of training data prepared by the user.

[39]See footnote 15 and Cyrul et al. (2014).

The use of immune-like processing for computer-aided legislation need not only provide text processing support but also ensure data security. In particular, AIS can monitor user activity, support authorization/access control mechanisms,[40] examine file changes[41] and analyze and enforce established legislative procedures. For example, AIS can detect that the draft of a regulation is not coherent with or does not meet criteria defined in the text of a statute, on the basis of which it must be issued. As a consequence, it can block the promulgation of such a regulation until coherence is achieved or the statutory criteria are meet. However, the paper attempts only to outline the possible application of the idea of artificial immune systems as a tool for aiding the legal drafting process. In particular it investigates the application of an immune-paradigm in legal text processing.

Although the use of natural immune systems as inspiration for legal text processing is intended to create a completely new legal-text-processing paradigm/schema, such systems can be also exploited as a scheme for obtaining new information from the processed data, which are difficult or impossible to achieve with widely used algorithms, devoted to common language processing (see Pełech-Pilichowski et al. 2014) and to support currently used software solutions.

Depending on the data processing objectives and expectations regarding computer-aided legislation, the first stage in designing such a system design will involve establishing the shape of the cells. The goal is to represent available, collected and processed documents as structures, which in turn constitute specific data and/or information codes. The approach adopted with regard to encoding text-based content should provide for the ability to generate a number of self-cells in order to provide a relative high degree of cell differentiation.

The data and information codes can be expressed as strings of characters (letters, numbers). We assume that (for legal text processing purposes) cells are generated as structures composed of two components: (1) text-based content acquired from an original legal document, input (raw) data, and (2) attributes to describe as closely as possible the process of drafting a legal text related to a text-based content. Attributes may be treated as metadata associated with an analyzed object (for example, a cell) used to characterize them and to determine their properties. Attributes affect the results of computational analyses. They can be used to determine the activities of used algorithms, including detectors inspired by lymphocytes. Text-based content attributes can be used to retain information about time (including with regard to writing, editing, correcting, checking), user activity (reading, editing, modifying), time-dependencies, relations between processed documents (texts), statuses (for example, in progress, finished), legal domain (for example, civil law or criminal,

[40]Data stored in the system log on user activity can include information on the following: login session, names opened/edited documents (and related time), entered/deleted words/signs, additional file usage and printing. Such services can be supported by immune-inspired systems by, for example, analysing untypical user activity.

[41]Dedicated immune-like algorithms can provide advanced monitoring of changes in documents (normative acts) edited by the legislator, including punctuation marks, word order, untypical features, the time and intensity of changes and the related user's names.

state law or local) or scope (e.g. information security, digital signature, inheritance). It is essential that an encoding method combined with a detection algorithm make it possible to distinguish between selfs and non-selfs. In particular, this can be done by comparing text-based content (in different ways) and by analyzing attributes. The distinction between an analyzed cell and specific properties, schemas etc. can be found by calculating the similarity coefficient and then comparing it with a fixed threshold value. Such a cut-off value can be adapted to changing processing conditions, input data size, number of defined cells/used detectors or data properties.

The text component can collect encoded data representing a fixed part of the original text (sentence, provision of law, paragraph, chapter, book etc.), words extracted from the original text, language structures or logical dependencies. A representation of text-based content as an original text or words makes it possible to use term-document matrix (TDM) processing algorithms based on the relative frequency of term calculations in the entire document collection (Pełech-Pilichowski et al. 2014), which are widely used as common English language processing procedures. Results obtained directly in this way may be ambiguous and unsuitable for supporting legislation, owing to, among other things, difficulties arising from large data set processing.[42] It is important to note that values obtained for Polish legal texts with algorithms/formulae dedicated to common English language processing are difficult to analyse and validate. For example, analysis of similar provisions from the same body of law can produce contradictory results (values) for different analysed pairs of objects. Moreover, low similarity values can be obtained when analysing a provision in the original version and in a slightly modified version.

The numerical approach to processing legal texts, like that adopted in the present article, involves encoding input data (single regulation, sentence, provision) in the form of a set of numbers. Such a representation of text-based content can be studied using numerical methods, especially with algorithms for subsequent sample analysis (e.g. time series processing) and it enables the user to convert text (input data) to obtain additional information,[43] reduce noise,[44] unify[45] or homogenize.[46] Applied

[42]A large set of available legal documents includes normative acts that are binding on a normative act drafted by the legislator. A system used for supporting legislation should accurately capture incorrect references, definitions etc. in real time.

[43]For example, spectral analysis (Fourier analysis) used with time series allows for their representation as sines and cosines, thereby signalling decomposition into fast-variable and slow-variable components. In particular, it enables periodicity analysis.

[44]Noise reduction refers to the removal of useless (insignificant) information from the input data that impede reliable analysis. Considering the time series, trend extraction from data may allow for more accurate forecasts. In the case of text-based content, individual letters or punctuation marks can be statistically irrelevant for text analyses.

[45]The aim of unifying and standardising a diversified input data set is to enable the use of numerical procedures, calculations, transformations of the same type and to make information storage, search and retrieval.

[46]The goal is to obtain a homogenous, uniform, disambiguate data set which doesn't contain unimportant variables.

transformations can aim at original text classification, clustering or obtaining quantitative data from a text. Such methods can be enhanced by using additional data processing procedures to (de)emphasize specific data or information codes.[47] In addition, it is a promising way to handle selective processing of very large datasets where a pre-selection of data (objects) to be taken into account in further calculations should be made. This may be due to, for example, technical limitations, computational complexity or the completeness of the available data.

The increasing availability of large datasets of normative texts provides opportunities for acquiring information and knowledge from data. However, such datasets are redundant, which may affect the reliability of analyses performed. To reduce the dimensionality (size) of heterogeneous datasets, and thus to acquire relevant information (i.e. semantic relations) and ensure noise reduction, statistical procedures may be applied, i.e. Principal Component Analysis (PCA) (Jolliffe 2002). In the area of natural language processing Singular Value Decomposition method (SVD) (Deerwester et al. 1990) or Latent Semantic Analysis method (LSA) (Landauer and Dumais 1997) may be used (Pełech-Pilichowski et al. 2014).

Text-based content can be described by attributes to increase processing accuracy. The definition and assignment of attributes may be essential. Attributes may directly affect the possibility of an effective search and making further refinements to the system.

The goal is to provide, for a particular structure (cell), additional information on an encoded text or to weigh the importance of particular parts of a processed normative act.[48]

The cell structure (text component with attributes) should provide a distinction between self and non-self with lymphocyte-inspired detectors.[49] In natural immune systems, during the maturation process lymphocytes involved in recognizing self-cells are removed from the set of cells. This mechanism makes it possible to identify and categorize unknown structures (text-based contents) with lymphocytes. To provide this functionality, expanded cell structures or a complex set of attributes with fixed schemas, profiles or other dependencies should be considered.

The next stage is to define a set of algorithms (detectors inspired by type T-lymphocytes) capable of comparing cells as important objects of a designed system, thereby identifying and categorizing nonselfs. Cells can be examined in a hybrid way: individually – via attribute validation (data format, values), linguistic correctness, compatibility, or in relation to other available objects. In the second case, a complex or selective comparison of self-cells with distance-based similarity detection algorithms is recommended.

[47]In many cases it is reasonable or necessary to increase or decrease the weight of attributes, specific data or dependencies. For example, small changes/differences between values can be enhanced by exponentiation, the importance of selected words can be weakened etc.

[48]The purpose of data processing and related assumptions imply the number of attributes and their complexity.

[49]According to the principle of negative selection, the detection process is based on pathogens (non-selfs) being recognized by lymphocytes.

Untypical, "*unknown*" structures can be identified with great accuracy through the number of diversified detection algorithms used that are capable of recognizing certain types of non-self-types. Referring to the legislation process, we can assume that the detection process can be formulated as an analysis of the similarity between texts[50] entered by the legislator and collected by the system. The similarity analysis consists in comparing encoded texts as a distance in a feature space.[51] In practice, the goal is to calculate a (dis)similarity rate by examining pairs of objects using a suitable distance-based (dis)similarity method. The selection depends on the representation of the text, the purpose of the analysis, the complexity etc. The computation can be performed on original or transformed data, in a moving or extending window width. Nevertheless, in the case of text dataset analysis, the Jaccard coefficient[52] and the Cosine distance[53] are widely employed. Computations are performed for a list of terms obtained from original document(s) and transformed into numerical values.[54] Note that these methods are intended for processing everyday (English) language, hence the use of algorithms. As a consequence, it would appear vital to design novel algorithms dedicated to normative text processing and written in a particular language.

A legitimate and valuable detection approach would be one based on nonself patterns being recognized by different types of lymphocytes. Identification based on detector complementarily relies on the use of algorithms (T-cells) capable of examining specific attributes of a text. In addition, a negative selection of T-lymphocytes results in the rejection of ineffective detectors, and thus the adaptation of the detection system. This corresponds to problems arising during the analysis and interpretation of normative acts.

Detectors have to be able to recognize nonselfs effectively. Due to possible changes in the set of legal texts, and thus the metadynamics of the system, the process of detector validation must be repeated (synchronously or asynchronously) to provide adaptability of the system.[55] Simultaneously, generating new sets of parameters for a detector class (text analysis, attributes validating etc.) or finding

[50]Such an analysis cay support a system or application for built-in data protection mechanisms (providing data authentication, confidentiality, integrity, availability).

[51]Feature space refers to the $n-$dimensions where variables (analysed objects) are considered. Variables are viewed as features.

[52]The Jaccard similarity coefficient is used for similarity analysis of sets A and B. For binary data it is calculated as the length of intersection of two input sets ($A \cap B$) divided by the length of the union of the sets ($A \cup B$). The Jaccard distance is calculated by subtracting the coefficient from 1.

[53]Cosine similarity is expressed as the normalized dot product of sets A and B (for text-based content matching: term frequency vectors): the dot product of A and B divided by the length of A multiplied by the length of B. For vector representation of documents, cosine similarity represents the cosine of the angle between documents. The value of the cosine distance equal to 1 indicates the same documents while a value equal to zero indicates no relationship between the documents.

[54]See Charikar (2002), Hand et al. (2001), and Pełech-Pilichowski et al. (2014).

[55]Non-efficient detectors are to be removed from the system through their deactivation, by changing the structure or by fixing the parameters.

new detectors (for example, with algorithms based on genetic programming) is strongly recommended to ensure (and maintain) diversity of detectors.[56]

The user is notified that an untypical/unknown structure[57] has been recognized by the system. We can assume that in such a situation the legislator should not be able to directly approve changes (incorrect legal text). For example, a reference to a non-existing provision or to a provision of a wrongly titled act would be blocked by the system until it is corrected. Moreover, such a system can validate the correctness of the structure of a drafted legal text to determine whether it remains in line with the requirements of the regulations on legal drafting.

A planned legal text represented as text-based content and attributes requires final approval by an authorized user(s). To make a system adaptive each newly added legal act, approved as corrected by the system, should be used to adjust the parameters of detectors and to enable the negative selection process and hence to maintain fixed detection accuracy.

To ensure greater accuracy in recognizing incorrect text structure as well as fast recognition of text structures, the concept of immune-like text processing can be used.[58] Two types of immune responses have been considered (Ademokun and Dunn-Walters 2010). We may assume that primary immune response occurs when a nonself is recognized by the detector[59] or a set of complementary detectors.[60] The detection process is performed with diversified detectors to identify occurring selfs (normative acts entered by the legislator) applied to new, unknown text structures. Information on the attributes of recognizing text structure should be categorized and retained in the system memory so to be usable when the cell of the same type (class) is encountered again. The immune-like memory can collect all relevant information on the detection process (false references, non-compliance with requirements of the new act etc.) and this makes the system adaptive.

An immune-like memory can ensure a system's ability to respond in a relatively short time. It is important to note that in this case fewer detectors can be utilized to confirm clearly a hypothesis or preliminary results. In addition, the immune memory can retain information on unreliable or incorrect detection profiles.

To ensure a relatively high degree of efficiency for system memory usage, its structure must be verified synchronously. The objective is threefold: (1) to

---

[56]The adaptation process must be repeated until there are no detectors binding the self-structures.

[57]Pathogen – referring to the immune paradigm.

[58]Although in such a case the detection scheme formulated above can be regarded as adequate so as to avoid examining system cells by *brute-force* methods as well as to utilize efficient and verified detection schemas (profiles), exploiting the system memory in the detection process seems to be valuable.

[59]To achieve a high level of accuracy and sensitivity in text processing, in many cases it may be necessary to perform time-consuming calculations or to ask the user (legislator) to confirm changes manually.

[60]A complementary detector set may consist of detectors designed to analyze specific, particular features of a text.

strengthen usable information by assigning more weights to useful, reliable and frequently used detection schemas; (2) to modify stored information mainly due to changes in the set of legal texts, and (3) to remove inefficient or unnecessary detection profiles.

The system outlined above can support the legislation process as a tool for assisting legislation according to the established rules of legislative technique and internal procedures of the legislative unit, which directly affects the properties of implemented algorithms.

20.2.3 An Example of AIS Design for Computer-Aided Legislation

The idea of immune-like processing of normative texts is intended as a support tool for the legislator. It was assumed that common tools used by the legislator to work on a text can be enriched through additional algorithmic/software solutions. The preliminary study outlined in this paper focuses on the basic principles and conditions of normative text processing with immune-like algorithms. The proposed idea is illustrated using the example of a limited sample set of normative texts.

To use an immune paradigm for legal text processing purposes selected functionalities and mechanisms derived from natural immune systems should be considered and described. This paper presents and discusses below a specific way of encoding legal texts stored in a system designed to support legislators together with detection schema based on comparing objects (legal texts). Outlined immune-like processing is aimed at analyzing similarities between objects (texts described by suitable attributes and entered by a legislator) and a database containing a fixed set of normative acts.

The proposed legal text processing draft is based on a comparison of a pair of objects (structures, cells) made with specially designed detectors. Its purpose is to identify similarities between processed system cells and then categorize them. The system's major components (cells, detectors, memory) are briefly described below.

The first stage in the system design process involves defining system cells (selfs, nonselfs) as a representation of processed normative texts. In the second stage detectors (lymphocytes) are defined. Finally, to improve search and detection quality and to make computation faster, a structure for storing information on (un)successful detection schemas (immune memory) should be proposed.

Let us consider Article 54 of the Polish Civil Code.[61] Text-based content may be expressed in numerical form by counting letters of the alphabet, either using

[61] Art. 54 *Pożytkami prawa są dochody, które prawo to przynosi zgodnie ze swym społeczno-gospodarczym przeznaczeniem.* (Civil Code, Journal of Laws of 1964, no. 16, item 93 with amendments.) Article 54. Proceeds which a right produces according to its social and economic purpose shall be profits from that right.

Table 20.1 Numerical form of article 54 of the Polish Civil Code. Frequency of characters

a	ą	b	c	ć	d	e	ę	f	g	h	i	j	k	l	ł	m	n	ń	o	ó	p	r	s	ś	t	u	w	y	z	ź	ż
6	**1**	**0**	**4**	**0**	**4**	**7**	**0**	**0**	**2**	**1**	**4**	**0**	**2**	**0**	**1**	**4**	**5**	**0**	**11**	**1**	**6**	**6**	**5**	**0**	**3**	**0**	**3**	**5**	**8**	**0**	**1**

Table 20.2 Numerical form of article 54 of the Polish Civil Code. Substrings of the length 2 (punctuation marks and spaces are included)

po	oż	ży	yt	tk	ka	am	mi	i	p	pr	ra	aw	wa	a	s	są	ą	d	do	oc	ch	ho	od
3	1	1	1	1	1	1	1	2	4	4	2	2	1	1	3	1	1	1	1	1	1	1	3
dy	y,	,	k	kt	tó	ór	re	e	wo	o	t	to	rz	zy	yn	no	os	si	z	zg	go	dn	ni
1	1	1	1	1	1	1	1	3	1	2	1	1	2	2	1	2	2	1	2	1	2	1	2
ie	ze	sw	wy	ym	m	Sp	oł	łe	ec	cz	zn	o-	-g	da	ar	rc	ez	na	ac	en	em	m.	
2	3	1	1	2	2	2	1	1	1	3	2	1	1	1	1	1	1	1	1	1	1	1	

Table 20.3 Data presented in Table 20.1 after unification by text length (the calculated values are multiplied by 10 to be presented clearly)

a	ą	b	c	ć	d	e	ę	f	g	h	i	j	k	l	ł
1.9	0.3	0	1.3	0	1.3	2.2	0	0	0.6	0.3	1.3	0	0.6	0	0.3
m	n	ń	o	ó	p	r	s	ś	t	u	w	y	z	ź	ż
1.3	1.6	0	3.4	0.3	1.9	1.9	1.6	0	0.9	0	0.9	1.6	2.5	0	0.3

additional characters (see Table 20.1) or counted text subsequences – for example, subsequent sub-strings containing two consecutive characters (see Table 20.2) calculated in a moving window.

To combine together orders of magnitude frequencies can be unified, e.g. by dividing by the length of the sentence or a fixed coefficient (for example, a standard deviation/variance). Data presented in Tables 20.1 and 20.2 after unification are shown in Tables 20.3 and 20.4.

Digital representation of information codes based on counting letters or sub-string frequencies, applied in original or unified form, can be further processed to extract specific, desired properties. For example, to assign additional weight to the word "*dochody*" (in English "*revenue*") simple mathematical operations may be applied to the frequencies. Such a new digital structure of the text of article 54 (based on data expressed in Table 20.2) as a result of exponentiation to the power 2 of values related to the term "*dochody*" is shown in Table 20.5.

The next stage involves defining, assigning and giving values to attributes. In this case (see Table 20.6), the following additional attributes and their values (flags) are specified as an example to be expressed: status S ("act in force" – sample code: *F*), date *D* ("23.04.1964" – code: *D*1), general type *T* ("provision" – code *P*), amended/modified (*AM*; "yes" – code *Y*), type *L* ("civil law" – code *C*), normative act with delegated legislations (*DL*; "yes" – code *Y*), last modification (*LM*; year 2011– code *D*6), legislative status *LS* ("not applicable" – code *N*). Note that, depending on the data processing conditions, different types of attributes and permissible values may be considered. For example, an attribute "*date*" can

Table 20.4 Substrings of the length 2 presented in Table 20.2 after unification by text length (calculated values are multiplied by 100 to be presented clearly)

po	oż	ży	yt	tk	ka	am	mi	i	p	pr	ra	aw	wa	a	s	są	ą	d	do	oc	ch	ho	od
4.2	1.4	1.4	1.4	1.4	1.4	1.4	1.4	2.8	5.6	5.6	2.8	2.8	1.4	1.4	4.2	1.4	1.4	1.4	1.4	1.4	1.4	1.4	4.2
dy	y,	,	k	kt	tó	ór	re	e	wo	o	t	to	rz	zy	yn	no	os	si	z	zg	go	dn	ni
1.4	1.4	1.4	1.4	1.4	1.4	1.4	1.4	4.2	1.4	2.8	1.4	1.4	2.8	2.8	1.4	2.8	2.8	1.4	2.8	1.4	2.8	1.4	2.8
ie	ze	sw	wy	ym	m	sp	oł	ł e	ec	cz	zn	o-	-g	da	ar	rc	ez	na	ac	en	em	m.	
2.8	4.2	1.4	1.4	2.8	2.8	2.8	1.4	1.4	1.4	4.2	2.8	1.4	1.4	1.4	1.4	1.4	1.4	1.4	1.4	1.4	1.4	1.4	

Table 20.5 Data presented in Table 20.3 after transformation. Values related to the term "dochody" are changed by exponentiation to the power 2

a	ą	b	c	ć	d	e	ę	f	g	h	i	j	k	l	ł
1.9	0.3	0	5	0	5	2.2	0	0	0.6	0.3	1.3	0	0.6	0	0.3
m	n	ń	o	ó	p	r	s	ś	t	u	w	y	z	ź	ż
1.3	1.6	0	37.8	0.3	1.9	1.9	1.6	0	0.9	0	0.9	16.3	2.5	0	0.3

Table 20.6 Sample general structure of a cell: text-based content (rows denotes as *Tx* – see 1st column, based on values presented in Table 20.2) and attributes (rows denoted as *A*)

<table>
<tr><td rowspan="6">Tx</td><td>po</td><td>oż</td><td>ży</td><td>yt</td><td>tk</td><td>ka</td><td>am</td><td>mi</td><td>i</td><td>p</td><td>pr</td><td>ra</td><td>aw</td><td>wa</td><td>a</td><td>s</td><td>są</td><td>ą</td><td>d</td><td>do</td><td>oc</td><td>ch</td><td>ho</td><td>od</td></tr>
<tr><td>3</td><td>1</td><td>1</td><td>1</td><td>1</td><td>1</td><td>1</td><td>1</td><td>2</td><td>4</td><td>4</td><td>2</td><td>2</td><td>1</td><td>1</td><td>3</td><td>1</td><td>1</td><td>1</td><td>1</td><td>1</td><td>1</td><td>1</td><td>3</td></tr>
<tr><td>dy</td><td>y,</td><td>,</td><td>k</td><td>kt</td><td>tó</td><td>ór</td><td>re</td><td>e</td><td>wo</td><td>o</td><td>t</td><td>to</td><td>rz</td><td>zy</td><td>yn</td><td>no</td><td>os</td><td>si</td><td>z</td><td>zg</td><td>go</td><td>dn</td><td>ni</td></tr>
<tr><td>1</td><td>1</td><td>1</td><td>1</td><td>1</td><td>1</td><td>1</td><td>1</td><td>3</td><td>1</td><td>2</td><td>1</td><td>1</td><td>2</td><td>2</td><td>1</td><td>2</td><td>2</td><td>1</td><td>2</td><td>1</td><td>2</td><td>1</td><td>2</td></tr>
<tr><td>ie</td><td>ze</td><td>sw</td><td>wy</td><td>ym</td><td>m</td><td>sp</td><td>o ł</td><td>ł e</td><td>ec</td><td>cz</td><td>zn</td><td>o-</td><td>-g</td><td>da</td><td>ar</td><td>rc</td><td>ez</td><td>na</td><td>ac</td><td>en</td><td>em</td><td>m.</td><td></td></tr>
<tr><td>2</td><td>3</td><td>1</td><td>1</td><td>2</td><td>2</td><td>2</td><td>1</td><td>1</td><td>1</td><td>3</td><td>2</td><td>1</td><td>1</td><td>1</td><td>1</td><td>1</td><td>1</td><td>1</td><td>1</td><td>1</td><td>1</td><td>1</td><td></td></tr>
<tr><td rowspan="2">A</td><td colspan="3">S</td><td colspan="4">D</td><td colspan="3">T</td><td colspan="3">AM</td><td colspan="3">L</td><td colspan="3">DL</td><td colspan="3">LM</td><td colspan="2">LS</td></tr>
<tr><td colspan="3">F</td><td colspan="4">D1</td><td colspan="3">A</td><td colspan="3">Y</td><td colspan="3">C</td><td colspan="3">Y</td><td colspan="3">D6</td><td colspan="2">N</td></tr>
</table>

be expressed directly (e.g. 22.12.2013[62]) or as codes which may represent the properties of a date (time intervals, limitations etc.).

Based on the cell structures designed for the system the next step in the system design process is to define the detectors. As outlined above (see Sect. 20.2.2) the detection process can be carried out using distance-like algorithms based on examining a pair of cells using a suitable similarity method.

The procedure for calculating the similarity between objects tends to transform input data into numerical values. Therefore, computation produces a real number. This makes it possible to interpret and compare results obtained with various algorithms and parameters, related to fixed threshold values or for different (heterogeneous) input data. In the present paper, simple methods of similarity analysis are used to clearly illustrate the proposed idea of immune-like processing.[63] In particular, two metrics – the Euclidean[64] and the Chebyshev[65] – widely used in the field of numerical data analysis are applied to calculate the distance between two objects, typically two points or vectors. A large distance between objects indicates little similarity.

[62]Directly encoding a date/time requires further data categorization or precise formulation of database queries.

[63]The methods discussed here and used for similarity analyses are applied in the field of text analysis relatively rarely.

[64]Calculated as the square root of the sum of the squares of the differences between corresponding points/vectors.

[65]Calculated as the greatest difference between points/vectors corresponding points/vectors.

Computation may be employed to compare all the unified frequencies of characters or to investigate particular sentences, language and logical properties.

The sample results of distance-based similarity analysis for the encoded and unified texts of the Articles 53,[66] 54,[67] 55,[68] 993[69] and 796[70] of the Polish Civil Law are shown in Tables 20.7, 20.8 (calculation using the Euclidean metric) 20.9 and 20.10 (calculation using the Chebyshev metric). Tables 20.8 and 20.10 illustrate values presented in Tables 20.7 and 20.9 normalized to minimum and maximum values to reveal differences between real numbers with relatively little variation. Values close to zero represent a high degree of similarity (a small distance) between texts (provisions of law) while higher values indicate texts with less similarity (greater distances).

It can be observed that the proposed encoding method based on expressing legal texts by letter counting and then unifying computed frequencies is capable of

[66] Art. 53. *§1. Pożytkami naturalnymi rzeczy są jej płody i inne odłączone od niej części składowe, o ile według zasad prawidłowej gospodarki stanowią normalny dochód z rzeczy. §2. Pożytkami cywilnymi rzeczy są dochody, które rzecz przynosi na podstawie stosunku prawnego.* Ustawa z dnia 23 kwietnia 1964 r. – Kodeks cywilny (Journal of Laws of 1964, no. 16, item 93 with amendments.) Article 53. *§1. A thing's produce and other component parts detached from it, as long as according to the principles of careful economic management they constitute the usual proceeds from the thing, shall be natural profits from the thing. §2. Proceeds which the thing produces on the basis of a legal relation shall be civil profits from the thing.*

[67] Art. 54 *Pożytkami prawa są dochody, które prawo to przynosi zgodnie ze swym społeczno-gospodarczym przeznaczeniem.* (Civil Code, Journal of Laws of 1964, no. 16, item 93 with amendments.) Article 54. *Proceeds which a right produces according to its social and economic purpose shall be profits from that right.*

[68] Art. 55. *§1. Uprawnionemu do pobierania pożytków przypadają pożytki naturalne, które zostały odłączone od rzeczy w czasie trwania jego uprawnienia, a pożytki cywilne - w stosunku do czasu trwania tego uprawnienia. §2. Jeżeli uprawniony do pobierania pożytków poczynił nakłady w celu uzyskania pożytków, które przypadły innej osobie, należy mu się od niej wynagrodzenie za te nakłady.* Wynagrodzenie nie może przenosić wartości pożytków. Ustawa z dnia 23 kwietnia 1964 r. – Kodeks cywilny (Civil Code, Journal of Laws of 1964, no. 16, item 93 with amendments.) Article 55. *§1. A person entitled to collect profits shall collect these natural profits which have been detached from the thing during his entitlement, and civil profits - in proportion to the period of this entitlement's duration. §2. If the person entitled to collect profits made expenses aimed at obtaining profits which have fallen to another person, he shall be entitled to the remuneration for these expenditures. The remuneration may not exceed the value of the profits.*

[69] Art. 993. *Przy obliczaniu zachowku nie uwzględnia się zapisów zwykłych i poleceń, natomiast dolicza się do spadku, stosownie do przepisów poniższych, darowizny oraz zapisy windykacyjne dokonane przez spadkodawcę.* Ustawa z dnia 23 kwietnia 1964 r. – Kodeks cywilny (Civil Code, Journal of Laws of 1964, no. 16, item 93 with amendments.) Article 993. *When calculating the reserved portion, ordinary legacies and instructions shall not be taken into account, unlike donations and specific bequests made by the decedent, which shall be added to the estate, pursuant to the below-mentioned provisions).*

[70] Art. 796. *Jeżeli przepisy tytułu niniejszego albo przepisy szczególne nie stanowią inaczej, do umowy spedycji stosuje się odpowiednio przepisy o umowie zlecenia.* Ustawa z dnia 23 kwietnia 1964 r. – Kodeks cywilny (Civil Code, Journal of Laws of 1964, no. 16, item 93 with amendments.) Article 796. *If the provisions of the present title or specific provisions do not provide otherwise, the provisions on on the contract of mandate shall apply accordingly.*

Table 20.7 Sample results of similarity analysis using the Euclidean distance method

	Article 53	Article 54	Article 55	Article 993	Article 796
Article 53	X	0.0725	0.0652	0.0664	0.1001
Article 54	0.0725	X	0.0988	0.092	0.1194
Article 55	0.0652	0.0988	X	0.0836	0.1082
Article 993	0.0664	0.092	0.0836	X	0.109
Article 796	0.109	0.1194	0.1082	0.109	X

Table 20.8 Sample results of similarity analysis with the Euclidean distance method normalized to the minimum and maximum values

	Article 53	Article 54	Article 55	Article 993	Article 796
Article 53	X	0.6072	0.5461	0.5561	0.8384
Article 54	0.6072	X	0.8275	0.7705	1
Article 55	0.5461	0.8275	X	0.7002	0.9062
Article 993	0.5561	0.7705	0.7002	X	0.9129
Article 796	0.9129	1	0.9062	0.9129	X

Table 20.9 Sample results of similarity analysis using the Chebyshev distance method

	Article 53	Article 54	Article 55	Article 993	Article 796
Article 53	X	0.2919	0.2888	0.3065	0.3942
Article 54	0.2919	X	0.4327	0.3973	0.4721
Article 55	0.2888	0.4327	X	0.3603	0.4226
Article 993	0.3065	0.3973	0.3603	X	0.3889
Article 796	0.3889	0.4721	0.4226	0.3889	X

Table 20.10 Sample results of similarity analysis using the Chebyshev distance method normalized to minimum and maximum values

	Article 53	Article 54	Article 55	Article 993	Article 796
Article 53	X	0.6183	0.6117	0.6492	0.835
Article 54	0.6183	X	0.9165	0.8416	1
Article 55	0.6117	0.9165	X	0.7632	0.8951
Article 993	0.6492	0.8416	0.7632	X	0.8238
Article 796	0.8238	1	0.8951	0.8238	X

producing interesting results. In addition, the encoding method was used directly (factors such as adjusting parameters, adaptation, data pre-processing are not considered) and it produces results of a quality not worse than commonly used algorithms for text processing purposes (as indicated by Pełech-Pilichowski et al. 2014). However, the results obtained in this way are also partially ambiguous. In general, according to processing conditions (depending on the algorithms and fixed parameters used) they note the greatest similarity between Articles 53 and 55 and the least similarity between Articles 796 and 54.

Table 20.11 Article 53 of the Polish Civil Law encoded as self-cell based on calculating the frequencies of single letters. The values presented in the tables have been unified and multiplied by 1,000 to ensure a clear view. For an additional description, see Table 20.6

T	a	ą	b	c	ć	d	e	ę	f	g	h	i	j	k	l	ł
	55.6	15.9	0	39.7	0	51.6	59.5	4	0	11.9	7.9	59.5	15.9	23.8	15.9	19.8
	m	n	ń	o	ó	p	r	s	ś	t	u	w	y	z	ź	ż
	19.8	55.6	0	79.4	7.9	23.8	43.7	39.7	4	27.8	15.9	31.7	47.6	51.6	0	7.9
A	S		D		T		AM		L		DL		LM		LS	
	F		D1		A		Y		C		Y		D6		N	

Table 20.12 Article 54 of the Polish Civil Law encoded as a self-cell. For an additional description, see Tables 20.11 and 20.6

T	a	ą	b	c	ć	d	e	ę	f	g	h	i	j	k	l	ł
	56.6	9.4	0	37.7	0	37.7	66	0	0	18.9	9.4	37.7	0	18.9	0	9.4
	m	n	ń	o	ó	p	r	s	ś	t	u	w	y	z	ź	ż
	37.7	47.2	0	103.8	9.4	56.6	56.6	47.2	0	28.3	0	28.3	47.2	75.5	0	9.4
A	S		D		T		AM		L		DL		LM		LS	
	F		D1		A		Y		C		Y		D6		N	

The great complexity of legal text processing suggests that the use of general procedures to analyze and compare texts limits the ability of the user (legislator) to search for information effectively. A detection method, configured and properly applied cannot be expected to provide an ability to analyze multiple attributes of processed texts simultaneously.

Considering the results of the similarity analyses presented in Tables 20.7–20.10, it can be clearly seen that different algorithms – in this case similarity methods – produce slightly different values (see the similarities between Articles 54 and 55, 53 and 54, 993 and 796). This indicates that – primarily – it is vital to select a suitable algorithm as well as pre-processing procedures, parameters adjusted to input data attributes and computation purposes or outline rules of adaptation.

The above may imply that the design and implementation of a legal-text processing system composed of dedicated[71] detection algorithms appears to be a promising way to achieve more reliable personalized search results. To ensure a relatively high degree of matching between processed texts and detectors, they should be adapted and parameter adjusted. To achieve this aim, the inspiration of a negative selection principle is recommended.

Let us assume that two system cells which collect encoded provisions of civil law (in force) encoded as shown in Tables 20.11 and 20.12 have been defined. They may cover texts of authorized normative acts during legislative drafting, Supreme Court decisions, legal comments and other bodies of domestic law.

[71] To achieve relatively high detection accuracy a detection algorithm should be suitable for input data properties, detailed data processing purposes, the intended use of the processing results etc.

Table 20.13 Art *N* encoded. For an additional description, see Tables 20.11 and 20.6

T	a	ą	b	c	ć	d	e	ę	f	g	h	i	j	k	l	ł
	56.6	9.4	0	37.7	0	37.7	66	0	0	18.9	9.4	37.7	0	18.9	0	9.4
	m	n	ń	o	ó	p	r	s	ś	t	u	w	y	z	ź	ż
	37.7	47.2	0	103.8	9.4	56.6	56.6	47.2	0	28.3	0	28.3	47.2	75.5	0	9.4
A	S		D		T		AM		L		DL		LM		LS	
	F		D1		A		Y		C		Y		D6		N	

Table 20.14 Results of a similarity analysis of vectors representing unified frequencies of characters, including the change in weights of the word *"kto"*, by two detectors based on the Euclidean distance method

	Article 53	Article 54	Article N
Article 53	X	0.0725 / 0.2920	0.0885 / 0.3513
Article 54	0.0725 / 0.2920	X	0.1092 / 0.4302
Article N	0.0885 / 0.3513	0.1092 / 0.4302	X

Table 20.15 Results of a similarity analysis of vectors representing unified frequencies of characters, including the change in weights of the word "kto", by two detectors based on the Chebyshev distance method

	Article 53	Article 54	Article N
Article 53	X	0.0725 / 0.2920	0.0885 / 0.3513
Article 54	0.0725 / 0.2920	X	0.1092 / 0.4302
Article N	0.0885 / 0.3513	0.1092 / 0.4302	X

To illustrate the detection process we can assume that a normative act, i.e. art 53 §1 of the Civil Code, should be amended by the legislator, which requires quoting the altered provision in the statute which amends it. This quotation (further labelled as Art. N): "*Kto jest uprawniony do pobierania pożytków odłączonych od rzeczy lub kto poczynił nakłady w celu uzyskania pożytków może domagać się wynagrodzenia*", has quite clearly been formulated incorrectly. Such a sentence is expressed as a cell, as shown in Table 20.13.

For the sake of analysis let us assume that provisions of the Civil Code very rarely begin with the word *"kto"*. Related detectors can be tuned to catch this specific characteristic. This can be done in the simplest way by strengthening the weight of certain words, sentences, letters, punctuation marks etc. In this example, the weights of the word "*kto*" is multiplied five times. The detection results are shown in Tables 20.14 and 20.15.

Detectors (based on the Euclidean and Chebyshev metrics) indicate differences between analyzed text-based content (see Tables 20.14 and 20.15). For a similarity threshold fixed at c.a. 0.08 for the Euclidean-based detectors and 0.03 or more for the Chebyshev detector, the system receives two positive signals from the two detectors of the same type. An additional true positive signal should be provided by detectors dedicated to validating attributes (the attribute for the type of formative act (t) is incorrectly encoded: code *R* instead of *A* – see Table 20.13).

The detection schema for computer aided legislation outlined above can rely on unknown structure recognition schemas retained in the system memory to provide a shorter detection lag time due to a smaller number of detectors involved. The memory may consist of fields which store information on encountered structures (the system cells containing information on a legal text) and related detectors (algorithms and their parameters).

In practice, the system memory may be represented as a matrix (structure) whose rows are like records in a database and columns are attributes corresponding to the essential features of individual or categorized nonselfs and the related detectors. When properly defined such a memory is able to retain information on logical relationships, the correctness of references or hierarchies. The memory framework may cover different structures of records (items) to enable comparisons between different types of detectors and categorized self-structures, thereby speeding up memory usage and then retrieving a suitable recognition profile.

An example of a memory record is shown in Table 20.16.

As is shown in Table 20.16, the record of a system memory can store encoded information on cells, related detectors and user(s) activities in a bid to catch detection profiles or patterns (see Table 20.16). A sample record describes an analyzed cell characterized by the assigned code *Cell ID (CL1045)*, general *type T* (in this case, *P* denotes a provision of law), date code *D* (equal to class/period labeled as *D1*), type of law *L* (*C* denotes civil law), last modification date code *LM* (after date/period coded as D5) and the related statistics calculated for numerical values and corresponding intervals: standard value 0.0273 with a precision of 0.007 (class marked as *A1*) and an average value 0.0265 with a precision of 0.002 (class *B4*). Furthermore, the record retains information concerning detectors used in the analysis of cell *CL1045*: detectors *ID (DE_O2, DP_11)* and their activities, including detection efficiency (number of successful and false detections/alarms). The memory record also stores information (logs) about users who have worked on the analyzed text-based content coded as cell *CL1045*. It contains information on the creation of the document (user, date), the last modification made, the last time it was accessed and the most active user (number of modifications, number of logins per day).

Although detailed information may be gathered, information stored as aggregated (classified) seems to be reasonable. As a consequence, this is a way to erase irrelevant information, statistically insignificant dependencies between cells and detectors, outliers, or apparently acceptable results.

The memory must be supported by mechanisms responsible for the maintenance of the system's metadynamics. This can be accomplished by algorithms based on an analysis of the accuracy, suitability and usefulness of information encoded in a record of the memory and continuous monitoring and validating of written data. In such a case, the effectiveness of the memory can be regarded as highly efficient nonself detection, which provides the lowest number of false alarms (detection failures) and an ability to avoid system oversensitivity.

Table 20.16 Example of a single record of a system memory structure, which stores the following information: cell type (ID), related attributes and statistics based on frequencies of characters; detector(s) type of and information on, detection accuracy; user(s) activities and document (file) attributes

No.	Data								
11	Cell					Statistics			
	Cell ID.	Attributes				Standard deviation		Average	
	CL1045	T	D	L	LM	Value/class	Acc.	Value/class	Acc.
		==“P”	**==“D1”**	**==“C”**	**>D5**	**0.0273 A1**	**0.007**	**0.0265B4**	**0.002**
	Detector 1			Detector 2			Detector N		
	L.ID	Alarms		L.ID	Alarms		L.ID	Alarms	
		FALSE	Succ.		FALSE	Succ.		FALSE	Succ.
	DE_O2	**1**	**14**	**DP_11**	**3**	**9**	…	…	…
	User/log								
	Creat. Date	Last mod.	Numb. of mod.	Last accessed	Acc./day	…	User 1	User 2	User N
	20131112	**20140122**	**85**	**20140124**	**8**	…	(log…)	(log…)	(log…)
	User	User	User	User	User	User			
	login1	**login2**	**login2**	**login3**	**login2**	…			
12	…								

20.3 Conclusions

The importance and complexity of legal drafting require different methods to analyze drafted texts in order to identify possible errors and, as a consequence, improve the quality of the process itself and its outcomes. For this reason the idea of developing immune-like algorithms for legislation is an attractive one, since it does not deny the utility of other solutions, but rather constitutes an attempt to design complementary tools. However, the advisability of seeking new algorithmic solutions supporting e-legislation is apparent on other grounds too. In particular, the specificity of many national legal languages requires the use of dedicated tools instead of solutions used for the English language (as developed in many research centers). Furthermore, it appears extremely useful to construct tools that enable a computer analysis of very large collections of text data, which use both semantic and syntactic search algorithms and have, in addition, an ability for self-learning, which is missing in most typical systems.

The immune paradigm enables the (semi) automatic creation of profiles/patterns of draft texts of normative acts, their categorization and the possibility of selective, syntactic-semantic searches for specific information. Identification of such profiles/patterns allows for, among other things, the use of advanced methods for analyzing similarities between information already contained in the databases of legal texts and information that the legislator plans to add to the database in the future as a result of the legislative process.

The search for new, alternative methods of representing information, in particular in numerical form, is an interesting and challenging task. It can result in a wide range of potential applications in algorithmic analyses of the potential impact of drafted regulations on an already existing body of legal texts. Some of these methods have been outlined in this paper, and the use of an immunological paradigm to support legal drafting is claimed to be promising. Although using such an approach as an inspiration for legal text processing requires mapping at least some mechanisms and activities of natural systems, it nevertheless allows specific, legally relevant information to be encoded into the cell of a system. In this approach, however, it is essential to define the cells and the basic structures of such an immune-like system. On this basis a system can classify all information either as known/correct (selfs) or pathogens (nonselfs), and also spot nonselfs. An artificial immune system enables the user to classify drafted texts as correct or incorrect based on information about, e.g., the correct structures/schemes of particular types of legal documents, relationships, references and concepts. From this perspective and inspired by the actions of T-lymphocytes, an invalid object (nonself-cell) is identified whenever something cannot be classified as a self-cell. In addition, the design and use of immunological memory, which updates and adapts itself to new (actual) conditions makes it possible to ensure a comprehensive analysis of drafted regulations more quickly, including in particular with regard to detecting faults or errors in both form and content. The immune-like systems have the ability to learn. As a result, it is potentially possible to ensure autonomous and automatic identification of specific characteristics of certain rules, their groups, types or objects of regulation. Respectively legislators when drafting a legal text could obtain information on the possible consequences of his proposal for the coherence of the text he is drafting. Moreover, the legislator can be informed whether the proposed form and content of the drafted provisions may influence their future interpretation or classification as provisions of a particular type or category i.e. *ius dispositivum* or *ius cogentis*. AIS also makes it possible to support the legislator by suggesting correct solutions (such a functionality can be inspired by the action of B-lymphocytes) or tracking and signaling the possible impact of the drafted provisions on the texts of legal acts or on references and the relationships already existing between them.

The application of artificial immune systems to assist legislators in their practices is also promising because it increases the accuracy of the search, the selectivity of the results (i.e. provides "targeted" results) and the detection of inconsistencies within a draft of a legal text or between drafted provisions and texts of legal acts collected in the system. Last but not least it offers new possibilities in the comparative analysis of legal texts and together with new paradigms for representing legal information it ensures efficient control of references between legal provisions. Therefore, we can expect that the implementation of such solutions will help both legislators and lawmakers to correctly evaluate information in the legislative process and can help decision-makers to control and supervise the legal drafting process.

To summarize, the implementation of AIS for normative text processing is a promising way to support legal drafting. It offers new tools for analyzing similarities between texts drafted by legislators and texts already collected in a legal source system. An example of such system design was outlined in the present paper. The results obtained during tests were encouraging. However, to confirm the validity of the proposed concept and to assess the accuracy of computations it is necessary to perform many more numerical tests and to compare the results already obtained with the results of using different detection algorithms and text encoding methods. Further research is planned, which will focus on the implementation of dedicated and adaptive algorithms for similarity analysis capable of processing large sets of legal texts.

References

Ademokun, Alexander A., and Deborah Dunn-Walters. 2010. Immune responses: Primary and secondary. In *eLS*, Wiley Oline Library. http://onlinelibrary.wiley.com/doi/10.1002/9780470015902.a0000947.pub2/full.

Ashby, F. Gregory, and Nancy A. Perrin. 1988. Toward a unified theory of similarity and recognition. *Psychological Review* 95:124–150.

Charikar, Moses S. 2002. Similarity estimation techniques from rounding algorithms. In *Proceedings of the thiry-fourth annual ACM symposium on theory of computing*, ed. John Reif, 380–388. New York: ACM.

Cyrul, Wojciech, Jerzy Duda, Janusz Opiła, and Tomasz Pełech-Pilichowski. 2014. *Informatyzacja tekstu prawa. Perspektywy zastosowania języków znacznikowych*. Warsaw: Wolters Kluwer SA.

Dasgupta, Dipankar. 2006. Advances in artificial immune systems. *IEEE Computational Intelligence Magazine* 1(4):40–49.

de Castro, Leonardo N., and Jonathan Timmis. 2002. *Artificial immune systems: A new computational approach*. London: Springer.

Deerwester, Scott, Susan T. Dumais, George W. Furnas, Thomas K. Landauer, and Richard Harshman. 1990. Indexing by latent semantic analysis. *Journal of the American Society of Information Science* 41(6):391–407.

Forrest, Stephanie, Alan S. Perelson, Lawrence Allen, and Rajesh Cherukuri. 1994. Self-nonself discrimination in a computer. In *Proceedings of the 1994 IEEE symposium on security and privacy*, 202. Washington, DC: IEEE.

Francesconi, Enrico. 2011. A review of systems and projects: Management of legislative resources. In *Legislative XML for the semantic Web*, ed. Giovanni Sartor, Monica Palmirani, Enrico Francesconi, and Maria A. Biasiotti, 173–188. Berlin/Heidelberg: Springer.

Glickman, Matthew, Justin Balthrop, and Stephanie Forrest. 2005. A machine learning evaluation of an artificial immune system. *Evolutionary Computation Journal* 13(2):179–212.

Gonzalez, Fabio, Dipankar Dasgupta, and Robert Kozma. 2002. Combining negative selection and classification techniques for anomaly detection. In *Proceedings of the congress on evolutionary computation*, (1), 705–710. Honolulu: IEEE.

Hand, David, Heikki Mannila, and Padhraic Smyth. 2001. *Principles of data mining*. Cambridge: MIT Press.

Hunt, John E., and Denise E. Cooke. 1996. Learning using an artificial immune system. *Journal of Network and Computer Applications* 19:189–212.

Jolliffe, Ian T. 2002. *Principal component analysis*. New York, Berlin, Heidelberg: Springer-Verlag.

Karakose, Mahmet. 2013. Reinforcement learning based artificial immune classifier. *The Scientific World Journal*. Hindawi. http://downloads.hindawi.com/journals/tswj/2013/581846.pdf. Accessed 15 Jan 2014.

Kumar, Akshat, and Shivashankar Nair. 2007. An artificial immune system based approach for English grammar checking. In *Artificial immune systems*, ed. de Castro and Leonardo N., et al. LNCS, vol. 4628, 348–357. Berlin/Heidelberg: Springer.

Landauer, Thomas K., and Susan T. Dumais. 1997. A solution to Plato's problem: The latent semantic analysis theory of acquisition. *Psychological Review* 104(2):211–240.

Mahmoud, Tarek M., and Ahmed M. Mahfouz. 2012. SMS spam filtering technique based on artificial immune system. *IJCSI International Journal of Computer Science Issues* 9(2):589–597.

Palmirani, Monica, and Fabio Vitali. 2011. Akoma-Ntoso for legal documents. In *Legislative XML for the semantic Web*, ed. Giovanni Sartor, Monica Palmirani, Enrico Francesconi, and Maria A. Biasiotti, 75–100. Berlin/Heidelberg: Springer.

Pełech, Tomasz, Jan T. Duda. 2005. Immune algorithm of stock rates parallel monitoring. In *Information systems and computational methods in management*, ed. Jan T. Duda J.T, 183–193. Krakow: AGH-UST Publishing.

Pełech-Pilichowski, Tomasz, Wojciech Cyrul, and Piotr Potiopa. 2014. On problems of automatic legal texts processing and information acquiring from normative acts. In *Advances in business ICT*, ed. Maria Mach-Król, and Tomasz Pełech-Pilichowski, 53–67. Cham: Springer.

Romero, Andres, Fernando Nino. 2007. Keyword extraction using an artificial immune system. In: *Proceedings of the 9th annual conference on Genetic and evolutionary computation*, 181. London: ACM.

Samsudin, Norlela, Mazidah Puteh, Abdul R. Hamdan, and Mohd Z.A. Nazri. 2012. Is artificial immune system suitable for opinion mining? In: *4th conference on data mining and optimization*, Langkawi, 131–136.

Sartor, Giovanni, Palmirani Monica, Francesconi Enrico, and Maria Angela Biasiotti. eds. 2011. *Legislative XML for the semantic Web*. Dordrecht: Springer.

Schadwinkel, Stefan, and Werner Dilger. 2006. A dynamic approach to artificial immune systems utilizing neural networks. In *Proceedings of the 8th annual conference on genetic and evolutionary computation*, 131–132. New York: ACM.

Somayaji, Anil, Steven Hofmeyr, and Stephanie Forrest. 1998. Principles of a computer immune system. In *Proceedings of the 1997 workshop on new security paradigms*, 75–82. New York: ACM.

Tang, Na, and V. Rao Velmuri. 2005. An artificial immune system to document clustering. In *Proceedings of the 2005 ACM symposium on applied computing*, ed. Hisham Haddad, Lorie M. Liebrock, Andrea Omicini, and Roger L. Wainwright, 918–922. New York: ACM.

Timmis, Jonathan, Mark Neal, and John Hunt. 2000. An artificial immune system for data analysis. *Biosystems* 55(1):143–150.

Timmis, Jonathan, Thomas Knight, Leonardo N. de Castro, and Emma Hart. 2004. An overview of artificial immune systems. In *Computation in cells and tissues: Perspectives and tools for thought*, ed. Ray Paton, Hamid Bolouri, Mike Holcombe, J. Howard Parish, and Richard Tateson, 51–86. Berlin, Heidelberg, New York: Springer Verlag.

Wierzchoń, Sławomir T. 2001. *Artificial immune systems. Theory and applications*. Warsaw, Poland: Akademicka Oficyna Wydawnicza EXIT.

Wolfram, Stephen. 1986. Approaches to complexity engineering. *Physica D* (22):385–399.

Index

M. Araszkiewicz, K. Płeszka (eds.), *Logic in the Theory and Practice of Lawmaking*, Legisprudence Library 2, DOI 10.1007/978-3-319-19575-9

MIX
Papier aus verantwortungsvollen Quellen
Paper from responsible sources
FSC® C105338

FSC
www.fsc.org

If you have any concerns about our products,
you can contact us on
ProductSafety@springernature.com

In case Publisher is established outside the EU,
the EU authorized representative is:
Springer Nature Customer Service Center GmbH
Europaplatz 3, 69115 Heidelberg, Germany

Printed by Libri Plureos GmbH
in Hamburg, Germany